AN INTRODUCTION TO
YOUNG
CHILDREN
WITH
SPECIAL
NEEDS

3rd
Edition

AN INTRODUCTION TO
YOUNG
CHILDREN
WITH
SPECIAL
NEEDS

Birth Through Age 8

Richard M. Gargiulo
Jennifer L. Kilgo

University of Alabama at Birmingham

WADSWORTH
CENGAGE Learning™

Australia • Brazil • Japan • Korea • Mexico • Singapore • Spain • United Kingdom • United States

WADSWORTH
CENGAGE Learning

An Introduction to Young Children With Special Needs: Birth Through Age 8
Richard M. Gargiulo and Jennifer L. Kilgo

Assistant Editor: Rebecca Dashiell

Publisher/Executive Editor: Linda Schreiber-Ganster

Marketing Manager: Kara Kindstrom

Marketing Coordinator: Dimitri Hagnere

Marketing Communications Manager: Martha Pfeiffer

Editorial Production Manager: Matt Ballantyne

Art Director: Maria Epes

Manufacturing Director: Marcia Locke

Manufacturing Buyer: Linda Hsu

Permissions Acq Manager, Image: Leitha Etheridge-Sims

Permissions Acq Manager, Text: Bob Kauser

Production Technology Analyst: Lori Johnson

Production Project Manager/CPM: Pre-Press PMG

Production Service: Pre-Press PMG

Cover Designer: Gia Giasullo

Cover Image: Ada Steinberg © 2007

Compositor: Pre-Press PMG

For product information and technology assistance, contact us at **Cengage Learning Customer & Sales Support, 1-800-354-9706**

For permission to use material from this text or product, submit all requests online at **cengage.com/permissions**
Further permissions questions can be emailed to **permissionrequest@cengage.com**

Library of Congress Control Number: 2010920458

ISBN-13: 978-0-4958-1315-6

ISBN-10: 0-4958-1315-X

Wadsworth
20 Davis Drive
Belmont, CA 94002
USA

Cengage Learning is a leading provider of customized learning solutions with office locations around the globe, including Singapore, the United Kingdom, Australia, Mexico, Brazil, and Japan. Locate your local office at: **international.cengage.com/region**

Cengage Learning products are represented in Canada by Nelson Education, Ltd.

For your course and learning solutions, visit **academic.cengage.com**

Purchase any of our products at your local college store or at our preferred online store **www.CengageBrain.com**

Printed in the United States of America
1 2 3 4 5 6 7 14 13 12 11 10

This book is dedicated with all my love to Emma. May your life be one of joy filled with boundless dreams and the courage to follow them.

I also dedicate this book to all of the teachers and service providers who steadfastly work to improve the lives of young children with special needs and their families. I respect and applaud your devotion.

RMG

August, 2009

This is dedicated to the following people:

Drs. Linda McCormick, Loretta Holder, Judy Wood, David Sexton, and Jerry Aldridge.

These individuals, each in their own unique way, have made significant contributions to my professional and personal development, and have enriched my life in countless ways. It was by chance that I met them professionally; it was my great fortune to have developed enduring relationships with each of them. The influence of these mentors, colleagues, and friends will be felt for the balance of my career and they will remain in my heart forever.

JK

August, 2009

Contents

PART 2

Assessment and Planning for Young Children with Special Needs | 95

CHAPTER 4
Assessment of Young Children with Special Needs | 96

CHAPTER 5

Delivering Services to Young Children
with Special Needs | 136

CHAPTER 6

Curriculum for Young Children with Special Needs | 180

1. Mission or Purpose for Writing This Book

As early intervention/early childhood special education (EI/ECSE) has developed over the past 30 years, it has become increasingly apparent that a comprehensive book is needed to present an overview of this field, which provides services to infants, toddlers, preschoolers, and early primary children with known or suspected disabilities and their families. As university professors, we have experienced the need for a comprehensive text to provide a strong foundation for the multifaceted components of the field of early intervention/early childhood special education. Some introductory special education texts focus exclusively on infants and toddlers, some on preschoolers, and some on children birth through age 5. Others cover children birth through age 21, with limited emphasis placed on the early years. Because the field of early childhood is recognized by the Division for Early Childhood (DEC) of the Council for Exceptional Children and the National Association for the Education of Young Children (NAEYC) as including children birth through age 8, this book is designed to specifically address children in this age range. As described in the title, *An Introduction to Young Children With Special Needs: Birth Through Age 8* offers a comprehensive overview and introduction to those professionals who will be serving young children, birth through 8 years old, with known or suspected disabilities and their families in a variety of settings.

It has long been recognized that the early years of a child's life constitute a critical period of development. Early interventionists/early childhood special educators, general early childhood educators, related services personnel, and other professionals who work with young children believe that what happens during the earliest years of a child's life significantly impacts later development and learning. A growing number of young children, however, encounter less than optimal situations and circumstances during the early years. Conditions such as congenital disabilities and developmental delays, environmental factors such as poverty, abuse, and neglect, and cultural and linguistic differences place some children at risk for future success. Early intervention/early childhood special education services were established based on supporting evidence that the earlier children receive special services and support, the better their outcomes, as well as evidence that families who receive special services and support earlier are better equipped to provide support for their children and advocate for them later in life.

As we have described, the topic of this book is young children from birth through age 8, some of whom have been identified as having disabilities, others who may be delayed in their development, as well as children who are at risk for problems in learning and development due to exposure to adverse genetic, biological, or environmental conditions. These children with known or suspected disabilities are members of families, programs, schools, communities, and society. They have the right to appropriate services, beginning with early intervention/ education designed to meet their individual needs and prepare them for a successful future. Hopefully, this book will provide the foundation for comprehensive, appropriate services for all young children and their families.

Throughout this text, we use "person first" language. This means that we discuss *children with disabilities* rather than *disabled children*. By placing the noun before the adjective, we hope to ensure that the reader realizes that the emphasis is correctly on the child, not the disability. This practice is in keeping with contemporary thinking and reflects our belief that young children with special needs are first and foremost children who are more similar to their typically developing peers than different.

2. Major Organizing Features and Benefits

There are four major parts to this book. Part I, *Perspectives, Policies, and Practices of Early Childhood Special Education,* provides a foundation to frame the field of early intervention/early childhood special education (EI/ECSE). Part I introduces the EI/ECSE field as well as its legal and historical basis. This part examines the multifaceted influences that have shaped the field of early intervention/early childhood special education. Part II, *Assessment and Planning for Young Children With Special Needs,* addresses the processes involved in assessment, planning, curriculum, and service delivery for young children with delays or disabilities. Part III, *Organization and Intervention for Young Children With Special Needs,* is composed of chapters that focus on designing, adapting, and organizing the learning environment and implementing instructional programs for young children with delays or disabilities. Part IV, *Contemporary Issues and Challenges in Early Childhood Special Education,* discusses the issues and challenges that exist in the field today, as well as future directions.

3. Pedagogical Aids and High-Interest Features

This edition has several unique features described below.

- Educational vignettes of three young children and their families help to illustrate how theory is translated to practice in the real world.
- A Making Connections feature throughout the text highlights the three young children and their families in the vignettes and provides insight into the services required to meet the unique needs of each child and family.
- A DEC standards integration grid connects the standards with topics in the text.
- This book is updated with current data, references, and research findings regarding services for young children with special needs and their families.
- The book includes suggestions for incorporating technology in the learning environment.
- New TeachSource Video Cases and TeachSource Videos, developed in box features and integrated into the text and available to view on the book's premium website, illustrate topics and recommended practices.
- A two-color design featuring an extensive use of tables, figures, and photographs helps to organize the information presented.

As you read this text, you will encounter certain recurring themes that reflect our professional beliefs and values about programs and services for young children with special needs and their families. These themes, along with certain basic premises, provide the theoretical and philosophical foundations for this book. The following list depicts those orientations that we consider requisites for delivering high-quality services. We value, support, and encourage the following:

- services in the natural environment
- family-based services
- a transdisciplinary service delivery model
- authentic assessment
- cultural responsiveness
- developmentally appropriate practices
- activity-based interventions
- evidence-based decision making, and
- coordinated and comprehensive services for young children with special needs and their families.

4. Substantial Content Changes to Each Chapter

As described previously, the third edition of this book has undergone significant changes. The greatest change has been the broader view of the field of early intervention/education to cover the birth-through-8 age range. The book is filled with more photos, examples, reflections, and applications, and new, updated references and resources have been added.

Chapter 1, The Foundations of Early Childhood Special Education, has been updated in a number of areas to provide a more comprehensive overview and basis for ECSE. The chapter includes updated references, new and revised tables and figures, and the CEC/DEC standards.

Chapter 2, The Context of Early Childhood Special Education, has been updated in the same way as Chapter 1. In addition, legislative information has been added with new and extensive coverage on Public Law 108-446. New content has been added on early primary students, ages 6 through 8 years of age.

Chapter 3, Family-Based Early Childhood Services, has been modified to reflect the contemporary American family. Greater emphasis is placed on family-driven services and families as contributing members of the team. Cultural responsiveness is emphasized throughout this chapter.

We combined Chapters 4 and 5 to address assessment in a more comprehensive, coordinated manner as suggested by recommended practices in the field today. Chapter 4, Assessment of Young Children with Special Needs, has expanded coverage of team-based and culturally responsive assessment practices. The emphasis is on the coordination of all phases of the assessment process.

Chapter 5, Delivering Services to Young Children with Special Needs, has been reorganized, and we've imposed a conceptually sound presentation of content. New coverage is included of cooperative teaching, 504 accommodation plans, and revised IFSP and IEP forms.

Chapter 6, Curriculum for Young Children with Special Needs, has been updated substantially to address the current practices in the field today related to appropriate curriculum development. Increased coverage includes the influence of the general education curriculum, students in the early primary grades, and a holistic approach to curriculum for young children with special needs.

Chapter 7, Designing Learning Environments for Young Children With Special Needs, has been reorganized to focus on birth to 3, preschool, and early primary students. The content is better organized and more conceptually sound. A number of Web resources are included.

Chapter 8 from the 2nd edition was expanded to two chapters to provide broader coverage of organization and intervention for young children with special needs. Chapter 8, Designing

Learning Environments for Young Children With Special Needs, and Chapter 9, Strategies for Teaching Young Children With Special Needs, provide a more in-depth focus on how instruction should be delivered for the birth through 8-year-old population based on recommended practices. Increased coverage of early primary students is a noticeable change to these chapters.

Chapter 10, Contemporary Issues and Challenges in Early Childhood Special Education, has been updated to more accurately reflect the most important issues and challenges in the field today. New references and resources are evidenced in this chapter, as well as future directions in early childhood special education.

5. Ancillaries to Accompany the Text

For the student

Premium Website (with videos)

The premium website offers access to the TeachSource Videos and Video Cases, including exercises, transcripts, artifacts, bonus videos, and other study tools and resources such as links to related sites for each chapter of the text, tutorial quizzes, glossary flashcards, and more. Go to www.cengage.com/login to register using the access code packaged with your new text. If your text does not include an access code card, you can go to www.ichapters.com to purchase an access code.

For the Instructor

Instructor's Manual and Test Bank

The updated Instructor's Manual includes learning outcomes, key terms, chapter outlines, activities, and additional discussion questions. The test bank, new to the third edition, includes multiple-choice, matching, true/false, short-answer, and essay questions.

Resources on the Premium Website

The instructor area of the premium website offers access to password-protected resources such as an electronic version of the instructor's manual and PowerPoint® lecture slides for each chapter.

WebTutor Toolbox

With WebTutor™ Toolbox for WebCT™ or Blackboard®, jumpstart your course with customizable, rich, text-specific content within your Course Management System. Robust communication tools—such as course calendar, asynchronous discussion, real-time chat, a whiteboard, and an integrated e-mail system—make it easy for your students to stay connected to the course.

6. Acknowledgements

Writing a textbook is a team effort, and this one is no exception. We wish to acknowledge with deep gratitude and much appreciation the contributions of Linda L. Brady (Chapters 8 & 9). Her ideas, expertise, and professionalism greatly added to the quality of this endeavor. We are grateful to Carrie Betcher for her careful editing and expert formatting. Her willingness to help with one revision after another helped to make this book a reality. We also wish to thank

Ora Owens for helping turn our jumbled ideas into well-designed tables, figures, and chapters. We are grateful to our team for their contributions to this textbook.

Appreciation is also extended to the wonderful team at Wadsworth/Cengage Learning who believed in the vitality of this book and offered us the opportunity to write a third edition. We wish to thank our editor, Linda Schreiber-Ganster, for his support, visionary ideas, and commitment to ensuring that *An Introduction to Young Children With Special Needs* is a market leader. Linda Stewart, our editorial assistant, answered countless questions, offered words of encouragement, and provided just the right amount of professional nudging. We were also blessed with a skillful copyeditor whose keen eyes and command of the English language ensured the accuracy and readability of this text. Thank you to the copyeditor, Kim Husband, and to Melena Fenn, who served as production coordinator and helped keep us attuned to various deadlines. A huge thank you is extended to all of you for your patience and commitment to this textbook.

Finally, we are indebted to our reviewers. These professionals provided invaluable input and helpful suggestions. Their thoughtful commentary and insights definitely helped to shape the direction of this edition. These individuals include

Stacia Cochems
Dowling College

Shelly Counsell
Idaho State University

Elaine Francisco
Skyline Community College

David Franks
University of Wisconsin–Eau Claire

Melanie McGill
Stephen F. Austin State University

Joanne Van Osdel
University of South Dakota

Richard M. Gargiulo
Jennifer L. Kilgo

AN INTRODUCTION TO
YOUNG
CHILDREN
WITH
SPECIAL
NEEDS

Perspectives, Policies, and Practices of Early Childhood Special Education

Part 1

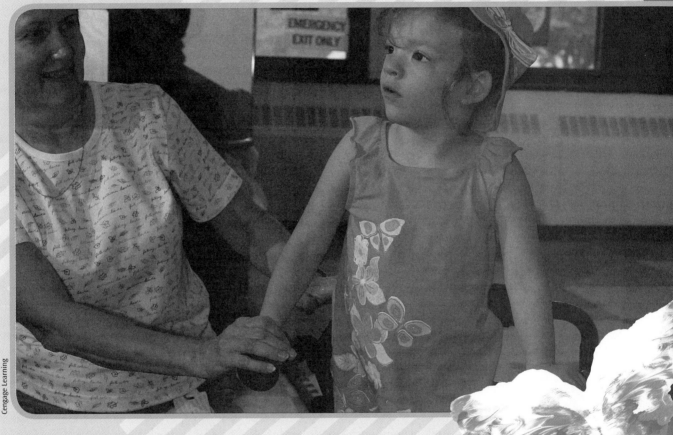

Cengage Learning

1 Foundations of Early Childhood Special Education

Key Terminology

Early intervention

Early childhood special education

Tabula rasa

Gifts

Occupations

Progressivism

Didactic materials

Sensitive periods

Prepared environment

Auto-education

Schema

Assimilation

Accommodation

Equilibration

Zone of proximal development (ZPD)

Scaffolding

Compensatory education

Project Head Start

Project Follow-Through

Home Start

Early Head Start

Learning Outcomes

After reading this chapter you will be able to:

- Describe the contributions of historical figures to the development of the field of early childhood general education.

- Discuss the evolution of educational opportunities for children with disabilities.

- Explain the concept of compensatory education.

- Describe the purpose of Head Start and related compensatory programs.

- List four long-term benefits of compensatory education.

Introduction

Before examining the origins of our field, it is perhaps best to define who is the focus of our attention. When we talk about **early intervention** and **early childhood special education,** we are referring to the period from birth to age eight. In educational terms, this includes early intervention, early childhood special education, and early primary special education. The individuals who require these services represent an especially heterogeneous group of children. The students you serve will vary in their chronological age, cultural, linguistic, ethnic, and socioeconomic backgrounds, as well as in the types and severity of their delays and disabilities. As early childhood special educators, you will encounter pupils with a wide range of physical, cognitive, communication, health, and social limitations (Kilgo, 2006). This textbook is designed to help you deliver an effective educational program to infants and young children with delays and/or disabilities who are receiving services in a variety of educational settings.

The Origins of Early Childhood Special Education

The last thirty-five years have witnessed a dramatic increase in awareness, services, and opportunities for young children with special needs. Legislative initiatives, litigation, public policy, and the efforts of advocacy groups are some of the factors that have helped to focus attention on this group of children. As a distinct field, early childhood special education is relatively young but rapidly emerging. The foundation for constructing developmentally and educationally appropriate experiences for young children with special needs is built upon three related fields. The origins of early childhood special education can be traced to trends and developments in early childhood general education, special education for school-age students, and compensatory programs like Head Start (Hanson & Lynch, 1995). In their own unique way, all the movements have played vital roles in the evolution of early childhood special education. Perhaps it is best to consider the field of early childhood special education as a hybrid built

FIGURE 1–1 The Foundations of Early Childhood Special Education

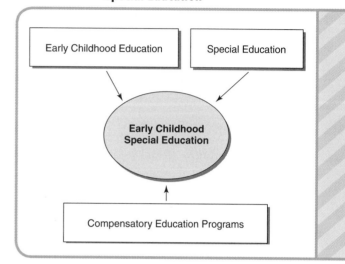

upon the evolving recommended practices of early childhood and special education, plus the research evidence from empirical investigations documenting the effectiveness of early intervention. Figure 1–1 illustrates this three-fold foundation of the field.

The Development of Early Childhood General Education

Early childhood education has a long history rich with tradition. The efforts of past religious leaders, reformers, educational theorists, and philosophers have helped to shape contemporary thinking about young children. The work of these individuals has also paved the way for many of the concepts and practices utilized with young children with disabilities and students who are at risk for future developmental delays or disabilities. It is important to note, however, that the value of children and their education reflects the social, political, and economic conditions of particular time periods.

Early Contributors

Although a significant historical religious leader, Martin Luther (1483–1546) is also remembered for advocating the importance of literacy and universal, compulsory education. He also was a firm believer in publicly supported schools for all children, including girls. Luther's legacy includes his visionary idea that family participation is a critical component of a child's education.

Another early religious leader and educational theorist was Jan Ámos Comenius (1592–1670). He was a strong believer in universal education, which ideally should begin in the early years due to the plasticity or malleability of the child's behavior. In *The Great Didactic* (1657), Comenius outlines his view that young children are like soft wax, capable of easily being molded and shaped. Schooling in the first six years of life should begin at home at the mother's knee ("School of the Mother's Knee") and progress throughout an individual's lifetime. Comenius also advocated that all children, including those with disabilities, should be educated (Gargiulo & Černá, 1992).

Many contemporary practices, as well as the thinking of later theorists such as Montessori and Piaget, can be found in Comenius's early ideas about children's learning and development. As an example, Comenius realized the importance of a child's readiness for an activity. He also stressed that students learn best by being actively involved in the learning process. Additionally, Comenius placed great emphasis on sensory experiences and the utilization of concrete examples.

John Locke (1632–1704) was a seventeenth century English philosopher and physician who also influenced thinking about young children. Locke is credited with introducing the notion that children are born very much like a blank slate (**tabula rasa**). All that children learn, therefore, is a direct result of experiences, activities, and sensations rather than innate characteristics. Locke was a strong advocate of an environmental point of view. What a person becomes is a consequence or product of the type and quality of experiences to which they are exposed.

Locke's belief in the domination of the environment is reflected in the behavioral theories of B. F. Skinner and other contemporary theorists as well as today's compensatory education programs aimed at remedying the consequences of a disadvantaged environment. Early school experience for children at risk, such as the popular Head Start program, is a prime example. Because Locke also stressed the importance of sensory experiences, his theorizing influenced Montessori's thinking about the significance of sensory training in early education.

One social theorist and philosopher who had a significant impact on education was Jean-Jacques Rousseau (1712–1778). Through his writings, in particular, *Emile* (1762), Rousseau described his views on child rearing and education. His ideas, radical for their time, included a natural approach to the education of young children. Rousseau urged a laissez-faire approach, one void of restrictions and interference, that would thus allow the natural unfolding of a child's abilities. Childhood was viewed as a distinct and special time wherein children developed or "flowered" according to innate timetables. Rousseau emphasized the importance of early education. He also believed that schools should be based on the interests of the child (Graves, Gargiulo, & Schertz, 1996).

Educational historians typically regard Rousseau as the dividing line between the historical and modern periods of education. He significantly influenced future reformers and thinkers such as Pestalozzi, Froebel, and Montessori, all of whom have contributed to modern early childhood practices.

Pioneers in Early Childhood Education

Johann Heinrich Pestalozzi (1746–1827), a Swiss educator, is credited with establishing early childhood education as a distinct discipline. Like Rousseau, Pestalozzi believed in the importance of education through nature and following the child's natural development. He also advocated developing school

Comenius believed that young children learn best by being actively involved in the learning process.

bilwissedition.com/bilwissedition Ltd. & Co. KG/Alamy

According to Rousseau, children develop according to innate timetables.

experiences centered on the interests of the student. Pestalozzi realized, however, that learning does not occur simply through a child's initiative and exploratory behavior; adult guidance is required. Teachers, therefore, need to construct "object" lessons to balance the pupil's self-guided experiences. Due to Pestalozzi's belief in the importance of sensory experiences, instructional lessons incorporated manipulative activities like counting, measuring, feeling, and touching concrete objects (Lawton, 1988).

Three additional ideas distinguish Pestalozzi's contributions to the field of early childhood education. First, Pestalozzi stressed the education of the whole child; second, he was a strong believer in involving parents in a child's early education; and, finally, he saw the merit of multiage grouping whereby older students could assist in teaching younger pupils.

Social reformer and entrepreneur Robert Owen (1771–1858) is recognized for establishing an Infant School in 1816. Influenced by the theorizing of Rousseau and Pestalozzi, Owen was concerned about the living and working conditions of the children and their parents who worked in textile mills. As the manager of a mill in New Lanark, Scotland, Owen was able to initiate his reform ideas. Very young children were prohibited from working at all and the working hours of older children were limited. Perhaps more important, however, was the establishment of a school for children between the ages of three and ten. He believed early education was critical to the

development of a child's character and behavior. The early years were the best time to influence a young child's development. By controlling and manipulating environmental conditions, Owen, like other Utopians, sought to construct a better society (Graves et al., 1996). Education was seen as a vehicle for social change.

Owen's Infant School was noted for its emphasis on the development of basic academics as well as creative experiences such as dance and music. This pioneer of early childhood education did not believe in forcing children to learn and was opposed to punishment, stressing mutual respect between teacher and learner. His ideas were immensely popular, and more than 50 Infant Schools were established by the late 1820s throughout Scotland, Ireland, and England. Several schools flourished in urban areas of the United States; yet, their influence diminished by the mid-1830s.

Owen's Infant Schools served as a forerunner of kindergartens. They were also seen as a way of immunizing children living in poverty from the evils of nineteenth-century urban living. This social reformer was visionary; he realized the important relationship between education and societal improvements. Owen believed, as did other reformers of that time, that poverty could be permanently eliminated by educating and socializing young children from poor families.

Graves and his colleagues (Graves et al., 1996) describe Friedrich Wilhelm Froebel[1] (1782–1852) as the one individual who perhaps had the greatest impact on the field of early childhood education. A student of Pestalozzi and a teacher in one of his schools, Froebel was a strong believer in the education of young children. He translated his beliefs into a system for teaching young children in addition to developing a curriculum, complete with methodology. His efforts have earned him the well-deserved title "Father of the Kindergarten."

Also influenced by the writings of Rousseau and Comenius, Froebel conceived an educational theory ("Law of Universal Unity") partly based on their thoughts as well as his own personal experiences and

---

[1] Information on Friedrich Froebel, John Dewey, Maria Montessori, and Jean Piaget is adapted from *Young Children: An Introduction to Early Childhood* by S. Graves, R. Gargiulo, and L. Sluder. St. Paul, MN: West Publishing, 1996.

religious views. His basic idea was essentially religious in nature and emphasized a unity of all living things—a oneness of humans, nature, and God. His notion of unity led Froebel to advocate that education should be based on cooperation rather than competition. Like Comenius and Pestalozzi, he also considered development as a process of unfolding. Children's learning should, therefore, follow this natural development. The role of the teacher (and parent) was to recognize this process and to provide activities to help the child learn whenever he or she was ready to learn (Graves, 1990).

Froebel used the garden to symbolize childhood education. Like a flower blooming from a bud, children would grow naturally according to their own laws of development. A kindergarten education, therefore, should follow the nature of the child. Play, a child's natural activity, was a basis for learning (Spodek, Saracho, & Davis, 1991).

Froebel established the first kindergarten (German for "children's garden") in 1837 near Blankenburg, Germany. This early program enrolled young children between the ages of one and seven. Structured play was an important component of the curriculum. Unlike many of his contemporaries, Froebel saw educational value and benefit in play. Play is the work of the child. Because he believed that education was knowledge being transmitted by symbols, Froebel devised a set of materials and activities that would aid the children in their play activities as well as teach the concept of unity among nature, God, and humankind. Education was to begin with the concrete and move to the abstract.

Froebel presented his students with "gifts" and "occupations" rich in symbolism. In his curriculum, **gifts** were manipulative activities to assist in learning color, shape, size, counting, and other educational tasks. Wooden blocks, cylinders, and cubes; balls of colored yarn; geometric shapes; and natural objects, such as beans and pebbles, are all examples of some of the learning tools used.

Occupations were arts-and-craft-type activities designed to develop eye-hand coordination and fine motor skills. Illustrations of these activities include bead-stringing, embroidering, paper folding, cutting with scissors, and weaving. Froebel's curriculum also used games, songs, dance, rhymes, and finger play. Other components of his curriculum were nature study, language, and arithmetic in addition to developing the habits of cleanliness, courtesy, and punctuality.

Megasquib/istockphoto.com

Froebel is considered to be the "Father of the Kindergarten."

According to Froebel, teachers were to be designers of activities and experiences utilizing the child's natural curiosity. They were also responsible for directing and guiding their students toward becoming contributing members of society (Graves, 1990). This role of the teacher as a facilitator of children's learning would later be echoed in the work of Montessori and Piaget.

Influential Leaders of the Twentieth Century

We believe that the thinking and educational ideas espoused by John Dewey, Maria Montessori, and Jean Piaget, along with his contemporary, Russian theorist Lev Vygotsky, have significantly influenced the field of early childhood general education. Many of the practices that are common in today's classrooms can trace their origins to the work of these four individuals.

John Dewey. The influence of John Dewey (1859–1952) can be traced to the early days of the twentieth century when conflicting points of view about young children and kindergarten experiences began to emerge. Some individuals professed a strong allegiance to Froebel's principles and practices. Other professionals, known as progressives, saw little value in adhering to Froebel's symbolism. Instead, they embraced the developing

Dewey founded a school of thought known as Progressivism.

child study movement with its focus on empirical study. Because of the work of G. Stanley Hall, the father of the child study movement, formal observations and a scientific basis for understanding young children replaced speculation, philosophic idealism, and religious and social values as a means for guiding the education of young children. Observations of young children led to new ideas about kindergarten practices and what should be considered of educational value for children.

Dewey, a student of Hall, was one of the first Americans to significantly impact educational theory as well as practice. He is generally regarded as the founder of a school of thought known as **Progressivism.** This approach, with its emphasis on the child and his or her interests, was counter to the then prevalent theme of teacher-directed, subject-oriented curriculum. According to Dewey, learning flowed from the interests of the child instead of from activities chosen by the instructor. Dewey, who taught at both the University of Chicago and Teachers College, Columbia University, coined the terms "child-centered curriculum" and "child-centered schools" (Graves, 1990). Consistent with Dewey's beliefs, the purpose of schools was to prepare the student for the realities of today's world, not just to prepare for the future. In his famous work, *My Pedagogic Creed,* this philosopher emphasized that learning occurs through real-life experiences and that education is best described as a process for living. He also stressed the concept of social responsibility. Basic

to his philosophy was the idea that children should be equipped to function effectively as citizens in a democratic society.

Traditionally, children learned predetermined subject matter via rote memory under the strict guidance of the teacher, who was in complete control of the learning environment. In Dewey's classroom, however, children were socially active, engaged in physical activities and discovering how objects worked. They were to be continually afforded opportunities for inquiry, discovery, and experimentation. Daily living activities such as carpentry and cooking could also be found in a Dewey-designed classroom (Graves, 1990).

Dewey (1916) advocated the child's interaction with the total environment. He believed that intellectual skills emerged from a child's own activity and play. He further rejected Froebel's approach to symbolic education.

Some have unfairly criticized Dewey as only responding to the whims of the child; this was a false accusation. Dewey did not abandon the teaching of subject matter or basic skills. He was merely opposed to imposing knowledge on children. Instead, he favored using the student's interest as the origin of subject matter instruction. Thus, curriculum cannot be fixed or established in advance. Educators are to guide learning activities, observe and monitor, and offer encouragement and assistance as needed. They are not to control their students.

Although Dewey's impact has diminished, his contributions to early childhood education in America and other countries are still evident. Many so-called traditional early childhood programs today have their philosophical roots in Dewey's progressive education movement.

Maria Montessori. As we examine the roots of modern early childhood special education, the work of Maria Montessori (1870–1952) stands out. Her contributions to the field of early childhood general education are significant. A feminist, she became the first female to earn a medical degree in Italy. (Montessori also held a Ph.D. in anthropology.) She began working as a physician in a psychiatric clinic at the University of Rome. It was in this hospital setting that she came into frequent contact with "idiot children," or individuals thought to be mentally retarded. At the turn of the century, mental retardation was, unfortunately, viewed as indistinguishable from

Montessori believed that children learn best by direct sensory experiences.

mental illness. A careful observation of these youngsters led her to conclude that educational intervention rather than medical treatment would be a more effective strategy. She began to develop her theories for working with these children. In doing so, she was following an historical tradition upon which the early foundation of special education is built—the physician turned educator. Dr. Montessori was influenced by the writings of Pestalozzi, Rousseau, Froebel, and the work of Edouard Seguin, a French physician who pioneered an effective educational approach for children with intellectual disabilities. She concluded that intelligence was not static or fixed, but could be influenced by the child's experiences. Montessori developed an innovative, activity-based sensory education model involving teaching, or **didactic materials.** She was eminently successful. Young children who were originally believed to be incapable of learning successfully performed on school achievement tests.

Montessori believed that children learn best by direct sensory experience. She was further convinced that children had a natural tendency to explore and understand their world. Like Froebel, she envisioned child development as a process of unfolding; however, environmental influences also had a critical role. Education in the early years is crucial to the child's later development. Montessori also thought children passed through **sensitive periods,** or stages of development early in life where they are especially able, due to their curiosity, to more easily learn particular skills or behaviors. This concept is very similar to the idea of a child's readiness for an activity.

To promote the children's learning, Montessori constructed an orderly or **prepared environment** with specially designed tasks and materials. Much like Froebel's gifts, these materials included items such as wooden rods, cylinders, and cubes of varying sizes; sets of sandpaper tablets arranged according to the degree of smoothness; and musical bells of different pitches (see Table 1–1). Dr. Montessori's program also emphasized three growth periods—practical life experiences, sensory education, and academic education. Each of these components was considered to be of importance in developing the child's independence, responsibility, and productivity.

Practical life experiences focused on personal hygiene, self-care, physical education, and responsibility for the environment. Examples of this last activity include tasks such as sweeping, dusting, or raking leaves utilizing child-size equipment. Sensory education was very important in Montessori's education scheme. She designed a wide variety of teaching materials aimed at developing the student's various senses. Her didactic materials are noteworthy for two reasons. They were self-correcting, that is, there was only one correct way to use them. Thus the materials could be used independently by the children and help them become self-motivated students. The sensory training equipment was also graded in difficulty—from easiest to the most difficult and from concrete to abstract. Her sensory training materials and procedures reflected her educational belief that cognitive ability results from sensory development. The final stage, academic instruction, introduced the child to reading, writing, and arithmetic in the sensitive period, ages two to six. Various concrete and sensory teaching materials were used in the lessons of this last stage (Montessori, 1965).

Montessori's classrooms were distinguished by their attractive and child-size materials and equipment. The furniture was moveable and the beautifully crafted materials were very attractive—appealing to the child's senses. Teaching materials were displayed on low shelves in an organized manner to encourage the pupil's independent use. Children worked at their own pace, selecting learning materials of their choice. They must, however, complete one assignment before starting another. Dr. Montessori fully believed in allowing children to do things for themselves. She was convinced that children are capable of teaching themselves through interaction with a carefully planned learning environment. She identified this concept as **auto-education.**

TABLE 1–1 Examples of Montessori's Sensory Materials

Material	Purpose	How It Is Used by Children
Wooden cylinders	Visual discrimination (Size)	Ten wooden cylinders varying in diameter, height, or variations of both dimensions. Child removes cylinders from wooden holder, mixes them up, and replaces in correct location.
Pink tower	Visual discrimination (Dimension)	Ten wooden cubes painted pink. Child is required to build a tower. Each cube is succeedingly smaller, varying from ten to one centimeter. Repeats activity.
Green rods	Visual discrimination (Length)	Ten wooden pieces identical in size and color but varying in length. After scattering rods, youngster arranges them according to gradations in length—largest to smallest.
Material swatches	Sense of feel	Matches identical pieces of brightly colored fabric (e.g., fine vs. coarse linen, cottons, and woolens). Initially performs task without blindfold.
Sound cylinders	Auditory discrimination	Double set of cylinders containing natural materials such as pebbles or rice. Child shakes cylinder and matches first according to similarity of sound and then according to loudness.
Tonal bells	Auditory discrimination	Two sets of eight metal bells, alike in appearance but varying in tone. Youngster strikes the bells with a wooden hammer and matches the bell on the basis of their sound; first according to corresponding sounds and then according to the musical scale.

SOURCE: Adapted from R. Orem (Ed.), *A Montessori Handbook: Dr. Montessori's Own Handbook* (New York: Putnam's Sons, 1965).

Teachers in Montessori classrooms are facilitators and observers of children's activities. By using skillfully crafted lessons, the teacher (or *directress* in Montessori terminology) slowly and carefully demonstrates concepts to the children. Ideas are presented to the students in small, sequential steps and build on previous experiences that form the basis for the next level of skill development. Teachers foster the development of independence in their students. A Montessori-designed classroom is typically focused on individual student activities rather than group work.

Many of Montessori's beliefs and concepts are directly applicable to young children with disabilities. Morrison (2009), based on the Circle of Inclusion Project at the University of Kansas, identified ten elements of Montessori's work that are relevant to teaching youngsters with special needs.

- *The use of mixed-age groupings.* The mixed-age groupings found within a Montessori classroom are conducive to a successful inclusion experience. Mixed-age groupings necessitate a wide range of materials within each classroom to meet the individual needs of children rather than the average need of the group.
- *Individualization within the context of a supportive classroom community.* The individualized curriculum in Montessori classrooms is compatible with the individualization required for children with disabilities. Work in a Montessori classroom is introduced to children according to individual readiness rather than chronological age.
- *An emphasis on functionality within the Montessori environment.* Real objects are used rather than toy replications whenever possible (e.g., children cut bread with a real knife, sweep up crumbs on the

Montessori classrooms are characterized by their attractive learning materials and equipment.

Cengage Learning

floor with a real broom, and dry wet tables with cloths.) In a Montessori classroom, the primary goal is to prepare children for life. Special education also focuses on the development of functional skills.

- *The development of independence and the ability to make choices.* Montessori classrooms help all children make choices and become independent learners in many ways; for example, children may choose any material for which they have had a lesson given by the teacher. This development of independence is especially appropriate for children with disabilities.
- *The development of organized work patterns in children.* One objective of the practical life area and the beginning point for every young child is the development of organized work habits. Children with disabilities who need to learn to be organized in their work habits and their use of time benefit from this emphasis.
- *The classic Montessori demonstration.* Demonstrations themselves have value for learners who experience disabilities. A demonstration uses a minimum of language selected specifically for its relevance to the activity and emphasizes an orderly progression from the beginning to the end of the task.
- *An emphasis on repetition.* Children with special needs typically require lots of practice and make progress in small increments.

- *Materials with a built-in control of error.* Materials that have a built-in control of error benefit all children. Because errors are obvious, children notice and correct them without the help of a teacher.
- *Academic materials that provide a concrete representation of the abstract.* Montessori classrooms offer a wide range of concrete materials that children can learn from as a regular part of the curriculum. For children with disabilities, the use of concrete materials is critical to promote real learning.
- *Sensory materials that develop and organize incoming sensory perceptions.* Sensory materials can develop and refine each sense in isolation. A child who cannot see will benefit enormously from materials that train and refine the sense of touch, hearing, and smell, for example (Morrison, 2009, p. 148).

Jean Piaget. Jean Piaget (1896–1980) is one of the major contributors to our understanding of how children think. He is considered by many to be the premiere expert on the development of knowledge in children and young adults.

Piaget studied in Paris, where he had the opportunity to work with Theodore Simon, who in conjunction with Alfred Binet was constructing the first test for assessing children's intelligence. While standardizing the children's responses to test questions, Piaget became extremely interested in the incorrect answers given by the youngsters. His careful observations led him to notice that they gave similar wrong answers. He also discovered that the children made different types of errors at different ages. This paved the way for Piaget to investigate the thinking process that led to incorrect responses.

According to Piaget's (1963, 1970) point of view, children's mode of thinking is qualitatively and fundamentally different from that of adults. He also believed that children's thought processes are modified as they grow and mature. Because Piaget's ideas about intellectual development are complex, only his basic concepts will be presented.

First, it is important to understand Piaget's (1963, 1970) view of intelligence. He was concerned with *how* knowledge is acquired. Piaget avoids stating a precise definition of intelligence; instead, he attempts to describe it in general terms. Piaget speaks of intelligence as an instance of biological adaptation. He also looks at intelligence as a balance or equilibrium between an individual's cognitive structures and the

Piaget is widely recognized for his ideas on the development of the intellect.

Bettmann/Corbis

environment. His focus is on what people *do* as they interact with their environment. Knowledge of reality must be discovered and constructed—it results from a child's actions within, and reactions to, their world. It is also important to note that Piaget is not concerned with individual differences in intelligence (Ginsburg & Opper, 1969).

Piaget's (1970) theory rests on the contributions of maturational and environmental influences. Maturation establishes a sequence of cognitive stages controlled by heredity. The environment contributes the child's experiences, which dictate how they develop. Thinking is a process of interaction between the child and the environment. Graves (1990) describes children as "active agents who interact with the social and physical world" (p. 198). Youngsters are self-motivated in the construction of their own knowledge, which occurs through activity.

One consequence of interaction with the environment is that the person soon develops organizing structures or **schema.** These schema, or mental concepts, become a basis from which later cognitive structures are established. Piaget developed three concepts that he believes individuals use to organize their personal experiences into a blueprint for thinking. He called these adaptive processes assimilation, accommodation, and equilibration.

Assimilation occurs when the child is able to integrate new experiences and information into existing schemes, that is, what the child already knows. Children will view new situations in light of previous experiences in their world. As an illustration, when a toddler first encounters a pony, she will most likely call it a dog, something the youngster is already familiar with.

Accommodation is Piaget's second process. It involves modifying existing cognitive structures so that new data can be effectively utilized. Current thought patterns and behavior are changed to fit new situations. Accommodation involves a change in understanding. For example, two-year-old Victoria visits Santa Claus at the mall. Later that day she is shopping with her mother and sees an elderly gentleman with a long white beard whom she calls Santa Claus. Victoria's mother corrects her daughter's mistake by saying that the man is old. When Victoria next meets a man with a white beard, she asks, "Are you Santa Claus or are you just old?" Victoria has demonstrated accommodation—she changed her knowledge base.

Assimilation and accommodation are involved in the final process of equilibration. Here an attempt is made to achieve a balance or equilibrium between assimilation and accommodation. Piaget believed that all activity involves both processes. The interaction between assimilation and accommodation leads to adaptation, a process of adjusting

TeachSource Video

Piaget's Preoperational Stage

Watch "Piaget's Preoperational Stage, available on the premium website for this text." After watching the video, answer the following questions:

1. What types of materials would you include in an activity center to help develop symbolic reasoning?
2. Why do preoperational children have difficulty with conversation tasks?

TABLE 1–2 Piaget's Stages of Cognitive Development

Approximate Age	Stage	Distinguishing Characteristics
Birth — 1½ – 2 years of age	Sensorimotor	• Knowledge constructed through sensory perception and motor activity. • Thought limited to action schemes. • Beginning to develop object permanence.
2 – 7 years of age	Preoperational	• Emergence of language and symbolic thinking. • Intuitive rather than logical schemes. • Egocentric in thought and action.
7 – 11 years of age	Concrete operations	• Beginning of logical, systematic thinking; limited however, to concrete operations. • Diminished egocentrism. • Understands reversibility and laws of conversation.
12 years of age – adulthood	Formal operations	• Abstract and logical thought present. • Capable of solving hypothetical problems. • Deductive thinking and scientific reasoning is possible. • Evidences concern about social issues, political causes.

to new situations. **Equilibration** is the tendency to reach a balance, which accounts for the formation of knowledge. Intellectual growth, according to Piaget, is achieved through the interplay of these three processes.

Four stages of cognitive development were identified by Piaget. Children pass through these stages in an orderly, sequential fashion. Each stage is a prerequisite for the next one. The ages identified in Table 1–2 are only rough estimates of when a youngster enters each stage. Children progress at their own rate, which is influenced by their experiences and existing cognitive structures, in addition to their maturation.

Lev Vygotsky. Russian psychologist Lev Semenovich Vygotsky (1896–1934) was a contemporary of Piaget and another influential contributor to present understanding of how children learn and develop.

A brilliant young man (he was literate in eight languages), Vygotsky entered Moscow University in 1914, where he studied law, one of the few vocations open to a Jew in tsarist Russia. Upon graduation in 1917, he returned to the city of Gomel, where he had spent most of his youth, and taught in several local institutions. The massive changes brought about by the Russian Revolution provided Vygotsky with the opportunity to teach at Gomel's Teacher's College. It was here that he became attracted to the fields of psychology and education, where his lack of formal training as a psychologist proved a distinct advantage. It allowed Vygotsky to look at the field of psychology as an outsider, someone with fresh perspectives and creative ideas about child development (Berk & Winsler, 1995). A visionary thinker, Vygotsky's theories and beliefs significantly shaped contemporary thinking about children's language, play, cognition, and social development.

In his book, *Mind in Society,* Vygotsky (1978) argues that people—children in particular—are the products of their social and cultural environments. Children's development is significantly influenced by their social and cultural worlds and the individuals they come into contact with such as parents, teachers, and peers. Social experiences were very important to Vygotsky because he believed that higher-order cognitive processes, such

RIA Novosti/Alamy

Vygotsky emphasized the importance of social interaction.

relationships, however, is contrary to the theorizing of Piaget. Recall that Piaget saw children as active yet solitary and independent discoverers of knowledge.

Perhaps the best-known Vygotskian concept is the **zone of proximal development (ZPD).** Simply described, it is a hypothetical region defined by Vygotsky (1978) as "the distance between the actual developmental level as determined by independent problem solving and the level of potential development as determined through problem solving under adult guidance or in collaboration with more capable peers" (p. 86). The ZPD exists between what a youngster can presently accomplish independently and what the child is capable of doing within a supportive environment. Support is typically viewed as coming from more mature thinkers like adults and competent peers, although, according to Hills (1992), it may be derived from materials and equipment. The ZPD is actually created, Tudge (1992) writes, through social interaction. It is the arena or "magic middle" (Berger, 2007) in which learning and cognitive development takes place. Figure 1–2 portrays Vygotsky's concept of ZPD.

Scaffolding is an idea related to Vygotsky's notion of a ZPD. It refers to the assistance given to a child by adults and peers that allows the individual to function independently and construct new concepts. Social interaction and collaboration with others typically provide youngsters with opportunities for scaffolding. One of the primary goals of scaffolding is to keep children working on tasks that are in their ZPD. This goal is generally obtained by providing the minimum amount of assistance necessary and then further reducing this aid as the child's own competence grows (Berk & Winsler, 1995). Within this context, the teacher's role is one of promoting and facilitating pupils' learning.

as language and cognition, necessitate social interaction. What begins in a social context is eventually internalized psychologically. In his writings, Vygotsky emphasized the link between the social and psychological worlds of the youngster. Learning and development occur via social interaction and engagement.

> Learning awakens a variety of developmental processes that are able to operate only when the child is interacting with people in his environment and in collaboration with his peers. Once these processes are internalized, they become part of the child's independent developmental achievement.
> (VYGOTSKY, 1978, p. 90)

Vygotsky (1978, 1986) believed that social interaction not only fosters intellectual development, but also is vital to the development of social competence. Vygotsky's emphasis on the reciprocity of social

TeachSource Video

Lev Vygotsky, the Zone of Proximal Development, and Scaffolding

Watch "Lev Vygotsky, the Zone of Proximal Development, and Scaffolding, available on the premium website for this text." After watching the video, answer the following questions:

1. How can an inclusive learning environment help develop the cognitive competence of a young child with a developmental delay or a disability?
2. What learning strategies would you use to enhance children's learning?

FIGURE 1–2 Vygotsky's Zone of Proximal Development

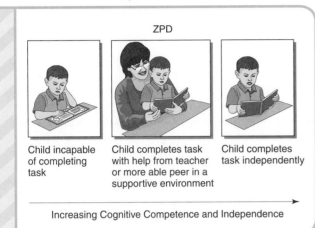

ZPD

Child incapable of completing task

Child completes task with help from teacher or more able peer in a supportive environment

Child completes task independently

Increasing Cognitive Competence and Independence

As we have just seen, collaboration and social interaction are key tenets in Vygotsky's sociocultural approach to understanding children's learning and development. For Vygotsky, learning leads to development rather than following it. Learning is not itself development; rather, structured learning experiences play a major role giving impetus to developmental processes that would be difficult to separate from learning (Tudge, 1992). According to Vygotsky, development and learning are neither identical nor separate processes; instead, they are interrelated and integrative functions. This perspective sees developmental change as arising from a child's active engagement in a social environment with a mature partner. Growth occurs, therefore, within this ZPD. His approach to education could accurately be described as one of assisted discovery, also known as guided practice or assisted performance (Berk & Winsler, 1995).

Vygotsky also spoke to the issue of children with disabilities. In fact, he enjoyed the title "Father of Soviet Defectology," which loosely translates to mean special education. Vygotsky (1993) was of the opinion that the principles that govern the learning and development of typical youngsters also apply to children with disabilities. He was firmly convinced that the optimal development of young children with special needs rested on fully integrating them into their social environment while ensuring that instruction occurs within their ZPD (Berk & Winsler, 1995). Children with learning problems should be educated, according

to Vygotsky, in the same fashion as their peers without disabilities.

One of the major difficulties encountered by children with disabilities is how the impairment modifies their interaction with, and participation in, their social environment and not the disability itself. A child's disability results in restricted interactions with adults and peers and this contributes to the creation of a secondary—yet more debilitating—social deficit. Potentially more harmful than the primary disability, Vygotsky believed that these cultural deficits are more amenable to intervention than the original disorder is.

Several contemporary practices in early childhood special education can be traced to Vygotsky's thinking. His conceptualizations suggest that young children with special needs should be included as much as possible in environments designed for typically developing learners. As an early advocate of integration, Vygotsky believed that a segregated placement results in a different social climate, thus restricting students' interactions and collaborative opportunities and thereby limiting cognitive development. Furthermore, educators should focus on students' strengths and abilities rather than their weaknesses. What a student can do (with or without assistance) is more important than what he or she cannot do. Finally, a student's learning (social) environment should be rich with opportunities for scaffolding, which is seen as assisting in development of higher-order cognitive processes.

Vygotsky's contributions to children's learning and development were not limited to children with disabilities. Many well-known instructional strategies are grounded in his theories. Teachers who engage in cooperative learning activities, peer tutoring, guided practice, reciprocal teaching, and incorporate mixed-age groupings or a whole-language approach can thank Vygotsky.

A Concluding Thought. Our brief examination of the historical roots of early childhood general education suggests two conclusions. First, efforts on behalf of young children were and are frequently constrained by the political and social realities of the times. Second, much of what we often consider new or innovative has been written about and tried before. Present services for young children with disabilities have been influenced significantly by the history of education for young children. As an illustration, many contemporary programs for young children with special needs emphasize parent involvement, a child-centered curriculum, and interventions based on practical applications of child development theory. These programs also recognize that early experiences impact later social, emotional, and intellectual competency (Meisels & Shonkoff, 2000).

Table 1–3 presents a brief summary of the contributions of key individuals to the development of the field of early childhood education. We now turn our attention to the contributions emerging from our second parent field—special education.

TABLE 1–3   Key Contributors to the Development of Early Childhood Education

Sixteenth Century	
Martin Luther	Strong believer in publicly supported schools. Advocate of universal, compulsory education.
Seventeenth and Eighteenth Century	
Jan Ámos Comenius	Advanced the notion of lifelong education, beginning in the early years. Realized the importance of a child's readiness for an activity. Stressed student's active participation in the learning process.
John Locke	Believed that children are similar to a blank tablet (tabula rasa). Environmental influences strongly impact a child's development. Sensory training is a critical aspect of learning.
Jean-Jacques Rousseau	Emphasized the importance of early education, which should be natural and allow for the unfolding of a child's abilities. School should focus on the interests of children.
Johann Heinrich Pestalozzi	Advocated education through nature and following the child's natural development. Early champion of the whole child and involving parents in the education process. Promoter of sensory education.
Nineteenth Century	
Robert Owen	Theorized that the early years were important in developing a youngster's character and behavior. Linked social change and education. His Infant Schools served as a forerunner of kindergartens.
Friedrich Wilhelm Froebel	Established first kindergarten. Believed in the educational value and benefit of play. Considered development as a natural process of unfolding that provides the foundation for children's learning.
Twentieth Century	
John Dewey	Founder of the school of thought known as Progressivism. Argued that learning flows from the interests of the child rather than from activities chosen by the teacher. Coined the phrases "child-centered curriculum" and "child-centered schools." Saw education as a process for living; stressed social responsibility.
Maria Montessori	Believed that children learn best by direct sensory experience; was also convinced that there are sensitive periods for learning. Designed learning materials that were self-correcting, graded in difficulty, and allowed for independent use. Classroom experiences were individualized to meet the needs of each pupil.
Jean Piaget	Developed a stage theory of cognitive development. Cognitive growth emerges from a child's interaction with and adaptation to his physical environment. Youngsters are self-motivated in the construction of their own knowledge, which occurs through activity and discovery.
Lev Semenovich Vygotsky	Russian psychologist who theorized that children's development is significantly influenced by their social and cultural environments and the youngster's interactions with individuals therein. Saw learning and development as interrelated and integrative functions. Originator of the concept of a zone of proximal development (ZPD).

The Development of Special Education: Historical Perspectives on Children with Disabilities

The history of special education provides a second point of departure for examining the evolution of early childhood special education. Society has chosen to deal with such individuals in a variety of ways. Oftentimes, programs and practices for individuals with special needs are a reflection of the prevailing social climate, in addition to people's ideas and attitudes about exceptionality. A change in attitude is often a precursor to a change in the delivery of services. The foundation of societal attitude in the United States can be traced to the efforts and philosophies of various Europeans. We now turn our attention to the historical contributions of these individuals with vision and courage.

People and Ideas

Present educational theories, principles, and practices are the product of pioneering thinkers, advocates, and humanitarians. These dedicated reformers were catalysts for change. Historians typically trace the roots of special education to the late 1700s and early 1800s. It is here that we begin our brief examination of early leaders in the field.

One of the earliest documented attempts at providing special education were the efforts of Jean Marc Gaspard Itard (1775–1838) to educate Victor, the so-called "wild boy of Aveyron." A French physician and expert on hearing impairment, Itard endeavored in 1799 to "civilize" and teach Victor through a sensory training program and what today would be known as operant procedures. Because this adolescent failed to fully develop language after years of instruction and only mastered basic social and self-help skills, Itard considered his efforts a failure. Yet Itard demonstrated that learning was possible even for an individual described by other professionals as a hopeless and incurable idiot. The title Father of Special Education is bestowed on Itard because of his groundbreaking work more than 200 years ago.

Another important pioneer was Itard's student, Edouard Seguin (1812–1880), who designed instructional programs for children his contemporaries

thought to be incapable of learning. He believed in the importance of sensorimotor activities as an aid to learning. Seguin's methodology was based on a comprehensive assessment of a youngster's strengths and weaknesses coupled with an intervention plan of sensorimotor exercises prescribed to remediate specific disabilities. Seguin also emphasized the critical importance of early education. He is considered one of the first early interventionists. His theorizing also provided the foundation for Montessori's later work with the urban poor and children with mental retardation.

The work of Itard, Seguin, and other innovators of their time helped to establish a foundation for much of what we do today in special education. Table 1–4 summarizes the work of European and American pioneers whose ideas have significantly influenced special education in the United States.

The Establishment of Institutions

Taking their cues from the Europeans, other American reformers such as Boston physician and humanitarian Samuel Gridley Howe (1801–1876) spearheaded the establishment of residential programs. A successful teacher of students who were both deaf and blind, Howe was instrumental in establishing the New England Asylum for the Blind (later the Perkins School) in the early 1830s. Almost two decades later, he played a major role in founding an experimental residential school for children with mental retardation, the Massachusetts School for the Idiotic and Feebleminded Youth. The first institution in the United States for individuals with mental retardation, it is now called the Fernald Developmental Center.

Residential schools for children with disabilities received additional impetus due to the untiring and vigorous efforts of social activist Dorothea Dix (1802–1887). A retired teacher, Dix was very influential in helping to establish several state institutions for people believed to be mentally ill, a group of individuals she felt to be grossly underserved and largely mistreated.

By the conclusion of the nineteenth century, residential institutions for persons with exceptionalities were a well-established part of the American social fabric. Initially established to offer training and some form of education in a protective lifelong environment, these institutions gradually deteriorated, for a variety of reasons, in the early decades of the

TABLE 1–4 Pioneering Contributors to the Development of Special Education

Contributors	Their Ideas
Jacob Rodrigues Pereine (1715–1780)	Introduced the idea that persons who were deaf could be taught to communicate. Developed an early form of sign language. Provided inspiration and encouragement for the work of Itard and Seguin.
Philippe Pinel (1745–1826)	A reformed-minded French physician who was concerned with the humanitarian treatment of individuals with mental illness. Strongly influenced the later work of Itard.
Jean Marc Gaspard Itard (1775–1838)	A French doctor who secured lasting fame due to his systematic efforts to educate an adolescent thought to be severely mentally retarded. Recognized the importance of sensory stimulation.
Thomas Gallaudet (1787–1851)	Taught children with hearing impairments to communicate via a system of manual signs and symbols. Established the first institution for individuals with deafness in the United States.
Samuel Gridley Howe (1801–1876)	An American physician and educator accorded international fame due to his success in teaching individuals with visual and hearing impairments. Founded the first residential facility for the blind and was instrumental in inaugurating institutional care for children with mental retardation.
Dorothea Lynde Dix (1802–1887)	A contemporary of S. G. Howe, Dix was one of the first Americans to champion better and more humane treatment of people with mental illness. Instigated the establishment of several institutions for individuals with mental disorders.
Louis Braille (1809–1852)	A French educator, who himself was blind, who developed a tactile system of reading and writing for people who were blind. His system, based on a code of six embossed dots, is still used today. This standardized code is known as Standard English Braille.
Edouard Seguin (1812–1880)	A pupil of Itard, Seguin was a French physician responsible for developing teaching methods for children with mental retardation. His training program emphasized sensorimotor activities. After immigrating to the United States, he helped found the organization that was a forerunner of the American Association on Intellectual and Developmental Disabilities.
Francis Galton (1822–1911)	Scientist concerned with individual differences. As a result of studying eminent persons, he believed that genius is solely the result of heredity. Those with superior abilities are born, not made.
Alfred Binet (1857–1911)	A French psychologist, Binet authored the first developmental assessment scale capable of quantifying intelligence. Also originated the concept of mental age with his colleague Theodore Simon.
Lewis Terman (1877–1956)	An American educator and psychologist who revised Binet's original assessment instrument. The result was the publication of the StanfordBinet Intelligence Scale. Terman developed the notion of intelligence quotient (IQ). Also famous for lifelong study of gifted individuals. Credited as being the grandfather of gifted education.

Institutions at one time were very common across the United States.

Jerry Cooke/Time & Life Pictures/Getty Images

twentieth century. The mission of the institutions changed from training to one of custodial care and isolation. The early optimism of special education was replaced by prejudice, unproven scientific views, and fear that helped to convert institutions into gloomy warehouses for the forgotten and neglected (Gargiulo, 2009).

Special Education in Public Schools

It was not until the latter part of the nineteenth century that special education began to appear in the public schools. In fact, in 1898 Alexander Graham Bell (1847–1922), a teacher of children who were deaf, advocated that public schools begin serving individuals with disabilities. Services for pupils with exceptionalities began slowly and served only a small minority of those who needed it. The first public school class was organized in Boston in 1869 to serve children who were deaf. Children thought to be mentally retarded first attended public schools about three decades later when a class was established in Providence, Rhode Island. The Chicago public schools inaugurated a class for children with physical impairments in 1899, quickly followed by one for children who were blind in 1900 (Gargiulo, 2009). By the mid-1920s, well over half of the largest cities in America provided some type of special education services. The establishment of these programs was seen as an indication of the progressive status of the school district. Still, these earliest ventures mainly served children with mild disabilities; individuals with severe or multiple impairments were kept at home or sent to institutions.

Meisels and Shonkoff (2000) assert that the economic depression of the 1930s and the ensuing world war led to the decline of further expansion of special education programs in public schools; instead, greater reliance was placed on institutionalization. The residential facilities, however, were already overcrowded and provided educationally limited experiences. The postwar years saw an increase in the recognition of the needs of Americans with disabilities. Impetus for the shift of societal attitude resulted from two related factors—the large number of men and women deemed unfit for military service and the large number of war veterans who returned home with disabilities.

With the Second World War behind the nation, the stage was set for the rapid expansion of special education. This growth has been described as a virtual explosion of services occurring at both the state and federal levels. Litigation at all levels, legislative activities, increased fiscal resources, and federal leadership, in addition to social and political activism and advocacy, are some of the factors that helped fuel the movement and revitalize special education (Gargiulo, 2009). Significant benefits for children with exceptionalities resulted from these efforts. For example, in 1948 approximately 12% of children with disabilities were receiving an education appropriate for their needs (Ballard, Ramirez, & Weintraub, 1982), yet from 1947 to 1972 the number of pupils enrolled in special education programs increased an astonishing 716% as compared to an 82% increase in total public school enrollment (Dunn, 1973).

The last decades of the twentieth century have also witnessed a flurry of activity on behalf of students with special needs. Evidence of this trend includes the 1975 landmark legislation PL 94-142, the Individuals with Disabilities Education Act (IDEA) (originally known as the Education for All Handicapped Children Act) and its 1986 Amendments—PL 99-457; they constitute one of the most comprehensive pieces of legislation affecting infants, toddlers, and preschoolers with special needs and their families. The growth of services for preschoolers who are at risk or disabled, infant and toddler programs, the transition initiative, and calls for full integration of pupils with disabilities (discussed in Chapter 6) are additional indications of a changing attitude and expansion of opportunities for children and youth with exceptionalities.

Compensatory Education Programs

The **compensatory education** movement of the 1960s also played a major role in the development of early childhood special education. As the name implies, this effort was designed to compensate for or ameliorate the environmental conditions and early learning experiences of youngsters living in poverty. Such children were thought to be disadvantaged or "culturally deprived" (a popular term in the 1960s). The goal of compensatory education programs was to assist these students "by providing educational and environmental experiences that might better prepare them for the school experience" (Gearheart, Mullen, & Gearhart, 1993, p. 385). The compensatory education movement had its foundation in the idealism and heightened social consciousness that typified America over four decades ago. It was also aided by the convergence of three distinct social issues: President Kennedy's interest in the field of mental retardation, President Johnson's declaration of a War on Poverty, and the emerging civil rights movement (Meisels & Shonkoff, 2000).

In addition to sociological reasons, the compensatory education movement was aided by solid theoretical arguments. The cogent and persuasive writings of J. McVicker Hunt (1961) and fellow scholar Benjamin Bloom (1964) raised serious questions about the assumption of fixed or static intelligence. The malleability of intelligence and the importance of the early years for intellectual development were recognized by scientists and policymakers alike. Thus the powerful contribution of early and enriched experiences on later development laid the cornerstone for programs like Head Start. It also set the stage for the concept of early intervention. It was thought that the deleterious effects of poverty could be remediated by early and intensive programming. The emphasis of preschool programs shifted from custodial caregiving to programming for specific developmental gains (Thurman & Widerstrom, 1990).

Representative Compensatory Programs

Project Head Start. **Project Head Start** came into existence as a result of the 1964 Economic Opportunity Act. Federally sponsored, Head Start was a critical component of a larger national agenda called the War on Poverty. As the first nationwide compensatory education program, Head Start was conceived as an early intervention effort aimed at reducing the potential for school failure in disadvantaged young children from low socioeconomic (impoverished) communities. Initiated in the summer of 1965 as an eight-week pilot program, Project Head Start served approximately 560,000 four- and five-year-old youngsters in more than 2,500 communities. Since its inception more than four decades ago, Head Start has served more than 25 million children and their families (Head Start Fact Sheet, 2008).

According to Zigler and Valentine (1979), the first volley on the War on Poverty was constructed around three fundamental ideas:

1. compensatory experiences initiated in the preschool years would result in successful adjustment to school and enhanced academic performance;
2. early intellectual growth and development is directly dependent upon the quality of care and type of experiences to which young children are exposed; and
3. socioeconomically impoverished environments include biological, environmental, and other risk factors, which can adversely affect chances of school success and impede intellectual growth.

Head Start was envisioned to be a comprehensive, multidimensional intervention effort aimed at the very roots of poverty in communities across America. It represented a coordinated federal effort at comprehensive intervention in the lives of young children (Zigler & Valentine, 1979). Head Start was unique in its emphasis on the total development of the youngster, on strengthening the family unit, and in its comprehensive nature of the services provided. The goals of the Head Start effort included increasing the child's physical, social, and emotional development; developing the youngster's intellectual skills and readiness for school; and improving the health of the child by providing medical, dental, social, and psychological services. Head Start was also unusual not only in its intent—to bring about a change for the child, her family, and the community—but also for its use of a multidisciplinary intervention model wherein the importance of seeing the whole child was recognized (Brain, 1979).

Head Start was the first nationwide compensatory education program.

Cengage Learning

- quicker screening of children suspected of needing special services;
- revised evaluation procedures for determining who might be eligible for special education and related services; and
- the establishment of a disability services coordinator who would be responsible for overseeing the delivery of services to preschoolers with special needs.

These goals are to be met through a detailed and comprehensive disabilities service plan, which outlines the strategies for meeting the needs of children with disabilities and their families. Among the several provisions are standards that call for the assurance that youngsters with disabilities will be included in the full range of activities and services provided to other children; a component that addresses the transitioning from infant and toddler programs into Head Start as well as exiting Head Start to the next placement; and a provision stipulating that eligible children will be provided a special education with related services designed to meet their unique needs. Currently, slightly more than 12% of the preschoolers enrolled in Head Start have an identified disability (Head Start Fact Sheet, 2008).

We consider Head Start to be a visionary program model. The framers of the project had the foresight to insist on comprehensive services, meaningful parent involvement, and a multidisciplinary approach to intervention. Many of these aspects can be found in contemporary programs and legislation. Head Start also served as a forerunner of other compensatory initiatives, which we will now briefly examine.

Parents played an unprecedented role in the Head Start program. Parents' involvement and their meaningful participation were considered vitally important. They had a key voice in the local decision-making process in addition to opportunities for employment in the program or for volunteering their expertise. The inclusion of training programs for low-income adults and the establishment of a career development ladder for employees and volunteers also distinguished the Head Start program.

It is important to remember that Head Start was not specifically directed at children with special needs, although many of the youngsters served would today be identified as an at-risk population. The enactment of PL 92-424 in 1972 did require, however, that the project reserve no less than 10% of its enrollment for children with disabilities.

Fortunately, thanks to changes in federal regulations regarding Head Start, this program is now able to play a larger role in the lives of young children with special needs. In January 1993, new rules for providing services to preschoolers with disabilities enrolled in Head Start were published in the *Federal Register*. Some of the many changes guiding Head Start agencies are the following requirements:

- a model designed to locate and serve young children with disabilities and their parents;
- the development of an individualized education program (IEP) for each youngster determined to be disabled;

Project Follow-Through. **Project Follow-Through** was developed in 1967 in response to controversy surrounding the effectiveness of the Head Start efforts. Some educational research data suggested that the cognitive gains of the Head Start experiment were not maintained once the children enrolled in elementary school (Cicerelli, Evans, & Schiller, 1969). Professionals quickly realized that a short-term intervention program was ineffective in inoculating young children against the deleterious effects of poverty. Follow-Through was introduced in an effort to continue the gains developed in Head Start. A new model was designed, which extended the Head Start concept to include children enrolled in kindergarten through the third grade. Like its predecessor, Project Follow-Through was comprehensive in its scope of services while maintaining the Head Start emphasis on creating change in the home and community. Unfortunately, a Congressional funding crisis precipitated a retooling of the project's original goals and objectives. According to Peterson's analysis (1987), the focus shifted from a service operation very much like Head Start to an educational experiment dedicated to assessing the effectiveness of various approaches aimed at increasing the educational attainment of young disadvantaged and at-risk students. Rather than offering a single model of early childhood education for low-income pupils, Project Follow-Through studied a variety of approaches and strategies, realizing that a singular model would not meet the needs of all children. Local public schools were free to adopt the program model that they believed best met the unique needs of their communities.

Home Start. In 1972 another program variation, **Home Start,** was created. Simply stated, this program took the education component typically found in Head Start centers into a child's home. The focus of Home Start was low-income parents and their preschool-aged children. Efforts were aimed at providing educational stimulation to the children in addition to developing and enhancing the parenting skills of adults. This task was accomplished through the utilization of home visitors who were skilled and trained residents of the community.

Early Head Start. Early Head Start emerged from a growing recognition among service providers, researchers, policymakers, and politicians of the need to extend the Head Start model downward to the birth-to-three age group. This awareness of the need for comprehensive, intensive, and year-round services for very young children resulted in **Early Head Start** (Halpern, 2000; Meisels & Shonkoff, 2000). The 1994 reauthorization of Head Start (PL 103–252) created Early Head Start, a program focusing on low-income families with infants and toddlers as well as on women who are pregnant. The mission of this program, which began in 1995, is to

- promote healthy pregnancy outcomes;
- enhance children's physical, social, emotional, and cognitive development;

- enable parents to be better caregivers and teachers to their children; and
- help parents meet their goals, including economic independence.

Early Head Start incorporates what its framers call a "four corner emphasis," which embodies child, family, community, and staff development (Allen & Cowdery, 2009). Services provided through this program include high-quality early education and care both in and out of the home; home visits; child care; parent education; comprehensive health services including services before, during, and after pregnancy; nutrition information; and peer support groups for parents. Since its beginning, Early Head Start has evolved into a nationwide effort of more than 730 community-based programs serving approximately 85,000 infants and toddlers (Early Head Start Research and Evaluation Project, 2009).

Research Activities

In addition to involvement and action by the federal government, individual scientists and researchers have also been concerned about the damaging consequences of poverty on young children and their families. Two representative intervention projects include the Carolina Abecedarian Project and the Perry Preschool Project. Both of these programs focus on improving the cognitive skills of young children, thereby increasing their chances for later scholastic success.

The Carolina Abecedarian Project attempted to modify environmental forces impinging upon the intellectual development of young children living in poverty. Designed in 1972 as a longitudinal experiment, Craig Ramey and his colleagues (Ramey & Campbell, 1977, 1984; Ramey & Smith, 1977) found that children enrolled in a center-based preschool intervention program who were exposed to intensive and stimulating early learning experiences achieved higher IQ scores when compared to matched age-mates who did not participate in the project. A follow-up of participants found that, at age twelve and fifteen, youngsters exposed to early intervention continued to outperform control subjects on standardized measures of intellectual development and academic achievement. Additionally, these individuals had significantly fewer grade retentions and special education placements (Campbell &

Ramey, 1994, 1995). As young adults, these individuals scored higher on measures of intellectual and academic achievement and were more likely to attend a four-year college (Campbell, Ramey, Pungello, Sparling, & Miller-Johnson, 2002). The Carolina program clearly demonstrates, as we noted earlier, the plasticity of intelligence and the positive effects of early environmental intervention.

Our second illustration is the Perry Preschool Project in Ypsilanti, Michigan. This program is one of the best examples of the long-term educational benefit of early childhood experiences. The Perry Preschool Project was designed as a longitudinal study to measure the effects of a quality preschool education on children living in poverty. Based on the work of Jean Piaget, it strongly emphasized cognitive development. More than 120 disadvantaged youngsters were followed from age three until late adolescence. The results of the investigation can be summarized as follows:

> Results to age 19 indicate long-lasting beneficial effects of preschool education in improving cognitive performance during early childhood; in improving scholastic placement and achievement during the school years; in decreasing delinquency and crime, the use of welfare assistance, and the incidence of teenage pregnancy; and in increasing high school graduation rates and the frequency of enrollment in postsecondary programs and employment.
> (BERRUETA-CLEMENT, SCHWEINHART, BARNETT, EPSTEIN, & WEIKART, 1984, P. 1)

Additional follow-up (Schweinhart, Barnes, & Weikart, 1993) demonstrated that, in comparison to a control group, individuals in their mid-20s who participated in this project as preschoolers had higher incomes, were more likely to own a home, had significantly fewer arrests, and had less involvement with community social service agencies.

Despite the methodological difficulties inherent in conducting early intervention research in a scientifically rigorous fashion, these two examples unequivocally illustrate that early intervention generates positive academic outcomes and significantly improves the quality of participants' later lives. We fully agree with Guralnick's (2005) observation that "the early years may well constitute a unique window of opportunity to alter children's' developmental trajectories" (p. 314).

A Concluding Thought. It is safe to conclude that, generally speaking, compensatory education programs do benefit young children at risk for limited success in school. The optimism exhibited by the early supporters of various intervention initiatives has been tempered, however, by a host of political, financial, and other factors. Reality has reminded educators, policymakers, and researchers that there are no quick or magical solutions to complex social problems like poverty. Yet we must not be overly pessimistic; education does remain an important vehicle for successfully altering the lives of young children and their caregivers.

Summary

Although early childhood special education is a relatively young field, the forces that have helped to shape its identity have a rich and distinguished history. Drawing upon the work of earlier educational theorists and writers such as Piaget, Vygotsky, Montessori, Dewey, and others, early childhood special education has evolved into a distinct field with its own identity and theoretical underpinnings. Yet it is interesting to note that many of the current practices in early childhood special education (for example, individualized instruction, parent involvement) and the values to which we subscribe are not especially contemporary. Perhaps there is truth to the maxim that "The past is prologue." Three distinct fields— early childhood general education, special education, and compensatory education—have contributed, in their own ways, to the emergence of a wide array of programs and services for young children with special needs and their families. Professionals recognize how very important the early years of a child's life are for later social, emotional, and cognitive growth and development.

Today's early childhood special education is perhaps best conceptualized as a synthesis of various theories, principles, and practices borrowed from each of its parent fields. It is a concept that continues to evolve. We are in a strong position to successfully build on the accomplishments and achievements of the past.

Check Your Understanding

1. Various religious leaders, philosophers, and educational theorists played major roles in the development of early childhood education. List five of them and their contributions found in contemporary early childhood programs.
2. Describe the "gifts" and "occupations" of Froebel's children's garden.
3. Explain Dewey's ideas about educating young children.
4. Identify the major elements of Montessori's approach to teaching young children.
5. How did Piaget believe intelligence develops?
6. Describe Vygotsky's concept of zone of proximal development (ZPD).
7. Why would Vygotsky be considered an early advocate of integration?
8. What role did Europeans play in the development of special education in the United States?
9. Define the term *compensatory education*.
10. What is the purpose of Project Head Start and Early Head Start?
11. List five significant events that have helped to shape the field of early childhood special education.

Reflection and Application

1. What evidence do you see of Dewey, Piaget, and Vygotsky in today's early childhood education settings? What are the strengths of each philosophy? Compare and contrast the three philosophies.
2. In what ways do you see contemporary educators building on the work of earlier philosophers? How does each of the philosophers mentioned in this chapter describe curriculum? What are their fundamental ideas about how children learn?
3. What influence does the environment have on infants, toddlers, and young children in today's society? What did Dewey say about the environment and its impact on teaching and learning? What did Piaget and Vygotsky say about the environment and early childhood learning?

4. How has the development of compensatory programs helped to strengthen today's children and families living in poverty? In what ways can early childhood special education programs make compensatory programs available to their children and families? Provide examples.

References

Allen, K., & Cowdery, G. (2009). *The exceptional child* (6th ed.). Clifton Park, NY: Thomson/Delmar.

Ballard, J., Ramirez, B., & Weintraub, F. (1982). *Special education in America: Its legal and governmental foundations.* Reston, VA: Council for Exceptional Children.

Berk, L., & Winsler, A. (1995). *Scaffolding children's learning: Vygotsky and early childhood education.* Washington, DC: National Association for the Education of Young Children.

Berrueta-Clement, J., Schweinhart, L., Barnett, W., Epstein, A., & Weikart, D. (1984). Changed lives: The effects of the Perry Preschool Project on youths through age 19. *Monographs of the High/Scope Education Research Foundation,* 8.

Bloom, B. (1964). *Stability and change in human characteristics.* New York: Wiley.

Brain, G. (1979). The early planners. In E. Zigler & J. Valentine (Eds.), *Project Head Start: A legacy of the war on poverty* (pp. 72–77). New York: Free Press.

Campbell, F., & Ramey, C. (1994). Effects of early intervention on intellectual and academic achievement: A follow-up study of children from low-income families. *Child Development, 65,* 684–698.

Campbell, F., & Ramey, C. (1995). Cognitive and school outcomes for high risk African-American students at middle adolescence: Positive effects of early intervention. *American Educational Research Journal, 32,* 743–772.

Campbell, F., Ramey, C., Pungello, E., Sparling, J., & Miller-Johnson, S. (2002). Early childhood education: Young adult outcomes from the Abecedarian Project. *Applied Developmental Science, 6*(1), 42–57.

Cicerelli, V., Evans, J., & Schiller, J. (1969). *The impact of Head Start on children's cognitive and affective development: Preliminary report.* Washington, DC: Office of Economic Opportunity.

Dewey, J. (1916). *Democracy and education.* New York: Macmillan.

Dunn, L. (1973). *Exceptional children in the schools* (2nd ed). New York: Holt, Rinehart & Winston.

Early Head Start Research and Evaluation Project. (2009). *About Early Head Start.* Retrieved January 27, 2009 from http://www.acf.hhs.gov/programs/opre/ehs/ehs_resrch/ehs_aboutus.html

Federal Register. (1993, January 21). Head Start program final rule. *58*(12), 5492–5518.

Gargiulo, R. (2009). *Special education in contemporary society: An introduction to exceptionality* (3rd ed.). Thousand Oaks, CA: Sage.

Gargiulo, R., & Černá, M. (1992). Special education in Czechoslovakia: Characteristics and issues. *International Journal of Special Education, 7*(1), 60–70.

Gearhart, B., Mullen, R., & Gearhart, C. (1993). *Exceptional individuals.* Pacific Grove, CA: Brooks/Cole.

Ginsburg, H., & Opper, S. (1969). *Piaget's theory of intellectual development.* Englewood Cliffs, NJ: Prentice-Hall.

Graves, S. (1990). Early childhood education. In T. E. C. Smith, *Introduction to education* (2nd ed., pp. 189–219). St. Paul, MN: West.

Graves, S., Gargiulo, R., & Sluder L. (1996). *Young children: An introduction to early childhood education.* St. Paul, MN: West.

Guralnick, M. (2005). Early intervention for children with intellectual disabilities: Current knowledge and future prospects. *Journal of Applied Research in Intellectual Disabilities, 18*(4), 313–324.

Halpern, R. (2000). Early childhood intervention for low-income children and families. In J. Shonkoff & S. Meisels (Eds.), *Handbook of early childhood intervention* (2nd ed., pp. 361–386). Cambridge, England: Cambridge University Press.

Hanson, M., & Lynch, E. (1995). *Early intervention* (2nd ed.). Austin, TX: Pro-Ed.

Head Start Fact Sheet. (2008). Retrieved December 28, 2008 from http://www.acf.hhs.gov/programs/ohs/about/fy2008.html

Hills, T. (1992). Reaching potentials through appropriate assessment. In S. Bredekamp & T. Rosegrant (Eds.), *Reaching potentials: Appropriate curriculum and assessment for young children* (Vol. 1, pp. 43–63). Washington, DC: National Association for the Education of Young Children.

Hunt, J. (1961). *Intelligence and experience.* New York: Ronald Press.

Kilgo, J., (2006). Overview of transdisciplinary teaming in early intervention and early childhood special education. In J. Kilgo (Ed.), *Transdisciplinary teaming in early intervention and early childhood special education* (pp. 9–15). Olney, MD: Association for Childhood Education International.

Lawton, J. (1988). *Introduction to child care and early childhood education.* Glenview, IL: Scott Foresman.

Meisels, S., & Shonkoff, J. (2000). Early childhood intervention: A continuing evolution. In J. Shonkoff & S. Meisels (Eds.), *Handbook of early childhood intervention* (2nd ed., pp. 3–31). Cambridge, England: Cambridge University Press.

Montessori, M. (1965). *Dr. Montessori's own handbook.* New York: Schocken Books.

Morrison, G. (2009). *Early childhood education today* (11th ed.). Upper Saddle River, NJ: Pearson Education.

Peterson, N. (1987). *Early intervention for handicapped and at-risk children.* Denver: Love.

Piaget, J. (1963). *Origins of intelligence in children.* New York: Norton.

Piaget, J. (1970). Piaget's theory. In P. Mussen (Ed.), *Carmichael's manual of child psychology* (3rd ed.) (Vol. 1, pp. 703–732). New York: Wiley.

Ramey, C., & Campbell, F. (1977). Prevention of developmental retardation in high risk children. In P. Mittler (Ed.), *Research to practice in mental retardation: Care and intervention* (Vol. 1, pp. 157–164). Baltimore: University Park Press.

Ramey, C., & Campbell, F. (1984). Preventive education for high risk children: Cognitive consequences of the Carolina Abecedarian Project. *American Journal of Mental Deficiency, 88,* 515–523.

Ramey, C., & Smith, B. (1977). Assessing the intellectual consequences of early intervention with high-risk infants. *American Journal of Mental Deficiency, 81,* 318–324.

Schweinhart, L., Barnes, H., & Weikart, D. (1993). *Significant benefits: The High/Scope Perry Preschool study through age 27.* Ypsilanti, MI: High/Scope Press.

Spodek, B., Saracho, O., & Davis, M. (1991). *Foundations of early childhood education* (2nd ed.). Englewood Cliffs, NJ: Prentice-Hall.

Thurman, S., & Widerstrom, A. (1990). *Infants and young children with special needs* (2nd ed.). Baltimore: Paul H. Brookes.

Tudge, J. (1992). Processes and consequences of peer collaboration: A Vygotskian analysis. *Child Development, 63,* 1364–1379.

Vygotsky, L. (1978). *Mind in society: The development of higher mental processes.* Cambridge, MA: Harvard University Press.

Vygotsky, L., (1986). *Thought and language.* Cambridge, MA: MIT Press.

Vygotsky, L. (1993). *The collected works of L. S. Vygotsky Vol. 2: The fundamentals of defectology.* New York: Plenum.

Zigler, E., & Valentine, J. (Eds.). (1979). *Project Head Start: A legacy of the War on Poverty.* New York: Free Press.

2

The Context of Early Childhood Special Education

Key Terminology

Exceptional children

Disability

Handicap

Developmental delay

At-risk

Established risk

Biological risk

Environmental risk

Early intervention

Early childhood special education

Least restrictive environment (LRE)

Individualized education program (IEP)

Individualized family service plan (IFSP)

Meta-analysis

Ecology

Microsystems

Mesosystems

Exosystems

Macrosystems

Chronosystem

Learning Outcomes

After reading this chapter you will be able to:

- Define the terms disability, handicap, developmental delay, and at-risk.

- Discuss how judicial decisions and legislative enactments have benefited young children with special needs.

- Summarize the major provisions contained in both PL 94-142 and PL 99-457.

- Identify at least four benefits of early intervention for young children with special needs.

- Explain the concept of ecology and its importance to the field of early childhood special education.

Early childhood special education is a relatively young field drawing upon the long history and rich legacy of both early childhood general education and special education in addition to the contributions from compensatory education. Yet early childhood special education is a distinct field having its own identity and purpose. In order to fully appreciate this discipline, several topics basic to the understanding of its development need to be explored. These issues will help provide a firm foundation for the later examination of programs and services for young children with special needs and their families. Attention will be focused on key terminology, the impact of litigation and legislation on the growth of the field, the prevalence of young children with special needs, the research evidence on the efficacy of early intervention, and the validity of an ecological approach for looking at the world of young children with special needs.

Young children with special needs are first and foremost children.

Definitions and Terminology

Early childhood teachers serve a wide range of students. An increasing number of these young children exhibit disabilities, some may have developmental delays, and others might be at risk for future school failure. What do these terms mean? Is a disability synonymous with a handicap? What is a developmental delay? What factors jeopardize a child's future academic success? Unfortunately, clear-cut answers to these basic questions are sometimes difficult to achieve. Confusion and misinterpretation are not unusual, even among professionals. Hence, the following descriptions are an attempt to clarify key terminology and provide a common foundation for understanding infants, toddlers, preschoolers, and early primary students with special needs.

Exceptional Children

Early childhood special educators will frequently identify the children they serve as being **exceptional children.** This inclusive term generally refers to individuals who differ from societal or community standards of normalcy. These children will, therefore, require early intervention or an educational program customized to their unique needs. Some exceptionalities are obvious, while others are less obvious, such

as an infant who is deaf. Furthermore, some young children may greatly benefit from their exceptionality in their daily lives—for example, a child who is intellectually talented—while in other situations an exceptionality may prove to be a significant problem.

Teachers must not lose sight, however, of the fact that a student with an exceptionality is first and foremost a child—a pupil who is more like his or her typically developing peers than he or she is different. The fact that a young child is recognized as exceptional should never prevent professionals from realizing just how typical the individual is in many other ways.

Disability and Handicap

All too often, professionals, as well as the general public, use the terms *disability* and *handicap* interchangeably. These terms, however, have distinct meanings and are not synonymous. When professionals talk about a **disability,** they are referring to the inability of an individual to do something in a certain way. A disability may be thought of as an incapacity to perform as other children will due to impairments in sensory, physical, cognitive, and other areas of functioning. A **handicap,** on the other hand, refers to the problems that a young child with a disability encounters as she attempts to function and interact in her environment. Mandy, for example, has cerebral palsy. This is a disability. If her disability prohibits her from becoming a professional ice skater, then we would say Mandy has a handicap. Stephen, a four-year-old who is legally blind (a disability), would have a handicap if his preschool teacher inadvertently used an overhead projector while explaining a cooking activity. A disability may or may not be a handicap depending upon the specific circumstances. For instance, a six-year-old child with braces on his legs might have difficulty walking upstairs but, in the classroom art center, his creativity and talents are easily demonstrated. We should only use the term *handicap* when explaining the consequences or impact imposed on a young child by his or her disability. Gargiulo (2009) urges educators to separate the disability from the handicap.

We have chosen to use the general term *children with special needs* to describe infants, toddlers, preschoolers, and early primary students with disabilities. We cannot stress enough the importance of remembering that a toddler, or any individual with a disability, is first and foremost a person. It is imperative that teachers focus on the child and not the impairment. Early childhood special educators should look for similarities between children with special needs and their typically developing peers, not differences. Attention should also be focused on the childrens' strengths and abilities, not their disabilities.

Federal Definition of Disability

As we previously noted, early childhood special educators serve a variety of young children with special needs; but who are these children? The federal government, via legislation, the Individuals with Disabilities Education Improvement Act Amendment of 2004 (IDEA) (PL 108-446), defines a student with a disability according to thirteen distinct categories listed in Table 2–1. The government's interpretation of these labels is presented in Appendix B. Individual states frequently use these federal guidelines to construct their own standards and policies as to who is eligible to receive early intervention and special education services.

Developmental Delay and At-Risk

Because of the adverse effects of early labeling, recommended practice suggests that young children with special needs be identified as being either developmentally delayed or in some instances at risk. These terms, in fact, are incorporated in PL 99-457.

TABLE 2–1 Federal Classification of Disabilities

Autism	Orthopedic impairment
Deaf-blindness	Other health impairments
Developmental delay*	Speech or language impairment
Emotional disturbance	Specific learning disability
Hearing impairment	Traumatic brain injury
Mental retardation	Visual impairment
Multiple Disabilities	

*Defined according to individual state guidelines

This significant enactment requires that local schools provide comprehensive services to children ages three to five with disabilities. The children, however, do *not* have to be identified with one of the federal disability labels found in Table 2–1. The 1991 amendments (PL 102-119) to the Individuals with Disabilities Education Act allow states to use a generic category like "children with disabilities." According to a national survey (Danaher, 2007), 17 states utilize a noncategorical description exclusively when classifying preschoolers with special needs. Examples of these generic labels include "preschool child [student] with a disability" (Colorado, Ohio, New York, South Carolina); "preschool special needs" (West Virginia); "individual with exceptional needs" (California); and "preschool disabled" (New Jersey). Many professionals believe that the use of a categorical disability label for most young children is of questionable value (McCollum & Maude, 1993), unfairly stigmatizes young children, and creates a self-fulfilling prophecy (Danaher, 2007). A noncategorical approach to serving young children with special needs is, therefore, perfectly acceptable as well as legal. Many early childhood special education programs offer services without categorizing children on the basis of a disability (McCollum & Maude, 1993; Spodek & Saracho, 1994a). Thus, instead of a categorical approach, we find that programs serving young children with special needs frequently use the broad terms *developmental delay* and *at-risk*.

As a result of the passage of PL 105–17 it is now permissible, at the discretion of the state and local education agency, to use the term *developmental delay* for children ages three through nine. The most recent reauthorization of IDEA, PL 108-446, reiterated the appropriateness of this term for children ages three to nine (or any subset of this group).

Developmental Delay. Congress realized that establishing a national definition of **developmental delay** would be an almost insurmountable task, and therefore, left the responsibility of developing a satisfactory definition to the individual states. One consequence of this action is the tremendous diversity of criteria found in the various meanings of this term. Many states, according to Shackelford's (2006) analysis, incorporate a quantitative approach when determining who is developmentally delayed. Typical of this strategy is a reliance on data derived from various assessment instruments. Shackelford noted three different kinds of quantitative definitions:

- a delay expressed in terms of standard deviations (SD) below the mean on a norm-referenced assessment (Georgia: 2 SD in one developmental area or 1.5 SD in two areas[1]);
- a delay expressed in terms of a difference between a child's chronological age and actual performance level (Alabama: 25% delay in one or more developmental areas); or
- a delay expressed in terms of performance—*n* number of months below child's chronological age (Texas: 2–12 months: 2-month delay; 13–24 months: 3-month delay; 25–36 months: 4-month delay).

Table 2–2 illustrates some of the various criteria used by the states when quantifying a developmental delay. Obviously, there is no one correct way to define this concept. Each approach has its advantages and disadvantages. In fact, 14 states allow for the use of a qualitative determination when considering whether or not a child is developmentally delayed (Danaher, 2007). Nebraska and New Mexico are but two examples of states that permit the use of professional judgment, informed team consensus, or the informed clinical opinions of members of a multidisciplinary team.

---

[1] Developmental areas include physical, communication, cognitive, social or emotional, and adaptive.

A qualitative determination is allowed due to the lack of valid and reliable dependent measures appropriate for infants and toddlers. The predictive validity of these assessment instruments is also suspect. As a result, the regulations accompanying IDEA require that informed clinical opinion be included as part of eligibility determination (Shackelford, 2006; Taylor, Smiley, & Richards, 2009).

There are several advantages to using the term *developmental delay.* First, because it suggests a developmental status rather than a category, it is anticipated that placement of students in developmentally appropriate classrooms will be more likely. Second, it is hoped that this concept will lead to services being matched to the needs and abilities of the child rather than having services decided by a categorical label. Third, professionals believe that the utilization of this term is likely to encourage inclusive models of service delivery instead of services being primarily driven by a disability label. Finally, the use of this label avoids the possibility of misidentifying a young child when the etiology or cause of the child's delay is not clearly evident (Division for Early Childhood, 1996, 2001).

At-Risk. When professionals talk about children being **at-risk,** they are speaking of children "who have not been formally identified as having a disability, but who may be developing conditions that will limit their success in school or lead to disabilities. This can be the result of exposure to adverse genetic, biological, or environmental factors" (Spodek & Saracho, 1994b, p. 16). This definition parallels an earlier description of risk factors identified by Kopp (1983). She defines risk as "a wide range of biological and environmental conditions that are associated with increased probability for cognitive, social, affective, and physical problems" (p. 1081).

In both of these definitions we see that exposure to adverse circumstances *may* lead to later problems in development and learning, but it is not a guarantee that developmental problems will occur. Risk factors only set the stage or heighten the probability that differences might arise. Many young children are subject to a wide variety of risks, yet they never evidence developmental problems. Table 2–3 presents some of the common factors and conditions that can place a child at-risk.

Our understanding of the at-risk concept has been greatly enhanced by the wide acceptance professionals have given to Tjossem's (1976) description of three

TABLE 2–2 Representative Examples of Definitions of Developmental Delay

State	Criteria
Arizona	50% delay in one or more areas
Florida	1.5 SD in one area or 25% delay in months of age in one area; or informed clinical opinion
Hawaii	consensus of multidisciplinary team; no quantitative data specified
Indiana	2.0 SD in one area or 25% below chronological age; 1.5 SD in two areas or 20% below chronological age in two areas; informed clinical opinion
Montana	50% delay in one area or 25% delay in two areas; informed clinical opinion
New Hampshire	atypical behaviors documented by qualified personnel; or 33% delay in one or more areas
South Dakota	25% below normal age range; 6-month delay; or 1.5 SD in one or more areas
Wisconsin	25% delay or 1.3 SD in one area; atypical development as determined by multidisciplinary team with informed clinical opinion

NOTE: SD = standard deviation.
Areas refers to physical, communication, cognitive, social or emotional, and adaptive areas of development.

SOURCE: Adapted from J. Shackelford. (2006). *State and Jurisdictional Eligibility Definitions for Infants and Toddlers with Disabilities Under IDEA*. (NECTAC Notes 21). Chapel Hill, NC: University of North Carolina, FPG Child Development Institute, National Early Childhood Technical Assistance Center.

at-risk categories. His tripartite classification scheme includes established, biological, and environmental risk categories. These categories are not mutually exclusive and frequently overlap. In some instances, a child identified as being biologically at risk due to prematurity may also be at risk due to environmental factors like severe poverty. As a result of this "double vulnerability," the probability for future delays and learning difficulties dramatically increases.

Established Risk. Children with a diagnosed medical disorder of known etiology and predictable prognosis or outcome are considered to manifest an established risk. Illustrations of such conditions would be a child born with cerebral palsy, Down syndrome, spina bifida, an inborn error of metabolism such as PKU (phenylketonuria), or severe sensory impairments. Young children identified with an established risk condition *must* be served if the state receives IDEA Part C monies.

Biological Risk. Included in this category are children with a history of pre-, peri-, and postnatal

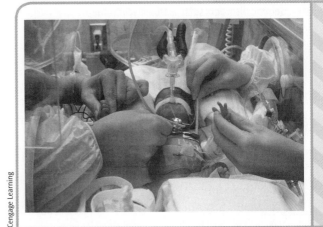

Cengage Learning

Some young children maybe at risk for future difficulties in learning and development due to biological risk factors.

TABLE 2–3 Representative Factors Placing Young Children At Risk for Developmental Problems

- Maternal alcohol and drug abuse

- Children born to teenage mothers or women over age 40

- Home environment lacking adequate stimulation

- Maternal diabetes, hypertension, or toxemia

- Exposure to rubella

- Chronic poverty

- Primary caregiver is developmentally disabled

- Infections such as encephalitis and meningitis

- Oxygen deprivation

- Child abuse and neglect

- Accidents and head trauma

- Inadequate maternal and infant nutrition

- Genetic disorders such as Down syndrome, phenylketonuria, and galactosemia

- Family history of congenital abnormalities

- Exposure to radiation

- Prematurity

- Rh incompatibility

- Low birth weight

- Ingestion of poisons and toxic substances by child

- Prolonged or unusual delivery

Note: Factors are not ranked in order of potential influence.

conditions and developmental events that heighten the potential for later atypical or aberrant development. Examples of such conditions or complications include premature births, infants with low birth weights, maternal diabetes, rubella (German measles), anoxia, bacterial infections like meningitis, and HIV (human immunodeficiency virus) infection.

Environmental Risk. Environmentally at-risk children are biologically typical, but their life experiences and/or environmental conditions are so limiting or threatening that the likelihood of delayed development exists. Extreme poverty, child abuse, absence of adequate shelter and medical care, parental substance abuse, and limited opportunities for nurturance and social stimulation are all examples of potential environmental factors. This risk category, as well as children who are biologically at risk, results in discretionary services. States may elect to provide early intervention if they wish to, but they are *not* mandated to serve infants and toddlers who are biologically or environmentally at risk. Currently, eight states have elected to serve infants and toddlers in these two risk categories (Shackelford, 2006).

Given the magnitude of factors that may place a child at risk for developing disabilities, the value of prevention and early intervention cannot be underestimated. Of course, prevention is better than remediation.

Early Intervention and Early Childhood Special Education

Finally, before leaving this section on terminology, we would like to clarify the terms *early intervention* and *early childhood special education*. Generally speaking, **early intervention** refers to the delivery of a coordinated and comprehensive set of specialized supports and services to infants and toddlers (birth through age two) with developmental delays or at-risk conditions and their families. This term can be found in federal legislation; specially, Part C of the Individuals with Disabilities Education Act (PL 99-457) commonly known as IDEA (to be discussed later in this chapter). Describing the nature of early intervention is not an easy task. Early intervention can be characterized according to type of service provided (physical therapy, vision services), location of service (home, special center), and even service provider (occupational therapist, nurse), to mention just some of the critical features of this concept (U.S. Department of Education, 2001).

The goal of early intervention is two-fold. One purpose is to minimize the impact or effect of a disability, while the second goal is to prevent the occurance of future learning and developmental difficulties in children considered to be at risk (Smith & Guralnick, 2007).

The label **early childhood special education** is typically used when talking about the provision of customized services uniquely crafted to meet the individual needs of young children three through eight years of age with disabilities. It is important to note that when describing special education, we are not talking about a particular location but rather a system of supports and services for young children with disabilities (Gargiulo, 2009; Walsh, Smith, & Taylor, 2000).

Litigation and Legislation Affecting Children with Special Needs

Key Judicial Decisions

Early childhood special education is an evolving discipline. In addition to drawing upon its three parent fields, judicial action has played a key role in the growth of the field. Litigation instigated by parents and interest groups has helped pave the way in securing numerous rights for children with disabilities and their families. Since the 1960s and early 1970s, a plethora of state and federal court decisions have continually shaped and defined a wide range of issues that impact contemporary special education policies and procedures. Table 2–4 summarizes some of the landmark cases affecting the field of special education. Many of the judicial remedies emanating from these lawsuits form the cornerstones of both federal and state legislative enactments focusing on children with special needs. Furthermore, many accepted practices in today's special education programs, such as nondiscriminatory assessments and due process procedures, have their roots in various court decisions.

Key Federal Legislation

Federal legislative intervention in the lives of persons with disabilities is of relatively recent origin. Prior to the late 1950s and early 1960s, little federal attention was devoted to citizens with special needs. When legislation was enacted, it primarily assisted specific groups of individuals such as those who were deaf or mentally retarded. The last 40 years, however, have witnessed a flurry of federal legislative activity, which has aided the growth of special education and provided educational benefits and other opportunities and rights to children and adults with disabilities.

Due to the multitude of the public laws (PL) affecting special education, discussion will be reserved for landmark legislation. We will examine seven

TABLE 2–4 A Synopsis of Selected Court Cases Influencing Special Education

Case	Year	Issue	Judicial Decision
Brown v. Board of Education	1954	Educational segregation	Segregation of students by race ruled unconstitutional. Children are being deprived of equal educational opportunity. Effectively ended "separate but equal" schools for white and black pupils. Used as a precedent for arguing that children with disabilities cannot be excluded from a public education.
Hobson v. Hansen	1967	Classifying students	Grouping or "tracking" of students on the basis of standardized tests, which were found to be biased, held to be unconstitutional. Tracking systems discriminated against poor and minority children. Equal protection clause of Fourteenth Amendment violated.

(continued)

TABLE 2–4 A Synopsis of Selected Court Cases Influencing Special Education *(continued)*

Case	Year	Issue	Judicial Decision
Diana v. State Board of Education	1970	Class placement	Linguistically different students must be tested in their primary language as well as in English. Students cannot be placed in special education classes on the basis of tests that are culturally biased. Test items were to be revised so as to reflect students' cultures. Group administered IQ tests cannot be utilized for placement of children in programs for the mentally retarded
Pennsylvania Association for Retarded Children v. Commonwealth of Pennsylvania	1972	Right to education	State must guarantee a free public education to all children with mental retardation, ages 6–21, regardless of degree of impairment or associated disabilities. Students were to be placed in the most integrated environment. Definition of education expanded. Case established the right of parents to participate in educational decisions affecting their children.
Mills v. Board of Education of the District of Columbia	1972	Right to education	Extended the Pennsylvania decision to include all children with disabilities. Specifically established the constitutional right of children with exceptionalities to a public education regardless of their functional level. Presumed absence of fiscal resources is not a valid reason for failing to provide appropriate educational services to students with disabilities. Due process procedures established to protect the rights of the child.
Larry P. v. Riles	1972, 1979	Class placement	A landmark case parallel to the Diana suit. African American students could not be placed in classes for educable mentally retarded (EMR) children solely on the basis of intellectual assessments found to be culturally and racially biased. The court instructed school officials to develop an assessment instrument that would not discriminate against minority children. The failure to comply with this order resulted in a 1979 ruling, which completely prohibited the use of IQ tests for identifying African American students for placement in EMR classes. Ruling applies only to the state of California.
Jose P. v. Ambach	1979	Timelines and delivery of services	A far-reaching class action lawsuit that completely restructured the delivery of special education services in New York City public schools. Judgment established (1) school-based support teams to conduct evaluations and provide services; (2) stringent timelines for completing evaluations and placement; (3) due process procedures; (4) guidelines for nondiscriminatory evaluation; (5) detailed monitoring procedures; and (6) accessibility of school facilities.

(continued)

TABLE 2–4 A Synopsis of Selected Court Cases Influencing Special Education *(continued)*

Case	Year	Issue	Judicial Decision
Armstrong v. Klein	1980	Extended school year	States' refusal to pay for schooling in excess of 180 days for pupils with severe disabilities is a violation of their rights to an appropriate education as found in PL 94-142. The court moved that some children with disabilities will regress significantly during summer recess and have longer recoupment periods; thus, they are denied an appropriate education if not provided with a year-round education.
Tatro v. State of Texas	1980	Related services	A U.S. Supreme Court decision, which held that catheterization qualified as a related service under PL 94-142. Catheterization not considered an exempted medical procedure as it could be performed by a health care aide or school nurse. Court further stipulated that only those services that allow a student to benefit from a special education qualify as related services.
Board of Education v. Rowley	1982	Appropriate education	First U.S. Supreme Court interpretation of PL 94-142. Court addresses the issue of what constitutes an "appropriate" education for a deaf student making satisfactory progress. Supreme Court ruled that an appropriate education does not necessarily mean an education that will allow for the maximum possible achievement; rather, students must be given a reasonable opportunity to learn. Parents' request for a sign language interpreter, therefore, was denied. An appropriate education is not synonymous with an optimal educational experience.
Honig v. Doe	1988	Exclusion from school	Children with special needs whose behavior is a direct result of their disability cannot be expelled from school due to misbehavior. If behavior leading to expulsion is not a consequence of the exceptionality, pupil may be expelled. Short-term suspension from school not interpreted as a change in pupil's individualized education program (IEP).
Daniel R. R. v. State Board of Education	1989	Class placement	A Fifth Circuit Court of Appeals decision that held that a segregated class was an appropriate placement for a student with Down syndrome. Preference for integrated placement viewed as secondary to the need for an appropriate education. Court established a two-prong test for determining compliance with the LRE mandate for students with severe disabilities. First, it must be determined if a pupil can make satisfactory progress and achieve educational benefit in a regular classroom through curriculum modification and the use of supplementary aids and services. Second, it must be determined whether the pupil has been integrated to the maximum extent appropriate. Successful compliance with both parts fulfills a school's obligation under federal law. Ruling affects LRE cases in Louisiana, Texas, and Mississippi, but has become a benchmark decision for other jurisdictions as well.

(continued)

TABLE 2–4 A Synopsis of Selected Court Cases Influencing Special Education *(continued)*

Case	Year	Issue	Judicial Decision
Oberti v. Board of Education of the Borough of Clementon School District	1992	Least restrictive environment	Placement in a general education classroom with the use of supplementary aids and services must be offered to a student with disabilities prior to considering more segregated placements. A pupil cannot be excluded from a regular classroom solely because curriculum, services, or other practices would require modification. A decision to exclude a learner from the regular education classroom necessitates justification and documentation. Clear judicial preference for educational integration established.
Agostini v. Fulton	1997	Provision of services	A U.S. Supreme Court decision that reversed a long-standing ruling banning the delivery of publicly funded educational services to students enrolled in private schools. Interpreted to mean special educators can now provide services to children in parochial schools.
Cedar Rapids Community School District v. Garret F.	1999	Related services	A U.S. Supreme Court decision that expanded and clarified the concept of related services. This case affirmed that intensive and continuous school health care services necessary for a student to attend school, and which are not performed by a physician, qualify as related services.
Arlington Central School District Board of Education v. Murphy	2006	Recovery of fees	At issue in this U. S. Supreme Court case is whether parents are able to recover the professional fees of an educational consultant (lay advocate) who provided services during legal proceedings. The Court ruled that parents are not entitled to reimbursement for the cost of experts because only attorneys' fees are addressed in IDEA.
Winkelman v. Parma City School District	2007	Parental rights	One of the more significant Supreme Court rulings. The Court, by unanimous vote, affirmed the right of parents to represent their children in IDEA-related court cases. Ruling seen as an expansion of parental involvement and the definition of a free and appropriate public education. Decision also interpreted to mean that IDEA conveys enforceable rights to parents as well as their children.

significant pieces of legislation that have dramatically affected the educational opportunities of infants, toddlers, preschool children, and school-age children with special needs. Our initial review will focus on PL 94-142, the Individuals with Disabilities Education Act (IDEA), or as it was previously called, the Education for All Handicapped Children Act. This change came about due to the enactment on October 30,

1990, of PL 101-476. Provisions contained in this legislation will be reviewed later.

Public Law 94-142. The Individuals with Disabilities Education Act is viewed as a "Bill of Rights" for children with exceptionalities and their families. It is considered by many individuals to be one of the, if not *the,* most important piece of federal legislation ever enacted on behalf of children with special needs. Some advocacy groups consider this enactment as a vital first step in securing the constitutional rights of citizens with disabilities (Allen & Cowdery, 2009). The intent of this bill was:

> to ensure that all handicapped children have available to them . . . a free, appropriate public education which emphasizes special education and related services designed to meet their unique needs, to ensure that the rights of handicapped children and their parents or guardians are protected, to assist States and localities to provide for the education of all handicapped children and to assess and ensure the effectiveness of efforts to educate handicapped children.
> (SECTION 601 (C))

In addition to these four purposes, there are six major components incorporated in this legislation:

1. *The right to a free appropriate public education (FAPE)—all* children, regardless of the severity of the disability, must be provided an education appropriate to their unique needs at no cost to the parent(s)/guardian(s). Included in this feature is the concept of related services, which requires that children receive, for example, as necessary, occupational and physical therapy, as well as speech therapy, among other services.

2. *The principle of* **least restrictive environment (LRE)**— children with exceptionalities are to be educated, to the maximum extent appropriate, with typical students. Placements must be consistent with the pupil's educational needs.

3. *An* **individualized education program (IEP)**—this document, developed in conjunction with the parent(s)/guardian(s), is an individually tailored statement describing an educational plan for each exceptional learner. The IEP is required to address (a) present level of academic functioning; (b) annual goals and accompanying instructional objectives; (c) educational services to be provided; (d) the degree to which the pupil will be able to participate in regular education programs; (e) plans for initiating services and length of service delivery; and (f) an annual evaluation procedure specifying objective criteria to determine if instructional objectives are being met.

4. *Procedural due process*—the Act affords parent(s)/guardian(s) several safeguards as it pertains to their child's education. Briefly, parent(s)/guardian(s) have the right to examine all records; obtain an independent evaluation; receive written notification (in parent's native language) of proposed changes to their child's educational classification or placement; and a right to an impartial hearing whenever disagreements occur regarding educational plans for their son/daughter.

5. *Nondiscriminatory assessment*—prior to placement, a child must be evaluated in all areas of suspected disability by tests, which are neither culturally nor linguistically biased. Students are to receive several types of assessments; a single evaluation procedure is not permitted.

6. *Parental participation*—PL 94-142 mandates parental involvement. Sometimes referred to as the "Parent's Law," this legislation requires that parents participate in the decision-making process that affects their child's education. IDEA regulations currently allow assistance to parents as part of a preschooler's IEP if such assistance is necessary for the child to benefit from special education. Parental training activities are also permissible as a related service.

Congress mandated by September 1, 1980, a free appropriate public education for all eligible children age three through twenty-one. The law, however, did *not* require services to preschool children with disabilities. An exception was contained in the legislative language:

> except that, with respect to handicapped children aged three to five and eighteen to twenty-one, inclusive, the requirements . . . shall not be applied . . . if such requirements would be inconsistent with state law or practice, or the order of any court, respecting public education within such age groups within the state.
> (SECTION 612(2) (B))

Since many states were not providing preschool services to typical children, an education for young children with special needs, in most instances, was not mandated. Although this legislation fails to require an education for our youngest students, it clearly focused attention on the preschool population and recognized the value of early education.

PL 94-142 did, however, contain benefits for children under school age. The enactment offered small financial grants (Preschool Incentive Grants) to the individual states as an incentive to serve young children with special needs. It also carried a mandate for schools to identify and evaluate children from birth through age twenty-one suspected of evidencing a disability. Finally, PL 94-142 moved from a census count to a child count, or the actual number of young children being served. The intent of this feature was to encourage the states to locate and serve children with disabilities.

Public Law 99-457. In October 1986, Congress passed one of the most comprehensive pieces of legislation affecting young children with special needs and their families—PL 99-457. This law, which was originally known as the Education of the Handicapped Act Amendments of 1986, changed both the scope and intent of services provided to preschoolers with special needs in addition to formulating a national policy for infants and toddlers at risk for, and with, identified disabilities.

Farran (2000) believes that one of the assumptions behind the enactment of PL 99-457 was that early intervention is cost-effective, a way of lowering future costs of special education. This rationale is vastly different from the thinking behind the passage of PL 94-142, which was rooted in the civil rights movement and saw an education for children with disabilities as a constitutional right. Thus, PL 99-457 was enacted primarily as a prevention measure.

Today, education for youngsters with a disability is a right, not a privilege.

AP Photo/Janet Hostetter

PL 99-457 contains several parts. Our attention will primarily focus on Part B, the preschool provision, as well as Part H (which is now known as Part C), a new section that allows for services to be provided to infants and toddlers with special needs.

As noted earlier, IDEA contains language that gave states the opportunity, through financial incentives, to provide an education and related services to preschool children with disabilities. This was a permissive or voluntary element of the Act, not a mandated requirement. Trohanis (1989) reported Congressional data, which revealed that less than 80% or 260,000 of the estimated 330,000 exceptional children ages three to five were being served. An estimated 70,000 preschoolers were, therefore, unserved. Koppelman (1986) found that 31 states and territories did not require special education services for preschoolers with special needs. PL 99-457 was enacted to remedy this situation.

Simply stated, Part C is a downward extension of PL 94-142, including all rights and protections. It requires that as of the 1991–1992 school year, *all* preschoolers with special needs, ages three to five inclusive, are to receive a free and appropriate public education. This element of the law is a mandated requirement. States will lose significant amounts of federal preschool funding if they fail to comply. The goal of this legislation was finally accomplished in the 1992–1993 school year, when all states had mandates in place establishing a free appropriate public education for all children ages three through five with disabilities. In fact, five states (Iowa, Maryland, Michigan, Minnesota, and Nebraska) have chosen to mandate services from birth, while Virginia begins a FAPE at age two. Table 2–5 shows the year that each state mandated a free and appropriate public education for children with special needs.

Other provisions of the earlier legislation remain the same, such as an education in the least restrictive environment (LRE), IEPs, due process safeguards, and confidentiality of records. Family services are also recognized as being vitally important; thus, family counseling and training are allowable as a related service. Depending on the needs of the child, service delivery models can either be home-based or center-based, full-time or part-time. As we noted earlier, states are not required to report to the U.S. Department of Education the number of children served according to a disability category. Thus, preschoolers do not have to be labeled with a specific disability, such as mental retardation.

TABLE 2–5 School Year in Which States Mandated a Free and Appropriate Public Education for Preschoolers with Disabilities

Year	State	Year	State
1973–1974	Illinois Michigan* Wisconsin	1990–1991	Montana Nevada Wyoming
1974–1975	Alaska Texas	1991–1992	Alabama Arizona Arkansas
1975–1976	Iowa* Virginia**		California Colorado Connecticut
1976–1977	Massachusetts Rhode Island South Dakota		Delaware Florida Georgia
1977–1978	Louisiana New Hampshire		Indiana Kansas Kentucky
1978–1979	Maryland*		Maine Mississippi
1979–1980	Nebraska		Missouri New Mexico
1980–1981	Hawaii		New York North Carolina
1983–1984	District of Columbia New Jersey		Ohio Oklahoma
1985–1986	North Dakota Washington		Pennsylvania South Carolina Tennessee
1986–1987	Minnesota*		Vermont West Virginia
1988–1989	Utah		
1989–1990	Idaho	1992–1993	Oregon

*Eligible for services beginning at birth.
**Eligible for services beginning at age two.

SOURCE: Adapted from A. Lazara, J. Danaher, and R. Kraus, *Section 619 Profile* (15th ed.), 2007. Chapel Hill, NC: University of North Carolina, FPG Child Development Institute, National Early Childhood Technical Assistance Center.

All states were required to modify their state plans and policies to ensure compliance with the law. Funding for serving these children has also dramatically increased.

Part C of PL 99-457 created the Handicapped Infants and Toddlers Program, a new provision aimed at children from birth through age two with developmental delays or disabilities. This component of the legislation is voluntary; states are not compelled to comply. Part C of this statute creates a discretionary program that assists states in implementing a statewide, comprehensive, coordinated, multidisciplinary, interagency program of services for very young children with developmental difficulties and their families. Each state that chose to participate was required to provide early intervention to children who evidence a physical or mental condition that has a high probability of resulting in a delay such as cerebral palsy or Down syndrome. At their discretion, states may also offer services to children who are medically or environmentally at risk for future delays. As of September 30, 1994, all states had plans in place for the full implementation of Part C (U.S. Department of Education, 1997).

The enactment of PL 99–457 reflects a major shift in thinking regarding public policy and service provision for infants and toddlers with special needs (Harbin, McWilliam, & Gallagher, 2000). This paradigm shift is reflected in Table 2–6, which illustrates pre- and post-IDEA service delivery.

There are several features of this law that are worthy of examination. Under this Act and its accompanying amendments, infants and toddlers are eligible for services if they meet the following conditions:

- they are experiencing developmental delays in one or more of the following areas: cognitive development, physical development, communication development, social or emotional development, or adaptive development;
- they have a physical or mental condition that has a high probability of resulting in a delay (for example, cerebral palsy, Down syndrome);
- or at the state's discretion, they are medically or environmentally at risk for substantial delay if early intervention is not provided.

Eligible children and their families must receive a multidisciplinary assessment conducted by qualified professionals and a written **individualized family service plan (IFSP).** Similar to the IEP, the IFSP is designed as a guide to the delivery of services to infants, toddlers, and their families. Developed by a multidisciplinary team, the IFSP, as promulgated in PL 99-457, must contain these components:

- a statement of the infant's or toddler's present levels of physical development, cognitive development, communication development, social or emotional development, and adaptive development;
- a statement of the family's resources, priorities, and concerns;
- a statement of major outcomes expected to be achieved for the infant or toddler and the family;
- a statement of specific early intervention services necessary to meet the unique needs of the infant or toddler and the family;
- the projected dates for initiation of services and the anticipated duration of such services;
- the name of the service coordinator;
- a description of the natural environments in which early intervention services will be provided; and
- the steps . . . supporting the transition of the toddler with a disability to services provided under Part B (preschool).

Unlike an IEP, the focus of the IFSP is on the family rather than the individual child, thereby resulting in a comprehensive and multidisciplinary plan. Parents are viewed as full-fledged partners with professionals. Their participation ensures that services occur within the context of the family unit and meet the unique needs of the child and his or her caregivers. This goal is clearly reflected in the IFSP statement, which addresses the issue of the "family's resources, priorities, and concerns." It is imperative for professionals to remember that while families may have a variety of needs (for example, informational, management, support), they also have strengths and resources that must not be overlooked. Best practice dictates that services should be individualized and responsive to the goals and preferences of the parents (caregivers) while supporting their role as primary decision maker.

A final noteworthy aspect of Part C of IDEA is the concept of service coordination. A service coordinator originally was a professional selected from the discipline closest to the child's primary problem, for example, a speech-language pathologist for toddlers with delayed language or a physical therapist for a young child with cerebral palsy. PL 102-119 not only changed the terminology from *case management* to

TABLE 2–6 Changes in Service Delivery for Infants and Toddlers Resulting from the Passage of Public Law 99-457 (IDEA)

Area	Pre-IDEA Services	Post-IDEA Services
Entitlement	Served only some of the eligible children	Serve all children
Eligibility	Served only disabled children and waited until children evidenced measurable delays	Serve children with diagnosed conditions regardless of whether measurable delays are present May serve at-risk children in order to prevent developmental delay
Early identification	Waited until children came to program	Find children as early as possible
Service array	Confined services to what program offered	Provide an array of services across programs
System	Provide separate, autonomous programs	Provide comprehensive, coordinated, interagency system of services
Focus	Child-centered	Family-centered
Individualization	Offered a package of services	Offer individualized services
Inclusion	Established segregated, self-contained programs	Establish inclusive programs and use of community resources
Disciplines	Disciplines worked autonomously	Disciplines working together to integrate all services (interdisciplinary, transdisciplinary)
Therapies	Provide separate and sometimes insufficient therapies	Provide sufficient integrated therapies
Procedural safeguards	Families had no recourse for complaints	Procedural safeguards in place
Transition	Unplanned traumatic transitions	Planned transition from infant and toddler program to preschool program
Funding	Single primary funding source	Coordinated and use all possible funding sources

Source: Adapted with permission from G. Harbin, R. McWilliam, and J. Gallagher, Services for Young Children with Disabilities and Their Families. In J. Shonkoff and S. Meisels (Eds.), *Handbook of Early Intervention,* 2nd ed. (Cambridge, England: Cambridge University Press, 2000). p. 388.

Cengage Learning

An individualized family service plan is developed by a multidisciplinary team.

service coordination and *case manager* to the less clinical term *service coordinator*, but it also broadened the category of service coordinator to *any* qualified professional who is best able to assist the family. Typically, their roles are to function as an advocate for the family, to ensure the coordination of early intervention services, to monitor the implementation of the IFSP, to assist in transition planning, and to foster family empowerment, among other duties. It is important to remember that the activities and responsibilities of the service coordinator are determined in conjunction with the child's family and are always individualized.

An IFSP must be reviewed every six months (or sooner if necessary) to assess its continual appropriateness. The infant or toddler is required by law to be reevaluated annually. Regulations further stipulate that an IFSP must be developed within forty-five days after a referral for services is made.

PL 99-457 is the culmination of many years of dedicated effort by both parents and professionals from various disciplines and agencies. It represents an opportunity to intervene and effect meaningful change in the lives of the nation's youngest and most vulnerable children.

Public Law 101-476. Arguably, one of the most important changes contained in this legislation was the renaming of PL 94-142 to the Individuals with Disabilities Education Act. The word "children" was replaced with the term "individuals" and "handicapped" became "with disabilities." This latter phrase also signifies a change in attitude to a more appropriate people-first point of view. We now realize that an individual's disability is but one aspect of his or her personhood.

PL 101-476 also required that adolescents have an individual transition plan (ITP) as part of their IEP while expanding the scope of the related services provision by adding two services—social work and rehabilitation counseling. A final element of this legislation was the identification of autism and traumatic brain injury as distinct disability categories. Previously, these disabilities had been subsumed under other disability labels.

Public Law 102-119. In 1991, IDEA was amended again by PL 102-119, the Individuals with Disabilities Education Act Amendment. As we noted earlier, PL 102-119 permits states to use a noncategorical label when identifying preschoolers with special needs. Amendments to Part C require that early intervention services are to be in "natural environments" with typically developing age-mates as appropriate for each child. Transition policies and procedures are to be established so that infants and toddlers receiving early intervention services can move smoothly, if eligible, to preschool special education. States are also allowed to use an IFSP as a guide for services for children ages three through five as long as IEP requirements are met. Additionally, states were permitted to use Part C monies for preschoolers with disabilities. Likewise, these amendments allow for the use of Part B funds to serve infants and toddlers with special needs. Finally, the amount of funds allocated by Congress increased from $1,000 to $1,500 per child.

Public Law 105-17. IDEA was reauthorized once again via the Individuals with Disabilities Education Act Amendments of 1997. This bill was signed into law by President Clinton on June 4, 1997. PL 105-17 restructures IDEA into four parts, revises some definitions, and revamps several key components ranging from funding to disciplining students with disabilities to how IEPs are to be developed. Highlights of this major retooling are as follows:

- Students with disabilities who bring weapons to school, possess or use illegal drugs, or pose a serious threat of injury to other pupils or themselves may be removed from their current placement and placed in an interim alternative educational setting as determined by the IEP team, but for no more than 45 days, after a due process hearing has been conducted. Students who are suspended or expelled are still entitled to receive a free and appropriate public education as addressed in their IEP.

- Pupils with disabilities who exhibit less serious infractions of school conduct may be disciplined in ways similar to children without disabilities (including a change in placement), provided that the misbehavior was not a manifestation of the student's disability. Additionally, either before taking disciplinary action, but no later than ten days after, the IEP team must conduct a functional behavioral assessment and develop (or implement) a behavior intervention plan.

- IEPs are now required to state how the student with disabilities will be involved with, and progress in, the general education curriculum. Other provisions stipulate that general educators will become part of the IEP team; short-term instructional objectives will no longer be required, rather, the emphasis will be on measurable annual goals; and lastly, the assistive technology needs of each learner must be considered by the IEP team.

- Orientation and mobility services for children with visual impairments are now included in the definition of related services.

- The present mandate of comprehensive triennial reevaluation of children with disabilities is lifted if school authorities and the student's parents both agree that this process is unnecessary.

- A new section on mediation requires states to offer mediation services to help resolve disputes as an alternative to using more costly and lengthy due process hearings. Parental participation is voluntary and parents still retain their right to a due process hearing.

- The eligibility category of *developmental delay* may now be used for describing children ages three through nine. The use of this term is at the discretion of the state and local education agency.

- Initial evaluations and reevaluations are not restricted to the use of formal, standardized tests. A variety of assessment tools and strategies are to be utilized in an effort to gather relevant, functional, and developmental information. Curriculum-based tests, portfolio reviews, parental input, and the observations of teachers and

related service providers may be considered in determining whether or not the student is eligible for services and in developing the content of the IEP. A student may not be considered eligible for a special education if their educational difficulties are primarily the result of limited proficiency in English or lack of adequate instruction in math and/or reading.

- A new mechanism for distributing federal monies will occur once the appropriations reach a threshold of $4.9 billion. Upon attaining this level, states and local school systems will receive additional funding based upon 85 percent of the population of children ages three to 21 and 15 percent of the number of children ages three through 21 who are in poverty. This switch to a census-based formula instead of the current enrollment-driven formula was due to a concern that some schools were overidentifying students in order to receive additional funding. No state would receive less than the amount of support it received in the year prior to the activation of this new scheme.

- The reauthorization of IDEA requires schools to establish performance goals for students with disabilities in an effort to assess their academic progress. Additionally, these children are to be included in state- and district-wide assessment programs or given alternative assessments that meet their unique needs.

- Early intervention services must be "family-directed" and, to the extent appropriate, these services are to be provided in noninstitutional settings such as the young child's home.

- Child Find requirements are extended to children with disabilities who are enrolled in private schools, including students attending parochial schools. A special education and related services may be provided on the premises of a private school (including parochial) to the extent permissible by law.

- IFSP requirements are modified to include a statement justifying the extent, if any, that early intervention services are not provided in the natural environment.

Public Law 108-446. The most recent of amendments to IDEA are incorporated in PL 108-446, the Individuals with Disabilities Education Improvement Act of 2004. This historic piece of legislation is commonly referred to as IDEA 2004. One of the goals of IDEA 2004 was to align this law with the **No Child Left Behind Act** (PL 107-110) enacted in 2001. The focus of PL 107-110 was to improve the academic performance of *all* students in reading and math (with science eventually being added) by the year 2014. Particular attention is paid to the achievement of pupils with disabilities, children from low-income families, English language learners, and individuals from racial and ethnic minority groups. The No Child Left Behind Act further requires that teachers are to be highly qualified professionals and that they incorporate scientifically validated practices in their instructional programs (Gargiulo & Metcalf, 2010).

The following summary[2] represents some of the significant issues contained in PL 108-446.

Individualized Education Program (IEP) Process

- Short-term objectives and benchmarks will no longer be required except for those pupils who are evaluated via alternate assessments aligned to alternate achievement standards.
- Assessment of the progress that a student is making toward meeting annual goals, which must be written in measurable terms, is still required. Reference, however, to the current requirement of reporting to the "extent to which progress is sufficient to enable the child to achieve goals by the end of the year" is eliminated. IEPs will now need to describe how the individual's progress toward achieving annual goals will be measured and when these progress reports will be made.
- PL 108-446 also requires that the IEP address the student's "academic and functional performance" instead of the previously used term "educational performance." This modification of terminology more closely aligns IDEA with the No Child Left Behind Act.

Identifying Students with Specific Learning Disabilities

Although young children are rarely identified with a learning disability, under IDEA '97, when identifying an individual for a possible learning disability, educators typically looked to see if the student exhibited a severe discrepancy between achievement and intellectual ability. IDEA 2004 removed this discrepancy

---

[2] Information adapted from *Teaching in Today's Inclusive Classrooms* by R. Gargiulo and D. Metcalf, Belmont, CA: Wadsworth/Cengage Learning, 2010.

provision. School districts will now be able, if they so choose, to use a process that determines if the pupil responds to empirically validated, scientifically based interventions, a procedure known as response-to-intervention (treatment). Under these guidelines, rather than comparing IQ with performance on standardized achievement tests, general education teachers can offer intensive programs of instructional interventions. If the child fails to make adequate progress, a learning disability is assumed to be present and additional assessment is warranted.

Highly Qualified Special Education Teachers

The language contained in IDEA 2004 concerning who is considered a "highly qualified" special educator is complementary to the standards promulgated in the No Child Left Behind Act of 2001.

- All elementary and secondary special education teachers must hold at least a bachelor's degree and be fully certified or licensed in the field of special education in order to be deemed "highly qualified." Special educators employed as of July 1, 2005, were required to meet this standard.
- Special educators who teach core subjects in elementary schools can obtain highly qualified status by passing their state's licensing or certification exam.
- This legislation does not address "highly qualified" requirements for early childhood special educators.

Discipline

- PL 108-446 stipulates that when a student is removed from his or her current educational setting, the pupil is to continue to receive those services that enable him or her to participate in the general education curriculum and to ensure progress toward meeting IEP goals.
- IDEA '97 allowed school authorities to unilaterally remove a student to an interim alternative setting (IASE) for up to 45 days for offenses involving weapons or drugs. IDEA 2004 now permits school officials to remove any pupil (including those with and without disabilities) to an IASE for up to 45 days for inflicting "serious bodily injury."
- Removal to an IASE will now be for 45 *school* days rather than 45 calendar days.
- Behavior resulting in disciplinary action still requires a manifestation review; however, language

requiring the IEP team to consider whether the pupil's disability impaired his or her ability to control his or her behavior or comprehend the consequences of his or her actions has been eliminated. IEP teams will now only need to ask two questions:

1. Did the disability cause or have a direct and substantial relationship to the offense?
2. Was the violation a direct result of the school's failure to implement the IEP?

- IDEA 2004 modifies the "stay put" provision enacted during the appeals process. When either the local education agency or school district (LEA) or parent requests an appeal of the manifestation determination or placement decision, the pupil is to remain in the current IASE until a decision is rendered by the hearing officer or until the time period for violation concludes. A hearing must be held within 20 school days of the date of the appeal.

Due Process

- Parents will encounter a two-year statute of limitations for filing a due process complaint from the time they knew or should have known that a violation occurred. Alleged violations might involve identification, assessment, or placement issues or the failure to provide an appropriate education.
- A mandatory "resolution session" is now required prior to proceeding with a due process hearing. (The parents or school district may waive this requirement and directly proceed to mediation.) School districts must convene a meeting with the parents and the IEP team members within 15 days of receiving a due process complaint. If

the complaint is not satisfactorily resolved within 30 days of the filing date, the due process hearing may proceed.

Eligibility of Students

- School districts will be required to determine the eligibility of a student to receive a special education and the educational needs to the child within a 60-day time frame. (This provision does not apply if the state has already established a timeline for accomplishing this task.) The 60-day rule commences upon receipt of parental permission for evaluation.
- Reevaluation of eligibility for special education may not occur more than once per year (unless agreed to by the school district and parent); and it must occur at least every three years unless the parent and school district agree that such a reevaluation is unnecessary.
- IDEA 2004 modifies the provision pertaining to native language and preferred mode of communication. New language in the bill requires that evaluations are to be "provided and administered in the language and form most likely to yield accurate information on what the child knows and can do academically, developmentally, and functionally, unless its is not feasible to do so or administer."

Assessment Participation

- PL 108-446 requires that *all* students participate in all state- and district-wide assessments (including those required under the No Child Left Behind Act) with accommodations or alternative assessments, if necessary, as stipulated in

---

TeachSource Video

Foundations: Aligning Instruction with Federal Legislation

Visit the premium website and watch "Foundations: Aligning Instruction with Federal Legislation." After watching the video, answer the following questions:

1. What is your opinion about the appropriateness of the No Child Left Behind Act for early primary students with disabilities?
2. What is the relationship between IDEA 2004 and the No Child Left Behind legislation?

the child's IEP. States are permitted to assess up to 1% of students (generally those pupils with significant cognitive deficits) with alternative assessments aligned with alternative achievement standards. IDEA 2004 further requires that assessments adhere to the principles of universal design when feasible.

Services for Infants and Toddlers with Disabilities

- Early intervention services are to be based upon peer-reviewed research.
- Individualized family service plans (IFSPs) are to include measurable outcomes for pre-literacy and language skills.
- IDEA 2004 permits states to provide early intervention services from age three until the youngster enters kindergarten.
- IDEA 2004 maintains the use of the label *developmental delay* for children three to nine years of age.

Section 504 of the Rehabilitation Act of 1973[3]. The six pieces of legislation that we just examined are representative special education laws. PL 93-112, the Rehabilitation Act of 1973, however, is a *civil rights* law. Section 504 of this enactment is the first public law specifically aimed at protecting children and adults against discrimination due to a disability. It said that no individual can be excluded, solely because of his or her disability, from participating in or benefiting from any program or activity receiving federal financial assistance, which includes schools (*CEC Today,* 1997). Unlike IDEA, this act employs a functional rather than a categorical model for determining a disability. According to this law, an individual is eligible for services if he or she:

1. has a physical or mental impairment that substantially limits one or more major life activities;
2. has a record of such impairment; or
3. is regarded as having such an impairment by others.

"Major life activities" are broadly defined and include, for example, walking, seeing, hearing, working, and learning.

Cengage Learning

Federal law requires that schools make reasonable accommodations for pupils with disabilities.

To fulfill the requirements of Section 504, schools must make "reasonable accommodations" for pupils with disabilities so that they can participate in educational programs provided to other students. Reasonable accommodations might include modifications of the general education program, the assignment of an aide, a behavior management plan, or the provision of special study areas (Smith, 2002; Smith & Patton, 1998). Students may also receive related services such as occupational or physical therapy if they are receiving a special education through IDEA.

Because the protections afforded by this law are so broad, an individual who is ineligible for a special education under IDEA may qualify for special

---

[3] Information from *Teaching in Today's Inclusive Classrooms* by R. Gargiulo and D. Metcalf, Belmont, CA: Wadsworth/Cengage Learning, 2010.

assistance or accommodations under Section 504. A second grader with attention deficit hyperactivity disorder (ADHD) or an adolescent with severe allergies, for example, would be eligible for services via Section 504, while those students are likely to be ineligible to receive services under IDEA (*CEC Today,* 1997). All students who are eligible for a special education and related services under IDEA are also eligible for accommodations under Section 504; the converse, however, is *not* true.

Similar to IDEA, there is a mandate contained within Section 504 to educate pupils with special needs with their typical peers to the maximum extent possible. Additionally, schools are required to develop an accommodation plan (commonly called a "504 plan") customized to meet the unique needs of the individual. This document should include a statement of the pupil's strengths and weaknesses, a list of necessary accommodations, and the individual(s) responsible for ensuring implementation. The purpose of this plan is to enable the student to receive a free, appropriate public education (Smith, 2002). We will examine 504 plans in greater detail in Chapter 5.

Prevalence of Young Children with Special Needs

The number of young children with special needs receiving services has increased dramatically over the past several years. This growth has been spurred on due to litigation, legislative enactments (especially IDEA and its amendments), and as we will shortly see, a greater awareness of the benefits of early intervention among other factors.

Infants and Toddlers

Recent data provided by the U.S. Department of Education (2009) reveals that 321,894 infants and toddlers birth through age two were receiving early intervention in the 2007–2008 school year. This statistic represents 2.5% of the entire birth-through-age-two population. Over the past several years, the number of infants and toddlers receiving early intervention services has steadily increased. Figure 2–1 illustrates this growth pattern. This trend reflects

FIGURE 2–1 Number of Infants and Toddlers Served Under IDEA in Representative Years

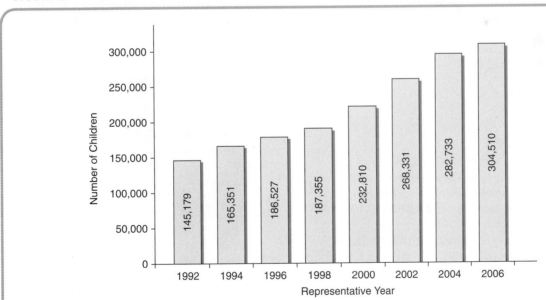

Source: U.S. Department of Education. (2005). *Twenty-sixth Annual Report to Congress on the Implementation of the Individuals with Disabilities Education Act, 2004* (Vol.1). Washington, DC: U.S. Government Printing Office, p. 5. Data also available at https://www.ideadata.org/PartCdata.aspp

TABLE 2–7   Increase in Number of Preschoolers Served under the Individuals With Disabilities Education Act (Part B)

| Ages | Representative Years | | | | | | Change 1986–2006 | |
	1986–87	1990–91	1994–95	1998–99	2002–03	2006-07	Numbers	%
3-year-olds	31,162	59,095	104,619	117,698	140,542	165,676	134,514	431.6
4-year-olds	62,327	111,787	179,825	199,924	246,751	246,980	184,653	296.2
5-year-olds	170,415	197,807	240,014	256,015	260,127	301,728	131,313	77.0
Total	265,814	368,689	524,458	573,637	647,420	714,384	450,480	169.4

NOTE: Data reported as of December 1 of each reporting year. Figures based upon data from the 50 contiguous states, Puerto Rico, the District of Columbia, and outlying areas.

SOURCE: U.S. Department of Education. (1991–2005). *Annual Reports to Congress on the Implementation of the Individuals with Disabilities Education Act.* Washington, DC: U.S. Government Printing Office, and data available from http://www.ideadata.org/PartBReport.asp

a 110% increase in the number of children served. This growth pattern is most likely due to greater public awareness, successful Child Find efforts, and program expansion. Currently, slightly more than half of the children (54%) receiving early intervention in 2007 were two years of age.

Preschoolers

Figures from the U.S. Department of Education (2009) reveal that more than 710,000 preschoolers ages three to five were served during the 2007–2008 school year under Part B of IDEA. (See Table 2–7.) This figure represents approximately 6.4% of the population of three- to five-year-old children in the United States. Figure 2–2 portrays the ages and the percentage of young children receiving services through IDEA, while Table 2–7 reflects the growth in the number of preschoolers receiving a special education.

Early Primary

Children ages six, seven, and eight who are receiving a special education are sometimes recognized under the developmental delay category, while in

FIGURE 2–2   Percentage of Preschoolers Receiving a Special Education and Related Services in the 2007–2008 School Year

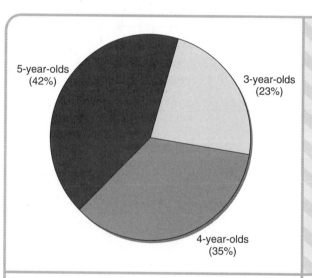

SOURCE: U.S. Department of Education. (2009). *IDEA data.* Available at https://www.ideadata.org/PartBReport.asp

other instances, a categorical label is used. The U.S. Department of Education (2009) reports that 85,130 children ages six through eight were eligible for services under the developmental delay category during the 2007–2008 school year. This figure represents about 6.9% of the more than 1.24 million students in this age range receiving a special education.

The Importance of Early Intervention/Education

Is early intervention effective? Does it benefit young children with special needs and their families? Unfortunately, these are not simple questions and their answers are equally, if not more, complex. It is perhaps best to respond to these queries by saying, "It depends." The reason we are so vague is that our initial inquiries only give rise to additional questions. For instance, What constitutes intervention? How early is early? Are we looking for short-term or long-term benefits? Who are the children we are talking about—infants and toddlers, young children who are environmentally at risk, children with suspected developmental delays, or preschoolers and early primary students with documented disabilities like Down syndrome or cerebral palsy? Obviously, the population we serve can affect the answer to the question.

Our initial concerns notwithstanding, we believe we can safely answer our primary questions in the affirmative. *Quality* early intervention/education programs *do* make a difference in the lives of young children with disabilities and their families. Guralnick (1998), in fact, considers early intervention to be "the centerpiece of our nation's efforts on behalf of vulnerable children and their families" (p. 337).

We will now review the reasoning for our position that early intervention/education is effective. We begin by establishing an understanding of what intervention is. Historically speaking, Fallen and Umansky (1985) describe early intervention as the process of intruding upon the lives of young children with disabilities and their families for the purpose of altering the direction and consequences of a disability or delayed development. These experts state that "the action required is individual, but it encompasses any modification or addition of services, strategies, techniques, or materials required to maximize the child's potential" (p. 160). Likewise, another early viewpoint

comes from Peterson (1987), who believes that the purpose of intervention for young children with special needs is to:

1. minimize the effects of a handicapping [disabling] condition upon a child's growth and development and maximize opportunities to engage in the normal activities of early childhood;
2. prevent, if possible, at-risk conditions or early developmental irregularities from developing into more serious problems that become deviant to the extent that they are labeled as handicapping [disabling];
3. prevent the development of secondary handicaps [disabilities] as a result of interference from a primary disability. . . . (pp. 72–73)

More recently, Hallahan, Kauffman, and Pullen (2009), in synthesizing the thinking of educators and researchers, echo these early perspectives. These writers offer the following rationale for early intervention:

- A child's early learning provides the foundation for later learning, so the sooner a special education program or intervention is begun, the further the child is likely to go in learning more complex skills.
- Early intervention is likely to provide support for the child and family that will help prevent the child from developing additional problems or disabilities.
- Early intervention can help families adjust to having a child with disabilities; give parents the skills they need to handle the child effectively at home; and help families find the additional support services they may need such as counseling, medical assistance, or financial aid. (p. 69)

Thus, we can state that, collectively, the aim of early intervention is to affect positively the overall development of the child's social, emotional, physical, and intellectual well-being. This whole-child approach is important because these aspects are interrelated and dependent on each other (Zigler, 1990).

Over the years, educators and social scientists (Hanson & Lynch, 1995; Howard, Williams, & Lepper, 2005; McCollum & Maude, 1993; Peterson, 1987; Raver, 1999) have identified a variety of reasons why early intervention is important for young children with disabilities and children at risk. Many of these reasons are derived from research evidence,

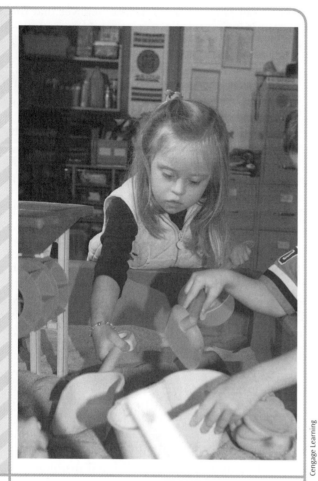

Cengage Learning

Early intervention has been shown to positively impact the lives of young children with disabilities.

theoretical arguments, expert opinion, and societal values. Frequently identified themes include:

- A belief that early environmental stimulation can positively facilitate subsequent development and readiness for learning.
- A critical periods hypothesis, which suggests that intervening during key periods in a child's life is vitally important if the child is to acquire more complex skills and competencies later on. The exclusivity of this notion, however, has been challenged by some professionals who advocate that the early years of a child's life are *not* the only crucial period of development; in fact, development continues across the lifespan (Clarke & Clarke, 1976). Similarly, Ramey and Ramey (1998) argue

that there is no compelling evidence to support the belief of an absolute critical period of development such that interventions introduced after a certain age are ineffective. Yet research does suggest that earlier enrollment in intervention programs produces the greatest benefit, implying that it is a matter of developmental timing (Hallahan et al., 2009).

- The intensity of these early intervention efforts can also substantially influence outcome effectiveness (Guralnick & Conlon, 2007; McCormick et al., 2006).
- An assumption that early intervention can minimize the impact of a particular disabling condition like the effect of a severe hearing loss on the development of speech and language and possibly prevent or attenuate the occurrence of secondary disabilities.
- The proposition that intervention programs can ameliorate learning deficits and problems frequently attributed to certain risk factors such as environmental conditions.
- Benefits that accrue to families of young children with special needs and children at risk. These children frequently present many new challenges and additional responsibilities for caregivers and can potentially impact the entire family constellation. Early childhood special education professionals can assist families by providing factual information, emotional support, and specific training as requested. A further role for professionals is to establish meaningful partnerships with parents guided by the principles of enabling and empowering parents (Dunst, Trivette, & Deal, 1988).
- Benefits that extend beyond the child and his or her family to society at large. Early intervention is cost effective. The effectiveness has been documented in terms of dollars saved and the reduced need for special education services at an older age (Guralnick, 2004).

In summary, early intervention/education for children with disabilities has definite advantages for society, the family, and, of course, the child. Early childhood special education can make a significant difference in the quality of life for young children with special needs and their families. In fact, early intervention as a strategy to prevent later problems has almost become conventional wisdom (Kamerman, 2000). Scientists have been able to consistently demonstrate that well-designed early intervention programs produce modest positive outcomes according to their intended purpose (Bailey, 2000; Guralnick & Conlon, 2007; Ramey & Ramey, 1998; Zigler, 2000). Thus, we are in full agreement with the Rameys' persuasive argument that "early intervention can improve the course of early human development . . . " (p. 118).

Representative Research Evidence on the Effectiveness of Intervention

During the past four decades there have been numerous investigations examining the effectiveness of early intervention with youngsters at risk and young children with documented disabilities. Many reviews and summaries of these efforts have been published (Casto & Mastropieri, 1986; Farran, 1990; Guralnick, 1997; Shonkoff & Hauser-Cram, 1987; White, Bush, & Casto, 1986). As might be expected, the analyses revealed, for a variety of reasons, contradictory findings. As a whole, however, the reports indicate positive outcomes for early intervention, especially when a distinction is made between statistical significance and clinical significance. A group of children who learn to accomplish specific self-help skills, like independently feeding themselves, might not evidence statistical significance due to small sample size, but this accomplishment is important for the youngsters and their families (Bailey & Wolery, 1992). While the research evidence does provide qualified support for the effectiveness of early intervention, several investigators and authors comment on the difficulty of conducting methodologically sound experiments (Bowe, 2007; Farran, 1990; Guralnick, 1988, 1991, 1998). Potential problems in interpreting the research literature lie with the appropriateness of the dependent measures; the absence of control groups; small sample sizes; improper sampling procedures; inappropriate statistical techniques; inadequate documentation of the treatment; the validity of the assessment instruments; and the variability within specific subject populations. Odom (1988) suggests that some of the research difficulties are due to the fact that early childhood special education is an applied discipline and given to answering pragmatic questions; researchers, therefore, have less control over variables in natural settings than in laboratory environments. Despite the shortcomings and the vulnerability of the research efforts, positive conclusions

about the efficacy of early intervention can be drawn. Guralnick (1998), for instance, emphatically states that, "comprehensive early intervention programs for children at-risk and for those with established disabilities reveal a consistent pattern of effectiveness" (p. 323). More recently, this expert in the field of early intervention noted that

> The thoughtful implementation of systematic, comprehensive, experientially based early intervention programs . . . will enhance the development of young children already exhibiting intellectual delays (of known or unknown etiology) both by altering their developmental trajectories and by preventing secondary complications from occurring. (GURALNICK, 2005, P. 314)

We will now review some of the research evidence.

We begin with the classic but methodologically controversial study conducted by Skeels and Dye (1939), which significantly influenced the then current thinking about intelligence. These investigators reported an experiment where 13 children under three years of age were removed from an orphanage and placed in an institution for the mentally retarded, where they received a great deal of care and attention from the female residents. A control group of 12 children remained at the overcrowded orphanage and was not exposed to individual stimulation or training. Intellectual assessments were conducted at the time of transfer. When the children were reevaluated 18 to 36 months later, significant differences were observed between the experimental and control subjects. The 13 children placed on the ward with the young women with intellectual disabilities demonstrated an average gain in IQ scores of 27.5 points, while the initially higher-IQ-scoring control children showed a loss of 26.2 points. Each of the children who transferred to the more enriched environment showed an increase in measured intelligence, while all except one of the controls suffered a loss; 10 children had a decrease in IQ score between 18 and 45 points.

Perhaps the most significant finding of this investigation is the long-term follow-up of the subjects into adulthood. Even as adults, the differences between the two samples are significant. Skeels (1966) reports that members of the treatment group maintained their gains and all were self-supporting. Their median grade level attainment was greater than twelfth grade, whereas the children who remained at the orphanage had a median educational attainment of less than third grade. Differences in occupational achievement were also noted, with the experimental subjects enjoying greater career accomplishment while the controls remained wards of the state or largely worked as unskilled laborers.

Although the methodology of the Skeels and Dye investigation has been criticized, the study did demonstrate that environmental conditions affect development as well as point out that the deleterious experiences of early childhood can be reversed. The work of Skeels and Dye, as Bailey and Wolery (1992) note, "remains as one of the few truly longitudinal studies of intervention effectiveness" (p. 6).

Another pioneering study is the work of Kirk (1958), who investigated the effects of preschool experiences on the mental and social development of children ages three to six with mental retardation. Eighty-one children with IQ scores ranging from 45 to 80 were assigned to either an intervention group or served as control subjects. Two experimental groups were established containing children who lived in the community or resided in an institution. The controls also lived either at home or in a residential environment. Both intervention groups who were exposed to two years of preschool experiences demonstrated significant gains on measures of intellectual and social functioning as compared to young children without the benefit of intervention. The performance of the control children decreased. Follow-up indicated that the experimental subjects retained their advantage until age eight. However, some of the community-based control subjects did catch up to the experimental children after one year of school.

Kirk's research, as well as the efforts of Skeels and Dye (1939), attests to the malleability of early development in addition to providing strong evidence of the effectiveness of early intervention. As we noted elsewhere, in the 1960s the social conscience of America was awakened. As a nation we became cognizant of the devastating effects of poverty and other social ills on the lives of young children and their families. One consequence of this heightened social awareness was the establishment of preschool intervention programs for poor children, or in contemporary terms, children who are environmentally at risk. The lasting effects of some of these projects were evaluated by the Consortium for Longitudinal Studies. Lazar and his colleagues (Lazar & Darlington, 1979; Lazar, Darlington, Murray, Royce, & Snipper, 1982) issued two major reports summarizing the

results of twelve comprehensive follow-up studies of children enrolled in cognitively oriented preschools established in the 1960s. None of the projects focused specifically on children with special needs, although several selected participants on the basis of low IQ scores (range 50–85). Using original data from each program, Lazar found that environmentally at-risk enrollees had higher achievement and intelligence test scores as compared to children who did not have the benefit of preschool intervention. Their analysis also revealed that early intervention experiences significantly reduced the number of young children placed in special education and retained in their current grade. In comparison to control groups, preschool graduates had more positive attitudes toward school and furnished more achievement-oriented responses in follow-up interviews. Lazar and his coworkers concluded that, overall, the projects produced lasting positive outcomes and were cost effective when compared to later remediation efforts or special class placement. Table 2–8, derived from a composite of empirical investigations, summarizes some of the short- and long-term benefits that result from participating in a well-run preschool program.

The efficacy of early intervention has also been examined with children manifesting an established risk. One population that has received considerable attention is young children with Down syndrome. An example is the work of Guralnick and Bricker (1987). Using

TABLE 2–8 Beneficial Outcomes of High-Quality Preschool Programs

- Enhanced scholastic achievement
- Less grade retention
- Higher IQ scores
- Decreased likelihood of receiving special education services
- More positive attitudes toward school and learning
- Greater likelihood of graduating from high school
- Less likelihood of accessing public assistance
- Greater possibility of securing meaningful employment

stringent criteria for inclusion, these investigators evaluated the outcomes of 11 projects. They concluded, based on the substantial number of "first generation" studies reviewed, that the documented decline in cognitive ability with advancing chronological age typically found in children with Down syndrome can be significantly reduced, prevented, and, to some extent, reversed as a result of early intervention. This significant outcome is consistent across a wide variety of programs incorporating diverse experimental designs.

The issue of maintenance of cognitive gains, however, is not clear-cut, due to limited information and contradictory findings. Equally difficult to answer is the question of when is the best time to begin early intervention. The research evidence is, once again, contradictory. Both of these issues await more extensive and systematic research that is skillfully designed to answer these questions. Despite these shortcomings, empirical investigations strongly speak to the positive benefits of early intervention with children with Down syndrome.

Another illustration of the efficacy of early intervention is the highly visible work of Casto and Mastropieri (1986). These investigators used a comprehensive statistical integration approach known as **meta-analysis.** In this method, all available research (both published and unpublished) incorporating a range of experimental designs is evaluated in an attempt to detect global statistical patterns, which yield an "effect size" reported as standard deviations (SD). Seventy-four studies of early intervention efforts of heterogeneous groups of children were analyzed. Criteria for inclusion were minimal. Overall, the meta-analysis outcomes supported the efficacy of early intervention. Modest gains were observed in children's test scores—typically standardized intelligence tests or other cognitive assessments. Cognitive measures yielded a mean effect size of .85 SD. When other dependent measures were included, such as motor and language assessments, the effect size was reduced to .68 SD. This means that the typical child with special needs in an early intervention program scored .68 of a standard deviation higher than a counterpart who was not receiving early services.

Casto and Mastropieri (1986) also reported that early intervention programs that are longer in duration and more intense usually demonstrate greater effectiveness. Two intriguing and controversial findings emerged, however, both of which were contrary to conventional wisdom and challenged two widely held beliefs of the field. First, Casto and Mastropieri found no support for the belief that the earlier the intervention commences ("earlier is better"), the greater its effectiveness. Second, their meta-analyses suggested that greater parental participation does not necessarily lead to enhanced program effectiveness.

As might be expected, professional reaction to these summary statements was swift and intense (Dunst & Snyder, 1986; Strain & Smith, 1986). Critics of the Casto and Mastropieri (1986) meta-analyses assailed the conclusions, claiming that the analysis was methodologically ("apples and oranges approach") and conceptually flawed. It must be remembered, however, that this investigation was based on an enormously heterogeneous group of children incorporating different intervention methods and procedures as well as employing diverse outcome measures. It would be prudent, therefore, to draw only limited conclusions.

A subsequent and better controlled meta-analysis using a subset of the original database focusing exclusively on children younger than three years of age yielded different and more positive results (Shonkoff & Hauser-Cram, 1987). This more selective analysis revealed that young children with mild disabilities had better outcomes with earlier enrollment, and higher levels of parent involvement were associated with greater child progress and performance.

Our final example is Guralnick's (1997) extensive examination of "second generation" research studies involving children at risk and children with a broad spectrum of established risks. This review examined the efficacy of early intervention and the variables that impede or enhance its effectiveness, such as child characteristics (type and severity of disability), family characteristics, and program features (curriculum, parent-child interventions, social support). Some of the conclusions gleaned from this work support the following generalizations—the outcomes of intervention are positive, albeit modest; the sheer number of deleterious variables affecting development may be more significant than any one factor; and finally, careful consideration should be given to ecological factors affecting child-caregiver and child-family relationships.

Despite the chronic problems in conducting efficacy evaluations, it is our opinion that early intervention does make a difference in the lives of young children with special needs. It would appear that the field of early childhood special education has moved beyond the global question of whether early intervention works (we believe it does) to more precise avenues of inquiry: for whom, under what conditions, and toward what outcomes (Guralnick, 1988). Like Bailey (2000), we believe that the debate will no longer be whether to provide early intervention, "but rather how much and what kind of intervention are children and families entitled to" (p. 74). A major task confronting the field will be to identify which early intervention programs work best and what elements are clearly essential to achieve maximum benefit (Zigler, 2000).

Early intervention research is not static, but rather an ongoing process. It can help guide researchers, policymakers, and educators in their quest to develop new models, programs, and services that benefit infants, toddlers, and preschoolers with special needs and their families.

An Ecological Perspective on Young Children with Special Needs and Their Families

One contemporary trend in early childhood special education is to view children as part of a larger social scheme wherein they influence, and are influenced by, various environments. This context, referred to as **ecology,** looks at the interrelationships and interactions of individuals within the environment. The primary advocate of this ecological model is Urie Bronfenbrenner (1977, 1979). From this ecological perspective, Bronfenbrenner attempts to understand the relationship between the immediate environments in which a young child develops and the larger context of those settings. A developing child, therefore, cannot be viewed in isolation but rather as part of a larger social system. We believe it is impossible to discuss children without also describing the context in which they develop and interact—their families and communities. As an illustration, early childhood professionals must have an appreciation for the child's total environment—home, school, community, and the larger society, in addition to the individuals encountered therein—parents, siblings, classmates, playmates, and therapists, among other people. Spodek and Saracho (1994a) support our viewpoint. They write that:

The influence of the classroom on the young child, many educators believe, cannot be separated

from the influence of the family or from the context in which both the classroom and family exist. Home, school, community, and culture are all linked to each other. (p. 80)

As we just noted, the foundation for our thinking emerges from the theorizing of Bronfenbrenner (1977), who defines the ecology of human development as:

the scientific study of the progressive, mutual accommodation, throughout the life span, between a growing human organism and the changing immediate environments in which it lives, as this process is affected by relations obtaining within and between these immediate settings, as well as the larger social contexts, both formal and informal, in which the settings are embedded. (p. 514)

We further accept his "unorthodox" belief (Bronfenbrenner, 1979) that development is grounded in the context in which it occurs. Basic to this notion is the idea that the contexts in which a person develops are nested, one inside the other, similar to a set of *matryoshka,* or Russian stacking dolls.

Bronfenbrenner identified four environments in which people develop:

- **Microsystems** are those immediate environments in which an individual develops.
- **Mesosystems** are identified as the relationships between various microsystems.
- **Exosystems** are social structures that have an influence on the development of the individual; however, the person does not have a direct role in the social system.
- **Macrosystems,** which are the ideological, cultural, and institutional contexts in which the preceding systems are embedded.

These nested relationships, as they relate to young children with special needs and their families, are portrayed in Figure 2–3. This ecological context provides us with a framework for understanding the world of young children and has led to the contemporary practice of viewing families as systems embedded within other systems. The *microsystem,* according to Bailey, Farel, O'Donnell, Simeonsson, and Miller (1986), looks at relationships within the crucial setting of the child's family in addition to the environments typically encountered by young children—child care centers, homes of relatives or friends, and in certain circumstances, institutional settings like

FIGURE 2–3 The Ecology of Human Development

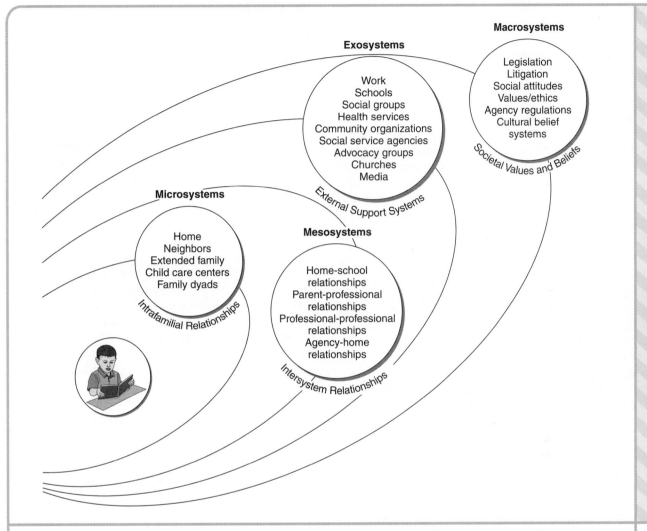

Source: Based on D. Bailey and M. Wolery, *Teaching Infants and Preschoolers with Disabilities* (New York: Macmillan, 1992).

hospitals. The second layer, or *mesosystem*, relates to the relationships, at a particular point in a child's life, between caregiver and teacher or physician as well as the interaction of one professional with another. The *exosystem* takes into consideration the social structures that impact family functioning. Early intervention programs as well as health/social service agencies are representative of this third setting (McLean, Wolery, & Bailey, 2004). The final context is the *macrosystem* and includes societal values and attitudes toward individuals with disabilities, in addition to legislative

enactments and judicial remedies, which in turn affect the lives of young children and their families. IDEA is a powerful example of a macrosystem in action.

Of course, the impact of time and history on the spheres of influence surrounding the developing child must also be considered. Bronfenbrenner and Morris (1998) refer to the interaction and influence of historical time on the four systems supporting the youngster as the **chronosystem**.

Kirk, Gallagher, Coleman, and Anastasiow (2009) embrace a concept very similar to Bronfenbrenner's ecological model. These writers also believe it is vital for early childhood professionals to consider the familial and social context encountered by children with disabilities. The child is seen as being at the center of successive layers of influence, with the family being the primary and frequently most influential context. Other orbits include the peer group (which may include typical and atypical children), schools, and society itself (see Figure 2–3). Like Bailey et al. (1986) and Odom and Wolery (2003), Kirk and his colleagues see the child with special needs in dynamic and complex interaction with many layers of environmental forces.

Recommended practices in early childhood special education (Sandall, Hemmeter, Smith, & McLean, 2005) rely heavily on the importance of the child's family. According to Kirk et al. (2009):

The trend toward early intervention (before the age of 5) increases the importance of the family. Much of the intervention with young children is directed toward changing the family environment and preparing the parent or parents to care for and teach their child. At the very least, intervention tries to generate more constructive parent-child interactions. (pp. 15-16)

The value of the family can be seen in the Head Start commitment to meaningful parent (caregiver) involvement and participation. It is also clearly evident in IDEA and its accompanying amendments.

Successful program planning and intervention, therefore, must take into consideration the fact that the child is part of a system that interacts reciprocally within his or her environment. Bronfenbrenner (1979) observes that accomplishment of a specific task or activity "may depend no less on how he [the child] is taught than on the existence and nature of the ties between the school and home" (p. 3). Vincent, Salisbury, Strain, McCormick, and Tessier (1990) also note that "a change in the child is dependent not just on professional skills or the child's disability, but also upon complex interrelationships among family values, intra- and extra-family supports, and the extent to which service is offered, match what families need and want" (p. 186).

The message is clear. Quality programs for young children with special needs demand that professionals see the child within the context of her family and, in turn, the family's interrelationships and interactions with other, larger social systems.

Summary

Early childhood special educators will serve a wide variety of young children in a diversity of settings. It is imperative, therefore, that early childhood special education teachers have a clear understanding of how children from birth through age eight qualify for special education services. Of equal if not greater importance is our belief that young children with special needs are more like their typically developing peers than they are different. Early childhood special educators should focus on the strengths of each child not their limitations; we need to separate the individual's abilities from his or her disabilities.

The growth of early childhood special education as a discipline has been aided by judicial action and federal legislation. In several instances, principles addressed in various judicial proceedings have found their way into both state and national legislation. Many contemporary special education policies, practices, and procedures are derived from court decisions of the 1960s and 1970s. Likewise, the rights, opportunities, and benefits presently enjoyed by young children with special needs and their families are the result of federal legislative activity.

A question typically encountered by early childhood special educators is, "Is early intervention effective, does it really make a difference in the lives of young children?" Perhaps the best way to answer this difficult query is to say, "It depends." One of the reasons we are so vague is due to the documented difficulty of conducting a methodologically sound investigation. In spite of this shortcoming, there is a very strong rationale for early intervention and the efficacy of these efforts, in our opinion, has been substantially demonstrated.

The number of young children receiving special education services has grown dramatically in the past several years. This growth is partially the result of litigation, legislation, and the benefits attributed to early intervention. In the 2007–2008 school year, more than 1.1 million young children from birth through age eight were enrolled in some type of early intervention or special education program.

Contemporary thinking in early childhood special education strongly suggests the validity of viewing children as part of a larger social system, wherein they influence and are influenced by various environments.

Children and their families need to be understood in the context in which they develop and interact. There is a reciprocal relationship among the various layers of environmental forces. This ecological perspective encourages early childhood professionals to be mindful of the child's total environment and the key people encountered within these several spheres of influence.

Check Your Understanding

1. What is the difference between a *disability* and a *handicap?*
2. List the advantages of using the developmental delay category in early childhood special education.
3. What is meant by the terms special education and related services?
4. Identify the significance of the following court cases:
    a. Pennsylvania Association for Retarded Children v. Commonwealth of Pennsylvania
    b. Mills v. Board of Education of the District of Columbia
    c. Larry P. v. Riles
    d. Board of Education v. Rowley.
5. List the major provisions of PL 94-142 and PL 99-457.
6. What is an individualized family service plan (IFSP)?
7. What is the role of a service coordinator?
8. Identify at least four benefits of early intervention for young children with disabilities and individuals considered to be at risk.
9. What general conclusions can be drawn from the efficacy research on early intervention?
10. According to Bronfenbrenner, how should early childhood special educators view young children and their families?

Reflection and Application

1. Trace the evolution of education law for children with disabilities. How have early childhood special educators become better prepared to meet the needs of young children with special needs as result of legislative activity?

2. How has the role of parents changed over the years? What evidence to you see that families/caregivers are involved in the early intervention/early education of their children?
3. How has the development of the IFSP/IEP process improved the education of young children with delays and disabilities? What types of information can an early childhood special educator contribute to an IFSP/IEP meeting? How are the IFSP and the IEP similar? Different?
4. In what ways do you see the philosophy of Bronfenbrenner being incorporated in early intervention programs or early childhood special education classrooms? Do you agree with the Bronfenbrenner's ideas?
5. Conduct a mock IFSP/IEP meeting and write a script that leads to developing a well written individualized family service plan or individualized education program. Be sure to include the family as a key partner in this process.

References

Allen, K., & Cowdery, G. (2009). *The exceptional child: Inclusion in early education* (6th ed.). Clifton Park, NY: Thomson/Delmar Learning.

Bailey, D. (2000). The federal role in early intervention: Prospects for the future. *Topics in Early Childhood Special Education, 20*(2), 71–78.

Bailey, D., Farel, A., O'Donnell, K., Simeonsson, R., & Miller, C. (1986). Preparing infant interventionists: Interdepartmental training in special education and maternal and child health. *Journal of the Division for Early Childhood, 11*(1), 67–77.

Bailey, D., & Wolery, M. (1992). *Teaching infants and preschoolers with disabilities* (2nd ed.). New York: Merrill.

Bowe, F. (2007). *Early childhood special education* (4th ed.). Clifton Park, NY: Thomson/Delmar Learning.

Bronfenbrenner, U. (1977). Toward an experimental ecology of human development. *American Psychologist, 32*(7), 513–531.

Bronfenbrenner, U. (1979). *The ecology of human development: Experiments by nature and design.* Cambridge, MA: Harvard University Press.

Bronfenbrenner, U., & Morris, P. (1998). The ecology of developmental processes. In W. Damon & R. Lerner (Eds.), *Handbook of child psychology* (5th ed., Vol. 1, pp. 993–1028). New York: Wiley.

Casto, G., & Mastropieri, M. (1986). The efficacy of early intervention programs: A meta-analysis. *Exceptional Children, 52*(5), 417–424.

CEC Today. (1997). What every teacher needs to know: A comparison of Section 504, ADA, and IDEA, *4*(4), 1, 3, 15.

Clarke, A., & Clarke, A. (1976). *Early experience: Myth and evidence.* New York: Free Press.

Danaher, J. (2007). *Eligibility policies and practices for young children under Part B of IDEA.* (NECTAC Notes 24). Chapel Hill, NC: University of North Carolina, FPG Child Development Institute, National Early Childhood Technical Assistance Center.

Division for Early Childhood. (1996). *Developmental delay as an eligibility category* (Concept paper). Reston, VA: Author.

Division for Early Childhood. (2001). *Developmental delay as an eligibility category* (Concept paper). Missoula, MT: Author.

Dunst, C., & Snyder, S. (1986). A critique of the Utah State University early intervention meta-analysis. *Exceptional Children, 53*(3), 269–276.

Dunst, C., Trivette, C., & Deal, A. (1988). *Enabling and empowering families: Principles and guidelines for practice.* Cambridge, MA: Brookline Books.

Fallen, H., & Umansky, W. (1985). *Young children with special needs* (2nd ed.). Columbus, OH: Merrill.

Farran, D. (1990). Effects of intervention with disadvantaged and disabled children: A decade of review. In S. Meisels & J. Shonkoff (Eds.), *Handbook of early intervention* (pp. 501–539). Cambridge, England: Cambridge University Press.

Farran, D. (2000). Another decade of intervention for children who are low income or disabled: What do we know now? In J. Shonkoff & S. Meisels (Eds.), *Handbook of early intervention* (2nd ed., pp. 510–548). Cambridge, England: Cambridge University Press.

Gargiulo, R. (2009). *Special education in contemporary society: An introduction to exceptionality* (3rd ed.). Thousand Oaks, CA: Sage.

Gargiulo, R., & Metcalf, D. (2010). *Teaching in today's inclusive classrooms.* Belmont, CA: Wadsworth/Cengage Learning.

Guralnick, M. (1988). Efficacy research in early childhood intervention programs. In S. Odom & M. Karnes (Eds.), *Early intervention for infants and children with handicaps: An empirical base* (pp. 75–88). Baltimore: Paul H. Brookes.

Guralnick, M. (1991). The next decade of research on the effectiveness of early intervention. *Exceptional Children, 58*(1), 174–183.

Guralnick, M. (1997). *The effectiveness of early intervention.* Baltimore: Paul H. Brookes.

Guralnick, M. (1998). Effectiveness of early intervention for vulnerable children: A developmental perspective. *American Journal on Mental Retardation, 102*(4), 319–345.

Guralnick, M. (2004). Family investments in response to the developmental challenges of young children with disabilities. In A. Kalil & T. Deleire (Eds.), *Family investments in children's potential* (pp. 119-137). Mahwah, NJ: Erlbaum.

Guralnick, M. (2005). Early intervention for children with intellectual disabilities: Current knowledge and future prospects. *Journal of Applied Research in Intellectual Disabilities, 18*(4), 313–324.

Guralnick, M., & Bricker, D. (1987). The effectiveness of early intervention for children with cognitive and general developmental delay. In M. Guralnick & F. Bennett (Eds.), *The effectiveness of early intervention for at-risk and handicapped children* (pp. 115–173). New York: Academic Press.

Guralnick, M., & Conlon, C. (2007). Early intervention. In M. Batshaw, L. Pelligrino, & N. Roizen (Eds.), *Children with disabilities* (6th ed., pp. 511–521). Baltimore: Paul H. Brookes.

Hallahan, D., Kauffman, J., & Pullen, P. (2009). *Exceptional learners* (11th ed.). Boston: Pearson Education.

Hanson, M., & Lynch, E. (1995). *Early intervention* (2nd ed.). Austin, TX: Pro-Ed.

Harbin, G., McWilliam, R., & Gallagher, J. (2000). Services for young children with disabilities and their families. In J. Shonkoff & S. Meisels (Eds.), *Handbook of early intervention* (2nd ed., pp. 387–415). Cambridge, England: Cambridge University Press.

Howard, V., Williams, B., & Lepper, C. (2005). *Very young children with special needs.* Upper Saddle River, NJ: Pearson Education.

Kamerman, S. (2000). Early childhood intervention policies: An international perspective. In J. Shonkoff & S. Meisels (Eds.), *Handbook of early intervention* (2nd ed., pp. 613–629). Cambridge, England: Cambridge University Press.

Kirk, S. (1958). *Early education of the mentally retarded: An experimental study.* Urbana: University of Illinois Press.

Kirk, S., Gallagher, J., Coleman, M., & Anastasiow, N. (2009). *Educating exceptional children* (12th ed.). Boston: Houghton Mifflin.

Kopp, C. (1983). Risk factors in development. In P. Mussen (Ed.), *Handbook of child psychology* (4th ed., Vol. II, pp. 1081–1088). New York: Wiley.

Koppelman, J. (1986). Reagan signs bills expanding services to handicapped preschoolers. *Report to Preschool Programs, 18,* 3–4.

Lazar, I., & Darlington, R. (1979). *Summary report: Lasting effects after preschool.* (DHEW Publication No. OHDS 80-30179). Washington, DC: U.S. Government Printing Office.

Lazar, I., Darlington, R., Murray, H., Royce, J., & Snipper, A. (1982). Lasting effects of early intervention: A report from the Consortium for Longitudinal Studies.

Monographs of the Society for Research in Child Development, *47,* (2–3, Serial No. 195).

McCollum, J., & Maude, S. (1993). Portrait of a changing field: Policy and practice in early childhood special education. In B. Spodek (Ed.), *Handbook of research in early childhood education* (pp. 352–371). New York: Macmillan.

McCormick, M., Brooks-Gunn, J., Buka, S., Goldman, J., Yu, J., Salganik, M., Scott, D., Bennett, F., Kay, L., Berbaum, J., Bauer, C., Martin, C., Woods, E., Martin, A., & Casey, P. (2006). Early intervention in low birth weight premature infants: Results at 18 years of age for the Infant Health and Development Program. *Pediatrics, 117*(3), 771–780.

McLean, M., Bailey, D., & Wolery, M. (2004). *Assessing infants and preschoolers with special needs* (3rd ed.). Upper Saddle River, NJ: Pearson Education.

Odom, S. (1988). Research in early childhood special education: Methodologies and paradigms. In S. Odom & M. Karnes (Eds.), *Early intervention for infants and children with handicaps* (pp. 1–21). Baltimore: Paul H. Brookes.

Odom, S., & Wolery, M. (2003). A unified theory of practice in early intervention/early childhood special education: Evidence-based practices. *Journal of Special Education, 37*(3), 164–173.

Peterson, N. (1987). *Early intervention for handicapped and at-risk children.* Denver: Love.

Ramey, C., & Ramey, S. (1998). Early intervention and early experience. *American Psychologist, 58*(2), 109–120.

Raver, S. (1999). *Intervention strategies for infants and toddlers with special needs* (2nd ed.). Upper Saddle River, NJ: Prentice Hall.

Sandall, S., Hemmeter, M., Smith, B., & McLean, M. (2005). *DEC recommended practices: A comprehensive guide to practical application.* Longmont, CO: Sopris West.

Shackelford, J. (2006). *State and jurisdictional eligibility definitions for infants and toddlers with disabilities under IDEA.* (NECTAC Notes 21). Chapel Hill, NC: University of North Carolina, FPG Child Development Institute, National Early Childhood Technical Assistance Center.

Shonkoff, J., & Hauser-Cram, P. (1987). Early intervention for disabled infants and their families: A quantitative analysis. *Pediatrics, 80*(5), 650–658.

Skeels, H. (1966). Adult status of children with contrasting early life experiences. *Monographs of the Society for Research in Child Development, 31,* (3, Serial No. 105).

Skeels, H., & Dye, H. (1939). A study of the effects of differential stimulation on mentally retarded children. *Proceedings and Addresses of the American Association on Mental Deficiency, 44,* 114–136.

Smith, B., & Guralnick, M. (2007). Definition of early intervention. In R. New & M. Cochran (Eds.), *Early childhood education: An international encyclopedia* (Vol. 2, pp. 329–332). Westport, CT: Greenwood Publishing Group.

Smith, T. (2002). Section 504: Basic requirements for schools. *Intervention in School and Clinic, 37*(5), 259–266.

Smith, T., & Patton, J. (1998). *Section 504 and public schools.* Austin, TX: Pro-Ed.

Spodek, B., & Saracho, O. (1994a). *Right from the start.* Needham Heights, MA: Allyn & Bacon.

Spodek, B., & Saracho, O. (1994b). *Dealing with individual differences in the early childhood classroom.* White Plains, NY: Longman.

Strain, P., & Smith, B. (1986). A counter-interpretation of early intervention effects: A response to Casto and Mastropieri. *Exceptional Children, 53*(3), 260–265.

Taylor, R., Smiley, L., & Richards, S. (2009). *Exceptional students.* New York: McGraw-Hill.

Tjossem, T. (1976). Early intervention: Issues and approaches. In T. Tjossem (Ed.), *Intervention strategies for high-risk and handicapped children* (pp. 3–33). Baltimore: University Park Press.

Trohanis, P. (1989). An introduction to PL 99-457 and the national policy agenda for serving young children with special needs and their families. In J. Gallagher, P. Trohanis, & R. Clifford (Eds.), *Policy implementation and PL 99-457: Planning for young children with special needs* (pp. 1–17). Baltimore: Paul H. Brookes.

U.S. Department of Education. (1997). *Nineteenth annual report to Congress on the implementation of the Individuals with Disabilities Education Act.* Washington, DC: U.S. Government Printing Office.

U.S. Department of Education. (2001). *Twenty-third annual report to Congress on the implementation of the Individuals with Disabilities Education Act.* Washington, DC: U.S Government Printing Office.

U.S. Department of Education. (2009). *IDEA data.* Retrieved March 22, 2009 from http://www.ideadata.org/PartBReport.asp

Vincent, L., Salisbury, C., Strain, P., McCormick, C., & Tessier, A. (1990). A behavioral ecological approach to early intervention: Focus on cultural diversity. In S. Meisels & J. Shonkoff (Eds.), *Handbook of early childhood intervention* (pp. 173–195). Cambridge, England: Cambridge University Press.

Walsh, S., Smith, B., & Taylor, R. (2000). *IDEA requirements for preschoolers with disabilities.* Reston, VA: Council for Exceptional Children.

White, K., Bush, D., & Casto, G. (1986). Learning from reviews of early intervention. *Journal of Special Education, 19*(4), 417–428.

Zigler, E. (1990). Foreword. In S. Meisels & J. Shonkoff (Eds.), *Handbook of early childhood intervention* (pp. ix–xiv). Cambridge, England: Cambridge University Press.

Zigler, E. (2000). Foreword. In J. Shonkoff & S. Meisels (Eds.), *Handbook of early intervention* (2nd ed., pp. xi–xv). Cambridge, England: Cambridge University Press.

MAKING CONNECTIONS

In order to help you understand programs and services for young children with special needs, we would like to introduce three children, Maria, T.J., and Cheryl. We will be talking about the educational needs of Maria, T.J., and Cheryl over the next several chapters. It is our wish that by getting to know these children, you will develop a better understanding of the diversity of services required for young children with disabilities and their families.

Maria Ramirez

Bubbly, outgoing, and affectionate with a constant smile are some of the terms Maria's interventionists use when describing her. This 30-month-old with Down syndrome is the youngest child of Bruce and Catherine Ramirez. Mr. Ramirez is an executive with a local bank. Maria's mother is employed as an intensive care nurse at the regional hospital. Her two older brothers enjoy their role as protector of their little sister. The Ramirez family lives in an affluent section of a small town approximately 50 miles from a large Midwestern city.

A service coordinator comes to Maria's home one morning a week in order to provide assistance with the achievement of her IFSP outcome statements. Due to her parents' work schedule and other commitments, Maria's grandparents provide child care and are prepared to work with her. Maria's entire family is committed to maximizing her potential.

Team members have recommended that Maria transition to an inclusive community-based program in order to receive Part B services. Although the family understands that with the approach of her third birthday, a change in service delivery is necessary, they are reluctant to agree to this recommendation. Maria's parents and grandparents have several concerns. Among their fears are issues of working with a new set of professionals, the length of her day, transportation to and from school, and Maria's interaction with typically developing peers.

Thomas Jefferson (T.J.) Browning

T.J. Browning is a rambunctious little boy who just celebrated his fourth birthday two months ago. He lives with his mother and a 12-year-old stepbrother, Willy. His mom has been separated from his dad for 14 months. The family lives in a large apartment complex for citizens with incomes at or below the poverty level. There are few playmates his own age in the complex. T.J. does not have a close relationship with his older brother; his mom has suspicions that Willy may be involved with a neighborhood gang.

T.J. has been attending the Epps Head Start Center for the past 15 months. In the center, T.J. has few friends. The staff observe that he has a short attention span, is easily distracted, and is overly aggressive. T.J. frequently uses his large size to get what he wants from the other children. Although well-coordinated, he has impairments with fine motor skills and his teachers suspect some cognitive deficits. T.J. receives integrated speech therapy twice a week from a speech-language pathologist. The director of the Epps Center and her staff are concerned about his readiness to attend kindergarten in the fall.

T.J.'s mother is a concerned parent who wants her son to be successful in school. Her job as a waitress limits her participation in center activities and from attending meetings and class field trips.

Cheryl Chinn

Cheryl is a petite first grader attending an elementary school located in a large metropolitan area. She is the youngest of four children. Her father is a senior project manager for a multinational corporation. Cheryl's mom, Elizabeth, does not work outside of the home.

(continued)

MAKING CONNECTIONS

Cheryl was an unplanned pregnancy. Elizabeth was 41 years old when Cheryl was born. Cheryl was born at 30 weeks gestation age and weighed slightly more than four pounds at birth. The first 10 days of Cheryl's life were spent in a neonatal intensive care unit. Developmental milestones were accomplished about six months later than normal. Other than recurring episodes of otitis media, the first few years of her life were unremarkable.

Cheryl was enrolled in a preschool program when she turned three. She attended this program three days a week for two years. Due to a late summer birthday, her parents considered delaying her entrance to kindergarten. She started kindergarten, however, with the other children from her neighborhood. Difficulty in following directions and instructions and with task completion, a short attention span, and social immaturity were soon observed. Cheryl required a "learning buddy" (peer helper) for her academic work. Because school officials were opposed to grade retention, Cheryl was promoted to first grade.

Many of the problems that Cheryl encountered in kindergarten were magnified in first grade. Shortly before a referral for special education services was to be made, Cheryl's pediatrician diagnosed her with attention deficit hyperactivity disorder (ADHD). Cheryl's teacher believes that a 504 accommodation plan would help Cheryl with her impulsivity, distractibility, and short attention span. The use of a peer helper was also continued.

Cheryl's parents are very involved in her education and fully support the development of a 504 accommodation plan. They were reluctant, however, to have their daughter referred for special education and possibly identified under the developmental delay category, especially since two of her older brothers are receiving services for children with gifts and talents.

3 Family-Based Early Childhood Services

Key Terminology

Collaboration

Nuclear family

Family

Culture

Hybrid family

Family systems theory

Family characteristics

Family interactions

Cohesion

Adaptability

Family functions

Family life cycle

Transition

Ecological perspective

Empowerment

Eco-maps

Family-centered practices

Family-based practices

Family-directed practices

Cultural responsiveness

Stereotyping

Communication

Learning Outcomes

After reading this chapter, you will be able to:

- Describe how the relationship between families and service providers in early intervention/early childhood special education (EI/ECSE) has changed over the years.

- Explain family systems theory and provide examples of each element of the approach.

- Discuss the importance of strong family–professional relationships in EI/ECSE.

- Describe the influences that have contributed to the emergence of a family-based orientation in EI/ECSE.

- Describe the key components of family–professional collaboration, as well as strategies to foster positive interactions between families and service providers.

- Explain cultural responsiveness and its importance in family–professional relationships.

- Explain the importance of ongoing, effective collaboration among families and professionals in EI/ECSE.

- Describe strategies for communicating with families, meeting with families, and conducting home visits.

In the field of early intervention/early childhood special education (EI/ECSE), practices associated with the concept of being family-based increasingly have been embraced by personnel from many disciplines concerned with the well-being, education, and care of young children with known or suspected disabilities and their families. Calls have become commonplace for early childhood personnel to adopt a family-based model, to provide support to families, and to appropriately address the needs of young children and families from diverse backgrounds. In fact, Bailey and his colleagues (1998) more than a decade ago recommended that a family-centered perspective should permeate all aspects of early intervention/ education services and include, but not be limited to, assessment, team meetings, program planning, intervention activities, service coordination, and transition.

A changing view of families and their participation in their children's EI/ECSE services has emerged over the last several decades. This view involves a true partnership in which families have a right to become involved in early intervention/education services and are encouraged to participate and engage in collaborative activities with professionals to the degree that they choose. A variety of research studies and program models have provided evidence in support of the mutual benefits of such **collaboration**, or working together, among families and professionals (Trivette & Dunst, 2005). Over the years, the roles of family members and professionals have changed to a marked degree and the rationale for building effective partnerships is more compelling than in the past. Further, there has been a dramatic increase in awareness, opportunities, services, and supports for families of young children with known or suspected disabilities. These and other factors related to family-based early childhood services will be examined in this chapter.

Historical and Legal Perspectives

It has long been recognized that the family is the fundamental social institution and the foundation of our society. The family is the primary arena in which a child, with or without a delay or disability,

is socialized, educated, and exposed to the beliefs and values of his or her culture. It is virtually impossible to overemphasize the importance of the development that takes place in the early years and the influence of the interactions that occur among young children and their families. Families play a critical role in facilitating and supporting a child's development, and it is the responsibility of service providers to help families realize the significance of their role. Thus, the importance of collaboration among professionals and families in EI/ECSE cannot be overstated. It is important to note, however, that family involvement in programs for children with known or suspected disabilities is not a new concept. In fact, the history of family involvement in the education of young children with disabilities has been described as an evolving process that has occurred over a number of years. As one early interventionist explained, "We've changed dramatically over the years. We've gone from trying to figure out how professionals can involve parents and provide training to them in areas we think are important to how can professionals provide support to parents in what parents consider important to their child and family." Table 3–1 provides a chronology of the family movement in early intervention/education.

Many factors contributed to the emergence of the emphasis on family involvement in the 1960s and 1970s, among them political, social, economic, and educational issues and events. Political movements, such as the civil rights and women's movements, advocacy efforts, and legislative actions led to the current emphasis that is now placed on the provision of quality programs for young children with special needs and their families. Influences have also come from the fields of general early childhood education, early childhood special education, and compensatory education (e.g., Head Start), as well as from professional organizations. Professional organizations such as the Division for Early Childhood (DEC) of the Council for Exceptional Children (CEC) (Sandall, Hemmeter, Smith, & McLean, 2005), the National Association for the Education of Young Children (NAEYC) (Copple & Bredekamp, 2009), and others have developed recommendations, standards, and policies concerning families. These documents emphasize that the benefits of family–professional collaboration during children's early years extend far beyond the early intervention, preschool, and early primary years.

TABLE 3–1 The Chronology of the Family Movement

1950s	Parents began to organize services and schools for children with disabilities in their communities. National organizations were formed and political action initiated.
1975	PL 94-142, the Education for All Handicapped Children Act (later incorporated into IDEA), established parents' roles as decision makers.
1980s	Grassroots support for parent-to-parent support groups increased.
1983	Legislation established a national program of Parent Training and Information Centers to provide assistance for families.
1986	PL 99-457 (later incorporated in IDEA) mandated that families were to be the focus of services.
1990s	Advocacy movements—early childhood, inclusion, transition, and self-advocacy—grew in numbers and influence.
1997	The 1997 IDEA Amendments placed greater emphasis on the involvement of parents in the eligibility, placement, and IEP processes.

SOURCE: Adapted from N. Flynn and C. Takemoto, The Family Perspective. 1997. In J. Wood and A. Lazzari, *Exceeding the Boundaries: Understanding Exceptional Lives.* Fort Worth, TX: Harcourt Brace College Publisher, p. 506.

Michael Ochs Archives/Getty Images

No longer is there a conventional perspective of a typical American family like the Cleaver family in 'Leave It to Beaver'.

The Changing American Family

As professionals attempt to provide appropriate services and support to families, the dramatic changes that have occurred in the composition of families over the last several decades are important to recognize. The **nuclear family** refers to a family group consisting of, most commonly, a father and mother and their children. The traditional American family was once viewed as: (a) two parents (a male and a female), who were married to each other and always have been; (b) two or more children from the parents' union; (c) two sets of grandparents, living within fifty miles; (d) the mother working in the home and caring for the children; and (e) the father working outside the home and interacting with the children in the evenings and on weekends. This description of the family is much like the television sit-com *Leave It to Beaver,* which was based on the lives of the Cleaver family—a traditional American family of the 1950s. Of course, no longer is it valid to think of a typical family today as a mom who is a full-time homemaker and a working dad along with their children who are all living together.

This conventional perspective of the nuclear family has definitely changed and is continuing to change. In fact, a limited number of families in the United States currently fit this description. The following statistics demonstrate some of the many ways in which the American family and American society have changed:

- Every 33 seconds, a child is born into poverty.
- Every 24 seconds, a child is born to an unmarried mother.
- Thirty-five percent of children are born to single parents.
- More than half of all marriages end in divorce.
- One out of two children will live with a single parent at some point during childhood.
- Twenty-three percent of children live with only their mothers, five percent live with only their fathers, and five percent live with neither parent.

- Of children under age six, 61.7% have all parents in the workforce.
- Thirty-four percent of the homeless population is made up of families with children. (Children's Defense Fund, 2008)

The preceding statistics strongly suggest that no longer is there a typical American family. In other words, the expression "The Cleavers don't live here anymore" is certainly accurate. It is only realistic to define families more broadly. In American families today, there may be many nuclear family configurations including single-parent families, teen parents, families with adopted children, families with foster children, grandparents raising grandchildren, and blended families, to name a few. The definition of **family** used in this chapter is a group of people related by blood or circumstance that rely upon one another for security, sustenance, support, socialization, and/or stimulation. When a young child was asked to draw a picture of his family, he explained that "A family means having someone to tuck you in bed at night."

American families have changed in many different ways. A major way in which families have changed is that they have become more culturally diverse. The term **culture** refers to "the foundational values and beliefs that set the standards for how people perceive, interpret, and behave within their family, school, and community" (Turnbull, Turnbull, Erwin, & Soodak, 2006, p. 19). Although some people limit their view of culture to race, national origin, or ethnicity, there are other influences on a family's cultural identity beliefs, such as religion, language, gender, age, geography, and income. Thus, culture determines how families think, feel, perceive, and behave (Gollnick & Chinn, 2009).

Also represented in today's society is the **hybrid family**, which Aldridge and Goldman (2007) describe as a "family who redefines itself and produces something new and different from the origins that created it" (pp. 184–185). An example of a hybrid family would be one in which each parent has a different ethnic and religious background. Rather than adopting the cultural and religious practices of one parent or the other, the family chooses to practice a blend of both cultures and a religion that is different from either of their families of origin. They have created a hybrid family that is different from either family of origin. As a result of the changes that have occurred in the families served, professionals face many unique challenges

Children come from diverse family structures and backgrounds, which calls for an individualized approach to effectively serve each child and family.

related to family diversity in the 21st century (Copple & Bredekamp, 2009; Kilgo, 2006).

The changes that have occurred and continue to occur in the structures and cultural backgrounds of families issue a call for the utilization of an extremely individualized approach in family–professional interactions. Each of these family configurations and backgrounds adds to the complexity of interactions among families and professionals. Many factors must be taken into consideration when working with diverse family structures and backgrounds, as well as the impact of these variations on family–professional relationships. Professionals must be sensitive to and aware of the unique characteristics of the families they serve. As families continue to change, professionals must carefully examine and discover the most effective methods of serving families.

Family Reactions to a Child with a Developmental Delay or Disability

When a child with a known or suspected disability becomes a member of the family, whether through birth, adoption, or later onset of the disability, the ecology of the family changes and often the entire family must make adjustments. Each parent or family member responds to a child's delay or disability in his or her own unique way, requiring an individualized approach to each family (Bailey et al., 2006; Winzer & Mazurek, 1998). In the same way that professionals realize that all children are individuals, they must also realize that families are also individual and unique entities. Reactions and feelings may be dramatically different from one family to another and from one parent to another (Cooper & Allred, 1992). Professionals, therefore, usually encounter a wide variety of behaviors and emotional responses on the part of parents and other family members.

In the past, some professionals made judgments about families based on a "stage theory" model of parental adjustment in response to having a child with a disability. In recent years, however, this theory has been strongly criticized (Vacca & Feinberg, 2000). The way in which this model evolved is surprising in that it began with a study conducted more than 35 years ago that was designed to assess parents' perceptions, feelings, and attachments to their children with disabilities (Drotar, Baskiewicz, Irvin, Kennell, & Klaus, 1975). Based on the results of this study, Drotar et al. developed a linear "stage theory" model of parental adjustment that followed a progression of acceptance beginning with shock and moving through denial and anger to a point of reorganization and acceptance. According to this model, parents are ready to deal with the responsibilities of their children with disabilities once they have moved through the various stages of acceptance and have dealt with guilt associated with having a child with a disability (Blacher, 1984). Later in the 1980s, stage theories were challenged by researchers who rejected the idea of families, all of whom are unique, going through the same specific stages of acceptance. Further, they disagreed with the idea of family reaction being judged and categorized according to this continuum. In fact, some researchers suggested that the stage theory of acceptance of a child's disability is a disservice to families and is an oversimplification of a complex process that families experience (Gallagher, Fialka, Rhodes, & Arceneaux, 2003).

Most professionals in the field of early intervention/ education today recognize that families respond differently to having a child with a disability based on a number of characteristics, resources, and supports that are unique to the individual family. Researchers have recognized that a variety of factors can interact to influence a family's reaction and subsequent adjustment to a child with a disability, which can

include personal characteristics of family members, patterns of family interactions, health and safety factors, and others. Stress factors or needs associated with disabilities also can affect family functioning and partnerships between professionals and families. For example, professionals who work with four-year-old T.J. must carefully consider the influences of his brother's gang-suspected activities, the neighborhood in which the family lives, his parents' separation, and other family dynamics. From a more positive perspective, some family characteristics could be considered strengths, such as having a large family or a family with effective coping skills, which may mitigate many of the stresses associated with a child with a delay or disability (Guralnick, 1998).

The needs of the parents reflect not only their ability to cope but also their child's developmental needs. For example, the demands placed on the professionals who initially break the news of a child's disability to a family may be very different from those placed on the professionals who help parents deal with the fears associated with the child's transition into a kindergarten classroom. Another example is that the needs of families of children with disabilities such as autism or complex medical disabilities may be different from the needs of the families of children with speech delays. Professionals must tailor their interactions and provide support based on the individual and ever-changing needs of families. Often families of young children with disabilities, especially those of young children with severe disabilities or medically complex conditions, face difficult issues, such as the following:

- Heavy expenses and financial burdens associated with hospitalization, medical treatment, surgery, and child care, as well as other needs such as special foods, equipment, or transportation;
- Frightening, energy-draining, often recurring crises, such as when a child stops breathing, experiences seizures, or faces life-threatening situations;
- Continuous day-and-night demands on families to provide routine but difficult care-giving tasks (e.g., feeding, suctioning, monitoring);
- Constant fatigue, lack of sleep, and little or no time to meet the needs of other family members or to participate in recreational or leisure activities;
- Difficulty locating qualified child care and respite care for children with severe disabilities, which can interfere with the parents' abilities to fulfill

work responsibilities, participate in social activities, etc.;

- Jealousy or feelings of rejection among siblings who may feel the child with a disability requires *all* the family's attention and resources; and
- Marital problems arising from finances, fatigue, and lack of time to devote to the relationship (Allen & Cowdery, 2009)

Professionals must remember that a team effort is required to understand and support each family according to its unique needs. Depending on each family's needs, team members may need to rely on the expertise of health care, mental health, and social service professionals. It is important to remember, however, that the effect of a child with a disability on the family may be positive, negative, or neutral (Turnbull et al., 2006) and can change over time. As emphasized in the American Indian proverb, "Never judge another man until you have walked a mile in his moccasins."

Family Systems Theory

Utilization of a family systems theory model has become the recommended approach in early intervention/early childhood special education. The fundamental belief underlying **family systems theory** is that a family is an interactional system with unique characteristics and needs. A family operates as an interrelated and interdependent unit; therefore, events and experiences that have an impact on particular family members also will affect the other members of the family or the entire family unit (Minuchin, 1988; Turnbull et al., 2006). Each family member may have his or her own set of needs that may or may not be congruent with the needs of other family members or with the needs of the family as a whole. Because of the relationship that exists among family members, professionals must consider the entire family unit as the possible focus of their attention. As described earlier, recommended practice suggests that professionals should apply family systems theory by individualizing their relationships with each family, just as they individualize their work with each child with a disability (Turnbull et al.).

Family systems theory was adapted by Turnbull, Summers, and Brotherson (1984) to focus specifically on families of young children with disabilities. Their family systems conceptual framework includes the following four key elements, which are interrelated.

1. Family characteristics are the attributes of a family, such as its cultural background, financial well-being, size, age, geographic location, abilities, and disabilities.
2. Family interactions refer to the daily relationships among family members.
3. Family functions are the needs and interests of family members met by the family, including social, emotional, educational, or physical needs such as health care or child care.
4. *Family life cycle* refers to all the changes that affect families and influence family resources, interactions, and functions.

Figure 3–1 provides a visual display of the components of the family systems theory model. What follows is a discussion of each component of the family systems theory model.

Family Characteristics

The first element of family systems theory is **family characteristics,** which are the dimensions that make each family unique (e.g., family size and form, cultural background, geographic location). Additionally, each family member's health status (both physical and mental), individual coping style, and the nature of the child's disability are included as personal characteristics. A final component includes special challenges that families can face, such as poverty, substance abuse, and parents who themselves have disabilities. Collectively, these variables contribute to each family's unique identity and influence interactional patterns among the members while also determining how the family responds to its child's disability McCormick, Stricklin, Nowak, & Rous (2008). It is easy to understand how a large family living below the poverty level in a rural location might adapt differently than an affluent suburban family with only one child with a disability. In both examples, the families may be successful in their adaptation; however, their responses, needs, and adaptive strategies may be very different.

FIGURE 3–1 Family Systems Conceptual Framework

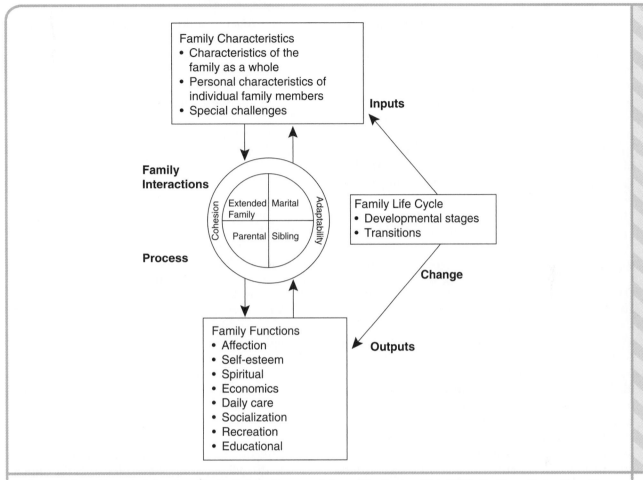

Source: Adapted by permission from Turnbull, A. P., Summers, J. A., and Brotherton, M. J. (1984). *Working with families with disabled members: A family systems approach* (p. 60). Lawrence, K S: University of Kansas, Kansas Affiliated Facility.

Family Interactions

The second component of family systems theory is **family interactions,** which is composed of the relationships that occur among and between the various family subsystems or subgroups. These subsystems include the following:

1. marital (husband–wife);
2. parental (parent–child);
3. sibling (child–child); and
4. extended family (nuclear family, friends, neighbors, larger community including professionals) (Turnbull et al., 2006).

How a particular family interacts depends, in part, on the degree of cohesion and adaptability in interactions. These two factors influence the quality of interactions and can only be interpreted within the context of the family's cultural background.

Cohesion that occurs in families is a type of emotional bonding that holds them together (Olson et al., 1989). It determines the degree of freedom and independence experienced by each member of the family unit. Cohesion occurs along a continuum of behavior ranging from enmeshment to disengagement. Highly enmeshed families are overly cohesive, which can impede the development of independence in individual family members. Families who are highly enmeshed are viewed as being overly protective and having weak boundaries between the subsystems. Conversely, rigid subsystem boundaries characterize disengaged families—believed to have a low degree of cohesiveness. In this situation, families are depicted as being under-involved, and the child with a disability may experience an absence of support (Minuchin, 1988). Ideally, well-functioning families seem to achieve a balance in cohesiveness in that the "boundaries between systems are clearly defined and family members feel both a close bonding and a sense of autonomy" (Seligman & Darling, 1997, p. 9).

Adaptability is the family's ability to change its power structure, role relationships, and rules in response to crises or stressful events occurring over a lifetime (Olson, Russell, & Sprenkle, 1980; Turnbull et al., 2006). Like cohesiveness, adaptability occurs along a continuum from rigidity to chaos and is influenced by the family's cultural background and other factors. When a stressful event occurs, rigid families respond according to prescribed roles and responsibilities and are often unable to adapt to the demands of the new situation. According to Seligman and Darling (1997), this type of behavior places a family at-risk for becoming isolated and disengaged. When a child with a severe disability becomes a member of a family, some form of accommodation or adjustment is usually required. Yet, in a rigid family with a clear hierarchy of power, the child care needs will more than likely become the responsibility of the mother with little or no assistance provided by other family members. On the other hand, how a chaotic family would respond to this situation is unpredictable due to few or inconsistent rules. Turnbull et al. (2006) describe chaotic families as being characterized by constant change and instability. In many situations, there is no family leader and the few existing rules are frequently altered, resulting in significant confusion, particularly for young children who need parental consistency and predictability. Most well-functioning families appear to maintain a balance between the extremes of high and low adaptability (Nichols, 2007; Taibbi, 2007).

Family Functions

The third element of the family systems theory is **family functions,** which refers to the eight interrelated activities that are necessary to fulfill the individual and collective needs of the family. These eight areas, with examples of each, are as follows.

1. *affection*—emotional commitments and display of affection
2. *self-esteem*—personal identity and self-worth, recognition of positive contributions

3. *spiritual*—needs related to church, religion, or God
4. *economics*—production and utilization of family income
5. *daily care*—day-to-day survival needs such as food, shelter, and health care
6. *socialization*—developing social skills, establishing interpersonal relationships
7. *recreation*—leisure time activities for both family and individuals
8. *educational*—involvement in educational activities and career choices

Turnbull et al. (2006) identify these nonprioritized functions as "outputs" and emphasize that it is impossible to discuss family functions without considering the other three main components of the family systems framework. While these tasks and activities are common to all families, they are likely to be affected by the presence of a child with a disability.

A concern of most parents today, particularly for those employed outside the home, is not having enough time to carry out family functions and meet the needs of the family. Further, families will be required to devote more time to addressing the needs of a child with a disability in most cases (Berry & Hardman, 1998; Brotherson & Goldstein, 1992). Figure 3–2 provides the words of Helen Featherstone, who is the author of the book *A Difference in the Family* (Featherstone, 1980). As the mother of a son with severe disabilities, Featherstone describes the difficulties she faces each day as she struggles with not having enough time to complete all the tasks required of her. In this passage, she writes about an occupational therapist asking her to add a 15-minute regimen to her daily routine, which she simply could not do due to lack of time. Although this took place many years ago, it illustrates the importance of professionals being sensitive to the extreme demands placed on families of children with disabilities.

In most cases, families have individualized priorities for each of the family functions. In one family, meeting the daily needs of having food and shelter is of utmost importance, while for another family, the emphasis may be on needs in the areas of education or recreation and leisure. A family living in poverty would probably place greater emphasis on daily needs. A teenage single mother may be focused on completing high school, as well as hanging out with friends. Berry and Hardman (1998) also note

FIGURE 3–2 Where Will I Find the Time?

I remember the day when the occupational therapist at Jody's school called with some suggestions from a visiting nurse. Jody has a seizure problem, which is controlled with the drug Dilantin. Dilantin can cause the gums to grow over the teeth; the nurse had noticed this overgrowth, and recommended innocently enough, that [his] teeth be brushed four times a day, for 5 minutes, with an electric toothbrush. The school suggested that they could do this once on school days, and that I should try to do it the other three times a day; this new demand appalled me; Jody is blind, cerebral palsied, and retarded. We do his physical therapy daily and work with him on sounds and communication. We feed him each meal on our laps, bottle him, bathe him, dry him, put him in a body cast to sleep, launder his bed linens daily, and go through a variety of routines designed to minimize his miseries and enhance his joys and his development. (All this in addition to trying to care for and enjoy our other young children and making time for each other and our careers.) Now you tell me that I should spend 15 minutes every day on something that Jody will hate, an activity that will not help him to walk or even defecate, but one that is directed at the health of his gums. This activity is not for a finite time, but forever. It is not guaranteed to help, but "It can't hurt." And it won't make the overgrowth go away but may retard it. Well, it's too much. Where is that 15 minutes going to come from? What am I supposed to give up? Taking the kids to the park? Reading a bedtime story to my eldest? Washing the breakfast dishes? Sorting the laundry? Grading students' papers? Sleeping? Because there is not time in my life that hasn't been spoken for, and for every 15-minute activity that is added one has to be taken away.

SOURCE: Excerpted from *A Difference in the Family* by Helen Featherstone. Copyright © 1980 by Basic Books.

that some families, particularly those with limited resources, may require assistance in several areas, while others may need support in only a few areas. The amount of support families request from professionals also will vary depending upon specific family circumstances.

Cengage Learning

Without appropriate planning, transitions encountered by young children with known or suspected disabilities and their families (e.g., graduating from preschool, beginning kindergarten) can cause increased stress.

Family Life Cycle

Family life cycle is the fourth element in the family systems theory framework. This component of the theory refers to developmental changes that occur in families over time. Most of these changes are fairly predictable, such as going to kindergarten; however, they can be non-developmental or unexpected, such as the untimely death of a family member, divorce or marriage within a family, or the unplanned birth of a child. These changes alter the structure of the family and, in turn, impact relationships, functions, and interactions. Researchers have identified as few as six to as many as twenty-four developmental stages that occur in families (Carter & McGoldrick, 1999). Regardless of the number of stages, each stage brings with it change, additional demands, and a new set of stressors. How the family responds to these situations determines, in part, the way in which the family functions. The movement from one stage to another and the accompanying adjustment period is considered to be a **transition**. Transitions tend to be stressful events for families, but especially for families of young children with disabilities. For many families, it is a time of challenge and uncertainty as to what the next stage holds for the child and family as well. For instance, when a child begins preschool or a preschooler moves to kindergarten, this can cause

TABLE 3–2 Potential Family Life Cycle Issues

Stage	Parental Issues	Sibling Issues
Early Childhood (Birth–Age 5)	• Obtaining an accurate diagnosis • Informing siblings and relatives of diagnosis • Seeking to find meaning in the disability • Clarifying a personal ideology to guide decisions • Addressing issues of stigma • Locating services • Participating in IFSP/IEP meetings • Identifying positive contributions of the disability • Setting expectations	Less parental time and energy for sibling needs Feelings of jealousy over less attention Fears associated with misunderstandings of the disability
School Age (Ages 5–8)	• Establishing routines to carry out family functions • Adjusting emotionally to educational implications • Clarifying issues of inclusion vs. special class placement • Participating in IEP meetings • Locating community resources • Arranging for extracurricular activities	• Division of responsibility for any physical care needs • Oldest female sibling may be at risk due to increased responsibilities • Limited family resources for recreation and leisure • Informing friends and teachers • Possible concern over surpassing younger sibling • Issues of inclusion into same school • Need for basic information about the disability

Source: Adapted from Barber, P. A., Turnbull, A. P., Behr, S. K., & Kerns, G. M. (1998). Family systems perspective on early childhood special education. In S. L. Odom & M. B. Karnes (Eds.), *Early intervention for infants and children with handicaps* (p. 194). Baltimore: Brookes.

heightened anxiety and significant stress. Transition plans are written as part of the IFSP for birth to three-year-olds and as part of the IEP for three- through eight-year-olds.

According to family systems theory, life cycle functions are highly age related. As a family moves through the life cycle, the priorities shift when the family encounters new situations (Seligman & Darling, 1997). Turnbull et al. (2006) discuss four major life cycle stages and the accompanying issues that the family of a child with a disability may encounter along the family's journey. The life cycle of a family typically includes the stages of the early childhood years, the school-age years, adolescence, and adulthood. In an earlier publication, Barber, Turnbull, Behr, & Kerns

(1998) describe the developmental issues that a child with a disability presents to his or her family during the early childhood years (birth through age eight) as presented in Table 3–2. Professionals must remember, however, that the way in which a family adapts to various stages throughout the life cycle is highly individualistic. Not all families successfully negotiate life cycle changes without support from professionals.

It is important to acknowledge that all families may experience a number of stresses at different points in time, and a family's behavior may seem extreme at times; however, most families eventually achieve a healthy balance. It is important to remain focused on the family's strengths and resources rather than the needs, challenges, and stresses it encounters.

Applications of Family Systems Theory

Understanding the family as a social and emotional unit embedded within other units and networks enables service providers to better grasp the complex nature of families and to work with them in more effective ways. Utilizing this view allows professionals to realize that events and changes in one unit may directly and indirectly influence the behavior of individuals in other social units. A systems perspective considers events within and between social units as supportive to the extent that they have positive influences on family functioning. Each family member is viewed as a system and as a part of many other systems, such as the early intervention program, school, community, and society.

Internally, as described earlier, the family system has basic functions that provide a broad framework through which a variety of roles and tasks are carried out. These functions change in response to developmental shifts in the family itself, as well as individual family member shifts. The structure of the family system and any changes in the structure may have an impact on all other elements.

In the family systems framework, the development of individuals and families is seen as a dynamic process of person–environment relationships. Therefore, the behavior of a child, a family, or a child and family is viewed as a part of a set of interrelated "systems" that powerfully influence one another. By understanding experiences and activities of families and assessing the influences on the family, professionals can work with families to design strategies to promote well-being in the family system. For example, if Maria's service coordinator realizes the close relationship Maria's brothers have with their 30-month-old sister, the brothers can be encouraged to participate in some of the learning activities and strategies designed to be used at home, which will benefit Maria.

Bronfenbrenner's (1979) **ecological perspective** emphasizes that power emerges from the nature and structure of human relationships. For example, an infant's need to develop trust is actualized within the primary relationship system of the family. This need may also be strongly influenced by other social systems, such as the neighborhood, child care program, and other systems. **Empowerment** is a concept used for many years by individuals in helping professions.

Most professionals would agree that it is much more accurate to describe this concept as a process rather than an end state. In early descriptions by Vanderslice (1984), family empowerment was defined as a process through which individuals increase their ability to influence those people and organizations that affect their lives, as well as the lives of their children and others they care about. Empowered individuals or families seek to have control over their lives and to take action to get what they need for themselves and their families (Dunst, Trivette, & Deal, 1988; Turnbull, Turbiville, & Turnbull, 2000). It is within the family ecology that children and parents develop their sense of power. Dunst, Trivette, & Deal (1988) remind us that empowered parents and families have three enabling characteristics:

1. the ability to access and control needed resources;
2. the ability to make decisions and solve problems; and
3. the ability to interact effectively with others in the social exchange process to gain the resources they need.

Because individual needs, interests, affective development, and perceptual orientation evolve within the family ecology, the underlying premises of a family systems model are highly related to the empowerment paradigm. These premises include the following (Swick & Graves, 1993):

1. behavior takes place in a systems context;
2. individual development is intimately interrelated with the family's development;
3. family development is systematic; and
4. events that influence any family member have some direct or indirect influence on the entire family system.

Within the family system, trust, attachment, self-esteem, social attitudes and behaviors, and many other processes and skills emerge in a nurturing, empowered family (Brubaker, 1993; Nichols, 2007; Taibbi, 2007). A sense of power or a sense of powerlessness is developed in the family ecology. It is important for professionals to remember that the concept of empowerment is dynamic, interactive, and process oriented. Professionals who embrace the empowerment paradigm share the assumption that all families have strengths. Professionals are in a strategic position to promote positive, empowering interactions

MAKING CONNECTIONS

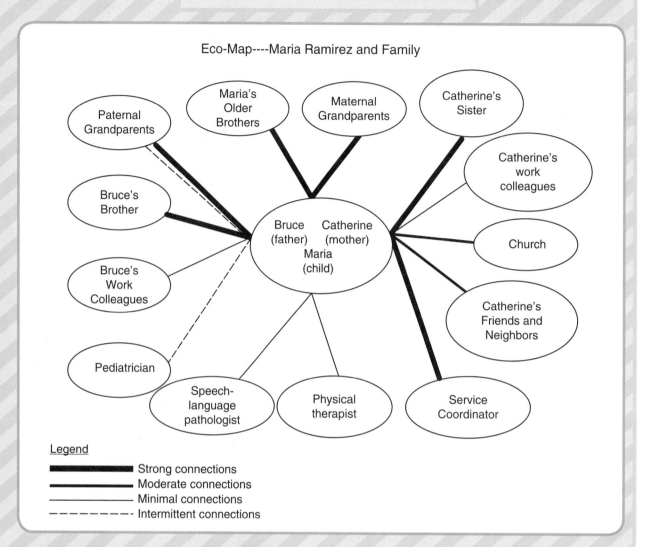

Eco-Map----Maria Ramirez and Family

with families by providing quality programs for young children, involving parents in partnerships, and supporting families in all aspects of early intervention/early childhood special education services.

One of the most important functions of empowerment is to provide skills that promote self-sufficiency. Empowerment may grow through a family's changes in self-perception, increased self-confidence, ability to set goals, acquisition of skills to attain goals, and the opportunity for supported practice (Dunlap, 1997). In most cases, empowerment means promoting access to resources, competence, and self-efficacy

(Bandura, 1997; Hanson & Lynch, 2004; Heflinger & Bickman, 1997; Nichols, 2007; Taibbi, 2007). Relationships between professionals and families can be fostered through family empowerment because families develop trust of professionals and professionals come to view families as part of an equal, reciprocal partnership (Swick, 1996; Turnbull et al., 2006). Families, with the support of professionals as needed, take actions to solve problems and get what they need for their child and family (Turnbull et al., 2006).

Many teams have found **eco-maps**, or family maps, to be useful in fostering collaboration among professionals and families and also in depicting and using important information such as family structure, strengths, and resources. According to McCormick, Stricklin, Nowak, & Rous (2008), eco-maps were "originally developed as a . . . visual representation of the family system at the beginning of intervention" (p. 18). Developing an eco-map requires specific steps: (1) identifying informal family supports, (2) identifying strengths and relationships, and (3) identifying formal family supports (Hartman, 1995). The eco-map can be used to link the IFSP or IEP goals/outcomes to support services for children and families and to review informal and formal family resources. The Making Connections feature provides an example of an eco-map developed with Maria's family to learn more about the family structure, examine needed services, and establish rapport with the Ramirez family. For example, the service coordinator who works with 30-month-old Maria must consider that Maria's interactions with her brothers, grandparents, friends from her affluent neighborhood, therapists who visit weekly, other significant people, and experiences in her life will have a profound influence on Maria.

A Family-Based Philosophy

Several themes have emerged for those who work with families of young children with disabilities to carefully consider. First, there is the recognition that families are all very different. They differ in their concerns, resources, priorities, and other areas; therefore, an individualized approach to working with families must be used to address each family's specific needs. Secondly, families should be partners with professionals in planning, providing services, and making decisions regarding issues such as the child's placement and the family's level of involvement in early intervention/education services. This relationship must include valuing and supporting the equality within the partnership. Finally, families are viewed as the ultimate teachers and decision makers for their children. A family-based perspective should be apparent in all aspects of early childhood services. An example of a family-centered early intervention philosophy, developed at the Frank Porter Graham Child Development Center, can be seen in Table 3–3. Early childhood programs all over the country have

embraced a family orientation that is the cornerstone of early intervention and early childhood special education (Turnbull et al., 2007)

As described previously, this family philosophy in early childhood special education has evolved over time. Dunst, Johanson, Trivette, and Hamby (1991) traced the history of the role of professionals in working with families of young children with special needs in the following order: professional-centered, family-allied, family-focused, family-centered, family-based, and family-directed. Most recently leaders in the field of early intervention and early childhood special education have espoused a family-directed model of early intervention/education as included in IDEA 2004.

The first model described by Dunst et al. (1991) is a professional-centered activity whereby the professional was the sole source and dispenser of expertise. Families were considered dysfunctional and incapable of resolving their own problems. The family-allied model came next—families served as teachers of their children, implementing family interventions prescribed by the professionals. This perspective gradually gave way to a family-focused emphasis. Service providers at this stage viewed families in a more positive light. Families were seen as competent and capable of collaborating with professionals; however, most professionals still believed that families needed their assistance. In the family-centered model, the family is the center of the service delivery system. As such, services are planned around the family, based on its individual needs. This approach is consumer driven—professionals are working for the family. Other terms that have been used in recent years include family-driven and family-directed. Regardless of the term used, early intervention/early childhood special education programs today believe that the family is the primary decision maker. Professionals provide support to families and assist them as needed in fulfilling their goals.

Using the view of the family as a system, the ecological and empathetic perspectives, and the empowerment paradigm, professional planners are acknowledging families as strong, unique, and able to identify their own concerns and resources. The concept of **family-centered practices** in this context refers to specific techniques and methods of working with families. As described by Dunst, Johanson, Trivette, and Hamby (1991), family-centered practices stress focusing on family strengths and enhancing family skills and competencies. Families are not

TABLE 3–3 Family-Centered Philosophy in Early Intervention

Family-centered	Professionals should recognize that the family is the constant in the child's life while the service systems and personnel within those systems may be involved only episodically.
Ecologically based	As professionals work with families, they need to consider the interrelatedness of the various contexts that surround the child and family.
Individualized	Since the needs of each child and each family may differ, services should be individualized to meet those unique needs.
Culturally sensitive	Families come from different cultures and ethnic groups. Families reflect their diversity in their views and expectations of themselves, their children, and professionals. Services should be provided in ways that are sensitive to these variations and consistent with family values and beliefs.
Enabling and empowering	Services should foster a family's independence, existing and developing skills, and sense of competence and worth.
Needs-based	Approach starts with a family's expressed interests and collaborates with families in identifying and obtaining services according to their priorities.
Coordinated service delivery	Families need access to a well-coordinated system of services.
Normalized	Programs should work to promote the integration or inclusion of the child and the family within the community.
Collaborative	Early intervention services should be based on a collaborative relationship between families and professionals.

Source: Adapted from The Carolina Institute of Research on Infant Personnel Preparation, Frank Porter Graham Child Development Center, The University of North Carolina at Chapel Hill.

mere recipients of services, but are active partners in planning and implementing service delivery processes (Kilgo & Raver, 2009). The goals of each program must contain elements that assist in supporting families as they strive to meet the needs of their children with special needs.

As Maria's mother noted when Maria was six months old, she still couldn't sit up and didn't smile, make sounds, and play like her brothers did. My pediatrician connected me with an early intervention program, and now Maria is receiving services that really help her. She is making lots of progress and we are learning what we can do to help her. We now know that we weren't doing anything wrong. Maria just doesn't do things as quickly as other children her age. But now she is making progress and we have lots of support.

In the *DEC Recommended Practice Guidelines,* Trivette and Dunst (2005) clarify the parameters of **family-based practices** (see Table 3–4). Ultimately, family-based practices supply the supports necessary for families to have the knowledge, skills, and resources to provide their children learning opportunities and experiences that promote child development. Thus, family-based practices potentially have child, parent, and family strengthening and competency-enhancing consequences. The *DEC Recommended Practice Guidelines* provide the foundation for high quality services for young children with disabilities and their families.

A longstanding belief held by professionals in the field of early intervention and early childhood special education is that families need both informal and

TABLE 3–4 DEC Recommended Practices: Family-Based Practices

Families and professionals share responsibility and work collaboratively.

F1.	Family members and professionals jointly develop appropriate family-identified outcomes.
F2.	Family members and professionals work together and share information routinely and collaboratively to achieve family-identified outcomes.
F3.	Professionals fully and appropriately provide relevant information so parents can make informed choices and decisions.
F4.	Professionals use helping styles that promote shared family/professionals responsibility in achieving family-identified outcomes.
F5.	Family and professionals' relationship building is accomplished in ways that are responsive to cultural, language, and other family characteristics.

Practices strengthen family functioning.

F6.	Practices, supports, and resources provide families with participatory experiences and opportunities promoting choice and decision making.
F7.	Practices, supports, and resources support family participation in obtaining desired resources and supports to strengthen parenting competence and confidence.
F8.	Intrafamily, informal, community, and formal supports and resources (e.g., respite care) are used to achieve desired outcomes.
F9.	Supports and resources provide families with information, competency-enhancing experiences, and participatory opportunities to strengthen family functioning and promote parenting knowledge and skills.
F10.	Supports and resources are mobilized in ways that are supportive and do not disrupt family and community life.

Practices are individualized and flexible.

F11.	Resources and supports are provided in ways that are flexible, individualized, and tailored to the child's family's preferences and styles, and promote well-being.
F12.	Resources and supports match every family member's identified priorities and preferences (e.g., mother's and father's may be different).
F13.	Practices, supports, and resources are responsive to the cultural, ethnic, racial, language, and socioeconomic characteristics and preferences of families and their communities.
F14.	Practices, supports, and resources incorporate family beliefs and values into decisions, intervention plans, and resources and support mobilization.

Practices are strengths and assets-based.

F15.	Family and child strengths and assets are used as a basis for engaging families in participatory experiences supporting parenting competence and confidence.
F16.	Practices, supports, and resources build on existing parenting competence and confidence.
F17.	Practices, supports, and resources promote the family's and professional's acquisition of new knowledge and skills to strengthen competence and confidence.

Source: "Recommended Practices in Family-Based Practices," by C. M. Trivette and C. J. Dunst, in *DEC Recommended Practices in Early Intervention/ Early Childhood Special Education* (pp. 45–46), by S. Sandall, M.L. Hemmeter, B. Smith, and M. McLean 2005, Longmont, CO: Sopris West.

FIGURE 3–3 Model of the Direct and Indirect Influences of Social Support and Intrafamily Factors on Families

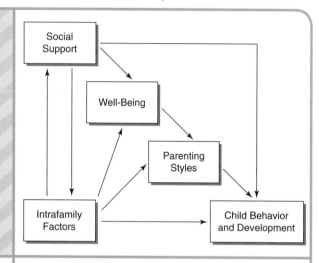

SOURCE: C. Trivette, & C. Dunst (2000). Recommended Practices in Family-Based Practices. In S. Sandall, M. McLean and B. Smith (Eds.) DEC Recommended Practices in Early Intervention/Early Childhood Special Education. Longmont, CO: Sopris West, p. 40.

formal resources and supports in order to have the knowledge and skills, as well as the physical and psychological energy and time, to engage in child rearing responsibilities and parenting activities that promote their children's development (Bronfenbrenner, 1979; Bronfenbrenner & Morris, 1998). In the *DEC Recommended Practice Guidelines,* Trivette and Dunst (2005) report research evidence that social support has positive effects on family well-being. Figure 3–3 contains a model they used to illustrate the direct and indirect influences of social support on personal and family well-being, parent–child interactions, and child behavior and development. According to this model, "social support and resources directly influence the health and well-being of parents, both support and health/well-being influence parenting styles; and support, well-being, and parenting styles directly and indirectly influence child behavior and development" (p. 108). Through this model, it is easy to recognize the far-reaching impact of family-based practices and the importance of utilizing such an approach.

A family-based approach can result in benefits to both the child and family (Guralnick, 1997). Benefits of a family-based approach include, but are not limited to, the following areas: (a) child functioning,

(b) parent skills and emotional well-being, (c) parents' view of service effectiveness and sense of control over their child's care, (d) problem-solving ability, (e) capacity of families to care for their child at home, (f) service delivery, (g) cost effectiveness, and (h) family empowerment (Beach Center on Families and Disability, 1997).

Evidence of the effectiveness of a family-based approach, as well as direct experience, has encouraged programs throughout the country to embrace family-based practices (Sandall et al., 2005). Finally, the most recent terminology used is **family-directed practices**. This term was included in the IDEA Amendments, which stated that early intervention services must be "family-directed".

To be successful, early childhood professionals, across disciplines and settings, must hold a set of values that place families at the center of the service delivery process and as the directors of the services for their children. This marks a dramatic shift from past practices when professionals focused solely on the child and designed interventions based on what they thought was best with little or no input from the family. Professionals have exchanged the role of expert for the role of partner in a relationship where professionals provide support for families. The focus is on the strengths and capabilities of families, with families making fully informed choices and decisions regarding services for their children. As one service provider explained, "We've come a long way from trying to get all families involved in their children's education in the same manner. Today families are at the center of services and we provide support to them as they deem appropriate".

Family–Professional Partnerships

One of the most important responsibilities of early childhood personnel is the development, nurturance, and maintenance of effective relationships with families. There is now a general acceptance and understanding that parents and families are the child's first and most important teachers. Recommended practice suggests that the best type of relationship that can develop between families and professionals is one in which families are viewed as full-fledged partners. This type of true collaboration requires shared trust and equality in the relationship. Like any relationship, family–professional partnerships take time and effort to sustain.

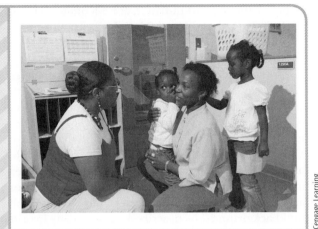

To build a positive relationship between service providers and families, trust must be established and ongoing communication should occur.

Cengage Learning

Early childhood programs with strong family components have contributed to children's later school success. For some time, effective professionals have been participants and supporters of parent–professional partnership efforts. Initial experiences and interactions of children, parents, and professionals in early childhood programs should be positive, nurturing, and caring. Professionals should learn as much as possible about each child and family in order to maximize the possibilities of the child's success. Service providers who are inviting and encouraging to families are much more likely to build a positive relationship with the family. It is the professional's responsibility to find ways, rather than excuses, to develop partnerships with family members. Young children with special needs are the ultimate beneficiaries of these partnerships. An understanding of each family from a systems perspective will provide insight and understanding that will help service providers approach families as partners in the early development and education of their young children.

The rationale for the development of collaborative partnerships between families and professionals has been emphasized in early childhood special education for many years. The rationale includes the following: (a) family members spend more time with a child who has a disability than anyone else; (b) parents have more information about the child than anyone else; (c) how a family "works" will determine what type(s) of intervention will "work" for the family and child; and (d) families have the ultimate control over the services provided for their children and themselves. "No matter how skilled professionals are, or how loving parents are, each cannot achieve alone what the two parties, working hand-in-hand, can accomplish together" (Peterson & Cooper, 1989, p. 208).

The foundation for building positive relationships between service providers and families must include a mutual understanding of their roles in supporting children's development and learning. This process of mutual understanding can allow both parties to empathize and discover ways to support one another in their roles. The early years are not only a formative period for young children, but also a critical and challenging time for families and professionals (Galinsky, 1990; Turnbull et al., 2006). Families often need and welcome support as they face the many challenges of family life during the early years of the life of a young child with a developmental delay or disability.

Key Components of Family–Professional Collaboration

As described throughout this chapter, families and professionals interact on a variety of levels to address the needs of young children with known or suspected disabilities. Effective family–professional collaboration is the foundation of early intervention/education. Some key components of family–professional collaboration include (a) cultural responsiveness, (b) communication, (c) meetings and conferences, and (d) ongoing support and information exchange. What follows is a discussion of each of these dimensions with suggested strategies.

Cultural Responsiveness

The influence of culture is one of the most critical effects on the relationships that develop among families and professionals. As described earlier in this chapter, culture is the blend of thoughts, feelings, attitudes, beliefs, values, and behavior patterns that are shared by ethnic, racial, religious, or social groups. Culture is especially relevant to relationships between families and professionals because culture includes many different factors that shape one's sense of group identity, including, but not limited to, geographic location, income status, gender, sexual orientation, language, disability status, value of education, and occupation. It is the framework within which individuals, families, or groups interpret their experiences and develop their visions of how they want to live their lives. As we examine the influence of culture on family–professional relationships in early intervention/education, Turnbull et al. (2006) emphasize the importance of considering the following aspects of culture, each of which may have a direct or indirect effect on the relationship between professionals and families:

- *Religion* and the beliefs and customs associated with religion are likely to influence such things as the holidays families celebrate and the appropriateness of professionals discussing with them associated activities (e.g., holiday events, schedules, traditions, and practices).
- *Language* can influence all aspects of communication with families if families do not speak English or are unable to read in English (or any other language).
- *Race,* which may influence the likelihood of families experiencing racism and discrimination, may foster skepticism about trusting others of a different race.
- *Ethnicity* may have an impact on families' feelings of belonging or perceptions of themselves as outsiders in early intervention/education programs.
- *Gender* may influence beliefs about the roles that various family members should assume in advocating for their children, as well as communicating with professionals.
- *Age* of the family members can influence the life experiences they have; for example, teenage mothers who have parental responsibilities or grandparents who are raising their grandchildren.
- *Geography* often creates certain opportunities and barriers to family–professional partnerships; for example, differences exist in rural settings where families live long distances from an early intervention/education program without public transportation or inner-city settings where families have to alter their lifestyle due to violence and crime.
- *Income* may influence the resources available to families and the extent to which their housing, medical care, and nutrition are adequate to meet the needs of children with delays, disabilities, or other special needs. (p. 10)

Professionals must understand that culture shapes a family's attitude about its child's disability, health and illness, child-rearing practices, communication style, choice of intervention goals, and view of professionals. It is also important to understand that culture is not a static concept. In fact, there is considerable variation within cultural groups that can change over time. Further, the influence of culture can vary from family to family even when families have similar cultural backgrounds. As described earlier, many hybrid families and cultures are served in early intervention/education in the 21st century (Aldridge & Goldman, 2007); therefore, professionals often face challenges related to cultural diversity (Bredekamp & Copple, 2009; Kilgo, 2006). *DEC Recommended Practices* (Sandall et al., 2005) suggest that family–professional relationship building should be individualized and accomplished in ways that are responsive to each family's cultural background.

Cultural responsiveness is a complex concept involving the awareness, acknowledgement, and acceptance of each family's culture and cultural values. Cultural responsiveness requires professionals to view each family as a unique unit that is influenced by, but not defined by, its culture. As such, professionals must avoid **stereotyping**, the generalized belief about members of a cultural group. Stereotyping occurs when assumptions are made that all individuals within a cultural group share the same perspectives or react in a predetermined manner. Such assumptions limit the ability to understand and develop relationships with families (Matuszny, Banda, & Coleman, 2007). We are not suggesting that professionals know everything there is to know about the culture of families they serve in early intervention/education. What we suggest, however, is that professionals gain an understanding of each family's cultural values, which will help facilitate effective interactions with families (Hains et al., 2005). After gaining general knowledge about a family's culture, more specific information can be learned by talking to the family, asking for clarification, and seeking the family's guidance in understanding. The following is an example of what could be said to a family in an attempt to seek clarification. "I read that people who practice the Sikh faith believe that all of life is sacred and that playing with food such as eggs is not appropriate. Is that true of your family? Since eating solid foods is a goal for your child, what should we know to assist with this?"

To effectively serve children and families representing diverse cultural backgrounds, the following strategies are recommended.

- Service providers should read as much as possible about the cultural backgrounds of the families with whom they work.
- Service providers must understand that there are many hybrid families and cultures.
- When professionals meet with the families, they should let them know that they are prepared and ready to learn from them.
- Service providers should ask appropriate questions and listen to what the families tell them.
- Based on what is learned from families, practices should be adapted as needed to ensure they respect and include the values, beliefs, and customs of families.
- Service providers should use multiple resources to become more culturally competent. For example, they should participate in ongoing staff development and learn from families, other service providers, policy makers, and members of the cultural communities served by the program.

When professionals and families have differing cultural beliefs and practices, these can serve as barriers to the development of their relationships (Harry, Kalyanpur, & Day, 1999). The importance of professionals understanding differences between their own perspectives and those of families from other cultures and ethnic groups cannot be overstressed. In order to do this, each service provider must carefully examine his or her own cultural background, beliefs, and values. In doing so, the provider will become more capable of understanding the individual perspectives that are unique to each family and how they differ from that provider's own background and beliefs. Service providers who fail to recognize values and beliefs of families are prone to make biased and faulty judgments about families that may weaken their relationships with them. Collaboration among families and professionals when there are cultural differences requires respect, trust, and cooperation. It

is the professional's responsibility to cope with and value differences in order to address these differences in positive ways.

Effective Communication

As we have come to realize, one of the most important elements in relationships between families and professionals is effective communication. To maximize learning and guide the child's development in positive ways, professionals and families must maintain an open, honest relationship, which of course is dependent on effective communication (Whitbread, Bruder, Fleming, & Park, 2007). Thus, communication skills rank among the most necessary of all the skills possessed by early childhood professionals.

In its most basic form, **communication** is the ability of two or more people to send and receive messages. Many forms of communication are used during interactions among families and professionals, both nonverbal and verbal. Not everyone has perfected his/her communication skills; however, it is important to point out that verbal and nonverbal communication skills and strategies can be learned and improved with practice.

Nonverbal communication involves body language that conveys information. Body language includes facial expressions, eye contact, posture, voice, physical proximity, and gestures. Desirable facial expressions, for example, could include eyes being at the same level as the parents', direct eye contact (except when culturally proscribed), warmth and concern reflected in facial expressions, and appropriately varied and animated facial expressions. Table 3–5 provides examples of desirable nonverbal communication skills.

Verbal communication refers to both oral and written language. Well-developed listening and observation skills are necessary for effective parent–professional relationships. Table 3–6 provides tips for using active listening and observation strategies. Table 3–7 provides examples of verbal communication skills that can be used to improve the effectiveness of communication. These strategies and skills can be practiced and perfected over time.

As in any relationship, effective communication between families and professionals involves a clear understanding and knowledge of the expectations, obligations, and responsibilities of each party in the relationship. It is important for the professional to

TABLE 3–5 Examples of Desirable Non-verbal Communication Skills

Facial Expressions

Comfortable eye contact

Warm, encouraging facial expressions

Occasional smiles (when appropriate)

Posture and Gestures

Use of appropriate gestures

Body leaning slightly forward (attentive, but relaxed)

Absence of repetitive movements (e.g., tapping fingers, shaking foot)

Voice

Can be heard clearly, but not loud

Warmth in voice tone

Natural speech tempo

Physical Proximity

Three to five feet between speakers (e.g., whether seated in chairs, sofa, or on floor)

communicate clearly about the policies and practices of the program. Professionals are advised to provide parents with information before they enter the program and review it on an ongoing and as–needed basis. Parents and other family members need to know about various aspects of the program such as the assessment process, related services, health and safety requirements, daily schedules, home visits, and other program features. Information can be provided via a program handbook, newsletter, and website. Having sufficient information about the program requirements helps to lay a positive foundation for an effective partnership.

Communication must be regular and useful to be effective. Communicating information that is not useful to families or communicating too infrequently will do little to facilitate the achievement of the family's goals for their child. A number of methods of communication should be available (e.g., notes, e-mails, meetings, telephone calls, communication notebook). Regardless of the method of communication or when it occurs, professionals must be willing to listen to and respect the families' points of view.

The way in which professionals communicate with and provide support to families plays a strong role in fostering positive parent–professional communication (Banks, Santos, & Roof, 2003). Professionals are encouraged to use responsive communication strategies, based on each family's unique characteristics, needs, and preferences. For example, specific strategies may be needed when families have linguistic differences. Depending on the family's primary language, different support may be required to enable communication. Bilingual and bicultural staff, mediators, and/or translators may be needed with some families.

The following list of suggestions (Gargiulo, 2009) for working with families is designed to facilitate effective communication, and ultimately, the development of a useful and meaningful relationship among families and professionals.

- *Listen to families!* In order for professionals to understand the family's vision for their child, communication is of the utmost importance. Professionals must often probe to solicit families' perspectives. In addition, they must practice active listening and make an effort to confirm the perceptions of the family's intent and meaning. Through interactive listening and observation, attempts can be made to understand what families are saying, what they are feeling, and what they want for their child. Acknowledgement of the family's vision and a willingness to follow the family's lead will help to establish the trust necessary for an ongoing working relationship.

- *Realize that the family knows its child better than anyone else.* Professionals must make every effort to learn from each family the relevant information about its child. Families know the most about the child, his or her needs, and how those needs should be met. Therefore, professionals should show respect for the families' knowledge and understanding, and convey a feeling of acceptance of the information they can offer. Further, opportunities should be created for parents and other family members to provide this type of meaningful information. Professionals should never underestimate the importance of communication and the power of their words in their relationships with families. According to reports from parents, some of the most helpful comments made by professionals include statements such as, "I value your input,"

TABLE 3–6 **Tips for Active Listening and Observation**

Stop talking.	Allow the person with whom you are communicating to formulate responses to your questions. Show that you want to listen and be helpful. Pay special attention to the feelings behind the facts and avoid preparing your next statement while the other person is talking.
Put the speaker at ease.	Relax and make the appropriate eye contact with the person with whom you are communicating. Remember, some cultures do not engage in direct eye contact.
Ask appropriate questions.	Ask open-ended questions, which will encourage the other person to answer with more than "yes" or "no" responses. Ask only one question at a time in a clearly phrased manner. Offer a chance for the other person to elaborate on his or her statements.
Make appropriate comments.	Be encouraging. Demonstrate attending skills (e.g., nodding, making neutral vocalization—"yes" or "oh").
Demonstrate reflection skills.	Use reflective paraphrasing by stating in your own words what you believe the speaker has said. The speaker can then either confirm or deny your understanding and contradictions may be cleared up. Be sure to also reflect on what you perceive to be the speaker's feelings as well. (e.g.," You sounded distressed when . . . " or "Were you relieved when . . . ?"
Exhibit openness.	Be willing to make statements in which you reveal something that may be personal or private to you. For example, "I was sad when . . . " or "I was frightened by . . ."
Share topic selection.	Allow the person with whom you are communicating to indicate his or her preference with regard to whether or not to discuss a certain topic. The individual may wish to postpone the topic until a later time.
Remain objective.	Work to avoid jumping to conclusions in conversations. Be on the lookout for negative feelings you may already have about the other person's point of view. Do not allow your emotions to interfere in your conversation. Accept his/her feelings and do not take ownership of them.
Attend to person's concerns.	Attend to the topics or issues that are important to the person with whom you are communicating. Try to listen as if you share his or her concerns.
Develop attention to detail.	Work on your skills at identifying physical characteristics of feelings. Although we generally associate facial expressions with certain feelings, you must really know the person with whom you are communicating. For example, they may smile most when they are the most hurt.
Focus.	Be sure to focus on the other person and focus out extraneous details. Surveying the room often gives the appearance of lack of interest and attention.

Source: Adapted from *Families and teachers of individuals with disabilities: Collaborative orientations and responsive practices (2001),* by D. J. O'Shea, L. J. O'Shea, R. Algozzine, D. J. Hammitte (Eds.). Boston, MA: Allyn & Bacon, pp. 260.

TABLE 3–7 Examples of Communication Skills

Listening Skills

Paraphrasing—Responding to basic messages.

"You are feeling positive about this approach, but you are confused as to the best way to implement it."

Clarifying—Restating a point or requesting restatement to ensure understanding. "I'm confused about this. Let me try to state what I think you have said."

Perception checking—Determining accuracy of feeling or emotion detected.

"I was wondering if the plan you chose is really the one you want. It seems to me that you expressed some doubt. Is this correct?"

Leading Skills

Indirect leading—Getting a conversation started.

"Let's start with you describing how things are going with the first strategy."

Direct leading—Encouraging and elaborating discussion.

"What do you mean when you say there is no improvement? Give me a recent example of an incident at home."

Focusing—Controlling confusion, diffusion, and vagueness.

"You have been discussing several problems with T.J.'s behavior at home. Which of these is most important to you?"

Reflecting Skills

Reflecting feelings—Responding to the emotion expressed.

"It sounds as if you are feeling very frustrated with this situation."

Reflecting content—Repeating ideas in new words for emphasis.

"His behavior is making you wonder about the effectiveness of these strategies?"

Summarizing Skills

Summarizing—Pulling themes together.

"Let's take a look at what we have decided thus far. We have agreed to try a different morning schedule and to use the same strategies for one more week."

Informing Skills

Advising—Giving suggestions and opinions based on experience.

"Based on my experience as a teacher, I can tell you that this approach has worked with many children."

Informing—Giving information based on expertise, research, and training.

"I recently attended a workshop series on positive behavioral support techniques for group situations. Perhaps some of these strategies would help make the groups in your classroom work more effectively."

SOURCE: From *The Helping Relationship: Process and Skills*, 4th ed. (pp. 66–67) by L. M. Brammer, 1988, Englewood Cliffs, NJ: Prentice Hall. Adapted with permission.

"I'll follow your lead," and "You're the expert on your child."

- *Use a two-step process when initially informing parents that their child requires early intervention/early childhood special education services.* After sharing diagnostic information, it is strongly suggested that families be given time to comprehend and absorb the information. Parental/family concerns must be dealt with prior to proceeding with matters such as intervention recommendations. These issues can be addressed in follow-up meetings according to the family's readiness.

- *Explain the terminology and avoid the use of jargon.* Most families have no previous experience with developmental delays or disabilities. This may be their first exposure to the terminology that is used in early intervention/early childhood special education. Their conceptualization of such terms as eligibility, developmental delay, or disability may be different from that of professionals; therefore, the terminology used should be made clear to families. Further, everyday language should be used when possible and professional jargon and acronyms (e.g., IEP, IFSP) should be kept to a minimum.
- *Keep families informed.* A variety of two-way communication techniques can be used when discussing a child's abilities and performance. Respect, concern, and a sincere desire to communicate and collaborate in all aspects of services must be demonstrated. Professionals should develop alliances with families based on the common goal to help the child.
- *Recognize that diverse family structures and parenting styles, as well as other factors, will influence each family's interactions and level of involvement.* Open communication with families allows professionals to understand the family dynamics and individual differences, which are part of each family. Professionals should respect the family's right to choose their level and style of participation in early intervention or early childhood special education services.
- *Support families in embracing realistic optimism.* In working with each family, professionals must work to achieve a balance between being optimistic and realistic about the future of each child. Children's strengths should be stressed, along with their needs. Families should be supported as they analyze, plan, and prepare for their child's future. As one mother stressed, "What families need most from professionals is hope and encouragement".
- *Be accountable.* Trust, consistency, and dependability increase the chances of an effective relationship developing. If service providers agree to assume specific responsibilities or gather information for the family, they must always follow through. Accountability demonstrates to the family that the family can depend on those professionals providing services.

Following these suggestions will not necessarily ensure a successful relationship with all families, but it can assist in helping to establish a mutually respectful tone in relationships.

Conferences and Meetings

Most early intervention and early childhood special education programs offer a variety of meaningful activities for coordinated planning such as group meetings, individual meetings, or conferences. In each of these activities, communication is critical. Perhaps the most utilized way of communicating with families is through individual meetings or conferences. These meetings or conferences can take place in a variety of settings, use a variety of formats, and occur for various reasons, including families' participation in the planning process. When possible, meetings should be conducted in family-friendly settings where families feel comfortable.

Effective meetings with families require advanced planning. Families should be contacted prior to the meeting to discuss the purpose of the meeting, what is to be accomplished, and the process that will be followed during the meeting. Input should be solicited from families regarding the specific topics they wish to discuss. The length of meetings should be established in advance. Further, families should be assured of the confidentiality of the information shared during meetings.

At the beginning, the purpose of the meeting should be reviewed, the amount of time allotted should be restated, and again confidentiality should be emphasized. During the meeting, professionals should share any information they have about the issues or topics and ask for any information or input that the family members might have. Professionals should try to keep the discussions focused on the issues or topics being discussed. All information should be synthesized during the meeting. Regardless of the issue or topic, families' input should be solicited and used to establish priorities and to develop a plan to address these priorities. Families appreciate professionals who are not rushed and who discuss specific tasks, behaviors, and abilities. Any meeting should conclude with a summary and consensus regarding next steps. When possible, meetings or conversations should end on a positive and encouraging note.

One of the major ways in which families are active participants in the program planning process is through the meetings that take place in the development of the individualized family service plan (IFSP) and the individual education program (IEP). The intent of the IFSP and IEP is to provide more accountability and to increase the level of family participation. As described in the previous chapter, IFSPs are written for birth to three-year-olds and IEPs for children three years and older. Detailed information about these individualized plans can be found in Chapter 5.

As also mentioned previously, a specific requirement of Part C of the Individuals with Disabilities Education Improvement Act 2004 is to enhance the capacity of families to assist in meeting each child's special needs. Much of the literature concerning the IFSP consists of recommended practices designed to guide the development of the IFSP and the delivery of services. Dunst, Trivette, and Deal (1994) state that the IFSP is the cornerstone of the family-based model.

Several conclusions have emerged from the literature on the outcomes and implementation of IFSPs. Gallagher and Desimone (1995) reported that there are a significant number of positive outcomes that provide confidence that the IFSP procedure, when implemented correctly, can result in parents and service providers having a clear picture of the child and the plans for intervention. Gallagher and Desimone offered the following suggestions for making the processes of using the IFSP more beneficial:

1. *Parents and professionals should be prepared.* Both parties need to be better informed about the plan and processes. Stakeholders needed to implement the plan. An orientation meeting and a videotape of a successful session could be most helpful to families.
2. *Sufficient time should be devoted to the process.* The development of an effective plan, with input from all parties, requires considerable time. Just like a the relationship between professionals and parents, time is needed for the development and maintenance of the plan.
3. *Reviews and updates are mandated.* The document must be reviewed regularly and checked for its effectiveness. Of course, the law requires a six-month review, but at least one person should assume the responsibility for regular ongoing reviews and updates.

Similar to the IFSP, the IEP process provides an opportunity for families and professionals to share information and concerns about the child. Both the family and professionals can reap benefits from positive partnerships. This process can also help the family better understand the program in which the child is enrolled, which in turn may boost the confidence of the parents in the way they view the program and staff. Another benefit of the IEP is that it is meeting the intended goal of providing information about the child's progress in academic and other areas of development. Effective use of IFSPs and IEPs can be a tremendous help to the service providers in delivering appropriate services and educational programs to young children with disabilities and their families.

Regardless of the type of meeting or conference that occurs between families and professionals, strategies are needed to facilitate coordinated planning and communication during conferences and meetings. Professionals should carefully select times for conferences and strive to plan times that are mutually agreeable. Some programs provide child care and assist with transportation. Being flexible in planning to meet families' needs demonstrates to families that the professionals are committed to involving them.

In planning for meetings or conferences with families, it is important to realize that families from diverse cultures may view time differently from how the professionals do and schedule meetings accordingly. If the family is linguistically diverse, arrangements must be made for native-speaking individuals (when needed) to make initial contacts and serve as a link between family and professionals. Also, there are times when trained interpreters must be used during conferences.

Home Visits

Home visits are another format through which coordinated planning and collaboration occur among families and service providers. Service delivery through home visiting is the keystone of family-centered intervention in Part C services for birth to three-year-olds with known or suspected disabilities. Home-based early intervention services are provided so that learning can take place in the natural environment. In addition, home-based services have a number of other benefits. Working with families and children in the natural environment provides for optimal carryover and generalization. It permits the parent–professional relationship to develop on a more informal and personal level. According to Hanson and Lynch (1995), families involved in home-based services develop more positive relationships with professionals with whom they work and are more likely to follow through on recommended activities as identified in

FIGURE 3–4 Example of a Family Scale to Evaluate their Early Intervention Experiences

Parenting Experiences Scale

Please circle how many times a staff member from your child's early intervention program has worked directly with your child during the past three months.

Not At All	1–2 Times	3–4 Times	5–6 Times	7–8 Times	9–10 Times	11–12 Times	More Than 12 Times

Please circle how many times a staff member from your child's early intervention program has worked with you to help you promote your child's learning and development during the past three months.

Not At All	1–2 Times	3–4 Times	5–6 Times	7–8 Times	9–10 Times	11–12 Times	More Than 12 Times

Thinking about all your contacts with your child's early intervention program staff, how often have the staff interacted with you in the following ways:

	Never	Some of the Time	About Half the Time	Most of the Time	All the Time
Give me information to make my own choices	1	2	3	4	5
Responded to my concerns and desires	1	2	3	4	5
Pointed out something my child or I did well	1	2	3	4	5
Worked with me in a way that fit my schedule	1	2	3	4	5

Parents often have different feelings and thoughts about being a parent. Please indicate the extent to which each of the following statements is true for you.

How true is each of the following for you:	Not At All True	A Little True	Some-times True	Mostly True	Always True
I feel good about myself as a parent	1	2	3	4	5
I enjoy doing things with my child(ren)	1	2	3	4	5
I am the best parent I can be	1	2	3	4	5

Thinking about your involvement in your child's early intervention program, how much influence can you have in terms of getting information and supports you want from the early intervention program?

No Influence At All					Influence About Half the Time					Influence All the Time
0	10	20	30	40	50	60	70	80	90	100

MAKING CONNECTIONS

Home Visit with Maria's Family

Based on the information presented in the vignette about Maria, the following is an example of the format for a home visit with the Ramirez family.

1. *Arrival and greeting.* The service coordinator is greeted by Maria's mother, Catherine, and Maria's grandparents. They exchange greetings and general information (e.g., important events that have occurred, what has been happening since the last home visit).

2. *Information exchange and review.* The service coordinator and Maria's family review and discuss the prior visit, the strategies or interventions that have been used, and the progress that has been made toward achieving the desired outcomes. Maria's mother explains that she is pleased with the strategies being used and comments on the progress Maria has made in several areas. The service coordinator observes Maria in order to review and reassess the appropriateness and success of the interventions and strategies in light of her progress.

3. *Development of new goals/outcomes and modification of strategies.* Based on the review of the prior goals/outcomes and family priorities, strategies or techniques can be modified.

   This phase may include an examination of family routines to determine how and when strategies will be used. Demonstration or modeling by the professional(s) will enable the family to understand why a strategy is selected and how it relates to the child's outcomes.

   Practicing the new strategies can be helpful with encouragement and specific feedback provided to the family. Time should be allowed for extensive discussions and questions by both the professional(s) and the parent or other family members. During this phase of the meeting, the home visitor should remain sensitive to the individual needs of the family and the circumstances in the home.

4. *Closure.* At the end of the home visit, the service coordinator summarizes the session to ensure mutual understanding of what has been accomplished and decisions that have been made. Mrs. Ramirez asks several questions to make sure that she understands all that has been planned. The service provider provides a record of the visit using pictures and instructions for the strategies for follow-up. They agree that the next home visit will take place the following week at the same time.

---

the IFSP. As McWilliam (1999) points out, "The child does not learn from home visits—the family does" **(p. 24)**. With thoughtful planning, flexible implementation, and frequent monitoring, home visiting can be a highly successful service delivery model with many benefits for families and service providers (Brady, Peters, Gamel-McCormick, & Venuto, 2004).

Because home visits require professionals to enter a family's home, special consideration should be given to honor the family's privacy and preferences regarding the logistics of the meeting (e.g., time of day, location). Families should be given choices in scheduling that are convenient and flexible. In some cases,

families may not want home visits to occur because they may feel that having service providers in their home is intrusive (Klaus, 2008). In such instances, other arrangements can be made for services to be provided (e.g., child care center, early intervention program). When conducting home visits, there are a number of practical factors to consider. Home visitor safety is an important consideration. When traveling in the community and entering homes, service providers should follow basic safety precautions.

Regardless of where the services are provided, careful planning must take place so that the family understands the expectations. The following are

Well-structured home visits have benefits for the child, family and service providers.

Cengage Learning

examples of decisions to be made prior to the visit so that the family will know what to expect:

- How long will the visit last?
- What will be the agenda and format of the visit?
- Will the family participate actively in the session?
- How will other family members (e.g., siblings, grandparents) be incorporated into the visit?
- How will progress be monitored and family satisfaction determined?

It is important to remember that the purpose of home visiting is to provide families with the skills and supports to meet the family priorities/outcomes identified on the IFSP or IEP. Therefore, it is more likely for the families to experience satisfaction if the expectations of the home visit are clear.

The Making Connections feature provides an example of the process that is followed during a home visit with the Ramirez family. Figure 3–4 provides a sample family evaluation form that was used to gain input from Maria's family about their experiences with early intervention services and the information and support they were provided.

Ongoing Support and Information Exchange

We have come to realize in the field of early intervention/early childhood special education, that families can be the best advocates for their children when they are provided with information, as well as encouragement, support, and optimism (Trivette & Dunst, 2004). Families who are supported and have the information they need are more likely to respond to early intervention/education services in a meaningful way. Professionals should be familiar with the various resources that are available and be ready to share this information with families. Some of the most widely used ways to share information with families of children with disabilities include pamphlets and other materials, newsletters, and online resources, as well as linking families to community resources. Modes of ongoing communication include classroom/program visits, group parent meetings, newsletters, Web pages, communication notebooks, phone calls, e-mails, audio recordings, and parent-professional conferences. Professionals must strive to provide information and support that is coordinated, coherent, and well-suited to each family's needs (Kaczmarek, 2007).

In addition to the information and support provided by early intervention/early childhood special education professionals, many families benefit from the support and guidance of other families who also have children with disabilities (Klemm & Schimanski, 1999). A family may establish a relationship with another family or families may become members of parent-to-parent organizations that exist on the local, state, or national levels. Many of these organizations have websites, listservs, chat rooms, and discussion boards. Networking with other families offers opportunities for them to problem-solve regarding various issues and creates opportunities for enrichment and learning from one another as well.

Summary

A specific requirement of IDEA is to enhance the capacity of families to meet the special needs of their children. This requirement explicitly acknowledges the families of young children with known or suspected disabilities as the central focus of early intervention/early childhood special education services and the primary decision makers in the service delivery process. Professionals are continuing to make changes in policy and practices in an attempt to move families to the center of the service delivery system.

As has been indicated throughout this chapter, a family-based philosophy is the cornerstone of recommended practice in early intervention/early childhood special education. Rather than asking families to adjust to programs' policies and needs, recommended practice suggests that programs must adjust services according to families' concerns, priorities, and resources. Families are seen as full partners in early intervention/early childhood special education programs.

A family-based approach is founded on a family systems model. That is, young children with special needs are viewed as part of their family system, which in turn is perceived as part of a larger network of informal and formal systems. What happens to one member of the family often affects all members, and each family member has his or her own needs and abilities. Thus, professionals must devise an individualized approach for each family served. To do this, professionals need a thorough understanding of how families operate and the impact that the birth of a child with a known or suspected disability, or the diagnosis of a child's disability, may have on how families function. Further, professionals must know how to engage in collaborative relationships with families and other professionals in meeting the needs of young children with disabilities.

The idea of strong relationships between families and professionals who work with young children with disabilities is proving to have many benefits. However, many changes have occurred in families, laws, and interactions between service providers and families. These changes contribute to a complex challenge for personnel in providing appropriate learning experiences and services for young children and their families. It is very important for service providers to consider the concerns, priorities, and resources of families and to view the family as a system with many interacting forces.

Here are some basic understandings in good family-professional partnerships:

- The relationship professionals develop with a family has a powerful effect on the child's learning.
- All families deserve to be valued, respected, understood, and appreciated.
- An open, trusting relationship between family members and service providers is essential to successful early intervention/education. This relationship develops over time.
- Professionals cannot make family members do things their way; pressure impedes relationship building.

- Start where the family is, listening to family members' points of view, reflecting on what they say, clarifying their thoughts and feelings.
- Professionals often think they are right; however, a family may have a solution the early interventionist/educator did not consider—that is the beauty of partnerships!

Check Your Understanding

1. How has the relationship between families and professionals changed in early intervention/early childhood special education changed over the years? What circumstances have influenced this process?
2. Describe the reactions of a family to a child with a developmental delay or disability.
3. What is the rationale behind the use of a family systems model?
4. Identify the four key elements of a family systems model. Explain the characteristics of each of these elements.
5. How does the concept of *cohesion* differ from *adaptability* in the family systems theory model?
6. What kinds of influences have contributed to an emergence of a family-based philosophy in programs for young children with special needs?
7. Discuss reasons why an effective family–professional relationship is critical to successful programs for young children with disabilities.
8. Discuss key components of family–professional collaboration and strategies to ensure successful implementation of each component: (a) cultural responsiveness, (b) effective communication, (c) conferences and meetings, (d) home visits, (e) ongoing support and information exchange.

Reflection and Application

1. Identify a family situation that you have experienced and discuss how the family systems theory could have been applied to your interactions with that family.
2. Observe in an early childhood special education setting. What evidence is there that families are a key part of the program's mission? How do

professionals work in partnership with families? What types of services are being provided to the families?

3. How might families be involved in meeting the needs of Maria, T.J., and Cheryl? What specific roles might the families play? How can the ECSE teacher help support families in the roles they play? In the development or implementation of an IEP, explain how the teacher could provide support to the families to encourage their involvement.

References

Aldridge, J., & Goldman, R. (2007). *Current issues and trends in education* (2nd Ed.). Boston: Allyn & Bacon.

Allen, E., & Cowdery, G. (2009). *The exceptional child: Inclusion in early childhood education* (6th ed.). Clifton Park, NY: Delmar.

Bailey, D., Bruder, M. B., Hebbeler, K., Carta, J., Defosset, M., Greenwood, C., Kahn, L., Mallik, S., Markowitz, J., Spiker, D., Walker, D., & Barton, L. (2006). Recommended outcomes for families of young children with disabilities. *Journal of Early Intervention, 28,* 227–251.

Bailey, D., McWilliam, R., Dykes, L., Hebeler, K., Simeonsson, R., Spiker, D., & Wagner, M. (1998). Family outcomes in early intervention: A framework for program evaluation and efficacy research. *Exceptional Children, 64*(3), 313–328.

Bandura, A. (1997). *Self-efficacy: The exercise of control.* New York: W.H. Freeman.

Banks, R., Santos, R., & Roof, V. (2003). Discovering family concerns, priorities, and resources: Sensitive family information gathering. *Young Exceptional Children, 6*(2), 11–19.

Barber, P. A., Turnbull, A. P., Behr, S. K., & Kerns, G. M. (1998). Family systems perspective on early childhood special education. In S. L. Odom & M. B. Karnes (Eds.), *Early intervention for infants and children with handicaps* (pp. 179–198). Baltimore: Paul H. Brookes.

Berry, J., & Hardman, M. (1998). *Lifespan perspectives on the family and disability.* Needham Heights, MA: Allyn & Bacon.

Blacher, J. (1984). Sequential stages of adjustment to the birth of a child with handicaps: Fact or artifact? *Mental Retardation, 22,* 55–68.

Brady, S., Peters, D., Gamel-McCormick, M., & Venuto, N. (2004). Types and patterns of professional-family talk in home-based early intervention. *Journal of Early Intervention, 26*(2), 146–159.

Bronfenbrenner, U. (1979). *The ecology of human development: Experiments by nature and design.* Cambridge, MA: Harvard University Press.

Bronfenbrenner, U., & Morris, P. (1998). The ecology of developmental processes. In W. Damon & R. Lerner (Eds.), *Handbook of child psychology* (5th ed., Vol. 1, pp. 993–1028). New York: Wiley.

Brotherson, M., & Goldstein, B. (1992). Time as a resource and constraint for parents of young children with disabilities: Implications for early intervention services. *Topics in Early Childhood Special Education, 12,* 508–527.

Brubaker, T. (Ed.). (1993). *Family relations: Challenges for the future.* Newbury Park, CA: Sage.

Carter, B., & McGoldrick, M. (1999). *The changing family life cycle* (3rd ed.). Boston: Allyn & Bacon.

Children's Defense Fund. (2008). *The state of America's children.* Washington, DC: Author.

Cooper, C., & Allred, K. (1992). A comparison of mothers' versus fathers' need for support in caring for a young child with special needs. *Infant-Toddler Intervention, 2,* 205–221.

Copple, C. & Bredekamp, S. (Eds.). (2009). *Developmentally appropriate practice in early childhood programs.* Washington, DC: National Association for the Education of Young Children.

Drotar, D., Baskiewicz, A., Irvin, N., Kennell, J., & Klaus, M. (1975). The adaptation of parents to the birth of an infant with a congenital malformation: A hypothetical model. *Pediatrics, 56,* 710–716.

Dunlap, K. M. (1997). Family empowerment: One outcome of cooperative preschool education. *Child Welfare, 76*(4), 501–519.

Dunst, C. J., Johanson, C., Trivette, C. M., & Hamby, D. (1991). Family-oriented early intervention policies and practices: Family-centered or not? *Exceptional Children, 58*(2), 115–126.

Dunst, C., Trivette, C., & Deal, A. (1988). *Enabling and empowering families: Principles and guidelines for practice.* Cambridge, MA: Brookline Books.

Dunst, C., Trivette, C., & Deal, A. (Eds.) (1994). *Supporting and strengthening families.* Cambridge, MA: Brookline Books.

Featherstone, H. (1980). *A difference in the family: Life with a disabled child.* New York: Basic Books.

Galinsky, E. (1990). Parents and teachers/caregivers: Sources of tension, sources of support. *Young Children, 43*(3), 4–12.

Gallagher, M. J., & Desimone, L. (1995). Lessons learned from implementation of the IEP: Applications to the IFSP. *Topics in Early Childhood Special Education, 15*(3), 353–378.

Gallagher, P., Fialka, J., Rhodes, C., & Arceneaux, C. (2003). Working with families: Rethinking denial. *Young Exceptional Children, 5*(2), 11–17.

Gargiulo, R. (2009). *Special education in contemporary society: An introduction to exceptionality* (3rd ed.). Thousand Oaks, CA: Sage.

Gollnick, D. M. & Chinn, P. C. (2009). *Multicultural education in a pluralistic society.* (8th ed.). Boston: Allyn & Bacon.

Guralnick, M. (1997). *The effectiveness of early intervention.* Baltimore: Brookes.

Guralnick, M. (1998). Effectiveness of early intervention for vulnerable children: A developmental perspective. *American Journal of Mental Retardation, 102*(4), 319–345.

Hains, A., Rhymer, P., McLean, M., Barnekow, K., Johnson, V., & Kennedy, B. (2005). Interdisciplinary teams and diverse families: Practices in early intervention personnel preparation. *Young Exceptional Children, 8,* 2–10.

Hanson, M. & Lynch, E. (1995). *Early intervention: Implementing child and family services for infants and toddlers who are at risk or disabled.* Austin, TX: Pro-Ed.

Hanson, M. & Lynch, E. (2004). *Understanding families: Approaches to diversity, disability, and risk.* Baltimore: Paul H. Brookes.

Harry, B., Kalyanpur, M., & Day, J. (1999). *Building cultural reciprocity with families. Case studies in special education.* Baltimore: Paul H. Brookes.

Hartman, A. (1995). Diagrammatic assessment of family relationships. *Families in Society: The Journal of Contemporary Human Service, 76*(2), 111–122.

Heflinger, C. A., & Bickman, L. (1997). A theory-driven intervention and evaluation to explore family caregiver empowerment. *Journal of Emotional & Behavioral Disorders, 5*(3), 184–192.

Kaczmarek, L. (2007). A team approach: Supporting families of children with disabilities in inclusive programs. In D. Koralek (Ed.), *Spotlight on young children and families* (pp. 28–36). Washington, DC: National Association for the Education of Young Children.

Kilgo, J. L., & Raver, S. A. (2009). Building partnerships in culturally/linguistically diverse settings. In S. Raver (Ed.), *Early childhood special education—0 to 8 Years: Strategies for positive outcomes.* Upper Saddle River, NJ: Pearson Education.

Kilgo, J. (Ed.). (2006). *Transdisciplinary teaming in early intervention/early childhood special education: Navigating together with families and children.* Olney, MD: Association for Childhood Education International.

Klaus, C. S. (2008). *Home visiting: Promoting healthy parent and child development* (3rd ed.). Baltimore: Paul H. Brookes.

Klemm, D., & Schimanski, C. (1999). Parent to parent: The crucial connection. *Exceptional Parent, 29*(9), 109–112.

Matuszny, R., Banda, D., & Coleman, T. (2007). A progressive plan for building collaborative relationships with parents from diverse backgrounds. *TEACHING Exceptional Children, 39,* 24–31.

McCormick, K., Stricklin, S., Nowak, T., & Rous, B. (2008). Using eco-mapping to understand family strengths and resources. *Young Exceptional Children, 11*(2), 17–28.

McWilliam, R. A. (1999). It's only natural . . . to have early intervention in the environments where it's needed. In S. Sandall & M. Ostrosky (Eds.), *Natural environments and inclusion* (Young Exceptional Children Monograph Series No. 2). Denver, CO: Council for Exceptional Children, The Division for Early Childhood.

Minuchin, P. (1988). Relationships within the family: A systems perspective. In R. A. Hinde & J. Stevenson-Hinde (Eds.), *Relationships within the families* (2nd ed., pp. 7–26). New York: Oxford University Press.

Nichols, M. (2007). *The essentials of family therapy* (3rd ed.). Boston: Allyn & Bacon.

Olson, D., Russell, C., & Sprenkle, D. (1980). Circumplex model of marital and family systems II: Empirical studies and clinical intervention. In J. Vincent (Ed.), *Advances in family intervention assessment and theory* (Vol. 1) (pp. 129–179). Greenwich, CT: JAI Press.

Olson, D. H., McCubbin, H. L., Barnes, H., Larsen, A., Muxem, M., & Wilson, M. (1989). *Families: What makes them work* (2nd ed.). Los Angeles: Sage.

Peterson, N., & Cooper, C. (1989). Parent education and involvement in early intervention programs for handicapped children: A different perspective on parent needs and parent–professional relationships. In M. Fine (Ed.), *The second handbook on parent education* (pp. 197–234). New York: Academic Press.

Sandall, S., Hemmeter, M., Smith, B., & McLean, M. (2005). *DEC recommended practices: A comprehensive guide to practical application in early intervention/early childhood special education.* Longmont, CO: Sopris West.

Seligman, M., & Darling, R. (1997). *Ordinary families, special children* (2nd ed.). New York: Guilford Press.

Swick, K. J. (1996). Building healthy families: Early childhood educators can make a difference. *Journal of Instructional Psychology, 23*(1), 75–82.

Swick, K. J., & Graves, S. B. (1993). *Empowering at-risk families during the early childhood years.* Washington, DC: National Education Association.

Taibbi, R. (2007). *Doing family therapy* (2nd ed.). New York: Guilford Press.

Trivette, C., & Dunst, C. (2005). DEC recommended practices: Family-based practices. In S. Sandall, M. Hemmeter, B. Smith, & M. McLean (Eds.), *DEC recommended practices: A comprehensive guide to practical application in early intervention/early childhood special education* (pp. 107–120). Longmont, CO: Sopris West.

Turnbull, A., Summers, J., & Brotherson, M. J. (1984). *Working with families with disabled members: A family systems approach.* Lawrence: Kansas University Affiliated Facility.

Turnbull, A., Summers, J., Turnbull, R., Brotherson, M., Winton, P., Roberts, R., Snyder, McWilliams, R., Chandler, L., Schrandt, S., Stowe, M., Bruder, M., DiVenere, N., Epley, P., Hornback, M., Huff, B., Miksch, P., Mitchell, L., Sharp, L., & Stroup-Rentier, V. (2007).

Family supports and services in early intervention: A bold vision. *Journal of Early Intervention, 29,* 187–206.

Turnbull, A., Turbiville, V., & Turnbull, R. (2000). Evolution of family–professional partnerships: Collective empowerment as the model for the early twenty-first century. In J. P. Shonkoff & S. J. Meisels (Eds.), *Handbook of early childhood intervention (pp. 630–648).* Cambridge, England: Cambridge University Press.

Turnbull, A., Turnbull, R., Erwin, E. & Soodak, L. (2006). *Families, professionals, and exceptionality: Positive outcomes through a partnership and trust* (5th ed.). Upper Saddle River, NJ: Pearson Education.

Vacca, J., & Feinberg, E. (2000). Rules of engagement: Initiating and sustaining a relationship with families who have mental health disorders. *Infants and Young Children, 13,* 51–57.

Vanderslice, V. (1984). Empowerment: A definition in progress. *Human Ecology Forum, 14*(1), 2–3.

Whitbread, K., Bruder, M. B., Fleming, G., & Park, H. (2007). Collaboration in special education: Parent–professional training. *TEACHING Exceptional Children, 39,* 6–14.

Winzer, M. A., & Maszurek, K. (1998). *Special education in multicultural contexts.* Upper Saddle River, NJ: Merrill.

Assessment and Planning for Young Children with Special Needs

Part 2

Cengage Learning

Chapter 4
Assessment of Young Children with Special Needs

Chapter 5
Delivering Services to Young Children with Special Needs

Chapter 6
Curriculum for Young Children with Special Needs

4 Assessment of Young Children with Special Needs

Key Terminology

Assessment

Screening

Eligibility

Program planning

Progress monitoring and evaluation

Multidisciplinary team

Standardized tests

Tests

Performance

Norm-referenced tests

Developmental age score

Percentile ranks

Criterion-referenced tests

Curriculum-referenced tests

Reliability

Validity

Content validity

Instructional validity

Construct validity

Concurrent validity

Predictive validity

Observational assessment

Play-based assessment

Interviews

Authentic assessment

Portfolio assessment

Developmental domains

Intelligence tests

Culturally biased assessment

Apgar Scale

PKU screening

Screening

Referrals

Child Find

Sensitivity

Specificity

False negative

False positive

Arena assessment

Program planning assessment

Ecological assessment

Protocol

Functional skill

Progress monitoring

Program Evaluation

Formative assessment

Summative assessment

Learning Outcomes

After reading this chapter, you will be able to:

- Explain the four primary purposes of assessment in early intervention (EI) and early childhood special education (ECSE) for children birth through age eight.

- Describe the types of assessment procedures used in EI/ECSE.

- Discuss issues associated with traditional assessment practices used with young children.

- List recommended practices for conducting appropriate assessments of young children.

- Differentiate between assessment for determining eligibility and assessment for program planning in EI/ECSE.

- Explain the importance of family involvement and family preferences being emphasized in the program planning process.

- Describe four methods that can be used to collect assessment information.

- Identify the steps in an ecological assessment process.

- Explain the importance of progress monitoring and evaluation.

The assessment of young children with disabilities is an integral component of early intervention (EI) and early childhood special education (ECSE) services for children birth through age eight. In order to implement recommended assessment practices for young children with delays or disabilities, professionals must consider the major purposes of assessment, guidelines for conducting appropriate assessments, and strategies for linking initial assessment with program planning and progress monitoring. In this chapter, an overview of assessment is provided; issues associated with the assessment of young children and recommended practices are identified; and assessments conducted for the purposes of screening, eligibility, program planning, and progress monitoring are described.

Assessment Purposes, Procedures, and Types

First, the definition of **assessment** must be considered in order to understand the comprehensiveness of the assessment process. McLean, Wolery, and Bailey (2004) describe assessment as the process of gathering information for decision making. Bagnato and Neisworth (1991) emphasize that early childhood assessment is a flexible, collaborative decision-making process in which teams of parents and professionals repeatedly revise their judgments and make decisions. Richard and Schiefelbusch (1991) describe assessment as "a multi-level process, beginning with screening procedures and continuing through diagnosis, planning of intervention, and program monitoring and evaluation" (p. 110). These definitions suggest that assessment is a dynamic, ongoing process allowing for various decisions to be made about children with delays, disabilities, or other special needs. In reality, many different types of assessment take place simultaneously and on several different levels.

Next, the origin of the word assessment should be considered. The word assessment can be traced to the Latin word *assidre*, which means to "sit beside." Assessment in ECSE is designed to be an experience through which professionals and families work together and exchange information to benefit the child's growth and development (Division for Early Childhood, 2007; Woods & McCormick, 2002).

Assessment, rather than referring to a "test," is a systematic process for obtaining information from a variety of sources (e.g., observations, interviews, portfolios, tests) to be used in making judgments about each child's characteristics, needs, and progress. Assessment should be viewed as a fact-finding and problem-solving process shared by families and professionals. Figure 4–1 illustrates the components of the assessment process in EI/ECSE. As can be seen, collaboration among professionals representing multiple disciplines and families is needed throughout each step of the assessment process.

Assessment Purposes

Assessment information is gathered to be used in making a decision in one or more of the following areas:

1. screening
2. eligibility
3. program planning, and
4. progress monitoring and evaluation.

McCormick (1997) noted "assessment, planning, intervention, and evaluation are overlapping activities" (p. 223). As illustrated in Figure 4–2, the areas of assessment are linked and each area of assessment is designed to answer specific questions and inform decisions made about young children (Botts, Losardo, Notari-Syverson, 2007). These various assessment purposes necessitate different instruments and procedures to be used by qualified professionals representing various disciplines.

General Assessment Considerations

As described previously, the Individuals with Disabilities Education Act (2004) requires that a **multidisciplinary team** be involved in the assessment of young children. A multidisciplinary team refers to the involvement of two or more professionals from different disciplines (e.g., physical therapy, special education, speech-language pathology) in early intervention/early childhood special education activities. Transdisciplinary teams, the type of team model often used in EI/ECSE, are composed of family members and professionals representing a variety of disciplines who address specific assessment questions. For example, children with sensory

FIGURE 4–1 **Components of a Collaborative Assessment Process in Early Intervention/Early Childhood Special Education Leading to Goals and Outcomes**

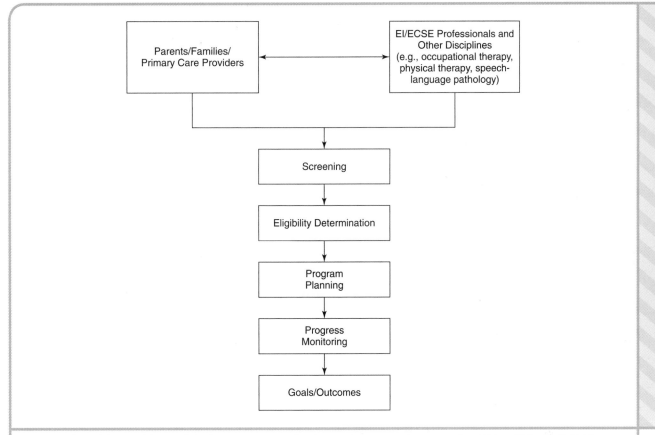

SOURCE: Adapted from Bricker, D. (2002). *Assessment, evaluation, and programming system for children* (Volume 1), Baltimore: Paul H. Brookes.

FIGURE 4–2 **Linked Assessment Process**

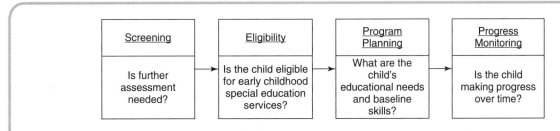

SOURCE: Adapted from Botts, D., Losardo, A., Notari-Syverson, A. (2007). Alternative assessment: The pathway to individualized instruction for young children. In E. Horn, C. Peterson, & L. Fox (Eds.), *Linking curriculum to child and family outcomes* (Young Exceptional Children Monograph Series No. 2). Missoula, MT: Council for Exceptional Children, The Division for Early Childhood. (p. 72).

needs (e.g., hearing or visual impairments) or children with developmental needs (e.g., visual impairments, communication delays, movement problems) require professionals on the team to have expertise in those areas (e.g., vision specialist, speech-language pathologist, physical therapist, occupational therapist). Although legislation and recommended practices call for assessments to be conducted by a team, which includes the family and professionals from a variety of disciplines, professionals must realize that a large number of team members may be confusing or overwhelming to family members. Professionals must be sensitive to family preferences and remember that the assessment process should be individualized and appropriate for each child and family.

Types of Assessment in Early Intervention/ Early Childhood Special Education

Because early childhood is a unique period of development, different types of assessment instruments and procedures have been developed specifically for young children. Common assessment procedures in EI/ECSE include: norm-referenced tests, criterion- or curriculum-based instruments, observations, interviews, and other measures. Because there are many purposes of assessment, tools designed for one purpose are in most cases inappropriate to use for a purpose other than that for which they were intended (Division Early Childhood, 2007; Grisham-Brown & Pretti-Frontczak, 2003). The instruments and procedures selected will depend on a number of factors such as the purpose of the assessment, state and program guidelines, and preferences of professionals and families (Andersson, 2004). In addition to standardized measures, informal assessment measures are recommended that are less prescriptive and more specific to the context in which they are used.

Assessment Instruments. Depending on the purpose of the assessment, different types of tests may be appropriate (Andersson, 2004). Of the different types of assessment measures used with young children, formal testing has been the procedure most frequently used during the initial phases of assessment (i.e., screening, eligibility determination). During formal testing, **standardized tests** are administered. It is important to remember, however, that **tests** are a predetermined collection of questions or tasks to

which predetermined types of responses are sought. A standardized testing instrument is one by which the individual child's **performance**, or the child's behavior that is exhibited while putting specific skills into action, is interpreted in relation to the performance of a group of peers of the same age group who have previously taken the same test—a "norming" group.

Norm-referenced tests provide a score that is relative to other children in a particular group—that is, the source of the norms (Cohen & Spenciner, 2003). Norm-referenced tools have certain advantages; they compare children to other children of the same age for eligibility purposes, report reliability and validity information, and can usually be administered in a short period of time. A disadvantage of norm-referenced tools, particularly for children with delays or disabilities, is that the administration of the tests usually takes place in unfamiliar settings (e.g., clinic, testing room) rather than the natural environment. Another problem is the lack of useful information they provide for determining functional, appropriate outcomes. Further, norm-referenced measures are often biased against children with disabilities and children from culturally or linguistically diverse backgrounds (Sattler, 2008).

Norm-referenced tests for children ages birth through five result in quantitative scores, often reported as **developmental age scores** (i.e., the average age at which 50% of the normative sample achieved a particular raw score) and **percentile ranks** (i.e., the percentage of the same-aged population that performed at or below a given score). The developmental age for children with delays or disabilities usually will differ from his or her chronological age depending on the effects of the child's delay or disability. For early primary-level students, ages five though eight, norm-referenced tests provide standard scores, percentile ranks, and grade-level equivalents in various subject areas (e.g., reading, math, science). This allows ECSE teachers to compare the child's performance to performances of other children of the same age (Sattler, 2008).

Criterion-referenced tests are used to determine whether a child's performance meets an established criteria or a certain level of mastery within various developmental domains (e.g., cognitive, motor, self-care), content areas (e.g., math, literacy), or within a detailed set of objectives. These tools provide information about a child's attainment of specific levels of competence. Specific strengths of criterion-referenced instruments are that they usually offer a continuum of skills linked to the curriculum that can be useful for program planning purposes and monitoring individual progress. Criterion-referenced measures may be administered in the natural environment, and they allow professionals to adapt or modify items to help children demonstrate competence. Limitations of criterion-referenced instruments are that they are time-consuming to administer and may include items that are not appropriate or functional for all children. Criterion-referenced measures may be biased against children with delays or disabilities, as well as children representing culturally or linguistically diverse backgrounds.

Curriculum-referenced tests are similar to criterion-referenced measures; however, curriculum-referenced tools are used to interpret a child's performance in relation to specific curriculum objectives. In most cases, curriculum-referenced tools are most relevant for program planning purposes (Cohen & Spenciner, 2003; Sattler, 2008). In recent years, curriculum-referenced tests have been used more frequently during the eligibility process because they provide useful information in making eligibility decisions (McLean, 2005).

Although a detailed description of the psychometric aspects of assessment instruments is beyond the scope of this chapter, it is important that these concepts be understood by those who are responsible for the selection of specific assessment tools to be used during any phase of the assessment process. Reliability and validity are two of the psychometric concepts that should be considered. **Reliability** refers to the consistency or dependability of an assessment tool. In other words, does the test measure what it is supposed to measure in a dependable manner? If T.J. was given the same test on different occasions, would his performance on the test be the same each time? If so, the examiner could assume with some confidence that the results were reliable or free of error. Or if several children were given the same test and received different scores on the tests, the test administrator would want to know that the variability in the scores was actually due to the differences in their abilities. The examiner needs to feel confident that the test is consistently measuring what it is designed to measure. Reliability is important for making generalizations about children's learning and development. Reliability is represented by a figure between .00 and 1.0, with values closer to 1.0 showing evidence of better reliability.

Another important psychometric property of an assessment instrument is **validity**, which is the extent to which an assessment instrument measures what it was designed to measure. Validity is represented by a figure between .00 and 1.0, such that values closer to 1.0 indicate better validity. Several different types of validity should be of concern to early childhood special educators, as well as professionals representing other disciplines. The first is **content validity**, which refers to how well the test represents the content it purports to measure. A second type of validity is **instructional validity**. This is the extent to which the information gained from an assessment instrument would be useful in planning intervention programs for young children with disabilities. A third type of validity, **construct validity**, focuses on the degree to which a test addresses the constructs on which it was based. A fourth type of test validity is **concurrent validity**. This type of validity is concerned with how well a test correlates with other accepted measures of performance administered close in time to the first. Finally, **predictive validity** focuses on the extent to which a test relates to some future measure of performance. When professionals are selecting an assessment measure, attention should be focused on the reliability and validity information reported in the manuals of the assessment instruments (Sattler, 2008).

Authentic Assessment. **Authentic assessment** is a comprehensive term used to represent the process of observing, recording, collecting, and otherwise

Assessment information is collected in a variety of ways to document the progress each child is making.

documenting what children do and how they do it for the purpose of making educational decisions (Losardo & Notari-Syverson, 2001). Assessment of behavior and interactions in familiar environments in which a child participates provides authentic information. This information can be gathered using a variety of processes and organized in such a way that it provides a comprehensive overview of a child's performance on authentic, meaningful tasks over time (Division for Early Childhood, 2007; Losardo & Notari-Syverson, 2001).

Observational assessment is a systematic process of gathering recordings of young children's behavior in real-life situations and familiar settings within their environments. Assessment procedures often include systematic observations of the interactions between children and their parents, primary caregivers, or peers. Several different strategies can be used to structure the observations and organize the information that is gathered such as checklists, rating scales, and structured observations (Division Early Childhood, 2007; Hanson & Lynch, 1995). **Play-based assessment** is an example of an observational procedure used frequently in early childhood education for infants, toddlers, and preschoolers. During play, children spontaneously and authentically demonstrate knowledge and skills. Play-based assessments provide a nonthreatening way to collect information regarding the level of development of young children (Linder, 2008). Play-based assessments support the observation of children in a play situation, which allows them to demonstrate behaviors that they typically exhibit under normal circumstances.

Interviews are forms of assessment that can be used to gather information regarding the areas on which to focus during the assessment process, specific information about the child (e.g., how a child responds to various situations), or other types of information that may be relevant to the assessment process. Because these interviews, or conversations, take place with a particular purpose in mind, it is important to have some structure to ensure that the intended goal(s) are achieved. Although suggested a number of years ago by Winton and Bailey (1988), the following phases are still recommended today for family interviews:

1. preliminary preparation (preparation for the meeting)
2. introduction (review of the purpose of the meeting)
3. inventory (discussion of the information and determination of the parents' perceptions)

4. summarizing (review of the options), and
5. closure (summary of what took place in the meeting)

Interviews, or conversations between the professionals and families or caregivers, require some structure; however, they should be flexible enough for everyone to feel comfortable with the process (Turnbull, Turnbull, Erwin, & Soodak, 2006).

Recent recommendations regarding assessment indicate a need for an increase focus on the *process* of assessment rather than just the *product* of assessment (McLean, Wolery, & Bailey, 2004; Neisworth & Bagnato, 2005). One recommended informal method through which this can be accomplished is an **arena assessment** process. An arena assessment is conducted by a group of professionals from various disciplines along with the child's family. This group of professionals and family members is referred to as a transdisciplinary team. As you may recall from the previous chapters, transdisciplinary teams plan and provide services within and across discipline boundaries to deliver integrated services. This team jointly collects information about specific developmental areas as well as the interrelatedness of these areas within the child. One or more of the team members usually conducts the assessment while other team members, including the parents, observe the assessment process. An integrated assessment report is then completed by the participating professionals, including input from the family. Figure 4–3 provides a visual example of the participants in an arena assessment, which include the child, family members, and professionals representing various disciplines as needed.

Considerations and Cautions in the Assessment of Young Children

Although each assessment instrument carries its own organizing framework, many are organized around **developmental domains**, which are the key areas typically addressed in comprehensive assessments of young children. Most assessment instruments for young children seek to measure development in one or more of the following skill domains: cognitive skills, motor skills, communication skills, social skills, and adaptive skills. These domains represent

FIGURE 4–3 **Example of Arena Assessment**

Adrienne Frank/Child Development Resources

SOURCE: From the *Example of Arena Assessment*, L.J. Johnson, et al (eds.), 1994. Paul H. Brookes.

interrelated areas of development that are usually the focus of assessments for young children. Assessment procedures should be comprehensive in coverage and focus on children's overall abilities rather than on one or two developmental areas alone. Although separate areas of development can be defined (e.g., motor, communication, cognition), these areas are not independent but interact in complex ways. Professionals must attempt to gain a holistic picture of children's abilities that cuts across all developmental domains (Division for Early Childhood, 2007). Each of these skill domains and content areas are described in greater detail in Chapter 6.

Problems with Traditional Assessment Practices

Much debate in recent years has focused on assessment approaches and procedures appropriate for young children with special needs and their families (Neisworth & Bagnato, 1996; 2000; 2005). One of the biggest issues has been the use of standardized, norm-referenced tests with young children. Bronfenbrenner (1977) cautioned against over-reliance on this type of assessment when he described the assessment of young children as "the science of the strange behavior of children in strange situations with strange adults for the briefest possible period of time" (p. 513). Conventional, standardized assessment instruments are

often inappropriate even for use with children experiencing typical development. The *inappropriateness* of such measures is even greater when used with young children with disabilities. As Bagnato, Neisworth, and Munson (1997) point out:

> Assessment of infants and preschoolers remains dominated by restrictive methods and styles that place a premium on inauthentic, contrived developmental tasks, that are administered by various professionals in separate sessions using small, unmotivating toys from boxes or test kits, staged at a table or on the floor in an unnatural setting, observed passively by parents, interpreted by norms based solely on typical children, and used for narrow purposes of classification and eligibility determination. (p. 69)

Assessment measures and practices must become compatible with, rather than at odds with, the behavior and interests of young children birth though age eight (Division Early Childhood, 2007; Neisworth & Bagnato, 2005).

Standardized, norm-referenced tests were designed to be used for screening, diagnostic, and eligibility purposes. Unfortunately, these tools too often are misused by professionals for purposes other than those for which they were intended, such as to design intervention goals and procedures (McLean, Wolery, & Bailey, 2004). In addition, standardized norm-referenced measures were designed to be used in conjunction with other sources of information. Too often, however, these measures are used exclusively. The real problem arises when the test results do not provide an accurate representation of a child's typical behavior or optimal performance.

As the field of early intervention/early childhood special education has evolved, it has become increasingly apparent that traditional assessment approaches should be replaced with procedures that are more appropriate for use with young children (Division Early Childhood, 2007). McLean (2005) called for a paradigm shift in assessment for young children due to the many issues and challenges associated with the assessment of young children, such as: (a) the problems associated with the use of intelligence tests for young children; (b) the limited number of appropriate instruments for young children with disabilities; (c) the nature and characteristics of young children and families; and (d) the cultural bias and lack of cultural sensitivity in traditional assessment procedures. Although there are other issues and challenges associated with the assessment of young children, these issues are highlighted in the following section.

Inappropriate Use of Intelligence Tests with Young Children

A problem that unfortunately continues to occur in early childhood is the over-reliance on **intelligence tests** to determine children's outcomes. An intelligence test is a standardized measure of intellectual functioning. Although the inappropriate use of standardized tests with young children has been criticized for a number of years, the misuse and abuse has continued (Neisworth & Bagnato, 1992; 1996; 2005). There are a number of possible explanations for the continued emphasis on intelligence testing with young children. Professionals who are responsible for assessment may be unfamiliar with more appropriate ways to determine a true estimate of the abilities of young children (McLean, Wolery, & Bailey, 2004). Another reason may be that an extensive amount of time is required to conduct a thorough assessment using authentic measures (e.g., observations, family interviews) across multiple settings (e.g., home or school). Due to limited professional knowledge, time constraints, and other factors, standardized testing continues to be used in inappropriate ways with young children with delays or disabilities. Based on what has been learned about assessment, professionals

must find ways to conduct thorough and appropriate assessments of young children (Division Early Childhood, 2007).

Limitations of Assessment Instruments for Young Children with Disabilities

Another assessment problem is the relatively small number of assessment instruments available that are appropriate for young children with disabilities. Most standardized tests are designed for children experiencing typical development and will not reflect the abilities and needs of children with disabilities. The presence of a disability can further complicate the task of accurately assessing the abilities of young children. For example, when a child has a physical, communication, or sensory disability, professionals must be extremely skilled in order to obtain an accurate assessment of the child's abilities. The most effective assessment protocols rely on sensitivity to the age of the child and the nature of the child's disability or delay.

A variety of strategies may be necessary to collect accurate information such as incorporating adaptations into the assessment, using alternative sensory modalities and/or methods of communication, and gaining information from families. In addition, the developmental impact of a disability must be taken into consideration. A child with a visual impairment or physical disability, for example, may not have experienced some of the same activities as nondisabled children (e.g., independent exploration of the environment, riding a tricycle or bicycle, or climbing a tree). Another problem, given the nature of many standardized assessment instruments, is that families are not able to participate as equal partners in the assessment process. Although a parent report is included as part of some standardized testing instruments, the parent reports often cannot be used for scoring purposes. Professionals must select assessment measures carefully to ensure that they are appropriate for the children and families with whom they are working.

Characteristics of Young Children and Their Families

The nature and characteristics of young children can be particularly challenging during the assessment process. In many cases, unfortunately, professionals have continued to rely on procedures utilized with older children even though the characteristics or nature of young children make the procedures inappropriate for them. Young children are poor candidates for traditional assessment procedures due to their short attention spans and the difficulty they have in following adult directions. Further, anxiety is often produced by children's interactions with unfamiliar adults and settings.

As we all know, young children are most comfortable with the people whom they are most familiar, such as their parents or primary caregivers. If possible, young children should not be separated from their parents during an assessment procedure. Often young children respond to separation by becoming more anxious and do not display optimal skills and behavior under these conditions. Assessment results will be more accurate if professionals allow time for children to become familiar with them. Familiar surroundings may help children feel more at ease and yield a more accurate portrayal of their abilities. If children do not feel comfortable, their performance often will not reflect their true ability. Assessments must be designed to make young children feel at ease in order to gain an accurate appraisal of their abilities and needs. The ultimate goal of assessment should be to elicit each child's typical pattern of behavior, the skills mastered, and the optimal level of performance (Division for Early Childhood, 2007).

Assessment of young children offers a unique opportunity to involve family members and other primary caregivers and gain their input and optimal information about each child (Division Early Childhood, 2007; Woods & McCormick, 2002). Families may be anxious about assessments and may not understand the purpose of each stage of the assessment process. As one parent commented following an assessment of her child, "I was concerned about my daughter passing the test. I didn't know if she would score high enough to get into the early intervention program." Another parent remarked that she went home from the assessment and made her child practice the skills he had missed. From these examples, it is clear that these mothers did not understand the purpose of the assessment process. They thought that the objective was to achieve a certain score that was high enough to get into a program. The professional's role is to provide information that will make families and caregivers fully aware of the purpose of each step in the assessment process. Pre-assessment planning is recommended as a way to provide opportunities for professionals to share information about the assessment process and for families to provide input to the professionals. Another important component of any assessment procedure is a period for explaining the process and answering parents' questions, usually before and after the assessment is conducted.

Culturally Biased Assessment Instruments

Young children who will potentially be eligible to receive early intervention or early childhood special education services are characterized by their diversity along a number of dimensions including culture, ethnicity, language, family structure, composition, values, socioeconomic status, etc. Professionals have struggled for many years with how to employ appropriate, nonbiased assessments of young children that do not penalize them based on their cultural background or experience. A **culturally biased assessment** is one that measures only skills and abilities valued by the dominant Western culture. Thus, those children from nondominant or non-Western cultures are placed at a unique disadvantage. Problematic situations often exist when traditional, standardized assessment measures that are culturally biased are used. An example of potential bias can be found in a commonly used screening tool that contains a test item that asks 4- to 6-year-old children to indicate "what a shoe is made of" with the acceptable answer being "leather." A child whose familiarity with shoes is limited to tennis shoes or sandals would not be given credit for providing the correct answer if he or she answered "rubber," "cloth," or "plastic." This item would be missed due to the child's lack of familiarity with leather shoes. It is easy to see the many potential problems associated with cultural bias in assessment tools and processes; therefore, professionals must strive for accurate and appropriate assessments of children from diverse backgrounds, which requires attention to the uniqueness of each child's culture and experience.

Recommended Assessment Practices and Procedures for Young Children with Disabilities

Driven by many years of experience and research demonstrating the limitations of traditional, single-dimensional assessment procedures, a number of recommended practices have emerged (Division Early Childhood, 2007; Sandall, Hemmeter, Smith, & McLean, 2005; Sandall & Schwartz, 2008; Taylor, 2009).

TABLE 4–1 Assessment Principles and Practices with Examples

Principles/Practices	Examples
Team-based assessment	Assessments should be conducted by a team, with equal status afforded to the family and to professionals.
Multidimensional assessment	Assessment information should be collected in a number of child and family domains.
Multimethod assessment	Assessment information should be collected using a variety of techniques, such as direct testing, observation, and interviews.
Multisource assessment	Assessment information should be collected from a number of sources knowledgeable about the child, including families, caregivers, and professionals.
Multicontext assessment	Assessment should occur across a number of environmental contexts, including the home, school, child care, or other relevant natural environments.
Culturally appropriate assessment	Assessment procedures should respect and be responsive to the unique culture of each child and family.
Proactive assessment	Assessment procedures should be designed to identify strengths, concerns, resources, needs, and priorities for intervention planning; emphasis should be placed on assessing resources, strengths and concerns, rather than deficits.
Ongoing information exchange and collaboration	The collection of assessment information should be an ongoing process that facilitates collaboration among families and professionals.

There is growing consensus that assessment should be considered a process, not a single procedure. Experts in the field of early childhood special education agree that "assessment should be an ongoing, collaborative process of systematic observation and analysis" (Greenspan & Meisels, 1994, p. 1). Table 4–1 contains a list of assessment principles and practices with examples provided of each. As can be seen in this table, assessment of young children should be multi- or transdisciplinary, multidimensional, multimethod, multisource, multicontext, culturally appropriate, proactive, and involve ongoing information exchange and collaboration.

Recommended Practices and Standards for Assessment

New directions and standards for the assessment of young children with delays or disabilities have been suggested (Division for Early Childhood, 2007;

Neisworth & Bagnato, 2005; Sandall et al., 2005). As described several years ago by Bagnato and Neisworth (1999), assessment must reflect essential qualities. Assessment must be useful, acceptable, authentic, collaborative, convergent, equitable, sensitive, and congruent. These qualities remain important today as important elements of recommended assessment practices in early intervention/early childhood special education (Sandall et al., 2005).

The Utility of the Assessment. Above all, the assessment information that is collected must be useful. The assessment of young children requires a careful subjective and objective appraisal of a child's performance in natural learning environments. Thus, a number of professionals from diverse backgrounds, as well as the child's family, are included in the process. This requires a blending of assessment models and an understanding of different methods and terminology used by professionals representing various disciplines so that the information will be useful to all members of the team. All assessment information must be combined, including information from families, to make important decisions about the child's need for services, individually targeted skills, and methods to be used in providing support to the child and family.

The Acceptability of the Assessment. To make the assessment process acceptable, it is recommended that the methods, styles, and materials for assessment must be mutually agreed upon by families and professionals (Neisworth & Bagnato, 2005). Assessment methods may range from separate assessments completed by EI/ECSE teachers and other professionals in a variety of settings to an arena format where all participants assess skills at the same time in the same setting. Assessment methods and styles may vary from direct testing to observations in natural contexts. Observational information may be more acceptable and may have more social validity due to the child's comfort level in performing skills in natural environments and within the context of play and everyday routines. In addition, the testing materials used must be acceptable and adaptable for children with various disabilities (e.g., physical, visual, cognitive); therefore, materials within the natural environment are usually most appropriate.

The Authenticity of Assessments. Establishing the authenticity of assessments may be especially important due to the number of professionals who may be involved and the diverse information gathered during the assessment process. Using multiple sources of information collected from those most familiar with the child (e.g., family members, child care providers, and teachers) and within natural contexts will ensure the authenticity of the information and result in information that is useful in determining the priorities for intervention.

Collaboration in the Assessment Process. The assessment of young children requires the highest degree of collaboration due to the number of professionals who may be involved along with the child's family. An initial assessment is completed by a number of professionals, along with the family, to determine if the child is eligible for services. Thereafter, the assessment team may vary in content due to the changing needs of the child. The use of the arena assessment

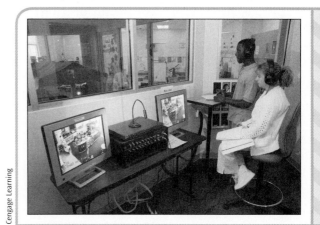

Cengage Learning

Observation of a child's performance during play and everyday routines can provide valuable information during the assessment process.

format and the presence of a facilitator make the assessment process more collaborative and, therefore, more understandable and useful to all participants. Collaboration is enhanced by the use of jargon-free language, especially when the terminology of various disciplines is combined.

Convergence of Assessment Information. Assessment requires the convergence of differing opinions that affect not only the child's progress in these skill areas but also the areas that are greatly affected by deficits in other areas. All information should be considered when the assessment team examines results and determines targeted skills for children across integrated developmental domains.

Equity. Equity in assessing young children with delays or disabilities can be a major issue when using standardized tests. Unfortunately, on a standardized test, the assessment instrument may not be valid if the materials are adapted. Children with disabilities or delays often take longer to complete a task and may not do as well in a "one-shot" testing situation; therefore, multiple observations yield more accurate and authentic results. Recommended practices suggest the use of additional measures, such as curriculum-based instruments and multiple observations in natural settings, to accurately determine each child's skill level.

Sensitivity of Assessment. Assessment instruments selected for children with significant delays or disabilities should be capable of reflecting some type of progress over time and after repeated administrations of the instrument. It would be insensitive to use inappropriate measures that repeatedly yield no developmental gains. More appropriate observational data that indicate small increments of change and progression of functional skills within the natural environment should be utilized.

Congruence. The DEC recommended practice guidelines assert that "early childhood assessment materials and methods must be developed specifically for infants and preschool children and match the styles and interests of typical young children" (Neisworth & Bagnato, 2005, p. 21), which applies to early primary-level students as well. In assessing the skills of young children with delays or disabilities, this may be interpreted to mean that materials and activities should be carefully selected to match children's chronological age rather than their developmental level so that the materials and activities focused on during the assessment process are congruent with those of their typically developing peers.

Cultural Considerations

As we have described, it is essential that the child's and family's cultural and linguistic backgrounds be considered in the assessment process to limit bias and promote communication and collaboration among the family and professionals (Division Early Childhood, 2007; Lynch & Hanson, 2004). In designing the process, the team must utilize the most effective strategies for gathering information based on each child's and family's unique background. Standardized instruments can be particularly problematic when they are not in the child's primary language or developmental expectations are different within the child's culture. Further, the child-rearing practices or patterns of adult-child interaction may be different in a child's culture, which may have a confounding influence in the assessment process.

Lynch and Hanson (2004) offer a number of suggestions for collecting information about children and families with diverse cultural and linguistic backgrounds. They suggest using alternative approaches to traditional assessment, such as conducting observations and interviews. In addition, Table 4–2 contains guidelines to be used in the assessment process with children representing diverse cultural and linguistic backgrounds.

Purposes of Assessment

The remaining portion of this chapter will focus on the purposes of assessment. The types of assessment will be discussed in the order of screening, eligibility, program planning, and progress monitoring and evaluation. Table 4–3 provides a definition of each type of assessment and describes the kind of information typically gathered, the type of decision made, and the time at which the information is gathered.

Assessment teams must consider the purpose of each assessment and gather initial information at the onset of the process. The following are some general considerations, which will vary depending on the purpose of the assessment.

- What is the purpose of this assessment or why is it being conducted (e.g., screening, eligibility, program planning, progress monitoring)?
- What are the characteristics of the child (e.g., age, physical abilities, communication skills, temperament, and special needs)?
- Who will take the lead or be in charge of coordinating the assessment (e.g., service coordinator, early childhood special educator, physical therapist)?
- Where will the assessment sessions take place (e.g., home, child care program, classroom, playground)?
- Who will be involved in the assessment (e.g., parents, other family members, early childhood special educator, related service professionals) and what roles will these individuals assume (e.g., facilitator, observer)?
- When will the assessment sessions take place (e.g., in the morning, after child's nap)?
- How will the assessment be conducted (e.g., formal testing, observation, interview)?

TABLE 4–2 Guidelines for Assessing Children from Diverse Cultural and Linguistic Backgrounds

Before the assessment

Learn about the child's and family's cultural and linguistic backgrounds.

   Talk directly to the family with an interpreter if necessary.

   Consult with others who are familiar with the culture.

Ask the following questions:

   What is the family's level of acculturation to the U.S. culture?

   What are the literacy practices in the home?

   Which languages can the child and family understand and speak?

During the assessment

Explain the purpose of and procedures for the assessment to the child and family members and others who will participate in the process.

Provide the child with meaningful and culturally appropriate learning experiences. Use culturally relevant materials and activities.

   Be aware of cultural differences in communication styles that may influence the child's responsiveness to the examiner's prompts and teaching strategies.

   Consider having a family member or an interpreter assist in the teaching if the child does not respond well to the examiners.

   Use visual nonverbal prompts and teaching strategies if the child has difficulty speaking English.

   If the child speaks more than one language or dialect, observe whether the child is aware of the differences between languages and can translate and explain words.

   Use simple words and sentences. Try to learn a few words and sentences in the child's and family's language.

After the assessment

Avoid making assumptions.

Take time to reflect on the information gathered during the assessment.

Ask caregivers for their opinions on the representativeness of the assessment results.

Solicit feedback from the family and/or the interpreter, if present, on the cultural appropriateness of communication and teaching styles.

Source: Adapted from: Losardo, and A. Notari-Syverson, (2001). *Alternative approaches to assessing young children.* Baltimore, MD: Paul H. Brookes (p. 190).

- What areas of development or domains will be assessed?
- What instrument(s) will be used (e.g., formal test, checklist, play-based measure)?
- How will the assessment area(s) be set up (e.g., amount of space needed, equipment or materials needed)?
- What skills or behaviors are important to the child's family (e.g., walking, talking, social skills, and independence)? What are the family's priorities (e.g., toilet training)?

- What skills or behaviors are important to the child in his environment (e.g., walking, communicating, toileting, turn-taking)?
- What adaptations are necessary for the child to display optimal skills (e.g., use of an alternative communication system, adaptive seating)?

A plan can be formulated regarding how the assessment process will be implemented for each child and family based on the answers to these questions and the family's preferences.

TABLE 4–3 Description of the Types of Assessment and the Decisions Made

Type of Assessment	Type of Information Gathered	Decision(s) Usually Made	When Information is Gathered
Screening A procedure designed to identify children who need to be referred for more in-depth assessment.	Potential for developmental disability or delay; vision; hearing; health and physical.	Whether a child should be referred for more in-depth assessment.	Prior to entry into a program.
Eligibility A comprehensive diagnostic process to determine if a child meets the criteria to be eligible for services.	Comprehensive diagnostic information that is standardized, norm-referenced, and comparative.	Whether a child is eligible for a program or services as specified in the state's criteria for eligibility.	Prior to entry into a program.
Program Planning A procedure used to identify desired goals/outcomes for the IFSP or IEP and how to design instruction.	Evidence of the child's skills and behaviors; family preferences and priorities; family resources and strengths; settings in which the child spends time and the demands of those settings.	What type of routines, activities, materials, and equipment to use with the individual child; style(s) of learning to use with the child; adult and peer interactions that may work best with the child.	Ongoing process; intensively at the beginning of a program year, during the first several weeks of entry in a program; during and immediately after any major changes in a child's life.
Progress Monitoring and Evaluation A process of collecting information about a child's progress toward outcomes, the family's satisfaction with services, and the program's effectiveness.	Evidence of the child's skills and behaviors in comparison to those skills at entry into the program; family satisfaction and indication of whether their priorities have been met; child's ability to be successful in the setting in which he/she spends time.	To determine the effectiveness of programming for an individual child or group of children; to determine changes in a child's skill and behaviors; to determine family satisfaction; to evaluate a program's overall effectiveness.	Ongoing to determine whether intervention is effective and if outcomes have been achieved; at the end of a program year or cycle; when dictated by administrative policy and funding sources.

Source: From Davis, M. D., Kilgo, J. K., and Gamel-McCormick, M., *Young children with special needs: A developmentally appropriate approach*. Copyright © 1998 by Allyn & Bacon.

Screening Young Children

In reality, the screening process begins immediately following birth. Routine examinations of infants serve as a means of predicting abnormalities. One of the first screenings experienced by infants and their families is the **Apgar Scale** (Apgar & James, 1962). Infants are screened at 1-minute and 5-minute intervals following their birth in the following areas: (a) heart rate, (b) respiration, (c) reflex response, (d) muscle tone, and (e) color (see Figure 4–4).

The 5-minute Apgar has been found to be an accurate predictor of future developmental progress

(Batshaw, 1997). A low Apgar score may indicate that further medical assistance is needed or that a referral should be made for a more in-depth assessment. Blood and urine tests are additional routine procedures used to detect metabolic disorders such as phenylketonuria (PKU), referred to as a **PKU screening**. Through early identification of PKU and appropriate intervention, which includes a restricted diet, many of the adverse outcomes associated with PKU, such as mental retardation, can be prevented.

Screening is the use of a process of gathering information designed to identify, from within a large population of children, those who need to be referred for further evaluation (Fewell, 2000). **Referrals** for screenings are usually made by professionals from various disciplines that come into contact with young children and suspect them of having delays in development. According to federal legislation, each state must establish a **Child Find** system of locating children who may have a developmental delay or disability, which makes them eligible for early intervention/early childhood

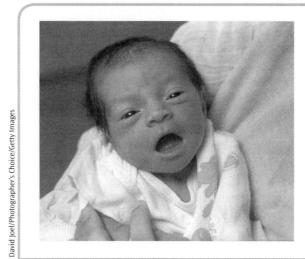

David Joel/Photographer's Choice/Getty Images

The screening process begins immediately after birth through routine examinations of newborns, using such measures as the Apgar Scale.

FIGURE 4–4 **The Apgar Evaluation Scale**

			1 min.	5 min.
Heart rate	Absent	0		
	Less than 100	(1)		
	100 to 140	(2)	1	2
Respiratory effort	Apneic	(0)		
	Shallow, irregular	(1)		
	Lusty cry and breathing	(2)	1	2
Reflex response	No response	(0)		
	Grimace	(1)		
	Cough or sneeze	(2)	1	2
Muscle tone	Flaccid	(0)		
	Some flexion of extremities	(1)		
	Flexion resisting extension	(2)	1	2
Color	Pale blue	(0)		
	Body pink, extremities blue	(1)		
	Pink all over	(2)	0	1
	TOTAL		4	9

special education services. Child Find requires community and interagency collaboration with professionals from a variety of disciplines and agencies (e.g., Head Start, education, social services, and public health) working together. Child Find teams are responsible for conducting public awareness campaigns to inform the community so that referrals for screening will be made. Advertisements often are disseminated through the local media, grocery stores, shopping malls or other places frequented by families of young children. Examples of the types of professionals who frequently make referrals are physicians, nurses, or other health professionals in high-risk nurseries, health clinics, or pediatricians' offices. As a result of extensive Child Find efforts, often families, other caregivers, and members of the community also make referrals.

Screenings can be accomplished by using a variety of procedures, including specific instruments or checklists, observations of the child, and parent interviews. Screening involves a quick look to see if a child's skills are adequate or whether there is a discrepancy from normal expectations that warrants further assessment. A screening procedure may last anywhere from 5 to 15 minutes. Although the Child Find process varies from state to state, many states offer screenings for preschoolers prior to entering kindergarten. In some states, screening is mandatory before children enter kindergarten. The purpose is to identify children with potential developmental issues, vision problems, hearing concerns, etc. As stated earlier, the results of screening determine whether children have the potential for a developmental delay or disability and should be referred for a comprehensive evaluation to determine if they are eligible for services. Table 4–4 contains sample instruments that are often used for screening purposes.

A screening tool should be selected based on a number of specific criteria. Accuracy, for example,

TABLE 4–4   Selected Screening Instruments Used in Early Intervention/Early Childhood Special Education

Instrument	Age range	Domains	Publisher
Ages and Stages Questionnaires (ASQ)	Birth–60 months	Communication Gross motor Fine motor Problem-solving Personal-social	Paul H. Brookes Publishing Co.
Battelle Developmental Screening Test (BDST)	Birth to 7 years, 11 months	Personal Social Adaptive Motor Communication Cognition	Riverside Publishing Company
Developmental Indicators for the Assessment of Learning-Revised (DIAL-3)	2–6 years	Motor Concepts Language Behavioral	Pearson Education
Denver Developmental Screening Test II (DDST-II)	2 weeks–6 years	Personal/social Fine motor Adaptive Language Gross motor	Denver Developmental Materials Inc.

FIGURE 4–5 Potential Outcomes for Screening

	Referred for evaluation	Not referred for evaluation
Eligible for special services	Sensitivity (accurate referral)	False negative (underreferral)
Not eligible for special services	False positive (overreferral)	Specificity (accurate nonreferral)

this is important for several reasons. Some children who need services may be missed, and are, therefore, not referred if a screening tool is not accurate. Sometimes children who do not need services are referred for evaluation and, therefore, overreferral is also a problem when a tool is not accurate. A screening tool's rate of under- and overreferral is related to its sensitivity and specificity. **Sensitivity** refers to a screening instrument's ability to identify children who need additional assessment. The less sensitive a screening instrument is, the greater the number of underreferrals or false negatives there will be from the results (see Figure 4–5). A **false negative** designates a child who needs special services but was not referred by the screening. **Specificity** refers to the capacity of a screening procedure to accurately rule out children who should not be identified. In other words, a test that is specific will not refer children who do not need further assessment. Losses in specificity result in an increased number of overreferrals or false positives. A **false positive** designates a child who has been referred by the screening but does not need special services. The levels of sensitivity and specificity measure the screening tool's validity, which tells us the extent to which a test measures what it says it measures. Data on the number of false positives and false negatives should be available and at an acceptable ratio. Great care should be taken when selecting screening tools to ensure that they are indeed valid and accurate. When an instrument is accurate, the likelihood of inappropriate referrals is minimized.

The simplicity of a screening tool is another important criterion. The administration and scoring of instruments should be quick, easy, systematic, and usable by professionals from a variety of disciplines. Another important criterion of a screening tool is that it should be comprehensive, focusing on multiple areas (e.g., educational, health, behavioral, and environmental concerns). Ideally, a screening instrument should be inexpensive to administer yet still be accurate.

Another criterion is that screening tools should provide for family input and involvement. Because of the wide range and variations in typical development and behavior during the early years, the screening process for infants and young children is often difficult. Parent involvement can alleviate some of these difficulties. Most screening tools typically include observations, parent reports, or some combination of the two. A comprehensive screening process includes the gathering of information about a wide range of children's abilities and, of course, parents have the most extensive information. A technique that has been used to gather information is a parent-completed screening questionnaire. Although parent-completed questionnaires provide important developmental information, not all parents are willing or able to complete independent questionnaires. This determination should be made based on each family's desire and ability, which may change over time. See the accompanying Making Connections feature for an example of how T.J.'s mom gradually became more comfortable with the assessment process.

Determining Eligibility for Services

After a young child is found to be in need of further assessment through the screening process, a comprehensive eligibility assessment should be conducted to determine whether infants, toddlers, preschoolers, and early primary-aged children do, in fact, meet the eligibility requirements for early intervention or early childhood special education services. This phase of the process is most often conducted by a team of qualified professionals from several disciplines (such as special education, speech-language pathology, physical therapy, and others as needed). Children are given a battery of assessment instruments to

MAKING CONNECTIONS

T.J.'s Mom and the Assessment Process

T.J.'s mother was initially reluctant to participate in the assessment process by completing questionnaires and answering all the questions about T.J.'s development. It wasn't because she didn't care about T.J.—that wasn't the case at all. She simply did not understand how useful this information could be and how important her role was in the assessment process. Although she was reluctant at first to have T.J. participate in the screening and be referred for a comprehensive assessment, she soon developed a relationship with the service providers, learned to trust them, and became more involved as a member of the team during the assessment process and beyond.

determine if they meet the eligibility requirements according to the Individuals with Disabilities Education Improvement Act Amendment of 2004 (IDEA).

Eligibility Criteria

Over the past several years, there has been much discussion regarding eligibility criteria and categories for infants and toddlers, preschoolers, and early primary-level children with known or suspected disabilities to receive early intervention and special education services. Recall from Chapter 2, according to federal legislation, each state determines the eligibility criteria for infants and toddlers. Through IDEA 1991, each state was given the option to use a developmental delay eligibility category for preschoolers. In the absence of an identified disability, children can be determined eligible for receiving services based on the particular eligibility criteria established within his or her state (for example, 25% delay in one or more developmental domains). Of course, this decision depends on state and local eligibility criteria that specify precisely how eligibility is determined in a particular program. For early primary-level children, the IDEA 1997 allowed for the developmental delay eligibility category to be extended to age nine if states desire. However, states and localities are still required by IDEA and its amendments to develop definitions of developmental delay thoughtfully so that the outcome will be eligibility procedures that are based on knowledge of young children with delays and disabilities and will ensure appropriate services for them and their families. Children within

the 3- to 9-year-old age range may also qualify for special education services by meeting the criteria for an IDEA disability category, such as visual impairment, hearing impairment, or autism. This is explained in greater detail in Chapter 2.

Eligibility Procedures and Instruments

To determine if young children meet the eligibility guidelines for early intervention or special education services, procedures must be used to determine if a child's skills are significantly different from a large group of children whose development falls within the typical range. This determination has traditionally been made by comparing a child's performance to the expected performance of children of the same age and, therefore, the assessment instruments are administered in a controlled manner. For example, the same materials, directions, and scoring procedures are used each time a tool is administered. Although norm-referenced tools have traditionally been required as the primary means for determining eligibility, many leaders in the field of early intervention/education have suggested the use of curriculum-based measures for eligibility purposes (Bagnato, 2005; McLean, 2005). As stated previously, recommended practice suggests that no major decision about a child's eligibility should be made based *solely* on the results of a single test. Decisions regarding eligibility should be based on multiple assessment measures.

A sample of the numerous instruments used for eligibility determination is included in Table 4–5. A number of other instruments are available,

TABLE 4–5 **Select Assessment Instruments for Determining the Developmental Status of Young Children**

Name of Instrument	Age range addressed	Developmental domain(s)	Results	Publisher
Battelle Developmental Inventory (2nd ed.) (BDI-2)	Birth to 7 years, 11 months	Personal social, adaptive, motor, communication, cognitive ability	Developmental levels in each domain	Riverside Publishing
Bayley Scales of Infant Development (2nd ed.) (Bayley-III)	Birth to 42 months	Cognitive, language, motor, social-emotional, adaptive	Standardized S scores for mental & motor development; descriptions of social-emotional & adaptive behavior	Pearson Assessment
Carolina Curriculum for Infants and Toddlers with Special Needs (3rd ed.) (CCITSN-3)	Birth to 36 months	Personal-social, cognition, cognition-communication, communication, fine motor, gross motor	Status in each curriculum domain	Brookes Publishing
Carolina Curriculum for Preschoolers with Special Needs (2nd ed.) (CCPSN-2)	2–5 years (i.e., developmental age)	Personal-social, cognition, cognition-communication, communication, fine motor, gross motor	Status in each curriculum domain	Brookes Publishing
Developmental Assessment of Young Children (DAYC)	Birth through 5 years, 11 months	Cognition, communication, social-emotional development, adaptive behavior, physical development	Standard scores, percentile ranks, and age equivalents in each curriculum domain; General Development Quotient (GDQ)	Pro-Ed Publishing
Hawaii Early Learning Profile Strands (Birth to age 3 years) (HELP Strands, 0–3)	Birth to 36 months	Regulatory/sensory, cognitive, language, gross motor, fine motor, social-emotional, self-help	Developmental age levels in each domain	VORT Corporation
Hawaii Early Learning Profile (Preschool) (HELP-P)	3–6 years	Cognitive, language, gross motor, fine motor, social-emotional, self-help	Developmental age levels in each domain	VORT Corporation
Learning Accomplishment Profile-Diagnostic (3rd-ed.) (LAP-D3)	30–72 months	Fine motor, gross motor, cognition, language	Child's skill level in comparison to normative scores	Kaplan Early Learning Company

Source: Adapted from: J. Taylor, J. McGowan, and T. Linder. The Program Administrator's Guide to Early Childhood Special Education: Leadership Development and Supervision Baltimore: Paul H. Brookes (2009) (p. 74).

depending on the age of the child, that allow professionals to evaluate strengths and needs in specific developmental domains (e.g., communication, social) and subject areas (e.g., language and literacy, mathematics). What these instruments have in common is that they all measure a child's skills and development as compared to a norm group of children who have previously completed the test. If a child's test scores fall significantly below the scores of the children in the norm group, this serves as a signal that he or she may have a developmental delay and be eligible for early intervention or early childhood special education services.

The team collaborates to determine a child's eligibility for services by reviewing the child's health records and medical history, determining the child's current level of functioning in major development areas, and assessing the child's individual strengths and needs. Observations and other assessment procedures should be used to support the findings from assessment instruments. By collecting additional information from the child's family and other caregivers and by observing the child's behavior in natural settings, examiners can make an informed decision about the presence of a developmental delay or disability and need for services. Parents and other family members can add valuable information to the eligibility decision by participating in the assessment process in a variety of ways. Parents can provide information informally through discussions with team members; they can complete questionnaires, checklists, or parent reports; and/or they can be present in the room with their child during the assessment. Often they can provide feedback regarding the skills or behaviors the child is demonstrating (e.g., whether this is typical behavior, other skills or abilities the child has demonstrated, or supplemental information).

Professionals are encouraged to be sensitive to families when discussing eligibility assessment information. Following are recommendations developed by Cohen and Spenciner (2003) for sharing eligibility information with families:

- Provide family members with an opportunity to receive the assessment report in a one-to-one setting rather than during a large team meeting (e.g., IFSP or IEP meeting), which allows the family time to ask questions and reflect on the information prior to the larger, full-staff meeting.

- Be honest and straightforward regarding the delay or disability and eligibility for services.
- Be sensitive to families if they are not ready to hear details.
- Allow time for families to express their feelings.
- Be willing to say when you do not know the answer to questions.
- Offer to provide additional information and suggest additional resources.
- Be available to the family for further discussions.
- Arrange to have a native-language interpreter available if families need assistance.

Assessment for Program Planning

In order to plan efficient, effective programs and interventions for young children with delays or disabilities, appropriate **program planning assessment** must occur. Assessment conducted for program planning purposes must be a continuous process that focuses on each child's skill level, needs, background, experiences, and interests, as well as the family's preferences and priorities. Ongoing assessment provides the basis for constructing and maintaining individualized programs for young children with disabilities. The initial assessment procedures used to determine eligibility are distinctly different from the assessment procedures necessary for program planning. Table 4–6 illustrates the major ways in which these two types of assessments differ.

Recommended practices in early intervention and early childhood special education recognize the importance of the link between assessment and curriculum to ensure that program content is meeting the needs of the child and the concerns of the family (Bagnato et al., 1997; Neisworth & Bagnato, 2005). As explained previously, in recent years, formal assessments have been found to be inappropriate for program planning, which has resulted in a shift away from the use of formal assessment measures toward the use of informal means of assessment (e.g., curriculum- or criterion-based instruments, observations, family reports, and play-based measures). Each of these methods will be discussed later in this chapter. Assessment procedures that are appropriate for

TABLE 4–6 Comparison of Assessment for Eligibility and Program Planning

Assessment for Eligibility	Assessment for Program Planning
Compares a single child to a large group of children.	Identifies the child's current levels of developmental skills, behaviors, and knowledge.
Uses instruments, observations, and checklists with predetermined items or skills.	Determines the skills and behaviors necessary for a child to function in the settings where he or she spends time.
Determines if a child's skills or behaviors fall below a specified cutoff level.	Determines those skills, behaviors, and knowledge that the child's family and primary caregivers have set as priorities for the child to learn.
Designed to differentiate children from one another.	Designed to determine the individual child's strengths and learning style.
Assessment instrument items do not necessarily have significance in the everyday lives of young children.	Assessment instrument items are usually criterion-based or focus on functional skills that may have importance in the everyday lives of young children.

Source: From Davis, M. D., Kilgo, J. K., and Gamel-McCormick, M., *Young children with special needs: A developmentally appropriate approach.* Copyright © 1998 by Allyn & Bacon.

determining a child's eligibility for services (standardized, norm-referenced instruments) should not be used in isolation and should not be relied upon to plan instructional programs or interventions for young children with disabilities (McLean, 2005; Neisworth & Bagnato, 2005).

In order to make an accurate appraisal of the child's strengths and needs, assessment for program planning purposes focus on the whole child within the context of his or her natural environment(s) (e.g., home, child care, or school settings). Collecting information of this nature is critical to designing individualized programs and planning appropriate interventions and supports for young children and their families.

Purpose of Assessment for Program Planning

The purpose of program planning assessment is to answer a number of questions related to the child's

Cengage Learning

Assessment is a process requiring a collaborative effort between families and professionals that occurs on an ongoing basis.

abilities, the desired child and family outcomes, the types of services to be provided, and the intervention strategies to be used. EI/ECSE professionals employ recommended practices for conducting program planning assessment when they do the following:

- Select assessment tools and practices that are individualized and appropriate for each child and family;
- Report assessment results in a manner that is both useful for planning program goals/outcomes and understandable and useful for families; and
- Rely on materials that capture the child's authentic behaviors in routine circumstances (Sandall et al., 2005).

Assessment information collected for program planning purposes is used to develop an individualized family service plan or individualized education program for each child and family. Recall from Chapter 1 that the IFSP and IEP are intended to be planning documents that are used to shape and guide the day-to-day provision of services to young children with developmental delays or disabilities. The IFSP is required for the provision of early intervention services for eligible infants and toddlers, age birth to three, and their families. The IEP is used for special education services delivered to eligible children ages three and older. IFSPs and IEPs contain individualized outcomes and goals that can be determined by conducting an inventory of the skills needed by the child to participate in a variety of natural environments as just described. This process, an ecological inventory, allows information to be gathered that has relevance to each child and family. When this method is used, the IFSP or IEP should be developed according to the family's routines (e.g., at home, school, and other environments) and priorities. Thus, goals and outcomes contained in the IFSP or IEP should be developed to reflect the necessary skills the child will need to participate in natural environments and routines within those environments (Noonan & McCormick, 2006).

When conducting assessments for the purpose of program planning for young children with disabilities, Bailey and Wolery (1992) suggest that the following goals be accomplished:

1. The identification of developmentally appropriate and functional goals/outcomes;
2. The identification of the unique styles, strengths, and coping strategies of each child;
3. The identification of parents' goals or outcomes for their children and the needs or priorities for themselves;

4. The formation and reinforcement of families' sense of competence and worth;
5. The development of a shared and integrated perspective among professionals and family members regarding the child's and family's needs and resources; and
6. The creation of a shared commitment to the collaboratively established goals/outcomes.

Through the accomplishment of these goals, the team members should be provided with the information necessary to make program planning decisions regarding the activities and strategies to meet the unique goals and outcomes of individual children and families.

Family Involvement in the Assessment Process

As stressed throughout this chapter, parents and other family members can provide a wealth of information about the child, as well as information about the family as a whole (Hendricks & McCracken, 2009). Although addressing family concerns, priorities, and resources is not a new concept in EI/ECSE, it has received increased attention in recent years due to the emphasis on IFSPs for families with children under age three and an increased emphasis on family-based practices in all aspects of services for young children with special needs ages three through eight. Thus, it is most important that family members be encouraged to become active members of the assessment team. If family members are willing and able to play an active role in the assessment process, their involvement will ensure the validity of the established goals and outcomes.

An approach that has been used for many years to help make certain that the family has input into the assessment process is referred to as "top-down" or "outcome-driven" assessment (Campbell, 1991). This model suggests using family-identified outcomes for the child as the starting point of the assessment. In other words, the family's vision for the child becomes the central focus of the assessment process (Turnbull et al., 2006). At what level would the family like to see the child functioning in terms of skills and abilities (e.g., in the next six months, year, three years)? What are the family's priorities? For example, one family's top priority might be for the child to be able to communicate and feed herself, while another family might want the child to be toilet trained and develop friendships with peers. In what environments would the family like the child to be able to participate? For example, does the family want the child to be in an inclusive preschool or kindergarten program?

An effective early childhood special educator recognizes the uniqueness of each family and realizes the importance of families having opportunities to provide input into the assessment process and serving as integral members of the team. Assessment information should be collected from families on an ongoing basis, be an integral part of the planning process, and be a collaborative effort; therefore, it is essential for families to be confident that the assessment process will maintain privacy and confidentiality.

A family-based approach suggests that families participate in the assessment process at the level they feel is appropriate for them. Regardless of the degree to which the family chooses to participate in the assessment process, the manner in which it participates, or the format in which it provides information, the family's participation and the information it provides serve invaluable purposes in program planning. According to Turnbull et al. (2006), families should be offered options for participating in the assessment process. Some of the areas in which families can provide input include the following:

- Collaborate with professionals in planning the assessment process (where, when, and how it will take place, who will be involved);
- Determine to what extent they want to be a part of the assessment process;
- Provide information about their children's developmental history, play and interaction preferences, and daily routines and schedule;
- Provide information about the settings where their children spend time and the demands placed upon their children in those settings;
- Report on their children's current skills, where and how those skills are used by the children, and under what circumstances the skills are exhibited;
- Report on their children's strengths, abilities, and needs in multiple settings;
- Share information about their children that will not be gained through traditional measures;
- Share their priorities, resources, and concerns; and
- Share their visions for their children's future.

Each family's preferences must be considered before information is gathered. Some potential areas

in which information can be gathered from families include their need for support, information, education, and services, and so forth. Information can be collected from families in a variety of ways—through interviews, observational methods, parent reports, instruments, and other measures. An ongoing conversational approach with families, in lieu of formal family interviewing, is used in some programs to promote relaxed and natural conversation with families. Some families may prefer providing information through a written format, such as a family needs questionnaire or checklist. Informal tools are preferred in most instances (Banks, Santos, & Roof, 2003).

Along with the different instruments available to identify family concerns, priorities, and resources, some EI/ECSE programs have developed their own measures. Regardless of the measures used, families should be encouraged to identify their concerns and resources and determine their priorities for their children and the family as a whole. Gathering information from families about their concerns, priorities, and resources is an important component of the assessment process (Kilgo & Raver, 2009). Professionals should realize that the range of concerns families may have is considerable. Families of young children with known or suspected disabilities often feel overwhelmed and unsure of where to begin. Professionals can provide information to help them sort out their concerns and make decisions about their priorities. It is likely, however, that their concerns and priorities will change over time. (Turnbull et al., 2006). Examples of possible family concerns include how their children's medical needs can be met or how their children will be treated when they begin preschool. Family priorities, for example, might be how to learn more about the child's disability or how to communicate with the child. Family resources might include reliable transportation, relatives who live nearby, and community support.

Ecological Assessment

For assessment information to be useful, emphasis must be placed on the context in which children develop and the influence of the environment on skill acquisition. It is essential that the environment(s) in which a child functions and the skills needed to be successful in those environments are considered during the assessment process (Vanderheyden, 2005). Thus, **ecological assessments** are increasingly being used to replace traditional assessment practices when planning interventions for young children with disabilities. An ecological assessment provides for functional goals and objectives to be generated within the natural environment. McCormick (1997) emphasizes the twofold purpose of an ecological assessment:

1. To generate information about the social, educational, and functional activities and routines in natural environments where the child is to be an active and successful participant; and

2. To determine the resources and supports needed for the child to participate in and receive maximum benefits from activities and routines in the environments. (p. 237)

Bronfenbrenner's (1979) theory of human ecology stresses that the interconnections between environments (e.g. the connection between home and school) influence what actually takes place within an environment (e.g., a child's learning within the home, child care, school, or community). Figure 4–6 shows that

FIGURE 4–6 Assessment in the Context of the Environment

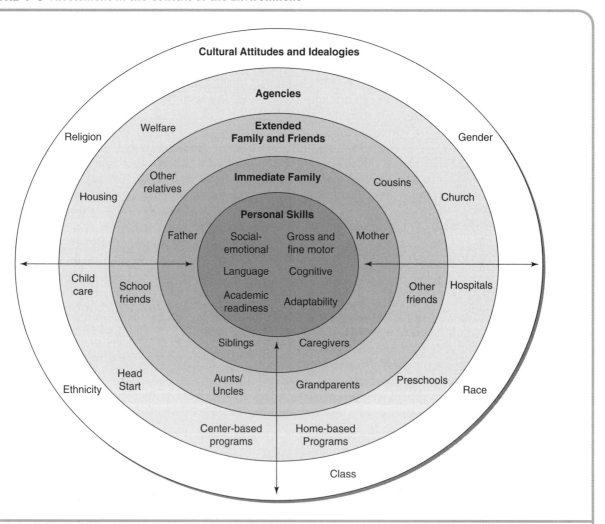

Source: From Introduction (pp. 1–8) by E. V. Nuttall, K. Nuttall-Vazquoz, and A. Hempel, in *Assessing and screening preschoolers: Psychological and educational dimensions.* E. Vazquoz Nuttall, I. Romero, and J. Kalesnik (Eds.). 1999. Needham Heights, MA: Allyn & Bacon.

the focus of assessment should be on a child's skills and abilities within the context of his environments.

As discussed previously, children's skills are not developed or displayed in isolation. Instead, each child's development is strongly influenced by the demands or expectations of his or her environment. For example, some environments require strong social or communication skills, while others call for advanced levels of independence. Several important aspects of a child's environment must be considered in program planning:

1. the expectations of the family or primary caregivers
2. the cultural parameters, and
3. the expected level of participation based on the child's age and ability

The demands placed upon children by the contextual aspects of the environment can have a tremendous influence on their development and the skills or behaviors they display. For example, if T.J. lives in a neighborhood in which all of the children learn to ride bicycles at an early age, then he might be motivated to learn to ride his bike at a young age. Or if a family lives in a warm climate and goes to the beach or pool on a frequent basis as a family activity, then the children may be likely to learn to swim or participate in water sports at an early age.

An ecological assessment considers the skills needed by a child to participate in his or her environment throughout the day. The specific environments, expectations, and levels of participation are defined by the child, his or her family and other primary caregivers, the community, and the family's culture. This type of assessment is distinctly different from the type of traditional child assessment in which the child's skills are observed and recorded. The product of an ecological assessment is not the skill level at which a child is functioning; however, it provides a greater understanding of the context and expectations that are important for the child. For example, when an ecological assessment takes place for T.J. at a Head Start center, the observer notices that there are several times in which the children are required to make transitions from one activity to another during the morning routine when prompted by the teacher. These transitions are an important part of this particular environment. Based on this observation, the team learns that these transitions are important requirements within the environment in which T.J. will be participating. With this information, the team conducting the assessment will know to focus on T.J.'s ability to make transitions like the ones that occur in his early childhood program.

The contexts, conditions, and expectations identified through an ecological assessment assist the team members in identifying those skills that should be examined during the assessment process. Furthermore, the ecological assessment allows the assessment team to determine the skills necessary for the child to be successful in his current settings. In other words, the result of the ecological assessment is a **protocol**, or assessment format, that can be followed to decide the skill areas on which to focus and the specific skills to be observed during the assessment.

An ecological assessment regards the family members and other primary caregivers as critical contributors to the assessment process. Family members and caregivers may include parents, siblings, grandparents, child care providers, or other significant people in a child's life, such as neighbors. These individuals, in addition to teachers, occupational therapists, physical therapists, speech-language pathologists, and others, will determine which of the individual child's skills are important to focus on during the assessment. Conducting ecological assessments of children within their natural environments requires a step-by-step approach. By assessing the environments in which children live and the expectations associated with those environments, the skills to be targeted can be better determined. Program planning can logically grow from the assessment information that is collected.

Conducting an ecological assessment will help members of the assessment team in determining the location of the assessment. The best place to determine if a child has a **functional skill** is in the environment(s) where he or she uses that skill. A functional skill is a basic skill that is required on a frequent basis (e.g., eating, toileting, requesting assistance, turn taking) in the natural environment. For example, if eating independently during meal time is an important skill for a particular child, the assessment team will know to conduct some portion of the assessment during a meal, either at home, at school, or in another setting. An ecological assessment approach usually will result in a more precise child assessment. The assessment team will know what skills on which to focus, what materials or activities the child prefers, and the setting(s) in which to conduct the assessment. The result of a thorough ecological assessment is a road map for the program planning phase of the assessment process.

Methods and Procedures for Collecting Information

The *DEC Recommended Practice Guidelines* (Sandall et al., 2005) suggest standards to address when gathering useful information for planning intervention. The whole child should be considered when planning programs for young children with disabilities rather than segmenting their abilities in the various developmental areas. In Maria's case, for example, she has a diagnosis of Down syndrome with delays in several developmental domains (e.g., communication, self-care, cognitive skills). In order to meet her multiple needs, program planning assessment should address all areas of development, which must function together to perform most tasks. As we all know, most activities or tasks require the combined use of several different skill areas. Thus, in order for program planning assessments to focus on the whole child, a variety of measures (such as criterion- and curriculum-referenced tools, observations, and interviews) should be used in a variety of settings (home, child care, school, playground, etc.). Using an arena assessment format, as described earlier in this chapter, provides optimal opportunities for families and professionals to cooperatively plan intervention goals from the same perspective using an appropriate assessment instrument whose purpose is to link assessment with intervention.

The types of measures most often used are curriculum-referenced or criterion-referenced instruments, which can provide the team with useful information to assist in program planning (Bagnato, Neisworth, & Munson, 1997; Neisworth & Bagnato, 2005). As described previously, a criterion-referenced assessment is one in which an individual child's response(s) is compared to a predetermined criterion or level of performance in an area of knowledge or skill, rather than to a group of children or normative group. Results are typically reported as levels of proficiency, such as an emerging skill or mastery of a skill. The criteria used to determine if a child has acquired a skill are often flexible ones that can have different interpretations for different settings. On curriculum-referenced measures, each assessment item relates directly to a specific educational objective in the program's curriculum. Curriculum- and criterion-referenced measures provide a level of flexibility that is not available with standardized,

norm-referenced instruments. Because the skills being assessed are within a natural context, represent specific skills that have been determined by the child's family and other team members to be valuable to his or her development, and are generally listed in a developmental sequence, they often can be very useful in program planning. On a cautionary note, it is important to remember that many curriculum- or criterion-referenced instruments are drawn from items on standardized tests, thus decreasing their relevance to the child's unique needs and to the necessary program planning to meet those needs. Curriculum-referenced measures do allow team members to determine how important skills are within the context (environment) in which they are used.

One of the recommended practices for assessment noted by Neisworth and Bagnato (2005) is that the EI/ECSE team use only those measures that have high treatment validity (i.e., link assessment, individual program planning, and progress evaluation). In order to ensure that the entire process is linked, the selection of appropriate instruments and measure is of critical importance. Criterion- or curriculum-based instruments are recommended for program planning and establishing a link between assessment and intervention (Bagnato et al., 1997).

Table 4–5 includes examples of widely used curriculum-referenced instruments that provide a strong linkage to program planning and implementation. The *Assessment, Evaluation, and Programming System (AEPS)* (Bricker & Waddell, 2002) is one example of a comprehensive instrument designed to use observational techniques to obtain assessment information within the context of the natural environment. The *AEPS* and other curriculum-based measures usually are multidomain instruments that subdivide major developmental milestones into smaller increments. For example, the *AEPS* subdivides fine motor skills into three strands: reach, grasp, and release, and functional use of fine motor skills. Each of the strands is further divided into goals and objectives that link the assessment process to the preparation of an educational plan to guide intervention.

The items on the *AEPS*, as is usually true with curriculum-based measures, follow a typical developmental progression. The curriculum activities that correspond to test items are designed to teach skills related to the identified needs of the individual child. Another example of a curriculum-based instrument is the

Carolina Curriculum (Johnson-Martin, Attermeier, & Hacker, 2004a; Johnson-Martin, Hacker, & Attermeier, 2004b), which provides developmental markers for assessing young children across developmental domains. The *Carolina Curriculum* also provides suggestions for modifying test items for children with motor or sensory impairments. Another instrument, the *Hawaii Early Learning Profile (HELP)* (Parks, 2007; VORT, 2004) provides developmental assessment and curriculum activities for home and preschool environments. For early primary-level students, ages five through eight, a variety of curriculum- and criterion-referenced assessment instruments are available in various content areas (e.g., language and literacy, mathematics, science, social studies).

Criterion- and curriculum-referenced tools are examples of measures that can be used to collect information for program and intervention planning. Other methods include: informal, teacher-made checklists or tests, play-based measures, observations, and interviews with the family or other primary care providers. The accompanying Making Connections feature contains a description of the characteristics of program planning assessment and examples of the various types of information that can be gathered to plan programs for young children with delays or disabilities. In program planning for T.J., the team could use a criterion-referenced instrument to measure his abilities in cognitive, communication, and motor development. They could devise situations to determine how T.J. performs particular skills in the context of the natural environment(s), such as riding a tricycle or eating a meal. More than likely, the team would also observe social interactions during a play situation with his peers.

Progress is monitored for each child in different areas of development within the context of the natural environment.

Cengage Learning

Progress Monitoring and Program Evaluation

The final purpose of assessment to be discussed involves **progress monitoring** and **program evaluation**. As previously described, the efficacy of early intervention and early childhood special education has received much attention during recent years with the result being an increased awareness of the importance of ongoing progress monitoring and evaluation as it relates to the improvement and expansion of services for young children with special needs and their families. Progress monitoring of outcomes helps ensure continuous feedback that is necessary to inform decision making about all aspects of early intervention/education services.

EI/ECSE programs must have a set of procedures for collecting and using data to monitor the effectiveness of program efforts (Sandall, Schwartz, & Lacroix, 2004). A comprehensive evaluation plan in EI/ECSE services should represent the scope of the most important components of intervention: the child, the family, and the program. Without this critical feedback regarding all of these interlocking components, EI/ECSE can never fully meet the desired

MAKING CONNECTIONS

Program Planning for T.J.

The chart below shows characteristics of program planning assessment, a description of the procedures that are used, and what was used during T.J.'s assessment process.

Characteristic	Description	Example
Assessment should include a variety of measures in a variety of settings.	The assessment procedures include the use of curriculum-referenced tests, teacher-devised and informal tests, direct observation in natural settings (e.g., home, classroom), and interviews with people who know the child best.	The teacher uses developmental scales to assess T.J.'s communication, motor, and cognitive development. She devises some testing situations to determine how he performs particular skills. She observes him during play sessions with other children to note his social interaction, play, and language skills. She observes him at lunch and in the bathroom to identify his self-care skills. She interviews his parents, former teachers, and therapists to secure additional information.
Assessment results should provide a detailed description of the child's functioning.	The results include a description of (a) the child's developmental skills across all relevant areas, (b) what the child can and cannot do, and (c) what factors influence the child's skills/abilities.	The teacher analyzes the results of her assessment activities, summarizes what T.J. can and cannot do in each area, and describes what factors appear to influence his performance (e.g., what toys he appears to like, which children he interacts with, what help he needs on different tasks, and what appears to motivate his behavior).
Assessment activities should involve the child's family.	The family should receive information from professionals, observe the assessment activities, provide information about the child's development and needs, gather new information, and validate the assessment results.	The teacher plans the assessment with the family. She asks them about how T.J. performs different skills, how he spends his time, and what concerns and goals they have for him. She allows them to observe the testing. She asks them to gather information on some skills at home. She reviews the results with them and asks them to confirm, modify, and qualify, and—if necessary—refute the findings.
Assessment activities should be conducted by professionals from different disciplines.	Frequently, assessment from the following disciplines is needed; speech/language therapy, physical therapy, audiology, social work, health (e.g., nurses, physicians), psychology, nutrition, special education, and possibly others.	The teacher coordinates the assessment activities of the team. Because of T.J.'s communication delays, a speech/language pathologist assesses him. An audiologist assesses his hearing, a physical therapist and an occupational therapist assess his motor skills, and the special education teacher assists the kindergarten teacher in assessing his social and cognitive skills.

(continued)

MAKING CONNECTIONS

Characteristic	Description	Example
Assessment activities should result in a list of high-priority objectives.	Assessment activities will identify more skills than are possible to teach; therefore, those of most value are identified. All team members, including the family, are involved in this decision. Skills are selected to be focused on if they are useful to the child, have long-term benefits, and/or are important to the family.	After the results have been analyzed, the team (including the parents) meets to review the findings. They discuss which skills T.J. needs to learn, which ones will be most useful, which will result in long-term benefits, and which are most important to his family. The most important skills are listed as goals on his individualized educational program (IEP).

Source: Adapted from M. Wolery, P. Strain, and D. Bailey, Reaching Potentials of Children with Special Needs, in *Reaching Potentials: Appropriate Curriculum Assessment for Young Children* (Vol. 1). Edited by S. Bredekamp and T. Rosegrant, (Washington, DC: The National Association for the Education of Young Children, 1990), p. 100.

outcomes for young children with disabilities and their families. Table 4–7 shows the questions, purposes, and procedures that are the focus of assessment conducted for program monitoring and evaluation.

As suggested for many years, evaluation in early childhood programs must be multidimensional and comprehensive (Johnson & LaMontagne, 1994; Neisworth & Bagnato, 2005). For children receiving EI/ECSE services, the measurement procedures should match the specific outcomes for which they are designed. This usually includes information that reflects the children's attainment of targeted skills documented on the IFSPs and IEPs, state and/or program standards, and global outcomes. In addition, the outcomes of various family variables (e.g., family satisfaction; family outcomes) should be measured. Last, specific aspects of the overall program should be evaluated using the recommended practice standards promulgated by the major professional organizations, such as the Division for Early Childhood (DEC) of the Council for Exceptional Children and the National Association for the Education of Young Children (NAEYC).

An ongoing evaluation plan is recommended that encompasses a schedule of data collection.

This schedule includes initial program planning assessment, ongoing monitoring of IFSP and IEP outcomes/goals, family outcomes, evaluation of program effectiveness, and annual evaluation across all program participants. Ongoing examination of child outcomes provides the team with realistic feedback about child progress. In addition, systematic data-based evaluations hold professionals accountable not only to themselves but also to the children and families they serve. All measures should be conducted on a schedule that includes a **formative assessment** (during program operation) and a **summative assessment** (at the completion of services). Formative assessment examines children's learning for the purpose of improving the quality of teaching and overall learning rather than for evaluating individual children. These types of assessments are often conducted at the beginning of the year and are ongoing. Summative assessments summarize learning to gauge if children as a whole have met overall program goals and outcomes. Most standardized measures are summative and are not designed to provide feedback during the learning process. These types of assessments are usually conducted at the end of the program or school year.

TABLE 4–7 **Program Monitoring and Program Evaluation: Assessment Questions, Purposes, and Procedures**

Assessment Questions	Purposes	Procedures
• Once intervention or instruction begins, is the child making progress? • Should the intervention or instruction be modified?	• To monitor the child's program • To understand the appropriate pace of intervention • To understand what the child is capable of doing prior to and following intervention	• Curriculum- or criterion-referenced assessments • Observations • Interviews • Checklists • Family reporting • Portfolios • Permanent product samples • Journals
• Has the child met the goals of the IFSP or IEP? • Has the child made progress? • Has the program been successful for the child and family? • Does the child continue to need services? • Has the program achieved its goals?	• To determine whether the program was successful in meeting the child and family goals (IFSP) • To determine if the program was successful in meeting the child's IFSP/IEP goals • To determine if the child continues to need services • To evaluate program effectiveness	• Curriculum- or criterion-referenced assessments • Observations • Interviews • Questionnaires • Family reporting • Surveys

SOURCE: Adapted from Cohen, Libby G., & L. J. Spenciner (2003). *Assessment of young children*, White Plains, NY: Longman.

Monitoring Child Progress and Outcomes

Collecting individual, child-focused information can serve as a valuable monitoring tool to provide input about child outcomes and program effectiveness. Data should be collected regularly and systematically and used in making intervention decisions. A variety of methods should be used to ensure a collection of reliable, valid, and useful progress-monitoring data (Branscombe, Castle, Dorsey, Surbeck, & Taylor, 2003; Wolery, 2004) and adequate time to review and interpret the data to inform and change practice (Grisham-Brown & Pretti-Frontczak, 2003; McAfee & Leong, 2002). Such data may be collected through direct observation of specific child behaviors; the use of curriculum- or criterion-referenced measures; permanent product samples (e.g., videotapes); ongoing performance data collection; and family reporting. Regardless of the methods used, it is critical for data to be linked to a child's goals and be used to adjust the intervention and program activities in accordance with changes in a child's development and progress made toward achieving the goals. As

described many years ago, child evaluation serves the following distinct, yet complementary, functions in early intervention/early childhood special education programs:

1. It guides the development of individual programming;
2. It provides feedback about the success of individual programming; and
3. It provides a system for determining the value of an intervention system designed to benefit groups of children (Bricker & Littman, 1982).

There are many ways to collect data and record children's progress (Hojnoski, Gischlar, & Missall, 2009). Table 4–8 provides a description of some of the different methods or monitoring procedures that can be used.

The Making Connections features provide examples of how observational data are collected to monitor T.J.'s and Maria's progress, which includes anecdotal recording, interval recording, and time sampling. One example shown in the Making Connections feature is anecdotal recording. By using this

TABLE 4–8 Methods of Recording Data for Monitoring Progress

Monitoring Method	Description of Data Collection Procedure
Event recording (frequency count)	Each occurrence of the target behavior is recorded, and at the end of the observation, a total number of occurrences is calculated, yielding the number or frequency of behaviors. Best used with behaviors that are short in duration and have a clear beginning and end (e.g., positive behaviors, such as requests and social initiations, or negative behaviors, such as hitting or calling out). Uses some indicator of the occurrence of the behavior, such as tally marks on a recording form.
Time sampling	Specific time intervals (e.g., 30 seconds, 2 minutes) are selected and used in observing and recording the target behavior. Sampling methods yield an approximation of the frequency of behavior as opposed to a precise recording of actual frequency.
Partial-interval time sampling	A predetermined time interval is used, and the target behavior is recorded if it occurs during any part of the interval, yielding a percentage of total intervals (or percentage of observation) that the behavior is observed. Occurrence of the target behavior is recorded only once during an interval regardless of whether there are additional occurrences of the behavior. Best used with frequently occurring behaviors.
Whole-interval time sampling	A predetermined time interval is used, and the target behavior is recorded if it occurs and is maintained during the entire interval. If the behavior begins and ends before the interval has elapsed, the target behavior is not recorded as occurring. This method yields a percentage of total intervals (or percentage of observation time) that the behavior is observed. Best used with behaviors that are longer in duration; otherwise, the method will underestimate the occurrence of the behavior.
Momentary time sampling	Interval is divided into a "rest" part and a "watch" part. Observation of the target behavior occurs only for a portion of the predetermined time interval or during the "watch" part of the interval (e.g., last 5 seconds or a 15-second interval). The target behavior is recorded as occurring only if it occurs during the "watch" part of the interval. This method yields a percentage of total intervals (or percentage of observation time) behavior is observed and is best utilized with high-frequency behaviors or behaviors that are longer in duration.
Duration	The elapsed time between onset and offset of the target behavior is recorded. Duration data can be summarized by each occurrence or by the total duration of the behavior during the period of observation. Observer starts the stopwatch when the behavior begins and stops the watch when the behavior ends. Best used with behaviors with a clear beginning and end, where the dimension of interest is how long behavior lasts and where the behavior is longer in duration (e.g., on-task, pro-social, or out-of-area behaviors).
Latency	The elapsed time between the prompt of request for behavior and the performance of the target behavior is recorded. Observer starts the stopwatch when the prompt or request is given and stops the watch when the target behavior is initiated. Latency data can be summarized by each occurrence. Best used with behaviors that have a clear beginning and are signaled by some type of prompt (e.g., compliance).

Source: Hojnoski, R., Gischlar, K., & Missall, K. (2009). Improving child outcomes with data-based decision making: Collecting data. *Young Exceptional Children, 12*(3), p. 39.

MAKING CONNECTIONS

Monitoring T.J.'s Progress

T.J.'s teacher observed him in the classroom setting to monitor his progress in the area of fine motor skills. Below are two examples of the data collection methods she used, anecdotal recording and time sampling.

Example of Anecdotal Recording

Child's name: T.J. Date: 1/22 Time: 9:20 a.m.
Observer's Name: *J.K.* Location: *Preschool Classroom*

Anecdote:
T.J. was playing with the small blocks. He was putting one block on top of another. He was having difficulty balancing the blocks on top of each other. He attempted to build a tower of 3 blocks. His teacher approached him and he turned away. Just then A.K., another child in the room, walked over to where T.J. was playing. T.J. picked up the blocks and started to take A.K.'s blocks. A.K. began to retrieve the blocks. Teacher noticed this incident and encouraged A.K. to move to another part of the room.

Comment:
Need to find out why he was having difficulty balancing the blocks.
Why did T.J. turn away from his teacher? Need to observe T.J. in other settings.

Example of Time Sampling

Child's name: *T.J.*   Date: *3/19* Time: *11:10*
Observer's Name: *J.K.* Location: *Preschool Classroom*

Time	Observation	Comment:
11:10	Watching block building	
11:12	Watching A.K. color	Switches hands
11:14	Writing name	
11:16	Moves to block area	
11:18	Playing with blocks	
11:20	Playing with blocks	Switches from right hand to left, right again
11:22	Playing with blocks	

format, teachers can make notes about significant events concerning a child's behavior and activities or record observations of the child's physical or emotional state on a given day, which may be factual or an interpretive form of data. If information recorded is a teacher's subjective interpretation, this should be made clear in the written narrative. Anecdotal records may entail written notes on specific behaviors, including events that preceded and followed each behavior observed (e.g., skill development for a child in a specific domain, what words a child uses during certain activities, and in what situations a child engages in spontaneous verbalizations). Anecdotal records may involve more lengthy written narratives in some instances, describing the sequence of events when a child exhibits a certain behavior (e.g., temper tantrum, seizure, accident involving the child). Anecdotal records usually focus on the content or style

MAKING CONNECTIONS

Monitoring Maria's Progress

Maria's service coordinator developed a system to monitor her progress in toilet training and participation in play activities. Below are two examples of the data collection methods she used, anecdotal recording and time sampling.

Example of Time Sampling

Name: Maria   Date: 2-17-10
Objective: Maria will urinate when placed on potty
Key: D = dry   W = wet   V = vocalized   P = placed on potty
              + = urinated in potty   − = did not urinate in potty

Time	Monday	Tuesday	Wednesday	Thursday	Friday
8:00	D	D	D	D	D
8:30	W	W	P−	VP+	P+
9:00	D	D	W	D	D
9:30	D	D	D	D	D
10:00	D	VP−	D	D	D
10:30	VP−	D	D	VW	VP+
11:00	W	W	VP+	D	D
11:30	D	W	D	D	D

An Interval Record Using One-Minute Intervals

Interval

Behavior	Child	Total	Percentage	1	2	3	4	5	6	7	8	9	10
Requests help	Maria	9	90%	X	X	X	X	X	X	X	X	X	0

of behavior or situations in which behavior occurs rather than the frequency or duration.

Another frequently used method to monitor progress is through the collection of samples of a child's work at regular intervals for qualitative comparisons of the child's progress over time (e.g., drawings of a person, writing name or numbers, art work, sample worksheets on pre-academic work). Audio recordings of a child's speech or video recordings of a child's skills represent other methods of data collection that can be especially useful in providing concrete evidence to show parents and other team members what the child can do and the progress he or she is making.

A recommended format to keep a record of children's progress is through the use of a **portfolio assessment** process, a type of authentic assessment system widely used in early childhood education. A portfolio assessment is a means to provide a comprehensive overview of a child's performance on authentic, meaningful tasks in natural environments over time (Losardo & Notari-Syverson, 2001). More specifically, a portfolio is a systematic and organized record of children's work and behaviors that can be used to monitor their knowledge, skills, and achievements over time (Artel & Spandel, 1991; Jarrett, Brown, & Wallin, 2006; Lynch & Struewing, 2001). A portfolio may simply be a container for carrying documents such as a notebook or pizza box covered in contact paper (LaBoskey, 2000), or it may be created using an electronic format. No specific rules dictate a portfolio's appearance; however, a portfolio should be well organized so that relevant materials can be located with minimal effort. These collections are used as evidence to monitor the growth of the child's skills, behavior, knowledge, and even his or her interests, attitudes, or personal reflections. Table 4–9 provides guidelines for developing and implementing a portfolio assessment process.

In addition, portfolios can serve as a record of teachers' and other team members' observations and comments about children's activities and behaviors; video or audiotapes of significant activities; checklists of skills (for example, vocabulary words used spontaneously); photographs of children's work or activities in which they have engaged; a wide selection of the child's work (such as art work, writing samples); summaries of teacher observations; anecdotal records of specific events; information shared by parents or family members; and any other evidence of children's skills and progress. The information and materials that are included in a portfolio can be selected by any member of the team—the teacher, therapists, paraprofessionals, family members, or even the child (Shores & Grace, 1998). Depending on the specific purpose, the portfolio can be divided into different sections according to IFSP or IEP goals, types of documents (e.g., photographs, drawings, anecdotal notes, test results), developmental or curriculum areas, sources of information (e.g., teachers, specialists, family), or context (e.g., classroom, home, community).

The information that is collected via the portfolio assessment process meets many of the criteria required in program planning and progress monitoring. That is, it is collected over time; it relies on multiple sources of information; it collects information from many different individuals about children's skills; and most importantly, it collects skill information in the setting where the child has demonstrated the skill.

The information collected is used to document progress that is being made toward the accomplishment of each child's individual outcomes.

Family Input in the Monitoring Process

If collected properly, family input is invaluable in monitoring child and family status within the larger context of determining program effectiveness. As IFSPs and IEPs are implemented, information should be collected from families regarding the appropriateness of the goals and outcomes, the success of the plan in meeting the child's needs, and the family's concerns and priorities. The IFSP or IEP should be modified based on the feedback provided by the family or upon the family's request. In addition to families having opportunities to evaluate the effectiveness of the IFSP or IEP, they should also have multiple opportunities to provide input into the overall effectiveness of the early intervention/early childhood special education program and the services they are receiving. Information can be collected regarding their perceptions of the program staff, the policies and procedures, the team process, and so on.

Overall Program Effectiveness

Program evaluation has been defined as an objective, systematic process for gathering information about a program, or set of activities, which can be utilized for the following purposes:

1. to ascertain a program's ability to achieve the originally conceived and implemented goals;
2. to suggest modifications that might lead to improvement in quality and effectiveness; and
3. to allow well informed decisions about the worth, merit, and level of support a program warrants.

In order for evaluation to be effective, it must be designed with a specific purpose in mind. Early childhood programs must have well developed purposes and evaluation plans prior to the beginning of services to increase the programs' ability to document outcomes.

Early childhood programs that serve young children with disabilities and their families must consider a number of issues when designing evaluation plans. Several years ago, Bailey and Wolery (1992) posed several questions to provide insight into the overall quality of a program. These questions are still relevant today in determining overall program quality.

TABLE 4–9 Guidelines for Implementing Portfolio Assessment

- Start portfolios at the beginning of the year.

- Caregivers and other team members should identify in advance the purpose for the portfolio, as well as expectations for children's work.

- Children should be told the purpose of their portfolios.

- Establish types of documentation for each goal and criteria for evaluating work.

- Develop plan for when and how data will be collected and by whom.

- Date all work promptly.

- Determine who will evaluate the portfolio.

- Identify ways to involve the child and family in work selection and evaluation.

- If necessary, teach children the skills needed to participate in this process.

- Portfolio contents should be representative of children's work, growth, and accomplishments.

- Explain to caregivers and children the reasons for selecting samples.

- Decide how to organize the portfolio.
  - Content areas
  - IEP goals
  - Themes
  - Chronological order of work

- Decide who owns the portfolio and where it will be stored.

- Establish clear, agreed-on guidelines to manage access to the portfolio and ensure confidentiality.

- Determine criteria for monitoring children's progress.

- Practitioners can schedule quarterly conferences with children, family, teachers, and other team members to review the portfolio. At these meetings, discuss team member observations and documentation to check for subjectivity and bias. Daily debriefings with other team members can help track the various types of documentation being gathered.

- Criteria for evaluating the portfolio may include:
  - Quantity, quality, and diversity of items,
  - Organization of the portfolio,
  - Level of student involvement,
  - Meaningfulness of caption statement,
  - Quality of summary statements about growth and change.

Source: Adapted from A. Losardo, & A. Notari-Syverson, (2001). *Alternative approaches to assessing young children.* Baltimore, MD: Paul H. Brookes Publishing.

1. Can the program demonstrate that its methods, materials, and overall service delivery represent recommended practices?

2. Can the program demonstrate that the methods espoused in the overall philosophy are implemented accurately and consistently?

3. Can the program demonstrate that it attempts to verify empirically the effectiveness of interventions or other individual program components for which recommended practice has yet to be verified?

4. Can the program demonstrate that a system is in place for determining the relative adequacy of client progress and service delivery?

5. Can the program demonstrate that it is moving toward the accomplishment of program goals/ outcomes?

6. Can the program demonstrate that the goals, methods, materials, and overall service delivery system are in accordance with the needs and values of the community and clients it serves?

These answers can provide a clear and realistic framework for understanding and monitoring the operations and effectiveness of early intervention/ early childhood special education programs.

Summary

Assessment of young children with disabilities or delays is a comprehensive process with overlapping components rather than a single procedure. Assessments of young children are conducted to help professionals and families to make informed, evaluative decisions at several levels. The type of decision to be made will determine the purpose of the assessment as well as the assessment tools to be used or the processes that will be followed. Depending on the purpose of the assessment, the assessment process can be formal and/or informal and can include testing, observations, interviews, portfolios, and/or other procedures.

Conducting appropriate assessments of young children has been the topic of discussion and debate for several years. Some of the issues have included the following:

1. the overreliance on intelligence testing

2. the limited number of tools appropriate for young children

3. the nature and characteristics of young children and families

4. culturally biased assessments

Recommended assessment practices have dramatically changed over the last several years. Because of the limitations of standardized and formal assessment tools, informal procedures are more widely used with young children. It is important to remember that the key component of an appropriate assessment is for the assessment team members to gain an accurate representation of the child's current abilities and behaviors in the context of his natural environment as he interacts with adults and peers.

Assessment must be useful, acceptable, authentic, collaborative, convergent, equitable, sensitive, and congruent. Because assessment is an ongoing process that begins with screening and continues with diagnosis, eligibility, and program planning, as well as progress monitoring and evaluation, assessments are conducted for three different purposes that have been described in this chapter. *Screenings* are conducted to identify children who may have a delay or disability. Through screenings, the determination is made if children should undergo more in depth assessment procedures. *Eligibility assessments* determine if children meet the requirements of a given program or service. *Program planning assessment* is designed to collect information about the child's intervention needs.

In order to determine the effectiveness of intervention, children's progress towards the attainment of their individual goals and outcomes, as well as family outcomes, must be monitored. Progress monitoring should be conducted regularly and frequently and should take place in authentic, naturalistic settings. This will provide a record of children's progress and indicate whether any interventions should be changed. Furthermore, information must be collected regarding family satisfaction and overall program effectiveness.

Check Your Understanding

1. Provide a definition of assessment in early intervention/early childhood special education.

2. Identify and describe the four purposes of assessment in EI/ECSE.

3. Describe four types of assessment procedures commonly used in EI/ECSE.

4. Discuss problems or issues associated with the assessment of young children and provide suggestions for addressing them.
5. List at least five recommended procedural guidelines for conducting appropriate assessments of young children.
6. Describe how professionals can ensure that assessments are culturally appropriate.
7. Differentiate between assessment conducted for screening purposes and assessment designed to determine eligibility.
8. Describe the difference between assessment to determine eligibility and assessment for program planning purposes.
9. Explain the importance of considering family preferences in the program planning process.
10. Describe strategies for including families in the assessment process and discuss the advantages for including them in the assessment of young children.
11. Describe four different methods that can be used to collect assessment information.
12. Provide a rationale for considering (as part of the assessment process) the environments or settings where children spend time and the demands placed on them in those environments.
13. Explain how each of the following levels of evaluation should be addressed in the overall evaluation plan of an early childhood program in which children with disabilities are served: (a) child level, (b) family level, and (c) program level.
14. Explain the importance of monitoring the progress of young children with disabilities.

Reflection and Application

1. Observe the assessment process in an early intervention/early childhood special education setting. What was the purpose of the assessment? Who was involved in the process? Where did it take place? What was done to prepare the environment prior to the assessment? How was rapport established with the child and family prior to the assessment?
2. Discuss with an early interventionist or educator his/her role in each component of the assessment process (i.e., screening, eligibility, program planning, and progress monitoring).
3. Examine several assessment instruments used in early intervention/education. Compare and contrast the instruments in terms of purpose, age range, domains, cost, administration, psychometric properties, inclusion of family, cultural and linguistic considerations, and usability of results for individualized program planning.
4. Review systems used to monitor progress within an early intervention, preschool, and early primary settings. How are they similar and how do they differ? Interview an early childhood special education teacher for recommendations on monitoring progress.
5. How might the families of Maria, T.J, and Cheryl be involved in the assessment process? What specific roles might the families play? How can the EI/ECSE teacher help support families in the roles they play? In assessment for program planning and progress monitoring, explain how the teacher could provide support to the families to encourage their involvement.

References

Andersson, L. (2004). Appropriate and inappropriate interpretation and use of test scores in early intervention. *Journal of Early Intervention, 27*(1), 55–68.

Apgar, V., & James, L. (1962). Further observation on the Newborn Scoring System. *American Journal of Diseases of Children, 104*, 419–428.

Bagnato, S. (2005). The authentic alternative for assessment in early intervention: An emerging evidence-based practice. *Journal of Early Intervention, 28*(1), 17–22.

Bagnato, S., & Neisworth, J. (1991). *Assessment for early intervention: Best practices for professionals.* New York: Guilford.

Bagnato, S., & Neisworth, J. (1999). Collaboration and teamwork in assessment for early intervention. *Child and Adolescent Psychiatric Clinics of North America, 8*(2), 347–363.

Bagnato, S., Neisworth, J., & Munson, S. (1997). *Linking assessment and early intervention: An authentic curriculum-based approach.* Baltimore, MD: Brookes.

Bailey, D., & Wolery, M. (1992). *Teaching infants and pre-schoolers with disabilities* (2nd ed.). New York: Merrill.

Banks, R., Santos, R., & Roof. (2003). Discovering family concerns, priorities, and resources: Sensitive family information gathering. *Young Exceptional Children. 6*(2), 1–7.

Batshaw, M. J. (1997). *Children with disabilities* (4th ed.). Baltimore: Brookes.

Botts, D., Losardo, A., Notari-Syverson, A. (2007). Alternative assessment: The pathway to individualized instruction for young children. In E. Horn, C. Peterson, & L. Fox (Eds.), *Linking curriculum to child and family outcomes* (Young Exceptional Children Monograph Series No. 2). Missoula, MT: Council for Exceptional Children, The Division for Early Childhood.

Branscombe, N. A., Castle, K., Dorsey, A. G., Surbeck, E., & Taylor, J. B. (2003). *Early childhood curriculum: A constructivist perspective*. Boston: Houghton Mifflin.

Bricker, D., & Littman, D. (1982). Intervention and education: The inseparable mix. *Topics in Early Childhood Special Education, 1*, 23–33.

Bricker, D. & Waddell, M. (2002). *Assessment, evaluation, and programming system (AEPS): Vol. 4, Curriculum for three to six years* (2nd ed.). Baltimore: Paul H. Brookes.

Bronfenbrenner, U. (1977). Toward an experimental ecology of human development. *American Psychologist, 32*(7), 513–531.

Bronfenbrenner, U. (1979). *The ecology of human development: Experiments by nature and design*. Cambridge, MA: Harvard University Press.

Campbell, P. (1991). Evaluation and assessment in early intervention for infants and toddlers. *Journal of Early Intervention, 15*(1), 36–45.

Cohen, L. G., & Spenciner, L. J. (2003). *Assessment of children and youth with special needs*. White Plains, NY: Longman.

Division for Early Childhood (DEC) (2007). *Promoting positive outcomes for children with disabilities: Recommendations for curriculum, assessment, and program evaluation*. Missoula, MT: Author.

Fewell, R. (2000). Assessment of young children with special needs. *Topics in Early Childhood Special Education, 20*(1), 38–42.

Greenspan, S., & Meisels, S. (1994). Toward a new vision for the developmental assessment of infants and young children. *Zero to Three, 14*(6), 1–8.

Grisham-Brown, J., & Pretty-Fontczak, K. (2003). Using planning time to individualize instruction for preschoolers with special needs. *Journal of Early Intervention, 26*(1), 31–46.

Hanson, M., & Lynch, E. (1995). Early intervention: *Implementing child and family services for infants and toddlers who are at risk* (2nd ed.). Austin, TX: PRO-ED.

Hojnoski, R., Gischlar, K., & Missall, K. (2009). Improving child outcomes with data-based decision making: Collecting data. *Young Exceptional Children, 12*(3), 39.

Hendricks, M., & McCracken, T. (2009). Screening, evaluation, and assessment in early childhood special education. In J. Taylor, J. McGowan, & T. Linder (Eds.), *The program administrator's guide to early childhood special education: Leadership, development, & supervision* (pp. 63–80). Baltimore: Paul H. Brookes.

Jarrett, M., Browne, B., & Wallin, C. (2006). Using portfolio assessment to document developmental progress of infants and toddlers. *Young Exceptional Children, 10*, 22–23.

Johnson, L., & LaMontagne, M. (1994). Program evaluation: The key to quality programming. In L. Johnson, R. Gallagher, M. LaMontagne, J. Jordon, J. Gallagher, P. Hutinger, & M. Karnes (Eds.), *Meeting early intervention challenges: Issues from birth to three* (pp. 185–216). Baltimore, MD: Paul H. Brookes.

Johnson-Martin, N., Attermeier, S., & Hacker, B. (2004a). *The Carolina curriculum for infants and toddlers with special needs* (3rd ed.). Baltimore, MD: Paul H. Brookes.

Johnson-Martin, N., Hacker, B., & Attermeier, S. (2004b). *The Carolina curriculum for preschoolers with special needs* (3rd ed.). Baltimore, MD: Paul H. Brookes.

Kilgo, J. L., & Raver, S. A. (2009). Building partnerships in culturally/linguistically diverse settings. In S. Raver (Ed.) *Early childhood special education—0 to 8 Years: Strategies for positive outcomes*. Upper Saddle River, NJ: Pearson Education.

LaBoskey, V. K. (2000). Portfolios here, portfolios there . . . Searching for the essence of 'educational portfolios.' *Phi Delta Kappan, 81*(8), 590–595.

Linder, T. (2008). *Transdisciplinary play-based assessment and transdisciplinary play-based intervention (2nd ed.)*. Baltimore: Paul H. Brookes.

Losardo, A., & Notari-Syverson, A. (2001). *Alternative approaches to assessing young children*. Baltimore, MD: Paul H. Brookes.

Lynch, E., & Hanson, M. (2004). *Developing cross-cultural competence: A guide for working with children and their families*. Baltimore: Paul H. Brookes.

Lynch, E., & Struewing, N. (2001). Children in context: Portfolio assessment in the inclusive early childhood classroom. *Young Exceptional Children, 5*(1), 2–10.

McAfee, R., & Leong, D. (2002). *Assessing and guiding young children's development and learning* (3rd ed.). Boston: Allyn & Bacon.

McCormick, L. (1997). Ecological assessment and planning. In L. McCormick, D. Loeb, & R. Schiefelbusch (Eds.), *Supporting children with communication difficulties in inclusive settings: School-based language intervention* (pp. 223–256). Boston: Allyn & Bacon.

McLean, M. (2005). Using curriculum-based assessment to determine eligibility: Time for a paradigm shift? *Journal of early Intervention, 28*(1), 23–27.

McLean, M., Wolery, M., & Bailey, D. (2004). *Assessing infants and preschoolers with special Needs*. (3rd ed.). Upper Saddle River, NJ: Merrill/Prentice Hall.

Neisworth, J., & Bagnato, S. (1992). The case against intelligence testing in early intervention. *Topics in Early Childhood Special Education, 12*(1), 1–20.

Neisworth, J., & Bagnato, S. (1996). Assessment for early intervention: Emerging themes and practices. In S. Odom & M. McLean (Eds.). *Early intervention/early childhood special education: Recommended practices.* (pp. 23–58). Austin, TX: PRO-ED.

Neisworth, J., & Bagnato, S. (2000). Recommended practices in assessment. In S. Sandall, M. McLean, & B. Smith (2000). *DEC recommended practices for early intervention/early childhood special education.* pp. 17–27. Longmont, CO: Sopris West.

Neisworth, J., & Bagnato, S. (2005). DEC recommended practices: Assessment. In S. Sandal, M.L. Hemmeter, B. Smith, & M. McLean (Eds.), *DEC recommended practices: A comprehensive guide to practical application in early intervention/early childhood special education* (pp. 45–69). Longmont, CO: Sopris West.

Noonan, M., & McCormick, L. (2006). *Young children with disabilities in natural environments: Methods and procedures.* Baltimore: Paul H. Brookes.

Parks, S. (2007). *Hawaii Early Learning Profile (HELP) Strands (0–3).* Palo Alto, CA: VORT Corporation.

Richard, N., & Schiefelbusch, R. (1991). Assessment. In L. McCormick & R. Schiefelbusch (Eds.), *Early language intervention.* Columbus, OH: Merrill.

Sandall, S., McLean, M. E., & Smith, B. J. (2000). *DEC recommended practices for early intervention/early childhood special education.* Longmont, CO: Sopris West.

Sandall, S., Hemmeter, M. L., Smith, B., & McLean, M. (Eds.). (2005). *DEC recommended practices: A comprehensive guide to practical application in early intervention/early childhood special education.* Longmont, CO: Sopris West.

Sandall, S., Schwartz, I., & Lacroix, B. (2004). Interventionists' perspectives about data collecting in integrated early childhood classrooms. *Journal of Early Intervention, 26*(3), 161–174.

Sandall, S. & Schwartz, I. (2008). *Building blocks for successful early childhood programs: Strategies for including all children.* Baltimore, MD: Paul H. Brookes.

Sattler, J. (2008). *Assessment of children: Cognitive foundations* (5th ed.) La Mesa, CA: Jerome M. Sattler.

Shores, E. & Grace, C. (1998). *The portfolio book: A step-by-step guide for teachers.* Beltsville, MD: Gryphon House.

Taylor, R. (2009). *Assessment of exceptional students: Educational and psychological procedures* (8th ed.). Boston: Pearson.

Turnbull, A., Turnbull, R., Erwin, E, & Soodak, L. (2006). *Families, professionals, and exceptionality: Positive outcomes through a partnership and trust* (5th ed.). Upper Saddle River, NJ: Pearson Education.

Vanderheyden, A. (2005). Intervention-driven assessment practices in early childhood/early intervention: Measuring what is possible rather than what is present. *Journal of Early Intervention, 28*(1), 28–33.

VORT Corporation (2004). *Hawaii early learning profile (HELP) for preschoolers—Assessment strands.* Palo Alto, CA: Author.

Woods, J., & McCormick, K. (2002). Toward an integration of child and family centered practices in the assessment of preschool children: Welcoming the family. *Young Exceptional Children, 5*(3), pp. 2–11.

Wolery, M. (2004). Monitoring child progress. In M. McLean, M. Wolery, & D. B. Bailey (Eds.), *Assessing infants and preschoolers with special needs* (3rd ed., pp. 545–584). Englewood Cliffs, NJ: Prentice Hall.

5

Delivering Services to Young Children with Special Needs

Key Terminology

Natural environments	Multidisciplinary
Mainstreaming	Interdisciplinary
Normalization	Transdisciplinary
Least restrictive environment (LRE)	Cooperative teaching
Regular education initiative (REI)	Individualized family service plan (IFSP)
Full inclusion	Individualized education program (IEP)
Home-based programs	504 accommodation plan
Center-based programs	Section 504
Combination programs	Transition

Learning Outcomes

After reading this chapter you will be able to:

- List five benefits of providing services in inclusive settings.

- Define the concept of least restrictive environment.

- Identify the advantages and disadvantages of center-based and home-based service delivery models.

- Explain the differences between multi-, inter-, and transdisciplinary team models.

- Describe the various cooperative teaching models.

- List the required components of an individualized family service plan (IFSP) and an individualized education program (IEP).

- Describe the purpose of a 504 accommodation plan.

- Outline the steps needed to ensure effective transitions.

A goal of early intervention and early childhood special education efforts is to provide at-risk and young children with special needs with the best possible beginning. As a field, early childhood special education has been driven by the recognition of the importance of providing services and interventions to young children with disabilities "as early and comprehensively as possible in the least restrictive setting" (Carta, Schwartz, Atwater, & McConnell, 1991, p. 4). One of the issues this chapter will address is how to provide appropriate services in the natural environment. The literature strongly suggests that segregated settings are not called for (Noonan & McCormick, 2006; Sandall, Hemmeter, Smith, & McLean, 2005; Sandall & Ostrosky, 2000). The challenge to early childhood professionals, as Carta and colleagues note, is to develop delivery systems that provide services in integrated environments. This leads us to our second issue, which also provides a framework for this chapter—how to best design services for young children with disabilities and those at risk in a manner that is responsive to the individual needs of each child and their family's goals and priorities.

The primary objective of this chapter is to examine the variety of placement options or models available for providing interventions. Our attention will also focus on the importance of professional collaboration and cooperation. Teamwork is absolutely necessary if programs are to effectively function and meet the needs of young children with special needs and their families. We will also look at the vehicles for delivering services—that is, individualized family service plans (IFSPs), individualized education programs (IEPs), and Section 504 accommodation plans. Finally, the importance of carefully planned transitions will be considered.

Inclusion

With the advent of IDEA (and its reauthorizations), along with support from the Americans with Disabilities Act (PL 101-336), options for delivering services to infants, toddlers, and preschoolers with special needs has dramatically changed. Services for infants and toddlers are required to be provided in **natural environments**. This provision is generally interpreted to mean those settings that are typical or natural for

Cengage Learning

Today, services for young children with special needs are often provided in inclusive learning environments.

the young child's peers who are not disabled and includes a wide variety of community placements (see the Parent Voices feature). Services for preschoolers with special needs and students in the early primary grades with delays or disabilities are under the jurisdiction of the public schools, who are mandated to serve these children according to the provisions of IDEA—including providing services in the least restrictive environment (LRE). While there is growing support for providing services in the natural environment, we must remember that where early intervention and education are provided, they must be appropriate to the needs of the child and in concert with the goals, values, and priorities of the child's family.

Many communities provide services for young children with special needs in inclusive settings. The idea of providing services to young children with special needs in normalized settings is not new. Early childhood special educators have been challenged by this issue for many years. Many professionals and parents have long advocated for the provision of services in natural environments that

Parent Voices

It is difficult to imagine how it feels to call an early childhood program and rather than inquiring about what kind of curriculum they have or types of activities, you first have to ask them if they accept children with disabilities. Because of inclusion, the dream of my child having the opportunity to go to the same early childhood program and to develop friendships with her typically developing peers has finally been realized.

Source: M. Davis, J. Kilgo, and M. Gamel-McCormick, *Young Children with Special Needs* (Needham Heights, MA: Allyn & Bacon, 1998), p. 52.

include both typically developing children and those with special needs (Cavallaro & Haney, 1999; Harbin, MWilliam, & Gallagher, 2000). Unfortunately, one of the problems with the implementation of this principle is the absence, in some communities, of appropriate placements or settings for infants, toddlers, and preschoolers with disabilities (Downing, 2008). To fully appreciate this contemporary practice, we need to review its conceptual evolution and understand key terminology.

The 1970s saw the establishment of a strong foundation for merging early childhood programs that integrated young children with and without disabilities (Guralnick, 1994). The decade of the 1980s, according to Guralnick (1990), witnessed the repeated demonstration that integrated early childhood programs could effectively be implemented. The challenge facing professionals in the 1990s was to construct program models that would allow for services to be delivered in nonspecialized or natural settings (Carta et al., 1991). Currently, in the early years of the 21st century, the most common programs for infants, toddlers, and preschoolers with special needs are those environments that are primarily designed for typical children. Across the United States, there is a growing recognition that it is essential to provide intervention for children with special needs as early as possible in the most normalized setting (Carta et al.).

More than 30 years ago, Bricker (1978) and more recently, Cavallaro and Haney (1999), identified social–ethical, legal–legislative, and psychological–educational arguments supporting the educational integration of young children with disabilities. In recent years, these arguments have been reinforced by an expanding research knowledge base, judicial

decisions, and legislative enactments. Today, many professionals and parents alike appreciate the benefits and opportunities that have accrued to young children with and without special needs and their families (see Table 5–1). They are the result of many years of arduous effort. Still, in spite of these gains, there are some professionals (and parents too), who believe that we have not done enough in advocating for the full inclusion of all children with disabilities into all aspects of society—but especially into educational programs. We see this call for full inclusion as having a potentially significant impact on the field of early childhood special education.

The debate surrounding the full inclusion movement is an emotionally and value-laden one with the potential for polarizing the field of special education. Across the country, advocates of this movement view it as the next great revolution in special education, while opponents see it as the start of the return of the "dark ages" of special education—namely, the pre-PL 94-142 era (Gargiulo, 2009). We suspect that the truth lies somewhere between these two extremes. The intensity of this debate is fueled by several factors, one of which is the inconsistent use of key terminology. As frequently happens in arguments, people are often saying the same thing, only they are using different words. Therefore, we offer the following interpretations, which are frequently encountered in describing this movement.

Mainstreaming

The first potentially confusing term is **mainstreaming**, or in contemporary language, inclusion. We define this term as the social and instructional integration

TABLE 5–1 **Benefits of Preschool Integration**

Beneficiary	Benefit
Children with disabilities	• They are spared the effects of separate, segregated education—including the negative effects of labeling and negative attitudes fostered by lack of contact with them. • They are provided with typically developing peer models that allow them to learn new adaptive skills and/or learn and how to use their existing skills through imitation. • They are provided with typically developing peers with whom to interact, and thereby learn new social and/or communicative skills. • They are provided with realistic life experiences that prepare them to live in the community. • They are provided with opportunities to develop friendships with typically developing peers.
Children without disabilities	• They are provided with opportunities to learn more realistic and accurate views about individuals with disabilities. • They are provided with opportunities to develop positive attitudes toward others who are different from themselves. • They are provided with opportunities to learn altruistic behaviors and when and how to use such behaviors. • They are provided with models of individuals who successfully achieve despite challenges.
Communities	• They can conserve their early childhood resources by limiting the need for segregated specialized programs. • They can conserve educational resources if children with disabilities, who are included at the preschool level, continue in regular, as compared to special education, placements during the elementary school years.
Families of children with disabilities	• They are able to learn about typical development. • They may feel less isolated from the remainder of their communities. • They may develop relationships with families of typically developing children who can provide them with meaningful support.
Families of children without disabilities	• They may develop relationships with families of children with disabilities and thereby make a contribution to them and their communities. • They will have opportunities to teach their children about individual differences and about accepting individuals who are different.

Source: M. Wolery and J. Wilbers, Introduction to the Inclusion of Young Children with Special Needs in Early Childhood Programs, in *Including Children with Special Needs in Early Childhood Programs,* M. Wolery and J. Wilbers (Eds.), (Washington, DC: National Association for the Education of Young Children, 1994), p. 11. Reprinted by permission.

of children with disabilities into educational programs whose primary purpose is to serve typically developing individuals. The term *mainstreaming* represents the popularized version of the principle of educating children with disabilities, including preschoolers and early primary students, in the least restrictive environment. Interestingly, neither the term *mainstreaming* nor *inclusion* appears in any piece of federal legislation.

The idea of mainstreaming has been woven into the fabric of American education for more than 30 years. Despite significant barriers and obstacles to implementing integrated programs at the preschool level, many successful programs have been established across the United States partly due to the Americans with Disabilities Act. Examples of these programs include Head Start, university child development centers, cooperative preschools, and family day care settings, among other options. Eighteen states currently have policy guidelines/statements addressing the inclusion of preschoolers (Lazara, Danaher, & Kraus, 2007).

Fortunately, as a result of litigation and legislation, parents no longer have to prove that their son or daughter should be included; rather, early childhood programs and schools must justify their position to exclude and justify that they have made a good faith effort at integration or present strong evidence that an inclusionary setting is unsatisfactory (Yell, 2006). IDEA 2004 currently supports this thinking.

The key to understanding mainstreaming (integration) is that it must provide the student with an appropriate education based on the individual needs of the child. According to Rose and Smith (1993), "mainstreaming is meant to enhance the child's education through provision of a normalized social context for learning" (p. 62). The framers of IDEA never envisioned that mainstreaming would be interpreted to mean that *all* young children with special needs must be placed in integrated placements; to do so would mean abandoning the idea of determining what is the most appropriate placement for a particular child. IDEA clearly stipulates that, to the maximum extent appropriate, children with disabilities are to be educated with their typical peers. We interpret this provision to mean that, for some young children, an inclusive setting, even with supplementary aids and services, might be an inappropriate placement due to the child's unique characteristics. A least restrictive environment does *not* automatically mean

placement with typical learners. Special educators need to make the distinction between the concepts of appropriateness and restrictiveness (Gargiulo, 2009).

The notion of mainstreaming flows from the principle of **normalization**, which advocates providing services in as culturally normative a fashion as possible (Wolfensberger, 1972). Accordingly, individuals with disabilities should be integrated, to the maximum extent possible, into all aspects of daily life, including educational opportunities. Yet just because a young child with special needs receives services in a normalized setting, such as a for-profit child care center, does not mean that he or she will be provided with an appropriate education. Parents and professionals alike must carefully assess the setting into which a youngster is placed. Merely placing children with disabilities into typical early childhood facilities does not guarantee that the needs of the child will be fulfilled.

Least Restrictive Environment

The terms *mainstreaming* and **least restrictive environment (LRE)**, while closely linked, should not be used interchangeably. Their meanings are educationally distinct. As we have just seen, mainstreaming refers to the integration of pupils with disabilities into general education programs. LRE, on the other hand, is a legal term interpreted to mean that young children with special needs are to be educated in settings as close as possible to a regular or general education environment. "Mainstreaming is one means of meeting the LRE requirement; but IDEA does not require mainstreaming in all cases" (Osborne & DiMattia, 1994, p. 7). The goal of the LRE principle is to prevent the unwarranted segregation of students with disabilities from their typical classmates. An LRE is not a place but a concept.

The determination of the LRE is individually defined for each child. It is based on the student's educational needs—not his or her disability. The LRE mandate applies equally to preschoolers and the school-age population. The provision for educating preschoolers with disabilities as much as possible with typical children also requires that service delivery options be available. A continuum of educational placements has been devised to meet the LRE requirements. Figure 5–1 portrays an example of one possible option.

FIGURE 5–1 **A Continuum of Service Delivery Options**

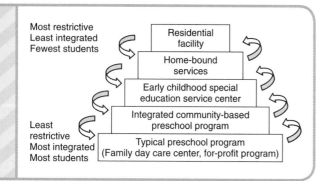

Cengage Learning

The least restrictive environment is individually determined for each child.

The continuum illustrated in Figure 5–1 reflects varying degrees of restrictiveness, which refers to the amount of available contact with typical learners. Being only with children with special needs is considered restrictive, while placement with individuals who are nondisabled is viewed as least restrictive. As we ascend the continuum, the environments provide fewer and fewer opportunities for interaction with typically developing age-mates; hence, greater restrictiveness. While contact with typical students is highly desirable, it must be balanced by the requirement of providing an education appropriate to the unique needs of the child.

Consequently, an integrated environment may not always be the most appropriate placement option. Each situation must be individually assessed and decided on a case-by-case basis. Furthermore, an educational placement is meant to be fluid. As the needs of the pupil change, so can the setting in which he or she receives services (Gargiulo, 2009).

The idea of a continuum of service delivery options allows for, in limited situations, the removal of a child from integrated environments if it is in the best educational interest of the student. Segregation, while not desirable, might be necessary in some situations in order to provide an appropriate education as outlined in the pupil's IEP or IFSP (Yell, 2006). As an example, Bricker (1995) contends that placement in a nonintegrated setting may be the placement of choice, especially if it increases the child's chances for future placement in a general education program. Judicially speaking, the courts have allowed, under certain circumstances, segregated placements for students with disabilities (Yell, 2006). Yet we recognize, as do many other special educators, that maximum integration with typically developing children is highly desirable and should be one of our major goals. The

TeachSource Video

Bobby: Serving a Student with Special Needs in an Inclusive Elementary Classroom

Visit the premium website and watch "Bobby: Serving a Student with Special Needs in an Inclusive Elementary Classroom." After watching this video, answer the following question:

1. Young children with cognitive disabilities should not be taught in the general education classroom. Agree or disagree with this statement. Support your position.

question, then, as posed by Gargiulo (2009), is when, where, with whom, and to what extent are young children with special needs to be integrated?

Regular Education Initiative

The third concept that requires attention is the **regular education initiative (REI)**. While not directly aimed at young children with special needs, REI is an important link in the evolution of the full inclusion movement and is conceptually relevant. The term was introduced in 1986 by former Assistant Secretary of Education (Office of Special Education and Rehabilitative Services) Madeline Will, who questioned the legitimacy of special education as a separate system of education and called for a restructuring of the relationship between general and special education. She endorsed the idea of shared responsibility or a partnership between regular (general) and special education, resulting in a coordinated delivery system (Will, 1986b). Her comments have been interpreted in many ways that have contributed to the current debate about the roles of special and general educators in delivering services to children with disabilities, as well as to students enrolled in remedial and compensatory programs. At one end of the spectrum are those who consider regular and special education as unnecessary dual systems (Wang & Reynolds, 1985) and thus advocate the elimination of special education as a distinct delivery system (Gartner & Lipsky, 1987; Stainback & Stainback, 1987). Some professionals believe that *all* children, including those with severe impairments, should be educated in general education classrooms (Downing, 2008). This proposal, of course, would radically reform special education as we presently know it and is genuinely counter to the basic tenets of special education.

Part of the difficulty in understanding the complexities of REI is that it has been misrepresented and, therefore, misunderstood. Some of the problem arises from the fact that Will (1986b) fails to clearly define what she means by a partnership between general and special educators, thereby providing the impetus for diverse interpretations of her call. A careful reading of her position finds that Will (1986a) does not suggest that special education be consolidated into general education. A question also arises regarding at which population REI is aiming. Will (1986b) talks about students with learning difficulties, the educationally disadvantaged, and those who learn slowly;

she does not describe a particular disability group for whom REI would be appropriate. Some interpret her remarks to mean that *all* children, regardless of the severity of their disability, should be educated in one consolidated delivery system (Gartner & Lipsky, 1989; Stainback & Stainback, 1984). Lieberman (1990) observes that the goal of these educators is to fully integrate "any and all children into regular classrooms regardless of condition, disability, fragility, vulnerability, or need" (p. 561). Professionally speaking, we question the wisdom of such a plan and wonder, as does Kauffman (1989), if a child's right to an appropriate education in the LRE would be abused by such an explanation. What Will does advocate is bringing services for children with special needs into inclusive environments. She writes, "The basic issue is providing an educational program that will allow them [children with learning problems] to learn better" (Will, 1986b, p. 21). Will (1986b) believes that educators must also "visualize a system that will bring the program to the child rather than one that brings the child to the program" (p. 21). As early childhood special educators, most of us can embrace this idea. Furthermore, few would argue that special education services would be enhanced if there were greater coordination and cooperation between general and special educators.

Full Inclusion

We see the movement toward full inclusion as an extension of REI and earlier thinking about where children with disabilities should be educated. Figure 5–2 illustrates the evolution of this thought process.

As we noted in the introduction to this section, the issue of full inclusion is a potentially explosive concept with vocal supporters as well as detractors. It has emerged as one of the most controversial and complex practices in the field of early childhood education. As with other controversial topics, an agreed-upon definition is difficult to develop. We offer the following succinct interpretation: **full inclusion** is a belief that *all* children with disabilities should be taught exclusively (with appropriate supports) in general education classrooms located in their neighborhood schools, that is, the same school and classrooms they would otherwise attend if they were not disabled. This will most likely require extensive curricular modifications along with professional collaboration and teaming between general and special

FIGURE 5–2 The Evolution of Placement Options for Children with Special Needs

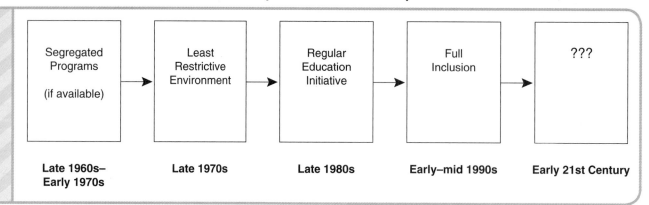

educators (Noonan & McCormick, 2006). Recall that Will (1986b) originally proposed this call for partnership in her REI. While the trend in judicial interpretations is toward inclusionary placement (Yell, 2006), the LRE mandate of IDEA does *not* require all pupils to be educated in regular classrooms, nor does the legislation require that students be educated in their neighborhood schools.

Advocates of full inclusion believe, according to Gargiulo (2009), that the current pull-out system of serving students with special needs is ineffective. Children are labeled and stigmatized, their programming fragmented, and general educators typically assume little or no ownership for students receiving a special education. Placement in a general education classroom, with a true partnership between special education teachers and general education teachers, would result in a better education for children with and without special needs, and it would occur within the LRE. See Table 5–2 for a summary of the key components of most full-inclusion models.

When correctly instituted, full inclusion is characterized by its virtual invisibility. Students with disabilities are not segregated but dispersed into classrooms they would normally attend if they were not disabled. "They are seen," Gargiulo (2009) writes, "as full-fledged members of, not merely visitors to, the general education classroom" (p. 78). Special educators provide services in the regular classroom alongside their general education colleagues.

Full inclusionists essentially advocate for the elimination of a continuum of service delivery options such as those illustrated in Figure 5–1. The concept of LRE, however, is not an all-or-nothing proposition.

Only if a full continuum of settings is available can one reasonably ensure that an appropriate placement will be made. The true litmus test for advocates of full inclusion is whether this model is more effective than the programming options presently available.

Like other professionals, we believe that *some* students with special needs will require intensive instruction if they are to achieve academic progress (Kauffman, Landrum, Mock, Sayeski, & Sayeski, 2005; Zigmond, 2007). Typically, this means instruction is delivered in a more restrictive setting such as a resource room. Of course, simply placing a pupil in a special education setting does not automatically mean that he or she will receive the specialized instruction needed (Gallagher & Lambert, 2006). Likewise, placement in a general education classroom does not guarantee that the student will receive an appropriate education. Regardless of where a learner receives an education, it must be effective. Perhaps the more appropriate question for educators to ask is not *where* instruction is provided but rather *how* is the instruction delivered and *what* is being taught. According to Zigmond (2003), "place is not what makes special education 'special' or effective. Effective teaching strategies and an individualized approach are the more critical ingredients in special education and neither of these is associated solely with one particular environment" (p. 198).

Hallahan, Kauffman, and Pullen (2009) also remind us that IDEA, as presently interpreted, gives parents the right to choose which environment they, not the full inclusionists, believe is most appropriate and least restrictive for delivering services to their son or daughter. The notion of making decisions based

TABLE 5–2 Key Elements of Full-Inclusion Models

- **"Home School" Attendance.** Defined as the local school the child would attend if nondisabled.

- **Natural Proportion at the School Site.** The percentage of special-needs children enrolled in a particular school is in proportion to the percentage of exceptional pupils in the entire school district; in regular education classes, this would mean approximately two to three students with disabilities.

- **Zero Rejection.** All students are accepted at the local school, including those with severe impairments; pupils are not screened out or grouped separately because of their disability.

- **Age/Grade-Appropriate Placement.** A full-inclusion model calls for serving children with special needs in regular classrooms according to their chronological age rather than basing services according to the child's academic ability or mental age.

- **Site-Based Management Coordination.** Recent trends in school organizational reform suggest a movement away from central office administration for special education programs to one where the building principal (or other administrator) plays a large role in planning and administering programs for all children in the school.

- **Use of Cooperative Learning and Peer Instructional Models.** Instructional practices that involve children learning in a cooperative manner rather than in a competitive fashion and using students to assist in the instruction of classmates with disabilities can be effective strategies for integrating exceptional learners in the regular classroom.

Source: W. Sailor, M. Gerry, and W. Wilson, "Policy Implications for Emergent Full Inclusion Models for the Education of Students with Disabilities," in W. Wang, H. Wolberg, and M. Reynolds (Eds.), *Handbook of Special Education*, Vol. 4 (New York: Pergamon Press, 1991). pp. 175–193; S. Stainback and W. Stainback, "Schools as Inclusive Communities," in W. Stainback and S. Stainback (Eds.), *Controversial Issues Confronting Special Education: Divergent Perspectives* (Boston: Allyn & Bacon, 1992), pp. 29–43.

TABLE 5–3 Recommendations and Suggestions for Educational Placement Decision Making

- Remember that program appropriateness is the primary IDEA mandate and the least restrictive environment provision is secondary.

- Make available a continuum of various alternative placements, including resource rooms, special classes, and special schools, so children with disabilities can learn in the environment that is appropriate for them based on their individual needs.

- Ensure that placement decisions are made by the IEP team that includes the student's parents.

- Ensure that each child is educated with and otherwise participates with children without disabilities to the maximum extent appropriate.

- Do not remove a child from the general education classroom unless his or her disability is such that an appropriate education cannot be achieved, even with the use of supplementary aids and services.

- Do not place a student on the basis of his or her disability. Regardless of the disability category, placement decisions must be based on the student's individualized education program.

Source: Adapted from B. Bateman and M. Linden, *Better IEPs: How to Develop Legally Correct and Educationally Useful Programs*, 4th ed. (Verona, WI: Attainment Company, 2006), pp. 27, 29.

on the individual needs of the child is fundamental to the foundation of special education. Yet advocates of full inclusion summarily dismiss the idea of individualized decision making by the very nature of their advocacy for full integration (Lieberman, 1990). To assert "that *all* [italics added] students must be educated in integrated settings," Yell (1995) writes, "is as discriminatory as educating all students with disabilities in segregated settings" (p. 400). Table 5–3 offers suggestions for making appropriate educational placement decisions.

Young Children and Full Inclusion. Full inclusion has implications for serving young children with special needs. Of particular interest to early childhood special educators are proposals where full inclusion is advocated for very young children with disabilities. For example, in a position paper crafted by Sexton, Snyder, Sharpton, and Stricklin (1993), the Association for Childhood Education International (ACEI) affirms their support for full inclusion for the very youngest of children with disabilities. ACEI believes that young children with special needs should be served in settings designed for their age peers without disabilities. A single inclusive system of care, intervention, and education is considered best for all children and their families.

The Division for Early Childhood (DEC) of the Council for Exceptional Children (CEC) also advocates for inclusion; however, DEC's position statement on inclusion (see Table 5–4) reflects an interpretation broader than simply inclusive educational services.

TABLE 5–4 The Division for Early Childhood Position Statement on Inclusion

A Joint Position Statement of the Division for Early Childhood (DEC) and the National Association for the Education of Young Children (NAEYC) April 2009

Today an ever-increasing number of infants and young children with and without disabilities play, develop, and learn together in a variety of places—homes, early childhood programs, neighborhoods, and other community-based settings. The notion that young children with disabilities and their families are full members of the community reflects societal values about promoting opportunities for development and learning, and a sense of belonging for every child. It also reflects a reaction against previous educational practices of separating and isolating children with disabilities. Over time, in combination with certain regulations and protections under the law, these values and societal views regarding children birth to age 8 with disabilities and their families have come to be known as early childhood inclusion. The most far-reaching effect of federal legislation on inclusion enacted over the past three decades has been to fundamentally change the way in which early childhood services ideally can be organized and delivered. However, because inclusion takes many different forms and implementation is influenced by a wide variety of factors, questions persist about the precise meaning of inclusion and its implications for policy, practice, and potential outcomes for children and families.

The lack of a shared national definition has contributed to misunderstandings about inclusion. DEC and NAEYC recognize that having a common understanding of what inclusion means is fundamentally important for determining what types of practices and supports are necessary to achieve high quality inclusion. This DEC/NAEYC joint position statement offers a definition of early childhood inclusion. The definition was designed not as a litmus test for determining whether a program can be considered inclusive, but rather, as a blueprint for identifying the key components of high quality inclusive programs....

Definition of Early Childhood Inclusion

Early childhood inclusion embodies the values, policies, and practices that support the right of every infant and young child and his or her family, regardless of ability, to participate in a broad range of activities and contexts as full members of families, communities, and society. The desired results of inclusive experiences for children with and without disabilities and their families include a sense of belonging and membership, positive social relationships and friendships, and development and learning to reach their full potential. The defining features of inclusion that can be used to identify high quality early childhood programs and services are access, participation, and supports.

NOTE: Full statement available at http://www.dec-sped.org/

Service Delivery Models

There are a variety of administrative options for providing services to young children with special needs and their families. These arrangements are usually referred to as service delivery approaches—where intervention or education is provided. The location of service delivery is frequently dependent on the age of the child (infant vs. preschooler), geographical considerations (rural vs. urban), child characteristics (severity and type of disability), and community resources as well as child/family goals and objectives (Graves, Gargiulo, & Sluder, 1996). Additionally, the philosophy and beliefs of the agency, program, or school regarding the inclusion of children with special needs with their typical peers may also influence where intervention/education is rendered.

Earlier in this chapter, we noted that contemporary thinking strongly supports the notion that intervention and other services for infants and toddlers with disabilities should occur in natural environments—that is, those locations viewed as typical for children of similar chronological age without disabilities. These locations might include child care settings, the child's home, or a neighborhood play group. Places viewed as "unnatural" include, for example, hospitals, clinics, or therapists' offices. This preference for offering services in the natural environment parallels the concept of LRE or inclusive settings for preschoolers and school-age students with disabilities—to the extent appropriate, children with disabilities must be educated alongside their typically developing peers (Gargiulo, 2009; Walsh, Rous, & Lutzer, 2000).

Traditionally, programs for young children with special needs are identified as center-based, home-based, or combination models. Like many other professionals, we agree with this conventional classification scheme. Yet it should be remembered that there is no single, accepted standard regarding where young children with special needs should be served. Furthermore, we believe that a decision as to where services are provided primarily resides with the child's family. They should be the primary decision makers. Noonan and McCormick (2006) suggest that the location of services should also reflect the "family's cultural values, the intensity of services that the child needs, and geographical accessibility for the family" (p. 14).

Even though there is no one best model, recommended practice guidelines for the delivery of early intervention and special education services have been formulated. Regardless of where services are provided, McDonnell and Hardman (1988) suggest that programs include the following dimensions:

- *Inclusive placements*: systematic contact with typical developing peers.
- *Comprehensive*: full range of services available.
- *Normalized*: age-appropriate skills and intervention strategies; instruction across a variety of settings.
- *Adaptable*: flexible procedures meeting individual needs of the child.
- *Peer and family referenced*: parents perceived as full partners; curriculum geared toward child, family, peers, and community (that is, an ecological approach).
- *Outcome-based*: developing skills with present and future usefulness; preparation for inclusive settings.

These suggestions hold true today. In fact, current recommendations based on empirical evidence (Odom & Wolery, 2003) strongly suggests that services for young children with special needs should be provided in inclusive settings along with appropriate and individualized supports. A child who receives services in an inclusive environment is afforded opportunities to develop more advanced social, linguistic, and cognitive skills that will aid in achieving success in integrated learning communities.

We need to keep in mind that the practices identified by McDonnell and Hardman (1988) and others are simply recommended indicators of quality. As such, they should be used as guidelines for early childhood special education programs. The needs of individual children with disabilities and their families dictate where, how, and what services are provided.

Home-Based Programs

For some young children, especially infants and toddlers, the most appropriate location for providing services is in their homes. Here, interventions can individually be provided by the primary caregiver in the child's most natural environment (Graves et al., 1996). The primary caregiver, typically a parent, works cooperatively with various professionals on implementing specific intervention strategies developed by an interdisciplinary team with the parents as members of the team. Service providers make regular and frequent visits to the home to work directly with the child, to assist and support the parent and other family members, and to monitor the child's progress. Forming meaningful partnerships with parents and families is crucial to the success of **home-based programs**. Although service providers are primarily concerned with advancing the developmental status of the child, they are also concerned with enhancing the well-being and competency of the family.

The Division for Early Childhood of the Council for Exceptional Children has developed a set of recommended practice guidelines for early intervention and early childhood special education programs (Sandall et al., 2005). Examples of these recommendations that are appropriate for home-based programs include the following four examples: Interventions should be embedded in naturally occurring daily activities such as snack and meal time, bathing, play activities, or bedtime.

- Interventions address family members' identified priorities and preferences.
- Interventions include all family members who desire to participate.
- Professionals and family members work collaboratively to achieve family-identified outcomes.

Delivering services in the child's home has multiple advantages. The primary advantage is that services are provided in a setting that is familiar to the child and by the child's first teacher—the parent. Parents also have the opportunity to intervene on an ongoing basis as behaviors naturally occur. Furthermore, skills learned in a child's natural environment are easier to maintain. Finally, disruption to the child's and family's routines are frequently minimized. With home-based programs, costs may be less, transportation is not a concern, and services are responsive to family needs. The potential for family involvement with the interventions is also greater. This model is especially appropriate for children living in rural or sparsely populated communities and, as we noted earlier, a home-based model is appropriate for infants and toddlers. Eighty-five percent of infants and toddlers receiving early intervention are provided these services in their home (U.S. Department of Education, 2009).

There are certain disadvantages to home-based models. A commonly noted drawback is the commitment required by, and the responsibilities placed

Cengage Learning

Services for infants and toddlers with delays or disabilities are often provided in their homes.

upon, the parent or primary caregiver. Not all parents are capable of providing effective intervention, nor is it a role they wish to assume. Providing intervention in a child's home also dictates that professionals demonstrate cultural sensitivity according to the values, beliefs, and customs of each family (Hanson, 2004). Furthermore, in some situations, the implementation of this model may be challenged due to family circumstances such as a single-parent household, conditions of poverty, and other risk factors. Opportunities for social interaction with other children are sometimes also absent in home-based models. Finally, a considerable amount of the professional's time is usually spent traveling from one home to another.

Center-Based Programs

As the name implies, **center-based programs** are located away from the child's home. Settings may be churches or synagogues, child care centers, preschools, public schools, Head Start centers, or other accessible locations. Center-based models are fairly common settings for preschoolers with special needs. Children are typically transported to the site where they receive intervention from professionals representing a variety of disciplines such as physical and occupational therapists or speech–language pathologists. The primary direct service provider for preschoolers with disabilities, however, is frequently the child's teacher. Center-based programs typically stress the acquisition of developmental, social, cognitive, and self-help skills necessary for success in elementary school (Hooper & Umansky, 2009).

Children usually attend a program for several hours each day. Some young children participate in daily programs, while others attend only two or three times a week. (See the Parent Voices feature for one mother's experience with a center-based program serving infants and toddlers.)

Recommended practice guidelines published by the DEC (Sandall et al., 2005) for center-based learning environments include the following representative examples:

- Classrooms are safe and clean environments, barrier free, and physically accessible for all children.
- Toys, learning materials, and activities are appropriate to the age and developmental needs of the children.
- Environments stimulate children's interactions and choice making while promoting high levels of engagement with peers and adults.

- Curriculum is consistent with developmentally appropriate practices and based on principles of child development.
- Professionals communicate with their colleagues and family members on a regular basis.

Center-based programs provide opportunities for parents to be central members of the team. Professionals consider the parents' participation to be necessary and beneficial. Parental involvement often increases the effectiveness of the interventions. According to Heward (2009), "virtually all effective programs for young children with disabilities recognize the critical need to involve parents" (p. 558).

Center-based models have several advantages. Frequently identified aspects include the following:

1. the development of social skills plus opportunities for social interaction between typically developing children and those with special needs;
2. access to comprehensive services from specialists representing many different disciplines;
3. availability of specialized equipment and materials;
4. enhanced efficiency of staff time;
5. parental involvement and the chance to develop social networks with other parents; and
6. exposure to experiences and the development of skills that will aid in the transition to kindergarten programs.

Parent Voices

A Mother's Story

Our son Ryan was diagnosed with multiple handicaps [disabilities] at the age of five months and I was thrown into a world I would never have chosen. Not for him and not for us.

Ryan was seven months old when we enrolled him in the center's infant intervention program. For an hour a week, a therapist from the center would work with Ryan, using toys and rattles, mirrors and music in an attempt to elicit a response.

The center revolves around the philosophy that early intervention can substantially boost a child's development, especially a child whose disabilities may prevent him from interacting with his world the way other children can. Patiently, the therapist showed me how

(continued)

Parent Voice

to position Ryan to encourage the strengthening of certain muscles, how to recognize his responses that signaled his interest in a toy, and how to interpret other subtle signals from him.

I remember one of these days very vividly. Ryan was lying on the mat and the therapist was shaking and rattling toys in an attempt to get him to hold his head up and look at the object. While she tried toy after toy, he just lay there motionless. There were two graduate students observing and two therapists evaluating. The quiet in that room was deafening. In my head I kept saying over and over: *Please look at the rattle . . . please look at the rattle.* Silently I tried to will him to move—to do something astounding.

One of the therapists reached over and turned on a musical windmill and suddenly that little head popped up off the mat and looked all around trying to locate the sound. The therapist sitting closest to me laughed and said under her breath, "Why, you little stinker!" They had found a motivator—music is what they would use to urge Ryan to do the things that were so difficult for him.

When he turned a year old, he entered the infant/toddler classroom, attending school twice a week for three-hour sessions. During those sessions, he would receive motor and speech therapy.

Ryan's motor ability was, and still is, severely limited. To even bring a toy to his mouth was a monumental achievement, often requiring repeated attempts. So he was put on a motor program to help him improve in this area. As a first step, he was given a battery-operated toy, which was operated by a switch. Ryan's training would involve repeated attempts (under the direction of his therapist) to hit the switch and activate the toy. Soon, they were substituting tape recorded songs for the toy. In addition to developing a certain, consistent reach in Ryan that might be useful in operating a wheelchair, the activity allowed him to finally control something himself.

One day while I sat and cheered him on, a therapist came in to watch. I had never met her, but obviously she knew Ryan. She stood quietly watching as his arm swung out into a wide arc, attempting over and over to hit the switch. When at last he made contact she bent over and kissed the top of his head. "Good job, Ryan," I heard her say softly to him. I sat in the corner and cried over the very special encouragement my child had received. I knew that in this school, he would learn many things, perhaps the most important being that he was lovable and worthy of our best efforts.

It hurts to watch your child struggle so hard to do the things that come naturally to other children. By spring, in Ryan's infant/toddler classroom, the others were all walking or learning to. Ryan was unable to even sit alone by himself, and sometimes activities that were perfect for the rest of the class seemed inappropriate for Ryan. One day I came in and found his teachers had placed him on the floor on his back and formed a circle around him with all the children. They sang "Ring-Around-the-Rosie" as they skipped around him. Ryan loved it, watching each face as it passed and squealing happily to the music.

As I watched him, I realized that while Ryan's disabilities were severe, it didn't need to limit him. He was as much a part of the class that day as any other child in the room. I will always be grateful to his teachers, Margo and Dawn, for finding ingenious ways to involve Ryan and for helping me to see that Ryan didn't have to sit back and watch life go by—he could be a part of it.

SOURCE: M. Hunt. A mother's story. *Children's Progress, 16*(2), 1988, pp. 4–6. Used by permission of Children's Hospital Medical Center of Akron.

Center-based programs are not without limitations and drawbacks. Disadvantages can include

1. the cost of transportation to and from the program (considered a related service according to IDEA)
2. extended periods of travel time to and from the program
3. the expense of maintaining the facility and its equipment
4. in comparison to a home-based delivery system, the possibility of limited opportunity for establishing meaningful working partnerships with parents.

In some situations, administrators of center-based programs are also confronted with the difficult task of providing services within a normalizing environment as mandated by IDEA. Unfortunately, too few public schools provide preschool programs for typical pupils; therefore, creative and alternative ways for serving young children with disabilities are being developed. A growing number of early childhood programs are including children with disabilities and are meeting their special needs by utilizing consultants or itinerant professionals for the delivery of specialized services (Sadler, 2003). Recent data provided by the U.S. Department of Education (2009) reveals that 48% of 3-, 4-, and 5-year-old children with disabilities are being served in a typical early childhood program. We suspect that this trend will continue.

In other instances, dual enrollments are being utilized. A young child with a disability, for example, might attend a program specifically for young children with disabilities in the morning, while in the afternoon care is provided in a proprietary setting like La Petite Academy or KinderCare. Thanks to the expanding influence of the Americans with Disabilities Act, young children with disabilities are enjoying greater access to programs designed for typically developing peers.

Combination Programs

Services to young children with disabilities and those who are at risk may require that program philosophies be merged in order to best serve and meet the unique needs of the child and his or her family. **Combination programs** provide this flexibility and reflect the advantages of both settings. A growing number of intervention programs include aspects of both

models. For example, in some instances a toddler with cerebral palsy may attend an inclusive child care center two mornings a week where she is the recipient of physical therapy while also receiving weekly home visits from a speech–language pathologist and an occupational therapist. Parent involvement and participation, however, remain a key component of this approach. In fact, because parent involvement is so crucial, many programs embrace a family-focused approach to providing services rather than the traditional child-focused approach. These programs aim to provide support and assistance to the entire family while building upon their strengths and resources.

Where services are delivered does not define the quality nor the effectiveness of an intervention program. A recommended practice approach suggests that a range of options be available so that parents may choose the service delivery option that best fits their needs and those of their son or daughter. Many special education professionals believe that what is most important is matching the services to the needs of the child while reflecting the priorities, needs, and values of the family. What is an appropriate program for one family may be inappropriate for another. Meyen (1996) believes that "the optimal model for service delivery depends on family and child characteristics and needs, intensity of services, and geographic characteristics of the service area" (p. 171). Cook and her colleagues (Cook, Klein, & Tessier, 2008) are in agreement with this argument. They too believe that no one location is best for all children and their families. They also remind us that any setting for delivering services must be culturally compatible with the values and child-rearing practices of the family.

Professional Teaming and Collaboration

The idea of professionals working together in a cooperative manner has been part of the fabric of special education for over 30 years. Since the implementation of PL 94-142, attention has been focused on how professionals from a variety of disciplines can work collaboratively in the planning and delivering of services to young children with special needs and their families. In fact, the concept of collaboration is an integral part of the philosophical foundation of

IDEA. It should be apparent that no one discipline, agency, or professional possesses all of the resources or clinical skills needed to devise appropriate interventions or construct appropriate educational plans for young children with disabilities, many of whom have complex needs. Furthermore, collaboration can be the vehicle by which services are provided in an integrated rather than fragmented fashion. Yet effective collaboration requires a high degree of cooperation and mutual respect among the various service providers.

A variety of disciplines are involved in delivering services to children with known or suspected disabilities. Examples of some of the professionals typically involved in the assessment and delivery of services to young children with special needs include early childhood special educators, physical therapists, speech–language pathologists, and psychologists in addition to a host of other professionals.

Teams differ not only in their composition but also according to their structure and function. Three types of team organizations are typically utilized in delivering services. The three most common approaches identified in the professional literature (Noonan & McCormick, 2006; McDonnell, Hardman, & McDonnell, 2003) include multidisciplinary, interdisciplinary, and transdisciplinary teams. These approaches are all interrelated and represent a historical evolution of teamwork. This evolutionary process can be portrayed as concentric circles with each model retaining some of the attributes of its predecessor (Gargiulo, 2009). Figure 5–3 illustrates these various configurations.

Multidisciplinary

The idea of a **multidisciplinary** team can be found in PL 94-142. This approach, whose origins are grounded on a medical model, utilizes the expertise of professionals from several disciplines, each of whom usually performs assessments and other tasks (e.g., report writing, goal setting) independent of the others. Each individual contributes according to his or her own specialty area with little regard for the actions of other professionals. There is a high degree of professional autonomy and minimal integration. It is viewed as a team only in the sense that all members share a common goal. There is very little coordination or collaboration across discipline areas (Gargiulo & Metcalf, 2010). Friend and Cook (2007) characterize

FIGURE 5–3 Multidisciplinary, Interdisciplinary, and Transdisciplinary Team Models

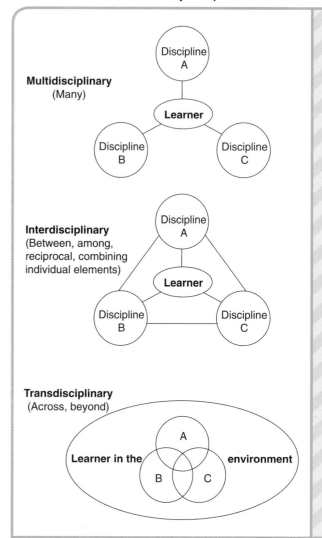

SOURCE: M. Giangreco, J. York, & B. Rainforth, 1989. Providing Related Services to Learners with Severe Handicaps in Educational Settings: Pursuing the Least Restrictive Option, *Pediatric Physical Therapy, 1(2)*, p. 57. Reprinted by permission.

this model as a patchwork quilt whereby different, and sometimes contrasting information, is integrated but not necessarily with a unified outcome.

Families often meet with each team member individually. They are generally passive recipients of information about their son or daughter. Because information to the parents flows from several sources, some parents may encounter difficulty synthesizing all of the data and recommendations from the various experts. We do not consider the multidisciplinary model to be especially family-friendly.

Interdisciplinary

PL 99-457 stresses the concept of interdisciplinary collaboration. With an **interdisciplinary** team, members perform their evaluations independently; however, program development and recommendations are the result of information sharing, joint planning, and mutual decision making. Significant cooperation exists among the team members, leading to an integrated plan of services. Coordination and collaboration are the hallmarks of this model. Direct services, however, such as physical therapy, are usually provided in isolation from one another. Families typically meet with the team or its representative; for the infant or toddler with special needs, this role is fulfilled by the service coordinator.

In addition to the potential for professional turf protection among team members, Noonan and McCormick (2006) call attention to another possible flaw with this model. They observe that information generally flows in one direction—from the various professionals involved in the assessment to the service provider. There is no mechanism in this model for the provider to give feedback as to the appropriateness of the intervention recommendations; for example, are they practical, functional, and meeting the needs of the child and the family?

Transdisciplinary

The **transdisciplinary** approach to providing services builds upon the strengths of the interdisciplinary model. It is distinguished, however, by two additional and related features: role sharing and a primary therapist. Professionals in the various disciplines conduct their initial evaluations; yet they relinquish their roles (role release) as service providers by teaching their skills to other team members, one of whom will serve as the primary interventionist. For young children with special needs, this role is usually filled by an early interventionist or an early childhood special educator. This individual relies heavily on the support and consultation provided by his or her professional peers. Discipline-specific interventions are still available, although they occur less frequently (Gargiulo & Metcalf, 2010).

"The primary purpose of this approach," according to Bruder (1994), "is to pool and integrate the expertise of team members so that more efficient and comprehensive assessment and intervention services may be provided" (p. 61). The aim of the transdisciplinary model is to avoid compartmentalization and fragmentation of services. It attempts to provide a more coordinated and unified or holistic approach to assessment and service delivery; team members function as a unit. Professionals from various backgrounds teach, learn, and work together in order to accomplish a common set of goals (Kilgo, 2006). Individuals who embrace this approach, however, need to be cautious that they do not overstep the boundaries of their professional competency and expertise.

A transdisciplinary service delivery model encourages a whole-child and whole-family approach (Raver, 2009). Families are full members of the team and share in the decision-making process. This model is currently the recommended model in early intervention and early childhood special education (Horn & Jones, 2005; Kilgo, 2006; Sandall et al., 2005).

"A transdisciplinary model," according to Davis and his colleagues (Davis, Kilgo, & Gamel-McCormick, 1998), "lends itself to integrated therapeutic services in the natural environment" (p. 57). This approach is recommended over a "pull-out" model whereby children are removed from a normalized setting in order to receive various services. Young children learn best through interactions and experiences that occur in their natural environment (Sandall et al., 2005). Integrated therapies that incorporate the child's typical routines and natural activities result in increased skill acquisition (Bruder, 1994).

The transdisciplinary model is equally appropriate for infants and toddlers with delays or disabilities and young children with special needs due to its emphasis on family involvement and cross-disciplinary collaboration. It is also recommended as the vehicle for ensuring mutual decision making and effective inclusionary practices (Bruder, 2001; Kilgo, 2006).

In conclusion, we predict that, for a variety of reasons (economics, personnel shortages, complexity of child/family needs), there will be a growing recognition of the importance of integrating interventions across developmental domains in spite of the difficulties inherent with interprofessional collaboration. Professional teaming will become the key to delivering services in a judicious fashion. Parents and professionals will increasingly find themselves linked

FIGURE 5–4 Characteristics of Team Models

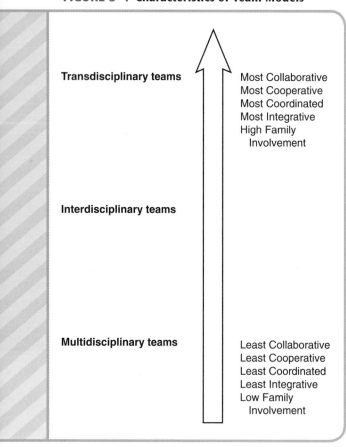

Transdisciplinary teams   Most Collaborative
                                 Most Cooperative
                                 Most Coordinated
                                 Most Integrative
                                 High Family
                                   Involvement

Interdisciplinary teams

Multidisciplinary teams   Least Collaborative
                                 Least Cooperative
                                 Least Coordinated
                                 Least Integrative
                                 Low Family
                                   Involvement

together as program partners. Figure 5–4 highlights, in hierarchical fashion, some of the characteristics of each team model we discussed, while Table 5–5 compares various components of each teaming model.

Cooperative Teaching[1]

In addition to the three models of professional teaming just examined, cooperative teaching is another example of collaborative efforts. It is not unusual to find general educators working in concert with early childhood special educators. Cooperative teaching is becoming an increasingly common service delivery approach for expanding instructional options for young children with disabilities. With this strategy, general education teachers and early childhood special educators work together in a collaborative and cooperative manner, with each professional sharing in the planning and delivery of instruction to a heterogeneous group of students.

Hourcade and Bauwens (2003), define **cooperative teaching** as

> direct collaboration in which a general educator and one or more support service providers voluntarily agree to work together in a co-active and coordinated fashion in the general education classroom. These educators, who possess distinct and complementary sets of skills, share roles, resources, and responsibilities in a sustained effort while working toward the common goal of school success for all students. (p. 41)

Likewise, Friend and Cook (2007) see cooperative teaching as a special form of teaming, a service delivery option whereby substantive instruction is jointly provided by one or more professionals to a diverse group of learners within the general education classroom.

Cooperative teaching is a service delivery approach based on collaboration. It is an instructional model that fosters shared responsibility for coordinating and delivering instruction to a group of children with unique learning needs. Essentially, cooperative teaching is about a true partnership and parity in the instructional process.

The aim of cooperative teaching is to create options for learning and to provide support to *all* learners in the general education classroom by combining the content expertise of the general educator with the instructional accommodation talents of the early childhood special educator (Murawski & Dieker, 2004; Wilson & Michaels, 2006). Cooperative teaching can be implemented in several different ways, as there are multiple versions of this instructional strategy. These arrangements, as identified by Friend and Cook (2007), typically occur for set periods of time each day or only on certain days of the week. Some of the more common instructional models for cooperative teaching are depicted in Figure 5–5. The particular strategy chosen often depends on the needs and characteristics of the children, curricular demands, amount of professional experience, and teacher preference, as well as such practical matters as the amount of space available. Many educators use a variety of arrangements depending upon their specific

---

[1] Information adapted from *Teaching in Today's Inclusive Classrooms* by R. Gargiulo and D. Metcalf, Belmont, CA: Wadsworth/Cengage Learning, 2010.

TABLE 5–5 **A Comparison of Multi-, Inter-, and Transdisciplinary Team Models**

	Multidisciplinary	Interdisciplinary	Transdisciplinary
Assessment	Separate assessments by team members	Separate assessments by team members	Team members and families conduct a comprehensive developmental assessment together
Parent participation	Parents meet with individual team members	Parents meet with team or team representative	Parents are full, active, and participating members of the team
IFSP/IEP development	Team members develop plans for their discipline	Team members share their separate plans with one another	Team members and the parents develop a service plan based on family priorities, needs, and resources
IFSP/IEP responsibility	Team members are responsible for implementing their section of the plan	Team members are responsible for sharing information with one another, as well as implementing their section of the plan	Team members are responsible and accountable for how primary service provider implements the plan
IFSP/IEP Implementation	Team members implement the part of the service plan related to their discipline	Team members implement their section of the plan and incorporate other sections, where possible	A primary service provider is assigned to implement the plan with the family
Communication style	Informal lines	Periodic case-specific team meetings	Regular team meetings where continuous transfer of information, knowledge, and skills occurs among team members
Guiding philosophy	Team members recognize the importance of contributions from other disciplines	Team members are willing and able to develop, share, and be responsible for providing services that are a part of the total service plan	Team members make a commitment to teach, learn, and work together across discipline boundaries to implement unified service plan

Source: Adapted from G. Woodruff and M. McGonigel, Early intervention team approaches: The transdisciplinary model. In J. Jordan, J. Gallagher, P. Hutinger, and M. Karnes (Eds.), *Early Childhood Special Education: Birth to Three*, (Reston, VA: Council for Exceptional Children, 1998), p.166. Reprinted by permission.

circumstances. We will now briefly describe some of the more common cooperative teaching options.

One Teach, One Observe. In this version of cooperative teaching, one teacher presents the instruction to the entire class while the second educator circulates gathering information (data) on a specific child, a small group of students, or targeted behaviors across the whole class such as productive use of center time. Although this model requires a minimal amount of joint planning, it

FIGURE 5–5 Cooperative Teaching Arrangements

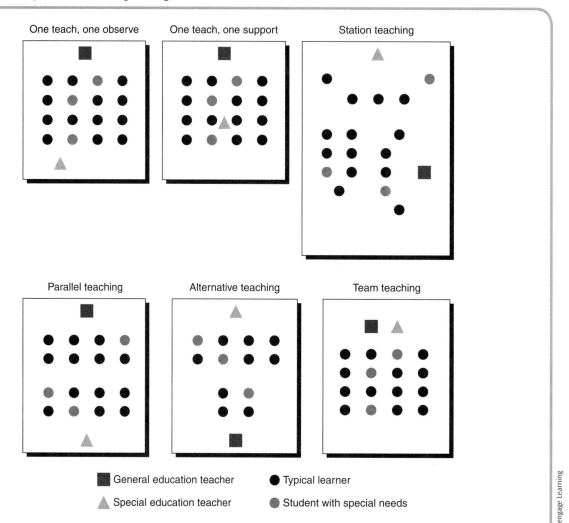

SOURCE: Adapted from M. Friend and L. Cook, *Interactions: Collaboration Skills for School Professionals*, 5th ed. (Boston: Pearson Education, 2007), p. 121. Reprinted by permission.

is very important that teachers periodically exchange roles to avoid one professional being perceived by children, and possibly parents, as the "assistant teacher."

One Teach, One Support. Both individuals are present, but one teacher takes the instructional lead while the other quietly provides support and assistance to the children. It is important that one professional (usually the early childhood special educator) is not always expected to function as the assistant; rotating roles can help to alleviate this potential problem. It is

also recommended that this model be used sparingly or as one of several approaches in order to prevent students from becoming overly dependent on additional assistance as well as jeopardizing the credibility of one of the teachers.

Station Teaching. In this type of cooperative teaching, the lesson is divided into two or more segments and presented in different locations in the classroom. One teacher presents one portion of the lesson while the other teacher provides a different portion. Then

---

TeachSource Video

Developmental Disabilities in Middle Childhood

Visit the premium website and watch "Developmental Disabilities in Middle Childhood." After watching this video, answer the following question:

1. Do you think it is a good idea for a general education teacher and a special educator to jointly work in the same classroom? Support your position.

---

the groups rotate, and the teachers repeat their information to new groups of children. Depending on the class, a third station can be established where students work independently or with a learning buddy to review material. Station teaching has been shown to be effective at all grade levels and it affords both teachers the opportunity to instruct all of the pupils, albeit on different content.

Parallel Teaching. This instructional arrangement lowers the teacher/pupil ratio. Instruction is planned jointly but is delivered by each teacher to one-half of a heterogeneous group of children. Coordination of efforts is crucial. This format lends itself to drill-and-practice activities rather than initial instruction or projects that require close teacher supervision. As with station teaching, noise and activity levels may pose problems.

Alternative Teaching. Some children benefit from small-group instruction; alternative teaching meets that need. With this model, one teacher provides instruction to a heterogeneous group of learners while the other teacher interacts with a small group of children. Although commonly used for remediation purposes, alternative teaching is equally appropriate for enrichment as well as preteaching activities and indepth study. Teachers need to be cautious, however, that children with delays or disabilities are not exclusively and routinely assigned to the small group; all members of the class should participate periodically in the functions of the smaller group.

Team Teaching. In this type of cooperative teaching, which is the most collaborative of our six models, both teachers equally share the instructional activities for the entire class. Each teacher, for example, may take turns leading a discussion about eating healthily, or

one teacher may talk about the parts of speech while the coteacher gives several examples illustrating this concept. Students view each teacher, therefore, as having equal status. This form of cooperative teaching, sometimes called interactive teaching (Walther-Thomas, Korinek, McLaughlin, & Williams, 2000), requires a significant amount of professional trust and a high level of commitment. Compatibility of teaching styles is another key component for successful teaming.

Advantages and disadvantages of cooperative teaching options are summarized in Table 5–6.

Delivering Individualized Services

Effective programs for infants, toddlers, preschoolers, and early primary students with special needs require that professionals and parents work together as a team. Perhaps nowhere else is this linkage more crucial than in the development of an **individualized family service plan (IFSP)**, an **individualized education program (IEP)**, or a **504 accommodation plan**. By mandate of federal law, each young child identified as being eligible for special education is required to have an individualized program plan of specially designed instruction that addresses the unique needs of the child and his or her family. The design and delivery of customized services and instruction is guided by one of these documents.

Individualized Family Service Plan

Recall from Chapter 2 that the IFSP is the blueprint behind the delivery of early intervention services to

TABLE 5–6 Advantages and Disadvantages of Representative Cooperative Teaching Arrangements

Instructional model	Advantages	Disadvantages
Team teaching (whole class)	• Provides systematic observation/ data collection • Promotes role/content sharing • Facilitates individual assistance • Models appropriate academic, social, and help-seeking behaviors • Teaches question asking • Provides clarification (e.g., concepts, rules, vocabulary)	• May be job sharing, not learning enriching • Requires considerable planning • Requires modeling and role-playing skills • Becomes easy to "typecast" specialist with this role
Station teaching (small group)	• Provides active learning format • Increases small-group attention • Encourages cooperation and independence • Allows strategic grouping • Increases response rate	• Requires considerable planning and preparation • Increases noise level • Requires group and independent work skills • Is difficult to monitor
Parallel teaching (small group)	• Provides effective review format • Encourages student responses • Reduces pupil/teacher ratio for group instruction or review	• Hard to achieve equal depth of content coverage • May be difficult to coordinate • Requires monitoring of partner pacing • Increases noise level • Encourages some teacher-student competition
Alternative teaching (large group, small group)	• Facilitates enrichment opportunities • Offers absent students catch-up times • Keeps individuals and class on pace • Offers time to develop missing skills	• May select same low-achieving students for help • Creates segregated learning environments • Is difficult to coordinate • May single out students

Source: Adapted from C. Walther-Thomas, L. Korinek, V. McLaughlin, and B. Williams, *Collaboration for Inclusive Education* (Needham Heights, MA: Allyn & Bacon, 2000), p. 190. Reprinted by permission.

infants and toddlers who are at risk or disabled. While primarily focusing on children younger than age three, changes in thinking now allow the document to be used with preschoolers who require a special education. In an effort to minimize the differences between early intervention and preschool special education services, the government has encouraged states to establish "seamless systems" designed to serve children birth through age five (Stowe & Turnbull, 2001). As a result of this policy decision, states now have the authority to use IFSPs for preschoolers with special needs until the child's sixth birthday. States are reminded that when a free and appropriate public education is provided by an IFSP, the Part B rights and protections still apply (U.S. Department of Education, 1994). As of 2007, three states are studying the feasibility of using IFSPs for their preschool population; Oregon uses IFSPs as statewide policy; 16 additional states allow local discretion in using the IFSP for delivering preschool services (Lazara et al., 2007).

The shift in policy is partly derived from a belief that similarities in service delivery for individuals birth through age five are greater than the differences. Additionally, the needs of children are generally best met with a single system of service. While there are several exchangeable features of IEPs (which we will discuss shortly) and IFSPs, a few distinguishable components stand out; for example, the IEP is silent regarding the issue of service coordination and transition planning for young children. Another difference is the IFSP acknowledgment of the family as the focal point of services in contrast to the emphasis in the IEP on the individual child and his or her educational needs.

The IFSP is developed by a team consisting of professionals and the child's parents, who are the key members of the team. Additionally, parents may invite other family members, as well as an advocate, to participate. Typically, the service coordinator who has been working with this family, those professionals involved in the assessment of the child, and the service providers constitute the remainder of the group charged with the responsibility of writing the IFSP.

An IFSP is to be developed within a reasonable period of time. The U.S. Department of Education interprets this requirement to mean within 45 days of referral. The following required components are the result of the enactment of PL 108-446:

- A statement of the infant's or toddler's present levels of physical development, cognitive development, communication development, social or emotional development, and adaptive development based on objective criteria.
- A statement of the family's resources, priorities, and concerns...
- A statement of measurable results or outcomes expected to be achieved for the infant or toddler and the family, including preliteracy and language skills, as developmentally appropriate for the child, and the criteria, procedures, and timelines used to assess progress toward achieving the results or outcomes...
- A statement of early specific intervention services, based on peer-reviewed research, necessary to meet the unique needs of the infant or toddler and the family, including the frequency, intensity, and method of delivering services. (See Table 5–6 for a list of representative early intervention services.)
- A statement of the natural environments in which early intervention services shall be provided... or justification if services are not provided in said environment.
- The projected dates for initiation of services and the anticipated duration of such services.
- The identification of the service coordinator.
- The steps . . . supporting the transition of the toddler with a disability to preschool or other appropriate services.

TABLE 5–7 Representative Early Intervention Services Available to Infants/Toddlers and Their Families

Assistive technology devices and services
Audiology
Family training and counseling
Health services
Medical services (only for diagnosis and evaluation)
Nursing services
Nutrition services
Occupational therapy
Physical therapy
Psychological services
Service coordination
Social work services
Special education
Speech–language pathology
Transportation services
Vision services

The IFSP, which is to be reviewed at least every six months, is intentionally designed to preserve the family's role of primary caregiver. Well-constructed IFSPs fully support the family and encourage its active and meaningful involvement. (See Appendix C for an IFSP completed for Maria Ramirez and her family.) This thinking is in keeping with an empowerment model, which views families as capable (with occasional assistance) of helping themselves (Gargiulo, 2009). This point of view allows parents to retain their decision-making role, establish goals, and assess their needs, among other functions. It is also in keeping with our support of an ecological perspective that argues that one cannot look at a child without considering the various systems and spheres of influence that provide support—in this instance, the infant's or toddler's family and community.

Various features of the IFSP reflect a family focus. One feature in particular, however, stands out: the assessment of the family's resources, priorities, and concerns. Although IDEA encourages early intervention programs to gather this information, family assessment is to be a voluntary activity on the part of the families. While a personal interview with key family members is one way to gather information, there are questions among professionals about the most appropriate strategies to use for obtaining information about the family (Noonan & McCormick, 2006). Furthermore, any information obtained must be gathered in a culturally sensitive fashion and reflect the family's perception of their resources, priorities, and concerns.

Bruder (2001) urges professionals to carefully listen to what families have to say so that they may better understand what is important for the family. We fully agree with this thinking and encourage service providers to appreciate the concerns and understand the priorities of the family from the family's perspective. We would like to reiterate our earlier point: families need to be the primary decision makers about what is best for them and their sons or daughters. Our job is to help them in this effort.

Information obtained from the family and data about the infant's developmental status are used to generate outcome statements or goals for the child and his or her family. Practitioners are increasingly emphasizing real-life or authentic goals for infants and toddlers (as well as preschoolers) with special needs (Pretti-Frontczak & Bricker, 2004). These goals are reflected in the ISFP's required outcome statements.

Recommended practice suggests that these statements focus on the priorities and concerns of the family.

Interventionists no longer teach skills in isolation; rather, goals are developed that are relevant to the daily activities and routines of the child and his or her family. These statements need to be practical and functional, reflecting authentic situations that occur in the natural environment. Contemporary thinking encourages service providers to structure learning opportunities that emphasize the acquisition of competence in natural settings. According to Notari-Syverson and Shuster (1995), five components are necessary for meaningful goals:

1. *Functionality*—skills necessary for independently interacting within the daily environment.
2. *Generality*—general vs. specific skills that are adaptable to meet the individual needs of the child.
3. *Ease of integration*—skills that can be used in a variety of natural environments such as the home, classroom, or playground.
4. *Measurability*—skills must be capable of being measured such as their frequency or duration.
5. *Hierarchical relationship*—complex skills need to be logically sequenced, building upon earlier behaviors.

Table 5–8 provides a checklist constructed by Notari-Syverson and Shuster for determining whether or not the IFSP statements fulfill the preceding criteria.

Individualized Education Program

The IEP is part of an overall strategy designed to deliver needed services appropriate to the individual preschooler (and older students). By the time we reach the IEP stage, the appropriate permissions have been gathered, assessments conducted, and an eligibility determination has been made. We are now at the point where the IEP is to be developed, followed by placement in the most appropriate and least restrictive setting with reviews occurring at least annually. (Parents may request a review prior to the annual review.) A complete reevaluation of the pupil's eligibility for special education must occur every three years. PL 105–17 waives this stipulation, however, if both parents and school officials agree that such a review is unnecessary.

Bateman and Linden (2006) make a very important point about *when* the IEP is developed. They

TABLE 5–8 Checklist for Writing IFSP (and IEP) Goals and Objectives for Infants and Young Children

Functionality

1. Will the skill increase the child's ability to interact with people and objects within the daily environment?
   The child needs to perform the skill in all or most of environments in which he or she interacts.
   Skill: Places object into container.
   Opportunities: Home—Places sweater in drawer, cookie in paper bag.
   School—Places lunchbox in cubbyhole, trash in trash bin.
   Community—Places milk carton in grocery cart, rocks and soil in flower pot.

2. Will the skill have to be performed by someone else if the child cannot do it?
   The skill is a behavior or event that is critical for completion of daily routines.
   Skill: Looks for objects in usual location.
   Opportunities: Finds coat on coat rack, gets food from cupboard.

Generality

3. Does the skill represent a general concept or class of responses?
   The skill emphasizes a generic process, rather than a particular instance.
   Skill: Fits objects into defined spaces.
   Opportunities: Puts mail in mailbox, places crayons in box, puts cutlery into sorter.

4. Can the skill be adapted or modified for a variety of disabling conditions?
   The child's sensory impairment should interfere as little as possible with the performance.
   Skill: Correctly activates simple toy.
   Opportunities: Motor impairments—Activates light, easy-to-move toys (e.g., balls, rocking horse, toys on wheels, roly-poly toys).
   Visual impairments—Activates large, bright, noise-making toys (e.g., bells, drums, large rattles).

5. Can the skill be generalized across a variety of settings, materials, and/or people?
   The child can perform the skill with interesting materials and in meaningful situations.
   Skill: Manipulates two small objects simultaneously.
   Opportunities: Home—Builds with small interlocking blocks, threads lace on shoes.
   School—Sharpens pencil with pencil sharpener.
   Community—Takes coins out of small wallet.

Instructional Content

6. Can the skill be taught in a way that reflects the manner in which the skill will be used in the daily environments?
   The skill can occur in a naturalistic manner.
   Skill: Uses object to obtain another object.
   Opportunities: Use fork to obtain food, broom to rake toy; steps on stool to reach toy on shelf.

7. Can the skill be elicited easily by the teacher/parent within the classroom/home activities?
   The skill can be initiated easily by the child as a part of daily routines.
   Skill: Stacks objects.
   Opportunities: Stacks books, cups/plates, wooden logs.

(continued)

TABLE 5–8 **Checklist for Writing IFSP (and IEP) Goals and Objectives for Infants and Young Children**
(continued)

Measurability

8. Can the skill be seen and/or heard?
   Different observers must be able to identify the same behavior.

   Measurable skill: Gains attention and refers to object, person, and/or event.

   Nonmeasurable skill: Experiences a sense of self-importance.

9. Can the skill be directly counted (e.g., by frequency, duration, distant measures)?
   The skill represents a well-defined behavior or activity.

   Measurable skill: Grasps pea-sized object.

   Nonmeasurable skill: Has mobility in all fingers.

10. Does the skill contain or lend itself to determination of performance criteria?
    The extent and/or degree of accuracy of the skill can be evaluated.

    Measurable skill: Follows one-step directions with contextual cues.

    Nonmeasurable skill: Will increase receptive language skills.

Hierarchical Relation Between Long-Range Goal and Short-Term Objective

11. Is the short-term objective a developmental subskill or step thought to be critical to the achievement of the long-range goal?

    Appropriate: Short-term objective—Releases object with each hand.

                    Long-range goal— Places and releases object balanced on top of another object.

    Inappropriate: 1. The short-term objective is a restatement of the same skill as the long-range goal with the addition of an instructional prompt.

                    2. The short-term objective is not conceptually or functionally related to the long-range goal.

Source: Adapted from A. Notari-Syverson and S. Shuster, 1995. Putting Real-Life Skills into IEP/IFSPs for Infants and Young Children, *Teaching Exceptional Children*, 27(2), p. 31. Reprinted by permission.

feel that IEPs are often written at the wrong time. Legally, the IEP is to be developed within 30 days following the evaluation and determination of the child's disability but *before* a placement recommendation is formulated. Placement in the LRE is based on a completed IEP, not the other way around (see Figure 5–6). A commonly noted abuse is developing the IEP on the basis of available placements or simple administrative convenience. Although professionals frequently follow this procedure, it is illegal. What often happens is that we wind up fitting children into programs rather than planning programs to meet the

TeachSource Video

Bobby: Serving a Student with Special Needs in an Inclusive Elementary Classroom

Revisit the "Bobby: Serving a Student with Special Needs in an Inclusive Elementary Classroom" video on the premium website and answer the following question:

1. What can professionals do to encourage parent–professional collaboration in the IEP process?

FIGURE 5–6 Correct Route for IEP Placement Decision Making

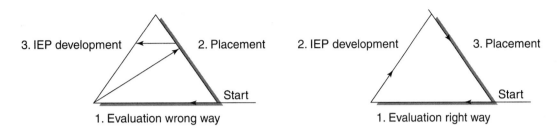

3. IEP development   2. Placement

Start

1. Evaluation wrong way

2. IEP development   3. Placement

Start

1. Evaluation right way

Source: Adapted from B. Bateman and M. Linden, *Better IEPs: How to Develop Legally Correct and Educationally Useful Programs*, 4th ed. (Verona, WI: Attainment Company, 2006). p. 91. Reprinted by permission.

needs of the students. The IEP is not to be limited by placement options or the availability of services.

The benchmark of early childhood special education is individualization. Instead of fitting the child into the program (curriculum), a curriculum is tailored that meets the individual needs of the student. One of the cornerstones of constructing appropriate curricula for young children with special needs is the IEP. Based upon a multidisciplinary educational evaluation of the pupil's strengths and needs, an individualized plan of learning activities and goals is prescribed. It is perhaps best to envision the IEP as a management tool or planning vehicle that ensures that children with disabilities receive an individualized education appropriate to their unique needs. According to Gargiulo (2009), the IEP "stipulates *who* will be involved in providing a special education,

IEPs and IFSPs are written by a team.

Cengage Learning

what services will be offered, *where* they will be delivered, and for *how long*. In addition, an IEP gauges *how successfully* goals have been met" (p. 68).

Like the IFSP, IEPs are written by a team. At a minimum, participation must include one or both parents/guardians; the child's teachers (including a special educator and at least one general education teacher); an individual capable of interpreting evaluation results; and a representative from the school district. When appropriate, the student and other professionals whose expertise is desired may participate at the discretion of the parent or school.

Parents have a legal right to meaningfully participate in this planning and decision-making process; they serve as the child's advocates. While IDEA mandates a collaborative role for parents, it does not stipulate the degree or extent of their participation. The parents choose the extent to which they wish to be involved. They alone define their role on the team. Professionals must respect the parents' right to choose their level of involvement and participation.

The role of the general and special education teacher is crucial in the IEP development process; these professionals are usually ultimately responsible for implementing the team's decisions. Contemporary thinking suggests that both the special educator and early childhood teacher should equally be viewed as the child's teacher. Their role in developing the IEP is complementary and mutually supporting.

Table 5–9 illustrates the required content of an IEP according to IDEA 2004. These elements must be in effect at the beginning of each school year. In addition, federal regulations require that the IEP team also consider the following factors when developing a child's IEP.

TABLE 5–9 Elements of a Meaningful IEP

- *Current performance.* A statement of the student's present levels of educational and functional performance, including how pupil's disability affects his or her involvement and progress in the general education curriculum, or for preschoolers, how the disability affects participation in age-appropriate activities

- *Goals.* A statement of measurable annual goals (both functional and academic) that addresses the student's involvement and progress in the general education curriculum as well as the student's other education needs; short-term objectives or benchmarks are required for pupils who take alternate assessments aligned to alternate achievement standards

- *Special education and related services.* A statement of special education, related services, and supplementary aids and services (based on peer-reviewed research) to be provided, including program modifications or supports necessary for the student to advance toward attainment of annual goals; to be involved and progress in the general education curriculum, extracurricular, and nonacademic activities; and to be educated and participate in activities with other children both with and without disabilities

- *Participation with typical students.* An explanation of the extent, if any, to which the student will *not* participate in the general education classroom

- *Participation in state- and district-wide assessments.* A statement of any individual modifications needed for the student to participate in state- or district-wide assessment; if student will not participate, a statement of why the assessment is inappropriate and how the pupil will be assessed

- *Dates and places.* Projected date for initiation of services; expected location, duration, and frequency of such services

- *Transition services.* Beginning at age 16, a statement of needed transition services identifying measurable postschool goals (training, education, employment, and, if appropriate, independent living skills), including a statement of interagency linkages and/or responsibilities

- *Measuring progress.* A statement of how progress toward annual goals will be measured and how student's parents (guardians) will be regularly informed of such progress

- *Age of majority.* At least one year before reaching age of majority, information regarding transferral of rights to student upon reaching age of majority

Source: R. Gargiulo, *Special Education in Contemporary Society*, 3rd ed. (Thousand Oaks, CA: Sage, 2009), p. 68. Reprinted by permission.

- If a pupil's behavior impedes his or her learning or that of classmates, the use of proactive behavioral supports.
- For a student with limited English proficiency, consider the language needs of the child as those needs relate to the IEP.
- For a child who is blind or visually impaired, provide for instruction in Braille and the use of Braille unless the IEP teams determines that instruction in Braille or the use of Braille is inappropriate.
- For a child who is deaf or hard of hearing, consider the child's language or communication needs, including his or her preferred mode of communication.
- The need for assistive technology devices and services (Noonan & McCormick, 2006; Walsh, Smith, & Taylor, 2000).

Unfortunately, the preceding elements do not contain any provision for family goals and services as found in an IFSP. Yet there is no rationale for excluding this component. In fact, it could reasonably be argued that this element is equally important for preschool children with disabilities and their families as it is for infants and toddlers. The DEC Recommended Practices Task Force (Sandall et al., 2005) also believes that services for young children with special needs should be family centered, reflecting family priorities rather than strictly academic priorities.

One possible remedy for this situation would be to use an IFSP (as permitted by state law) instead of an IEP until the child's sixth birthday.

For a comparison of the required components of an IEP and IFSP, see Table 5–10.

TABLE 5–10 Comparable Components of an IEP and an IFSP

Individualized Education Program	Individualized Family Service Plan
• A statement of child's present levels of academic achievement and functional performance, including involvement and progress in the general education curriculum; for preschool children, how the disability affects participation in age-appropriate activities	• A statement of the infant's or toddler's present levels of physical, cognitive, communication, social/emotional, and adaptive development
• No comparable feature	• A statement of the family's resources, priorities, and concerns
• A statement of measurable annual goals, including benchmarks or short-term instructional objectives, for children who take alternate assessments aligned to alternate achievement standards	• A statement of measurable results or outcomes expected to be achieved for the infant or toddler and the family
• A statement indicating progress toward annual goals and a mechanism for regularly informing parents/guardians of such progress	• Criteria, procedures, and timelines used to determine the degree to which progress toward achieving the outcomes or results is being made
• A statement of specific special education and related services and supplementary aids and services, based on peer-reviewed research, to be provided and any program modifications	• A statement of specific early intervention services, based on peer-reviewed research, necessary to meet the unique needs of the infant or toddler and the family
• An explanation of the extent to which the child will not participate in general education programs	• A statement of the natural environments in which early intervention services will appropriately be provided, or justification if not provided
• Modifications needed to participate in state- or district-wide assessments	• No comparable feature
• The projected date for initiation of services and the anticipated duration, frequency, and location of services	• The projected date for initiation of services and the anticipated duration of services
• No comparable feature	• The name of the service coordinator
• At age 16, a statement of transition services needed, including courses of study in addition to measurable postsecondary goals	• The steps to be taken to support the child's transition to other services at age 3

Source: Adapted from Individuals with Disabilities Education Improvement Act of 2004, Title 20 U.S. Code (U.S.C.) 1400 *et seq*, Part B Section 614 (d) (1) (A), and Part C Section 636 (d).

The IEP serves as the basis for constructing a tailor-made plan of instruction for each preschooler and student with a disability who is in need of a special education. IEPs are not constructed, however, to be so detailed or complete that they serve as the entire instructional agenda (Gargiulo, 2009), nor are they intended to prescribe curriculum (Goodman & Bond, 1993). IEP goals are designed, according to Cook et al. (2009), "to target remediation of particular developmental lags or to accelerate learning" (p. 129). These goals, listed by priority, form the foundation from which daily instructional plans can be developed within developmental domains. Typical areas might include speech and language, motor skills, social development, cognitive activities, or self-help skills.

Based on the pupil's present level of performance, goals are drafted that represent reasonable estimates of the child's progress. Goal setting is a complex process. It is exceedingly difficult to project accomplishments for preschool children who exhibit cognitive, social, and emotional disabilities (Goodman & Bond, 1993). Priorities for determining measurable annual goals are formulated on the basis of critical needs—what the child needs in order to meaningfully participate in present and future environments (Noonan & McCormick, 2006). Educational goals for preschoolers with delays or disabilities should reflect skills that are relevant to everyday functioning, focus on authentic or real-life situations, and occur within naturally existing activities and routines.

Goals statements are intentionally broad. Their intent is to provide long-range direction to a child's educational program and not to define exact instructional tasks. The business of guiding instruction is the role filled by short-term objectives, typically one to three months in duration. These statements, written after goals have been crafted, describe the sequential steps the pupil will take to meet the intent of the goals statement(s). IDEA 2004 only requires objectives, however, for school-age students who take alternate assessments aligned to alternate achievement standards—typically individuals with very serve disabilities. Instructional objectives are usually written by the child's teacher.

Criteria for effective short-term objectives, commonly called benchmarks, include three components: a description of the behavior using observable and measurable terminology; a statement of conditions under which the behavior will be exhibited; and finally, a standard or performance criterion for assessing the adequacy of the student's accomplishment (Lignugaris/Kraft, Marchand-Martella, & Martella, 2001). Writing meaningful instructional objectives is not an easy task. Teachers are sometimes confused about what constitutes a useful objective. Recall that Notari-Syverson and Shuster (1995) believe that high-quality objectives should be functional, measurable, generalizable, and easily integrated into daily routines, as well as being conceptually related to the goal statements. These indicators of quality are equally appropriate for developing IEPs and IFSPs.

In conclusion, the quality of an IEP largely depends on having well written and appropriate goals that address the unique needs of the child. The IEP should be viewed as a "living" or dynamic document, guiding the delivery of special education services to young children with special needs. It is not something to be filed away and forgotten until the end of the academic year approaches. IEPs are the vehicle for ensuring that a specially designed educational

TeachSource Video

Preschool: IEP and Transition Planning for a Young Child with Special Needs

Visit the premium website and watch "Preschool: IEP and Transition Planning for a Young Child with Special Needs." After watching this video, answer the following questions:

1. How might a teacher's attitude affect his or her perception of a child's capabilities?
2. Why is it important for parents, teachers, and other professionals to work in a collaborative fashion? Identify five steps you would use to increase parent involvement.

program is provided. (See Appendix D for a typical IEP developed for four-year-old T.J. Browning.)

Section 504 Accommodation Plan[2]

Recall from Chapter 2 that **Section 504** of the Rehabilitation Act of 1973 (PL 93-112) is a civil rights law designed to prohibit discrimination against individuals with disabilities. The intent of this legislation, according to Smith (2002), is to create equal opportunities for persons with disabilities. Far-reaching in its intent and coverage, this law holds great significance for educators. Section 504 provides, among other things, that students with disabilities (who are otherwise qualified) have equal access to programs, activities, and services that are available to pupils without disabilities. This provision includes, for example, field trips, extracurricular activities, and academic courses (with appropriate accommodations) in addition to physical accessibility. Interestingly, because this law is an antidiscrimination statute, federal funds are not available to help schools meet the various requirements of Section 504. As this law pertains to education, PL 93-112 requires schools adhere to the following provisions:

- Annually identify and locate all children with disabilities who are unserved.
- Provide a "free, appropriate public education" to each student with a disability, regardless of the nature or severity of the disability. This means providing general or special education and related aids and services designed to meet the individual educational needs of persons with disabilities as adequately as the needs of nondisabled persons are met.
- Ensure that each student with disabilities is educated with nondisabled students to the maximum extent appropriate.
- Establish nondiscriminatory evaluation and placement procedures to avoid the inappropriate education that may result from the misclassification or misplacement of students.
- Establish procedural safeguards to enable parents and guardians to participate meaningfully in

decisions regarding the evaluation and placement of their children.
- Afford children with disabilities an equal opportunity to participate in nonacademic and extracurricular services and activities. (Office for Civil Rights, Department of Education, 1989, p. 8.)

Who Is Protected by Section 504? Although 504 protections are afforded to persons with disabilities across their lifespans, our focus here is on school-age individuals, particularly early primary students. As we noted in Chapter 2, all students eligible for services under IDEA are also protected by Section 504. The converse of this statement is not true, however. Some examples of pupils eligible for services under Section 504 include

- a student referred for special education services but who does not qualify under IDEA;
- individuals who are no longer eligible for services under IDEA or who transition out of a special education program;
- students with a history of substance abuse;
- victims of abuse and neglect;
- pupils with health needs, such as diabetes, asthma, severe allergies, hemophilia, or communicable diseases; and
- someone with a low IQ but who is not considered intellectually disabled.

Obviously, due to the broader scope of the definition of a disability incorporated in Section 504, significantly greater numbers of students are eligible to receive a free, appropriate public education via Section 504 than would be afforded services under IDEA.

Accommodation Plans. Once a student has been found eligible for Section 504 services, an accommodation plan must be developed. Section 504 accommodation plans should be simple, inexpensive, and easy to use. The majority of accommodations will occur in the general education classroom. It is important to note that special educators are not liable for Section 504 accommodations; this responsibility belongs to general education teachers. Designed for an individual pupil, these plans should include the information necessary to enable the individual to have equal access to educational and extracurricular activities while also providing an equal opportunity to be successful (Smith, 2002). Many of the accommodations

---

[2] Information adapted from *Teaching in Today's Inclusive Classrooms* by R. Gargiulo and D. Metcalf, Belmont, CA: Wadsworth/Cengage Learning, 2010.

are common sense and will vary depending on the needs of the learner. Examples include

- preferential seating
- extended test time
- rest periods during the school day
- tape-recorded lessons
- modified attendance policies
- oral testing options
- peer note-taker
- outlines and study guides
- textbooks kept at home

MAKING CONNECTIONS

Section 504 Accommodation Plan

Name: Cheryl Chinn   **Birthdate:** August 1, 2004
School: Tuggle Elementary   **Grade:** 1st
Teacher: Jane Newman   **Date:** November 10, 2010
Review Date: At the end of the 6-week grading period
General Strengths: Cheryl has above-average intellectual ability. Although socially immature, she is popular with her classmates. Discipline is generally not a problem. Supportive and concerned parents.
General Weaknesses: Cheryl exhibits ADHD. She has difficulty concentrating (except for brief periods of time) and is easily distracted. Classroom assignments and homework are frequently not completed. Recent evidence of growing frustration and loss of self-esteem.

Specific Accommodations

Accommodation #1
Class: All classes
Accommodation(s): Worksheets will be modified so less material is presented on each page. Allow extra time for completion if necessary
Person Responsible for Implementation: Mrs. Newman

Accommodation #2
Class: All classes
Accommodation(s): Cheryl will be given access to a study carrel when working on classroom assignments or taking tests.
Person Responsible for Implementation: Mrs. Newman

Accommodation #3
Class: All classes
Accommodation(s): Cheryl will record daily homework activities in assignment notepad. Teacher will check for accuracy and parents will sign notepad and return it to school.
Person Responsible for Implementation: Mrs. Newman

Accommodation #4
Class: All classes
Accommodation(s): Cheryl will receive praise and recognition for task completion and appropriate behavior. Teacher to provide immediate feedback whenever possible.
Person Responsible for Implementation: Mrs. Newman
General Comments: Weekly progress reports to parents via telephone or e-mail.

(continued)

MAKING CONNECTIONS

Accommodation Plan Team Members:

Name	Team Member's Signature	Position/Title
Ms. Elizabeth Chinn	Elizabeth Chinn	Parent/Guardian
Mr. Robert Johnson	Robert Johnson	Assistant Principal/504 Coordinator
Ms. Nancy Washington	Nancy Washington	School Counselor
Mr. Samuel Oden	Samuel Oden	Resource Teacher
Ms. Jane Newman	Jane Newman	General Educator

Copies: Parent
Classroom Teacher(s)
Cumulative File
Other: _____
_____

Source: Form adapted from T. Smith and J. Patton, *Section 504 and Public Schools: A Practical Guide* (Austin, TX: Pro-Ed, 1998), p. 45.

Accommodation plans do not have mandated components like IEPs do. The format of these plans will, therefore, greatly vary. At a minimum, this document should identify the pupil's strengths and needs, the type of accommodation required, the individual(s) responsible for implementation, and team members. See the accompanying Making Connections feature for an example of a 504 plan completed for Cheryl Chinn.

Transition

Change is inevitable in the lives of young children with special needs. Each year thousands of youngsters move from one type of early childhood program to another. The most common reason for this transition is the age of the child (Allen & Cowdery, 2009). When this movement occurs, it generally affects the children, their caregivers, and service providers. Change also brings with it the potential of stress due to the disruption of patterns of behavior and fearfulness of new situations and environments. Yet a typical dimension in the lives of infants, toddlers, and preschoolers with delays or disabilities and their families is change, or transition, to new service programs. We succinctly define **transition** as the process of moving from one type of placement to another. Examples of transition can range from moving from a hospital neonatal intensive care unit to home-based services, from an early intervention program to a community-based inclusive preschool program, or from a Head Start program to kindergarten. A transition can also occur within a particular program and is exemplified when a child begins working with a new teacher or is placed in a different classroom. Regardless of the type of transition that occurs, key elements of this process include planning, coordination, cooperation, and followup.

One of the main goals of both early intervention and early childhood special education programs is successful transitions. If accomplished, it presents to the children and their families opportunities for growth and development. It can also be an enabling experience. Poorly orchestrated transitions, however, may lead to stress, anxiety, frustration, and confusion.

Transitions may occur at any time during the early childhood years. They can be characterized as either vertical or horizontal transitions (Winter, 2007). Vertical transitions occur across settings within the same time frame. For example, for preschoolers with disabilities, it occurs upon entering a preschool special education program and exiting from it. Young children may enter from day care, early intervention programs, or from being at home, and they leave to be placed in kindergartens or other appropriate educational settings. A horizontal transition refers to the provision of multiple services typically offered by different providers and delivered at different locations. For instance, a four-year-old boy with Down syndrome might attend an inclusive preschool program in the mornings and an after-care facility in the afternoon while receiving physical therapy once a week at his therapist's office.

Inherent in the concept of transition is allegiance to the philosophy of normalization. An attempt is usually made to place a child in a program less restrictive or more normalized than the preceding one. Our goal should always be to serve the child in the most natural and normalized setting (Noonan & McCormick, 2006).

One of the goals of the primary objectives of transition planning is to enable the child to be as successful as possible in future environments (Howard, Williams, & Lepper, 2005). In concert with this aim, the DEC Task Force on Recommended Practices (1993) identified three goals of the transition planning process.

1. to ensure continuity of service;
2. to minimize disruption of the family system; and
3. to promote the individual's functioning in the natural environment.

The need for effective transitioning is clearly articulated in IDEA and its accompanying rules and regulations. The legislation is very specific about this issue. Part C, which focuses on infants and toddlers, specifies that the IFSP must include a transition plan that outlines the procedures to be undertaken as infants and toddlers move from early intervention to preschool special education programs. Language in Part B, the preschool grant program, also emphasizes the importance of carefully planned transitions. Yet there is no legislative mandate for transition planning as students move from preschool special education programs to kindergarten. The intent, however, is undeniable—there must be a continuity of services. A few states have even developed, or are in the process of constructing, policies and agreements that will guide and provide for a seamless system of services for children birth through age five (Lazara et al., 2007).

When a transition occurs, it impacts more than the toddler or preschooler. Recall that we assert that change also effects families and professionals as well. It is a crucial time for all involved. Bronfenbrenner (1977) supports this idea and contends that transitions produce "ripple effects" within systems. Like a pebble being dropped in a pond, when a young child moves from an infant program to a preschool program or from a preschool special education program to a kindergarten, this change in ecology disturbs the existing ecological structure. Obviously, the child's microsystem is changed. Parents will establish new parent–professional relationships; thus, the mesosystem is also modified. Furthermore, involvement with a variety of new and different agencies (ecosystems) is possible, and encounters with different regulations, rulings, and even values (macrosystem) are very likely. Professionals must be sensitive to how families react to these changes. The more existing behavior patterns and routines are disrupted, the greater the likelihood that stress and anxiety will develop. One remedy for this problem is careful and skillful preparation for transitioning. A smooth transition relies on proactive and comprehensive planning. Preparation, by necessity, involves the child, family, and service providers. We now turn our attention to strategies for meaningfully involving key team members.

Child Involvement

A critical component of successful transition is the preparation of the child. A smooth transition depends, in a large part, on the child demonstrating the skills and behaviors required in the new environment. This information is usually gathered by future environment surveys, which describe behaviors needed in the receiving program. Generally speaking, there should be a match between the skills in the child's repertoire and the requirements and expectations of the new placement (DEC Task Force on Recommended Practices, 1993). This typically requires an assessment of the individual's strengths and needs

Planning is crucial for successful transitions.

and subsequent instruction in the essential social, behavioral, and academic requirements of the new environment. Identifying and teaching critical skills and routines will enable the student to participate with greater independence and success in the new setting (Cavallaro & Haney, 1999). Knowing what skills are expected in the new learning environment also facilitates the transition process (Downing, 2008).

Noonan and McCormick (2006) note that early childhood educators generally do not consider skills associated with academic readiness as crucial as those associated with independence such as following directions, adhering to classroom rules and routines, and participating in group activities. It is important to remember, however, that in any discussion, essential skills and behaviors are seen as optimal goals, *not* prerequisites for placement in a new setting (Allen & Cowdery, 2009). A child's failure to demonstrate

specific skills should not prohibit movement to a new placement. Rather, it is a starting point for identifying needed adaptations, supports, and initial intervention targets, and for preparing the child for a successful transition experience (Downing, 2008; Noonan & McCormick).

Family Involvement

The family of a young child with special needs plays a vital role in the transition process. Recall that in Chapter 2, we argue for professionals to see the child within the context of the family and the family in interaction with larger social systems. A transition from an early intervention program to a community-based inclusive preschool provides us with a good example. An effective transition requires that professionals not only prepare the child but also fully involve and prepare the family for movement (see the Making Connections feature). A change in programs can be especially stressful for families—routines and schedules are altered, new relationships are established, and old ones relinquished. Attendance at meetings is often necessary as well as helpful in establishing new goals and expectations for the child. An active role in the decision-making process and meaningful involvement can minimize the adverse effects of change. Families must be integrally involved in the transition planning. Professionals must view the child's family as an equal member of the transition team (Sandall et al., 2005).

While parents have much to offer professionals, as well as much to gain by their involvement in the transition process, professionals must be sensitive to the needs, priorities, and expectations of the individual family. Each family has its own preferred level of involvement. Professionals need to ascertain what the optimal level of involvement is for each family. Teachers and other service providers should not assume that all families want to be involved in the transition process, nor are all families prepared for the responsibility (Allen & Cowdery, 2009).

Cavallaro and Haney (1999) point out that family members will often require support and information in order to actively participate in the transition process. Successful transitions require adherence to what we identify as the four essential Cs: *C*ollaboration, *C*ooperation, *C*ommunication, and *C*omprehensive planning with families.

Professional Involvement

The third component of our tripartite strategy for ensuring smooth transitions requires the involvement of a variety of service providers. Professionals from the program the child is exiting (sending program), as well as providers from the program the child is entering (receiving program), must be involved. Team members will most likely include general and special educators, administrators, physical and occupational therapists, speech–language pathologists, service coordinators, and a host of other professionals involved in providing services to the child with disabilities and his or her family. It is very important that professionals from both the sending and receiving programs work together and understand one another's goals and procedures (Noonan & McCormick, 2006). Cooperative and collaborative planning between groups will help to facilitate a smooth transition. Formal program/agency policies and procedures will also aid in the transition process. Joint involvement is important due to the number of logistical and programmatic issues that need to be addressed. Examples of these concerns include the identification of program exit criteria, coordination responsibilities, transfer of records, and discussion of placement options. Figure 5–7 provides a flowchart/checklist of transition activities necessary for facilitating effective transitions.

MAKING CONNECTIONS

Family Participation in Transition Planning

With the approach of Maria Ramirez's third birthday, her early intervention team members have recommended to Mr. and Mrs. Ramirez that Maria transition from her home-based program to an inclusive, community-based program in order to begin receiving Part B services. Her parents and grandparents are very reluctant to agree to this recommendation. They have expressed their concerns to their service coordinator. Among their worries are working with a whole new staff, the length of Maria's school day, her involvement with typical playmates, her social readiness, transportation difficulties, and other potential problems.

We offer the following suggestions illustrating specific activities that may assist Mr. and Mrs. Ramirez in understanding the transition process, in addition to diminishing their anxieties about their daughter's success in a new setting. Remember, successful transitions depend, in part, on being sensitive to the needs and concerns of the parents.

- Service coordinator schedules meeting with parents (and grandparents if desired) to discuss their preferences, explain transition process and rationale, review legal rights, and ascertain parents' need for support.
- Arrange for Maria and Mr. and Mrs. Ramirez (and grandparents) to visit the facility. Opportunity for parents to meet staff, teachers, and related service providers. Maria visits her classroom and meets other children and staff.
- As desired by Maria's parents, service coordinator arranges meeting with parents of other children enrolled in the class and/or provides Mr. and Mrs. Ramirez with appropriate written materials.
- At least 90 days prior to Maria's third birthday, her service coordinator, in cooperation with Maria's parents, other early intervention team members, and professionals from the program jointly develop a transition plan.
- With parents' permission, service coordinator arranges for program staff to observe Maria's therapy sessions to ensure continuity of service and to answer parents' questions.
- Service coordinator arranges for Maria to visit her classroom on several different occasions. Parents (and grandparents) are provided an opportunity to qualitatively assess impact of attendance on their daughter.

FIGURE 5–7 **Flowchart/Checklist of Transition Steps**

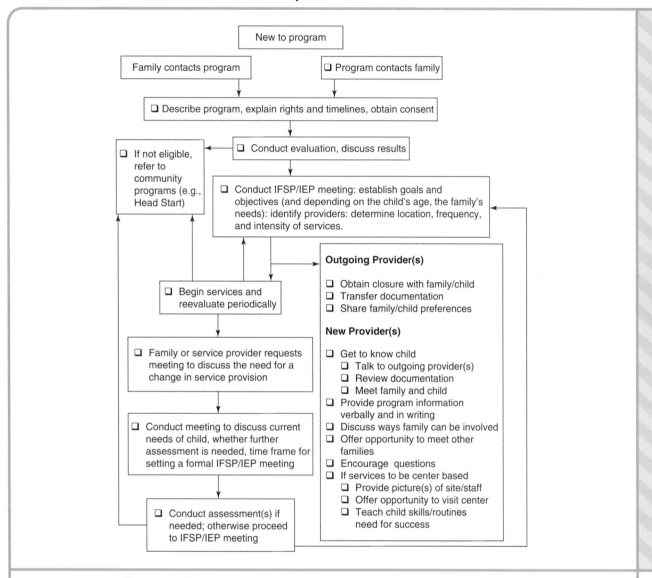

Source: B. Hussey and H. Bernstein, Transitions and Service Coordination in Early Childhood and Early Childhood Special Education, in *The Program Administrator's Guide to Early Childhood Special Education*, J. Taylor, J. McGowan, and T. Linder (Eds.), (Baltimore: Paul H. Brookes, 2009), p. 178. Reprinted by permission.

Parents should perceive the transition process as routine and predictable. Services should be minimally interrupted, if at all. Unfortunately, this often is not the case. Although effective transition policies are seen as crucial to the development of a coordinated system of transitioning children from one service delivery system to another, families frequently perceive the process as frustrating and traumatic (Harbin et al., 2000).

Noonan and McCormick (1993) recommend that service providers attempt to minimize the differences between sending and receiving environments. If at all possible, the transition should be gradual rather than abrupt and should commence anywhere from 6 to 12 months before the toddler or preschooler exits his or her current program. Children in transition need time to adjust to the demands and expectations of the new setting. These experts offer the following five steps that teachers from the sending program can undertake to facilitate movement to the new program—in this example a kindergarten.

1. *Field trips to the "new" school.* Ideally such tours would include lunch in the cafeteria, some time for play on the playground, and participation in a few kindergarten activities.
2. *Reading stories about the fun of new adventures and new friends.* Read (or make up) stories about new experiences.

3. *Helping the children create a scrapbook about kindergarten.* Each child's scrapbook could include photos taken during the field trip, as well as pictures of kindergarten activities created by the child.
4. *Role playing "going to the new school."* In the course of role-play sessions, encourage the children to express their feelings about the new experiences.
5. *Invite kindergarten teachers to visit the class.* Try to arrange for each receiving kindergarten teacher to visit the preschool class. The goal is for the kindergarten teachers to get to know the children in familiar setting. (p. 370)

TABLE 5–11 Steps in Planning Transitions

1. Form a transition team—including parents, current program staff, and staff of the most likely receiving programs.

2. Schedule meetings—the first meeting will be to develop an initial written plan; the later meetings will consider specific transition tasks.

3. Identify possible receiving settings.

4. Identify basic transition tasks—what will be necessary to implement the transition?

5. Agree on assignments—specifically, who will perform each of the different transition tasks.

6. Establish timelines—including the referral date and dates for preplacement activities.

7. Decide communication procedures—including transfer of records and other information.

8. Agree on preplacement activities—such as
   a. Parent visits to potential receiving environments.
   b. Information sharing between teaching staff in sending and receiving agencies.
   c. Observations in the receiving setting to determine needed adaptations.
   d. Arrangements for whatever family support will be provided.
   e. Therapy and other special services.
   f. Future consultative interactions.

9. Plan for follow-up activities—should be planned and carried out between the family and the agencies involved.

10. Place the child—after needed environmental adaptations have been completed.

11. Provide consultation and therapy services.

12. Follow up and evaluate.

SOURCE: M. Noonan and L. McCormick, *Early Intervention in Natural Environments* (Pacific Grove, CA: Brooks/Cole, 1993). p. 359.

These steps provide an excellent illustration of the type of activities T.J. Browning's teachers could use to facilitate his movement from the Epps Head Start Center to kindergarten.

Steps for Planning Effective Transitions

Smooth transitions don't just happen; they demand extensive preparation on the part of everyone involved. Effective transitions require adherence to a series of well planned steps. Utilizing the following strategies and recommendations can help to minimize the disruption of services; reduce stress for the child, parents, and service providers; and ensure that movement from one program to another progresses as smoothly as possible. The intent of transition planning is to maximize the students' chances for success in their future environment.

Noonan and McCormick (2006) believe that transitions involve three distinct phases: preparation, implementation, and followup. Each of these elements is evident in Table 5–11. These steps are equally appropriate when planning transitions from an early intervention program to a preschool program in addition to offering suggestions on transitioning from a preschool special education placement to a kindergarten.

Effective transition planning, however, does not terminate upon a child's entry into the receiving program; rather, it is an ongoing process. Transition team members should continue to serve as resources for the family and each other even after the child transitions.

For additional information on transition planning, we recommend that early childhood professionals consult the website of the National Early Childhood Transition Center at the University of Kentucky, http://www.hdi.uky.edu/nectc.

Summary

One subject that has sparked considerable debate among professionals is the movement toward full inclusion of preschoolers with special needs into early childhood programs designed for typically developing children. Portrayed as an evolving concept, this issue has its vocal advocates as well as opponents. Calls for full inclusion represent a radical departure from present-day service delivery models. While we fully endorse the principle of maximum integration, we believe that any placement decision should be formulated based on the child's best interest, while also respecting the wishes of the parent(s). There is no one ideal placement capable of meeting the needs of *all* learners.

Young children with special needs receive services in a variety of locations. Traditionally, these settings have been identified as center-based, home-based, or combination programs; yet no one service delivery approach is necessarily superior to another. The delivery of services must be tailored to the individual needs of the infant, toddler, or preschooler and his or her family. The field is presently experiencing a thrust toward more integrated and normalized environments for young children with disabilities. Our challenge is to develop models that allow for the delivery of comprehensive services in the most integrated setting.

Young children with special needs typically receive services from a multitude of professionals. The idea of professionals from various disciplines working together is a well established aspect of early childhood special education. No one discipline, agency, or professional possesses all of the skills or resources needed to develop appropriate educational experiences for infants, toddlers, and preschoolers with disabilities. Professionals need to work together, usually forming teams. Three common team structures typically encountered by young children with special needs and their families are multidisciplinary, interdisciplinary, and transdisciplinary models. Each model has its own unique features and serves a specific function. We see value in the importance of teaming and professional collaboration. It serves as the foundation for delivering services in a judicious fashion.

Cooperative teaching, in its multiple forms, is a special type of professional teaming. It is a service delivery approach based on collaboration whose purpose is to create options for learning and offer support to *all* children in the general education classroom.

States have been encouraged to develop seamless systems for providing services to children with special needs birth through age five. One consequence of this shift in government policy is that individualized family service plans (IFSPs) can be used to guide the delivery of services to preschoolers with disabilities as well as to infants and toddlers. We see this as a commendable effort at providing for continuity and minimizing the disruption of services to young children with special needs and their families.

The IFSP is the driving force behind the delivery of services to infants and toddlers who are disabled or at risk. The IFSP acknowledges the child's family as the focal point of services. This focus is clearly evident in the required statement of the family's resources, priorities, and concerns. A well-developed IFSP encourages the parents' full and meaningful involvement while supporting their role as primary decision makers for their son or daughter.

An individualized education program, more commonly referred to as an IEP, is the vehicle that ensures that preschoolers and school-age students with disabilities receive an individualized education appropriate to their unique needs. Written by a team, it is the basis for constructing a customized plan of instruction. At the heart of an IEP are well written goals. An IEP is not developed solely for compliance purposes; rather, it is a dynamic document and the primary tool for providing a specially designed educational program.

Section 504 accommodation plans are frequently developed for students who have special needs but are not eligible for a special education under IDEA. Developed by general educators, these plans are designed to ensure that these individuals have equal access to programs, services, and activities that are available to pupils without disabilities.

Movement or transitioning from one type of placement to another is an important element of early intervention and early childhood special education programs. Successful transitions are enabling experiences for both the child and the family. The intent is to provide for continuity of services. Smooth transitions dictate comprehensive planning and collaboration in addition to ongoing communication among all parties involved. The preparation for transitioning must involve the child and the parent(s), as well as both current and new service providers.

Check Your Understanding

1. What are normalized environments for young children with disabilities?
2. Describe the evolution of the movement toward full inclusion.
3. Take a position either for or against full inclusion. Support your viewpoint.
4. Identify some of the advantages and disadvantages of center-based and home-based service delivery models.
5. What are the similarities and differences between multidisciplinary, interdisciplinary, and transdisciplinary team models?
6. Why is a transdisciplinary approach to providing services currently viewed as recommended practice?
7. Describe cooperative teaching. What are the advantages and disadvantages of this instructional option?
8. What is the rationale for using IFSPs for preschool children with special needs?
9. List the required components of an IFSP.
10. Identify at least five types of early intervention services available to infants/toddlers and their families.
11. What are the reasons for including families in the development of an IFSP?
12. What is the purpose of an IEP?
13. How does an IEP differ from an IFSP?
14. Describe the function of a 504 accommodation plan.
15. What roles do the child, parents, and service providers play in the transition process?
16. List five outcomes or goals of the transition process.

Reflection and Application

1. Compare and contrast home-based and center-based models as appropriate intervention settings for young children with special needs. How can the quality of related support services be ensured in each model?
2. Examine each of the three teaming models discussed in this chapter. What is the role of the family in each model? How might the role of the family be strengthened in each model?
3. Visit early childhood facilities and public schools in your area that engage in cooperative teaching. What form of cooperative teaching did you observe? How do the teachers feel about this form of teaming? What do they see as the advantages and disadvantages of cooperative teaching?

4. Locate a preschooler with a disability who attends an inclusive center-based program. Talk to the child's teacher and parents to determine what they see as the advantages and disadvantages of this setting. What do the parents desire for their child's future environment? Develop a transition plan that will effectively prepare him or her for this new placement.

References

Allen, K., & Cowdery, G. (2009). *The exceptional child* (6th ed.). Clifton Park, NY: Thomson/Delmar.

Bateman, B., & Linden, M. (2006). *Better IEPs: How to develop legally correct and educationally useful programs* (4th ed.). Verona, WI: Attainment Company.

Bricker, D. (1978). A rationale for the integration of handicapped and nonhandicapped preschool children. In M. Guralnick (Ed.), *Early intervention and the integration of handicapped and nonhandicapped children* (pp. 3–26). Baltimore: University Park Press.

Bricker, D. (1995). The challenge of inclusion. *Journal of Early Intervention, 19*(3), 179–194.

Bronfenbrenner, U. (1977). Toward an experimental ecology of human development. *American Psychologist, 32*(7), 513–531.

Bruder, M. (1994). Working with members of other disciplines: Collaboration for success. In M. Wolery & J. Wilbers (Eds.), *Including children with special needs in early childhood programs* (pp. 45–70). Washington, DC: National Association for the Education of Young Children.

Bruder, M. (2001). Inclusion of infants and toddlers. In M. Guralnick (Ed.), *Early childhood inclusion: Focus on change* (pp. 203–228). Baltimore: Paul H. Brookes.

Carta, J., Schwartz, I., Atwater, J., & McConnell, S. (1991). Developmentally appropriate practice: Appraising its usefulness for young child with disabilities. *Topics in Early Childhood Special Education, 11*(1), 1–20.

Cavallaro, C., & Haney, M. (1999). *Preschool inclusion.* Baltimore: Paul H. Brookes.

Cook, R., Klein, M., & Tessier, A. (2008). *Adapting early childhood curricula for children in inclusive settings* (7th ed.). Upper Saddle River, NJ: Pearson Education.

Davis, M., Kilgo, J., & Gamel-McCormick, M. (1998). *Young children with special needs: A developmentally appropriate approach.* Needham Heights, MA: Allyn & Bacon.

DEC Task Force on Recommended Practices. (1993). *DEC recommended practices: Indicators of quality in programs for infants and young children with special needs and their families.* Reston, VA: Council for Exceptional Children.

Downing, J. (2008). *Including students with severe and multiple disabilities in typical classrooms.* Baltimore: Paul H. Brookes.

Friend, M., & Cook, L. (2007). *Interactions: Collaboration skills for school professionals* (5th ed.). Needham Heights, MA: Allyn & Bacon.

Gallagher, P., & Lambert, R. (2006). Classroom quality, concentration of children with special needs, and child outcomes in Head Start. *Exceptional Children, 73*(1), 31–52.

Gargiulo, R. (2009). *Special education in contemporary society* (3rd ed.). Thousand Oaks, CA: Sage.

Gargiulo, R., & Metcalf, D. (2010). *Teaching in today's inclusive classrooms.* Belmont, CA: Wadsworth/Cengage Learning.

Gartner, A., & Lipsky, D. (1987). Beyond special education: Toward a quality system for all students. *Harvard Educational Review, 57,* 367–395.

Gartner, A., & Lipsky, D. (1989). New conceptualizations for special education. *European Journal of Special Needs Education, 4*(1), 16–21.

Goodman, J., & Bond, L. (1993). The individualized education program: A retrospective critique. *Journal of Special Education, 26*(4), 408–422.

Graves, S., Gargiulo, R., & Sluder, L. (1996). *Young children: An introduction to early childhood education.* St. Paul: West.

Guralnick, M. (1990). Major accomplishments and future directions in early childhood mainstreaming. *Topics in Early Childhood Special Education, 10*(2), 1–17.

Guralnick, M. (1994). Mothers' perceptions of the benefits and drawbacks of early childhood mainstreaming. *Journal of Early Intervention, 18*(2), 163–168.

Hallahan, D., Kauffman, J., & Pullen, P. (2009). *Exceptional learners* (11th ed.). Boston: Pearson Education.

Hanson, M. (2004). Ethnic, cultural, and language diversity in service settings. In E. Lynch & M. Hanson (Eds.), *Developing cross cultural competence* (3rd ed., pp. 3–18). Baltimore: Paul H. Brookes.

Harbin, G., McWilliam, R., & Gallagher, J. (2000). Services for young children with disabilities and their families. In J. Shonkoff & S. Meisels (Eds.), *Handbook of early childhood intervention* (2nd ed., pp. 387–415). Cambridge, England: Cambridge University Press.

Heward, W. (2009). *Exceptional children* (9th ed.). Upper Saddle River, NJ: Pearson Education.

Hooper, S., & Umansky, W. (2009). *Young children with special needs* (5th ed.). Upper Saddle River, NJ: Pearson Education.

Horn, E., & Jones, H. (2005). Collaboration and teaming in early intervention and early childhood special education. In E. Horn & H. Jones (Eds.), *Interdisciplinary teams* (Monograph No. 6, pp. 11–20). Longmont, CO: Sopris West.

Hourcade, J., & Bauwens, J. (2003). *Cooperative teaching: Rebuilding and sharing the schoolhouse* (2nd ed.). Austin, TX: Pro-Ed.

Howard, V., Williams, B., & Lepper, C. (2005). *Very young children with special needs* (3rd ed.). Upper Saddle River, NJ: Pearson Prentice Hall.

Kauffman, J. (1989). The regular education initiative as Reagan-Bush education policy: A trickle-down theory of education of the hard-to-teach. *Journal of Special Education, 23*(3), 256–278.

Kauffman, J., Landrum, T., Mock, D., Sayeski, B., & Sayeski, K. (2005). Diverse knowledge and skills require a diversity of instructional groups: A position statement. *Remedial and Special Education, 26*(1), 2–6.

Kilgo, J. (Ed.). (2006). *Transdisciplinary teaming in early intervention/early childhood special education.* Olney, MD: Association for Childhood Education International.

Lazara, A., Danaher, J., & Kraus, R. (Eds.). (2007). *Section 619 profile* (15th ed.). Chapel Hill, NC: University of North Carolina, FPG Child Development Institute, National Early Childhood Technical Assistance Center.

Lieberman, L. (1990). REI: Revisited . . . again. *Exceptional Children, 56*(6), 561–562.

Lignugaris/Kraft, B., Marchand-Martella, N., & Martella, R. (2001). Writing better goals and short-term objectives or benchmarks. *Teaching Exceptional Children, 34*(1), 52–58.

McDonnell, A., & Hardman, M. (1988). A synthesis of "best practices" guidelines for early childhood services. *Journal of the Division for Early Childhood, 12,* 328–341.

McDonald, J., Hardman, M., & McDonald, A. (2003). *Introduction to persons with moderate and severe disabilities* (2nd ed.). Needham Heights, MA: Allyn & Bacon.

Meyen, E. (1996). *Exceptional children* (3rd ed.). Denver: Love.

Murawski, W., & Dieker, L. (2004). Tips and strategies for co-teaching at the secondary level. *Teaching Exceptional Children, 36*(5), 52–58.

Noonan, M., & McCormick, L. (1993). *Early intervention in natural environments.* Pacific Grove, CA: Brooks/Cole.

Noonan, M., & McCormick, L. (2006). *Young children with disabilities in natural environments.* Baltimore: Paul H. Brookes.

Notari-Syverson, A., & Shuster, S. (1995). Putting real-life skills into IEP/IFSPs for infants and young children. *Teaching Exceptional Children, 27*(2), 29–32.

Odom, S., & Wolery, M. (2003). A unified theory of practice in early intervention/early childhood special education. *Journal of Special Education, 37*(3), 164–173.

Office for Civil Rights. (1989). *The civil rights of students with hidden disabilities under Section 504 of the Rehabilitation Act of 1973.* Washington, DC: Author.

Osborne, A., & DiMattia, P. (1994). The IDEA's least restrictive mandate: Legal implications. *Exceptional Children, 61*(1), 6–14.

Pretti-Frontczak, K., & Bricker, D. (2004). *An activity-based approach to early intervention.* Baltimore: Paul H. Brookes.

Raver, S. (2009). *Early childhood special education—0 to 8 years.* Upper Saddle River, NJ: Pearson Education.

Rose, D., & Smith, B. (1993). Preschool mainstreaming: Attitude barriers and strategies for addressing them. *Young Children, 48*(4), 59–62.

Sadler, F. (2003). The itinerant special education teacher in the early childhood classroom. *Teaching Exceptional Children, 35*(3), 8–15.

Sandall, S., & Ostrosky, M. (2000). *Natural environments and inclusion.* Longmont, CO: Sopris West.

Sandall, S., Hemmeter, M., Smith, B., McLean, M. (2005). *DEC recommended practices: A comprehensive guide to practical application.* Longmont, CO: Sopris West.

Sexton, D., Snyder, P., Sharpton, W., & Stricklin, S. (1993). Infants and toddlers with special needs and their families. *Childhood Education, 69*(5), 276–286.

Smith, T. (2002). Section 504: What teachers need to know. *Remedial and Special Education, 37*(5), 259–266.

Stainback, S., & Stainback, W. (1987). Integration versus cooperation: A commentary on "Educating children with learning problems: A shared responsibility." *Exceptional Children, 54*(1), 517–521.

Stainback, W., & Stainback, S. (1984). A rationale for the merger of special and regular education. *Exceptional Children, 51*(2), 102–111.

Stowe, M., & Turnbull, H. (2001). Legal considerations of inclusion for infants and toddlers and preschool-age children. In M. Guralnick (Ed.), *Early childhood inclusion: Focus on change* (pp. 69–100). Baltimore: Paul H. Brookes.

U.S. Department of Education. (1994). *Sixteenth annual report to Congress on the implementation of the Individuals with Disabilities Education Act.* Washington, DC: U.S. Government Printing Office.

U.S. Department of Education. (2009). *IDEA data.* Available at https://www.ideadata.org

Walsh, S., Rous, B., & Lutzer, C. (2000). The federal IDEA natural environments provision. In S. Sandall & M. Ostrosky (Eds.), *Natural environments and inclusion* (pp. 3–15). Longmont, CO: Sopris West.

Walsh, S., Smith, B., & Taylor, R. (2000). *IDEA requirements for preschoolers with disabilities.* Reston, VA: Council for Exceptional Children.

Walther-Thomas, C., Korinek, L., McLaughlin, V., & Williams, B. (2000). *Collaboration for inclusive education.* Needham Heights, MA: Allyn & Bacon.

Wang, M., & Reynolds, M. (1985). Avoiding the "catch-22" in special education reform. *Exceptional Children, 51*(6), 497–502.

Will, M. (1986a). Educating children with learning problems: A shared responsibility. *Exceptional Children, 52*(5), 411–415.

Will, M. (1986b). *Educating students with learning problems: A shared responsibility.* Washington, DC: U.S. Department of Education, Office of Special Education and Rehabilitative Services.

Wilson, G., & Michaels, C. (2006). General and special education students' perceptions of co-teaching: Implications for secondary-level literacy instruction. *Reading and Writing Quarterly, 22*(3), 205–225.

Winter, S. (2007). *Inclusive early childhood education.* Upper Saddle River, NJ: Pearson Education.

Wolfensberger, W. (1972). *Normalization: The principle of normalization in human services.* Toronto: National Institute on Mental Retardation.

Yell, M. (1995). Least restrictive environment, inclusion, and students with disabilities: A legal analysis. *Journal of Special Education, 28*(4), 389–404.

Yell, M. (2006). *The law and special education* (2nd ed.). Upper Saddle River, NJ: Pearson Education.

Zigmond, N. (2003). Where should students with disabilities receive special education services? Is one place better than another? *Journal of Special Education, 37*(3), 193–199.

Zigmond, N. (2007). Delivering special education is a two-person job: A call for unconventional thinking. In J. Crockett, M. Gerber, & T. Landrum (Eds.), *Achieving the radical reform of special education: Essays in honor of James M. Kauffman* (pp. 115–137). Mahwah, NJ: Erlbaum.

6 Curriculum for Young Children with Special Needs

Key Terminology

Curriculum

Outcomes

Developmental domains

Scope

Sequence

Cognitive skills

Gross motor skills

Fine motor skills

Communication

Language

Speech

Receptive language

Expressive language

Social skills

Adaptive skills

Universally designed curriculum

Developmental approach

Developmental-cognitive approach

Academic (or Preacademic) approach

Behavioral approach

Functional approach

Curriculum model

Developmentally appropriate practice (DAP)

Age appropriateness

Individual appropriateness

Cultural appropriateness

Activity-based intervention

Learning Outcomes

After reading this chapter, you will be able to:

- Provide a definition of curriculum in early intervention/early childhood special education.

- Describe the interrelated developmental domains and content areas of curriculum.

- Explain how curriculum has evolved in early intervention/early childhood special education as a result of historical, legislative, and philosophical influences.

- Discuss the influence of various curriculum approaches on curriculum development for young children with disabilities.

- Provide examples of well known curriculum models with advantages and disadvantages of each and the applicability to young children with delays or disabilities.

- Describe developmentally appropriate practice (DAP), including the three components.

- Discuss the similarities and differences between DAP from general early childhood education (ECE) and recommended practices from early childhood special education (ECSE).

- Explain a model for blending recommended practices from ECE and ECSE.

- Describe a framework for curriculum development for young children with disabilities.

- Provide examples of curriculum resources for young children with disabilities.

In recent years, the fields of general early childhood education (ECE) and early childhood special education (ECSE) have placed increased attention on curriculum for young children. This chapter provides an overview of curriculum development for young children with delays or disabilities, birth through age eight. After curriculum is defined and the developmental domains of curriculum are described, a brief description follows of the historical, legal, and philosophical influences on curriculum. The major theoretical perspectives that have shaped curriculum in early intervention and early childhood special education and well known curriculum models that are used in programs today also are described. A discussion follows of recommended practices from the fields of general ECE and ECSE. ECE and ECSE address the needs of young children in the same age range, birth through age eight. Emphasis is placed on the similarities and differences in ECE and ECSE practices and how these perspectives can be blended to best meet the needs of young children with disabilities and their families. The chapter provides a comprehensive framework for curriculum and the process used to develop curriculum in programs serving young children with disabilities.

Overview of Curriculum

Curriculum is one of a number of program features that contribute to the effectiveness of early intervention/early childhood special education for children with disabilities (Bruder, 1997). Many definitions of curriculum can be found in early childhood literature. In the past, the term *curriculum* represented, at least to some, a purchased package of materials, objectives, and activities designed to guide instruction. This, of course, is an extremely narrow view of curriculum. In this chapter, we move beyond this limited view of curriculum and recognize the historical, legislative, and philosophical influences on curriculum development. We also highlight the importance of the child's unique needs and interests, the child's environment, the family's priorities, and the desired child outcomes. **Outcomes** are defined as what is to be taught to young children with delays or disabilities (Carta & Kong, 2009).

Professionals in general early childhood education today view curriculum in terms of a theoretical model reflecting beliefs about what should be taught and in what sequence. Copple and Bredekamp (2009) describe curriculum as consisting of "the knowledge, skills, abilities, and understandings children are to acquire and the plans for the learning experiences through which those gains will occur" (p.20). According to this definition, curriculum is viewed as everything that a child should learn in an early childhood setting.

For young children with disabilities, this perspective must be coupled with their individual needs, the environmental demands placed on them, and what will be necessary for them to be successful in their environments. Approximately 30 years ago, Dunst (1981) defined curriculum for young children with disabilities as consisting of

> A series of carefully planned and designed activities, events, and experiences intentionally organized and implemented to reach specified objectives and goals, and which adhere and ascribe to a particular philosophical and theoretical position, and whose methods and modes of instruction and curriculum content are logically consistent with the perspective from which it has been derived. (P. 9)

More recently, the Division for Early Childhood (DEC) (2007) provided a similar comprehensive definition of curriculum: "A complex idea containing multiple components including goals, content, pedagogy, and instructional practices . . . a comprehensive guide for instruction and day-to-day interactions with young children" (p. 3).

Similar to these definitions, we believe that curriculum is comprehensive and provides the theoretical and philosophical foundation on which programming is based. Curriculum supplies a basis for the content to be taught and serves as the guide for all that occurs during instruction and interactions with young children (Branscombe, Castle, Dorsey, Surbeck, & Taylor, 2003; Davis, Kilgo, & Gamel-McCormick, 1998; Dodge, Trister, & Bickart, 2003; Hitchcock, Meyer, Rose, & Jackson, 2002; Sandall & Schwartz, 2008; Wolery & Sainato, 1996).

As McCormick (1997) suggests, it is easier to define curriculum in terms of what it is not rather than what it is. She states that " . . . curriculum is *not* a set of activities: It is *what* is to be learned" (p. 268). In this chapter, the primary focus is on child outcomes and *what* is to be learned by young children with disabilities. Chapters that follow address the intervention and instructional methods to be used in teaching (or *how* to teach) young children with disabilities, birth through age eight.

Interrelated Developmental Domains and Content Areas of Curriculum

Curriculum for young children, both with and without disabilities, focuses on the whole child and emphasizes development in all areas rather than on only one aspect of learning (Morrison, 2009). To better understand curriculum in early intervention/early childhood special education (EI/ECSE), it is helpful to consider the interrelated developmental curriculum domains. **Developmental domains** are the key skill areas addressed in early childhood special education curriculum: cognitive, motor, communication, social, and adaptive skills. Content areas from different disciplines also form the basis for early childhood curriculum: literacy, math, science, social studies, the arts, technology. Standards from these areas help to provide curriculum content. In curriculum development, the terms *scope* and *sequence* are used to describe what is to be taught and the order in which it is to be taught. **Scope** refers to the developmental skill areas (e.g., cognitive, motor, communication, adaptive, social) and content areas (e.g., literacy, math, science). **Sequence** is the order in which the content is taught (e.g., ages, stages, or grade levels) and is often specified in a developmental progression—from easier to more difficult (DEC, 2007). The interrelated developmental domains and content areas of EI/ECSE are described in the section that follows.

Cognitive Skills

Cognitive skills refer to a child's evolving mental and intellectual ability. An infant's cognitive behavior is primarily reflexive with a tremendous amount of progress being made during the first two years of life. Cognitive skills during this period include the concepts of object permanence, spatial relationships, imitation, means–end, causality, and object

usage. Cognitive development occurs and is evidenced when children attend to stimuli; integrate new information with existing knowledge and skills; and perform increasingly complex problem-solving tasks. In addition, cognitive skills are assessed that include the child's capacity to predict occurrences, the use of short- and long-term memory, the ability to sequence activities, the ability to detect differences among objects and events, and the capacity to plan what they will do in the future. During the preschool years, cognitive skills are focused on preacademic skills, which include literacy, math and science skills, letter recognition, counting, and sorting. Cognitive development during the early primary years addresses more advanced preacademic or academic skills. At this point, children's cognitive abilities have become more sophisticated as evidenced by their knowledge of concepts, ability to tell short stories in sequence and their quantitative abilities (Morrison, 2009).

Motor Skills

In the motor, or physical, skill domain, skills are typically divided into gross and fine motor abilities. **Gross motor skills** are described as the ability to move and get around the environment. Gross motor skills involve the movement and control of large muscle groups used for rolling, sitting, crawling, standing, walking, throwing, and jumping. **Fine motor skills** refer to the ability to use small muscle groups such as those in the hands, feet, and face. Fine motor skills are used in reaching for, grasping, and releasing a toy; building towers; tying shoes; cutting; and writing.

Infants' motor skills are solely reflexive at birth. As the brain matures and the muscles strengthen, the ability of young children to control their movements and to move about their environment improves. Not only do most young children gain increased control of their movements, but they also gain increased coordination and complexity as their motor skills develop. They improve in general strength, flexibility, endurance, and eye–hand coordination. Between the ages of two and six, children learn to perform a variety of motor tasks with more refinement such as walking, balancing, running, and performing many fine motor tasks with more precision (e.g., scribbling, cutting with scissors, buttoning, writing). An eight-year-old who is experiencing typical development usually has mastered gross motor skills such as tumbling, roller skating, bicycle riding without training wheels, and ball handling (e.g., throwing accurately). In the area of fine motor skill development, most eight-year-olds have refined their handwriting skills so that they can print most words, draw pictures with details, and can use puzzle pieces, blocks, or other small objects. Motor skill development is focused on both gross and fine motor areas with emphasis placed on the quality and accuracy of the child's motor skills and how they actually use these skills in the context of their daily routines (Cook & Kilgo, 2004).

Communication Skills

In the area of communication skills, there are three aspects of development to consider: communication, language, and speech. **Communication** refers to the exchange of messages between a speaker and a listener. **Language** refers to the use of symbols (that is, letter sounds that are used in various combinations to form words), syntax (rules that guide sentence structure), and grammar (the way sentences are constructed) when communicating with one another. **Speech** is the oral–motor action used to communicate. The communication skill domain addresses both receptive and expressive language. **Receptive language** refers to the child's ability to understand and comprehend both verbal and nonverbal information. **Expressive language** is the ability to communicate thoughts or feelings and may involve vocalizations, words, gestures, and other behaviors used to relay information.

The most critical period for communication and language development is before the age of five. The communication of infants is usually unintentional in the beginning; however, by the age of three, most children have acquired all of the major components of a system of communication. Language development has been conceptualized as developing through a series of stages that begin in infancy. When communication skills are delayed, the focus is on communicative intent, which means that attention is given to what a child is attempting to communicate using a variety of means (e.g., gestures, eye gaze, vocalizations). By the time children enter school, they are usually using all of the sentence types produced by adults (Owens, 2010).

Social Skills

Social skills, or social–emotional skills, refer to a range of behaviors associated with the development of social relationships (Brown, Odom, & McConnell, 2008). This domain includes how children react in social situations, interact with others, initiate communication, and respond to interactions initiated by others. When children interact with adults, they usually need skills such as how to participate in reciprocal interactions. When they interact with peers, children often need skills such as how to play cooperatively, share toys, or request a turn. Emotional skills are children's abilities to identify and communicate feelings, as well as their capacity to act on their emotions while respecting the rights of others. Skills in this area include how to control one's impulses or temper and how to resolve conflicts. During infancy, the foundation is laid for the development of long-term social relationships with others. As children age, their personalities are defined by their early childhood experiences.

Adaptive Skills

Adaptive skills, or self-care skills, usually focus on the areas of eating and personal care (e.g., toileting, grooming, and dressing). As children mature in the other skill areas (gross and fine motor for example), the skills from these areas become integrated so that children are able to perform self-care and adaptive skills at more advanced levels of independence. In early infancy, the adaptive skill, or self-care, areas that predominate are sleeping and eating. However, as children mature and spend greater amounts of time interacting with their environment, they usually acquire greater independence in the areas of eating and personal care. Eating skills typically progress from an infant's suck-swallow response to a toddler's finger feeding and cup drinking to a preschooler's independent feeding with appropriate utensils. Toileting, hand-washing, tooth brushing, and hair combing are examples of personal care skills, which also become more refined as young children practice and gain increased independence. Similarly, in most preschool children, dressing skills progress from cooperation in undressing and dressing to independent dressing skills. By the time children reach kindergarten and the early primary grades, they can usually perform all or most of the basic adaptive or self-care skills with some assistance on some of the more difficult tasks (e.g., like buttons or snaps on blue jeans). Gradually, children increase their ability to function with greater independence across a variety of tasks (e.g., selecting clothing, fastening seatbelt) in various environments (e.g., home, school, and community). Emphasis is placed on precision in performing more advanced adaptive skills, as well at a higher level of independence.

In this section, we have provided a brief overview of the interrelated developmental domains and content areas that are usually the focus of skill attainment within the curriculum for young children. During the early childhood period, development cannot realistically be separated into isolated skill domains. This is because the developmental areas are interdependent and interact in complex ways. In fact, a direct functional relationship exists between changes in one area of development and those that occur in another area of development. When a young child learns to walk, for example, he or she is afforded new experiences that will more than likely influence skill development in other areas (such as cognitive, social, and language skill development). Knowledge of each of the developmental domains and content areas can be helpful in understanding the child as a whole. Typical development can be useful as a general guide and reference point to consider when determining each child's individual strengths, needs, and progress. However, it is important to remember that the learning that occurs in early childhood is episodic and uneven with great variability among children (Copple & Bredekamp, 2009; Morrison, 2009). This is particularly true for those children with developmental delays or disabilities. To learn more about curriculum in EI/ECSE, it is helpful to consider the historical, legislative, and philosophical influences on curriculum for young children, which are addressed in the section that follows.

Historical, Legislative, and Philosophical Influences on Curriculum

Curriculum for young children with disabilities, age birth through eight, is influenced by a number of complex factors. Early intervention and early childhood special education and the various approaches to curriculum for young children with disabilities have developed from three different fields of education: general early childhood education, special education (e.g., for older children), and compensatory education (e.g., Head Start) (Peterson, 1987). Each of these areas represents a different point of view about young children and their development and learning. The field of general ECE, for example, underscores the young child's need to construct his or her own knowledge through active engagement with and exploration of the environment (Copple & Bredekamp, 2009). On the other hand, special education emphasizes the use of remedial instruction and the provision of related services to facilitate skill acquisition. Compensatory education is founded on the perspective that early intervention/education can help to minimize or alleviate the effects of environmental influences such as poverty and other risk factors. Figure 6–1 shows how the fields of general early childhood education, special education, and compensatory education overlap to produce curriculum in ECSE.

In addition to these influences, research in the field of child development has provided an opportunity to broaden the focus of intervention for young children to include children's care-giving environments. The transactional view of child development

FIGURE 6–1 Influences on Early Intervention/Early Childhood Special Education Curriculum

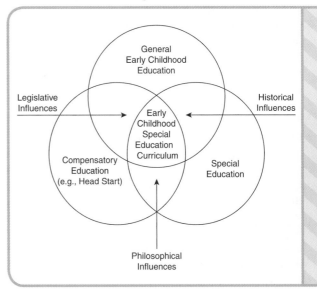

(Sameroff & Chandler, 1975), developed many years ago, proposes that a child's developmental status varies as a function of the transactions occurring between the child's biological characteristics and the environmental or contextual conditions in which he or she lives. The emphasis placed on a child's relationship with his or her family and other primary caregivers has greatly influenced early childhood curriculum.

The designation of recommended practice in curriculum development for infants and young children with disabilities has evolved over a period of years due to the different fields of education and federal legislation, in particular the Individuals with Disabilities Education Act (IDEA). In fact, the explicit requirements of the individualized family service plan (IFSP) and individualized education program (IEP) have altered the nature of curriculum. In most instances, a broad-based application of curriculum is used in EI/ECSE. The IEP and IFSP goals/outcomes, which are relevant to each child within the context of his or her home and community, are used to individualize the experiences of children with disabilities (Cook, Klein, & Tessier, 2008; Grisham-Brown, Hemmeter, & Pretti-Frontczak, 2005; Noonan & McCormick, 2006).

Perhaps the most dramatic influence has been the input from both the general early childhood education and early intervention/early childhood special education fields related to the inclusion of young children with special needs. The 2004 amendments to IDEA require that all children, regardless of ability, have access to the general curriculum and have the opportunity to participate, as well as make progress, in the general curriculum. Rather than young children with disabilities simply being placed in child care programs, preschools, or early primary classrooms, children have access to and participation in the general curriculum. All aspects of an accessible curriculum (i.e., assessments, goals, content, environment, instructional methods, interactions, and materials) invite active participation of *all* children (Division for Early Childhood, 2007. p. 4), referred to as **universally designed curriculum.**

There have been a number of other significant influences on curriculum. One important influence has been the federal emphasis on measuring child outcomes. In 2006, the Office of Special Education Programs (OSEP) required that programs for young children document and report the progress that children make annually toward achieving the following three global outcomes:

1. Positive social–emotional skills (including social relationships);
2. Acquisition and use of knowledge and skills (including early language, communication, and literacy); and
3. Use of appropriate behavior to meet needs (Early Childhood Outcome Center, 2007).

It should be noted that these global outcomes represent an integrated set of behaviors and actions that are meaningful to young children in the context of everyday life. These outcomes for children are to be documented along with the individual goals and outcomes on the IFSPs and IEPs. Another important influence on curriculum is the early learning standards that most states have in place to define the desired outcomes and content of early education.

Taking the aforementioned factors and influences on curriculum into consideration, a suggested framework for curriculum development to which all children have access is presented later in this chapter. In the sections that follow, we describe the theoretical influences on curriculum and widely used curriculum models in the field of early childhood today.

Theoretical Influences on Curriculum Development

As described previously, most professionals in early childhood agree that an integral component of any curriculum is the theoretical perspective on which it is based. A number of theoretical perspectives have been identified in early intervention/early childhood special education (Bailey & Wolery, 1992; Hanson & Lynch, 1995; Noonan & McCormick, 2006; Odom, Horner, Snell, & Blacher, 2009) as having influenced the development of curriculum. These curriculum perspectives include (a) developmental, (b) developmental–cognitive, (c) academic (or preacademic) skills, (d) behavioral, and (e) functional perspectives. It is important to note that, in practice, most early childhood programs rely on a combination of theoretical approaches. That is, different components of any one or more of the various theoretical perspectives are combined to match the needs of a given group of children, which is often referred to as an *eclectic approach* to curriculum development in early childhood. This is not surprising, however, due to the fact that the field of EI/ECSE has such a diverse background of historical, legislative, and theoretical influences.

Developmental Perspective

The most traditional early childhood curriculum models seem to primarily reflect a developmental focus. The **developmental approach** is a a traditional curriculum model based on theories of typical child development (Morrison, 2009). The sequence of skills in this model include physical development (i.e., gross motor and fine motor), adaptive development (e.g., self-care and daily living skills), social development, and communication and language development (e.g., receptive and expressive language) based on well known child growth and maturation studies dating back many years (Gesell & Amatruda, 1947). According to the developmental model, children's development is genetically predetermined, suggesting that children who are experiencing typical development usually acquire skills in a fairly predictable sequence. For instance, in the gross motor area, children usually learn to roll over, sit, crawl, and stand before they learn to walk. By using a developmental model, it was originally assumed that teaching the same sequences of skills to young children with disabilities, although at a slower rate, would help them to overcome many of their developmental delays or disabilities. The implication of this perspective is that curriculum outcomes for children with special needs should be focused on the mastery of skills that follow a typical developmental sequence (Carta & Kong, 2009).

Curriculum based on the developmental model contains a sequenced list of developmental milestones organized into a common set of domains with accompanying activities to facilitate the skill development. The skills in a developmental model are determined by and compared to the age-related norms of children who are experiencing typical development. The model is not determined by whether the child has or has not acquired them. Children's active interaction with the physical and social aspects of the environment is thought to be critical to the acquisition of more advanced developmental skills. Thus, children are supported as active participants in the learning process. Intervention strategies are designed to simulate activities engaged in by typically developing children (Morrison, 2009).

The developmental focus in early childhood curriculum may be partly due to the eligibility criteria for EI/ECSE services that emphasize a discrepancy between a child's chronological age and his or her developmental abilities. Although a development focus is prevalent, it is important to realize that a developmental approach has a number of limitations when designing curriculum for young children with disabilities. A curriculum based on a linear model of development is problematic for children with disabilities because, rather than focusing on the actual skills needed to be successful in the natural environment, it tends to focus on the skills that children need to develop in comparison to age-related norms of typically developing children (Carta & Kong, 2009; Rainforth, York, & MacDonald, 1992). A developmental curriculum does not reference the natural environments and expectations of those environments for children with disabilities (Noonan & McCormick, 2006). For example, the skills required to be successful during group time at T.J.'s child care program (e.g., raising his hand to have a turn) would not be addressed in a developmental curriculum. Further, it is unlikely that individual differences and family preferences would be given appropriate consideration.

Developmental–Cognitive Perspective

Another major influence on curriculum development for young children is the developmental–cognitive perspective. The **developmental–cognitive approach** is a theory-driven model that is based on the work of Piaget (Noonan & McCormick, 2006; Morrison, 2009). As discussed in the first chapter, Piaget (1952) theorized that cognitive development occurs as a result of physiological growth and the child's interaction with the environment. The developmental–cognitive model is defined by the content that is covered and the instructional methods that are used. The content of the developmental–cognitive model is very similar to the developmental model; however, the cognitive skill domain is emphasized. The cognitive domain consists of skill sequences derived from Piaget's description of the various periods of intellectual development, like the sensorimotor period (Piaget, 1952). The instructional approach utilized in a developmental–cognitive model, like the one used in a developmental model, focuses on children's interaction with a stimulating, well planned environment (Hanson & Lynch, 1995).

The criticisms of a developmental–cognitive model are similar to those of the developmental

A variety of curriculum approaches are used in programs for young children with known or suspected disabilities.

model. The major drawback is that children's functional skills are not addressed in this model. Functional skills are those skills that will be useful to the child and will be used often by the child in his natural environment (examples include greeting others, eating independently). It is easy to understand why functional skills are important to children with disabilities. Because the developmental–cognitive model does not address functional skills, it has limited utility in designing curriculum for children with disabilities (Noonan & McCormick, 2006).

Academic (or Pre-academic) Perspective

Closely related to the developmental and developmental–cognitive curriculum models is the basic academic (or preacademic) skills perspective. The **academic** (or preacademic) **approach** makes the assumption that the development of nondisabled children is based on a group of core skills that are typically taught to children during the preschool years (usually referred to as preacademics) and the early primary years (academics). There are a number of disadvantages in applying this preacademic or academic approach to curriculum for young children with disabilities. First, a preacademic or academic curriculum primarily focuses on the traditional subject areas of literacy, math, and science. Nonacademic skills that children with disabilities need to acquire, such as appropriate social skills (e.g., greeting others, turn-taking behaviors) and adaptive or self-care skills

(e.g., dressing, toileting), may not be addressed. Second, preacademic or academic skills are often taught in isolation during separate time periods of the day with separate materials and tasks. Yet participation in most activities within the natural environment requires that young children be able to perform several different skills within the same activity (for example, playing a board game usually requires fine motor, cognitive, communication, and social skills, as well as some basic academic skills such as reading or counting). Another concern is that children with disabilities will be unable to generalize skills learned in isolation to the functional context in which they are actually performed in daily life. As one mother commented, "My son learned to count to 20 and to recognize coins, but he never learned to pay for his own hamburger at McDonald's." Third, the basic preacademic or academic skills that are taught may be different from those needed by children with disabilities to perform functional tasks in natural contexts (for example, rather than just counting money out of context, they need to learn all the skills necessary to use money to buy things within their natural environment).

Behavioral Perspective

The **behavioral approach** is based on the learning principles of behavioral psychology. Behaviorists (such as Skinner, Bijou, and Baer) believe that children are extrinsically motivated and describe child development and learning as resulting from environmental factors. From a behavioral point of view, emphasis should be placed on the activities in which a child engages within his environment and the skills that are necessary to participate in those activities in an age-appropriate manner. According to a behavioral approach, skills are important only to the extent to which they are adaptive and related to increasing children's independence. A curriculum that is based on a behavioral model emphasizes direct instruction through a prescribed sequence of instructional activities (Hanson & Lynch, 1995). According to this approach, antecedent events and consequences related to behavior (i.e., what precedes and follows the behavior) are examined and then direct instruction and reinforcement are applied to change the behavior. Instructional procedures such as prompting, shaping, or reinforcing are used to facilitate children's acquisition of skills. Skill acquisition is then monitored through frequent data collection. Based on the amount of progress that the children make, modifications are made in instructional activities (Janney & Snell, 2008).

Instead of following a developmental sequence for curriculum content, behavioral interventionists apply remedial logic to the selection of skills. The focus is on the identification of targeted behaviors with the application of direct instructional techniques designed to increase or decrease certain behaviors. The major problem with a behavioral curriculum approach is the degree of structure and precision required in the implementation. Furthermore, this approach is more difficult to blend with the theoretical perspectives espoused in most general early childhood programs (Strain & Hemmeter, 1997).

Functional Perspective

There is also a **functional approach** to curriculum which is somewhat related to the behavioral model (Carta & Kong, 2009; Owens, 2010; Rainforth et al., 1992; Strain, McConnell, Carta, Fowler, Neisworth, & Wolery, 1992). In recent years, many early interventionists/early childhood special educators have adopted a functional skills approach to developing curriculum for young children with disabilities, especially for children with more severe disabilities. Within this perspective, functional skills or behaviors that are useful for the child to adapt to current or future anticipated environmental demands are identified and facilitated. Thus, skills having immediate relevance to a child are emphasized, such as interacting in a typical manner based on the demands of the environment and performing skills required for daily tasks such as dressing, eating, and many other functional skills performed at home, child care, school, and all other community settings. Developmental age is of less importance than is the child's proficiency in acquiring important age-appropriate skills. Functional skills geared toward daily living activities, rather than developmental or academic sequences, are the focus. In some cases, relevant skills are task-analyzed into a sequence of observable and measurable subskills. For example, a skill such as eating with a fork would be broken down into steps, beginning with picking up the fork, stabbing the food with the fork, and, finally, returning the fork to the plate.

A functional approach has several advantages over developmental and other theoretical approaches for children with disabilities (Carta & Kong, 2009; Noonan & McCormick, 2006, Owens, 2010). First, the curriculum is based on functional and age-appropriate skills needed by children in a variety of natural settings within the community. Learning to perform these skills usually enables children to function more independently in a variety of settings. When children with disabilities perform in a competent manner, those observing often raise their expectations of them. A second advantage of the functional curriculum approach is that many of the skills taught are performed by nondisabled children. By learning many of the same day-to-day tasks performed by typically developing children, the opportunities increase for children with disabilities to be successfully included within the natural environment. Third, the use of task analysis as a strategy to identify specific responses to be taught facilitates individualization. A particular task may be analyzed into any number of discrete steps, based on the unique strengths and needs of the child (Bailey & Wolery, 1992).

A major disadvantage of the functional skills approach is that it lacks a clear organizational framework. Because there are no universal or generally accepted criteria for determining what skills are functional and relevant for children, the potential exists for idiosyncratic curriculum content that is specific to each child. Difficulty can arise when teachers attempt to address the unique skills that each and every child needs (Noonan & McCormick, 2006; Rainforth et al., 1992).

This description of the various theoretical perspectives that have influenced curriculum development models is an extreme oversimplification. Most early childhood special educators recognize that the perspectives described above are not necessarily mutually exclusive approaches. There is rarely a strict adherence to any one curriculum model in early childhood programs, and, in fact, many would agree that a combination of approaches might be most effective for young children with disabilities (Carta & Kong, 2009; Odom & Wolery, 2003). Hanson and Lynch (1995) explain that curriculum content is most often based on developmental, cognitive, and/or functional theoretical approaches. Instructional strategies, on the other hand, are often derived from a behavioral theoretical approach.

A number of factors differentiate the various approaches to curriculum. Bailey (1997) points out that one of the primary features to distinguish curriculum approaches is the role of the teacher (or sometimes the parent) in relation to the child. Approaches that are directive or adult-centered emphasize teacher planning of curriculum activities, setting objectives for children, and engaging in planned instructional activities. On the other hand, approaches considered to be responsive or child-centered emphasize the child as the initiator of interactions with the adult responding to children's interests in a facilitative manner. Each early interventionist or early childhood special educator must select an approach to curriculum development that is appropriate for the individual child and the group of children being served. The perspectives described above and the dichotomies that exist as defining characteristics of curriculum approaches (developmental versus functional approaches to curriculum content; directive versus responsive approaches to teaching) serve as the focus of much discussion in the field of early childhood education.

In addition to subscribing to a particular theoretical perspective, curriculum can vary along a variety of dimensions. Curriculum can focus on one or more developmental domains or content areas. The focus can be more on broad-based, integrated constructs such as play (Linder, 2008). The target of curriculum can differ as well, with the target being the child only, the family only, or both. This dimension also varies according to the focus of the intervention (e.g., direct intervention vs. relationship-oriented), the age of the child, etc. Curriculum also can vary according to the contexts in which it is implemented, such as when directed toward the home or community environment. The implementation of the curriculum can range from highly structured, teacher-directed learning episodes to more naturalistic activities (Wolery & Sainato, 1996, Noonan & McCormick, 2006). Further, it must be emphasized that these dimensions are neither mutually exclusive nor exhaustive (Bruder, 1997).

Curriculum Models

A **curriculum model** refers to a conceptual framework and organizational structure, combining theory with practice, that describes what to teach and how to teach (Aloi, 2009). Because early intervention and childhood special educators work with young children with disabilities in a variety of settings, it is important to be familiar with the different curriculum models used in early childhood programs today. High-quality early childhood programs require a curriculum

TABLE 6–1 Features of Curriculum in High-Quality Programs for Young Children with Disabilities

- Based on research
- Age appropriate
- Individually appropriate
- Culturally appropriate
- High value on play
- Active learning
- Integrated activities across domains
- Balance between teacher-directed and child-directed activities
- Appropriate level of teacher support and guidance
- Engaging interactions
- Responsive environment
- Easily adapted for young children with disabilities
- Meaningful involvement for families

model that is based on research showing it to be effective, as well as a number of other important features (please see Table 6–1). Although these features are necessary, they may not be sufficient to meet the needs of young children with delays or disabilities (Sandall & Schwartz, 2008). Curriculum models may be adjusted in many different ways to meet the needs of young children with special needs.

Theories of child development and learning form the foundation of curriculum models; the variations in curriculum models represent the differences in values about what is important for young children to learn, *how* children learn, and the manner in which they should be taught. Some of the well known curriculum models today include *The Creative Curriculum,* Bank Street Curriculum, High/Scope Curriculum, Montessori Curriculum, Reggio Emilia, and theme-based models. Although these curriculum models vary in their underlying premises, the following are some of the best known and most widely used curriculum models available today. It is important to remember that these models were developed primarily for typically developing children. These curriculum models must be supplemented with a variety of methods and strategies to ensure that young children with special needs learn important skills in their early learning environments, which will be discussed later in this chapter.

The Creative Curriculum Model

The Creative Curriculum is directed toward programs serving infants and toddlers, preschoolers, and children in the primary grades (Dodge, Colker, & Heroman, 2002). This curriculum is described as an assessment and curriculum system that is inclusive of all children. As such, it is used in many different types of early childhood programs, particularly in Head Start programs throughout the United States (Dodge, 2004). Based on research on how children learn, *The Creative Curriculum* provides thorough guidance for early childhood educators by helping them to understand how to work with children of varying abilities. It claims to be an assessment and curriculum system that is inclusive of all children (Aloi, 2009). Specific indoor interest areas are recommended in the curriculum with high-quality materials (i.e., blocks, dramatic play, toys and games, art, library, discovery, sand and water, music and movement, cooking, and computers). A parent component of *The Creative Curriculum* is also available with guides and resources to help early childhood educators build relationships with families (Dodge, Trister, & Bickhart, 2003).

Bank Street Curriculum Model

Another model is the Bank Street Curriculum, also known as the Developmental Interaction Approach, which is based on the theories of Jean Piaget, Erik Erikson, and John Dewey, among others. In this model, the curriculum is flexible within a planned framework encompassing developmentally appropriate knowledge and skills. The emphasis is on open education in which the classroom provides children with direct and rich interactions with a wide variety of materials, ideas and people in their environment. Because it is a child-initiated and child-directed approach that aims for actively involving children

in acquiring competence, children spend most of their time exploring, discovering, and engaging in hands-on activities. The teacher's role within the Bank Street Curriculum is to serve as a guide and facilitator of learning by creating a stable, organized environment, providing an array of materials, and creating opportunities for experiences from which children are to choose. Children participate actively, supported by adults who help to expand, elaborate on, and interpret the meaning of their experiences. Teachers play a vital role in this model, analyzing child behavior, child–adult interaction, and the social and physical setting of the classroom. Teachers look for opportunities to promote cognitive development by creating a climate that encourages questioning, exploration, and children's growing understanding of patterns and relationships in the ideas and environment around them (Cufarro, Nager, & Shapiro, 2005).

High/Scope Curriculum Model

The High/Scope Curriculum is a well known model based on Piagetian theory of child development The High/Scope approach, as described in Chapter 2, was developed by David Weikart and his colleagues to be used with the Perry Preschool Program in the 1960s. The Perry Preschool Project, a longitudinal study to demonstrate that early education could prevent future school failure in disadvantaged children, is now known as the High/Scope Research Foundation (Goffin & Wilson, 2001; Hohmann & Weikart, 2002). A key component of the High/Scope Curriculum is the belief that children should be actively involved in learning. The role of the teacher is to support learning as children make choices about materials and activities within the learning environment. The materials typically found in a High/Scope program are manipulated by children through a hands-on approach rather than a teacher-directed approach. Another key component of High/Scope is that children are active learners who learn best from activities they plan, carry out, and reflect upon, which is known in High/Scope as the plan-do-review process.

The five curriculum content areas that are the focus of the High/Scope Curriculum include the following:

1. approaches to learning
2. language, literacy, and communication
3. social and emotional development

4. physical development, health, and well-being, and
5. arts and sciences (math, science and technology, social studies, and the arts)

The framework for curriculum of the High/Scope model is based on 58 developmental indicators (previously referred to as key experiences) that guide the teacher in supporting and extending the child's development and learning (Hohmann & Weikart, 2002).

Montessori Curriculum Model

The Montessori Curriculum Model is based on the work of Maria Montessori, described in detail in Chapter 2. The model is child directed and the role of the teacher is to serve as a guide who takes his or her lead from the children. In a Montessori classroom, children are actively engaged in the learning process within a well prepared environment. Carefully selected and ordered materials are available that allow each child to decide if he or she wants to engage in an activity. The materials are concrete, intriguing, and usually self-correcting, which means that they can only be used in one way, to prevent errors, promote mastery through repetition, and build confidence through competency (Goffin & Wilson, 2001; Morrison, 2009). The Montessori curriculum model focuses on five areas with interest centers in the classroom focused on these areas:

1. practical life (e.g., self-care skills)
2. sensory awareness
3. language arts
4. mathematics and geometry
5. culture

Montessori classrooms are made up of mixed age groups so that older children can serve as teachers and role models for the younger children.

Reggio Emilia Model

The Reggio Emilia Model, developed in the villages around Reggio Emilia, Italy, is a unique and innovative approach in many ways. The Reggio Emilia curriculum is described as one that is emergent, or one that builds on children's interests, and is based on the theory that children learn best by doing and when they are interested in the topic. Thus, teachers are encouraged to let the children's interests guide the curriculum. Projects are built on children's interests, with the teacher's role being that of a learner alongside the children as they work together to plan and carry out long-term projects. The classroom environment also is considered an important and essential component of the learning process, with carefully organized space for small and large group projects, as well as common space for all children to learn together (e.g., dramatic play areas, work tables, discovery areas). Teachers use documentation, similar to portfolios, as a tool in the learning process. Proponents of Reggio Emilia resist the tendency to define the approach as a curriculum model because they believe the designation goes against the program's dynamic and emergent characteristics (Edwards, Gandini, & Forman, 1993; Goffin & Wilson, 2001).

Theme-Based Model

A theme-based model, commonly used with infants, toddlers, and preschoolers, focuses on topics found in events, culture, and the shared environment of young children. Teachers usually use developing themes focused on topical areas that are relevant and of interest to young children (e.g., animals, holidays, transportation, and special events such as the circus). An array of activities and learning experiences are built around that topical area or central idea. Several factors should be considered when integrated thematic topics are selected (Davis, Kilgo, & Gamel-McCormick, 1998; Kostelnik, 1991). The topic should

- be broad enough to address the wide range of abilities of the children;
- be generated based on the interests and experiences of the children;
- be selected based on the availability of resources and materials necessary;
- be designed based on the interests of the teacher and other team members;
- relate directly to children's real-life experiences and should build on what they know;
- represent a concept or topic for children to discover more about;
- integrate content and processes of learning; and
- allow for integration of several subject areas in the program.

Themes provide a way to integrate curriculum, as well as unify topics, so that they are relevant to young children. Depending on the thematic units selected, curriculum activities can be planned to address multiple areas of development and address children's special interests and needs.

An extension of a theme-based approach is a project approach, which involves an in-depth investigation of a topic selected by the teacher based on the children's and his/her interest, curriculum, and availability of local resources. A topic "web" is then organized by the teacher as a structure to guide the project. Children engage in investigation by gathering information on the chosen topic. Projects have a structure with a beginning, middle, and end, which helps the teacher organize the activities according to the development of the children's interests and progression with the topic of study. A project approach is often used during preschool and the early primary years. When a theme-based or project approach is used with early primary-level students, this method is often referred to as unit teaching. Teachers integrate material from several subject areas to create one unified plan, which includes preassessment, integrated objectives, and evaluation of learning performance. As Jenkins (2005) described, unit teaching focuses on group learning, is project oriented, and is motivating to students who are difficult to engage in academic learning.

As we have described, multiple curriculum models exist in early childhood education with advantages and disadvantages associated with each model. For the selected models described, Table 6–2 shows the advantages, disadvantages, and applicability to young children with disabilities. The Making Connections feature contains a description of the array of curriculum models often used in early childhood programs serving young children with disabilities.

TABLE 6–2 Advantages and Disadvantages of Curriculum Models and Their Applicability to Young Children with Disabilities

Curriculum Model	Advantages	Disadvantages
The Creative Curriculum	<ul><li>Children learn by doing</li><li>The environment plays an important role in learning</li><li>Integrates all areas of learning</li><li>Includes assessment tool</li></ul>	<ul><li>An expensive model</li><li>Must be followed correctly and adults must be well trained in the model</li></ul>
Bank Street	<ul><li>Child-initiated and -directed approach</li><li>Teachers guide and facilitate learning</li><li>Stimulating environment</li></ul>	<ul><li>Requires well trained teachers that may not be available</li><li>Interests of children with disabilities may be overlooked</li><li>Children with disabilities may require more direction</li></ul>
High/Scope	<ul><li>Encourages creative exploration</li><li>Emphasizes active learning</li><li>Promotes socialization</li><li>Establishes consistent routine, including plan-do-review process</li></ul>	<ul><li>Teachers may be unsure of their roles</li><li>May not be enough teacher- directed activities for some learners</li><li>Less structured environment</li></ul>

(continued)

TABLE 6–2 **Advantages and Disadvantages of Curriculum Models and Their Applicability to Young Children with Disabilities** *(continued)*

Curriculum Model	Advantages	Disadvantages
Montessori	<ul><li>Emphasis on sensory learning</li><li>Highly organized environment</li><li>Carefully sequenced and ordered materials that are self-correcting</li><li>Teachers require extensive training in the approach</li><li>Active learning and independence are encouraged</li></ul>	<ul><li>Materials designed to be used in only one way and to prevent errors</li><li>Requires well trained teachers although few programs have them</li><li>Limited opportunity for pretend play</li><li>Majority of time spent in independent activities</li><li>Children with disabilities often need more direction and support</li><li>Used infrequently with children with disabilities</li></ul>
Reggio Emilia	<ul><li>Teachers let children's interests guide the curriculum</li><li>Long-term projects designed to stimulate children's curiosity</li><li>Much attention placed on the organization of the environment</li><li>Advocates that children learn by doing</li><li>Encourages cooperation and collaboration among children and teacher</li><li>Children with disabilities or "special rights" are welcomed</li></ul>	<ul><li>Complex approach</li><li>Requires well prepared teachers who may not be available</li><li>Less exposure to this model in the United States</li><li>Often difficult for teachers to allow children to make decisions about what to investigate</li><li>Children with disabilities may not be able to independently choose what to investigate</li></ul>
Theme-based Model	<ul><li>Integrates all areas of learning</li><li>Helps children connect learning with things in the environment</li></ul>	<ul><li>Preplanned activities or lessons on topics selected by teacher</li><li>Often time consuming to prepare thematic units</li><li>May be difficult to address the interests of all the children</li><li>Lacks organizational structure</li></ul>

Source: Adapted from J. Taylor, J. McGowan, and T. Linder, *The Program Administrator's Guide to early childhood special education.* (Baltimore: Paul H. Brookes, 2009), p. 12.

Early interventionists and early childhood special educators must be aware of recommended practices and stay current with changing curricular trends in order to determine appropriate curriculum models and approaches for the children they serve. Further, they must be able to determine how to supplement methods and strategies as needed for young children with delays or disabilities to learn important skills and experience success in their early learning environments.

MAKING CONNECTIONS

Curriculum Models in Programs for T.J. and Other Preschoolers

T.J.'s early childhood special education teacher, Ms. Harnish, works with young children with disabilities in a variety of settings. T.J. is in a Head Start Program where *The Creative Curriculum* is used. The other children on her caseload are served in programs that are based on several different curriculum models and approaches. One program implements a Montessori model, another uses the Bank Street Curriculum Model, another utilizes a theme-based model, and another program is based primarily on a behavioral approach. It is easy to see why it is so important for Ms. Harnish to be familiar with the different curriculum models in order to meet the needs of her students who are served in various early childhood classrooms and programs. Regardless of the curriculum model or approach, Ms. Harnish is responsible for ensuring that T.J.'s and the other students' individualized goals are addressed. She, along with the other team members, determines the supplement methods and strategies needed for T.J. and the other children to achieve their individual goals and be as successful as possible within their learning environments.

Influences of ECE and ECSE Recommended Practices on Curriculum

As described previously, the designation of recommended practice in curriculum development for young children with disabilities continues to evolve. When we think about curriculum that will optimize development for young children with disabilities, it is important to look to all guidelines and standards that help to provide quality services to young children and their families. Within the two disciplines of ECE and ECSE, professionals representing the major professional bodies have constructed documents that represent contemporary thought regarding practices that should be used in the education of young children, both with and without special needs. The question that arises is how to reconcile the apparent pedagogical and philosophical differences between these two approaches. We believe that common ground must be established with the increased legislative and educational emphasis on including children with disabilities in programs alongside their typically developing peers. In order to provide adequate support for a blended approach to curriculum development and implementation in programs serving children with disabilities, the recommended practices from ECE and ECSE must be explored and followed by an analysis of the applicability of the DAP guidelines to young children with special needs.

Recommended Practices in General Early Childhood Education (ECE)

One of the most widely used descriptors of recommended practice in early childhood curriculum is **developmentally appropriate practice (DAP)** (Copple & Bredekamp, 2009). DAP is a set of guidelines established by the National Association for the Education of Young Children (NAEYC) to articulate appropriate practices for the early education of young children, birth through age eight. The idea of constructing a statement of DAP was inaugurated in 1987 as a vehicle for providing information to early childhood programs seeking accreditation through NAEYC (Bredekamp, 1987). The document also served as a reactionary statement to the growing fears of the increasing emphasis on academic demands and the expectations encountered by young children in preschool and early primary programs (Carta et al., 1991; Udell, Peters, & Templeman, 1998). Many professionals in the early childhood community, as well as parents, were concerned that too many early childhood programs were focusing on academic preparedness and not providing young children with sufficient opportunities to engage in play-based activities and other less structured activities that typify the early childhood period of development. As one mother explained, "although I'm not a teacher, I know from experience that four-year-olds should not be expected to sit at a table and complete work sheets for an hour at a time! No one should be expected to do the same task for that long without getting bored and misbehaving!"

The DAP guidelines were developed to promote high-quality programs for all children and their families. Some mistake DAP for a curriculum model; however, DAP does not meet the criteria to be considered a curriculum model. Rather than being a thoroughly developed curriculum model, the DAP guidelines were designed to be used as a tool to help distinguish between appropriate and inappropriate practices with young children regardless of what curriculum model is used (Kostelnik, Soderman, & Whiren, 2007).

After a decade of extensive dissemination, the 1987 position statement became the most widely recognized guidelines for recommended practice in the field of early childhood education. The DAP guidelines were conceived as a living document and not as educational dogma. They were also conceptualized as a dynamic and evolving statement of recommended practices that were designed to be subject to change and amenable to revisions as thinking and recommended practices (which are necessarily time-bound) change. NAEYC published revised guidelines in 1997 titled *Developmentally Appropriate Practice in Early Childhood Programs: Serving Children from Birth through Age 8* (Bredekamp & Copple, 1997) and published a third edition of the DAP guidelines in 2009 (Copple & Bredekamp, 2009).

A longstanding fundamental premise of DAP is the belief that "early childhood programs should be tailored to meet the needs of children, rather than expecting children to adjust to the demands of a specific program" (Bredekamp, 1987, p. 1). According to the most recent NAEYC publication, Developmentally Appropriate Practices are defined as:

> those that result from the process of professionals making decisions about the well-being and education of children based on at least three important kinds of information or knowledge: [1] what is known about child development and learning; . . .

> [2] what is known about each child as an individual; . . .
> [3] and what is known about the social and cultural contexts in which children live.
>   (COPPLE & BREDEKAMP, 2009, PP. 9–10)

Based on the above definition, DAP is often described in terms of three components that are the focus of the assessment and program planning processes: age appropriateness, individual appropriateness, and cultural appropriateness (Copple & Bredekamp, 2009). These areas of knowledge about each child are central to the concept of DAP, as well as the role of the child and teacher in the learning environment. In addition, another key aspect of DAP is that teaching must take place in the child's natural context rather than in any artificial environment.

- The first dimension, **age appropriateness,** refers to the universal nature of the course of human development during the early childhood years. According to research in child development, there are universal, predictable sequences of growth and change that occur in young children during the first nine years of life across various development domains (physical, emotional, social, and cognitive, etc.). Based on their knowledge of typical development in children, teachers are able to prepare the learning environment and plan appropriate experiences.
- **Individual appropriateness,** the second dimension, refers to the uniqueness of children. Children have individual patterns and timing of growth, as well as individual personalities, strengths, interests, backgrounds, and experiences. According to the DAP guidelines, for the learning environment and curriculum to be responsive to the individual differences, teachers must design to meet the needs of each child.
- The third dimension of the DAP guidelines, **cultural appropriateness,** refers to the teacher's ability to understand each child and his or her unique social and cultural contexts. The curriculum and meaningful learning experiences, which are relevant to individual children, can be planned when the teacher has firsthand knowledge of each child's social and cultural background.

When applying these concepts to curriculum development, the goals underlying curriculum content and activities should reflect what professionals know about the typical sequence of child development and, at the same time, should be responsive to the individual variances in development, personality, ability, interest, learning style, and culture. Curriculum is age appropriate when knowledge of typical child development is used to plan experiences that are based on the ages of the children in the program. Curriculum is individually appropriate when it is responsive to unique differences in children. Curriculum is culturally and socially appropriate when learning experiences are designed based on the social and cultural contexts in which children live. In addition, curriculum is flexible, allowing for content that meets a wide range of abilities, interests, and backgrounds of the children (Bredekamp & Rosegrant, 1992; Copple & Bredekamp, 2009).

Recommended Practices in Early Childhood Special Education (ECSE)

The field of ECSE did not have a set of guidelines comparable to the DAP guidelines until 1993, when the Division for Early Childhood (DEC) of the Council for Exceptional Children (CEC) published the first document to provide recommendations for programs serving young children with special needs and their families and indicators of quality in these programs (DEC Task Force on Recommended Practices, 1993). In 2000 and in 2005, DEC published a set of guidelines titled *DEC Recommended Practices in Early Intervention/ Early Childhood Special Education* (Sandall, McLean, & Smith, 2000; Sandall, Hemmeter, Smith, & McLean, 2005) that synthesizes the knowledge found in the scientific/professional literature and the knowledge from experience of parents, practitioners, and administrators about those practices that produced the best outcomes for children. Further, and perhaps most important to this discussion, the guidelines contain many recommendations that have relevance to curriculum development and implementation. In designing early childhood curriculum for young children with disabilities and their families, it is important to consider the principles underlying the DEC recommended practices and quality indicators that support the goals of early childhood special education.

Principles Underlying DEC Recommended Practices.

- *Educational experiences should be family–based.* This means that the curriculum should be responsive to families' goals and priorities for their children.

As described in Chapter 3, a dramatic shift in advocated practices has occurred in early childhood special education over the years, from a solely child-oriented approach to a family-based approach. Although federal legislation is largely credited with providing the rationale for basing services on the family, the law put into policy what had been an already burgeoning movement. Family participation is now guided by the goal of a partnership of equals being built between the family and the EI/ECSE service system (such as a family-based service delivery model). The spirit of this family movement is based on the belief that the vision families have for their children should provide the foundation for program planning. Family preferences play a vital role in planning the curriculum content and strategies. Thus, family input is encouraged and supported, and families' rights to make decisions about their children's experiences are respected.

- *Educational experiences should be evidence–based.* Buysse, Wesley, Snyder, and Winton (2006) define evidence-based practices as "a decision-making process that integrates the best available research evidence with family and professional wisdom and values" (p. 3). That is, specific strategies that early childhood special education professionals use should have some empirical support or be wisdom and value driven (supported by current wisdom or values held by professionals in the field and the family). This implies that professionals must continually examine their current practices and procedures to ensure their effectiveness and social validity.

- *Educational experiences should provide for cultural responsiveness.* Appropriate educational experiences should reflect the diverse values, backgrounds, and experiences of children and families served within a program, acknowledging the individuality of children and families. The cultural backgrounds of the children and families should help to guide curriculum development.

- *Educational experiences should provide for multidisciplinary input.* Because children with disabilities often have a need for services such as physical therapy, speech–language therapy, occupational therapy, and/or other related services, there are often many different professionals who work with the child and family. Practices should reflect a team approach whereby all team members share information and expertise, communicate

Cengage Learning

Curriculum for young children with known or suspected disabilities must be individually tailored to meet each child's unique needs.

frequently, and participate in joint decision making. Input from the various disciplines should be integrated into the design of the curriculum.

- *Educational experiences should be developmentally and individually appropriate.* As stressed throughout this chapter, the DAP guidelines may not be sufficient when addressing the needs of children with disabilities (Wolery et al., 1992; Carta & Kong, 2009). The key to developing appropriate educational experiences (for any child) is to create a match between the unique, individual needs of the child and the curriculum. Making this match for children with disabilities may require taking individualization to a higher level by paying attention to the physical and social environment, adapting or using specialized equipment and materials, and/or utilizing specialized instructional strategies and techniques to support each child's development and learning.
- *Educational experiences should be normalized.* As described previously, Nirje (1976) defined normalization as making available to all persons with disabilities ". . . the patterns of life and conditions of everyday living which are as close as possible to the regular circumstances and ways of life of society" (p. 231). Normalization is often narrowly interpreted to mean that children with disabilities should be placed in inclusive settings. While that is one application of normalization, placement within inclusive settings does not ensure that the

normalization principle is being addressed. When applied to young children with disabilities, it includes examining a number of different aspects of each child's educational placement to include educational programming, teaching strategies, the physical and social environment, and family-based practices.

Potential Benefits of EI/ECSE. The underlying premises of DEC recommended practices support the general goals of early educational experiences for young children with disabilities (Bailey & Wolery, 1992; Sandall et al., 2005) utilizing the DEC recommended practices provides potential benefits for participants in early intervention/education services.

- *Families are supported in achieving their goals.* Children with disabilities may have complex needs that are better understood when professionals interact with families and learn about the priorities that parents have for their children. As the mother of a three-year-old with cerebral palsy told her child's teacher, "All I want is for my child to learn to walk." Thus, this mother's priority became the major focus of intervention. Although the child never actually learned to walk, he did learn to use an electronic wheelchair to get from place to place independently. If professionals do not have knowledge of the families' priorities, the likelihood of success will be diminished. It is critical for professionals to understand that families function as a system. Thus, they must develop rapport with families, have ongoing interactions with them, and support them in achieving the goals they have for their children (Turnbull, Turnbull, Erwin, & Soodak, 2006).
- *Child engagement, independence, and mastery are supported.* Through the EI/ECSE curriculum, each child's engagement with people, materials, and activities in his or her natural environment (e.g., home, child care, school) is supported, which enables him or her to master the demands associated with each of these environments. A mother of a four-year-old child who has Turner's Syndrome with accompanying delays in all developmental areas encouraged professionals to examine the routines and demands of the general early childhood program where her daughter was enrolled in order to determine the focus of intervention. In order for the child, Kathryn, to become more independent and to be successful in this setting,

the focus of her program needed to be on what was expected of her within this setting. As stressed for many years, efforts should be made to "promote active engagement (participation), initiative (choice making, self-directed behavior), autonomy (individuality and self-sufficiency) and age-appropriate abilities in many normalized contexts and situations" for young children with disabilities (Wolery & Sainato, 1996, p. 53).

- *Development is promoted in all areas.* Experiences for young children with disabilities should be designed to promote progress in each of the key areas of development as described earlier in this chapter. Many activities in which young children participate require the integrated use of skills from various domains. For example, when Maria is participating in a snacktime activity, she is using skills from several areas, including fine motor, communication, social, and adaptive skills. Often, young children with disabilities are behind their typically developing peers and, therefore, individual goals are targeted for each child and instructional strategies are used that lead to rapid learning in order to help children with disabilities make progress in achieving desired outcomes (Wolery & Sainato, 1996; Sandall et al., 2005).

- *The development of social competence is supported.* Most would agree that social skills (e.g., developing relationships, getting along with peers, playing cooperatively) are among the most important skills for young children to learn (Brown, Odom, McConnell, 2008). Young children with special needs reportedly engage in less sophisticated and less frequent social interactions than their nondisabled peers (Guralnick, 1990). Therefore, many children with disabilities have difficulty developing these skills and must be taught to interact effectively and properly (Goldstein, Kaczmarek, & English, 2001). As a result, one of the primary benefits of EI/ECSE is that the social competence of young children with disabilities is often further developed. As one mother noted,

  > "My son needed to learn the social expectations of the general education classroom. His kindergarten teacher didn't seem to mind that he couldn't write his name, but she did expect him to walk in a line with his classmates to the lunchroom and to stay in his seat during group time." The generalized use of skills is emphasized. Skill generalization is especially important

when teaching young children with disabilities who have extreme difficulty with generalizing or applying what they learn to different situations, people, and materials (Drew, Logan, & Hardman, 1992). Bethany is a four-year-old with Down syndrome who learned to communicate at preschool by using sign language along with a few words. After her initial success communicating at preschool, the emphasis of her program was expanded to using her communication skills at home, the after–school program, and other environments. As Wolery and Sainato (1993) point out, "Early interventionists should not be satisfied if children learn new skills; they should only be satisfied if children use those skills when and wherever they are appropriate" (p. 54).

- *Children are provided with, and prepared for, "normalized" life experiences.* Because IDEA and its amendments reflect the normalization principle (previously discussed), services for young children with disabilities should be provided to the greatest extent possible in settings that are as similar as possible to the typical settings in which young children without disabilities play and learn (Cook, Klein, & Tessier, 2008). Therefore, a primary purpose and potential benefit of early education for young children with disabilities is to provide a "normalized" curriculum, which should prepare them for "normalized life experiences." Some of the normalized learning environments for a two-year-old child might be a play group with other children in the neighborhood, a child care program, or a babysitter's house. Some normalized life experiences for T.J. might be going to church, attending birthday parties, or eating at McDonald's. The literature describes the benefits of placements in inclusive settings and suggests strategies for effective inclusive early childhood programs (Guralnick, 2001; Sandall et al., 2005; Sandall & Schwartz, 2008).

- *The emergence of future problems or disabilities is prevented.* A final benefit of the EI/ECSE curriculum is to prevent the development of additional problems in young children with disabilities. For example, Audrey is a four-year-old with cerebral palsy who spends most of her day in a wheelchair or other adaptive seating devices that provide trunk support. Without the trunk support and continued physical therapy, she probably will develop scoliosis (i.e., a curvature of the spine). Jimmy is a three-year-old who is blind. As a result of his visual impairment, he does not receive the same visual stimulation as other children his age, does not move around to explore his environment, and exhibits few social initiations. Without encouragement and support to explore his surroundings and initiate interactions with others, Jimmy may develop delays in related areas such as cognitive, social, and/or motor development. In each of these examples, the child has a primary disability that will lead to secondary problems unless he/she is provided with a curriculum that meets his/her individual needs (including attention to the environment, materials, equipment, and instruction).

The principles and potential benefits undergird curriculum content and experiences for young children with disabilities. Based on the DEC guidelines, a number of strategies can be used by professionals who develop and implement appropriate curriculum for young children with disabilities. The questions that emerge include the following: (a) Are the DAP guidelines appropriate for and do they meet the needs of young children with disabilities? and (b) How can recommended practices from both NAEYC (general ECE) and DEC (ECSE) be combined to effectively meet the needs of children with differing abilities?

Curriculum based on the DAP guidelines alone is not likely to be sufficient for young children with special needs. Appropriate curriculum requires that the DAP guidelines serve as the foundation with adaptations applied as needed for young children with special needs.

Cengage Learning

NAEYC's Developmentally Appropriate Practice (DAP) Guidelines have utility for young children with disabilities; however, adaptations and instructional techniques must be tailored to each child's individual needs.

The Relevance and Sufficiency of the DAP Guidelines for Children with Disabilities

Over the years, there has been much debate in the literature over the applicability of NAEYC's Developmentally Appropriate Practice guidelines for children with disabilities (Carta & Kong, 2009). Within the field of ECSE, most professionals agree that curriculum models emphasizing DAP are desirable but are usually insufficient without adaptations and instructional techniques individually tailored to meet the needs of children with disabilities (Carta, 1994; Carta et al., 1991; Johnson, 1993; Sandall et al., 2005; Wolery & Bredekamp, 1994;). As Wolery et al. (1992) pointed out, "a program based on the guidelines alone is not likely to be sufficient for many children with special needs" (p. 106). Carta and her colleagues also share this viewpoint. Their analysis of the DAP guidelines revealed the following inadequacies as it pertained to young children with disabilities:

- Programs serving young children with disabilities must offer a range of services that vary in intensity based on the needs of the children.
- Assessment must be derived from many sources, be carried out across settings, and be frequent enough to monitor children's progress toward their individual goals and objectives.
- Programs serving young children with disabilities must develop individualized teaching plans consisting of goals and objectives that are based on a careful analysis of the child's strengths, needs, and interests, as well as the skills required for future school and nonschool environments.
- Instructional methodologies and procedures for teaching young children with disabilities should be effective, efficient, functional, and normalized.
- The instructional procedures employed by the teacher should result in high levels of active involvement and participation in activities.
- Programs serving young children with disabilities should focus on strengthening the abilities of families to nurture their children's

development and to promote normalized community adaptation.

- Programs serving young children with disabilities must be outcome–based, with specific criteria, procedures, and timelines to determine if individual children progress toward stated outcomes.

Carta et al. (1991) explained that the preceding statements represent basic premises of ECSE; they also serve as indicators of deficiency in the DAP guidelines. Carta and colleagues clearly acknowledge that the DAP guidelines have much in common with the underlying principles of the field of ECSE, yet they provide several illustrations for each of their points where the DAP guidelines are considered insufficient for meeting the needs of young children with disabilities and their families. Our interpretation of the Carta et al. position is that DAP is not necessarily *wrong;* it just does not go far enough as a vehicle for guiding the development of curriculum and the delivery of instruction to young children with disabilities.

But perhaps the biggest challenge in applying the DAP guidelines to the education of young children with disabilities is a difference in the purpose or focus of instruction. Carta et al. (1991) explain that essentially, typically developing young children require a "safe, carefully planned environment that encourages . . . cognitive and social interaction" (p. 8). DAP is also an opponent of unwarranted acceleration of academic progress in typically developing children. Early childhood special education, on the other hand, is driven by an environmentalist rather than a constructivist position, which attempts to accelerate developmental progress and the acquisition of skills that typically would not occur without the benefit of direct intervention or instruction. This, in fact, is the explicit mission of ECSE. We, therefore, seem to be confronted with something of a dichotomy. On one side, we have a present-oriented, teacher-facilitated, and child-initiated philosophy. The other side contains a structured, teacher-led, skill-focused, future-oriented philosophy (Safford et al., 1994). Are these positions that far apart? Is it at all reasonable to expect a blending of viewpoints? Do we have a true dichotomy or is it a continuum of approaches? We believe that the apparent difference between these two positions is due, in a large part, to myths and misconceptions about DAP.

Commonly accepted misconceptions about DAP exacerbate differences between early childhood special educators and professionals in general early childhood education (Kostelnik et al., 2007). Bredekamp (1993a) examined the status of the relationship between what she believes to be the two complementary fields of ECE and ECSE. Her analysis revealed that while diversity exists in both fields, there is a need to resolve the pedagogical and philosophical differences. Bredekamp identifies three misconceptions that have a direct bearing on serving young children with disabilities. Her first example focuses on the NAEYC position regarding direct instruction of children. The DAP guidelines identify the following practice as inappropriate for typically developing children: "using highly structured, teacher-directed lessons almost exclusively" and using "large group, teacher-directed instruction most of the time" (Bredekamp, 1987, p. 54). Unfortunately, this has been interpreted as suggesting that teachers should never use direct instruction with individual learners or in small groups. This representation is simplistic and unproductive (Burton, Hains, Hanline, McLean, & McCormick, 1992) while contributing to the disbelief that teachers in a DAP classroom do not teach and their students control the room (Bredekamp, 1993b). NAEYC advocates that the *exclusive* use of teacher-directed instruction is inappropriate for any child—partly because it denies opportunities for social interaction with peers that research has validated to be vitally important for young children with disabilities (Bredekamp, 1993a; Copple & Bredekamp, 2009).

Curriculum in a classroom utilizing developmentally appropriate practices is construed as solely emerging from children's interest. This is an inaccurate portrayal, which has contributed to confusion about the role of goals (outcomes) in DAP. Goals are emphasized in DAP programs but not to the same degree as found in ECSE classrooms. Because DAP is—by definition—age, individually, and culturally and socially appropriate, a teacher could not possibly address individual appropriateness without assessment of a student's individual interests and needs and careful planning (Copple & Bredekamp, 2009). Bredekamp believes that some of the confusion surrounding this issue is due to a difference in interpretation of individualization. Early childhood educators look at individualization as responding to the interests of their children while their colleagues

Activity-based instruction promotes skills from several domains within a routine or planned activity.

Cengage Learning

in ECSE interpret the term in relationship to IFSP and IEP goals and outcomes. This difference is one of language rather than substance as both ECE and ECSE address the individual needs and interests of their students. Hopefully, we have cleared up some of the confusion that surrounds the issue of the relevance and sufficiency of developmentally appropriate practices for young children with disabilities.

Blending ECE and ECSE Recommended Practices

As we have described, much discussion has occurred across and within general ECE and ECSE fields regarding the similarities and differences in the guidelines of NAEYC and DEC related to philosophical origins, language, and emphases within practices used with young children. Nonetheless, both the fields of ECE and ECSE have provided excellent

guidelines that should be utilized when creating educational experiences for young children with disabilities (Bredekamp & Rosegrant, 1992; Copple & Bredekamp, 2009; Sandall et al., 2005). An effort has been underway for some time now to determine how ECE and ECSE practices can be blended or used in combination, while remaining true to what is recommended in their respective fields.

As stated previously, the growing interest in blending ECE and ECSE recommended practices has emerged in recent years and can be attributed primarily to the inclusion movement. This movement has been spurred by public laws (for example, the IDEA amendments and the Americans with Disabilities Act) and the belief that services for young children with disabilities should be provided in settings they would be in if they did not have a disability. As we saw in Chapter 5, young children with disabilities increasingly are being served in the natural environment. The provision of services to children with disabilities in the natural environment has had and will continue to have a tremendous impact on curriculum development.

We support the notion that greater collaboration is needed between general ECE and ECSE professionals. Most of the philosophical and pedagogical differences have been resolved (Bredekamp, 1993a). As Burton and her colleagues (1992) emphasized, working partnerships must be established as the demand for services outstrips available resources in both fields. Goodman (1994) also notes that as greater numbers of young children with disabilities are being served in inclusive settings, "the theoretical divide between special education and regular education becomes increasingly problematic" (p. 113). According to this authority, a merging of practices is necessary that does justice to the diversity of children, instructional objectives, and instructional methods. We are inclined to agree with the analysis of Burton et al. (1992) that differences between ECE and ECSE are merely reflections of different developmental pathways and not an expression of deep philosophical differences.

DAP has been championed as an approach for working with *all* young children, including those with disabilities (Bredekamp, 1993a; Bredekamp & Rosegrant, 1992; Copple & Bredekamp, 2009; Kostelnik et al., 2007). Current consensus is that the DAP guidelines do not conflict with practices recommended for children with disabilities by the DEC of the Council for Exceptional Children (Sandall et al., 2005). We also find that strategies valued by professionals in ECSE are compatible with what is viewed as important for teaching typically developing children. Similarities have been documented across both DAP and the DEC guidelines in a number of areas (Fox et al., 1994) including:

- the importance placed on individualization,
- the de-emphasis of standardized assessment,
- the integration of assessment and curriculum,
- the importance of child-initiated activities,
- the importance of a child's active engagement with the environment,
- the emphasis on social interaction, and
- the importance of cultural diversity.

In fact, there appear to be no areas of major disagreement in practices advocated by either general early childhood educators or early childhood special educators (McLean & Odom, 1993). The two fields share much common ground. When differences do emerge, they are typically differences of intensity or emphasis and not an indication of conflict. Differences are found in the application and emphasis of certain guidelines within each field. In particular, these differences include: (a) the role of the family, and (b) the models of service delivery. As emphasized earlier, current consensus is that DAP is a necessary condition for programs serving all young children, including those with disabilities (Fox & Hanline, 1993; Guralnick, 1993). However, leaders in the field of early intervention/early childhood special education have cautioned that DAP may be insufficient for children with disabilities (Carta & Kong, 2009; Fox et al., 1994; Wolery, 1991).

A conceptual model, developed at the Teaching Research Early Childhood Program at Western Oregon University, views DAP as the foundation on which individualized programs are built. Early childhood special education practices are added as needed for individual children. According to Udell et al. (1998), both DAP and ECSE practices can exist within the same setting. Their analysis illustrates a conceptual base for dealing with the issue of combining recommended practice from ECSE and DAP. In Figure 6–2, a builder is shown who is trying to construct a program or school by combining DAP and ECSE practices. Figure 6–3 shows how the builder reconciles this issue by having DAP guidelines serve as the foundation and ECSE practices as the material to complete the structure. Udell and his colleagues encourage professionals to recognize that the ECE and ECSE practices are different types of resources to be used appropriately with individual children.

For DAP to serve as the foundation for programs serving young children with disabilities, several steps must be taken. First and foremost, ECE and ECSE professionals must have a clear understanding of what constitutes recommended practice in their respective fields. Furthermore, they must understand the congruencies and differences between ECE and ECSE philosophies and practices, which will help them move toward a model in which DAP is the foundation upon which appropriate programming for any child can be built. Finally, early childhood programs must incorporate ECSE practices into developmentally appropriate programs. The result should be stimulating programs

FIGURE 6–2 Builder with Two Sets of Materials: ECSE and DAP

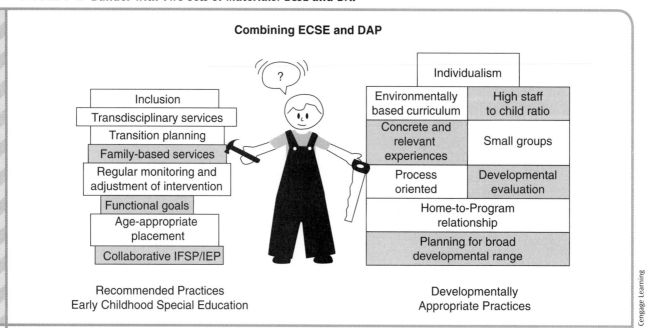

SOURCE: T. Udell, J. Peters, & T. P. Templeman, 1998. From philosophy to practice in inclusive early childhood programs. *Teaching Exceptional Children, 30*(3), p. 48.

that meet the needs of *all* young children and their families.

We believe that the DAP guidelines are indeed appropriate for young children with disabilities. Yet we must remember to gauge the appropriateness of suggested practices by how well they meet the needs of the *individual* child (Carta, 1994). Effective practices associated with the field of ECSE within the DAP framework neither prohibit nor inhibit their use (Fox et al., 1994). However, ECSE programs that are *exclusively* constructed around DAP guidelines are likely to be insufficient for meeting the needs of many young children with disabilities (Carta & Kong, 2009; Wolery et al., 1992). Programming that reflects the recommended practices of both ECE and ECSE is likely to result in appropriate services for all children. Our task as early childhood professionals is "to identify the practices that are relevant for all children and to understand when, and under what conditions, differences and adaptations of practices are required" (Wolery & Bredekamp, 1994, p. 335).

Curriculum Framework in Early Intervention/Early Childhood Special Education

As described throughout this chapter, curriculum in early intervention/early childhood special education is influenced by a number of complex factors. A comprehensive curriculum framework is needed to ensure: (a) access to and full participation by all children; (b) that the individual needs of children and families are met; and (c) accountability to federal requirements and state standards. The DEC of the Council for Exceptional for Exceptional Children (2007) summarizes recommended practices regarding curriculum for children with disabilities as follows:

To benefit all children, including those with disabilities and developmental delays, it is important to implement an integrated, developmentally

FIGURE 6–3 Builder Successfully Combines DAP and ECSE

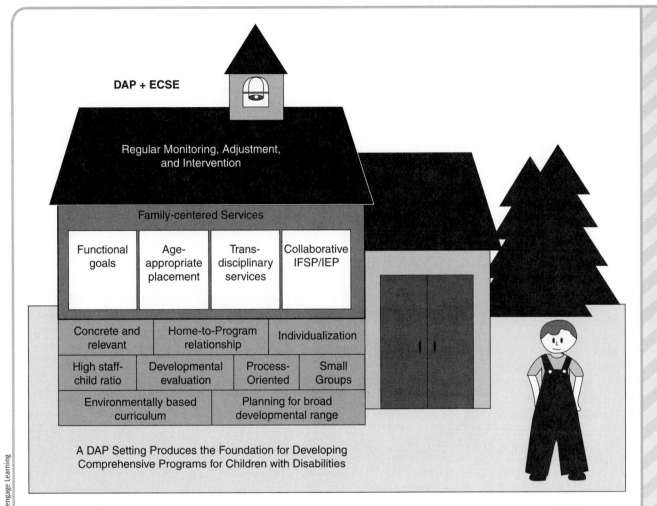

SOURCE: T. Udell, J. Peters, & T. P. Templeman, 1998. From philosophy to practice in inclusive early childhood programs. *Teaching Exceptional Children, 30*(3), p. 49.

appropriate, universally designed curriculum framework that is flexible, comprehensive, and linked to assessment and program evaluation activities. Such a curriculum framework can help ensure successful access, which in turn facilitates participation and learning of all children and families regardless of need, ability, or background. (P. 3)

The purpose of this section is to describe a comprehensive curriculum framework that ensures access, participation, and progress for all learners. Early intervention/early childhood special education is an evolving field. Each decade brings new

challenges and new ideas for curriculum development. Much research is needed in order to determine the appropriateness and effectiveness of various curriculum models and practices in an ever-changing field.

According to Division for Early Childhood (2007), a comprehensive curriculum for early intervention, preschool, and early primary programs encompasses four specific elements:

1. assessment to identify curriculum content (involves assessing children's strengths, needs, interests, etc.);

FIGURE 6–4 Curriculum Framework

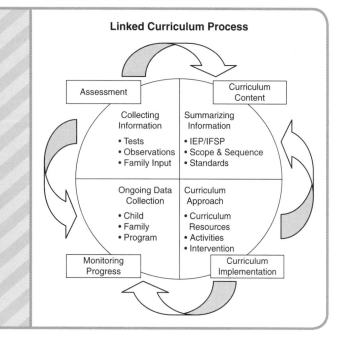

current skills and abilities. As described in Chapter 4, ongoing assessment can be used to help the team determine the targets of intervention by examining child characteristics, environmental demands, and the necessary skills to be successful in their environments. A variety of procedures may be used to identify suitable and meaningful curriculum such as curriculum-referenced tests, observations, family input, and other measures.

Curriculum Content

The content of the curriculum for young children with disabilities usually includes a broad range of skills that would be relevant and appropriate for most young children with disabilities (Division for Early Childhood, 2007; Wolery & Sainato, 1996). As described previously, the scope is the broad, interrelated areas of development and/or content areas and the sequence is the order (ages/stages/grade levels) in which the content will be taught and learned, which is often specified in a developmental progression or by grade level. In the last few years, most states and programs have developed standards for early childhood that include the skills that all children are expected to learn. These broad standards often serve as the scope and sequence for all young children in a state or program (Division for Early Childhood).

Within the broad standards, or scope and sequence, of curriculum, young children with identified delays or disabilities will have individually targeted skills based upon the unique needs of each child, which are stated in their individualized family service plans or individualized education programs (Grisham-Brown, Hemmeter, & Pretti-Frontczak, 2005). Skills on the IEP or IFSP "should not be simply a restatement of what is being addressed for all learners, but rather the underlying, earlier, or prerequisite skills that are necessary for a child [with a delay or disability] to have access to and participate fully in the curriculum" (Division for Early Childhood, 2007, p. 7). Although these individually targeted skills remain aligned with common standards for all children, team members must work together to adapt the curriculum as needed to address each child's individually targeted skills stated on their IFSPs or IEPs. They often require substantial modifications. The scope of early intervention/education services often includes information and support for the family in addition to services for the child.

2. curriculum content, which includes the scope (what is to be taught) and sequence (the order in which it is taught);
3. activities and intervention strategies; and
4. progress monitoring (determining if planned activities are resulting in desired outcomes for children).

For early childhood special educators to address the elements of the curriculum framework, collaboration with other members of the team is required (Pretti-Frontczak et al., 2007). Figure 6–4 provides a representation of a curriculum framework featuring the elements of a linked curriculum process. Each of these elements is described in the subsequent sections.

Assessment to Identify Curriculum Content

Ongoing assessment of child performance is a key element of curriculum development. Identifying the content of the curriculum that will be the target of intervention for each child with a disability is an ongoing process. To determine the targets of intervention and develop appropriate learning opportunities, the curriculum process must have a mechanism for early childhood special educators, family, and other team members to gain a clear understanding of children's

Curriculum Implementation

Curriculum Resources. In addition to collecting information specific to each child and family in designing the curriculum, there are a number of curriculum resources organized in a sequenced format that are used in early childhood programs serving young children with disabilities. Many of these curriculum resources promote functional and individually appropriate activities for young children. Often these guides are referred to as curriculum-based assessment systems because they usually contain an assessment scale and an accompanying curriculum guide.

Most early interventionists and early childhood special education teachers find curriculum guides, or curriculum-based assessment systems, to be helpful in planning activities in early childhood programs. Selected curriculum-referenced assessment systems are described in Chapter 4. Some widely used curriculum systems in early intervention and preschool include the following:

- Assessment, Evaluation, and Programming System (AEPS) Curriculum for Birth to Three Years and Curriculum for Three to Six Years (Bricker & Waddell, 2002);
- Carolina Curriculum for Infants and Toddlers with Special Needs and Carolina Curriculum for Preschoolers with Special Needs (Johnson-Martin, Attermeier, & Hacker 2004a; Johnson-Martin, Hacker, & Attermeier, 2004b); and
- Hawaii Early Learning Profile Strands (Birth to age three years) (Parks, 2007) and Hawaii Early Learning Profile (Preschool) (VORT, 2004).

For the early primary level, a number of curriculum resources are available, including some that are specific to content areas such as literacy, math, and science.

As an example of how these measures are used, the *AEPS Curriculum for Birth to Three Years* and *AEPS Curriculum for Three to Six Years* (Bricker & Waddell, 2002) is divided into two volumes. The AEPS allows professionals to match the child's established IFSP/IEP goals and objectives with age-appropriate, activity-based interventions that correspond to the six areas scored on the *AEPS Test.* Because the test and curricula use the same numbering system, users can easily locate activities in the curriculum that correspond to specific goals and objectives identified with the test—a feature that also helps with ongoing evaluation. In both volumes, professionals are provided with instructional sequences, sample teaching strategies, recommendations for environmental arrangements, and suggestions for incorporating the activities into the child's daily routine. To reflect the individual learning styles many children acquire by ages three to six, the *Curriculum for Three to Six Years* is more flexible in that it provides general intervention considerations and suggested activities rather than specific instructional sequences.

There are many different curriculum resources from which to choose. Hanson and Lynch (1995) developed questions for early childhood special educators and other team members to consider when evaluating the quality and appropriateness of curriculum resources. These questions can be asked about any curriculum model or curriculum-referenced assessment system being considered for young children with delays or disabilities.

- Is the curriculum organized around a theoretical rationale? Is this philosophical approach clearly stated? And is the philosophical approach consistent with or appropriate to the EI/ECSE program's approach and the population to be served?
- Does the curriculum include a wide range of items/activities (scope), such that the needs of the full range of children in the program will be met?
- Are items appropriate for use with children with different disabilities (if so, which ones?) and of different ages? Has the curriculum been tested on the populations for which it was designed? Are the validation data present?
- Are the curricular items sequenced in a developmentally appropriate order? Can items be further "branched" or broken down to accommodate children for whom items may be too difficult? Are instructions for this branching provided?
- Do items meet the test of being both developmentally and functionally appropriate for young children? Are the curricular items culturally appropriate and nonbiased?
- Is family a central focus of the curriculum? Are professionals from different disciplines involved? Can families, care providers, and other team members implement the curriculum?
- Is the selection of curricular items integrally linked with assessments and observations of child behavior? Are the goals and objectives clearly stated so that the child's progress can be assessed?

- Are the goals and activities written in a jargon-free manner so that they can be easily and consistently used? Are the teaching techniques and areas of expertise required to implement the curriculum consistent with those of the teacher and other team members? Are the directions for curriculum use clearly and specifically stated?

- Is the amount of time needed to implement the curriculum appropriate to the needs of the program? Can it be used with various group sizes and, if so, is it appropriate for the group size(s) of the program? Are the target environments or settings in which the curriculum is to be implemented appropriate to the goals and needs of the program?

- Is the cost of the curriculum package reasonable and economically feasible for the program? Are special materials or equipment needed? If so, are these readily available to early childhood teachers and other team members, including family members?

- Can the curriculum be used in formative and summative evaluations of child progress? Can the effectiveness of the curricular approach be evaluated as part of program evaluation? (p. 199)

Curriculum Activities and Intervention. There is an increased recognition that the concept of curriculum is much broader than the traditional view of a packaged set of goals and activities. As described throughout this chapter, curriculum is, or at least is highly influenced by, the entire set of experiences provided in an early intervention or early childhood special education program, including the degree of structure, types of activities, teacher roles, therapy services, physical environment, and peers. We embrace a broad view of curriculum to include curriculum planning and the full range of activities experienced by young children participating in EI/ECSE programs.

The use of daily routines and activities as the context for learning in a universally designed curriculum framework ensures that standards and individually targeted skills are addressed in a manner that expands, modifies, or is integral to the activity in a meaningful way (Pretti-Frontczak & Bricker, 2004). High-quality learning contexts that incorporate the principles of universal design serve as the foundation for intervention planning for all children. For children with disabilities who need additional support, accommodations are provided to help ensure progress towards meeting their desired outcomes (Sandall & Schwartz, 2008).

In implementing the curriculum, the team must consider each child's individual characteristics and unique needs, the necessary adaptations and modifications to activities, the amount and type of support required, and the therapy services to be provided (e.g., physical therapy, occupational therapy, speech-language pathology) for all children to participate within the environment. A method frequently used to teach targeted skills is **activity-based intervention** (Pretti-Frontczak & Bricker, 2004), which embeds instruction on a child's individual IFSP or IEP goals and outcomes into the many naturally occurring events and opportunities that exist in a young child's daily routine as intervention opportunities in the home, classroom, and other settings. Activity-based intervention and other types of instructional strategies are described further in Chapter 9.

The curriculum content is addressed by embedding intervention and integrating therapy into activities and routines in the home, childcare, and classroom environments. Figure 6–5 shows a model developed by Robin McWilliam (2008) illustrating how integrated therapy and embedded interventions provide opportunities for teachers and families to address curriculum content at home, in the classroom, and in other environments. In addition to children making progress in achieving desired outcomes, families often benefit from this approach as they develop feelings of competence and confidence in their abilities to provide support for their children's development and learning.

FIGURE 6–5 Curriculum Implementation in Home and Classroom Environments

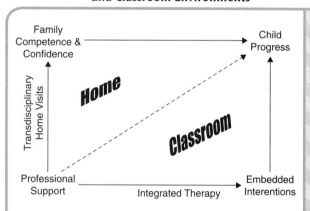

R. A. McWilliam (2008). "Working With Families Not Too Much, Not Too Little" (presentation)

Monitoring Curriculum Progress

The early interventionist or early childhood special educator and other team members must regularly monitor child progress to determine how each child is responding to the supports provided. This ongoing data collection is used to monitor progress, which helps ensure continuous feedback that is necessary to inform and change practice, guide interactions and the selection of materials, and inform decision making regarding all aspects of an early intervention/education program. As discussed in Chapter 4, this requires the use of a variety of methods to ensure collection of reliable, valid and useful progress monitoring data (Branscombe, Castle, Dorsey, Surbeck, & Taylor, 2003; Wolery, 2004). Adequate and collaborative time to review and interpret the data to inform and change practice is also needed (Dodge, 2004; Grisham-Brown & Pretti-Frontczak, 2003; Helm & Gronlund, 2000; McAfee & Leong, 2002).

Curriculum implementation must include documentation regarding the children's progress in relation to the broader curriculum goals, as well as each child's individual goals and outcomes. It is important that teams conduct ongoing monitoring of all children's development and learning. Record keeping and reevaluation are important for meeting the changing needs of children as well as families. Regular communication about children's progress should be maintained with families using methods selected by families. When children with disabilities are included in the same environments as their nondisabled peers, the family, along with the general early childhood, early childhood special education, and related service professionals, can discuss ways to coordinate their communication about children's progress.

Understanding families from a systems perspective allows professionals to approach them as partners in fostering the devleopment and education of their children.

Cengage Learning

Families should have opportunities to be involved in the curriculum process as much as possible.

Collaboration in the Curriculum Process

An effective curriculum process requires that early childhood special educators and other team members work together through the process of collaboration at several levels. Collaboration and partnerships among program personnel and families serve as the foundation of the curriculum framework. Collaborative efforts or partnerships are formed on individual levels between early childhood teachers and teaching assistants, home visitors and families/caregivers, child care providers and early childhood special education teachers, related service personnel and teachers, and many others. These types of partnerships are required routinely for most, if not all, young children with special needs. In implementing the curriculum, collaboration is required at another level on an ongoing basis among team members representing multiple disciplines and family members. Collaboration is essential to the curriculum process to help children with special needs move toward their desired goals and outcomes.

Summary

In this chapter, we have provided an overview of curriculum in early childhood with an emphasis on determining curriculum content to be addressed in programs serving young children with disabilities. Because curriculum focuses on children as a whole, the developmental areas cannot realistically be separated into isolated skill domains. The developmental domains (cognitive, motor, communications, social, and adaptive skills) are interdependent and interact in complex ways. The multiple theoretical perspectives on curriculum such as the developmental perspective, developmental–cognitive perspective, academic (or preacademic) perspective, behavioral perspective, and functional perspective form the foundation of curriculum models and how children learn. The most widely known curriculum models are *The Creative Curriculum* model, Bank Street model, High/Scope model, the Montessori Curriculum model, the Reggio Emilia model, and the theme-based model. Each approach and model has its own advantages and disadvantages when applied to young children with delays or disabilities.

In addition to the different approaches and models, organizations that support the education of young children offer guidelines on curriculum. There has been much discussion of the developmentally appropriate practice (DAP) guidelines (Copple & Bredekamp, 2009) published by the National Association for the Education of Young Children (NAEYC) regarding their application to curriculum development for young children with disabilities. The Division for Early Childhood (DEC) published a similar set of guidelines (Sandall et al., 2005) with recommended practices for young children with disabilities. Both guidelines offer input on how to develop appropriate curriculum for young children with disabilities.

Over the last several years, the dialogue that has emerged between ECE and ECSE has served a number of important functions in that many misconceptions have been clarified and an increased understanding of the unique perspectives of both fields has been the result. For programs serving young children with disabilities, many professionals suggest a curriculum approach that merges practices from ECE and ECSE. The DAP guidelines have laid the groundwork for a widely accepted definition of what represents quality early childhood programs for young children. Many professionals suggest that the DAP guidelines should provide the foundation for all early childhood programs and that strategies and adaptations from ECSE should be applied as needed for young children with disabilities.

The framework for curriculum development in early childhood special education involves determining (a) assessment, (b) the curriculum content to be addressed, (c) the curriculum implementation process to be followed, and (d) the curriculum evaluation procedures to be used. Any evaluation of a particular curriculum guide or approach should take into consideration additional curriculum components when making judgments about its effectiveness. Professionals must make decisions regarding curriculum based on the unique abilities, needs, backgrounds, and interests of the children and families they serve.

Check Your Understanding

1. Define *curriculum* as it applies to programs serving young children with disabilities.
2. (a) Name the theoretical perspectives that have influenced curriculum development in early

intervention/early childhood special education. (b) Discuss the advantages and disadvantages of each perspective when applied to curriculum development for young children with disabilities.

3. List and describe several well-known curriculum models and discuss the advantages and disadvantages of their use with young children with disabilities.

4. (a) Describe what is meant by *developmentally appropriate practice*. (b) Explain how the components of age appropriateness, individual appropriateness, and cultural appropriateness influence curriculum in early childhood.

5. Describe the conclusions that have been drawn in the fields of general ECE and ECSE regarding the applicability of the DAP guidelines to young children with disabilities.

6. Describe a model for blending recommended practices from ECSE and ECE.

7. Describe a framework for curriculum development in ECSE including the four elements.

8. Describe important features of commercially available curriculum resources to be used with young children with special needs.

Reflection and Application

1. Observe an early intervention program, a preschool classroom, and an early primary classroom where children with disabilities are receiving services. How does the concept of curriculum change depending on the age group—infants and toddlers, preschoolers, or children in early primary special education?

2. Examine several commercially available curriculum resources described in this chapter. Evaluate them using the questions developed by Hanson and Lynch (1995) that are included in the chapter.

3. Of the curriculum models described in this chapter, what model do you think would be most appropriate for Maria? For T.J.? For Cheryl?

4. Review the descriptions of NAEYC's Developmentally Appropriate Practice (DAP) guidelines (Copple & Bredekamp, 2009) and the Division for Early Childhood (DEC) Recommended

Practice guidelines (Sandall et al., 2005). Why do you think both are important to consider in meeting the needs of the children described in the vignettes of Maria, T.J., and Cheryl?

References

Aloi, A. Program planning in preschool (2009). In J. Taylor, J. McGowan, & T. Linder. (Eds.), *The program administrator's guide to early childhood special education: Leadership, development, & supervision* (pp. 117–146). Baltimore: Paul H. Brookes.

Bailey, D. (1997). Curriculum alternatives for infants and preschoolers. In M. J. Guralnick (Ed.), *The effectiveness of early intervention* (pp. 227–247). Baltimore: Paul H. Brookes.

Bailey, D., & Wolery, M. (1992). *Teaching infants and preschoolers with disabilities* (2nd ed.). Columbus, OH: Merrill.

Branscombe, N., Castle, K., Dorsey, A., Surbeck, E., & Taylor, J. (2003). *Early childhood curriculum: A constructivist perspective.* Boston: Houghton Mifflin.

Bredekamp, S. (Ed.) (1987). *Developmentally appropriate practice in early childhood programs serving children from birth to age 8* (Exp. ed.). Washington, DC: National Association for the Education of Young Children.

Bredekamp, S. (1993a). The relationship between early childhood education and early childhood special education: Healthy marriage or family feud? *Topics in Early Childhood Special Education, 13,* 258–273.

Bredekamp, S. (1993b). Myths about developmentally appropriate practice: A response to Fowell and Lawton. *Early Childhood Research Quarterly, 8*(1), 177–120.

Bredekamp, S., & Copple, C. (1997). *Developmentally appropriate practice in early childhood programs* (Rev. ed.). Washington, DC: National Association for the Education of Young Children.

Bredekamp, S., & Rosegrant, T. (1992). *Reaching potentials: Appropriate curriculum and assessment for young children.* (Vol. 1). Washington, DC: National Association for the Education of Young Children.

Bricker, D. & Waddell, M. (2002). *Assessment, evaluation, and programming system (AEPS):Vol. 4. Curriculum for three to six years* (2nd ed.). Baltimore: Paul H. Brookes.

Brown, W., Odom, S., & McConnell, S. (2008). *Social competence of young children: Risk, disability, and intervention.* Baltimore: Paul H. Brookes.

Bruder, M. (1997). Curriculum for children with disabilities. In M. Guralnick (Ed.), *The effectiveness of early intervention* (pp. 523–548). Baltimore: Paul H. Brookes.

Burton, C., Hains, A., Hanline, M., McClean, M., & McCormick, K. (1992). Early childhood policy, practice, and personnel: The urgency of professional unification. *Topics in Early Childhood Special Education, 11,* 53–69.

Buysse, V., Wesley, P., Snyder, P., & Winton, P. (2006). Evidence-based practice: What does it really mean for the early childhood field? *Young Exceptional Children, 9*(4), 2–11.

Carta, J. (1994). Developmentally appropriate practices: Shifting the emphasis to individual appropriateness. *Journal of Early Intervention, 18*(4), 342–343.

Carta, J., & Kong, N. (2009). Trends and issues in interventions affecting preschoolers with developmental disabilities. In S. Odom, R. Horner, & M. Snell, & J. Blacher (Eds.), *Handbook of developmental disabilities.* New York: Guilford Press.

Carta, J., Schwartz, I., Atwater, J., & McConnell, S. (1991). Developmentally appropriate practice: Appraising its usefulness for young children with disabilities. *Topics in Early Childhood Special Education, 11,* 11–20.

Cook, M. & Kilgo, J. (2004). Motor assessment of infants and young children. In M. McLean, D. Bailey, & M. Wolery (Eds.) *Assessment of infants and young children with special needs.* (3rd ed.) (pp. 307–344). Upper Saddle River, NJ: Merrill/Prentice Hall.

Cook, R., Klein, M., & Tessier, A. (2008). *Adapting early childhood curricula for children in inclusive settings* (7th ed.). Upper Saddle River, Pearson Prentice Hall.

Copple, C. & Bredekamp, S. (Eds.). (2009). *Developmentally appropriate practice in early childhood programs.* Washington, DC: National Association for the Education of Young Children.

Cufaro, H., Nager, N. & Shapiro, E. (2005). The developmental-interaction approach at Bank Street College of Education. In J. Roopnarine & J. Johnson (Eds.) *Approaches to early childhood education* (4th ed.). Upper Saddle River, NJ: Pearson Education.

Davis, M., Kilgo, J., & Gamel-McCormick, M. (1998). *Young children with special needs: A developmentally appropriate approach.* Needham Heights, MA: Viacom.

Division for Early Childhood (DEC) Task Force on Recommended Practices. (1993). *DEC recommended practices: Indicators of quality in programs for infants and young children with special needs and their families.* Reston, VA: Council for Exceptional Children.

Division for Early Childhood (DEC) (2007). *Promoting positive outcomes for children with disabilities: Recommendations for curriculum, assessment, and program evaluation.* Missoula, MT: Author.

Dodge, D. (2004). Early childhood curriculum models: Why, what, and how programs use them? *Child Care in Information Exchange.* (January/February), 71–75.

Dodge, D., Colker, L., & Heroman, C. (2002). *The creative curriculum for preschool.* Bethesda, MD: Teaching Strategies.

Dodge, D., Trister D., & Bickart, T. (2003). Curriculum, assessment, and outcomes: Putting them all in perspective. *Children and Families, 17*(1), 28–32.

Drew, C., Logan, D., & Hardman, M. (1992). *Mental retardation* (5th ed.). New York: Merrill/Macmillan.

Dunst, C. J. (1981). *Infant learning: A cognitive–linguistic intervention strategy.* Hingham, MA: Teaching Resources Corp.

Early Childhood Outcome Center. (2007). *Demonstrating results for infants, toddlers, and preschoolers with disabilities and their families.* Retrieved June 14, 2009, from http://www.fpg.unc.edu/~eco/pages/fed_req.cfm

Edwards, C., Gandini, L., & Forman, G. (1993). *The hundred languages of children: The Reggio Emilia approach to early childhood education.* Norwood, New Jersey: Ablex.

Fox, L., & Hanline, M. F. (1993). A preliminary evaluation of learning within developmentally appropriate early childhood settings. *Topics in Early Childhood Special Education, 13*(3), 308–327.

Fox, L., Hanline, M. F., Vail, C., & Galant, K. (1994). Developmentally appropriate practices: Applications for young children with disabilities. *Journal of Early Intervention, 18*(3), 243–257.

Gesell, A., & Amatruda, C. (1947). *Developmental diagnosis* (2nd ed.) New York: Harper & Row.

Goffin, S., & Wilson, C. (2001). *Curriculum models and early childhood education: Appraising the relationship* (2nd ed.). Upper Saddle River, NJ: Merrill/Prentice Hall.

Goldstein, H., Kaczmarck, L. A., & English, K. M. (2001). *Promoting social communication: Children with developmental disabilities from birth to adolescence.* Baltimore: Paul H. Brookes.

Goodman, J. (1994). "Empowerment" versus "best interests": Client-professional relationships. *Infants and Young Children, 6*(4), vi–x.

Grisham-Brown, J., Hemmeter, M., & Pretti-Frontczak, K. (2005). *Blended practices for teaching young children in inclusive settings.* Baltimore, MD: Paul H. Brookes.

Grisham-Brown, J. & Pretti-Frontczak, K. (2003). Preschool teachers' use of planning time for the purpose of individualizing instruction for young children with special needs. *Journal of Early Intervention, 26*(1), 31–46.

Guralnick, M. (1990). Major accomplishments and future directions in early childhood mainstreaming. *Topics in early childhood special education, 10*(2), 1–17.

Guralnick, M. (1993). Developmentally appropriate practice in the assessment and intervention of children's peer relations. *Topics in Early Childhood Special Education, 13*(3), 344–371.

Guralnick, M. (2001). *Early childhood inclusion: Focus on change.* Baltimore, MD: Paul H. Brookes.

Hanson, J., & Lynch, E. (1995). *Early intervention: Implementing child and family services for infants and toddlers who are at-risk or disabled.* (2nd ed.). Austin, TX: Pro-Ed.

Helm, J. & Gronlund, G. (2000). Linking standards and engaged learning in the early years. *Early Childhood Research & Practice, 2*(1). Retrieved May 29, 2009, from http://ecrp.uiuc.edu/v2n1/helm.html

Hitchcock, C., Meyer, A., Rose, D., & Jackson, R. (2002). Providing new access to the general curriculum: Universal design for learning. *Teaching Exceptional Children, 35*(2), 8–17.

Hohmann, M., & Weikart, D. (2002). *Educating young children: Active learning practices for pre-school and child care programs* (2nd ed.). Ypsilanti, MI: The High/Scope Press.

Janney, R., & Snell, M. (2008). *Teachers' guides to inclusive practices: Behavioral support.* Baltimore: Paul H. Brookes.

Jenkins, R. (2005). Interdisciplinary instruction in the inclusionary classroom. *TEACHING Exceptional Children, 37*(5), 42–48.

Johnson, C. (1993). Developmental issues: Children infected with human immunodeficiency virus. *Infants and Young Children, 6*(1), 1–10.

Johnson-Martin, N., Attermeier, S., & Hacker, B. (2004a). *The Carolina curriculum for infants and toddlers with special needs* (3rd ed.). Baltimore: Paul H. Brookes.

Johnson-Martin, N., Hacker, B., & Attermeier, S. (2004). *The Carolina curriculum for preschoolers with special needs* (3rd ed.). Baltimore: Paul H. Brookes.

Kostelnik, M. (Ed.) (1991). *Teaching young children using themes.* Glenview, IL: Scott, Foresman.

Kostelnik, M., Soderman, A., & Whiren, A. (2007). *Developmentally appropriate curriculum: Best practices in early childhood education* (4th ed.). Upper Saddle River, NJ: Prentice Hall.

Linder, T. (2008). *Transdisciplinary play-based assessment (TPBA2)* (2nd ed.). Baltimore: Paul H. Brookes.

McAfee, R., & Leong, D. (2002). *Assessing and guiding young children's development and learning* (3rd ed.). Boston: Allyn & Bacon.

McCormick, L. (1997). Ecological assessment and planning. In L. McCormick, D. Loeb, & R. Schiefelbusch (Eds.), *Supporting children with communication difficulties* (pp. 223–256). Boston, MA: Allyn & Bacon.

McLean, M., & Odom, S. (1993). Practices of young children with and without disabilities: A comparison of DEC and NAEYC identified practices. *Topics in Early Childhood Special Education, 13*(3), 274–292.

Morrison, G. (2009). *Early childhood education today* (11th ed.). Upper Saddle River, NJ: Pearson Education.

Nirje, B. (1976). The normalization principle. In R. Kugel & A. Shearer (Eds.), *Changing patterns in residential services for the mentally retarded.* Washington, DC: President's Committee on Mental Retardation.

Noonan, M., & McCormick, L. (2006). *Young children with disabilities in natural environments: Methods and procedures.* Baltimore: Paul H. Brookes.

Odom, S., Horner, R., Snell, M., & Blacher, J. (2009). *Handbook of developmental disabilities.* New York: Guilford Press.

Odom, S. & Wolery, M. (2003). A unified theory of practice in early intervention/early childhood special education. *Journal of Special Education, 37*(3), 164–173.

Owens, R. (2010). *Language disorders: A functional approach to assessment and intervention,* (5th ed.). Boston: Allyn & Bacon.

Parks, S. (2007). *Hawaii early learning profile (HELP) strands (0–3).* Palo Alto, CA: VORT Corporation.

Piaget, J. (1952). *The origins of intelligence in children.* New York: Norton.

Peterson, N. (1987). *Early intervention for handicapped and atrisk children.* Denver: Love.

Pretti-Frontczak, K., & Bricker, D. (2004). *An activity-based approach to early intervention* (3rd ed.). Baltimore: Paul H. Brookes.

Pretti-Frontczak, K., Jackson, S., Gross, S., Grisham-Grown, J., Horn, E., Harjusola-Webb, S., Lieber, J., & Matthews, D. (2007). A curriculum framework that supports quality early childhood education for all young children. In E. Horn, C. Peterson, & L. Fox (Eds.), Young Exceptional Children Monograph Series No. 9: *Linking curriculum to child and family outcomes* (pp. 16–28). Missoula, MT: The Division for Early Childhood.

Rainforth, B., York, J., & McDonald, C. (1992). *Collaborative teams for students with severe disabilities.* Baltimore: Paul H. Brookes.

Safford, P., Sargent, M., & Cook, C. (Eds.). (1994). Instructional models in early childhood special education: Origins, issues, & trends. In P. Safford (Ed.), *Early childhood special education* (pp. 96–117). New York: Teachers College Press.

Sameroff, A., & Chandler, M. (1975). Reproductive risk and the continuum of care-taking casualty. In F. D. Horowitz, M. Hetherington, S. Scarr-Salapatek, & G. Siegel (Eds.). *Review of child development research* (Vol. 4) (pp. 187–244). Chicago: University of Chicago Press.

Sandall, S., McLean, M. E., & Smith, B. J. (Eds.) (2000). *DEC recommended practices in early intervention/early childhood special education.* Reston, VA: Council for Exceptional Children. Division for Early Childhood.

Sandall, S., Hemmeter, M. L., Smith, B. J., & McLean, M. (2005). *DEC recommended practices: A comprehensive guide for practical application.* Missoula, MT: DEC.

Sandall, S. & Schwartz, I. (2008). *Building blocks for successful early childhood programs: Strategies for including all children.* Baltimore, MD: Brookes.

Strain, P., & Hemmeter, M. L. (1997). Keys to being successful when confronted with challenging behaviors. *Young Exceptional Children, 1*(1), 2–8.

Strain, P., McConnell, S., Carta, J., Fowler, S., Neisworth, J., & Wolery, M. (1992). Behaviorism in early intervention. *Topics in Early Childhood Special Education, 12*(1), 121–141.

Turnbull, A., Turnbull, R., Erwin, E., & Soodak, L. (2006). *Families, professionals, and exceptionality: Positive outcomes through a partnership and trust* (5th ed.). Upper Saddle River, NJ: Merrill/Prentice Hall.

VORT Corporation (2004). *Hawaii early learning profile (HELP) for preschoolers—assessment strands.* Palo Alto, CA: Author.

Udell, T., Peters, J., & Templeman, T. (1998). From philosophy to practice in inclusive early childhood programs. *Teaching Exceptional Children,* Jan./Feb., 44–49.

Wolery, M. (1991). Instruction in early childhood special education: Seeing through a glass darkly. . . knowing in part. *Exceptional Children, 58*(2), 127–135.

Wolery, M. (2004). Monitoring child progress. In M. McLean, M. Wolery, & D. B. Bailey (Eds.), *Assessing infants and preschoolers with special needs* (3rd ed.) (pp. 545–584). Englewood Cliffs, NJ: Prentice-Hall.

Wolery, M., Ault, M. J., & Doyle, P. M. (1992). *Teaching students with moderate to severe disabilities.* New York: Longman.

Wolery, M., & Bredekamp, S. (1994). Developmentally appropriate practices and young children with disabilities: Contextual issues in the discussion. *Journal of Early Intervention, 18*(4), 331–341.

Wolery, M., & Sainato, D. (1993). General curriculum and intervention strategies. In Division for Early Children, Council for Exceptional Children (Ed.), *DEC recommended practices: Indicators of quality in programs for infants and young children with special needs and their families.* Denver, CO: Author.

Wolery, M., & Sainato, D. (1996). General curriculum and intervention strategies. In S. Odom & M. McLean (Eds.), *Early intervention/early childhood special education: Recommended practices* (pp. 125–158). Austin, TX: PRO-ED.

Organization and Intervention for Young Children with Special Needs

Chapter 7
Designing Learning Environments for Young Children with Special Needs

Chapter 8
Adapting the Learning Environment for Young Children with Special Needs

Chapter 9
Strategies for Teaching Young Children with Special Needs

7 Designing Learning Environments for Young Children with Special Needs

Key Terminology

Environment

Activity areas

Stimulus-control

Premacking

Responsivity

Learned helplessness

Accessibility

Learning Outcomes

After reading this chapter, you will be able to:

- Describe the key characteristics of a well-designed indoor and outdoor learning environment.

- Outline the types of learning centers typically found in classrooms designed for infants/toddlers, preschoolers, and students in the early primary grades.

- List the requirements of an accessible learning environment.

- Describe a safe and healthy learning environment.

- Identify the factors to consider when purchasing classroom learning materials.

One of the most important responsibilities of an early childhood special educator is to construct an environment that facilitates the delivery of an effective instructional program. This role of classroom designer and architect has been referred to as "environmental engineering" (Neisworth & Buggey, 2005). It is important for teachers to be aware of the impact that the environment has on influencing the behavior of children. Educators must also be cognizant of how to manipulate the learning environment to enhance learning. Over the past 30 years, proponents of diverse theoretical models of learning such as behaviorism, constructivism, and social learning have increasingly stressed the importance of environmental elements in their learning and instructional paradigms. Maria Montessori, for example, through her concepts of auto-education and the "prepared classroom," emphasized environmental considerations in the educational process. The focus of her work was based on the premise that, during early development, an enriched learning environment could offset the effects of impoverished living conditions. The schools of Reggio Emilia in Italy, which are gaining in popularity across the world, have the "beautiful environment" as one of the three major components of their program. In these programs, the environment is seen as the "third teacher" (New & Kantor, 2009).

The main focus of this chapter will be on environmental arrangements for school and center-based programs primarily designed for preschoolers. Yet, many of the same principles and practices that are applied in these settings can be adapted to fit programs for toddlers, home-based programs, and early primary programs. The key is to provide environments that promote the growth, development, and learning of children with varying abilities and needs. We will investigate how to effectively arrange space, consider environmental factors that maximize learning, and discuss how to provide safe and accessible learning environments. But first we need to define the term *environment*. According to Gordon and Browne (2008),

> the **environment** is the sum total of the physical and human qualities that combine to create a space in which children and adults work and play together. Environment is the context teachers arrange; it is the atmosphere they create; it is the feeling they communicate. Environment is the total picture. . . .
> (P. 328)

These authorities go on to say that the environment speaks volumes to children and it has a powerful effect on their behavior as well as that of adults.

Another way to think about the classroom environment is to look at its various parts. According to Jalongo and Isenberg (2008), the learning environment consists of its physical attributes (space, room arrangement, equipment), the human dimension (the atmosphere and interactions among individuals) and the curricular environment (content, routines, goals). Each of these three components plays a key role in establishing a high-quality learning environment.

Organizing Your Classroom

Human learning is primarily based on experiences gained in interacting with the environment. The environment is constantly sending messages to children. If a child finds an experience pleasurable, he or she will seek to return to the conditions that provided that sensation. If an individual experiences discomfort or failure, however, that person typically will avoid the circumstances associated with that experience. In a sense, we become what we experience. If we can construct a classroom environment that communicates the messages "This is a safe place," "This is a fun, enjoyable place," and most importantly, "You can learn here and have a good time," then we will have set the stage for maximizing instructional efficiency.

The positive effects of a secure, pleasant working/ learning environment are many. By skillfully arranging and organizing the learning environment, teachers are often able to positively affect a variety of behaviors in young children, including those with delays or disabilities, such as encouraging learning, enhancing self-confidence, and minimizing disruptive actions. Knowledge of how the environment impacts children can be used to create learning environments that can maximize, and even magnify, a teacher's instructional effectiveness. A well-planned learning environment is also crucial to meeting the developmental needs of *all* children.

High-quality environments for young children are typically constructed around the following five research-based principles of environmental design. Jalongo and Isenberg (2008) believe that that learning environment should:

- be organized, challenging, and esthetically pleasing

- be capable of creating a caring community of learners that affirms diversity
- have clear goals that reflect a particular instructional emphasis
- protect the health and safety of the children
- allow all students equal access to age-appropriate materials and equipment

The design of your classroom should be based on a fundamental knowledge of learning theory, what we know about children's growth and development, advice from expert practitioners, recommended practice guidelines from professional associations, and research evidence. Effective environmental arrangements are also related to issues of:

- available space
- age of the children
- population density
- individual differences of the students
- visual appeal
- accessibility
- safety and health
- organization/scheduling
- budget
- student–teacher ratios

Consideration of these factors and other variables will help determine the look and feel of the learning environment you create.

Key Dimensions

Creating an effective learning environment for young children and early primary students with and without special needs is a tremendous undertaking. Building on your knowledge of child growth and development coupled with your understanding of the characteristics and needs of children with delays and disabilities, you will also need to consider a number of other factors such as space, lighting, and room arrangement in addition to materials and equipment, to mention only a few of the key elements. In some instances, various aspects of the learning environment, such as room design, are predetermined and established by the location of your classroom; for example, a public school building versus an office building or a religious facility. While some variables may not be under the teacher's control, how you structure other aspects of the learning environment are often a clear indication of the priorities, goals, and expectations you have for your children.

Designing a learning environment is not a one-time event; it is typically an ongoing process. As the needs of your children change, the classroom environment frequently requires modification. Our purpose here is to briefly review some of the important dimensions of arranging your classroom.

Space. The ratio of classroom size (area) to the child population is an important factor in designing the learning environment. The National Association for the Education of Young Children (NAEYC) (2005) recommends that preschools should maintain 35 square feet of space per child for indoor settings (50 square feet is desirable) and 75 square feet for outdoor spaces. Many states have adopted these figures for inclusion in their licensing regulations and specifications for early childhood programs. Dimension requirements for infant and toddler programs tend to be slightly lower due to the more limited mobility of the children. As stated above, the square footage provided per child may not be as significant a factor as the way in which the available space is arranged.

Other Variables. Environmental conditions strongly influence the learning environment. It is important for teachers to be alert to the effects of such things as sound, light, color, and temperature (Graves, Gargiulo, & Sluder, 1996). Sounds are a natural by-product of children' interactions and exploration of their classroom. Excessive noise, however, is uncomfortable, and negatively affects children's ability to communicate, interact socially, and concentrate while impeding their ability to learn (Readdick, 2006). Table 7–1 presents some suggestions for minimizing classroom noise pollution.

Appropriate lighting is another important classroom variable. Light has been shown to affect the emotional well-being of children (Graves et al., 1996). Classrooms should have as much natural light as possible. Art areas should always be located near windows. If natural light is insufficient, soft lighting from floor lamps is often recommended instead of harsh fluorescent lighting.

Color contributes to the ambience of the classroom. Color selection should be stimulating but not agitating or distracting. While soft colors are often seen as restful to adults, they may be viewed as uninteresting to the students. Because children spend a large portion of their day in classrooms, their classrooms need to be esthetically pleasing (Graves et al., 1996).

TABLE 7–1   Ten Suggestions For a Quieter and Attractive Environment

1. *Use carpet, throw rugs, or carpet squares.* These items absorb sounds and can be used to suggest a special place such as a reading or home activity center.

2. *Hang curtains or drapes on the windows or display children's art on the windows.* Capable of influencing the available lighting as well as softening the sounds of the room.

3. *Lower high ceilings by using permanent mobiles, drop signs from the ceiling to announce the names of the learning centers, or hang children's artwork from strings.*
   Visually attractive, minimizes echoes, and communicates where things are to students and visitors alike.

4. *Arrange plants throughout the classroom.* Absorbs sounds, filters the air, and provides opportunities for children to learn and care about plants.

5. *Include pets.* Pets soften the environment on several levels—children often lower their voices to nurture pets while they learn to care for their animals.

6. *Scatter pillows around the room.* Bean bags, throw pillows, and stuffed animals absorb vibrations and offer a cozy, warm environment.

7. *Use teacher's influence.* Use a soft voice when addressing class, use visual signals to cue to for quiet.

8. *Provide books, magazines, and paper.* These materials promote literacy as well as absorbing sound.

9. *Use baskets.* Using baskets as containers and transports for learning tools provides an attractive and soundproofing alternative to other containers.

10. *Add bulletin boards.* Cloth-covered bulletin boards absorb sound. If the room has limited display space, provide portable boards or make space by securing cloth to walls.

SOURCE: Adapted from S. Graves, R. Gargiulo, and L. Sluder, *Young Children* (St. Paul, MN: West, 1996), p. 213.

Finally, if a classroom is too hot or too cold, children will find it difficult to concentrate and learn. An optimal room temperature is generally between 68 and 72 degrees Fahrenheit (20 to 22 degrees Celsius).

Feeney and her colleagues (Feeney, Moravcik, Nolte, & Christensen, 2010) offer the following suggestions for producing an esthetically pleasing classroom that is functionally organized and pleasing to the eye.

- Choose soft, neutral colors. Use light colors for walls and ceilings. If color selection is not possible, try to coordinate with the color of the walls.
- Display children's artwork. Mount and display the students' artwork at eye level. Use shelf tops to display photographs, sculptures, and plants.
- Incorporate natural objects and materials. Use plants, stones, seeds, and shells as learning materials and to enhance the beauty of the classroom.
- Pay attention to storage. Storage should be functional, organized, and attractive. An organized learning environment helps to maintain order. Baskets and wooden bowls make attractive storage containers.
- Avoid clutter; rotate materials. Crowded shelves and storage areas look unattractive. Rotate materials instead of placing all items out for use at once. If a new item is brought out, put something away.
- Label shelves. Students will become more self-sufficient if they know where to put things away. Shelves and containers can be labeled with pictures for infants and toddlers. Silhouettes of materials can also be used.

TeachSource Video

Infants and Toddlers: Creating an Optimal Learning Environment

Visit the premium website and watch "Infants and Toddlers: Creating an Optimal Learning Environment." After watching this video, answer the following questions:

1. How would your knowledge of child development affect the organization of learning centers for infants and toddlers with delays or disabilities?
2. How would you structure learning centers to enhance the cognitive development of infants and toddlers with delays or disabilities?

Creating Activity Areas

Many teachers divide their classroom space into activity or interest areas. There can be a permanent site in the classroom for such centers as reading (literacy), arts and crafts, gross motor, and fine motor, while centers can also be temporary or rotating such as in a "discovery" or science area. Centers or areas tend to give a sense of order to the room and can serve as the focal points of daily scheduling and programming. Center content also may vary depending on the age and abilities of the children.

Infants and Toddlers

Activity areas for infants and toddlers must be safe, secure, esthetically pleasing, and stimulating. Safety and cleanliness are of paramount importance. Because developmental changes occur so rapid in the early years, the learning environment must be designed so as to account for varying levels of stimulation and challenge (Essa, 2007). Young infants (birth to 9 months), for example, seek security, mobile infants (8 to 18 months) engage in exploration, while toddlers (16 to 36 months) continue to develop their identity (Copple & Bredekamp, 2009). Activity areas must consider each of these developmental stages.

Recall that infants and toddlers are at the sensorimotor stage of intellectual development (Piaget, 1963). They learn about their world through touch, taste, sight, smell, and hearing. Accordingly, an appropriate learning environment should be a responsive environment—a setting that supports and encourages exploration and discovery through interactions with individuals, materials, and activities (Allen & Cowdery, 2009). Therefore, activity areas for infants and toddlers typically include a rattle area, a reaching and manipulation center, a sensory stimulation area, a water table, an exercise mat, an interaction-game area, a puppet theater, and a dollhouse structure.

A large part of an infant's day is structured around predictable routines—eating, sleeping, and toileting; therefore, areas must be provided that allow for changing, sleeping, and feeding, as well as quiet and active play.

Infants with developmental delays or disabilities may have much of their program prescribed by specialists such as physical or occupational therapists. Inclusive infant/toddler care environments, however, will often structure their programs around activities of daily living such as dressing, eating, or going to the bathroom. These tasks are just as important for youngsters with delays and disabilities as they are for typically developing children (O'Brien, 2001).

Due to the increased mobility and developing cognitive skills of toddlers, centers can become increasingly complex and varied. Environments for toddlers are often developed around developmentally appropriate activity areas similar to those suggested for older youngsters (Copple & Bredekamp, 2009). Typical areas include music, creative play, construction and blocks, personal identity, problem solving, sand/water play, and fine and gross motor activities. Spaces for role playing, outdoor play, and privacy should also be provided. Figure 7–1 provides one example of an infant/toddler classroom arrangement.

FIGURE 7–1 Representative Design of an Infant/Toddler Classroom

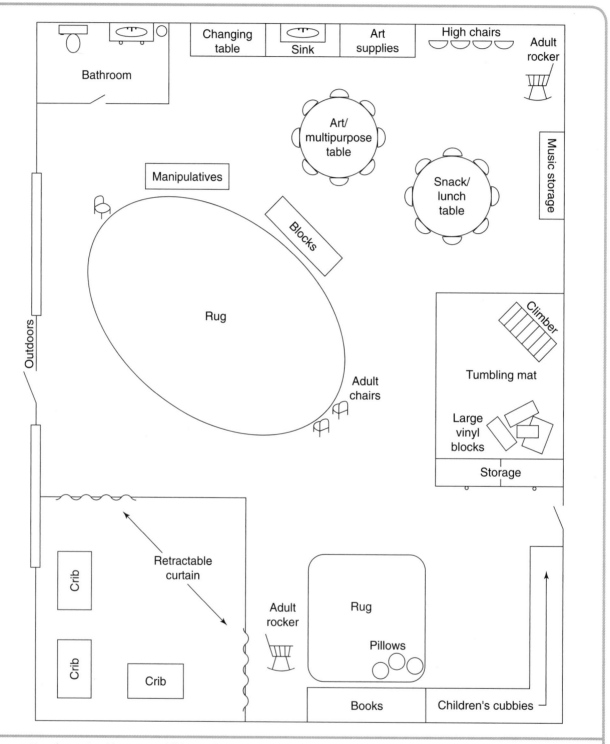

Source: Henninger, *Teaching Young Children, Infant/Toddler Classroom*. Reprinted by permission of Pearson Education, Inc.

Preschoolers

A question that often arises when planning the space for preschoolers is whether to construct open- or closed-plan facilities. Open plans tend to have undivided internal spaces within a large room, while closed-plan facilities usually entail several self-contained rooms connected by corridors or hallways. Each design has its advantages and disadvantages. Designers often suggest the use of both large and small activity sites that provide youngsters with some protection from distraction while allowing them to be able to view other areas in the room and the activities available to them.

Several years ago Olds (1987) suggested the use of "fluid boundaries" for separating areas of the preschool. This recommendation is still valid today. Fluid boundaries consist of environmental clues that a change of area has occurred while placing no physical barriers to impair mobility. For example, an activity site may be differentiated from other areas by lowering the ceiling with a parachute canopy rather than surrounding the area with bookcases or storage units. Painted lines on the floor (or colored tape if the floor is carpeted) can form effective boundaries, as can different carpet colors.

It is safe to say that at least several activity centers will be present in most preschool classrooms. Common areas in many preschool settings include, for example, a block area, gross motor center, literacy area, music area, and a quiet area. Typically these areas

are designed to accommodate small groups and a teacher, although some areas such as a circle area for introductory or circle time/sharing activities may be designed to accommodate the entire class.

Learning activities must be organized so as to encourage the meaningful participation of pupils who exhibit a wide range of skills and abilities. The preschool classroom should include centers that are age, ability, and interest appropriate while also being linked to individual outcomes and goals as outlined on the youngster's individualized family service plan (IFSP) or individualized education program (IEP). Selection of materials and the arrangement of learning centers should reflect age appropriateness and individual appropriateness (Copple & Bredekamp, 2009). A skillful matching of the individual needs of the child with the organization of the classroom often leads to equitable learning opportunities for all students while ensuring that pupils with delays or disabilities are fully integrated (Winter, 2007).

The National Association for the Education of Young Children (2005) recommends that space be divided to facilitate a range of small-group and individual activities including block building, sociodramatic play, art, music, science, math, manipulative, and quiet reading. Feeney and her colleagues (Feeney et al., 2010) recommend the addition of computer, writing, and sensory play/stimulation areas. Within these general areas, an almost endless number of specific centers can be arranged. The quiet, calm area may include the literacy (reading) language center, a private space, a listening center, and a nap area. During the day, an area's use may change, taking on dual or triple roles. For example, the quiet, calm area may first be used for language activities, then as a listening center with a tape recorder with multiple headphones, and then as the nap area. The discovery area could have rotating centers based on the theme of the week or special projects. This is a good site for hands-on science activities and as a home for classroom pets.

The dramatic play area should have activities that promote creative expression and real-life simulations. Materials should be provided to stimulate role playing such as dress-up clothes, mirrors, play kitchen, and store. Also, human figures or dolls representing various ages, ethnic backgrounds, and occupations should be provided. Although this may be considered an area devoted to creative play, there is much a teacher can do in this area to promote learning of

Activity centers for preschoolers should be attractive and encourage learning.

Cengage Learning

TeachSource Video

Preschool: Appropriate Learning Environments and Room Arrangements

Visit the premium website and watch "Preschool: Appropriate Learning Environments and Room Arrangements." After watching this video, answer the following question:

1. How does the physical arrangement of the classroom affect young children's learning and behavior?

new language behaviors and social behaviors such as tolerance for differences, sharing, and working through disputes.

The range of activities provided in the arts and crafts area should be limited only by the media available through the school's budget; and even then, the creative teacher can often work around this limitation. If possible, this area should be located in proximity to the bathroom or a sink to ease cleanup and the flooring should be slip-proof tile or linoleum. Child-size easels are recommended and space should be provided for the display of the children's work. Besides traditional coloring and painting, other activities might include woodworking projects, clay or play dough pottery, collage making, basketry, sewing (for example, class patchwork quilts), and printmaking. In classes with students with motor and physical disabilities, it is particularly important to have a variety of media available so that all children can be working at a project appropriate for their skills and specific abilities.

A question that frequently arises is whether to have a separate area for interventions or therapies. There is a rapidly increasing body of empirical evidence that suggests that for therapies (interventions) to be effective, they should be delivered during naturally occurring, ongoing, routine events (Downing, 2008; Harbin, McWilliam, & Gallagher, 2000; Noonan & McCormick, 2006). This thinking is also in keeping with the contemporary preference for service delivery in inclusive settings. The inclusion of speech–language therapy, for example, in the natural environment can usually be accomplished with minimal adaptations. Although environmental arrangements are important for certain language interventions, major adaptations to the environment are rarely needed. The introduction of physical or occupational therapy within a classroom setting, on the other hand, may require the addition of adaptive equipment that necessitates additional space for use

and storage. Teachers and related service providers using naturalistic approaches generally want to limit the amount of adaptations necessary to accommodate the needs of the children. There are two reasons for this. One is a social consideration of limiting the amount of undue attention given to the youngster with a disability. The second reason is functional—children with disabilities must learn to navigate and communicate as much as possible within the constraints of a normalized environment (Noonan & McCormick, 2006).

Another consideration is the preschooler's need for individual or private areas. Early childhood educators often suggest that time and space be provided for individual private areas (Brewer, 2007) both in terms of social time (or lack thereof) and privacy for storage and care of belongings. Children's sense of independence and need for privacy can be managed by providing them with individual "cubbies" for storage of personal items and attractive and comfortable areas designed specifically for individuals to have private time as an option. It is important that these areas be viewed by the children as positive or neutral areas.

When designing classroom space, it is also important to consider factors related to the needs of the adults. Just as children should be provided space for private time, so should adults. An adult area can be used for parent meetings and for storage of files and records. Amenities such as a refrigerator, microwave, and sofa will make the environment more teacher friendly and serve to enhance the total teaching experience.

Over time, many teachers change the environment based on their own experiences and the needs of the children presently in the class. Once again, the teacher acting as an "environmental engineer" must weigh the benefits of providing a consistent environment against the need for new opportunities for exploration. Figure 7–2 presents a representative diagram of a preschool learning environment.

FIGURE 7–2 Sample Preschool Classroom

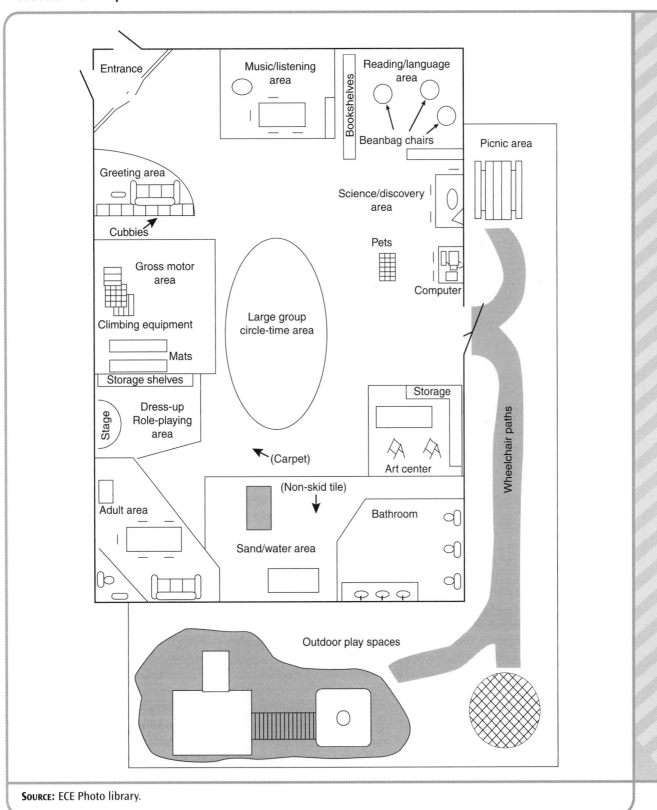

SOURCE: ECE Photo library.

Early Primary Grades

Classrooms for children in the early primary grades (ages six through eight) are typically filled with students who are excited and curious about learning. They enjoy exploring, reasoning, and problem solving. At this age, according to Tomlinson (2009), children "delight in their new intellectual prowess, social skills, and physical abilities" (p. 257). Developing an enthusiasm for learning is a major goal for this age group. At this point in time, children learn best through concrete experiences, so they need to see the relevance of what they are learning and the connections across various learning domains (Tomlinson).

Likewise, young children with delays or disabilities learn best when they are fully engaged and involved in their learning (Pretti-Frontczak & Bricker, 2004). The learning environment for these students should encourage self-initiation, personal responsibility, and self-regulation (Raver, 2009). Teachers, therefore, must carefully organize their classrooms to support these various goals, which often coexist in inclusive programs.

Many early primary grade classrooms are designed around the following eight developmentally appropriate practices (Copple & Bredekamp, 2009).

- Teachers arrange tables or flexible groupings of desks to enable children to work alone or in small groups.
- Teachers provide a safe environment and age-appropriate supervision as children are gradually given more responsibility.
- Teachers anticipate and prevent situations where children might be hurt while supporting children's risk-taking behavior within safe boundaries.
- Teachers foster a learning environment that encourages exploration, initiative, positive peer interaction, and cognitive growth. They choose materials that comfortably challenge children's skills.
- Various types of spaces are provided for silent or shared reading, working on construction projects, writing, playing math or language games, and exploring science.
- Teachers organize the daily schedule to allow for alternating periods of physical activity and quiet time.
- Teachers give children advance notice of transitions and, when possible, allow them to complete what they are working on before moving on to the next thing.
- Teachers plan the curriculum, schedule, and environment so that children can learn through active involvement in various learning experiences with each other, with adults, and with a variety of materials.

The physical environment of early primary grade classrooms typically shows a decreased use of activity centers. Desks, however, are often arranged in clusters so as to allow for small-group work and cooperative learning activities. When activity centers are incorporated into the design of the classroom, their focus is frequently on mathematics and literacy—centers where students can develop academic skills linked to the school's curriculum. Some teachers still appreciate the importance of activity centers for this age group. It would not be uncommon, therefore, to find dramatic play, art, and music centers (Henniger, 2009). Figure 7–3 presents one type of room arrangement for an early primary grade classroom.

It is very likely that your classroom will include children with special needs, thereby requiring adaptations to the learning environment. In many cases, the adaptations are relatively minor. Children with physical disabilities, for example, might require wider doorways, aisles, and pathways in order to successfully maneuver around the classroom. Learning materials may have to be placed on lower shelves so students can independently access them. Desks may need to be raised to accommodate a child in a wheelchair. Additional storage areas might be necessary to house specialized equipment or adaptive seating devices.

Some children with visual impairments may need preferential seating, clear pathways for movement, different types of lighting, and distinguishable landmarks so they can easily orient themselves in the classroom (Gargiulo, 2009).

Students with learning or emotional disorders may need a private, quiet area of the room where they can work alone or seek shelter from noise and stimulation.

Teachers have an obligation to be responsive to the individual needs of *all* their pupils. Everyone should feel welcomed. Recall that earlier in this chapter, we stated that the learning environment speaks volumes to children. What do you want *your* classroom to say about you and what happens in it?

FIGURE 7–3 Representative Design of an Early Primary Grade Classroom

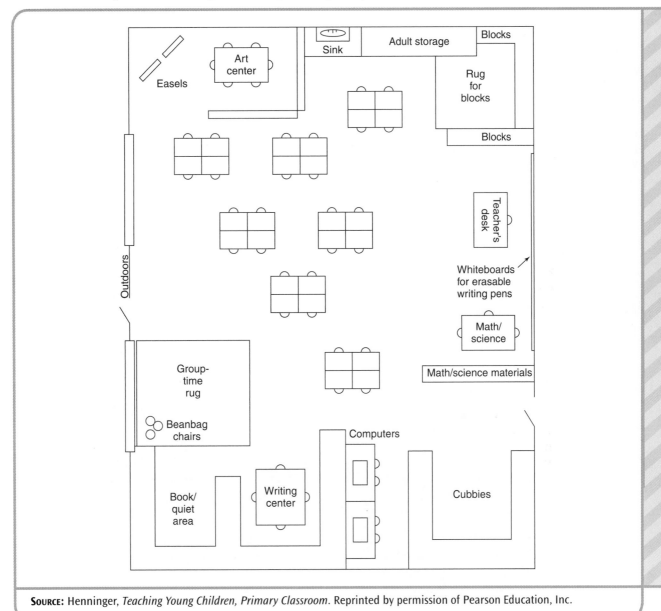

SOURCE: Henninger, *Teaching Young Children, Primary Classroom.* Reprinted by permission of Pearson Education, Inc.

Outdoor Learning Environments

Most early childhood programs have some form of outdoor play space. In fact, many teachers view the playground as an outdoor classroom. "Outdoor environments stimulate children's thinking, ability to solve problems, make decisions, socialize, and try new ideas in ways that are often different from indoor environments" (Jalongo & Isenberg, 2008, p. 207). Outdoor play is an integral part of any child's natural environment and provides children the opportunity to receive the health benefits associated with sunshine and fresh air as well as providing breaks for both children and adults from the indoor routines. Properly designed outdoor settings not only benefit the youngster's physical development but also support the child's cognitive, language, and social–emotional development as well. Outdoor play is also an essential component of developmentally appropriate practices for young children (Copple & Bredekamp, 2009). The American Academy of Pediatrics (2002), in conjunction with other professional associations, recommends that all children, including infants and toddlers, should have daily opportunities to play outdoors. Yet is unfortunate that some children, particularly those in early primary grades, no longer have a scheduled recess. Due to growing concerns about meeting academic standards, recess is sometimes eliminated in favor of increased instructional time (Elkind, 2006).

Ideally, a large, accessible, grassy area (the National Association for the Education of Young Children, [2005] advises 75 square feet per child) with interactive and exploratory equipment, plus traditional swings and slides, is generally recommended.

Playground designers also suggest that children have access to climbers, balance beams, a sandbox, and other fixed equipment in addition to a gardening area when feasible. The addition of playhouses provides opportunities for socialization and role-playing activities. For toddlers and other youngsters who are developmentally unable to safely participate, adaptive equipment appropriate to the abilities of the children should be available.

Space for outdoor eating should also be available and the entire area should be fenced in for safety purposes. Paved surfaces connecting equipment and play areas will allow for wheelchair accessibility. Areas under the play equipment should be lined with bark, pea gravel, sawdust, or sand to cushion any falls. The material should be deep enough to prevent serious injury. The U.S. Consumer Product Safety Commission (2009) recommends 12 inches of material to be effective. Safety concerns should always be your priority when planning a playground.

The number of accidents requiring medical attention that occur on playgrounds is alarming.

Outdoor play is an important component of developmentally appropriate practices.

Emergency rooms report more than 200,000 cases of children who are hurt on playgrounds each year (U.S. Consumer Product Safety Commission, 2009). The majority of these accidents occur with swings, slides, and climbing equipment. A contributing factor to these numbers may be that children are engaged in risk-taking behavior involving activities or equipment that are beyond their developmental levels. If the outdoor space involves a mix of toddlers and preschoolers or preschoolers and early primary age students, the design should incorporate activities and equipment developmentally appropriate for each group. In situations with varying levels of students, scheduling of separate outdoor play time for each group based on developmental level is advised. We tend to equate playgrounds with "equipment"; however, we should not undervalue the use of open, natural outdoor spaces. A natural space with several height levels and simple material to develop balance and other gross motor skills might be just as effective as more complex designs, especially in terms of safety and cost. According to White and Coleman (2000), developmentally appropriate outdoor environments provide children with a variety of natural and commercially produced landscape elements.

Young Children with Special Needs

All children, including those with delays and disabilities, profit from playing outdoors. Play, which is the work of the child, can be the vehicle through which children, regardless of individual differences, grow, develop, and learn; it provides a natural opportunity for inclusive experiences. Yet some children with delays or disabilities might require modeling, additional encouragement, and reinforcement in order to maximize their playground experience (Henniger, 2009).

In some circumstances, the outdoor environment must be modified to accommodate the child with special needs with accessibility and safety—two of the primary concerns. Pathways, for example, need to be 5 feet wide for use by children in wheelchairs or walkers, handrails may need to be installed, wider gates might be necessary, and playground surfaces must be designed to be accessible by children with motor impairments.

The U.S. Access Board (2005) has developed specific guidelines for playgrounds that are in compliance with the Americans with Disabilities Act. Examples include:

1. *Ground-level playground equipment.* One type of each piece of equipment (for example, swings or slides) must be accessible.
2. *Elevated structures.* Fifty percent of elevated play components must be accessible.
3. *Dramatic play equipment.* Structures such as a playhouse can easily be made accessible simply by locating them adjacent to accessible walkways.
4. *Play tables.* Tables used for board games, for sand and water play, or merely as a gathering place must be on an accessible route and meet minimum wheelchair knee requirements.
5. *Water play, sandboxes, and garden areas.* These items should be located at the edge of pathways and raised to be wheelchair accessible.

Table 7–2 offers an example of the type of outdoor play adaptations often necessary to accommodate children with disabilities. The intent of these suggestions is to ensure that young children with special needs have the opportunity to meaningfully participate with their peers to the maximum extent possible.

See Figure 7–4 for an example of an inclusive outdoor playground. Feature 7–1 identifies several play resources specific to children with special needs.

Designing the Learning Environment

When designing a learning environment for young children with and without delays or disabilities, teachers must consider multiple factors. Some of these variables include making the classroom accessible and safe while also maintaining a healthy environment. In addition, early childhood special education professionals must ensure that the students exhibit appropriate behavior when working in various activity areas of the room. How you structure the learning environment will significantly affect your students' involvement with the environment and the learning that occurs therein. We will now examine various components of an effective learning environment.

TABLE 7–2 **Planning Guide for Outdoor Play Adaptations**

Activities	For a Child Who Is Blind	For a Child with AutismSpectrum Disorder
Transition to playground	Upon entering playground, give child verbal directions about where friends and equipment are located; use sighted guide (peer or teacher) to help child move to area of choice.	Prior to entering playground, tell child he or she is going to the playground next; give him or her a ball to carry outside and repeat, "We are going outside now."
Gardening	Orient child to garden area verbally and physically; describe other children's activities (watering, digging) and offer choices for participating.	Create a physical boundary around garden area (fence or other physical structure); establish for child a specific area in which to dig, plant, and water.
Water table	Tell child which materials are in water table, where materials are located, which friends are present, and what they are doing.	Model ways to use materials and describe what you are doing or what child is doing.
Balls	Use adapted ball with beeper noise inside; place ball under child's hands rather than pulling child's hands to ball.	Communicate rules and boundaries clearly when playing with balls and repeat in different ways, as needed.
Climbing equipment	Alert child to any potential safety concerns (bumping head) and describe the location of possible danger.	No modification necessary (but monitor activity for safety).
Sandbox	Tell child which materials are available and who is playing; be aware of potential need to facilitate child's entering and maintaining play with peers.	Limit number of toys/materials available to those specifically of interest to child.

SOURCE: Adapted from L. Flynn & J. Kieff, 2002. Including Everyone in Outdoor Play. *Young Children,* 57(3), p. 23. Reprinted by permission of *NAEYC.*

Environmental Arrangement

An important principle related to environmental arrangement is that of stimulus-control. **Stimulus-control** refers to the fact that certain behaviors are more likely to occur in the presence of stimuli present while the behavior is being reinforced. Thus, physical prompts in the learning environment can be used to cue desired behaviors. For example, many homes are designed so that rooms fill a specific purpose. The den or study is decorated and furnished to promote quiet, studious pursuits. A fireplace, bookshelves, and comfortable seating all serve to stimulate behaviors related to quiet study. If one places other items in the room such as a television or pool table, the mood is changed and other types of behaviors are promoted. Each room exerts power over the person based on the experiences that individual associates with a particular environmental arrangement. For example, why do we often lower our voices to whispers when entering a church or library?

Obviously, the contingencies of these environments have modified our speaking behavior.

In a similar manner, teachers often manipulate stimulus-control when designing learning environments (Wolery, 2000). The reading center, for instance, might be decorated with letters, posters of children reading, and attractive book covers, which all serve as prompts for looking at picture books and other reading materials. In this manner, stimulus-control also can be used to promote and hold engagement. Classroom management can be facilitated by color coding the areas. Brightly colored free play and gross motor areas can cue the children that louder noise levels are permissible. Softer, pastel hues in the reading and math areas can serve to prompt quiet behavior. In order to limit distractions and interference, quiet areas should not be in proximity to noisier areas. Movement within the classroom can be cued by using functional objects. A simulated stop sign or red light can cue children that an area is

FIGURE 7–4 Example of an Inclusive Outdoor Playground

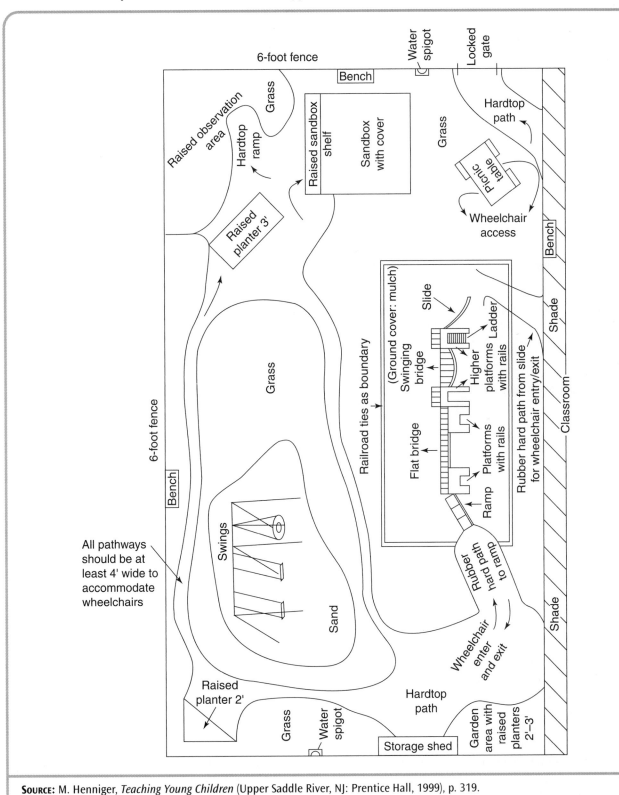

Source: M. Henniger, *Teaching Young Children* (Upper Saddle River, NJ: Prentice Hall, 1999), p. 319.

FEATURE 7–1

Play Resource Websites for Children with Delays and Disabilities

- **AblePlay** www.ableplay.org
  Independent ratings and reviews of toys for children with special needs

- **Guide to Toys for Children with Special Needs 2008**
  www.afb.org/Section.asp?SectionID=82
  An educational guide to toys for children with special needs

- **Toys for Kids with Disabilities**
  www.disabilityresources.org/TOYS.html
  A resource for locating toys specifically designed for children with physical, cognitive, and sensory impairments

- **Toys and Playtime Tips for Children with Special Needs**
  www.fisher-price.com/us/special_needs
  Toys and playtime tips for children with specific types of impairments. Developed in conjunction with the Let's Play! Projects, a federally funded program that supports family play experiences and activities for children with special needs

SOURCE: Adapted from A. Watson and R. McCathren, 2009. Including Children with Special Needs, *Young Children, 64*(2), p. 26.

---

off limits for the time being. A green light can signal areas children may visit. By allowing the environment to provide cues about classroom routine and rules, the teacher can save him- or herself time and energy. Children will tend to monitor peer behavior and there will be less temptation for students to test limits when a visual prompt is present.

Reinforcement and Responsivity

Elements of the learning environment can also serve as reinforcers for children's behavior. Activity areas can be manipulated so that children receive immediate feedback and reinforcement. For example, a child working in the math activity center who successfully completes a task may be rewarded with time to work on the class computer or another activity that has high value to the child. Activity centers can easily be designed so that they permit flexible sequencing of child activities. The Premack principle (Alberto & Troutman, 2009), also known as Grandma's Law, is a method that can be used for scheduling activities so that children

move from less desirable to more desirable activities. **Premacking** involves sequencing activities so that less-probable or low-probability activities are followed by high-probability (motivating) activities (i.e., you don't get your dessert until after you eat your broccoli). College students also apply this principle when they interrupt periods of tedious studying by inserting an activity that allows them to relax or unwind. If a child is uninterested in the reading area and highly motivated by the gross motor area, time in the gross motor area can serve as a reinforcer following participation in the reading center. Likewise, if a child enjoys the dress-up center, he or she can attend this area contingent on completion of prescribed activities in a less desirable setting such as the listening center.

Related to the idea of reinforcement is the concept of **responsivity.** Researchers have identified responsivity as an environmental factor closely linked to academic gain (Wolery, 2000). A responsive environment is one that provides the learner with predictable and immediate outcomes from any environmental interaction. Toy manufacturers make great use of responsivity in the production of material for infants. Crib-hanging learning centers and mobiles provide the infant with a visual or auditory response for any action done to them. For instance, push a rubber bulb and you get a ding, run a hand across a cylinder and you get a spinning, jingling response. The infant's verbal and facial reactions to these types of immediate feedback indicate the strength of responsivity to promote engagement. The child will return again and again to these stimuli because he or she understands that his or her actions can influence the environment.

A setting that provides immediate and consistent reinforcement of behaviors will permit children to acquire a sense of power and security in controlling their environment. This sense of empowerment can be an important motivator for young children with disabilities and serves to encourage them to explore the next nook or cranny. The antithesis to the concept of empowerment, **learned helplessness,** is typical of many students with special needs. Children develop this sense of helplessness when their interactions with the environment prove futile or produce inconsistent results (Gargiulo, 2009). Children may shy away from risk and new experiences because they are unsure of the results their actions will bring.

Self-correcting materials are a good example of instructional technologies that can provide immediate feedback. Because self-correcting materials can be completed by the child or a small group of students with or without the teacher being present, children will also develop independence. Montessori preschools have long used self-correcting material in their preschool designs. Many computer software programs developed for preschool-aged children and students in the early primary grades use a self-correcting format. An animated creature will appear on the screen and say "good work" or will provide a soft form of correction and urge the child to try again.

Teachers can make use of the same procedures when constructing their own self-correcting instructional materials. Windows and flaps that conceal the correct response or a picture of the correct response can be easily incorporated into either two-dimensional or three-dimensional manipulative materials constructed from cardboard or posterboard. Some examples of these materials are presented in Figure 7–5.

FIGURE 7–5 Examples of Self-Correcting Manipulatives

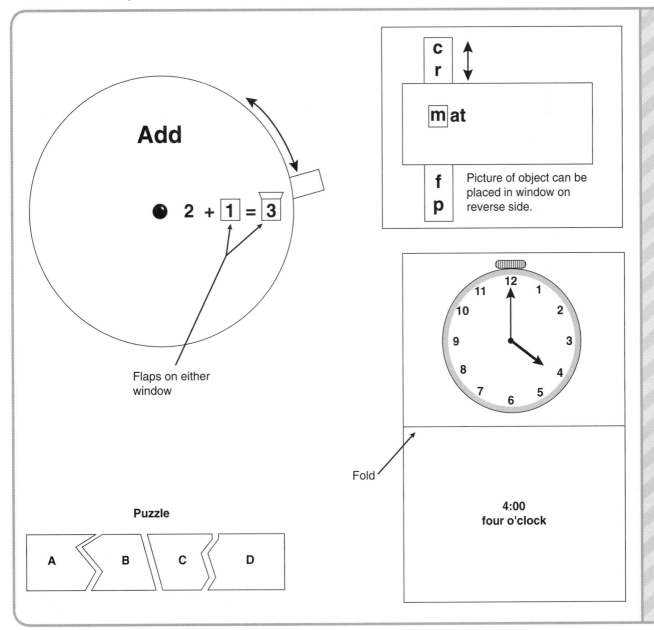

Responsivity can be greatly facilitated when working with children with physical or multiple disabilities through the use of switches and adapted materials. Any battery-operated toy can be easily adapted to operate when pressure is applied to a connected switch. Switches come in a variety of shapes and sizes to fit the specific mobility abilities of the student. They can be placed on a lap board on a child's wheelchair for hand use, on the top side of the wheelchair for response to head movement, and can even be connected to sip-and-puff devices that respond to air pressure.

For a child who is nonverbal, augmentative or alternative communication (AAC) devices can be used that allow a child to use a switch to scan possible responses to center activities. For example, during storytime, the teacher may be reading a Beatrix Potter story. Beforehand a paraprofessional records the terms "Peter," "Flopsy," and "Mopsy" into the device and places corresponding pictures in spaces provided. When the teacher asks comprehension questions, the child can scan the device by pressing the switch and, by pressing again, can stop the scan on the answer she wishes to give. The answer will then be stated verbally. With the emergence of adaptive equipment and advancing technology, it is now possible for just about all children with disabilities to meaningfully participate and interact with their learning environments and their peers.

An Accessible Environment

The Americans with Disabilities Act requires that reasonable accommodations be made to ensure that public facilities, including child care centers, preschool programs, and schools are accessible to individuals with disabilities. Accessibility of the learning environment is crucial if inclusion of young children with special needs is to be successful (Downing, 2008; Odom & Wolery, 2003). Developmentally appropriate practices also call for the inclusion of *all* children (Copple & Bredekamp, 2009).

While the term **accessibility** often is used in the context of providing equal opportunity to enter into an environment, this term is more encompassing in education circles. Accessibility in educational contexts includes adaptations necessary to ensure successful goal attainment by children with disabilities. This may require changes in the communication methods as well as the physical arrangements. Programs that cater to individual needs will be relatively easy to adapt for children with sensory or physical

disabilities. In these programs, modifications to meet the needs of students are part of the presentation of daily activities. Programs that are more freeform, relying on child-directed activities, will need more adaptation to accommodate children with special needs. We recommend that early childhood programs conduct accessibility assessments.

As a rule, adaptations to an environment to accommodate a child should be kept to a minimum. In other words, adaptations should be as subtle and unobtrusive as possible to minimize pointing out the differences in the child with the disability. Examples of classroom adaptations include:

- lowered or raised desktops and work tables of varying sizes and shapes
- adjustable shelves containing books, supplies, and learning materials
- adequate pathways and turn-around space for students using walkers, wheelchairs, or other mobility devices
- lowered sinks and water fountains (or the use of a cup dispenser)
- restrooms designed to accommodate individuals with physical disabilities

Generally speaking, adaptations to the physical environment are arranged so as to enhance learning, social interactions, communication, and independence. Teachers should only modify the learning environment if the child is unable to participate or access an activity without modification (Noonan & McCormick, 2006). The adaptations required will depend on the type and severity of the pupil's disability. A second grader with physical disabilities, for example, will most likely need additional space for maneuvering his or her mobility device and may require various pieces of adaptive equipment to use in therapy and assist in accessing the school program. Equipment often used in this context includes wedges, wheelchairs, prone standers, sidelyers, posture chairs, and support bars. The purpose of a wedge, for example, is to give the lower trunk and torso support so that head, arms, and hands are free to manipulate objects. A child using a wedge may freely participate in activities such as block play, art, and role playing with human figures and dolls. Sidelyers and prone standers serve the same purpose for youngsters with a variety of physical disabilities. Examples of adaptive equipment used to assist students with physical disabilities are presented in Figure 7–6.

Adaptations to the communication environment may require the adoption of AAC devices. This may

FIGURE 7–6 Examples of Adaptive Equipment

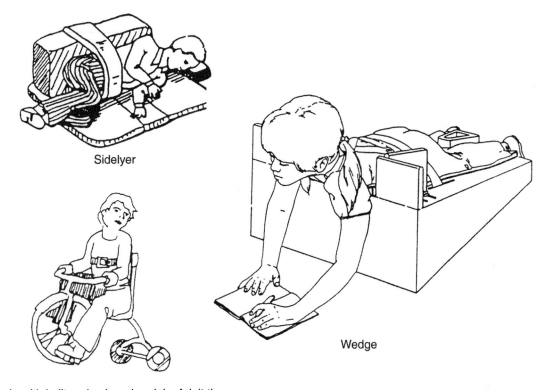

Sidelyer

Wedge

Tricycle with built-up back and pedals. Adult three-wheeled bikes are available for larger children and adolescents.

Source: S. Best, K. Heller, and J. Bigge, *Teaching Individuals with Physical or Multiple Disabilities* (5th ed.) (Upper Saddle River, NJ: Pearson Education, 2005), p. 198.

include a range of low-tech materials and methods such as sign language or flip-picture cards to high-tech devices like electronic communication boards or scanning computer keyboards that can be operated with switches adapted for a particular disability. It may also be necessary to modify bulletin boards and other classroom materials to accommodate low-tech alternative forms of communication. The use of signs or symbols with the printed word on materials may facilitate learning of these techniques by all class members, thus improving accessibility for children who are nonverbal by providing a universal method of classroom communication.

TeachSource Video

Preschool: Appropriate Learning Environments and Room Arrangements

Revisit the "Preschool: Appropriate Learning Environments and Room Arrangements" video on the premium website and answer the following question:

1. What procedures would you incorporate in your classroom to ensure accessibility of the learning environment?

Some young children communicate via alternative means.

Cengage Learning

Finally, when thinking about adapting your classroom to include children with special needs, it would be helpful to remember the following three key concepts: accessibility, usability, and developmental appropriateness. Remember, it is not always necessary for children with delays and disabilities to participate in an activity to the same degree as their typical classmates for the activity to be enjoyed. The concept of "partial participation states that, regardless of severity of disability, individuals can be taught to participate in [a] variety of activities to some degree, or activities can be adapted to allow participation" (Sheldon, 1996, p. 116). Adaptations to activities can increase opportunities for interaction and enhance the quality of participation so that the environment is exciting and interesting for *all* youngsters.

Table 7–3 offers a checklist of environmental adaptations typically needed to accommodate children with diverse abilities. Feature 7–2 provides a list of Web resources for obtaining adaptive toys and equipment.

A Safe Environment

Keeping children safe and healthy is job number one. Regulations governing these two critical areas are found in all licensing and accreditation standards. It is imperative that teachers are committed to the safety and well-being of their pupils. While keeping youngsters safe is a matter of common sense, the responsibility for a safe environment resides with the teacher. Educators must be especially vigilant when caring for infants and toddlers who are particularly vulnerable (Feeney et al., 2010).

The teacher's task of providing a safe environment for young children with special needs has been made easier due to the development of safer toys and equipment and by the production of safer building materials. Many early childhood programs are now equipped with slip-proof linoleum with a rubber underlining to help prevent breakage. This product can be essential in making bathrooms, wet areas, and art areas safer for children.

As matters of safety and efficiency, learning areas can be partitioned by using shelving or dividers that are approximately 3 feet high (2 feet for toddlers). This allows the teacher to have a clear field of vision across the classroom, provides a sense of privacy to the areas, and places storage of materials adjacent to the site where they will most likely be used.

Consumer protection groups have worked diligently to ensure that toys and materials are nontoxic and fire retardant. Most children's toys now carry labels and warnings concerning age appropriateness and possible safety problems experienced by infants and toddlers. Although these improvements have decreased potential dangers, teachers must be ever vigilant to identify environmental conditions that may put children at risk of injury. For example, a throw rug used in a high-traffic area of the room will invariably lead to an unplanned tumble. This arrangement will also tend to limit accessibility for a child with a visual or motor impairment.

A particularly frightening source of accidents in the preschool is electrical shock and resulting burns. The effects of burns are always painful and often irreparable. The effect of electrical shock is often heart failure. It is much easier to work on preventative measures than to initiate treatment after the accident. Wall sockets are very attractive to young children wishing to explore a newfound cranny. In new construction, wall outlets should be teacher height, approximately 5 to 6 feet off the floor. Extension cords should be used with extreme care or be completely excluded from preschool settings (American Academy of Pediatrics, 2002). Young children can easily separate an extension cord and place the exposed end in their mouth. This can cause severe burns to the

TABLE 7–3 Checklist for an Accessible Environment

Physical Environment

Questions to think about:
- How do different children use their bodies or the space around them for learning?
- How can we enhance or adapt the physical environment for children who have difficulty moving (or who move too much)?
- How can we capitalize on the physical environment for children who learn by moving?

Accessing the environment safely:

❑ Are doorway widths in compliance with local building codes?

❑ Ramps in addition to or instead of stairs?

❑ Low, wide stairs where possible (including playground equipment)?

❑ Hand rails on *both* sides of stairs?

❑ Easy handles on doors, drawers, etc.?

❑ At least some kids' chairs with armrests?
- "Cube" chairs are great!
- Often a footrest and/or seat strap will provide enough stability for a child to do fine motor activities.

❑ When adapting seating, mobility, and/or gross motor activities for a specific child with physical disabilities, consult a physical therapist.

Learning through the environment:

❑ Do the environment and equipment reflect variety?
- Surface, heights (textured, smooth, low, high, etc.)
- Space for gross motor activity (open spaces, climbing structures, floor mats)
- Quiet/comfort spaces (small spaces, carpet, pillows)
- Social spaces (dramatic play area, groups of chairs or pillows, etc.)

❑ Are toys and equipment physically accessible?
- Glue magnets to backs of puzzle pieces and attribute blocks and use on a steel cookie tray.
- Attach large knobs or levers to toys with lids and movable parts.
- Attach tabs to book pages for easier turning.

❑ An occupational therapist can provide specific suggestions for adapting materials and activities so a child with physical disabilities can participate.

Visual Environment

Questions to think about:
- How do different children use their vision for learning?
- How can we enhance the visual environment for a child with low or no vision?
- How can we capitalize on the visual environment for children who learn by seeing?

Accessing the environment safely:

❑ Are contrasting colors used on edges and when surfaces change (e.g., tile to carpet, beginning of stairs)?

❑ Can windows be shaded to avoid high glare?
- Also consider darker nonglossy floors and tabletops.
- Some children's behavior and learning may improve dramatically once a strong glare is eliminated.

❑ Is visual clutter avoided on walls, shelves, etc.?
- Visual clutter can interfere with learning, predictability, and safety.

❑ Is "spot lighting" (e.g., swing arm lamp) in a dimmer room available?
- Spot lamps help some children pay attention and work better on table tasks.

❑ Orientation and mobility specialists help children with visual impairments learn to navigate the environment.

(continued)

TABLE 7–3 Checklist for an Accessible Environment *(continued)*

Learning through the environment:

❑ Are objects and places in the environment labeled ("door," "chair," etc.)?

❑ Are the size and contrast of pictures and letters adequate for the children with visual impairments in your program?

❑ Are visual displays at the children's eye level?

❑ Are large-print materials, textured materials, and auditory materials available (e.g., big books, sandpaper letters, books on tape)?

❑ Is the daily schedule represented in words and pictures?
  • A Velcro schedule that allows children to post the schedule and then remove items as activities are completed can help children to stay focused and transition more easily from one activity to the next.

❑ Are children with low vision seated close to the center of activity and away from high glare?

❑ Teachers for the visually impaired assist in selecting and adapting materials for children with low vision.

❑ Children who are blind may need a running commentary of events, places, etc. Pictures in books and food on plates, for example, should be described.

Auditory Environment

Questions to think about:
  • How do different children use their hearing for learning?
  • How can we enhance the auditory environment for a child who is deaf, is hearing impaired, or has poor auditory discrimination skills?
  • How can we capitalize on the auditory environment for auditory learners?

Accessing the environment safely:

❑ Does background noise (from indoor or outdoor sources) filter into the area?

❑ Is there a way to eliminate or dampen background noise (using carpeting, closing windows and doors)?
  • Some kids are unable to do the automatic filtering out of background noises that we do so unconsciously.

❑ Is "auditory competition" avoided?
  • Raising one's voice to compete with a roomful of noisy children is rarely as effective as "silent signals," such as holding up a peace sign or encouraging children who notice to do the same until the room is full of quiet children holding up peace signs.

❑ Are nonauditory signals needed to alert a child with a hearing impairment?
  • Turning the lights on and off is a common strategy.
  • Ask the child's parents what strategies are used at home.

Learning through the environment:

❑ Are auditory messages paired with visual ones (e.g., simple sign language, flannel boards, picture schedules)?

❑ Are children with hearing impairment seated so they can see others' faces and actions?

❑ Teachers for the hearing impaired can provide strategies for modifying activities for children with hearing impairments.

❑ A child who is deaf will need a teacher or aide who uses sign language.

Social Environment

Questions to think about:
  • How do different children use social cues for learning?
  • How can we adapt the social environment for children with impulsive behavior, attention deficits, or behavior problems?
  • How can we capitalize on the social environments for children who learn by relating to others?

(continued)

TABLE 7–3 Checklist for an Accessible Environment *(continued)*

Accessing the environment safely:

❑ Is the schedule predictable? Are children informed of schedule changes?

❑ Does the schedule provide a range of activity levels (e.g., adequate opportunities for physical activity)?

❑ School psychologists and behavior specialists can help analyze misbehavior and modify the environment or schedule to minimize problems for children with attention deficits or behavior problems.

Learning through the environment

❑ Does the environment have a positive impact on self-esteem?
  • Allows all children to feel safe?
  • Invites all children to participate?
  • Maximizes all children's opportunities for independence?

❑ Do learning materials and toys include representations of all kinds of people, including children and adults with disabilities?
  • People with disabilities should be represented in active and leadership roles, not just as passive observers.

❑ Does the schedule include opportunities for a variety of groups (pairs, small groups, whole class) as well as quiet time or time alone?
  • Pairing or grouping children with complementary abilities eases the demands on the teacher and enables children to help one another.
  • When given a chance, peers often come up with the most creative ways for children with disabilities to participate.
  • Creative use of staffing may be needed to provide additional support for some children during some activities.

❑ Does the schedule provide both structured and open activity times?
  • Children who have difficulty with a particular type of activity may need extra support at those times.

Additional Strategies When Adapting the Environment for Individual Children

❑ Make use of the diverse strengths of the various people on the child's team.
  • Early childhood educators are among the most sensitive and creative when it comes to developing multisensory, inclusive activities that take individual children's skills and needs into account!
  • Be on the lookout for how kids modify environments and activities for themselves and their peers. They often come up with the most creative solutions!
  • Include parents when making accommodations for children with special needs. Parents know their own children better than anyone else.
  • Some children qualify for special education services through state-wide infant or preschool intervention services. The specialists in these programs can assist in assessing a child's needs and providing suggestions and/or parameters for modifying the environment (and instructional strategies).

❑ Respect for each child's strengths and needs is the most important ingredient in creating appropriate environments for all children.

Source: Adapted from CCIE in K. Haugen, *Using Your Senses to Adapt Environments* (114, pp. 50, 55–56). Reprinted by permission of Exchange Press.

FEATURE 7–2

Representative Web Resources for Adaptive Toys and Equipment

• **Abilitations** www.abilitations.com
• **Flaghouse, Inc.** www.flaghouse.com/Special-Populations/Recreation-and-Play-PN=1
• **Letotek** www.lekotek.org/
• **Rifton** www.rifton.com

tongue, lips, and other soft parts of the oral cavity and, in some instances, can be fatal. Although we believe that all teachers should be trained in first aid and CPR, an ounce of prevention will better serve the children.

A final topic related to safety is classroom orderliness and organization. A cluttered room is not safe; thus, a cleanup time between activities is important. Not only is cleanup desirable for safety factors, but it also promotes good work habits and responsibility among the students.

We recommend that early childhood special educators consult the following resource manual for guidance on establishing a safe and secure learning environment.

- *Stepping Stones to Using Caring for Our Children* (National Resource Center for Health and Safety in Child Care, 2003).

Table 7–4 details specific suggestions for maintaining a safe classroom while Table 7–5 offers the "golden rules" for selecting safe learning materials and toys.

A Healthy Environment

Cleanliness is an important factor in maintaining a healthy learning environment. Classrooms should be cleaned daily and accumulated trash should be removed. Frequently used equipment should be

TABLE 7–4 Classroom Safety Suggestions

1. Check the environment, both inside and outside, for any hazards. Check electrical outlets and cords; make sure children cannot pull over any equipment (television sets, DVD players); remove dangerous plants; cover sharp edges; make sure fences are sturdy and exit gates are childproof; and eliminate any other hazards to children's safety.

2. Practice emergency procedures on a regular basis. Children's and teachers' responses to fire drills (and in some areas, tornado and earthquake procedures) must become automatic.

3. Make sure that the classroom contains a fire extinguisher and that all staff know how to use it.

4. All teachers and staff members should be trained in first aid and cardiopulmonary resuscitation (CPR). At minimum, one person with such training should be present at all times. Staff should be required to have special training in CPR for infants if the program accepts children that young.

5. Post a list of the names of all children and a map of fire exit routes near each exit.

6. Each classroom should be equipped with a well stocked first aid kit. Keep it in a specific location so staff members can quickly find it. A second kit should be available for use on field trips and outdoor outings.

7. Keep cleaning agents, insecticides, and other such items (including medications) out of the reach of children—preferably in a locked cabinet.

8. Maintain an up-to-date list of emergency phone numbers (parents, relatives, doctors, and hospitals) for each child. Take a copy of this information with you when going on field trips or other excursions.

9. Keep the number for the poison control center posted near the telephone.

10. Post a list of children's allergies (including reactions to ant, wasp, or bee stings, or certain foods) and check it before planning any food experiences or outdoor activities.

11. Keep a list by the door of the adults authorized to pick up each child. Do not release a child to any unauthorized person.

12. Make all posted information readily available to substitute teachers.

SOURCE: Adapted from J. Brewer, *Introduction to Early Childhood Education* (6th ed.). (Boston: Pearson Education, 2007), pp. 98–100.

TABLE 7–5 Creating a Safe Learning Environment for Young Children

1. Choose toys and art materials that are labeled nontoxic. Crayons and paints should say "ASTM D-4236" on the package. This means that the item has been tested and evaluated by the American Society for Testing and Materials.

2. Choose water-based paints, glue, and markers.

3. Avoid battery-operated or electrical toys that may cause shock.

4. Do not use toys with strings or cords longer than 10 inches.

5. Check all toys regularly to ensure that they are in good repair with no cracks, rips, sharp edges, or loose parts.

6. Avoid materials with small removable or loose parts that could easily be swallowed. For youngsters under the age of 3, choose toys that are larger than 1.75 inches and balls that are larger than 1.75 inches in diameter.

7. Avoid toy chests or similar storage facilities that might trap children or pinch fingers.

SOURCE: Adapted from S. Feeney, E. Moravcik, S. Nolte, and D. Christensen, *Who Am I in the Lives of Children?* 8th ed. (Upper Saddle River, NJ: Pearson Education, 2010), p. 219.

conditions, or chronic illnesses. Infectious diseases that tend to be of particular concern with infants and young children include hepatitis A and B, cytomegalovirus (CMV), herpes simplex Type 1, and AIDS (Aronson & Shope, 2004; Heller, Forney, Alberto, Best, & Schwartzman, 2009). CMV will produce only flulike symptoms in children but can be devastating if transmitted to a teacher or parent who is pregnant. Both hepatitis B (the more virulent form of hepatitis) and herpes simplex are incurable and can be spread through bodily fluids. Herpes simplex Type 1 and CMV are probably the most infectious of these diseases because they can be spread through airborne effects of coughing and sneezing. AIDS has the least likelihood of transmission because of the need for semen or blood transference (Heller et al.). (The issue of children with AIDS is discussed in Chapter 10.)

The spread of these and other communicable diseases can be controlled by applying good health practices such as frequent hand washing, which is considered by many health care professionals to be the most effective way of controlling the spread of disease and illness. This hygiene practice, commonly referred to as "universal precautions," also requires that the cleansing of materials and surfaces with disinfectant become a regular part of an adult's duties in the classroom. Surfaces such as diaper changing areas, toilet seats, positioning boards, wheelchair trays, and eating areas should receive special attention. Toys and materials should be washed after use and adults should pay special attention to material handled by children with runny noses and to toys placed in or near the mouth. A rule in the classroom could be that anything touching the mouth is immediately taken and placed in a tub to be cleaned. Adults should always wash their hands following any contact involving bathroom assistance, positioning, feeding, or diaper changing. A good practice is to wear disposable latex-free gloves during these duties. Any open cuts or sores noticed on adults or children should be covered with bandages. Adapting these hygiene procedures into the daily routine not only helps to prevent the spread of disease but also serves as a model of safety behavior for children. Lastly, because it is always better to prevent an illness, many teachers find it beneficial to provide hand sanitizers and tissues throughout their room.

sanitized periodically, and dramatic play items (dress-up clothes), personal blankets, and fabric toys all require regular laundering.

Another critical aspect of establishing a healthy environment is protecting children from the spread of communicable diseases. Teaching good personal hygiene habits is a central element of many early childhood and elementary school programs and is often an integral component of a functional curriculum. Some children with disabilities are particularly at risk for certain infections due to related problems with immune systems, heart

Selecting Learning Materials

Effective teachers must think from the child's point of view about what materials will be most appealing. A consistent source of dismay among parents at gift giving times, such as Christmas or birthdays, is when their toddler spends hours playing with the cardboard box and wrapping paper and ignores the bright, expensive toy contained within. Early childhood professionals must be good consumers and consumer advocates, not always deciding on purchasing that which is widely advertised and neatly packaged. The money that is spent on resources for our programs must be spent wisely, as the amount of money typically available seems to decrease every year. An outline of representative considerations for purchasing activity area/classroom materials is offered in Table 7–6.

A key consideration when purchasing or creating material is to ensure its durability. Almost all two-dimensional materials can and should be laminated or covered with clear plastic to facilitate cleaning and promote longevity. Young children can be rough on materials, especially materials used frequently. Even materials designed specifically for teacher use such as curricula, kits, teacher idea books, or thematic units can receive a lot of wear in a short time.

Because most commercially made materials can be costly, it is highly recommended that teachers accumulate their own teacher-made materials. Not only will this save on expense, but it is also much easier for teachers to create materials geared to specific student needs. Many teachers find the making of materials worthwhile for intrinsic reasons. Having one's own materials in the classroom provides a sense of investment and self-fulfillment. The concept of personal pride and investment can also be applied to the activities of children and their parents. An investment in the physical design of the classroom may promote parent involvement and child interest. In addition to being an environmental engineer, the teacher often must take on the role of architect and interior design expert.

Before the purchase of any materials such as prepackaged kits or curricula, the early childhood special educator should examine any available information on its development and field-testing. Information obtained can be helpful in determining whether this material is suitable for a specific group and the specific purposes behind its development. The appropriateness of material in terms of both age and ability becomes especially relevant when dealing with children with developmental delays or disabilities. Material field tested with populations that did not include children with disabilities may turn out to be inappropriate for similar-aged populations with disabilities and delays.

TABLE 7–6 Considerations for Purchasing Instructional Materials

I. General Considerations
1. Safety
2. Cost and durability
3. Target population
4. Skill level(s) required
5. Esthetically attractive
6. Necessity of adult supervision
7. Reflective of children's individual differences (avoid racial/cultural stereotypes)

II. Instructional Considerations
1. Is the item developmentally appropriate?
2. Does the item allow for versatility and flexibility of use (age and ability levels)?
3. Is corrective feedback provided?
4. Is the item aligned with specific learning goals/objectives?
5. Does the item allow for individual and/or group work?

Summary

Environmental arrangements are critically important in the education of young children with special needs. Teachers must become environmental engineers in their own classrooms to maximize the impact of their instruction. Development of this ability is dependent on a basic understanding of children's growth and development and how the environment affects the learning process. Variables such as room arrangement, effective use of space, color, lighting, and even room temperature are all key dimensions of an effective learning environment.

Most early childhood (and some early primary) classrooms today are organized around activity areas or interest centers. The number and type of the centers used is frequently dependent on the age of the children and their developmental needs. Regardless of the focus of the activity area (literacy, fine motor, dramatic play), interest centers must be individually and developmentally appropriate and able to meet the needs of *all* children.

Outdoor play is essential to the overall development of young children and an integral component of daily activities. Play is the work of the child and a natural mechanism for facilitating inclusive experiences. Two factors of utmost importance for the early childhood special educator are the safety of the children as they interact with the environment and the issue of accessibility—no child should be denied meaningful participation because of a lack of appropriate adaptations.

Teachers must carefully consider how they design their classrooms. The physical arrangement of the room and the organization of materials significantly influences children's behavior. Of course, it goes without saying that the teacher's primary responsibility is keeping the children safe and healthy. Equally important is the requirement that the learning environment be readily accessible so children with different types of delays and disabilities can access it.

Instructional materials, whether teacher-made or commercially available, must be not only durable but also developmentally appropriate and keyed to the unique needs of the students.

Check Your Understanding

1. Discuss how interactions with the environment can help shape a child's learning and development.
2. What are some of the key dimensions to consider when designing a classroom?
3. Identify the various types of activity centers typically found in most classrooms for infants and toddlers, preschoolers, and early primary students. Describe the components of each.
4. What steps would you take to ensure that an outdoor learning environment is accessible for children with disabilities?
5. How can stimulus-control enhance learning?
6. Describe the concept of Premacking.
7. Why is responsivity important for learning in young children with disabilities?
8. List the steps you would take to ensure an accessible, safe, and healthy learning environment for young children with special needs.
9. What are some of the factors to consider when selecting instructional materials?

Reflection and Application

1. Observe an outdoor learning environment at an area preschool and an elementary school. Prepare a report for your class. Some of the issues to address in your presentation include:
   - a sketch of the playground
   - the kinds of activities the children were engaged in
   - the types of equipment available—did you observe a difference in the equipment at each location?
   - Was the equipment being used appropriately by the children?
   - Was the environment accessible by children with delays and disabilities? What types of adaptations did you observe?
   - Were safety standards maintained?
   - What was the role of the teacher during outdoor play?
   - suggestions for improving the outdoor experience
2. You have been asked by a local benefactor of young children to submit a proposal for establishing an inclusive preschool program in your community. She has requested that your proposal include the following points:
   - a sketch of the floor plan, including room design and planned activity areas
   - supplies and instructional materials, including their cost
   - plans to make the program accessible

- an outdoor learning environment, including needed equipment
- health and safety requirements

3. What other items would you include in your prospectus?

References

Alberto, P., & Troutman, A. (2009). *Applied behavior analysis for teachers* (8th ed.). Upper Saddle River, NJ: Pearson Education.

Allen, K., & Cowdery, G. (2009). *The exceptional child* (6th ed.). Clifton Park, NY: Thomson/Delmar Learning.

American Academy of Pediatrics. (2002). National health and safety performance standards: Guidelines for out-of-home child care programs (2nd ed.). Elk Grove Village, IL: Author.

Aronson, S., & Shope, T. (Eds.). (2004). *Managing infectious diseases in child care and schools.* Elk Grove Village, IL: American Academy of Pediatrics.

Brewer, J. (2007). *Introduction to early childhood education* (6th ed.). Boston: Pearson Education.

Copple, C., & Bredekamp, S. (2009). *Developmentally appropriate practices in early childhood programs* (3rd ed.). Washington, DC: National Association for the Education of Young Children.

Downing, J. (2008). *Including students with severe and multiple disabilities in typical classrooms* (3rd ed.). Baltimore: Paul H. Brookes.

Elkind, D. (2006). *The power of play.* Cambridge, MA: Da Capo Press.

Essa, E. (2007). *Introduction to early childhood education* (5th ed.). Clifton Park, NY: Delmar/Cengage Learning.

Feeney, S., Moravcik, E., Nolte, S., & Christensen, D. (2010). *Who am I in the lives of children?* (8th ed.). Upper Saddle River, NJ: Pearson Education.

Gargiulo, R. (2009). *Special education in contemporary society* (3rd ed.). Thousand Oaks, CA: Sage.

Gordon, A., & Browne, K. (2008). *Beginnings and beyond* (7th ed.). Clifton Park, NY: Thomson/Delmar Learning.

Graves, S., Gargiulo, R., & Sluder, L. (1996). *Young children.* St. Paul, MN: West.

Harbin, G., McWilliam, R., & Gallagher, J. (2000). Services for young children with disabilities and their families. In J. Shonkoff & S. Meisels (Eds.), *Handbook of early intervention* (2nd ed., pp. 387–415). Cambridge, England: Cambridge University Press.

Heller, K., Forney, P., Alberto, P., Best, S., & Schwartzman, M. (2009). *Understanding physical, health, and multiple disabilities* (2nd ed.). Upper Saddle River, NJ: Pearson Education.

Henniger, M. (2009). *Teaching young children* (4th ed.). Upper Saddle River, NJ: Pearson Education.

Jalongo, M., & Isenberg, J. (2008). *Exploring your role* (3rd ed.). Upper Saddle River, NJ: Pearson Education.

National Association for the Education of Young Children. (2005). *NAEYC early childhood program standards and accreditation criteria.* Washington, DC: Author.

National Resource Center for Health and Safety in Child Care. (2003). *Stepping stones to using caring for our children* (2nd ed.). Elk Grove Village, IL: American Academy of Pediatrics.

Neisworth, J., & Buggey, T. (2005). Behavior analysis and principles in early childhood education. In J. Roopnarine & J. Johnson (Eds.), *Approaches to early childhood education* (4th ed., pp. 186–210). Upper Saddle River, NJ: Pearson Education.

New, R., & Kantor, R. (2009). Reggio Emilia's approach to early care and education. In J. Roopnarine & J. Johnson (Eds.), *Approaches to early childhood education* (5th ed., pp. 287–311). Upper Saddle River, NJ: Pearson Education.

Noonan, M., & McCormick, L. (2006). *Young children with disabilities in natural environments.* Baltimore: Paul H. Brookes.

O'Brien, M. (2001). Inclusive child care for infants and toddlers. In M. Guralnick (Ed.), *Early childhood inclusion: Focus on change* (pp. 229–251). Baltimore: Paul H. Brookes.

Odom, S., & Wolery, M. (2003). A unified theory of practice in early intervention/early childhood special education. *Journal of Special Education, 37*(3), 164–173.

Olds, A. (1987). Designing settings for infants and toddlers. In C. Weinstein & T. Edward (Eds.), *Spaces for children: The built environment and child development* (pp. 117–138). New York: Plenum Press.

Piaget, J. (1963). *Origins of intelligence in children.* New York: Norton.

Pretti-Frontczak, K., & Bricker, D. (2004). *An activity-based approach to early intervention* (3rd ed.). Baltimore: Paul H. Brookes.

Raver, S. (2009). *Early childhood special education—0–8 years.* Upper Saddle River, NJ: Pearson Education.

Readdick, C. (2006). Managing noise in early childhood settings. *Dimensions of Early Childhood, 34*(1), 17–22.

Sheldon, K. (1996). "Can I play too?" Adapting common classroom activities for young children with limited motor abilities. *Early Childhood Education Journal, 24*(2), 115–120.

Tomlinson, H. (2009). Developmentally appropriate practice in the primary grades—ages 6–8. In C. Copple & S. Bredekamp (Eds.), *Developmentally appropriate practice in early childhood programs* (3rd ed., pp. 257–326). Washington, DC: National Association for the Education of Young Children.

U.S. Access Board. (2005). *A guide to the ADA accessibility guidelines for play areas.* Retrieved May 2, 2009 from http://www.access-board.gov/play/guide/intro.htm

U.S. Consumer Product Safety Commission. (2009). *Public playground safety checklist.* (Document # 327). Retrieved May 12, 2009 from http://www.cpsc.gov/cpscpub/pubs/327.html

White, C., & Coleman, M. (2000). *Early childhood education.* Upper Saddle River, NJ: Prentice Hall.

Winter, S. (2007). *Inclusive early childhood education.* Upper Saddle River, NJ: Pearson Education.

Wolery, M. (2000). Behavioral and educational approaches to early intervention. In J. Shonkoff & S. Meisel (Eds.), *Handbook of early childhood intervention* (2nd ed., pp. 179–202). Cambridge, England: Cambridge University Press.

8

Adapting the Learning Environment for Young Children with Special Needs

Contributed by Linda L. Brady, Director, Exceptional Children's Program, Vestavia Hills (Alabama) City Schools

Key Terminology

Evidence-based practices	Mobility
Embedding	Auditory trainer
Generalization	FM system
Task analysis	Sound field system
Scaffolding	Cochlear implant
Functional behavior analysis	Hypotonic muscle tone
Positive behavior supports	Hypertonic muscle tone
Time out	Orthotic devices
Echolalic speech	Prosthetic devices
Orientation	

Learning Outcomes

After reading this chapter, you will be able to:

- Identify adaptations in the home and school environments for children with cognitive delays, social and emotional delays, communication and language delays, sensory delays, motor delays, and health impairments.

- Identify and adapt appropriate materials and equipment for working with young children with special needs in both the home and the educational environment.

- List appropriate assistive technologies for children with special needs.

- Summarize instructional strategies for children with special needs in each specific domain area.

Over the past few decades, state and federal laws have focused attention on the participation of young children with special needs in their natural environments or least restrictive educational settings. This model, known as inclusive education, is now widely accepted as an effective way to meet the educational needs of young children with special needs. Children with special needs are now common in child care centers, preschools, Head Start programs, and public schools, learning along side their typically developing peers. Some children will be successful with minimal supports from general education teachers, special educators, and related service professionals. Most children with delays or disabilities, however, will require some adaptations, accommodations, and modifications to the curriculum, learning environment, or personnel. Collaborative teams of parents and professionals are charged, therefore, to work together to create a plan that will meet the individual needs of each learner.

Including young children with special needs in the natural environment or least restrictive educational setting often requires that the early childhood special educator modify his or her instructional tactics. It is axiomatic that young children with delays or disabilities are individuals; thus, teachers need to customize their teaching to meet the unique needs of each learner. When determining *how* to teach the young child with special needs, early childhood special educators should partly base their decision on what is commonly known in the field as **evidence-based practices.** Simply defined, this means "a decision-making process that integrates the best available research evidence with family and professional wisdom and values" (Buysse, Wesley, Snyder, & Winton, 2006, p. 3). The Individuals with Disabilities Education Improvement Act of 2004 (IDEA 2004) also speaks to this issue. According to this law, services for young children are to be constructed around scientifically based research. In other words, teachers should incorporate research-based practices in their instruction. Another commonly heard term is *recommended practices.* The Division for Early Childhood offers guidelines for early intervention and early childhood special education specifically developed around recommended practices (Sandall, Hemmeter, Smith, & McLean, 2005). In fact, it is suggested that "practitioners' decisions and work should not be based solely on their experiences and beliefs, rather, clear guidance is available from the [professional] literature for making many critical decisions and for using particular practices" (p. 73). Collectively, this thinking suggests that early childhood special educators should attempt to incorporate evidence-based practices whenever possible into their daily instructional routines (Cook, Klien, & Tessier, 2008). We fully embrace this position.

This chapter provides suggestions for adapting and modifying the environment, materials, and instructional delivery to young children with special needs. For ease of communication, young children are discussed using noncategorical descriptors. Where appropriate, children will be discussed using more traditional categorical terminology, as some young children already meet guidelines for specific disabilities (for example, visual impairment or hearing impairment).

Adapting the Home and School Environment, Materials, and Instruction

Young Children with Delays in Cognitive Development

Children with cognitive delays represent a diverse population. Children with cognitive delays may learn at a slower rate, experience a high rate of forgetting, and have difficulty regulating their own behavior and transferring (generalizing) learning to new events, situations, or people (Hallahan, Kauffman, & Pullen, 2009). They may require more adult guidance and direct instruction, activities that are concrete versus abstract, and they may not readily understand lengthy verbal instructions. Because these characteristics are variable from one child to the next, it would be a mistake to assume that all children with cognitive delays exhibit the same characteristics or learning difficulties. Hickson, Blackman, and Reis (1995) describe two main goals applicable to young children with cognitive delays. First, early intervention and early childhood special education programs should focus on furthering development in all developmental domains in order to reduce or minimize the impact of the delay on normal development. Second, professionals should support the family's efforts to achieve desired outcomes and independence level in the developmental domains.

Adapting the Home and Classroom Environments. Creating a rich and stimulating environment for children with cognitive delays is critical to their development. As with all children, teachers and parents should capitalize on the interests of children. Children should be observed or parents should be asked about what toys, foods, or activities they like. Using the child's interest will ensure that some aspect of the tasks and activities is reinforcing to the child. For example, Matt, a five-year-old with Down syndrome, enjoys playing with racecars. The teacher incorporated the racecars into the center for color, number, and letter identification. Each car was a different color and had a letter or number attached to it. While at the car center, children raced the cars, then identified the winning cars by color and letter/number. The use of a child's interest offers multiple learning opportunities across the child's day in the early childhood environment. Professionals often recommend embedding instruction into typical classroom activities and routines (Noonan & McCormick, 2006; Sandall & Schwartz, 2008; Wolery, 2005). **Embedding** is defined as

> identifying times and activities when a child's goals and the instructional procedures for those goals can be inserted into children's on going activities, routines and transitions in a way that relates to the context. It involves distributing opportunities to learn goals and apply instructional procedures for those goals across different activities, routines, and transitions of the day. (Wolery, p. 94)

When teachers embed effective instruction into activities that are fun and motivating for children, learning occurs more quickly. The children learn the skills in a natural setting. With embedded objectives, the classroom activities and routines become the structure for supporting the child's learning in the early childhood classroom. For example, Lauren, a second grader with cognitive delays, participates in the writing workshop daily with her peers. Lauren's task is modified by her general education teacher. Lauren works with the teacher initially to verbalize her thoughts using a specified writing prompt such as "My Favorite Food." Lauren's teacher writes down her thoughts in sentence form. Lauren and the teacher review her story. Lauren then copies her story onto her specially lined paper. Lauren does her written work with a peer partner. Several goals

were embedded in this instruction. The teacher and Lauren worked on her language and sentence formation. They worked on the identification of familiar words and sight words. Lauren practiced fine motor and writing skills. Lauren worked with a peer using appropriate social skills and practiced using her attention skills by staying on task and finishing her writing.

As with all young children, consistency in the routine provides the child with security and promotes self-assuredness ("I know what I am supposed to be doing here."). This is especially important for the young learner with cognitive delays. A consistent routine facilitates memory for a child who may have difficulty remembering items or activities that occur out of sequence. Establishing a routine, remaining faithful to the routine when possible, and preparing the child for changes in the routine when necessary are possible strategies. In addition, teachers should ensure that there is adequate time to finish tasks within the established routine for the child who may take a little longer to complete activities.

Unlike typically developing children, a child with cognitive delays does not necessarily acquire cognitive, language, or social skills during social interactions and play with others without support to promote these skills (Brown & Bergen, 2002). Therefore, it is important for teachers to examine the schedule to determine if there are multiple opportunities in the day for socialization and speech/language production at home and at school. Structured play with typically developing peers is an excellent strategy for providing models for language development and socialization.

Adapting Materials and Equipment. As much as possible, hands-on, concrete materials should be available for a young child with cognitive delays. Especially when teaching abstract concepts (up, down, in, out) or common preacademic skills (letter recognition, numbers, colors, shapes), it is critical for teachers to have multiple ways of presenting these abstract concepts in concrete ways. Using predictable games with an infant or toddler is an ideal way to address this issue. During play, a parent lifts the toddler up saying, "Up, up, up!" followed by "Down, down, down!" as the child is lowered. In this way the abstract concepts (up, down) are embedded within an enjoyable, predictable game sequence.

Substituting favorite toys within the same routine extends the play routine with the same concepts, encourages generalization, and sustains interest. With a preschooler or early primary-age child, the use of real pennies (instead of toy money) when counting, real food when measuring, or talking about colors of clothing when matching socks are all examples of concrete learning materials/activities. Not only are these more hands-on ways to promote skills acquisition, they are also activities that relate learning to the child's real world (Copple & Bredekamp, 2009) and increase the likelihood of generalization of skills.

A variety of materials may be needed to accommodate young children with diverse cognitive abilities. Blocks of different sizes or busy boxes with a variety of switches (representing different levels of difficulty) might enable a toddler to have some successes and some challenges. Puzzles with varying degrees of difficulty could be available in the free play corner or books with different levels of difficulty in the reading corner. Likewise, it is important to select materials or toys that are more likely to increase social interactions (Copple & Bredekamp, 2009; McLean, Bailey, & Wolery, 2004). Children with cognitive delays may exhibit memory deficits, requiring visual cues to prompt behavior. For example, when photographs are placed above each cubby, children can find their photograph when trying to locate their cubbies. Pictures of the steps to washing hands can be placed by the sink at the children's eye level to support independence in hand washing.

Adapting Instruction. Every child has strengths—even children with cognitive delays have some areas in which they excel. It is critical to capitalize on the child's strengths when planning activities in order to increase the likelihood of success, promote self-esteem, maintain interest, and diminish frustration. For example, Martha, a child with Down syndrome, exhibited cognitive and language delays but excelled in gross motor activities. Her mother reported that as a toddler, she sat independently, crawled, and walked early, but she did not use words until she was three years old. As a preschooler, she enjoys outdoor play equipment (slide, swings) and the obstacle course. Her parents and teachers often incorporate language skills within a gross motor activity where Martha finds success and enjoyment. When she is on the swing,

Teachers should capitalize on a child's strengths when planning activities.

waiting for someone to push her, the teacher waits for Martha to indicate or communicate what she wants. Initially even an approximation of "pu" for "push" is accepted, and later, the desired vocalization is modeled: "Say *push*" and, expanded, "Say *push swing*." (These models are consistent with activity-based intervention and incidental teaching, topics that will be presented in Chapter 9.)

Children with cognitive delays may have a smaller vocabulary, use less complex sentence structures, use language less frequently, and sometimes have difficulty making friends (Gargiulo, 2009). As mentioned previously, play with typically developing classmates is an excellent context for promoting these skills. However, even within these structured play opportunities, children need to be frequently monitored and supported (by using prompts or praise) in their interactions to maximize socialization and communication. Without such supports, children may engage in fewer social interactions and less mature social behavior, may be rejected by peers, and may ultimately have difficulty developing social relationships (McPhee, Favazza, & Lewis, 2004). In addition, to expand the child's communicative and social attempts, language should be integrated into all aspects of the curriculum, including transition activities ("Where are we going next?"), self-help activities ("Tell me what you are doing"), and play activities ("James, ask Francie to help you"). The assistance of a speech–language pathologist is often sought for suggestions on how to insert language goals into daily activities.

Because children with cognitive delays often have memory problems, it is not unusual for them to have difficulty transferring or generalizing knowledge or skills acquired in one context to a new or different setting (Gargiulo, 2009). **Generalization** is a phase of learning. It refers to learning to use a skill outside of the context in which it was initially acquired. This is often thought of as performing a skill in a different setting, with other people, or with materials different from the ones used in the initial instruction (Wolery, 2005). Some suggested strategies for promoting generalization are the following:

- *A variety of adults can be involved when teaching skills.* For example, periodically a classroom assistant or volunteer can teach a particular skill so that a child becomes accustomed to different people. It is important that the directives and expectations for the child are consistent across people. This implies that communication and collaboration should occur among teachers, parents, and other caregivers to ensure consistency across settings.

- *Skills can be embedded into naturally occurring activities.* For example, if putting socks on and off is a skill area that the child needs to focus on, instruction should occur during the dressing and undressing routines during the day (such as before/after nap). The use of a pincer grasp can be promoted during snack time (eating crackers or cheese cubes), during art (picking up tissue squares or pebbles to glue on art project), and during dressing routines (button, unbutton, or zip). For an example of an activity that is embedded into a naturally occurring activity, please see the Making Connections feature vignette about Maria, a young child with cognitive delays.

- *Activities can be created in the instructional setting that are as similar as possible to the generalization setting.* The greater the differences between the educational setting and other settings, the less likely the generalization will occur. For example, if the child is learning to drink from a two-handled cup at home, the same type of cup should be used at school.

- *The instructional setting should be varied.* By expanding the settings and activities in which the children utilize targeted skills and the people they utilize them with, teachers can increase the probability of the generalization of skills can.

MAKING CONNECTIONS

Implementing an Embedded Learning Opportunity for Maria

The implementation of an embedded learning opportunity is one of the strategies that Maria's teachers use to practice individual goals and objectives that are meaningful and interesting to her. The teachers embed the learning activities using the natural routine across the activities, people, and materials in the inclusive classroom. Using the daily routine at snack time, when Maria's glass is empty, she signs "more." The teacher asks Maria, "More what?" Maria signs "more" again. The teacher uses the opportunity to model for Maria. She signs, "more drink" and gives Maria a questioning look. Maria imitates and signs, "more drink" and receives more juice. At the block center, Maria needs more blocks for the tower she is building. She asks the teacher for "more blocks" and receives them. This is an example of an embedded objective that crosses activities throughout Maria's day. Later at free play, Maria asks the teacher for "more toys" and receives them. In this example, the embedded learning objective has crossed to other adults in the classroom environment. Maria's objective was practiced within the natural routine, with different activities, with different adults, and with different materials within her classroom setting.

An instructional strategy often used with children with cognitive and delays is **task analysis.** Task analysis involves breaking down a skill or activity into smaller, more manageable steps. Alberto and Troutman (2006) offer the following guidelines for conducting a task analysis:

1. Identify the long-term objective.
2. Break the behavior into smaller steps.
3. Eliminate unnecessary and redundant behaviors.
4. Sequence the steps for teaching.
5. Specify the prerequisite behaviors that must be acquired before teaching the behavior.

With younger children, pictures of each step can be provided to support the child in independent completion of a particular task. For example, pictures of each step used in washing hands could be placed near the sink area at the child's eye level. In this way, an unobtrusive prompt serves as a reminder for all children. Teaching young children phrases or songs that accompany daily activities is another strategy for providing the steps to a task. It is not only enjoyable, but it is also functional because the child can use the phrase or song wherever he/she goes. For example, creating a phrase or song to accompany the motions or steps for tying shoes can be used over and over by a young child at school or at home. (See Table 8–1 for a sample task analysis).

Task analysis can also be individualized with younger toddlers using backward chaining. For example, for a toddler who offers no assistance in dressing or undressing, the parent or teacher could complete all of the steps of a task analysis (for pulling up pants) and leave the last step for him to complete, such as pulling pants from mid-thigh to hips. In this way, the child begins to assist in dressing, successfully completes the new skill, and is off to an enjoyable (and reinforcing) activity (for example, play or snack). Once this step is achieved with consistency, the parent or teacher can raise the expectation that he should pull his pants from the knees, from the ankles, and so on. This example of backward chaining starts with the last step of a task analysis. It is typically used with younger children or children who are lower functioning because they can successfully complete the last steps(s) and are immediately reinforced by moving on to the next enjoyable activity.

One final strategy for children with cognitive and adaptive delays is **scaffolding.** This technique helps children become independent, proficient problem

TABLE 8–1 Task Analysis for Washing Hands[1] (Sequenced by order in which to be performed)

1. Step on the stool to reach the sink.
2. Place hands on faucet handles.
3. Turn water on (faucets automatically turn off).
4. Place hands under the water.
5. Squeeze the soap on both hands.
6. Rub hands together with soap.
7. Rub hands together and over back and front.
8. Rinse hands in sink.
9. Turn the faucets to the off position.
10. Reach for a paper towel.
11. Dry hands on paper towel.
12. Put paper towel in the trashcan.
13. Step down from stool.

[1] This activity is easily adapted to use picture symbols if needed for visual prompt.

solvers. In this teacher-directed strategy, various forms of support are provided as the child initially engages in learning a new task or skill. As the student becomes competent, the supports or "scaffolds" are gradually removed. This instructional strategy begins with what the child knows and attempts to connect new information with previously learned material. New information is presented in a logical sequence building on the child's knowledge base. Pupils are given the opportunity to apply and practice the new skill (Gargiulo, 2009).

For links to websites containing more information about young children with cognitive impairments, see the text's accompanying premium website.

Young Children with Delays in Social and Emotional Development

The term *behavior disorder* is frequently used to describe a wide variety of social and emotional challenges that include, but are not limited to, conduct disorders (aggressiveness and disruptive or destructive behaviors), difficulty with interpersonal relationships, depression, or anxiety disorders (overanxiousness, withdrawal). At least four characteristics are common to most definitions of individuals with

TeachSource Video

Scaffolding the Hiding Assessment for a Child with Special Needs

Visit the premium website and watch "Scaffolding the Hiding Assessment for a Child with Special Needs." After watching this video, answer the following questions:

1. Why would scaffolding be an appropriate instructional adaptation to use with a child with special needs?
2. How would you incorporate this instructional strategy in your classroom?

emotional or behavioral disorders. These dimensions include the following:

1. the frequency or rate of occurrence of the behavior;
2. the intensity of the behavior;
3. the duration of the behavior (over a period of time); and
4. the age appropriateness of the behavior (Coleman & Webber, 2002; Wickes-Nelson & Israel, 2006).

Typically, very young children are not given specific labels but might exhibit some early signs that may later develop into behavioral problems. Because of the diversity of children who have delays in this area of development, it is critical to individualize strategies used with each child. However, there are some issues and considerations that may be applicable across children who exhibit problems in social and emotional development when adapting the environment, materials, and instruction.

Adapting the Home and Classroom Environments. Parents and teachers should think about several issues when considering environmental modifications for children with challenging behaviors. Adults should make note of when and where the behavior occurs. Some questions that might be asked include: Are there aspects of the home or school environment that trigger inappropriate behavior? For example, is the schedule realistic or is there too little time to complete activities? Are activities too long, and if so, are there planned activities for the child to move on to when his attention is waning? Is there too little or too much space for each child? It is important to compare the number of children and amount of space to determine if space is contributing to unwanted behaviors. Are there enough materials or has the lack of materials lead to problems? Are

the expectations realistic? (Remember, young children often have not yet learned to share. Therefore, it is not uncommon to have some problems when materials are limited.) Does the inappropriate behavior always involve the same children or the same activity? Do problems occur at the same time of the day (when the child is overtired, seated next to a specific peer, or after snack time)? Is there something happening in the home setting that is contributing to problems at school (birth of a sibling, move to a new house, or other transition events)?

Sandall and Schwartz (2008) offer several ways to structure the environment for success.

They recommend these strategies:

- *Provide a balance between child-directed and adult-directed activities.* Provide opportunities for children to make choices throughout their day.
- *Provide a variety of areas within the classroom that have boundaries and are easily viewed.* The teacher should be able to view all areas of the classroom easily. Children should learn to recognize the boundaries of their learning areas.
- *Ensure materials are organized and in good working order.* Materials should be engaging and attractive to children. Organize the materials in a fashion that tells the children where they belong.
- *Offer activities that provide many ways for children to respond.* Consider children's current skills and interests. Plan activities that allow choices and different ways to respond.

For a child with behavior problems, it is critical that he or she has a predictable, consistent environment. Rules should be established and maintained for the class *with* the children, and the rules should be consistently applied. A routine should be established and children should be prepared for changes in the routine.

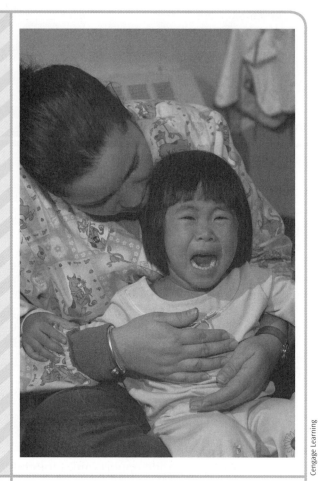

Cengage Learning

Environmental factors can sometimes contribute to inappropriate behaviors.

strategies that allow all young children to feel secure, knowing what is happening throughout their day.

Adapting Materials and Equipment. The use of classroom materials can often guide a child's behavior. For instance, are materials available that encourage self-expression (modeling clay, paints, play dough, writing supplies, and tape recorders)? One kindergarten teacher provided a tape recorder and drawing materials to children who acted out. While they were pulled aside to "sit and watch" others engaging in appropriate play, the child would tell what happened using either the art supplies or the tape recorder before talking with the teacher about the incident. The tape or picture was then passed on to the parents to keep them informed of behaviors at school. Another teacher had the child dictate what happened, which was then sent home to the parents.

Are learning materials safe and do they promote the kind of interactions that should be encouraged? Some materials and activities may suggest aggressive themes. Even with toddlers, it may become apparent that a particular toy or activity (such as toy guns or books or cartoons with aggressive themes) is involved when disruptive behavior occurs. It is important for teachers and parents to observe children at play, removing the objects that are associated with problems or discontinuing exposure to books or programming that lead to imitations of aggressive play behavior. It is equally as important for teachers to provide toys and materials in the classroom that promote appropriate social interaction as well those that encourage cooperation and opportunities to share (Gestwicki, 1999).

Are there enough materials? Teachers must judge the amount of materials needed in the classroom. On the one hand, teachers need to promote sharing among preschool-age children; on the other, they want to avoid conflicts over limited resources. Is recreational equipment available that naturally promotes cooperative play? Seesaws, rocking boats, and wagon rides are all examples of equipment that rewards cooperative play as they require children to play together. Are the materials (and activities) reinforcing (high-interest, motivating) to children? It is critical that children have choices of materials that are of interest, especially if access to preferred materials or activities is contingent on behavior.

Transitions can be a difficult time during the day for many children. Transitions are unpredictable and hard for some children to understand. Teachers should consider preparing children for transitions. Be specific in teaching children what to do during transitions. Using picture cues or social stories may be helpful. Some children may require specific teaching as to the routine for the transition. If students have difficulty leaving one activity for another, begin the activity with just a few children. If the new activity is interesting and engaging, the other child may join those children who made the transition quickly. Warning signals (bell, music, or singing a "clean-up" song) can be provided to give notice that a transition is about to happen. These are simple environmental

Adapting Instruction. One of the first steps for instruction is to determine, with the parent's help, the cause of a behavior problem, noting when, where, and with whom a particular inappropriate behavior occurs. This process of gathering information and data about the particular behavior is called a **functional behavior analysis.** Is the behavior something that can be ignored? Or is it a behavior that warrants attention (it is interfering with performance or it is not safe for the child or others)? Are there environmental elements that are contributing to problem behaviors? For example, almost daily, Amy exhibits disruptive behavior when it is time to transition to another activity such as nap or snack. When she was given a little more time to complete activities, the disruptive behavior subsided.

If it is determined that the behavior warrants attention, an individualized behavior plan with positive behavioral supports can be created to address the behavior problems. **Positive behavior supports** is a comprehensive approach focusing on facilitating appropriate behaviors while reducing or preventing challenging behaviors (Gargiulo, 2009; Sandall & Schwartz, 2008). Specific strategies can be discussed with the family and other professionals (paraprofessionals, related service providers) to ensure consistency across people in the home and school setting. Strategies can be selected for reinforcing desired behaviors that include activities, materials, and people that are reinforcing to the child.

Children learn and persist in inappropriate behaviors because they are motivated to do so. Teachers and parents using positive behavioral supports are encouraged to look at discovering the function of the behavior. Four possible reasons or functions of behaviors in young children may be described as sensory seeking, escape behaviors, attention getting, and the need for tangible reinforcers. For example, if adult attention is sought by Micki, a child who exhibits frequent tantrums, the teachers should make sure she receives adequate adult attention for desired behaviors ("That's a great picture; tell me about it." "I like the way you and Roman are playing together.") while withholding adult attention for undesired behavior. A child whose function for inappropriate behaviors is sensory seeking may be highly motivated by touch, smell, taste, visual, or hearing. Roman, a first grader with autism, exhibits behaviors such as waving his hands in a flapping manner, rocking, and loud shouts. The teacher and occupational therapist designed a series of sensory activity breaks for Roman to engage in daily. These breaks are embedded within his daily schedule. Among these activities

are jumping on a small trampoline, rolling on a therapy ball, brushing, swinging, and spending time with toys that light up and make repetitive noises.

When possible, provide choices for children instead of placing demands on them. For example if T.J. refuses to leave the block area to come to the small-group circle, the teacher may give him choices by saying, "T.J., we need to sit for circle time. You may bring a red or blue block to the circle area with you." Or, "You can hop like a bunny or jump like a frog to the circle." In this way, T.J. has the choice of the way he comes to the circle and the teacher has accomplished the desired behavior.

Multiple opportunities should be provided for choice making throughout the day (centers, art supplies, snack, or toys) so that children have a sense of control over some aspects of the environment. Opportunities should be provided for self-expression (art, music, or social dramatic play) that serves as a channel for appropriate self-expression for a child who might have difficulty expressing himself in acceptable ways. When creating small-group activities, peers should be carefully selected who can serve as appropriate models for behavior, socialization, and communication.

Teachers should set clear, consistent, and fair limits for the classroom. Children will have an easier time meeting expectations if they know what is expected and what behaviors are appropriate. A limited number of rules is recommended for both preschool and early primary classrooms. Having the rules posted in the classroom or revisiting (reminding children) of the rules throughout the day is a positive approach to build in repeated presentations of the expected behaviors. Many early primary teachers include the children in the creating and discussing classroom rules. In this way, the children have a better understanding of the rules and limits.

Redirection is another strategy that leads children to more acceptable behaviors. Redirection can often keep a small problem from escalating into a large one. Sometimes redirection can be embedded into an established behavioral pattern. For example, Kevin is a 5-year-old kindergartener who does not separate from his mother at the classroom door without crying and throwing a tantrum. The teacher and parent engaged in many discussions over the first 3 weeks of the school year to brainstorm ways to make the transition easier for all. During one discussion, the teacher discovered that Kevin has a preference for building with blocks. The next morning, the teacher and two of Kevin's peers were sitting outside the classroom door playing with a new set of colored blocks. Kevin quickly separated from his mother to join in his classmates. His crying and tantrums gradually diminished over the next few days. The teacher had successfully embedded a redirection to a preferred activity for Kevin.

Time out has been used to address a wide range of inappropriate behaviors across a variety of educational environments. Parents report using this strategy in their homes. Providing a child with a time out when aggressive behavior occurs has been shown to be effective when dealing with aggression (Alberto & Troutman, 2006). **Time out** is a strategy that involves removing a child to a location a way from reinforcing conditions. The child is briefly removed (1 minute for each year of chronological age) from rewarding activities (including attention from people). Table 8–2 offers guidelines for using time out appropriately in the learning environment.

There is some concern, however, about the appropriateness of time out with young children, as it has the potential to be overused and misused. Examples of misuse include the following:

- being placed in time out too frequently and without the child understanding the reasons
- being placed out of view of teachers
- use without other strategies that promote desired behavior (that is, without talking about the behavior with the child)
- use as the first and only option when dealing with behavior problems
- use without the knowledge or consent of parents
- placement in time out for long periods of time

When thoughtfully used, time out can be one of many valuable strategies for dealing with problem behavior. It provides children (and sometimes adults) with a chance to control their own emotions. It separates the aggressor from the victim. It is best applied briefly, immediately, and in a matter-of-fact fashion without anger or reprimands. Explaining to children

TABLE 8–2 Guidelines for Using Time Out Successfully

1. Immediately go to the child and say calmly, "You were _____" (tell the child what he/she did that was a misbehavior—for example, hitting). "That is not allowed. You must go to time out."

2. Don't say more. Don't get into the conversation trap! Take the child to time out. Use a timer. Set the timer for no longer than 2 minutes. Do not talk or make eye contact with the child during the time out. In some cases it may be necessary the first few times to use a gentle arm across the child's lap to keep him/her in time out. Providing a location near the continuing class activities can sometimes be effective in allowing the child to observe the other children engaging in appropriate behavior.

3. When the timer goes off, immediately say to the child, "Time out is over. You can go." Direct the child to the appropriate activity. "Remember that [the misbehavior] is not allowed."

4. Quickly help the child engage in positive behavior that you can praise and reinforce.

Points to Remember

1. Time out should not be the major behavior management strategy you use. It is only a supplement to a plan that provides positive behavioral supports.

2. Remember, time out only teaches the child what not to do. It is essential to teach and reinforce positive behaviors.

3. Always have a plan.

4. Always keep records. Something is wrong if time outs are not becoming less frequent.

Source: M. Davis, J. Kilgo, and M. Gamel-McCormick, M. *Young Children with Special Needs: A Developmentally Appropriate Approach* (Boston: Allyn & Bacon, 1998), p. 222.

which behaviors will result in time out and why will enable them to understand that it is one way to help them learn to change their behavior. Teachers and parents can demonstrate time out procedures, showing children that they are provided a space and time to compose themselves before rejoining the group. One alternative to the traditional time out is to have a child "sit and watch." In this way, the child can step aside briefly, watch other children at play or work, and learn from children who are demonstrating appropriate behaviors (Noonan & McCormick, 2006).

A young child with behavior problems may lack the communication skills and/or social competence needed to negotiate the interactions in her world (Coleman & Webber, 2002). For example, some children may not have the words to express their emotions of anger or anxiety; others may lack the appropriate social skills necessary for asking for a toy from a peer; some may lack self-control in a conflict situation. Some youngsters may require direct instruction (of words and/or social skills), while others may need prompts for appropriate self-expression ("Show me what you want." "Use your words." "Tell Jo Ann how you feel." "Tell him that it's your turn with the truck."). Likewise, a student may benefit from opportunities to interact with children who model appropriate communication and social skills. If the lack of communication skills is contributing to the problem, explore alternative ways of communicating (for example, use picture cards to express feelings). See the Making Connections feature for an application of using positive behavioral strategies in working with T.J., a child with behavioral problems, and Cheryl, a student with ADHD and a Section 504 plan.

For links to websites containing more information about young children with delays in social emotional development, see the text's accompanying premium website.

MAKING CONNECTIONS

Strategies for Providing Positive Behavioral Support for T.J.

Based on the information presented in the vignette on T.J. (see page 60) and the information on characteristics of young children with behavioral problems, there are several strategies that could be utilized to address T.J.'s unique needs. For example, because of his aggressive behavior, it would be important to create an individualized plan to address behavioral issues. The parent is very concerned about her son and can provide useful information about him. She can be asked what kinds of strategies she has used at home to mediate behavior, including the ones that are successful as well as those that have been unsuccessful. It is important to pay attention to *when* the aggression typically occurs, if it is directed at *specific individuals* or preceded by *predictable events*. A plan of action can be created with the mother and T.J. so that he understands what is expected of him, understands the consequences of his actions, has opportunities for success and praise throughout his day, and sees that his mother is working closely with the teacher to help him.

T.J. should be provided with alternatives to aggressive behavior such as being encouraged to "use his words;" should be provided with opportunities for choices and self-expression through art, music, social dramatic play; or should have the option of having peer-mediated social interventions used, whereby appropriate social skills are modeled and taught. In addition, it would be important for T.J. to hear praise for the things he is doing well, instead of receiving adult attention (in the form of reprimands) solely for inappropriate behavior.

It would be important for an examination of his social network to occur. Does he have friends and social relationships that are rewarding to him? It may be necessary for some of the strategies for promoting acceptance (see Chapter 9) to be utilized if he does not have a social network within the class. Moreover, to address his problems with distractibility, it would be important to determine his interest in materials and toys to ensure that high-interest items are available for instruction. Environmental factors (too much noise, too much visual simulation, close proximity to others) that may be contributing to the distractibility should also be examined.

MAKING CONNECTIONS

A Positive Behavioral Support Plan for Cheryl

Cheryl Chinn was introduced in Chapter 2 (see pages 60–61) as a first grader with a diagnosis of attention deficit hyperactivity disorder. In Chapter 5, we learned that Cheryl's teachers and parents collaborated to create a Section 504 Plan to address difficulties with concentration. Cheryl is easily distracted and her classroom assignments are often not completed. In this vignette, Cheryl's parents and classroom teacher, Mrs. Newman, have discussed the use of positive behavioral supports to help Cheryl be successful in the classroom. They have decided to implement a daily contract with Cheryl to increase her time on task without distraction and work to complete her assignments.

Goal # 1: Cheryl will increase her time on task in her classroom daily.

Goal # 2: Cheryl will complete her class assignments.

Environmental Supports:

1. Cheryl will be seated near the teacher (proximity seating) and close to attentive peers. She will have designated space on the carpet marked by tape for small-group and calendar activities.
2. Cheryl and a peer will help keep her desk clean and uncluttered. Mrs. Newman will check her desk at dismissal time daily.
3. Cheryl will have the classroom rules printed at the top of her daily checklist. They will be clear and concise. The teacher will alert Cheryl if a change in the daily schedule is going to occur.

Academic Supports:

1. Mrs. Newman will make directions to the class in brief statements. Directions will be both oral and visual (see daily checklist).
2. The teacher will break Cheryl's activities into small parts. She will be given extended time if needed (example: math facts sheet cut into halves).
3. Mrs. Newman will model the activities and use Cheryl as the helper as much as possible.
4. Cheryl will be assigned a peer helper if needed.

Behavioral Supports:

1. Mrs. Newman will give Cheryl frequent specific verbal praise and encouragement for desired behaviors.
2. Cheryl will be given verbal and visual reminders of the class rules and expectations throughout the day.
3. If needed, Mrs. Newman will repeat and model the desired behaviors for the whole class in a nonthreatening manner.
4. Mrs. Newman will review Cheryl's daily checklist with her (conference) prior to dismissal.

Cheryl Chinn's Daily Checklist

Classroom Rules:

1. Look at and listen to the teacher.
2. Stay in my seat or place.
3. Raise my hand.
4. Respect others.
5. Finish my work.

Daily Schedule:

Warm-up: Journal Writing
Math meeting–calendar time
Math
Math centers
Recess
Spelling
Reading
Lunch
Library
Science—hands-on activity
Clean-up/daily conference
Dismissal

Did I pay attention to the teacher?	YES	NO
Did I stay in my seat?	YES	NO
Did I finish my work?	YES	NO
Did I earn my reward?	YES	NO
Cheryl's choice reward? _____		

(determined by Cheryl and Mrs. Newman)

Young Children with Delays in Communication and Language Development

Communication refers to the exchange of messages between a speaker and a listener. Language refers to the use of symbols (letter sounds that are used in various combinations to form words), syntax (rules that guide sentence structure), or grammar when communicating with one another. Speech is the oral–motor action used to communicate (Gargiulo, 2009). The federal definition found in IDEA 2004 refers to children with a communication disorder such as stuttering, impaired articulation, a language impairment, or voice impairment that adversely affects a child's education performance. In this area of development, a young child could have difficulty with one or more of these aspects of development. Moreover, there are many potential causes of problems in language development. A language delay could be related to cognitive delays, sensory impairments (hearing loss or visual impairment), emotional problems, autism or pervasive developmental disorders, motor impairments (such as cerebral palsy), linguistic and cultural

differences, and so on. Because the delay in communication and language development may be tied to a variety of etiologies, the early indicators could vary widely. For example, a young child with pervasive developmental delay may use **echolalic speech** patterns (repeats what is said instead of generating an original sentence), a child with a cognitive delay may develop language at a slower pace and may not progress in his use of more complex language structures, or a child with a hearing loss may have difficulty following directions or exhibit poor articulation. Because of the interrelated nature of a communication or language delay with other disorders, the early indicators must be examined very carefully, keeping in mind that all children do not acquire language at the same pace and that many young children exhibit difficulty with articulation or fluency as they are developing language

Adapting the Home and Classroom Environments. Adapting the home or school setting will depend, in part, on the cause of the language delay. However, some general guidelines would include the following.

● *Provide a language-rich home or classroom setting.* Children should be exposed early on to music, conversation, and printed language (books). Children need immense amounts of stimulation to challenge their intellectual, social, and emotional development. A language-rich setting provides models for speech production, language structures, and social exchanges.

- *Children's nonverbal and verbal communications should be responded to by teachers and caregivers.* Infants and toddlers communicate often through cries, gestures, eye gaze, and sound and word production. It is critical that infants and toddlers have a responsive caregiver (one who responds to early communicative efforts).
- *Turn-taking games should be used to have "conversations" with young children.* Simple games such as peek-a-boo or pat-a-cake can be used to support turn-taking behavior that is a necessary component of communication.
- *Actions and objects in the child's surroundings should be labeled.* For example, as Mom is dressing her toddler, she could say, "Now, let's put on your socks and shoes. Socks go on. Shoes go on." In this way, the child is given labels for the actions and the objects in her surroundings. One mom commented that after doing this on a regular basis during dressing routines (with her son with Down syndrome), he began bringing the socks and shoes to her in anticipation of the dressing routine. Clearly, the labeling activity had an impact on her child's language development.

Adapting Equipment and Materials. Materials should spark children's interest and expand their development. Keep the following in mind when choosing materials.

- *Select materials and activities that are appealing to his/her unique interests.* For example, the parents of Andrea (who has a language delay) noted their child's keen interest in animals. They purchased many toys and books that depicted animals. Many of the toys had a feature that allowed the child to activate the animal sounds. Some of the first sounds Andrea made were imitations of these animals. She later went on to imitate other sounds and words in her environment. Likewise, activities that the child is interested in will be more enjoyable for her or him, will maintain attention, and will have greater potential for language production.
- *Place materials in a location where the child can see them but is unable to access them.* This strategy provides a visual incentive for the child to request the materials he/she wants. While it may be easier to place all materials out for children, following this strategy creates a natural opportunity for children with language delays to use language.
- *Limit the materials or equipment.* When preparing lunch, place the child's cup on the table without his favorite juice while you fill your own cup with juice. In this way, the child will note something is missing and need to request the missing item. Again, this intentional limitation of materials creates a natural opportunity for the child to use language.
- *Use materials for choice-making opportunities.* If you provide the child with multiple choices throughout her school and home routines, she gains more control and autonomy in her world and is supported in communication attempts.

Adapting Instruction. Every activity should be viewed as an opportunity for developing language. Routine activities such as going to the grocery store, washing the dishes, playing after breakfast, taking daily walks in the neighborhood, and getting dressed are all opportunities to expose a young child to language. Times should be selected across the day at home and school where language skills can be addressed. The following illustrations represent strategies that are often useful in promoting the development of language.

Imitate the child's actions and sounds. Imitation of early actions and vocalizations is an ideal way to reinforce a toddler's motor and verbal movements. For example, Jonathan and his mother are playing with sand. His mother drops sand from her hand while saying, "ba, ba, ba." Pairing vocal models with physical imitation may encourage a child to use more complex and frequent vocalizations during play. When Jonathan pushes his fingers into the sand, his mother can imitate by pushing her fingers into the sand while adding the vocalization "da." Adults can model conventional gestures such as pointing to objects out of reach, shrugging one's shoulders, upturning the palms, nodding the head to indicate yes or no, waving, and making the "shhh" gesture. Imitation is a strategy that is effective for teaching turn-taking behaviors and teaches the use of communication to regulate others' behaviors. For example, Susan and her mother are rolling a ball back and forth. One day, instead of rolling the ball back, Susan's mother waits. After Susan looks at her mother and vocalizes "ba," her mother rolls the ball back to her.

Expand the language that a child uses. For example, if Alina says "down" when the ball falls down, the parent or caregiver could say, "ball down" or "ball fell down." In this way, teachers and parents can capitalize on her initiation (and interest), imitate (reinforce) her vocalization, and provide a model for expanding her vocalization. Elaborative modeling is an effective procedure used when a child has not yet acquired independent production of language. For example, Stacy is playing with the teacher in the doll center. She says "bottle" while reaching for the baby bottle. The teacher gives her the bottle as she says, "Say, 'I want bottle.'" Stacy responds with "Want bottle." The teacher then provides the corrective model by saying, "*I* want bottle." Stacy then imitates, "I want bottle," and receives the bottle. The teacher follows with feedback and compliance with Stacy's request by expanding the language, saying, "Yes, here is the bottle for your baby!"

Couple vocalizations with gestures if necessary. For example, a caregiver could say "no" while shaking her head and "yes" while nodding her head. This provides a visual cue as well as a vocal directive. Another example would be pointing to the door while saying, "Go to the door." Again, it provides the child with visual and auditory input while labeling the action as it occurs.

Use pauses (verbally and physically) to provide an opportunity to communicate. This seems like such an obvious strategy, but when trying to communicate with a child who has limited verbal skills, it is easy for caregivers to talk so much that the child does not have an opportunity to talk. Likewise, it is easy for caregivers to provide children with all of the materials before they have indicated a need for them. This strategy requires the teacher or parent to make a conscious effort to slow down his or her own communication or sit back and wait to allow the child a chance to communicate what he/she wants.

Teachers should collaborate with related service personnel (such as the speech–language pathologist). It is critical that everyone working with the child use the same strategies and have the same expectations for addressing individualized language goals for each child. Collaboration will ensure consistency across settings and people and increase the likelihood of the generalization of skills. Moreover, the selection of effective strategies is highly dependent on the unique needs of each child. For example, if the child has a visual impairment, the strategies used to adapt instruction

that will be used to facilitate language development may be different than those selected for a child with a hearing impairment. Also, the related service personnel who are involved may vary. Therefore, it is important for teachers to look at each child individually and collaborate with the appropriate related service professional. There are many more ways to adapt instruction that will be discussed in detail in Chapter 9. In particular, teachers should pay attention to monitoring communicative input, peer initiation intervention, cooperative learning strategies, routine-based strategies, and milieu strategies.

For links to websites containing more information about young children with delays in communication and language development, see the text's accompanying premium website.

Young Children with Sensory Impairments: Vision

Children with visual impairments are generally identified as partially sighted or blind. The Individuals with Disabilities Education Improvement Act of 2004 (PL 108-446) defines visual impairment as an impairment in vision that, even with correction, adversely affects an individual's educational performance. The impact of a visual impairment depends on the age of onset, the amount of functional vision, the etiology, mobility, and the presence of other disabilities. The presence of a visual impairment has the potential of having adverse effects on social (D'Allura, 2002), language, cognitive, and perceptual motor development if the child's needs are not met at an early age. Cox and Dykes (2001) identify several areas that may require additional attention when working with young children with visual impairments. These include attention to locomotion (crawling, walking), fine motor skills, classification, social interaction, communication, and sensory coordination.

Adapting the Home and Classroom Environments. First and foremost, the child with a visual impairment should be encouraged to use whatever vision he or she has. The home and class settings should have good lighting and the child should be seated away from glares, shadows, or flickering lights. Making the area brighter or dimmer according to the child's need should be considered in the home or classroom (Gould & Sullivan, 1999). Poor lighting or changing lighting may interfere with the limited vision that the child does have. Centers or stations (block area, reading corner, etc.) should have high-quality lighting. The noise level should be monitored to ensure that it does not interfere with the child's ability to use auditory cues. For example, Tameka, a 5-year-old child with a visual impairment, relies heavily on auditory cues to know where to go, what is happening next, and what she is supposed to be doing. Each morning, Lisa, a 2-year-old with limited vision, relies on the auditory cues from the kitchen (Mommy removing the dishes from the cabinet, refrigerator humming, Dad listening to the morning news on the television) to navigate her way to the kitchen. Refer to Table 8–3 for a list of common environmental adaptations for students with visual impairments.

TABLE 8–3 Environmental Adaptations for Students with Visual Impairments

Lighting	Color and Contrast	Size and Distance	Time
What to observe: • Variety of lighting situations • Lighting at different times of day • Low-vision devices used	**What to observe:** • Contrast between object and background • Color contrast • Tactile tasks such as locker for books	**What to observe:** • Placement and size of objects near or far	**What to observe:** • Time for completion of visual discrimination during tasks
What to do: • Light sensitivity: shades, visors, tinted spectacles • Low light: lamp or illuminated low-vision device • Room obstructions: preferential seating, furniture placement • Glare: nonglare surface on areas such as chalkboards, computer screens, desktop, paper, maps, globes	**What to use:** • Bold-line paper • Black print on white background • Dark markers • One-sided writing on paper • Dark placemat for contrast during eating • Floor contrast for mobility ease • Tactile markings for outline discrimination • Contrast to define borders on walls • Lock-and-key is preferred over combination locker	**What to do:** • Enlarged materials • Preferred seating • Electronic devices • Magnification • Optical character recognition • Adjustment of desks, tables, and chairs • Additional storage space for Braille, large-print books, low-vision devices near each work station	**What to do:** • Verbal cues for actions in classroom • Increase time for task completion • Call student by name • Announce when entering or leaving room • Encourage participation in demonstrations • Provide opportunity to observe materials prior to lesson • Use authentic manipulative objects • Schedule instructional time in early part of day • Convenient use and storage of materials
Desired results: • Better posture • Greater concentration • Less fatigue	**Desired results:** • Better visual efficiency • Less fatigue • Safer travel	**Desired results:** • Ease of viewing • Appropriate adaptations for specific vision loss	**Desired results:** • Less fatigue • Inclusion in class activities • Time efficiency

Source: R. Gargiulo, *Special Education in Contemporary Society,* 3rd ed. (Thousand Oaks, CA: Sage, 2009), p. 472.

Attention must be given to the layout and arrangement of the environment. The child needs to orient herself to the home as she is learning to crawl/walk and to the classroom setting prior to placement. In both settings, she needs to demonstrate that she has access to all aspects of the class. Marking the home or classroom areas with easily identifiable tactile cues is an important adaptation. The teacher or parent should enlist the assistance of an orientation and mobility specialist who can work with the child to enhance her mobility and level of independent movement about the home or classroom. (Orientation and mobility refers to a related service available to children with visual impairments.) **Orientation** is defined as being aware of where you are, where you are going and which route you will use to get there. **Mobility** is moving from one place to another (Gargiulo, 2009). Orientation and mobility training uses sensory awareness and motor development to help a child move independently through the environment. The use of orientation and mobility skills will facilitate movement within the current environments, and support total independence in future settings.

Adapting Materials and Equipment. Adaptations for children with visual impairments fall into several categories. They are visual aids and the use of hands-on real life situations, tactile methods and the use of Braille, and auditory strategies and aids. Additionally, students with visual impairments should be taught self-awareness as well as mobility and orientation skills (Turnbull, Turnbull, & Wehmeyer, 2007). Examples of visual aids include glasses, magnifiers, bookstands, bold-line paper, closed-circuit television, high-intensity lamps, large-print materials, an abacus, beeper balls, and toys with auditory output devices. When using visual aids, the main focus is to create a contrast. For example, when offering the child a choice (of toys, clothing, etc.), dark items should be against light backgrounds and vice versa. Or, if the toddler is eating in a high chair that is light, dark dishes should be used to assist him in finding the food. When working/playing with printed material, dark lines should be used around pictures or items in the books to guide the child using the material.

Tactile aids allow a child to obtain information through the sense of touch. Examples of tactile aids include Braille books, Braille writers (a machine used to type materials in Braille), raised-line paper, abacuses (for math calculations), and tactual maps.

Toys with interesting tactile components include fabric balls with different textures and dominoes that require the child to match different textures. In addition, the use of Braille readiness materials is recommended. These would include materials that require the child to match raised line patterns, match textures, identify big/small shapes, and so on. *Tactual* symbols could also be placed throughout the child's school and home environment to mark personal belongings or differentiate between similar items (such as different cans of food). Texture changes underfoot assist children in identifying different locations (for example, the carpeted area is the living room, the tile is in the kitchen). Teachers could also use carpet runners to assist the child in following specific paths across an open room (from doorway to play area, from doorway to bathroom, etc.).

Auditory aids allow children to obtain information through the sense of hearing. Examples of auditory aids include toys with auditory signals (for example, bells within a ball), talking books, clocks with auditory signals, tapes, or synthetic speech (computerized production of sound). It is important for a very young child with visual impairments to learn to reach, move toward, or follow a sound source. This skill will be critical as he learns to move independently about his home or other environments. For example, as he learns to associate sounds in his surroundings (the kitchen has the refrigerator sound, the television in the family room, etc.), he will begin to understand the direction in which he must move in order to get where he wants to go. In addition to sounds that naturally occur in the environment, artificial sounds can be created to facilitate the location of specific objects. Placing a wind chime over the toy box and a music box at the dresser will enable the toddler to learn the location of objects in the room while he is in his crib. Creating a sound library can help the child to learn sounds associated with different places and activities. This involves recording sounds that might be heard in different environments such as sounds from school, sounds at the grocery store, sounds of a city bus, and so on. The use of auditory aids will support the child's understanding of the auditory signals in the environment and ultimately lead to greater engagement and independence.

When developing printed materials or visual media (such as posters, charts), attention should be given to the edging paperwork, and the use of too much detail should be avoided. A child with partial vision may use tactile cues from the edging of the paper to determine where to begin writing (or even from the edging of furniture to determine where to place objects). Using bright or fluorescent colors in activities or to modify toys encourages children to use their vision (Gould & Sullivan, 1999). For a child who is partially sighted, too much detail may clutter printed material, making it more difficult for the child to focus on the most critical aspects on the paper or poster (Amerson, 1999). The vision consultant within the local school district will be a valuable resource in determining the kind of adapted materials needed. The vision specialist will be able to advise families and other personnel on the many recent technological advances that have created many products that are advantageous for young children with visual impairments. Equipment is available that helps children by "reading" printed material, providing a Braille printout of what is displayed on a computer monitor, and converting Braille to print. A scanner with optical character recognition (machines that "read") or speech synthesis is a technology that "talks" or speaks aloud anything on a computer disk. Television and video programming is made accessible to viewers with blindness or low vision by video description. Brief, spoken descriptions of on-screen action are inserted into the video when no dialog is occurring, allowing the viewer to follow the story (Hallahan et al., 2009). Adaptations and changes in instructional materials should occur only when necessary and should be based on the individual needs of the child. It would be a mistake to think that every child with a visual impairment requires the same adaptations. For a description of available technology for students with visual impairments, see the accompanying Teacher Technology Tips feature.

Teacher Technology Tips

Technology for Children with Sensory Impairments: Visually Impaired and Blind

Technology plays a vital role in the lives of children who are visually impaired. Examples of tools are listed below.

Adaptive Hardware	Braille writer refreshable Braille displays screen enlargements speech synthesizers printers Braille embosser electronic note-taker voice output device Braille input/output devices
Adaptive Software	Braille translation software screen readers screen enlargement software speech recognition software
Use of Adapted Output Systems	enhanced imaged system synthesized speech systems use of a Braille printer
Use of Adapted Input Systems	Braille input devices use of voice recognition systems use of optical character recognition system

Adapting Instruction. Gould and Sullivan (1999) offer some guidelines for working with young children with visual impairments. Some of their suggestions include the following:

- *Use consistent labels for objects.* Using different words for the same object ("jacket," "overcoat," "parka," or "cat" and "kitty" etc.) may be confusing for the child who cannot see.

- *Actively assist a child to explore the environment.* Give the child the opportunity to explore new environments with adult help initially. If a child has bumped or tripped over something, go back and allow the child to explore the obstacle visually and tactilely. If a child is startled by a loud noise, help the child investigate the source and cause.

- *Work from behind the child, putting him through the movements of what is expected of him while providing verbal feedback.* A child with vision can observe the movements of others, monitor and change his actions, and understand what is expected of him. Because a young child with a visual impairment does not have this input, it is necessary to demonstrate what is expected using a hand-over-hand approach and to provide feedback about what he is doing right and what he needs to do differently. When demonstrating, the teacher should work from behind the child. In this way the teacher, provides a sense of security and allows the child to feel the natural fluidity of movement. Furthermore, it enables the teacher to be more responsive to the child. However, as with any assistance, it is important that the level of assistance be gradually decreased in order to increase independence in the child.

- *Listen and explain everyday environmental sounds and visual information.* Individuals with sight take in so much with their vision. Sight enables individuals to connect a sound with a sound source by seeing something happen, understand what sound belongs to what source, and locate the direction from which the sound came. By identifying sounds (for example, the cabinet doors opening and closing, or the humming of the air conditioner), parents and teachers can provide the child with an understanding of the sounds in his environment and enable him to use the auditory cues as landmarks for organizing his environment. In addition, whenever visual information is presented, auditory input should also be provided. For example, a teacher may say out loud *what* he is doing while he is doing it ("I am tying your shoe." "I am peeling your orange."). In this way, *all* children within the class have access to visual information.

- *Teach self-care skills in the places and at the times where they naturally occur.* For example, a child who is toilet trained on a potty chair in the kitchen and then must transition to toileting in the bathroom The two environments have very different smells and sounds, and may be confusing for a child who cannot see. This approach is consistent with activity-based instruction (Pretti-Frontczak & Bricker, 2004), which stresses embedding skills within the natural environment or daily routines to promote skill acquisition and generalization.

- *Present objects before the instruction.* Teachers using models, manipulative toys, or other equipment should introduce students with visual impairments to the materials before teaching the lesson. If children have the opportunity to explore the materials before the activity begins, they will be more able to concentrate on the concept being taught rather than on the equipment (Cox & Dykes, 2001).

According to Noonan and McCormick (2006), there are some considerations when teaching a young child with a corrected visual impairment. Before, during, and after instruction, teachers must be attentive to whether the optical aids or glasses are correct for the child. An incorrect prescription could cause eye damage, result in headaches, or cause eye fatigue. If changes in child behavior occur (such as complaints of headaches or rubbing of eyes after use of new optical aids), the parent should be notified to determine if a follow-up examination is needed.

Teachers should be attentive to the length of time the pupil wears glasses. When a child first wears glasses or there is a change in the prescription, the child may be required to wear the glasses for a specified length of time. In addition, the child may have an adjustment period associated with the way the glasses feel or look and may be reluctant to wear the glasses. It may be necessary to provide incentives for wearing glasses or optical aids and to create a need to see. High-preference activities should be provided that require him or her to wear the new glasses in order to participate. This would be one way of creating a need to see that might be highly reinforcing to

Cengage Learning

Children with visual impairments can experience success within their learning environment with appropriate adaptations.

a young child. For preschoolers or early primary children, it may also be necessary to provide a unit on feelings, providing children with an outlet for talking about self-awareness and feelings related to the way they look in their new glasses.

Another instructional consideration is the modality of input. A young child with a visual impairment may need the parent, teacher, and peers to provide information that utilizes other senses. For example, Mary Kate, a 6-year-old who is blind, relies on her sense of hearing and smell to navigate her way around the classroom. By noticing an olfactory cue (an apple, bowl of potpourri, or flowers) on the teacher's desk, she is readily able to locate the teacher's desk using her sense of smell. Placing the cage for the pet gerbil by the door to the playground provides an olfactory cue (and sometimes audible cue) to where the door is located for Joyce, who is enrolled in a half-day early intervention program. Coupling a verbal directive, such as "Put your cups here," with auditory cues such as tapping on the tabletop, enables the child to place the cups in the designated location. The unobtrusive nature of these adaptations makes them particularly appealing since they do not single out the child with a disability.

Teachers must recognize that for a child with a visual impairment, learning may require more adaptations, repeated presentations and more intensive direct instruction. This is, of course, highly dependent on the individual. But it may require a teacher to find creative ways to reteach skills that were not achieved the first time around, to examine lessons presented to determine if a visual element to the lesson interfered with learning, and to allow sufficient time for the child to complete a task successfully.

For links to websites containing more information about young children with visual impairments, see the text's accompanying premium website.

Young Children with Sensory Impairments: Hearing

Children with hearing impairments can be classified as having a mild, moderate, severe, or profound hearing loss (Gargiulo, 2009). The federal definition describes deafness as a condition that adversely affects educational performance and is so severe that the child is impaired in processing linguistic information or communication through hearing, with or without amplification (hearing aids). Typically, a young child with a mild to moderate hearing loss is considered hard of hearing, while a child with a severe or profound hearing loss is considered deaf. A child who is deaf has a hearing loss that is so significant that he or she is unable to process spoken language without the use of amplified hearing devices (such as hearing aids or auditory trainers). A child who is hard of hearing has a less significant hearing loss and may be able to process spoken language (hear and speak) with or without the support of amplified hearing devices. Some children have a prelingual hearing loss (developed the hearing loss prior to language acquisition), while others exhibit postlingual hearing loss (developed a hearing impairment after they had acquired language). While children with hearing impairments represent a diverse group, there are some common issues and considerations related to adapting the environment, materials, and instruction.

Adapting the Home and Classroom Environments. Attention should be given to the light source in the home and classroom settings, making sure that there is adequate lighting and that the speaker is not standing in a shadow or location where a glare is present. The child may be using the visual cues of speech reading (lipreading), body language, facial expressions, sign language, or natural gestures to supplement hearing.

Attention should be given to seating and positioning. It may be necessary to seat a child with a hearing impairment directly in front of the teacher or to the left or right of the teacher if he is dependent on one ear for auditory input. All caregivers (parents, teachers, paraprofessionals) should be encouraged to position themselves at the child's level to allow easy access to visual cues given when speaking. Teachers should not talk with their backs to the child (for instance, while searching for items inside the closet) or obscure their lips with anything (for example, their hands, a book, the newspaper). The child with a hearing impairment may be heavily dependent on the movement of lips as the teacher is speaking. Teachers should remember to monitor classroom noise and background noise. When a student wears a hearing aid, all sounds in the environment are amplified.

Many young children with hearing impairments benefit from using assistive listening devices.

Spencer Grant/PhotoEdit

Adapting Materials and Equipment. There are several considerations related to using hearing aids. It is important to know how to manipulate the controls and how to troubleshoot minor problems—for example, what to do if and when the hearing aid whistles. Parents are excellent resources and can familiarize a teacher with their child's hearing device (such as knowing how to determine if the hearing aid is on or off and the volume controls). Even a young child may learn quickly how to turn the hearing aid off (and go about doing her own thing!). In addition, it is important to have a spare set of batteries on hand at home and at school and to frequently check them to ensure that they are still working. Teachers should make note if the hearing aid appears to fit improperly or has a damaged ear mold and notify the parent accordingly. A periodic visual examination of the ear (for redness or soreness), the cords of the hearing aid (to determine if they are worn and need replacing), and the mold (for split or broken pieces) takes very little time and can ensure that the child is properly fitted.

Current technologies have lead to improvements over previously available personal hearing aids. Assistive listening devices are frequently used by children with hearing impairments to enhance the use of auditory input. Many of these pupils benefit from using an **auditory trainer** or **FM system.** Gargiulo (2009) notes that these systems are often very effective and help manage acoustical problems found in the classroom. Some classrooms employ the use of a **sound field system.** With this system, the teacher wears a small microphone. The voice is then transmitted to speakers placed strategically around the room. These systems often benefit students with a minimal hearing loss.

Young children with hearing impairments and deafness are sometimes surgically implanted with a cochlear implant. A **cochlear implant** is not a hearing aid but a tiny array of electrodes implanted in the cochlea of the inner ear. It is attached to a tiny transmitter behind the ear. The child wears a microphone and speech processor connected by wiring and held in place by a magnet over the implant site behind the ear. Children with cochlear implants will frequently require the services of an audiologist and a speech–language pathologist. The audiologist can provide training for the parent and teacher in the usage and maintenance of the external parts of the implant equipment. The speech–language pathologist can provide intensive intervention in speech and language in order to further enhance the child's developing communication skills.

Technology often plays important part in developing the auditory and communication skills of young children with hearing impairments or deafness. See the Teacher Technology Tips feature for more information on available technologies for students with hearing impairments and deafness.

Adapting Instruction. Young children with hearing impairments may exhibit delays in communication development as language becomes more intertwined with other areas such as social or cognitive development, and because they have been denied auditory input necessary for development. For example, a 2-year-old with a hearing impairment may not be producing sounds, word approximations, or words as other peers would be at this same age. Young children who are deaf typically have less language interaction during play and appear to prefer groups of two rather than groups of three or more. These patterns may be attributed to the difficulty of dividing their attention, which is visual in nature, and their poorer knowledge of language appropriate for play situations. They also engage in less pretend play, possibly because language deficits impede their ability to script elaborate imaginary situations.

Children who are deaf spend less time in cooperative peer play (Gargiulo, 2009). The implication for the teacher is to utilize other modalities (tactile or visual methods or materials such as photos, pictures, charts, or gestures) and to provide multiple opportunities for social interaction.

One of the largest concerns for parents and teachers of young children with hearing impairments is

Teacher Technology Tips

Technology Tips for Children with Sensory Impairments: Hearing

Technology is an important component in the lives of individuals with disabilities. Nowhere are the effects of technological advances more evident than in the lives of students with hearing impairments. Examples of technology for students with hearing impairments are listed below.

Amplification of Auditory Information
- personal hearing aids
- assistive listening devices
- auditory training devices or FM systems
- sound field systems
- cochlear implants

Computers
- specialized software for speech drill, auditory training, speechreading, and sign language instruction
- synthesized speech from keyboards to input and transcribe speech onto a printed display screen

Alerting Devices
- wristwatches with vibratory alarm devices
- doorbells, fire alarms, and alarm clocks with vibratory mechanisms or flashing lights

Captioning Devices
- provides captioning for many current television programs, movies, and video

Telecommunication Devices
- A telecommunication device for the deaf (TDD) is a small keyboard with an electronic modem. Messages are typed onto the keyboard and carried as different sets of tones over the telephone to the other party's telephone, which must be linked to another TDD.
- amplified telephones

the choice of the communication mode for the child. Also of great concern is the method or educational approach that is chosen to use when teaching the child who is hard of hearing or deaf. Three possible educational approaches are ***auditory–oralism*** bilingual–bicultural, and total communication. *Auditory–oralism* is an educational approach that emphasizes the development of speech, speechreading, and listening with appropriate amplification. Neither sign language nor gesture is used with this approach. *Bilingual–bicultural* is an approach that emphasizes the early use of American Sign Language (ASL) because it is thought to be the natural language that permits children who are deaf to advance through the normal stages of language acquisition. ASL is used as the language of instruction, and English is taught by reading and writing. Both English and ASL are valued as educational tools in this method. *Total communication* focuses on using the individual child's preferred modes of communication. It includes oral, auditory, speechreading, sign language, finger spelling, writing, and gestures as methods for teaching. For a detailed view of the educational approaches used when working with students with hearing impairments, see Table 8–4.

TABLE 8–4 Educational Approaches Often Used When Working with Children with Hearing Impairments

Bilingual–bicultural	
Basic position	Considers American Sign Language (ASL) to be the natural language of the Deaf culture and urges recognition of ASL as the primary language choice with English considered a second language.
Objective	Provide a foundation in the use of ASL with its unique vocabulary and syntax rules.
	ASL instruction provided for English vocabulary and syntax rules.
Method of communication	ASL (American Sign Language).
Total communication	
Basic position	Supports the belief that simultaneous use of multiple communication techniques enhances an individual's ability to communicate, comprehend, and learn.
Objective	Provide a multifaceted approach to communication to facilitate whichever method(s) works best for each individual.
Method of Communication	Simultaneous combination of sign language (accepts the use of any of the sign language systems), fingerspelling, and speechreading.
Auditory–oral	
Basic position	Supports the belief that children with hearing impairments can develop listening/receptive language and oral language expression (English) skills with the emphasis placed on using residual hearing (the level of hearing an individual possesses), amplification (hearing aids, auditory training, etc.) and speech/language training.
Objective	Facilitate the development of spoken (oral) English.
Method of communication	Spoken (oral) English.

SOURCE: Adapted from R. Gargiulo, *Special Education in Contemporary Society*, 3rd ed. (Thousand Oaks, CA: Sage, 2009), p. 422.

Consulting with the speech–language pathologist enables the teacher to learn first hand about the mode of communication that is supported by the family and therapist. Likewise, peers and adults who interact with the child should know how to communicate in the child's preferred mode. Professionals recommend that everyone use the same communication mode when interacting with a child with a hearing impairment.

A normal voice, gestures, and touch (when appropriate) should be used in communicating with a child with a hearing impairment (Heward, 2009). For example, a light touch on the shoulder (to gain the child's attention) or gestural motion (pointing to the door) is a subtle visual cue that allows the child to understand what is happening or where to go. For a list of classroom adaptations and accommodations for children with hearing impairments, refer to Table 8–5.

For links to websites containing more information related to young children with hearing impairments and deafness, see the text's accompanying premium website.

TABLE 8–5 Suggestions for Teaching Students with Hearing Impairments and Deafness

Suggestion	How to Do It
Promote acceptance of your students. Your student will benefit from a classroom where he/she feels accepted and where modifications are made without undue attention.	• Welcome the student to your class. Your positive attitude will help other students accept him/her. • Discuss your student's hearing loss with him/her; let him/her know you are willing to help. • As appropriate, have your student, the audiologist, or another person explain the student's hearing loss to your entire class. • Make modifications seem as natural as possible so the student is not singled out. • Accept your student as an individual; be aware of his/her assets as well as his/her limitations. • Encourage your student's special abilities or interests.
Be sure hearing aids and other amplification devices are used when recommended. This will enable your student to use his/her hearing maximally.	• Realize that hearing aids make sounds louder, but not necessarily clearer. Hearing aids don't make hearing normal. • Be sure your student's hearing aids or other devices are checked daily to see that they are working properly. • Encourage the student to care for his/her hearing aid(s) by putting it on, telling you when it is not functioning properly, etc. • Be sure your student always has a spare battery at school. • Know who to contact if your student's device is not working properly.
Provide preferential seating. Appropriate seating will enhance your student's ability to hear and understand what is said in the classroom.	• Seat near where you typically teach. It will be helpful if your student is at one side of the classroom so he/she can easily turn and follow classroom dialogue. • Seat where your student can easily watch your face without straining to look straight up. Typically the second or third row is best. • Seat away from noise sources, including hallways, radiators, pencil sharpeners, etc. • Seat where light is on your face and not in your student's eyes. • *If* there is a better ear, place it toward the classroom. • Allow your student to move to other seats when necessary for demonstrations, classroom discussions, or other activities.

Increase visual information. Your student will use lipreading and other visual information to supplement what he/she hears.	• Remember, your student needs to see your face in order to lipread.
	   ○ Try to stay in one place while talking to the class so your student does not have to lipread a moving target.
	   ○ Avoid talking while writing on the chalkboard.
	   ○ Avoid putting your hands, papers, or books in front of your face when talking.
	   ○ Avoid talking with your face turned downward while reading.
	   ○ Keep the light on your face, not at your back. Avoid standing in front of windows where the glare will make it difficult for your student to see your face.
	• Use visual aids, such as pictures and diagrams, when possible.
	• Demonstrate what you want the student to understand when possible. Use natural gestures, such as pointing to objects being discussed, to help clarify what you say.
	• Use the chalkboard—write assignments, new vocabulary words, key words, etc. on it.

Minimize classroom noise. Even a small amount of noise will make it very difficult for your student to hear and understand what is said.	• Seat your student away from noisy parts of your classroom. • Wait until your class is quiet before talking to them.
Modify teaching procedures. Modifications will allow your student to benefit from your instruction and will decrease the need for repetition.	• Be sure your student is watching and listening when you are talking to him/her. • Be sure your student understands what is said by having him/her repeat information or answer questions. • Rephrase, rather than repeat, questions and instructions if your student has not understood them. • Write key words, new words, new topics, etc., on the chalkboard. • Repeat or rephrase things said by other students during classroom discussions. • Introduce new vocabulary to the student in advance. The speech–language pathologist or parents may be able to help with this. • Use a buddy to alert your student to listen and to be sure your student has understood all information correctly.
Have realistic expectations. This will help your student succeed in your classroom.	• Remember that your student cannot understand everything all of the time, no matter how hard he/she tries. Encourage him/her to ask for repetition. • Be patient when student asks for repetition. • Give breaks from listening when necessary. Your student may fatigue easily because he/she is straining to listen and understand. • Expect student to follow classroom routine. Do not spoil or pamper your student. • Expect your student to accept the same responsibilities for considerate behavior, homework, and dependability as you require of other students in your classroom. • Ask the student to repeat if you can't understand him/her. Your student's speech may be distorted because he/she does not hear sounds clearly. Work with the speech–language pathologist to help your student improve his/her speech as much as possible. • Be alert for fluctuations of hearing due to middle ear problems. • Request support from the audiologist, the speech–language pathologist, or others when you feel uncertain about your student and what is best for him/her.

SOURCE: Adapted from C. Johnson, P. Benson, and J. Seaton, *Educational Audiology Handbook* (San Diego, CA: Singular, 1997), pp. 370–371.

Young Children with Delays in Motor Development and Health Impairments

Children with physical and/or health impairments represent a very diverse group with children having health impairments such as asthma, cystic fibrosis, leukemia, or diabetes or physical impairments such as spina bifida, cerebral palsy, muscular dystrophy, and spinal cord injury (Gargiulo, 2009). (See Appendix A for the federal definitions associated with physical and health impairments.) Because young children with physical and health impairments reflect a wide range of etiologies and disabilities, early signs or indicators vary, as does the age of onset. However, children with physical or health impairments may share some common issues and considerations related to adapting the environment, instruction, and materials.

Adapting the Home and Classroom Environments. Because the child may be using adaptive equipment (wheelchair, walker, adaptive seating, etc.), ample space is needed for the child to move independently about the classroom. Prior to the child coming to the class, it must be determined how accessible the travel paths are within the classroom and doorways.

Determine if there any changes in the layout of the home or class setting that are necessary to facilitate mobility. All areas (toy shelves, bookcases, coat racks, sensory tables, activity centers and so forth) should be accessible to all children. Railings may be needed, especially in the restroom and along ramps. The match between the height of the work surface and the child's seating should be examined to ensure that the child has access to all of the tabletop activities. Materials should be presented at the child's eye level and should be stored at child height to promote independence in retrieving and replacing items. Depending on the child's abilities and his/her goals, location of objects and materials needs careful attention. For example, Mike is a right-handed toddler with cerebral palsy who has a limited range of motion in his right hand and arm, but has excellent grasping ability. If a goal for Mike is to promote independent play or eating, it would be important to place objects such as toys, food, and drink within his reach. Or, if his goal is to increase cross-midline reaching, objects should be placed on the left side of his lapboard to encourage cross-midline reaching.

The accessibility and architectural specifications of the home or school should be examined to determine if the child will need adaptations (for example, the use of ramps or railings) to gain access to restrooms, water fountains, and doorways, as well as passageways within the classroom. Table 8–6 offers some suggestions on how to modify the learning environment for children with orthopedic or health impairments.

Proper seating and positioning can combat poor circulation, muscle tightness, and pressure sores and contribute to digestion, respiration, and physical development. In addition, proper seating can promote feelings of physical security and safety, positively affect the use of the upper body, and reduce the possibility of developing additional deformities (McEwen, 1995). Because of the importance of seating and positioning, several aspects of the environment need attention. There should be many seating options within the home and school, such as adaptive chairs, corner chairs, or prop sitting with pillows or wedges. See Figure 8–1 for various types of apparatus.

If necessary, an abduction block (a pummel, block, wedge, or cushion that the child's legs can straddle) can be used to prevent the child from sliding out of the chair. A seat belt and/or shoulder and chest strap may be necessary to maintain an appropriate upright position. In addition, to ensure maximum trunk control, adding a footstool may be warranted to ensure that the child's feet rest firmly on a flat surface. Prior to any changes in seating or prompting a young child to walk or move with or without adaptive equipment, an accredited specialist (physical or occupational therapist) should be consulted (Case-Smith, 2005).

A child may require medication or have specific nutritional needs. Therefore, when creating an environment that supports this child, attention is warranted regarding safety precautions and side effects associated with medication or nutrition. Written authorizations from the parents and physician are required related to the administration of medication or alternative nutritional needs of the child (such as a child with diabetes). At the school level, a determination must be made regarding who will administer medication, record medication administration, store medication in a secure, locked location, and monitor any changes in child behavior associated with nutritional or medication needs. In addition, teachers need to be aware of medication or special diets that the child is on while at home. For example,

TABLE 8–6 Suggested Classroom Checklist of Accommodations for Children with Orthopedic or Health Impairments

Child's Name: _____ Date of Birth: _____
Diagnosis: _____

Check any of the following that apply:
_____ has a difficult time remaining upright
_____ poor head control
_____ deformities that limit the child's ability to function
_____ tires easily
_____ abnormal reflexes
_____ abnormal muscle tone on just one side: _____right _____left
_____ abnormal muscle tone in the legs only
_____ abnormal muscle tone throughout the body
_____ low muscle tone/appears floppy
_____ high muscle tone/appears stiff
_____ problems with coordination and balance
_____ difficulty keeping lips closed; drooling
_____ tremors
_____ seizures
_____ unable to walk without help
_____ unable to sit without help
_____ joint pain
_____ bones break easily
_____ difficulty swallowing
_____ does not use verbal language in communicating

Check any of the following strategies that will help the child with physical and health impairments in your classroom.
_____ Position the child carefully so that he is sitting with his hips bent and head back in alignment.
_____ Make sure that tables and chairs are helping the child to stay upright.
_____ Stabilize learning materials with suction cups, clamps, or Velcro.
_____ Provide alternative methods of communication such as picture icons.
_____ Provide electric switches to activate toys, music, voice-activated output device.
_____ Make items easier to grasp by adding foam tubing.
_____ Position items on a tabletop easel to help maintain an upright position.
_____ Provide a chair with sides.
_____ Watch for signs of fatigue.
_____ Encourage the child to use two hands in activities.
_____ If the child has tight muscles, avoid resistive materials such a playing with stiff play dough.
_____ Warn the child before picking him up or moving him.
_____ Make sure the furniture in the room can support the weight of a child pulling to stand.
_____ Change the child's position frequently unless medically contraindicated.

Source: P. Gould and J. Sullivan, *The Inclusive Early Childhood Classroom* (Baltimore, Gryphon House, 1999), p. 17.

FIGURE 8–1 Alternative Seating Options

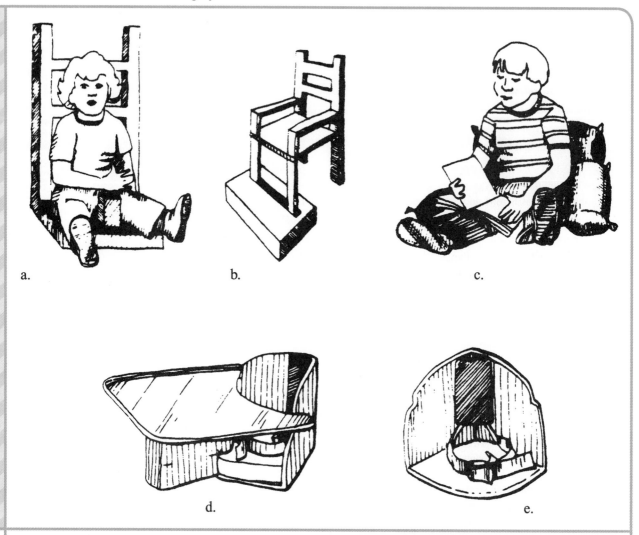

a.

b.

c.

d.

e.

Source: S. Best, K. Heller, and J. Bigge, *Teaching Individuals with Physical and Multiple Disabilities,* 5th ed. (Upper Saddle River, NJ: Pearson Education, 2005), p. 202.

medication administered at home could result in side effects (such as altered behavior) during school hours. Therefore, teachers and parents need to have regular communication about the nutritional and medication needs of the child.

Adapting Materials and Equipment. The physical and occupational therapist should work closely with the teacher and parents to provide the information and consultation that is necessary for each individual child. Specialized equipment for standing, sitting, and ambulation may be necessary because of abnormal muscle tone. **Hypotonic muscle tone** (floppy muscles) or **hypertonic muscle tone** (tight muscles) may thwart movement patterns and physical growth. Adaptive equipment and **orthotic devices** offer a variety of options to optimize learning potential of a young child with a physical or health impairment. **Prosthetic devices** support the child in the learning environment, but without careful attention, they can restrict range of motion, cause discomfort and abrasions, or interfere with circulation if not properly fitted. If special equipment such as a wheelchair is used, periodic inspections are necessary to ensure proper fit, comfort, and that the equipment is in good working order (Case-Smith, 2005). In addition, because of limited physical strength, it may be necessary to examine the weight of materials that the child will be expected to manipulate to determine if adaptations are warranted.

Teachers should always enlist the help of therapists (and parents) to adjust and adapt equipment or materials. It is important to remember that simple modifications of everyday materials are preferred, as they are less stigmatizing. For example, if a child cannot use the same materials (such as scissors or a drinking cup) as his classmates, adapted scissors or adapted cups can be provided or made from standard materials and equipment. Clothing with Velcro fasteners may increase independent dressing. Velcro straps added to a musical instrument may allow a child who has an unsteady grasp to hold the tambourine while playing it. A spoon handle built up with layers of tape may be enough of an adaptation for a student to grasp the handle and feed himself. Physical therapists and occupational therapists can also support the teacher by demonstrating effective techniques for using adaptive equipment or for positioning, lifting, carrying, and transfer strategies that can be utilized with confidence and without harm to the caregiver (Case-Smith, 2005). Assistive technology for students with physical and health impairments can be used to enhance communication, academic tasks, leisure activities, and socialization. For a list of available technologies, see the accompanying Teacher Technology Tips feature.

Adapting Instruction. Children with physical and/or health impairments may exhibit fatigue, have limited stamina and vitality, or require limited physical activity. This may require the teacher and parent to examine the schedule (at home and at school), the length of activities, and the pace of the curriculum. The teacher may need to determine the optimal time to schedule certain activities, adjust the length of activities, or create alternative ways for the less active child to participate.

For children who experience problems with fatigue and endurance, it is important that teachers plan for ambulation when setting up activities for the classroom. Teachers must think through the movements that will be needed, as well as equipment and materials necessary to maximize learning. Some questions that can be asked include these:

- Does the class really need to transition after this activity?
- How long will the transition take?
- Can the student make this transition within the time allotted, with enough time to move independently, or is the teacher (or assistant) always carrying him (and fostering dependence)?
- Is it better to do two activities at the same table or do you want to utilize the transition to another area to allow an opportunity for the child to use his/her new walker?
- Is time a factor? Mobilizing several children who are nonambulatory takes time. Therefore, before everyone is moved to new space, it is important that teachers be thoughtful about the transition.
- Is the wait time or transition movement utilized effectively—for example, to address fine motor and gross motor skills, language and listening skills?

TeachSource Video

Including Students with Physical Disabilities: Best Practices

Visit the premium website and watch "*Including Students with Physical Disabilities: Best Practices.*" After watching this video, answer the following questions:

1. What types of accommodations would you include in your classroom to make a student with a physical disability feel educationally as well as socially welcomed?
2. How would you prepare your typically developing students for the inclusion of a classmate who has a physical disability?

Teacher Technology Tips

Technology for Children with Delays in Motor Development and Health Impairments

Children with physical or health disabilities use technology for academic tasks, leisure, and socialization. Computers are widely used. Depending on the severity of the disability, many modifications can be made to individualize equipment use to the specific needs of the user. Examples of high- and low-technology solutions are listed below.

Activity	Low Technology	High Technology
Reading	• Book stand • Turn page with mouth stick • Ruler to keep place on page	• Electric page-turner • Software to scan book into computer or read text aloud
Writing	• Pencil with built-up grip • Wider-spaced paper • Mouth stick with attached pencil	• Computer with alternative input (switch or voice recognition)
Math	• Counter • Abacus • Money cards	• Graphing calculator • Software that positions the cursor for regrouping
Eating	• Spoon with built-up handle • Hand splint to hold spoon • Adaptive cup • Scoop dish	• Electric feeder • Robotic arm
Leisure	• Card holder • Larger baseball	• Sport wheelchair • Adapted bicycle • Computer games

SOURCE: R. Gargiulo, *Special Education in Contemporary Society*, 2nd ed. (Belmont, CA: Thomson/Wadsworth, 2006), p. 605.

• Is the child supported in his own planning related to movement? The child may need assistance with the thinking and reasoning skills related to his own independent mobility. For example, when it's time to go outside, Sam, age two, may need a verbal prompt from his caregiver, "Sam, what do you need to get to the door?" He replies, "My walker." She responds, "That's right, go get your walker."

Restrictions in movement, including locomotion and voluntary gross and fine motor actions, can occur and interfere with the mastery of other developmental skills. For example, a young child who has motor delays and is not able to freely explore his surroundings could exhibit delays in other areas such as speech, language, and social development due to limited exploration of new objects, limited vocabulary, or limited social experiences. The implication is for

Cengage Learning

For a young child with physical limitations, adaptations and accommodations are often needed for maximum participation in all aspects of the learning environment.

teachers and parents to provide a language-rich environment, integrating language into all areas of learning and ensuring that the child has as much mobility and accessibility as possible within stimulating home and school settings.

Within the class and home settings, there are many opportunities for children to take on responsibilities (assist in daily events and activities) or leadership roles. Allowing children to participate in this capacity promotes leadership, independence, and positive self-esteem. It would be important that the child with a physical or health impairment, who is typically on the receiving end of assistance, be included in the leadership roles available in the home and school. For example, Anna Kathryn, a 5-year-old with spina bifida, was selected to carry books to and from

the library using the tray that fit onto her wheelchair. In this way, she was provided with leadership opportunities like her classmates, and the use of the wheelchair tray has become an asset for her as opposed to something that separates her from her classmates. Even when she was three years old, she assisted at home by clearing the table and taking folded clothes to the hall closet using her lapboard (attached to her wheelchair). At a very early age, she was participating in family activities that supported her sense of belonging, positive self-esteem, and leadership abilities.

Frequent and/or prolonged absences are not uncommon among this population and warrant attention. For a young child, this may have a negative impact on various areas of development, such as the development of friendships and security in the school setting, as well as the parent–child relationship. In addition, the child may qualify for homebound or hospitalized educational services, depending on the guidelines within the local school district.

Adjustments and accommodations for a student with a physical and/or health impairment may present a unique set of issues for teachers, parents, and other family members. For example, one child may have a physical impairment that does not progress (such as spina bifida), while another may have a physical or health impairment that is progressive in nature (such as muscular dystrophy) or has episodic (recurring) events (seizures or asthmatic attacks). Still another youngster may be sensitive to his own body related to the use of a prosthesis. Other issues relate to stress from repeated hospitalizations, daily or crisis care events, or the anxiety related to life-threatening illness or accident (like muscular dystrophy, leukemia, or spinal cord injury). Parents and teachers alike may be overprotective or have difficulty balancing the amount of attention given to the child with the health problem versus siblings or other children in the class. Likewise, it may be difficult to promote independence in a student who has been sick and become dependent on adults and others for support and assistance. Because of these unique stressors, different types of support, such as counseling, may be required for a young child related to his health or physical impairment.

In addition, peers may have a need for counseling related to their friend with a disability. For example, Joe, a 3-year-old child with muscular dystrophy, was progressively losing control of his gross and fine motor abilities, which negatively impacted his ability to walk, play ball, color and paint, carry his belongings, or feed himself. Several of his peers expressed concern and anxiety about themselves ("Will I catch what he has"? "My leg hurts today. Does that mean I will be sick like Joe?"). Others expressed concerns about Joe as his illness progressed and resulted in frequent hospitalizations ("I feel sad about Joe. Is he going to ever walk again? Is he going to die?").

Teachers need to recognize signs of anxiety or stress that may warrant consultation with the school counselor. Likewise, parents and teachers may have counseling and support needs related to the death of a child with a disability. Therefore, it is critical that professionals understand the nature of the grief process and find healthy ways of addressing it if the situation occurs (Webb, 2002).

For links to websites containing more information related to young children with physical and health disabilities, see the text's accompanying premium website.

Summary

This chapter focused on adapting, accommodating, and modifying instruction, materials, and equipment as well as environments for young children with diverse abilities. Additionally, brief descriptors of young children with special needs were provided. It is important to realize that these are only possible characteristics or early indicators of a delay or disability. A disability may not manifest itself in the same way or at the same time for every child with the same disability. Additionally, the presence of one (or some) of these early indicators does not always indicate a delay.

Although this chapter delineated several ways to adapt environments, materials, and instruction for children with delays or disabilities, it is important to remember that children with disabilities are first and foremost children who are capable of learning. With the proper support and guidance from teachers and parents, these students will achieve. As discussed in this chapter, students with disabilities typically learn at different rates. They may learn through another modality or respond in a variety of different ways. Teachers, therefore, have to use different instructional strategies. The key is to be flexible and create collaborative, supportive teams between parents and professionals. This collaborative team

has the responsibility to create an appropriate match between the individual needs of the child and the environment, materials, and instruction.

Check Your Understanding

1. How can embedded instruction facilitate the learning of a young child with special needs?
2. Define the term *generalization* and provide examples of ways that it can be used to ensure the transfer of skills across environments.
3. Explain how you would use task analysis to teach a young child how to make a peanut butter and jelly sandwich.
4. What are positive behavioral supports? How can this strategy be used to modify a child's behavior?
5. A second grader with a visual impairment is placed in your classroom. Identify the adaptations you would use to ensure the social and instructional integration of this pupil.
6. How would you adapt the learning environment to accommodate a child with a hearing impairment?
7. What are some of the issues that might need to be addressed if a child with muscular dystrophy is placed in a preschool classroom?

Reflection and Application

1. Observe children with special needs and typically developing individuals between 30 months and 8 years of age in their natural environments. Record their conversations with family members, friends, peers, adults, and other significant individuals. In what ways were their language skills the same? Dissimilar? Were any particular strategies used by the adults to enhance the language skills of children with delays or disabilities? What particular steps could a teacher incorporate in the classroom to develop the language abilities of a child with cognitive delays?
2. Visit an inclusive kindergarten or an inclusive early primary grade classroom in your local school district. If possible, determine which student has special needs and observe this child for

about one hour. Did this individual exhibit any inappropriate behavior? How did the teacher respond to these actions? Were the intervention tactics successful? How did the classmates respond to this child's behavior? If this student was in your classroom, what intervention steps would you use to guide his or her behavior?

References

Alberto, P., & Troutman, A. (2006). *Applied behavior analysis for teachers* (7th ed.). Upper Saddle River, NJ: Pearson Education.

Amerson, M. (1999). Helping children with visual and motor impairments make the most of their visual abilities. *Re: View, 31*(1), 17–21.

Brown, M., & Bergen, D. (2002). Play and social interaction of children with disabilities at learning/activity centers in an inclusive preschool. *Journal of Research in Childhood Education, 17*(1), 26–37.

Buysse, S., Wesley, P., Snyder, P., & Winton, P. (2006). Evidenced-based practice: What does it really mean for the early childhood field? *Young Exceptional Children, 9*(4), 2–11.

Case-Smith, J. (2005). *Occupational therapy for children* (5th ed.). St. Louis, MO: Elsevier Mosby.

Coleman, M. C., & Webber, J. (2002). *Emotional and behavioral disorders: Theory and practice.* Boston: Allyn & Bacon.

Cook, R., Klien, M., & Tessier, A. (2008). *Adapting early childhood curricula for children with special needs* (7th ed.). Upper Saddle River, NJ: Pearson Education.

Copple, C., & Bredekamp, S. (Eds.). (2009). *Developmentally appropriate practice in early childhood programs: Serving students from birth through age 8.* Washington, DC: National Association for the Education of Young Children.

Cox, P., & Dykes, M. (2001). Effective classroom adaptations for students with visual impairments. *Teaching Exceptional Children, 33*(6), 68–74.

D'Allura, T. (2002). Enhancing the social interaction skills of preschoolers with visual impairments. *Journal of Visual Impairments and Blindness, 96*(8), 576–584.

Gargiulo, R. (2009). *Special education in contemporary society: An introduction to exceptionality* (3rd ed.). Thousand Oaks, CA: Sage.

Gestwicki, C. (1999). *Developmentally appropriate practice: Curriculum and development in early education.* Albany, NY: Delmar.

Gould, P., & Sullivan, J. (1999). *The inclusive early childhood classroom: Easy ways to adapt learning centers for all children.* Beltsville, MD: Gryphon House.

Hallahan, D., Kauffman, J., & Pullen, P. (2009). *Exceptional learners* (11th ed.). Boston: Pearson Education.

Heward, W. (2009). *Exceptional children* (9th ed.). Upper Saddle River, NJ: Pearson Education.

Hickson, L., Blackman, L., & Reis, E. (1995). *Mental retardation: Foundations of educational programming.* Boston: Allyn & Bacon.

McEwen, E. (1995). *Occupational and physical therapy in educational environments.* Binghamton, NY: Haworth Press.

McLean, M., Bailey, D., & Wolery, M. (2004). *Assessing infants and preschoolers with special needs* (3rd ed.). Upper Saddle River, NJ: Pearson Education.

McPhee, N., Favazza, P., & Lewis, E. (2004). *Sensitivity and awareness: A guide for developing understanding among children* (4th ed.). Hollidaysburg, PA: Jason & Nordic Publishing.

Noonan, M., & McCormick, L. (2006). *Young children with disabilities in natural environments.* Baltimore: Paul H. Brookes.

Pretti-Frontczak, K., & Bricker, D. (2004). *An activity-based approach to early intervention* (3rd ed.). Baltimore: Paul H. Brookes.

Sandall, S., Hemmeter, M., Smith, B., & McLean, M. (2005). *DEC recommended practices: A comprehensive guide for practical application.* Longmont, CO: Sopris West.

Sandall, S., & Schwartz, I. (2008). *Building blocks for teaching preschoolers with special needs.* Baltimore: Paul H. Brookes.

Turnbull, A., Turnbull, R., & Wehmeyer, M. (2007). *Exceptional lives: Special education in today's schools* (5th ed.). Upper Saddle River, NJ: Pearson Education.

Webb, N. (2002). *Helping bereaved children* (2nd ed.). New York: Guilford Press.

Wickes-Nelson, R., & Israel, A. (2006). *Behavior disorders of childhood* (6th ed.). Upper Saddle River, NJ: Pearson Education.

Wolery, M. (2005). DEC recommended practices: Child-focused practices. In S. Sandall, M. Hemmeter, B. J. Smith, & M. McLean (Eds.), *DEC recommended practices: A comprehensive guide for practical application in early intervention/early childhood special education.* Longmont, CO: Sopris West.

9 Strategies for Teaching Young Children with Special Needs

Contributed by Linda L. Brady, Director, Exceptional Children's Department, Vestavia Hills (Alabama) City Schools

Strategies for Including Young Children with Special Needs
  Teacher-Mediated Strategies
  Peer-Mediated Strategies
  Routine-Based Strategies
  Specific Naturalistic (Milieu) Strategies

Summary

Check Your Understanding

Reflection and Application

References

Key Terminology

Engagement

Teacher-mediated

Environmental arrangements

Prompts

Partial participation

Adapted participation

Peer-mediated strategies

Routine-based strategies

Play-based intervention (strategies)

Activity-based instruction

Milieu strategies

Learning Outcomes

After reading this chapter, you will be able to:

- Describe teaching strategies that facilitate inclusion of young children with special needs in natural, center-based, and school settings.

- Identify teacher-mediated strategies that focus on active engagement and differing levels of participation of young children with special needs, environmental arrangements, promoting acceptance, use of prompts and praise, and the monitoring of communication.

- Identify peer-mediated strategies, including cooperative learning.

- Describe routine-based, play-based, activity-based, and specific milieu strategies in the context of teaching young children with special needs from birth through age eight.

- List technology tools and strategies used to enhance the participation of young children with special needs in the educational environment.

Children with disabilities are first and foremost children. They can and do learn. They may learn at a different rate, use different strategies, or learn through another modality, but they do learn. They may learn through exploration and child-initiated activities or with the additional support of peers and direction from a teacher. The key in creating appropriate educational experiences for any child is to *create a match* between the individual needs of the child and the instruction. This may result in teachers and parents using a variety or combination of strategies to facilitate development and learning.

IDEA and its amendments stress that children be educated "to the maximum extent appropriate in the least restrictive environment (LRE)." These federal laws provide support for educational services for children between the ages of three and eight with disabilities, with the placement of choice being with typically developing children (Odom, 2000). This concept has been written about since the early 1970s and has emerged as the service delivery model of choice for children and families in recent years. The most common interpretation of this aspect of the law is that children should be placed in educational settings alongside typically developing peers. One current application of the least restrictive environment clause is referred to as *inclusion*. Within inclusive settings, children can be functionally included, achieve social integration, and engage in the typical classroom setting without support or with special educators providing an array of services and supports in the general education classroom (Carvallo & Hanney, 1999; Gargiulo, 2009). This level of participation requires that teachers examine the child in each setting to determine if he/she is actively engaged in all aspects of the environment.

This chapter provides suggestions for including young children with special needs in natural environments or inclusive settings for children from birth through age eight. It presents a wide range of strategies proven to be effective in promoting child engagement (Wolery, 2005). This chapter will focus on those selected strategies effectively used in center-based programs or inclusive classrooms. Teaching strategies from the field of early childhood and early childhood special education will be discussed including preschool and the early primary grades. Many of the strategies are appropriate for use with younger children who receive early intervention services in centers or at home.

Strategies for Including Young Children with Special Needs

For several years, educators have questioned the idea that students requiring intensive specialized services should receive them outside a general education setting. Federal law and the focus on providing access to the general education curriculum have resulted in a growing number of students with various special needs receiving services within the general education classroom environment (Gargiulo & Metcalf, 2010). Prompted by legislation and parent input, an increasing number of children with developmental delays participate in inclusive settings during preschool and the early primary grades (U.S. Department of Education, 2006). The placement of young children with disabilities in inclusive settings is a complex subject that involves many factors in the decision. Some key issues that professionals and parents should consider are the quality of the early childhood program, child characteristics, family goals, and experience of the staff (Sandall, Hemmeter, Smith, & McLean, 2005). Furthermore, inclusion is more than just the physical placement of children with disabilities in educational settings alongside typically developing children. It requires teachers to examine the child in each setting to determine if he/she is actively engaged in all aspects of the environment. For the purpose of this discussion, **engagement** will be defined as consistent, active involvement with the people (teachers, parents, classmates), activities (snack time, play time, group time participation, center selection/participation), and materials (use of toys, art supplies, water play materials) throughout the child's day that lead to goal achievement (Wolery, 2005). This chapter will focus on selected strategies that will be organized into the following four categories:

1. teacher-mediated strategies
2. peer-mediated strategies
3. routine-based strategies
4. naturalistic (milieu) strategies

While the discussion focuses on strategies used in center-based programs or inclusive classrooms, many of the strategies are appropriate for use with younger children who receive early intervention services in centers or at home.

Teacher-Mediated Strategies

The term **teacher-mediated** has typically been used to describe teacher-directed explicit interventions designed to promote social interaction by the teaching of a specific skill or skills set (Gargiulo, 2009; McEvoy, Odom, & McConnell, 1992). We will broaden the term *teacher-mediated* to include many techniques that an adult (teacher or parent) can implement before or during activities that promote child engagement with people, materials, or activities. Teacher-mediated strategies include arranging the environment, promoting acceptance, providing prompts and praise, accepting differential levels/types of participation, and monitoring communicative input.

Environmental Arrangements. *Environmental arrangement* is one of the least intrusive steps that teachers can take to promote engagement of children within their educational settings. Current guidelines are available with suggestions for the organization, structure, and operation of optimal learning environments for children with diverse abilities (Copple & Bredekamp, 2009; Wolery, 2005). Three strategies will be discussed that fit within these guidelines: the arrangement of physical space, the selection and use of materials, and the use of structured activities (Gargiulo, 2009).

The typical guidelines used when arranging any learning environment include the following: quiet areas that are located away from noisy areas; high-interest materials that are accessible to children; materials that are safe and stimulating; adequate space to provide easy movement throughout the classroom; and an environment that can be easily monitored by adults (Sandall & Schwartz, 2008). Research has shown that some additional environmental strategies are warranted when children with delays or disabilities are included within the educational setting. The physical environment may be used by teachers to develop individual goals for students in the classroom. A teacher may want to promote lunch- or snack-time conversation by the placement of certain children in proximity to the child working on social communication goals. A teacher working with a student who is highly distractible may design quiet, isolated play areas for the child and assign a friend to explore with away from the large group. Even within the designated space, other aspects of the environment warrant attention, including limiting the amount of materials available to children, attending to the specific considerations related to the individual child with the disability (such as use of walker or adaptive seating to maintain trunk control, or a wheelchair access), and monitoring the number of adults and their behavior (Gestwicki, 1999; Sandall & Schwartz).

Attention should be given to the selection and use of materials. Materials should be safe, multidimensional, and developmentally appropriate for the children within the classroom. In addition, teachers can select toys known to promote high levels of engagement, select toys based on the child's preference, monitor the child's access to materials, and adapt the use of toys or materials (Davis, Kilgo, & Gamel-McCormick, 1998).

Some toys or materials result in more isolated play, while others appear to result in more interactive play (Wolery, 2005). Toys that are more likely to result in higher social interactions are blocks, dolls, trucks and cars, social dramatic play (dress-up, cooking), and games that have multiple parts (such as Mr. Potato Head, farm or zoo animals). Materials that are more likely to result in solitary play include books, puzzles, and art activities (paints, paper and pencil drawing). Obviously, how a teacher structures the use of these more solitary materials will impact the level of interaction. For example, preschoolers can share a book, each taking turns reading, holding, and turning the pages. The selection of the materials should be driven by the goals of the teacher in the structured play setting. At times, the goal may be to promote interactive play, which involves more social and communicative exchanges, while at other times it may be to promote the use of appropriate toy play behavior.

Material selection should also be determined by the level of interest and preferences of the child. Young children with disabilities are more likely to engage with high-interest toys and materials. Preschoolers, for example, are more likely to show high levels of engagement and are less likely to engage in inappropriate behavior when participating in high-interest activities (Brown & Bergen, 2002). Asking parents, family members, or the child is an excellent way to ensure that the activities, materials, and toys are preferred by the child.

While child choice and preference are important, a teacher or parent may want to provide some guidance to youngsters who consistently select the same activities, materials, or toys. The teacher could observe the child as he makes choices of toys, materials, and activities across a specific period of time. Then, the adult could provide suggestions for play or introduce new materials with a high-preference toy as a way of expanding a child's choice to new, and perhaps more challenging activities. This could be done by coupling the child's choice with that of the adult's. For example, every day 3-year-old Analise selects blocks during play. One day the teacher adds farm animals, suggesting that together they build barns, corrals, and beds for the animals. On another day, the teacher adds zoo animals to the block activity and asks Analise, "What could we do with these animals and blocks?" Peter, age two, chooses to bang toy objects (blocks, pretend food, etc.) on a daily basis and appears to be reinforced by the noise he makes while playing. The teacher could add containers (with big spoons for stirring) to the activity and suggest that they cook. Later, dolls and bears could be added to the activity for a pretend snack time. In this way, the teacher has extended his play with the materials and still provided an auditory reinforcer as the blocks (or food) are stirred. In both of these examples, the teacher has still provided the child with a choice (using the preferred materials), while expanding the activity or the way the child uses the materials. In a home visit, a service provider could show an older sibling how to manipulate a preferred manipulative by giving cues on how to model building a house with blocks. The sibling asks the brother to "build one like hers" (Wolery, 2005).

Another environmental strategy that could enhance engagement is the provision of structure within the activity. Planned structured play activities embedded or integrated in the usual classroom activities or routines result in increased social interactions between children with and without disabilities (Sandall & Schwartz, 2008). Examples of planned embedded structure include setting rules for a specific activity, identifying child roles within the activity, asking children to generate ways that they could play within an activity, and identifying the theme for the play ("Let's make pizza with the play dough. What kind of pizza will you make today?"). Another way of structuring the activity is to analyze and monitor the accessibility of the materials. Infants or toddlers who have easy access to every toy may have a decreased need for communicating or socializing within their environments. Alternating the availability of some materials and toys

Cengage Learning

Peer-mediated strategies are often effective in promoting social and communication skills in young children with disabilities.

across the day or week may be an effective strategy for promoting engagement. In essence, the novelty of a toy is maintained through the regular rotation of materials. Restricting access to high-interest toys may result in higher levels of communicative attempts. By placing preferred materials within the child's field of vision, but out of reach, the result would be in increased child requests for preferred toys and snacks.

Promoting Acceptance. Promoting acceptance is a strategy that can be viewed as creating and preparing the social environment to be more accepting of a child with a disability. It is a strategy that supports engagement with peers and one that is easily overlooked when preparing a class for young children with disabilities.

While positive attitudes toward children with disabilities (and subsequent social relationships among children with and without disabilities) are an anticipated benefit of inclusion (Guralnick, 2001), empirical evidence is mixed. The classic research of Favazza and Odom (1996, 1997) demonstrates that children form perceptions and attitudes about persons with disabilities as early as four and five years of age. Across studies, it is apparent that the placement of children with disabilities alongside typical peers does not automatically ensure acceptance without adult mediation (that is, actively promoting understanding and acceptance of children with disabilities). However, children with delays or disabilities placed in inclusive or natural environments make developmental progress at least comparable to children with disabilities in segregated environments (Noonan & McCormick, 2006). In other words, children with disabilities in inclusive environments appear to learn as much as children in segregated environments. Promoting acceptance of children with disabilities may be one of the essential elements for achieving authentic inclusion in later years beyond the preschool setting.

Guidelines are available that provide suggestions for creating accepting environments for young children (Sandall & Schwartz, 2008). In addition, teachers can use specific strategies within the early childhood setting to actively promote acceptance of children with disabilities. Prior to the transition of a child with a disability into a general early childhood classroom, teachers can prepare typically developing children by providing information about the child with the disability (Lane, Stanton-Chapman, Jamison, & Phillips, 2007). Effective strategies for increasing understanding and promoting acceptance of children with diverse abilities include the use of cooperative activities, stories, and guided discussions that highlight similarities as opposed to differences (McPhee, Favazza, & Lewis, 2004), and structured social opportunities, or a combination of these activities (Favazza, LaRoe, Phillipson, & Kumar, 2000). Favazza et al. found that kindergartners who had contact with children with disabilities expressed low levels of acceptance of children with disabilities. After a 9-week intervention, the same kindergartners who were provided with stories and guided discussions about children with disabilities and opportunities for social interaction with children with disabilities had more accepting attitudes than children who did not have these types of experiences. The authors speculate that what contributed to acceptance was the children's exposure to these components as well as the fact that the stories and guided discussions (about children with disabilities) were also provided to the parents of the children without disabilities. In this way, teachers and parents alike were involved in promoting acceptance of children with diverse abilities.

In addition to actively promoting acceptance through interventions within a center-based program, teachers (and parents) can examine the environment to determine if children without disabilities are exposed to individuals with special needs. We recommend that teachers examine their classrooms to determine if children with disabilities are represented in toys, displays, materials, and media, and

how they are depicted (in ways that highlight similarities? as contributing members of society? in a variety of roles?). In addition, teachers need to be discriminating when selecting materials such as books about children with disabilities. It is important to select books that promote acceptance and emphasize similarities as opposed to differences and disabilities (see Table 9–1).

Research clearly indicates that placement alone will not guarantee acceptance. However, teachers and parents can actively promote acceptance and create more accepting environments by utilizing some of the previously mentioned strategies.

The Provision of Prompts and Praise. Teacher-mediated or direct instruction involves choosing the behavior to be taught. The teacher selects a specific time to teach the behavior directly to the child. Through discussion, instructions, demonstration, modeling, and use of concrete examples, the teacher provides direct instruction and practice opportunities. The teacher then follows the instruction with prompts and praise. Prompts and praise are strategies that teachers can employ to promote engagement within the inclusive preschool setting. Praise can be defined as a verbal reinforcement ("I like the way you are sharing those blocks") or a tangible reinforcement (stickers, access to desired activities, or "happy faces"). Praise is an effective technique for promoting child engagement among children who have special needs. **Prompts** are defined as any assistance or help given by another person (adult) to assist young children in knowing how to make a desired response or behavior (Sandall et al., 2005). A variety of prompts can be identified by the type of assistance they provide. Common prompts include direct and indirect verbal prompts, model prompts, partial or full physical prompts, spatial prompts, pictorial prompts, and cued prompts.

- *Direct verbal prompts* are simple statements that provide support for a child in his or her current task. For example, when a child is trying unsuccessfully to turn on the faucet, a teacher (or parent, adult, or peer) could say, "Try turning it the other way." This simple statement may be enough for the child to be successful as he/she attempts to turn on the faucet.
- *Model prompts* actually supply the child with the desired behavior. The model prompt can be verbal or gestural or a combination of the two. For

TABLE 9–1 Teacher Resource: List of Books on Disability Appropriate for Early Childhood and Early Primary Classrooms

Book	Disability Area
The ADDed Touch, Robyn Watson, Silver Star, 2000	ADHD
The Alphabet War, Diane Burton Warr, Whitman, 2004	learning disabilities
Crow Boy, Tako Yashima, Viking, 1955	autism
Dad and Me in the Morning, Patricia Laken, Whitman, 1994	deafness
Flying Solo, Ralph Fletcher, Clarion, 1998	communication
The Handmade Alphabet, Laura Rankin, Dial, 1998	deafness
Hooway for Wodney Wat, Helen Lester, Houghton-Mifflin, 1999	communication
Knots on a Counting Rope, Bill Martin Jr. and John Archambault, Holt, 1987	visual impairment
My Brother Sammy, Becky Edwards and David Armitage, Milbrook, 1999	autism
Susan Laughs, Jeanne Wills, Red Fox, 2000	orthopedic impairments
We'll Paint the Octopus Red, Stephanie Stuve-Bodeen, Woodbine, 1998	developmental disabilities

Source: Adapted from M. Prater & T. Dyches, 2008. Books That Portray Characters With Disabilities: A Top List for Children and Young Adults, *Teaching Exceptional Children, 40*(4), pp. 34–35.

example, a teacher may Velcro the child's shoe while saying, "I'll do this one, and you do the next one." In this way, the child is supported in the dressing activity by a modeled verbal and gestural prompt.

- *Physical prompts* can provide partial or physical support. Guiding a child's elbow as she lifts a spoon, cup, or lunch tray is an example of a partial physical prompt. A full physical prompt for the same behavior might involve hand-over-hand assistance with the teacher holding the child's hands as she is grasping the object (spoon, cup, or tray).
- *Spatial prompts* involve placing an object in a location that will more than likely increase a desired response. For example, placing paper towels (for wiping paint off of hands) near the sink and placing clips on the clothesline where children will go to hang their completed artwork are examples of spatial prompts.
- *Visual/pictorial prompts* involve providing assistance through the use of pictures (drawings, photographs, Rebus cue cards), colors, or graphics. Using different colors for different children or placing a red mark or the letter "C" on Cathy's cup are examples of visual prompts. Placing photographs depicting the steps to hand washing above the sink is a pictorial prompt.
- *Cued prompts* can be verbal and/or gestural and involve drawing direct attention to a specific aspect or dimension of a stimulus or task. Two examples of a cue are "Pick up your paint brush (or spoon)" and "It's time to paint (or eat)" while

pointing to the handle of the brush (or spoon). Cued prompts are used to focus on the most relevant characteristic or dimension of the stimuli.

There are several important points to remember when using praise and/or prompts (Sandall et al., 2005). These include the following:

1. Teachers should carefully plan for the provision of praise/prompts. They should not be applied when they are not necessary to support the child's behavior. Providing unnecessary prompts could result in a child becoming overly dependent on the adult and decreasing his/her own level of independence. When possible, prompts and/or praise should be faded or removed to promote independence in the child's behavior and to lessen his/her dependence on the adult.

2. Teachers should be certain that they have the child's attention when presenting a prompt/praise. The impact or effectiveness of a prompt or praise may be lost unless the child is paying attention.

3. Prompts should be selected and praise should be provided that are the least intrusive while at the same time are the most effective with that individual child. For example, a cued prompt (touching the paintbrush) or physical assistance (moving the child's hand to the brush) with a young child with a visual impairment may be less effective and more intrusive than a verbal prompt of, "We are going to paint. Everyone, find a paintbrush. Wow! Now we are ready to paint." Not only is the prompt (and subsequent praise) likely to be successful in assisting the child, it does not single him/her out from the rest of the group at the art table, and a spatial prompt (the paintbrush) has been provided for everyone.

4. The prompts/praise can be changed or faded as the situation warrants. Ideally, a child should perform a task with fewer and fewer prompts and less praise applied. This implies that the teacher should keep a careful watch on the effectiveness and necessity of prompts and praise to sustain the child's behavior. If a particular strategy is not effective or is not producing the desired results, teachers should shift to another prompt/praise strategy.

5. Teachers should always consult with the related service personnel (speech–language pathologist,

occupational therapist, physical therapist) before applying prompts or changing prompts that they have recommended. Changes in child prompts could be harmful to a child or counterproductive to the objectives that the various therapists have recommended. In addition, it is important to have the same expectation for the use of prompts/praise across all caregivers (teacher, assistants, parents).

Accepting Different Levels and Types of Participation. This teacher-mediated strategy allows a child with diverse abilities to become more engaged in a group activity. Children learn best in small groups (Harris & Gleim, 2008). The approach requires the teacher to make adjustments in his/her expectations about levels or ways a child participates in group activities. When a child is unable to participate at the same level as his peers in a group activity, the expectations for participation can be adjusted. When a child uses only a portion of the response, it is referred to as **partial participation.** Examples of partial participation include the following: In a game of Simon Says, the leader says, "Touch your toes." The child extends his hands downward, but does not touch toes. In another situation, the teacher accepts a single-word response as opposed to a whole or partial sentence response in a group discussion. For example, during sharing time, a teacher may have two children come to the front of the group. The teacher prompts the first child to ask the other child questions about an object brought for sharing time. The prompted questions could be, "What do you have?" "What do you do with it?" and "Where did you get it?" The questions for the second child could be shortened to his/her accepted level of participation with verbalizations like, "What have?" or "Have?" "What do?" or "Do?" and "Where get?" or "Get?"

Adapted participation is when a child may also use an alternative means to participate. Examples would be a youngster who orients his head or eye gaze instead of pointing or verbalizing, a child with speech delays who uses a communication board, or a child with a visual impairment who uses a sensory ball (that emits an auditory signal) when at play. These are all examples of adapted participation that enable a child with a disability to fully participate in group activities. For principles for integrating technology in the classroom for young children with special needs, see the Teacher Technology Tips feature.

Teacher Technology Tips

Principles for Integrating Technology in the Classroom

1. Start with the child. Technology should be considered for all students with special needs. Let the individual needs of the student and the demands of the curriculum drive the selection of the technologies and the ways they are used.

2. Consider all areas of development. Technology applications can be applied to natural learning opportunities and enhance participation in the general education environment. Consider the following areas: (a) motor, (b) communication/language, (c) cognitive, (d) social interactions, and (e) adaptive.

3. Consider technology to increase children's ability to participate in less restrictive environments. Use both high-tech and low-tech options such as voice output, picture and word cues, touch screens for tools for prewriting and early literacy, and making choices.

4. Consider age and developmental appropriateness for choosing technology for infants, toddlers, and preschool children. Ask for input from other professionals such as an occupational therapist or physical therapist.

5. Customize the technology. Features such as the ability to control the content and instructional parameters make it easy to adapt activities to the students' needs.

6. Monitor student work at the computer or with other technologies. Use performance data collected by the technology in making instructional decisions

7. Consider the functionality of the technology. Address the level of the student's independence when selecting the technology.

8. Consider the environment in which the technology will be used. Look for available supports if needed and address any challenges that might hinder successful use.

9. Teach students to use technology as a tool. Provide opportunities and encouragement for practice. Technology can help students compensate for disabilities and allow for achievement of greater levels of independence.

10. Extend the benefits of technology to teachers. Technology is an important tool for teachers well as students.

SOURCE: Adapted from: R. Gargiulo, *Special Education in Contemporary Society,* 3rd ed. (Thousand Oaks, CA: Sage, 2009). K. Stremel, Technology application. In S. Sandall, M. Hemmeter, B. J. Smith, & M. McLean (Eds.), *DEC Recommended Practices: A Comprehensive Guide for Practical Application.* (Longmont, CO: Sopris West, 2005). R. Lewis, *Special Education Technology: Classroom Applications.* (Pacific Grove, CA: Brooks/Cole, 1993).

Monitoring Communicative Input. This is another strategy that enables children with diverse abilities to participate in group activities. The adjustment of the timing and complexity of a teacher's communication can impact a child's ability to interact within group activities. Examples include the use of simple vocabulary and shorter sentence length, a variation in intonation and rate of speech, contingent responses, and scaffolding. For example, while young children learn word meanings of objects, people, and actions that are in their immediate surroundings, they can typically understand and attend to input that is slightly above their level of comprehension. Videotaping a group activity is an excellent strategy for examining the level of communication used when speaking to children. Is it understandable by all children? Does the teacher need to alter his communicative input (simplify the vocabulary or shorten the length of sentences in directives)? In this way, the adult matches the receptive and cognitive levels of the child and thus enhances the possibility of every child's participation in group activities. Likewise, videotaping a parent playing with his/her child is another way to use this strategy with younger children and provide consistency in communicative input across caregivers.

Varying the speaker's intonation level may provide cuing to certain tasks. For example, a teacher may state, "We are going outside today," with appropriate intonation and enthusiasm placed on the words *going* and *outside*. Providing verbal input to a child at a slower rate may allow for more processing time and provide more precise cues for relating language to actual events. For example, when giving directions to a child, a pause while the child is moving through steps enables the child to process each individual step along the way. In a hand washing activity, a teacher could say, "Go to the sink." (Pause as the child moves toward sink.) "Turn on the water." (Pause while the child reaches the sink and turns on the water.) "Wash your hands." (Pause while the child washes her hands.) This strategy could be coupled with task analysis when addressing self-care skills with younger children.

Peer-Mediated Strategies

Peer-mediated strategies are a collection of procedures that involve the use of peers to promote the learning and behavior of a child with disabilities (Wolery, 2005). This may involve having peers model specific behaviors. Peers may be taught how to initiate social interactions with the child with disabilities. It may involve teaching peers to respond to social interactions from children with delays or disabilities or in the role as a tutor. Peer-mediated strategies have been effective in promoting social and communication skills and accruing a positive outcome in young children with disabilities (Kohler & Strain, 1999). Peer-mediated strategies typically involve carefully selecting classmates (who are typically developing), teaching selected classmates specific ways to engage their peers with disabilities, encouraging the classmates to persist in their attempts with children with disabilities, providing structured opportunities for the children to interact with one another (so as to use the skills taught), and providing support (reinforcement and prompts by teachers) during the structured opportunities (Wolery). Two types of strategies that utilize peers to mediate learning will be discussed: peer-initiation interventions and cooperative learning.

Peer-Initiation Interventions. These interventions are among the most effective peer-mediated strategies used for increasing social behaviors such as initiating, responding, and sharing (Gillies & Ashman, 2000). A teacher selects typically developing classmates who are known to be highly social, attend school regularly, have little or no history of negative interactions, have adequate attention spans and the comprehension to participate in the training sessions, and have the willingness to participate in the special play groups. The teacher instructs the selected peers about ways to interact with children with disabilities, such as how to initiate an exchange ("Ask for a toy," or "Ask Sam to play with you.") or suggest a play theme ("Let's play grocery store. You be the clerk."). After practicing the strategies with the teacher and other typically developing peers, the children are then given brief structured play opportunities (10 to15 minutes in length) for using the strategies with peers with disabilities. When creating structured play sessions, the teacher carefully arranges the environment to promote interactions (see the previous section in this chapter on environmental arrangements). For example, during an art activity, the teacher provides the supplies and suggests that the children make a picture to hang in the classroom. The teacher then prompts the peers to model cooperative behaviors such as sharing ("Please give T.J. a paintbrush."); requesting materials ("Maria, say 'please give me the blue paint.'"); complimenting other children ("That's a colorful rainbow."); and making suggestions to the group ("You can add clouds to the sky, Sam."). During the structured play sessions, the teacher remains close by, providing prompts and reinforcement as needed. Instructional resources are available that provide guidelines for promoting social and communication skills such as sharing, initiating, responding, learning alternative ways to initiate, and utilizing persistence in social attempt. Carvallo and Haney (1999) and McConnell and Odom (1993) identify the following suggestions for teachers when planning naturalistic interventions with typically developing peers and children with disabilities. They suggest:

1. *Observe to identify peer models.* Pair a child with a disability with a more skilled partner.
2. *Set up a novel activity.* Children are attracted to things that are new and different in the classroom. Use small, well-defined play areas for activities like building, dramatic play, and computer use.

Young children with disabilities need learning environments that are accepting of all children.

3. *Invite a peer to join an activity.* Introduce and facilitate the play activity with both typical students and children with disabilities participating.
4. *Help children to enter activities.* Children with disabilities often do not know how to enter an activity. Teachers may model social skills, such as obtaining another's child's attention, responding to another child, requesting desired items, and negotiating during play.
5. *Position children to maximize interaction.* Pay attention to where the adults and children are seated. Make sure children are in close proximity to one another to maximize interaction opportunities. Place a peer with more advanced skills next to a child with disabilities.

Teachers should be encouraged to adapt strategies according to the individual needs of the children in their particular class. For example, children with delays and disabilities may need to be taught alternative means of communication (the use of a communication board), gestural methods of initiating (tapping a peer who has a hearing impairment, or waiting until the peer is looking before speaking).

Cooperative Learning. This is another strategy that can utilize peers to mediate learning and child engagement. *Cooperative learning* can be defined as an intervention strategy in which small groups of heterogeneous learners are actively involved in jointly accomplishing an activity (Gargiulo, 2009). The goals of cooperative learning are to foster cooperative interaction, to teach cooperative learning skills, and to promote positive self-esteem. Research has demonstrated the effectiveness of cooperative learning in promoting positive interactions and social interactions between children with and without disabilities. Cooperative learning can be used as a strategy for promoting social and communication skills of preschoolers with disabilities in a typical preschool setting. Preschool and early-primary children with disabilities will have more opportunities to practice skills in social and communication behaviors (taking turns, asking/offering assistance) when placed in cooperative learning situations across the classroom environment. Gargiulo believes that cooperative learning is an effective strategy for integrating learners with special needs into the general education classroom. McMasters and Fuchs (2002) note that cooperative learning as has grown in popularity and is considered a promising instructional approach.

According to Lewis and Doorlag (2006), cooperative learning has been shown to increase opportunities for students with disabilities to experience success in the school environment. Cooperative learning uses the social dynamics of the group to support social interactions and friendships, teaches children to encourage one another, and celebrates the success of peers. The four essential elements of cooperative learning include positive interdependence, communication (or face-to-face interactions), accountability of all members, and group process (with emphasis on interpersonal skills).

1. *Positive interdependence is promoted.* Members of small groups work together and depend on each other to complete the task.
2. *Communication is required.* To achieve the common goal, the teacher can encourage or facilitate interactions and communication among the group members as necessary. Materials can be strategically placed to require members to ask for them.
3. *Accountability is expected.* Every member of the group is responsible for contributing to the final product. Within the activity, each child with a disability could have his/her individual objectives embedded into the activity. While students may be working on a common project, the objectives may vary according to the needs of the individual child.

4. *Group process is expected.* As two or three children work together, they are expected to follow basic formats such as taking turns, listening, initiating, and responding.

In addition to these strategies, Noonan and McCormick (2006) provide several suggestions for adapting cooperative learning for use with young children. These experts recommend:

- A unit with clear objectives should be selected, listing the cooperative skills to be taught.
- A series of lessons or activities can be planned in which the embedded skills will be taught.
- Children can be assigned to dyads or three-member groups that remain intact for the duration of all lessons/activities within the unit. (One child with a disability should be within the dyad.)
- Cooperation should be encouraged by the way materials are distributed.
- Activities should be prefaced with specific explanations and demonstrations of what it means to be cooperative ("Sit next to your partner." "Take turns with the glue.").
- Children should be assisted and monitored carefully, providing prompts and praise as warranted.
- The child should be evaluated and provided with feedback ("Did you like working together?" "What was the hardest or easiest part?" "How does it feel when you help a friend?" "Who helped you?").

Cooperative learning may be better suited for older preschoolers or early primary-grade students, and the teacher may need to be more involved the first few times that it is used to ensure that children understand the nature and process of the activity. Clearly, more research is needed in this area to determine how cooperative learning in early childhood settings could better utilize peers as models, guides, and partners in learning. For an example of the use of cooperative learning strategies utilized within an early primary classroom, see the accompanying Making Connections feature.

MAKING CONNECTIONS

Using Cooperative Learning and Accommodations in a Primary Classroom

Cheryl Chinn is a first grader introduced to us in the vignette in Chapter 2. Cheryl is a child with a diagnosis of attention deficit hyperactive disorder. Her parents, teacher, and school staff team developed a Section 504 plan with accommodations designed to help her remain on task during instruction. Additionally, Cheryl needs extra time and less work per assignment. She has a homework notepad that goes home daily to increase the outcome of completed class work and homework assignments. In class, Mrs. Newman, Cheryl's teacher, has taken advantage of some other accommodations that have been successful for Cheryl. For example, during math meeting or reading circle time, Cheryl is most often seated close to Mrs. Newman. Having this environmental accommodation of proximal seating allows Mrs. Newman to monitor Cheryl's off-task behaviors quickly and quietly to keep her on task more often. Mrs. Newman uses Cheryl as the book holder or page turner to keep her actively involved with the instruction. Throughout the day, Mrs. Newman chooses a peer helper to work with Cheryl. In math centers or quiet reading time, Cheryl and her peer partner often go to a quiet part of the room. Mrs. Newman is careful when she chooses the peers and has three to five students that she routinely picks who are good role models for Cheryl. This peer intervention technique has been successful, as Mrs. Newman has noted that Cheryl will follow the peer's good model. Also, on the playground at recess, Cheryl has been observed to play consistently with these peer models in an age-appropriate manner. Finally, when working on class projects for science, social studies, or unit time, Mrs. Newman uses cooperative learning activities. She is careful in placing Cheryl in a group where she can contribute her talents and observe good work and study habits. All of the above strategies have had a positive effect on Cheryl's classroom performance.

Routine-Based Strategies

Routine-based strategies take advantage of already occurring events such as play (Linder, 2008), predictable routine activities such as snack time, diapering, or circle time (Pretti-Frontczak & Bricker, 2004) and transitions. Many routine-based strategies are appropriate for use with infants as well as toddlers, preschoolers, and early primary students.

For routine-based strategies to be successful, teachers and parents need to understand that daily activities that have a specific purpose (snack time is for eating) can also serve as an instructional time. For example, snack time could also be a time for promoting fine motor skills such as reaching or using the neat pincer grasp to eat raisins, Cheerios, or cheese cubes, as well as gross motor skills such as trunk control. The same activity could be used to promote communicative attempts such as requesting (verbally or gesturally) "more," making a choice when asked, "Do you want an apple or an orange?" and responding by pointing, signing, or saying "Apple." Therefore, before starting routine-based instruction, it would be important that all involved with the child (teachers, assistants, parents) are able to recognize the variety of skills that can be promoted within the same routine activity.

Play-Based Intervention (Strategies). Play is a logical and natural activity for incorporating skills of children with disabilities. Play provides an avenue for children to master their thoughts and actions and contributes to the child's cognitive, physical, and social/emotional development. Through play, children have opportunities for learning through exploration, self-expression, imitation and imagination, interpretation of situations, negotiation of relationships, and utilization of social and communicative behaviors such as turn-taking, sharing, initiating, and responding (Causton-Theoharis & Malmgren, 2005).

Linder (2008) has developed **play-based interventions (strategies)** for incorporating and promoting skill acquisition in the play arena. This approach utilizes a transdisciplinary model (see Chapter 5) whereby all service providers (teachers, assistant teachers, occupational therapist, speech–language pathologist, physical therapist) and parents observe and assess the child during play. Each service provider supplies information about the child related to his/her discipline area while watching the child at play with peers or an adult. The goals for the child are developed based on this transdisciplinary-based assessment and incorporated into the child's playtimes while at school. Using this approach, related service personnel provide support and consultation to teachers for promoting and supporting child goals in regularly occurring playtimes. The transdisciplinary approach is characterized by sharing of expertise through frequent, ongoing communication with all caregivers and training these caregivers to implement interventions. For example, if a toddler exhibits delays in fine motor skills, the occupational therapist would provide information and training to the parents and teachers on how to address these skill deficits during play activities at home and at the center the child attends.

Embedded child-directed play provides an excellent resource for teachers to integrate concepts and instructional goals of children with diverse abilities into play. For example, using wet and dry sand, fine motor skills (digging, shaking, grasping), as well as cognitive and communicative skills (vocabulary, concepts such as wet, dry, under, fast, slow, size, texture), are incorporated into sand play (see Figure 9–1). A teacher could examine typical play activities in the preschool setting (play dough, water play, dress-up, or transportation toys) and generate a variety of skills that can be addressed within the play setting (Pretti-Frontczak & Bricker, 2004). Likewise, the teacher can

Daily activities often provide instructional opportunities.

Cengage Learning

FIGURE 9–1 Play-Based Instruction

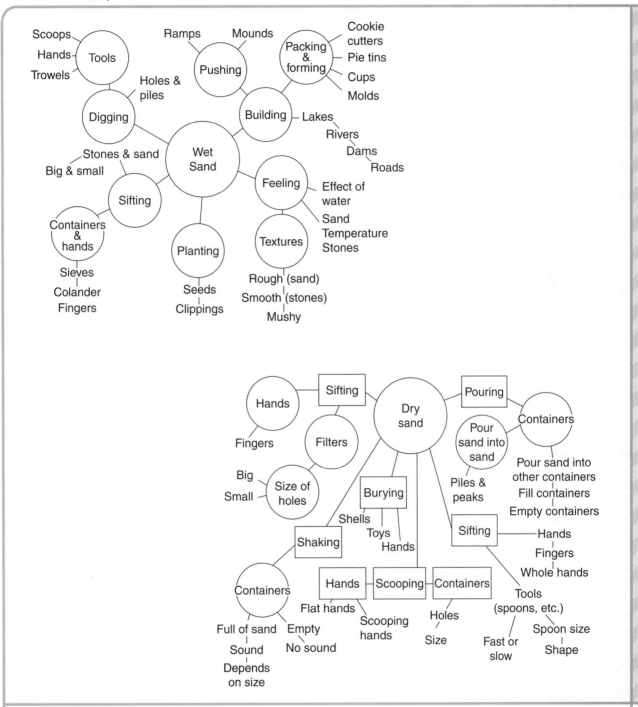

Source: K. Dolinar, C. Boser, & E. Holm, *Learning Through Play* (Clifton Park, NY: Delmar, 1994).

assist the parent in examining play materials at home, and together they can generate ideas for promoting skill acquisition.

When setting up activities, it is important to provide a range of difficulty in order to support active engagement. This strategy enables everyone to be successful by participating at his/her own level with a variety of materials. For example, providing some puzzles with pegs for easy grasp, others without knobs, some with two to three pieces, and others with seven to eight pieces allows many options for children with varying levels of fine motor abilities. During art, a variety of drawing implements (brushes with adaptive grips or of different sizes) can be provided, or within the social–dramatic play area, clothing of different sizes with a variety of fastening devices (snaps, buttons, zippers) and shoes that slip on, buckle, have Velcro straps, and shoestrings can be provided. In this way, teachers can structure an activity to address the diverse abilities of children that will ultimately challenge and provide success for all.

Activity-Based Instruction. Pretti-Frontczak and Bricker (2004) define **activity-based instruction** or intervention as "a child-directed, transactional approach where multiple learning activities are embedded into authentic activities and logically occurring antecedents and timely feedback are provided to ensure functional and generative skills are acquired and used by children" (p. 11). While it was designed to be used with children with disabilities, it can easily be adapted for use with all students in an inclusive setting. Activity-based instruction utilizes the child's interest while addressing goals and objectives in routine, planned, or child-initiated activities. Activity-based instruction takes advantage of naturally occurring antecedents and consequences to develop skills that are functional and generalize across people and settings. Two features of this approach are effective when working with young children. First, multiple goals from a variety of the developmental domains can be addressed in one activity. Additionally, the approach provides reinforcement for children for participating in planned activities that are motivating to them. It requires careful planning of the schedule to ensure that activities in which the child's goals can be addressed will occur throughout the child's day. Pretti-Frontczak and Bricker demonstrate how the schedule from a typical

preschool classroom can provide multiple opportunities to address a child's targeted goals. (See the accompanying Making Connections feature.)

This is an excellent strategy for infants and toddlers whose objectives can be embedded into daily routine activities at home and at center-based programs. In this way, the likelihood of generalization of skills is increased as instruction occurs across settings within activities where the behavior naturally occurs. For example, a parent can address grasping and across-the-midline reaching with an infant or toddler with cerebral palsy by careful placement of a cup of favorite juice during snack time or a favorite tub toy during bathtime. There are many aspects of activity-based instruction that make it appealing to programs that strive to be developmentally appropriate. Children with motor or communication delays who utilize forms of assistive technology in the home or classroom can benefit from an activity-based approach. Embedding the use of the various adapted toys, mobility items, and communication devices into the schedule assists with use in naturally occurring situations. In addition, an activity-based approach capitalizes on goals that are individually appropriate, utilizes naturally occurring events and reinforcers (as opposed to applying artificial activities or reinforcement), capitalizes on child-initiated transactions, and can be used by teachers and parents alike in addressing child goals. (See the Teacher Technology Tips feature.)

Changing the Content of an Existing Activity. Changing the content of an existing activity is another strategy for embedding child goals into routine activities. For example, appropriate expression of and response to affectionate behavior may be a goal for a young child with autism who has difficulty demonstrating and receiving affection (hugs, pats on back, or handshakes). Research suggests that the modification of well-known games/songs is effective in promoting affection activities because children are paired with peers in pleasurable, nonthreatening activities, and there appears to be a desensitization to peer interaction during the activity (Danko & Buysse, 2002). Teachers can incorporate typical group games and songs such as "The Farmer in the Dell" and "Simon Says" to incorporate affection activities (pat on the back, hug, handshake, high fives), and songs such as

MAKING CONNECTIONS

Activity-Based Instruction

Date: *January 24, 2010*
Teacher's Name: *Miss Linda*
Child's Name: *T.J. Browning*

Write the classroom schedule in the left-hand column. Write the child's learning objectives across the top row. Fill the appropriate cells with a brief version of the plan for embedding the objective into the daily schedule.

	Uses short phrases of 4–5 words	Verbally sequences 3 events in sequence (simple stories)	Correctly responds to "wh" questions	Shares or exchanges objects with peers	Follows adult instructions	Participates in activity for 10 minutes	Prints first and last name
Arrival	Greets adults, peers		Responds to "What did you do last night?"				
Planning		Use unit book for retelling	Use unit book for questions	Free play with 2 peers		Attends morning group	
Work	Requests materials			Use paired activities	Sort dishes, building toys	Utilize choice/preferred materials	Use raised line paper
Recall			Recall days of the week and weather				
Snack	Requests preferred snack	Retells steps to make snack			Follows adult direction for manners and cleanup		
Outside				Paired activities with 2–3 peers	Follows adult directions for safety and time to go		
Small-/large-group play	Facilitate verbal peer interactions			Paired activities	Follows center schedule		Puts name on writing center product
Departure	Says appropriate goodbyes						

SOURCE: Adapted from K. Pretti-Frontczak & D. Bricker, *An Activity-Based Approach to Early Intervention*, 3rd ed. (Baltimore: Paul H. Brookes, 2004).

Teacher Technology Tips

Using Assistive Technology With Infants, Toddlers, and Preschoolers

Assistive technology devices can be used to increase, maintain, or improve the abilities of all young children with disabilities. Using assistive technology to improve play abilities of young children is the goal of many early intervention and preschool special education programs. Some examples are listed below.

Adapted commercial toys	• Highlighters—outlines or emphasizes that help in focusing a child's attention • Extenders—foam or molded plastic that may help children press small buttons or keys • Stabilizers—Velcro or nonslip materials that will hold a toy in place or connecta communication device to a crib • Confinement materials—planter bases, hula hoops, box tops that keep toys from getting out of the child's field of vision
Positioning items	• Sling Seats, Boppys®, E-Z Lyers, wedges, floor tables, corner seats, Sassy Seats, and Exersaucers all support children so that their hands are free to interact with toys more readily
Mobility items	• Walkers such as toy shopping carts or activity centers with wheels that a child can stand at and push to allow them to explore the environment • Low rocking and riding toys
Switches, adapted battery-operated toys, and interfaces	• Switches that allow for *on* and *off* function, battery adapters, timers, latch devices, and series adapters
Computer hardware and software	• Single-switch connection reduces control to a single key • Use of a touch window where the child presses anyplace on the screen to operate the computer
Communication items	• Devices that use recorded messages to incorporate language into play or provide a way to use a voice to communicate, such as One-Step, Say It/Play It or Cheaptalk and Talk and Go

Source: Adapted from S. Lane & S. Mistrett, 2002. Let's play! Assistive Technology Interventions for Play, *Young Exceptional Children,* 5(2), pp. 19–27.

"When You're Happy and You Know It" that include such phrases as "Shake a friend's hand, give a friend a hug, pat your friend on the back." As a result of this change in the routine song, children interacted more with one another within the group activity and during the playtime the following day. At bathtime, one dad chose to sing to his toddler, "This is the way we wash our tummy, wash our tummy, wash our tummy (foot, hand, etc.) . . . early in the morning." The child's goal was to increase language. The dad was providing names of body parts and naming the behavior (washing) within an enjoyable routine activity.

Transition-Based Instruction. Transition-based instruction is another example of using daily routine as an opportunity for learning. In using this strategy, the adult presents an opportunity for participating within the group while children are transitioning to other activities (Sandall & Schwartz, 2008).

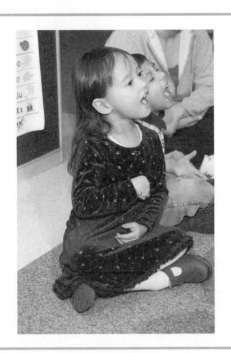

Cengage Learning

Embedding goals into routine activities is an effective instructional strategy.

There are several advantages to using routine activities/games/songs to incorporate skills. Examples of regularly occurring transitions might include going from free play to the snack table, lining up for outdoor play, or arrival and departure times. During this transition time, the teacher obtains the attention of the children and asks them to respond to questions ("What is this?" or "I spy something yellow, what could it be?") that match their level of functioning. It is an activity that is effective in teaching preacademic skills such as letter names, shapes, and colors, while utilizing the frequently occurring transitions in the child's daily routine. Some children may respond by saying the word, others may respond with a word approximation, and others may use an initial letter sound. Likewise, singing songs during transition times is a strategy that allows for group responding at a variety of levels. In addition, transitions provide an excellent vehicle for using fine motor skills (such as clean-up activities) or gross motor skills (mobility or ambulation) skills. They do not require using new materials or a change in the existing structure or routine of the day (at school or home). They do not require changes in personnel, except informing all personnel of how multiple skills can be incorporated in already occurring routines. The child with a disability can receive the attention needed without singling him or her out from the rest of the group. In addition, transition-based instruction may increase the likelihood of the generalization of skills when the instruction occurs in the place and time when the desired behavior typically occurs. However, to be effective, routine-based instruction does require preplanning, ongoing monitoring for changes that are needed, and coordination with all personnel involved with the child. It is an ideal way to incorporate skills that related service personnel (occupational therapist, physical therapist, speech–language pathologist, etc.) typically address when they take children out of the classroom for therapy. Through the use of routine-based instruction, related service personnel can consult with the teacher and parents, identifying times when child goals can logically be supported and promoted in daily routine activities.

Specific Naturalistic (Milieu) Strategies

Milieu strategies are ideal in early childhood settings in that they reflect developmentally appropriate practice (Copple & Bredekamp, 2009) by using procedures that are child directed and teacher guided. Milieu strategies are used to facilitate language skills (especially social interaction context) that take advantage of the natural environment (people, materials, activities) to support learning. Variations of these naturalistic strategies include the use of incidental teaching, models and expansions, the mand-model procedure time delay, and interrupted routines.

Incidental Teaching. Incidental teaching is a naturalistic strategy that has been effective in promoting communication skills in young children with diverse abilities (Wolery, 2005). Incidental teaching is the use of naturally arising situations to teach skills.

Incidental teaching is *always* child initiated. The environment is structured to increase the probability that the child will initiate to the adult or teacher. When the child initiates, the adult/teacher requests a more elaborate request for a certain behavior. If the more elaborated behavior is forthcoming from the child, the adult/teacher will praise and respond to the child's initiation. If the behavior does not appear to be forthcoming, the adult/teacher can prompt the child, then allow the child to respond. Finally, the adult/teacher will respond to the child's initiation. This strategy takes advantage of children's initiations to promote communicative attempts and model more sophisticated language. In addition to providing models, the teacher can incorporate expansions, mands, and time delays within incidental teaching. The steps for using incidental teaching include the following:

1. Identifying the communication goals of the child and activities or opportune times for addressing these goals.
2. Arranging the environment to increase the likelihood of initiations from the child. This could involve placing high-interest materials/toys within view, but out of reach, intentionally selecting materials with which the child will need assistance (such as opening the play dough can), selecting materials that are new or novel to the child, or intentionally providing materials that have some pieces/parts missing.
3. Being within close proximity of the child, watching, and waiting for his or her initiation.
4. When the child initiates, follow the steps below:
   a. Focus on precisely what it is the child is requesting.
   b. Ask for more elaborate language by saying, "Use your words," "What about the ball (swing, play dough, cup, etc.)?" "What do you need?"
   c. Wait expectantly for a more sophisticated response from the child. ("Want ball," "Yellow ball," "Push swing," "Top off.")
   d. If the child provides more language, praise her, expand her statement, and provide the desired object or action. ("You want the yellow ball." "Push swing, please." "You want the top off.")
   e. If the child does not respond adequately, provide a model coupled with an expectant look and wait again for her to respond. Once the child imitates the model, provide what is needed (that is, assistance or the desired object).

The Model and Expansion. The model and expansion technique involves providing a verbal or gestural model for the child and providing an expansion (new information). For example, after showing the child the desired object (ball, cup of juice), the adult would say, "Ball" or "Say 'ball.'" The adult would then pause expectantly, looking at the child. Once the child gives the desired response, the adult provides the desired object or action and provides an expansion of what the child said ("O.K., you want the *blue* ball.").

The Mand-Model. The mand-model technique involves observing the child's focus of attention and asking a non–yes/no question (a mand). The question presented is about the focus of the child's attention. The adult/teacher waits for a response. If no response is evident, then a model is provided. The mand model is a directive and therefore more intrusive technique that can successfully be used in conjunction with and to augment child-initiated activities. The mand model can easily be embedded into a child's play or interactions (Wolery, 2005). For example, when the child finishes the juice and obviously wants more (begins looking around for juice or looks inside cup), the adult would say, "Tell (or show) me what you want." The directive is always related to *exactly* what/where the child's attention is focused at the time. If the child responds, the child is given what he or she wants and is provided with a verbal confirmation and expansion. For example, using the previous example, if the child responds by saying "Juice," the adult could say "Oh, you want the *orange* juice," "Oh, you want *more* juice," or "You want the *delicious* juice." In this way, the adult has confirmed his/her response, provided the desired object, and provided an expansion of the response with an additional word or descriptor. If the child does not respond (or does not respond correctly), a model should be provided for the child followed by the desired object or action. The adult would say, "Say 'swing,'" then push her in the swing.

Time Delay. Time-delay procedures systematically employ a brief waiting period to teach the child to initiate an interaction. Time delay can refer to three different strategies. Wolery (2005) identifies the following:

1. an adult waiting for a child to initiate a behavior
2. constant time delay
3. progressive time delay

Simple time-delay procedures can occur throughout a child's natural routine. An adult simply waits for the child to initiate a behavior. An example could be a mother opening the refrigerator and waiting for the child to initiate communication by asking for juice. Constant time delay occurs when the adult initially provides a prompt for a child to perform and then on subsequent trials delays the assistance for a fixed period of time (constant number of seconds). Progressive time delay occurs when the adult provides a prompt for a child to perform and then on subsequent trials progressively increases the time before giving help. With the application of both constant time delay and progressive time delay, correct responses whether with or without a prompt are reinforced. Time delay is particularly effective in teaching language and response behavior to preschool children and older children with moderate and severe disabilities (Sandall et al., 2005). For example, a child may be presented with high-preference objects within view but out of reach at the snack table. Once the child shows an interest in an object (juice, food, spoon), the adult waits briefly for the child to emit a desired behavior (look expectantly at the adult, say "more," say "juice," orient eye gaze, reach, etc.). The desired behavior or range of desired behaviors is predetermined based on the child's individual goals. Some steps in a time delay approach include the following:

1. The adult should face the child with an expectant look. Have the desired object within the child's field of vision (favorite toy, snack items, paints, or water play pieces). Encourage eye contact.
2. The adult should wait a brief period of time (5 seconds, 10 seconds) for the child to initiate a request.
3. If the child responds, the adult provides the desired object.
4. If the child does not respond, the adult provides a verbal prompt ("Want juice"), or a physical prompt (hand-over-hand assistance in reaching toward the desired object) and reinforces the response by providing the desired object (Gomez, Walls, & Baird, 2007).

For an example of the use of a time-delay approach that is embedded within daily instruction, see the Making Connections feature.

Interrupted Routine. Interrupting a routine activity is another strategy that can be used to promote child engagement and to teach communication, social, cognitive, motor, and self-care skills (Pretti-Frontczak & Bricker, 2004). Daily routines include caregiving routines (diaper changing, snack time, dressing and undressing), social routines (greeting and departure times, waking up from naptime), and activity routines (specific steps or actions that typically occur with a song or game).

There are three ways of applying interrupted routines: the provision of an incomplete set of materials, withholding or delaying the provision of expected or high-interest items or events, and making "silly" mistakes. Many routines or activities require a set of materials such as clothing when dressing; food, drink, plates, and cups when having a snack; paints, brushes, and paper during art. The adult simply sets up the materials for the activity or routine, but does not provide all the needed materials in order to prompt an initiation by the child. The adult waits until the child says something about the missing item(s). For this procedure to be effective, the routine should be reinforcing, and it must require a known set of materials.

Withholding or delaying an expected action, event, or object is another way of applying interrupted routines. For example, during the finger play "Eensy Weensy Spider," the adult "forgets" to do the next action in the sequence of hand motions. Or during snack time, the adult passes out the napkins and juice cups (but withholds the crackers) and tells students, "Eat your crackers." The omitted action or object will likely result in a protest response from the child or children. Purposefully withholding the object from one student could also prompt other children to tell the child, "Tell Miss Micki that you did not get crackers."

Making "silly mistakes" involves violating the function of an object or what children know to be the correct action or word. Examples of "silly mistakes" while dressing include putting shoes on hands or hats on feet. Also, the dad who routinely sang as he bathed his toddler changed some of the words once the routine and words were familiar to the child. He would sing, "This is the way we wash our hands," while he was washing the tummy. As he made the silly mistake, he looked at the toddler with an expectant gaze (raised eyebrows, mouth and eyes wide open) waiting for the toddler's protest, "Tummy, Daddy!

MAKING CONNECTIONS

Plan to Embed and Distribute Time Delay for Maria's Goals

Steps for using time delay	Using words to request	Using words for actions	Increasing muscle strength and fine motor skills
Step 1: Identify the skills to be taught.	Naming food and drink items. Using "Want " or "Please" forms. Naming toys when given the choice between two.	Naming actions she is performing (e.g., stacking, pushing, drinking, building, drawing, eating).	Using utensils, (e.g., spoon, fork) and writing tools (e.g., crayons, markers).
Step 2: Identify the activities and routines for teaching.	Snack, lunch, and when given a choice of toys during free play.	Free play and during play on the playground.	Breakfast, lunch, or snack time and during art or writing activities.
Step 3: Decide how many and how often trials will be used.	Every time she makes a nonverbal request.	10 times per day. At least 2 minutes and no more than 10 minutes between trials.	About 4 times per day; every time she engages in art or writing activities at centers.
Step 4: Select an interval time delay procedure.	Constant time delay—response intervals are all the same length.	Progressive time delay—response time gradually increases over trials or days.	Constant time delay—response intervals are all the same length.
Step 5: Identify a task cue and controlling prompt.	Her nonverbal request (sign or gesture) and any choice she is given; the prompt is the verbal model.	Prompt is the verbal model: "Maria, what are you doing?"	Hand-over-hand at the center or prompt is physical guide.
Step 6: Select a reinforcer.	Receives the item she requested.	Continuing to play; praise for approximation or word Maria used.	Item and activity she enjoys and adult praise.
Step 7: Determine the number of 0-second trials to use.	4 days of 0-second trials.	4 days of 0-second trials.	4 days of 0-second trials.
Step 8: Determine the length of the response interval.	10 seconds	Increase by 1-second increments every 2 days; stop at 15 seconds.	10 seconds
Step 9: Select and use a monitoring system.	Count the number of requests, number of verbal requests using a prompt, number of nonverbal requests.	Count the number of questions, number of action words using a prompt, and number of no responses.	Count the number of steps before the prompt and number of steps wrong before the prompt.
Step 10: Implement the plan and monitor use and effects.	Record how many requests occur and if the steps of time delay were completed correctly.	Record how many questions were asked and if the steps of time delay were completed correctly.	Keep track of the number of opportunities of using utensils and art/writing tools in which she was taught and if the steps of time delay were completed correctly.

SOURCE: Adapted from M. Wolery, Embedding time delay procedures in classroom activities. In M. Ostrosky & S. Sandall (Eds.), *Teaching Strategies: What to do to Support Young Children's Development* (Denver, CO: Division for Early Childhood, 2001), pp. 84–85.

Including Students With High-Incidence Disabilities: Strategies for Success

Visit the premium website and watch "Including Students with High-Incidence Disabilities: Strategies for Success." After watching this video, answer the following questions:

1. What instructional strategies would you incorporate in your classroom for early primary-grade students who exhibit disabilities? Why did you select these particular teaching approaches?
2. Would you use these same strategies with typically developing children?

Tummy!" Another example with older children would be to give the wrong response in a counting or color identification activity. These types of exchanges can increase child engagement and communication, but require that the children know the correct or expected behavior. When considering routines in which to use the interrupted routine strategy, the following characteristics need attention: (a) the routine should be established so that the child can anticipate the steps in the routine; (b) the routine should involve a variety of high-interest objects; (c) the whole routine should be completed quickly to increase the potential for multiple interactions; and (d) the routine should be functional to increase the probability of generalization. (See the Making Connections feature.)

MAKING CONNECTIONS

Strategies for Using Maria's Goals in Naturalistic Settings

Based on the information presented in the vignette on Maria (see page 60) and the information on young children with cognitive delays, there are a variety of strategies that could be used to address the unique needs of Maria in the *home setting*. For example, Maria has the following goals: (a) to verbally request items that she wants, (b) to use words for actions she is doing (pushing, running, cooking, drawing), (c) to increase muscle strength and fine motor skills, especially her ability to use utensils (e.g., spoon, toothbrush) and writing tools (e.g., crayons). Based on these goals, Maria's daily schedule could be examined to determine opportunities for addressing these skills in her routine activities. Specifically, during breakfast, lunch, or dinner, Maria could use eating utensils and during an art activity she could use a paintbrush, markers, and crayons. (In a discussion with the family, they noted that one of her favorite activities is art.) Both of these activities could serve to strengthen her fine motor skills. Also, during each of these activities, materials could be withheld to encourage Maria to request the items she wants and needs. For example, she could be given the art paper without the paint or paintbrushes. The teacher could request that Maria name the action she is doing during the art activity. If Maria needs a model, the teacher could say, "You are drawing, Maria." Or "You are painting with the paintbrush." During mealtime, she could be given her cup without the juice. In this way, she would be provided with multiple opportunities to use the skills she is developing in a naturalistic setting (e.g., home) within routine activities.

Summary

Teaching strategies from the field of early childhood and early childhood special education have been discussed. Both fields have provided general guidelines for creating appropriate educational experiences for young children with diverse abilities. Research has shaped these guidelines, providing specific strategies that have proven to be effective when teaching children with delays or disabilities. Teachers have the responsibility to make thoughtful choices and use different strategies. The key is to be flexible and to create collaborative, supportive teams between parents and professionals. This collaborative team has the responsibility to create an appropriate match between the individual needs of the child and the strategies that will ensure success in meeting the individual goals of each student.

Current ideas about appropriate educational experiences for young children and strategies for creating less-restrictive environments for children with disabilities should be continually examined to ensure that educational practice is informed by ongoing research.

Check Your Understanding

1. Define "active engagement" when referring to young children with special needs in the educational environment.
2. What should teachers consider when making classroom environmental arrangements to promote engagement of children within the educational setting?
3. Describe the differences between the types of prompts and assistance given to assist young children.
4. What are some suggestions for planning naturalistic interventions for peer-mediated strategies for typically developing peers and children with disabilities in the educational or natural environment?
5. Describe the elements of cooperative learning.
6. What is the difference between a time delay and an interrupted routine?

7. Describe the kinds of strategies that can be used to prepare the social environment for children with special needs.
8. Give an example of the model-and-expansion milieu instructional procedure.

Reflection and Application

1. Each morning, a particular preschool classroom has circle time in class. Some children rarely or never participate in this activity. Describe two teacher-mediated strategies that could be used to increase the level of child engagement during this group activity.
2. A child with delays in cognitive development is in your class. She uses sign language to communicate. One of her goals is to indicate when she wants items (to request) using the sign "more." Provide an example of how activity-based instruction could be used to address this goal throughout the daily classroom routine.

References

Brown, M., & Bergen, D. (2002). Play and social interaction of children with disabilities at learning/activity centers in an inclusive preschool. *Journal of Research in Childhood Education, 17*(1), 26–37.

Carvallo, C., & Haney, M. (1999). *Preschool inclusion.* Baltimore: Paul H. Brookes.

Causton-Theoharis, J., & Malmgren, K. (2005). Increasing peer interactions for students with severe disabilities via paraprofessional training. *Exceptional Children, 71*(4), 431–444.

Copple, C., & Bredekamp, S. (Eds.). (2009). *Developmentally appropriate practice in early childhood programs: Serving students from birth through age 8.* Washington, DC: National Association for the Education of Young Children.

Danko, C., & Buysse V. (2002). Thank you for being a friend: Fostering friendships for children with autism spectrum disorder in inclusive environments. *Young Exceptional Children, 6*(1), 2–9.

Davis, M., Kilgo, J., & Gamel-McCormick, M. (1998). *Young children with special needs: A developmentally appropriate approach.* Boston: Allyn & Bacon.

Favazza, P., LaRoe, J., Phillipson, L., & Kumar, P. (2000). Representing young children with disabilities in classroom environments. *Young Exceptional Children, 3*(3), 2–8.

Favazza, P., & Odom, S. (1996). Use of the Acceptance Scale with kindergarten-age children. *Journal of Early Intervention, 20*(3), 232–248.

Favazza, P., & Odom, S. (1997). Promoting positive attitudes of kindergarten-age children toward children with disabilities. *Exceptional Children, 63*(3), 405–418.

Gargiulo, R. (2009). *Special education in contemporary society: An introduction to exceptionality* (3rd ed.). Thousand Oaks, CA: Sage.

Gargiulo, R., & Metcalf, D. (2010). *Teaching in today's inclusive classrooms: A universal design for learning approach.* Belmont, CA: Wadsworth/Cengage Learning.

Gestwicki, C. (1999). *Developmentally appropriate practice: Curriculum and development in early education.* Albany, NY: Delmar.

Gillies, R. M., & Ashman, A. F. (2000). The effects of cooperative learning on students with learning difficulties in the lower elementary school. *Journal of Special Education 34*(1), 19–27.

Gomez, C., Walls, S., & Baird, S. (2007). On the same page: Seeking fidelity of intervention. *Young Exceptional Children, 10*(4), 20–29.

Guralnick, M. (Ed.). (2001). *Early childhood inclusion: Focus on change.* Baltimore: Paul H. Brookes.

Harris K., & Gleim, L. (2008). The light fantastic: Making learning visible for all children through the project approach. *Young Exceptional Children, 11*(3), 1–14.

Kohler, F. W., & Strain, P. S. (1999). Maximizing peer-mediated resources in integrated preschool classrooms. *Topics in Early Childhood Special Education, 19*(2), 92–102.

Lane, L., Stanton-Chapman, T., Jamison, K., & Phillips, A. (2007). Teacher and parent expectations of preschoolers' behaviors: Social skills necessary for success. *Topics in Early Childhood Special Education, 27*(1), 86–97.

Lewis, R., & Doorlag, D. (2006). *Teaching special education students in general education classrooms* (7th ed.). Upper Saddle River, NJ: Pearson Education.

Linder, T. (2008). *Transdisciplinary play-based intervention* (2nd ed.). Baltimore: Paul H. Brookes.

McConnell, S., & Odom, S. (1993). *Play time, social time.* Tucson, AZ: Communication Skill Builders.

McEvoy, M., Odom, S., & McConnell, S. (1992). Peer social competence interventions for young children with disabilities. In S. Odom, S. McConnell, & M. McEvoy (Eds.), *Social competence of young children with disabilities: Issues and strategies for intervention* (pp. 113–133). Baltimore: Paul H. Brookes.

McMasters, K., & Fuchs, D. (2002). Effects of cooperative learning on the academic achievement of students with learning disabilities. *Learning Disabilities: Research and Practice, 17,* 107–117.

McPhee, N., Favazza, P., & Lewis, E. (2004). *Sensitivity and awareness: A guide for developing understanding among children* (4th ed.). Hollidaysburg, PA: Jason & Nordic Publishing.

Noonan, M., & McCormick, L. (2006). *Young children with disabilities in natural environments.* Baltimore: Paul H. Brookes.

Odom, S. (2000). Preschool inclusion: What we know and where we go from here. *Topics in Early Childhood Special Education, 20*(1), 20–27.

Pretti-Frontczak, K., & Bricker, D. (2004). *An activity-based approach to early intervention.* (3rd ed.). Baltimore: Paul H. Brookes.

Sandall, S., Hemmeter, M. L., Smith, B. J., & McLean, M. E. (Eds.). (2005). *DEC recommended practices in early intervention/early childhood special education.* Longmont, CO: Sopris West.

Sandall, S., & Schwartz, I. (2008). *Building blocks for teaching preschoolers with special needs* (2nd ed). Baltimore: Paul H. Brookes.

U.S. Department of Education. (2006). *Twenty-sixth annual report to Congress on the implementation of the Individuals with Disabilities Education Act.* Washington, DC: U.S. Government Printing Office.

Wolery, M. (2005). DEC recommended practices: Child-focused practices. In S. Sandall, M. Hemmeter, B. J. Smith, & M. McLean (Eds.), *DEC recommended practices: A comprehensive guide for practical application in early intervention/early childhood special education* (pp. 71–106). Longmont, CO: Sopris West.

A Look to the Future

Part 4

Chapter 10
Contemporary Issues and Challenges in Early Childhood Special Education

10

Contemporary Issues and Challenges in Early Childhood Special Education

Key Terminology

Culture

Ethnocentric behavior

Physical abuse

Neglect

Emotional abuse

Sexual abuse

Acquired immune deficiency syndrome (AIDS)

Human immunodeficiency virus (HIV)

Children with special health needs

Learning Outcomes

After reading this chapter, you will be able to:

● Discuss why early childhood special educators should demonstrate cultural awareness and sensitivity.

● Identify the four main types of child maltreatment.

● Summarize the responsibilities of schools for meeting the needs of young children with special health needs.

● Describe the rationale for an integrative personnel preparation program.

Few would argue that the field of early childhood special education has dramatically changed in the past 30 years. We can only speculate what the next decade will hold for young children with special needs and their families. The only safe assumption is that change will continue to occur, affecting service providers, caregivers, and the children themselves. We foresee change occurring in several different arenas. Issues such as the full-inclusion movement (which we fully discussed in Chapter 5), and our response to an increasingly diverse student population, in addition to questions about the professional preparation of early childhood special educators are only a few of the topics that will present a myriad of challenges to the field. Early childhood professionals must be prepared to respond to these issues and the impact they will have on the children and families we serve. The purpose of this chapter is to consider three topics we believe are individually important to the professional development of teachers and have meaning for the field as well.

Celebrating Cultural Diversity

The United States is an immensely diverse society. We live in a nation of many different people and cultures. We are rich in our diversity of national origins, languages, foods, music, folkways, values, religious practices, and traditions. As a nation, we greatly benefit from this mix—it is a strength of our country rather than a flaw (Graves, Gargiulo, & Sluder, 1996).

While we celebrate and value this richness of diversity, all too often, cultural differences generate stereotypes, misunderstandings, and in some instances, outright prejudice and discrimination. Our educational system is not immune to this faulty pattern of thinking. In fact, in the opinion of some educators, business leaders, and policymakers, the educational system confronting children from minority groups can be characterized as inadequate, damaging, and openly hostile (Quality Education for Minorities Project, 1990). It is truly regrettable that in some of our schools today, children from culturally and linguistically diverse backgrounds are viewed as less than capable and/or difficult to teach (Gargiulo, 2009). In our opinion, this viewpoint is completely unacceptable. As early childhood special educators working in an increasingly culturally pluralistic society, we need to model respect for and sensitivity to the cultural characteristics of our students and their families.

The makeup of America's population is rapidly changing. The number of children from culturally and linguistically diverse backgrounds is increasing at an extraordinary rate. Our classrooms in the coming years will become especially heterogeneous and evidence greater diversity than we find today. Changing demographics will present a multitude of new challenges to early intervention, early childhood, and early primary special education programs, as well as the professionals who work therein. Consider if you will the implications of the following statistics:

- By the year 2020, students of color are projected to make up 50% of all school-age youth (Gollnick & Chinn, 2009)
- Approximately 20% of the U.S. population over the age of five speaks a language other than English at home (U.S. Census Bureau, 2008)
- Currently, children of color make up the majority of students in several states and many of our urban centers (Howard, Williams, & Lepper, 2005; Lustig & Koestner, 2010; National Center for Education Statistics, 2008)

The effectiveness of our schools in meeting the needs of an expanding culturally diverse population will largely depend upon teachers' ability to be responsive to cultural differences.

While it is axiomatic that early childhood special educators are sensitive to the individual differences of their pupils, increasing emphasis is being placed on cultural and linguistic differences. The current DEC guidelines on recommended practices (Sandall, Hemmeter,

Early childhood special educators need to model respect for and sensitivity to cultural and linguistic differences.

Smith, & McLean, 2005) for young children with special needs and their families reflect the importance of cultural awareness and sensitivity as crucial components in the delivery of services. The guidelines call for professionals to acknowledge, honor, respect, and value the culture and language of *all* children and their families. Yet we must remember that families are influenced but not defined by their cultural and linguistic heritage.

Recognition of cultural diversity is also an important element of developmentally appropriate practice. One aspect of individual appropriateness is the various cultures that the youngsters bring to the classroom (Davis, Kilgo, & Gamel-McCormick, 1998). The key is to include this diversity in all aspects of the curriculum and to make our programs culturally relevant for all children (Odom & Wolery, 2003).

Culture

Perhaps we should offer our interpretation of the word **culture** before continuing this discussion. Simply defined, culture can be viewed as the attitudes, values, belief systems, norms, and traditions shared by a particular group of people that collectively form their heritage. A culture is transmitted from one generation to another. It is typically reflected in language, religion, dress, diet, social customs, and other aspects of a particular lifestyle.

Tiedt and Tiedt (2002) echo this thought. They write that culture

> denotes a complex integrated system of values, beliefs, and behaviors common to a large group of people. A culture may include shared history and folklore, ideas about right and wrong, and specific communication styles—the "truths" accepted by members of the group.   (P. 23)

These authors further state that every student grows up belonging to a particular culture. The cultural background of the student frequently influences his or her response to the educational process and must be considered when planning instruction.

"As educators working in increasingly culturally diverse environments, we need to model respect for sensitivity to the cultural and linguistic characteristics represented by our students and their families" (Gargiulo, 2009, p. 85). Consequently, we must always guard against generalizing and stereotyping when working with young children from various cultural groups. Even within specific groups, each child (and each family) is unique and special despite the fact that many share similar group characteristics. Stated another

way, teachers need to be cognizant of pupils' intraindividual differences regardless of shared cultural heritage. Two early primary students from the same racial group will most likely perform quite differently in the classroom irrespective of their common background.

Early Childhood Special Education and Cultural Diversity

For some children with special needs, entrance into an early intervention or early childhood special education program may be their first exposure to a culture and a language that is different from that of their home. The values of the child's home and the values of society typically confront each other for the first time in school (Kirk, Gallagher, Coleman, & Anastasiow, 2009). Thus, there is the potential for cultural conflict as roles, relationships, and expectations may clash. Hanson and Zercher (2001) write, if "preschool goals, and values for children's learning, social and behavioral expectations, and demands for interactional and communication abilities differ from those that the children and their families possess, then potential differences [conflict] may arise" (p. 418). Language, race, and ethnicity may potentially influence access to early intervention and special education services and supports (Sandall et al., 2005). Early childhood special educators must be alert to these possibilities. They must also communicate to the child and his or her family that they value and respect the child's cultural heritage. Effectiveness in working with culturally diverse students further requires that teachers understand and are comfortable with their own cultural background (Gollnick & Chinn, 2009).

One particular challenge confronting early childhood special educators is distinguishing between ethnicity and exceptionality. Professionals who work with young children and their families need to ensure that ethnicity is not mistaken for educational exceptionality (Hallahan, Kauffman, & Pullen, 2009). This can easily occur when teachers view their own cultural group as setting the standard against which other groups are to be measured. When this happens, teachers are guilty of exhibiting **ethnocentric behavior**, whereby they view their own cultural group characteristics as correct or superior and the ways of other groups are thought of as odd or inferior. Consequently, actions that are considered atypical or deviant by the early childhood special educator may, in fact, be fairly typical and adaptive within the child's culture (Hallahan et al.). It is important to recognize that we all view other people and the world around us through "culturally-tinted lenses" (Barrera, 2000); different cultural groups interpret behavior differently—it all depends on one's perspective.

It is vitally important that early childhood special education professionals do not generalize or stereotype on the basis of a child's cultural or linguistic heritage. Likewise, educators should not assume that all individuals within a particular cultural group will perform or react in a predetermined fashion. We must always view the child and his or her family as individuals. Remember, differences do *not* equate to dysfunction or deficits.

Cultural differences should not routinely translate into disabilities. Far too often, however, belonging to a particular racial/ethnic group results in an automatic assumption that the child will behave in certain ways. Possible reasons for this situation are that differences are sometimes not valued or are easily misunderstood, while in some cases it is the direct result of prejudice and stereotyping (Hallahan et al., 2009). This frequently leads to the overrepresentation of students from minority populations in some special education programs (such as those for individuals with mental retardation) and an underrepresentation in others (such as programs for the gifted and talented). The issue of over- and underrepresentation of children of color has been a longstanding concern among educators. While there are a myriad of possible reasons for this relationship, it is perhaps best understood as a relationship between family socioeconomic status and disability rather than being an issue of disability and minority group status per se (Gargiulo, 2009). Report after report and survey after survey routinely indicate an overrepresentation of minority groups living in poverty (Children's Defense Fund, 2008). Poverty contributes to limited access to health care, poor nutrition, and inadequate living conditions, among other adverse circumstances. All of these variables increase the probability of the young child being at-risk for future learning and development difficulties. Cultural and language differences only exacerbate the child's problems and heighten the likelihood of him or her needing special education services.

As the numbers of infants, toddlers, preschoolers, and early primary students with special needs continues to grow, one can reasonably anticipate a corresponding increase in the numbers of young children with special needs from culturally diverse groups. Unfortunately, the numbers of teachers who share a similar cultural heritage with these children are failing to expand. Almost 89% of teachers in this country are White, approximately 6% are African American, and about 5% are Hispanic or from other racial groups (National

Alison Wright/Documentary/Corbis

Poverty is one variable frequently associated with learning and developmental difficulties.

Center for Education Statistics, 2007). This means that teachers working in early intervention and early childhood special education programs, the majority of whom are White, will have to exhibit heightened cultural sensitivity as they work with an increasingly culturally diverse student population. This will present many unique challenges to early childhood special educators. Cultural differences may present themselves in several ways. Examples of some of the issues that may confront teachers include: cultural interpretations of the etiology of disability; the family's perception of the child with a disability; the perceived value of early childhood special education services; child-rearing practices; family coping strategies; medical practices and traditions; the role of family members; and the acceptance of "outsiders" who offer assistance with the child's care and education (Lynch & Hanson, 2004). It would not be uncommon for the best intentions of professionals to be misinterpreted due to their failure to consider the family's value system and cultural traditions.

Many years ago, Hanson, Lynch, and Wayman (1990) recognized the difficulty of the task confronting early childhood special educators as they work with families of culturally and linguistically diverse children. Their concerns are still valid today. These experts believe that teachers of young children with special needs must not only acknowledge different cultural perspectives, but they must also learn "how to work effectively within the boundaries that are comfortable for the family" (p. 117). This will require that service providers become ethnically competent. It is not necessary, however, for the professional to know everything about a particular culture to provide sensitive and appropriate services (Hanson, 2004). What is required, according to Hanson and Zercher (2001), is an attitude of openness and respect for the many beliefs, values, practices, and behaviors presented by the children and their families. Service providers who are open and eager to learn, respectful of differences, and willing to conduct honest and reflective self-examinations and make changes when necessary are capable of developing cultural competence.

We cannot emphasize enough the importance of early childhood special educators demonstrating cultural awareness and sensitivity. In future years, the success of our early intervention and early education efforts may well depend upon the ability of teachers to exhibit culturally sensitive behavior while providing culturally competent services.

Table 10–1 offers examples of strategies that may help early childhood special educators work effectively with culturally diverse families. We realize, of course,

America's classrooms are becoming increasingly culturally and linguistically diverse

TABLE 10–1 Recommendations for Providing Families With Culturally Sensitive Services

1. Provide information using the family's desired language and preferred means of communication—written notes, telephone calls, informal meetings, or even audiotapes.

2. When appropriate, recognize that extended family members often play a key role in a child's educational development. Give deference to key decision makers in the family.

3. Use culturally competent interpreters who are not only familiar with the language but also knowledgeable about educational issues and the special education process.

4. Seek cultural informants from the local community who can assist teachers in understanding culturally relevant variables such as nonverbal communication patterns, child-rearing strategies, gender roles, academic expectations, medical practices, and specific folkways that might affect the family's relationship with professionals.

5. Attend social events and other functions held in the local community.

6. With the help of other parents or volunteers, develop a survival vocabulary of key words and phrases in the family's native language.

7. Address parents and other caregivers as "Mr.," "Ms.," or "Mrs.," rather than using first names. Formality and respect are essential, especially when speaking with older members of the family.

8. In arranging meetings, be sensitive to possible barriers such as time conflicts, transportation difficulties, and child care issues.

9. Conduct meetings, if necessary, in family-friendly settings such as local community centers or houses of worship.

10. Invite community volunteers to serve as cultural liaisons between the school and the pupil's family.

Source: R. Gargiulo, *Special Education in Contemporary Society* (3rd ed.). (Thousand Oaks, CA: Sage, 2009), p. 131.

that no list of ideas can guarantee that services to young children with special needs and their families will be provided in a culturally sensitive fashion.

Emerging Populations of Young Children With Special Needs

The professional issues confronting early childhood special educators are many. We have identified only a select few of these challenges. Other issues, which seem to be a product of our times, are also affecting the lives of our youngest citizens and the professionals who serve them. It is indeed unfortunate that our children are not immune to the myriad of ills that are rampant in our society. Homelessness, child abuse, and children suffering the effects of parental/caregiver substance abuse are only some of the problems facing teachers. Consider the following portrait of contemporary life in the United States:

- Almost 40% of the homeless population is families with children.
- Fetal alcohol syndrome (FAS) is recognized as one of the leading causes of mental retardation in the United States.
- Every 35 seconds, a child is a victim of abuse or neglect.
- More than 20% of children younger than age 6, or more than 4.2 million youngsters, were living in poverty in 2007.
- One in nine children, or nearly 9 million, are without health insurance.
- Human immunodeficiency virus (HIV) is the leading infectious cause of pediatric mental retardation in America.
- One in 12 babies born in the United States is born at low birth weight (less than 5.8 pounds).
- In 2007, only 66% of 2-year-olds were immunized against preventable childhood illnesses.
- Between 3.3 and 10 million youngsters are exposed to domestic violence each year (Children's Defense Fund, 2008; Gargiulo, 2009; Shaw & Goode, 2008).

The preceding data are truly frightening, especially when one considers the implications for our educational system. Historically, schools have responded to the needs of society. The challenges that are now upon us dictate, therefore, that teachers have greater awareness of the magnitude of the crisis and are

positioned to deal effectively with changing societal conditions and the resulting changing clientele.

Our goal in this section of the chapter is to highlight a few of the areas of concern. Selected for brief review are the issues of homelessness, child abuse, and neglect, and young children with special health needs.

Homelessness

The problem of homelessness in America is growing. The homeless population is also changing. Traditionally, adult males were the primary group of citizens without permanent shelter. Today, however, families with children are the fastest growing segment of homeless Americans (National Coalition for the Homeless, 2008), accounting for more than 40% of the homeless population (Children's Defense Fund, 2008). More than 42% of the 1.55 million children who experience homelessness each year are under the age of six—approximately 650,00 youngsters (National Center on Family Homelessness, 2009). More than 8 out of 10 homeless families with children are female-headed households; a disproportionate percentage of these families are members of racial or ethnic minority groups (National Center on Family Homelessness, 2008). Of course, the transient status of these families leads to a significant problem of underreporting the actual incidence of homelessness.

In its simplest terms, a homeless child is any child who lacks a fixed, regular, and adequate nighttime residence (*CEC Today*, 2003). Codified in federal legislation (Title X, Part C, §1032 of PL 107-110 [No Child left Behind Act]) are some examples of inadequate living arrangements such as individuals and families who reside in abandoned buildings, parks, campgrounds, automobiles, bus/train stations, motels, or emergency/transitional shelters. Essentially, homelessness is a lack of permanent housing caused by a variety of reasons (Gargiulo, 2006).

The experience of being homeless is especially destructive for children. Due to their homelessness, they are frequently absent from school, and when they are able to attend, many of these children evidence academic problems and social/emotional difficulties (Gargiulo, 2006).

The consequences of homelessness are especially devastating for young children. Homelessness is portrayed as a breeding ground for disabilities. Many young children who are homeless often exhibit inattentiveness, frustration, aggression, and diminished academic achievement in addition to speech delays,

Families with children are the fastest growing group of homeless Americans.

Rob Crandall/PhotoLibrary

short attention span, poor impulse control, and withdrawal (Gargiulo, 2006; Morrison, 2009). Homelessness also takes a toll on young children physically as well as emotionally. This profile often makes these children eligible for special education services; however, the transient nature of their families' lifestyles frequently prohibits the delivery of needed services.

Children who are homeless also encounter numerous obstacles to educational services. Barriers confronting students who are homeless

> come in many forms, including school policies pertaining to residency requirements, immunization records, transportation issues, availability of school records, guardianship requirements, and in some instances, a disregard for federal mandates coupled with a lack of parental understanding of their child's educational rights.
>
> (Gargiulo, 2006, P. 359)

Educational Rights of Children Who Are Homeless.[1] The Stewart B. McKinney Homeless Assistance Act (PL 100-77) was the first, and remains the only, federal law focused specifically on the educational needs of children who are homeless. Enacted in 1987 as part of the reauthorization of the Elementary and Secondary Education Act, this legislation was intended to ensure that children who are homeless have access to a free and appropriate public education, including a preschool education. The McKinney Act did not establish separate educational programs for children who are homeless; rather it reinforced their right to participate in existing public school programs. In November 1990, the original legislation was amended by PL 101-645, which significantly strengthened the rights of children who are homeless to a public education. This amendment specifically addressed the obligations of state and local education agencies in assuring that the educational needs of children who are homeless were considered. It is interesting, however, that this legislation is silent regarding children with disabilities who are homeless. The McKinney Act was reauthorized and amended again in 1994 via the Improving America's Schools Act of 1994 (PL 103-382). Collectively, these amendments provide considerable protection to the educational rights of children who are homeless. In addition to mandating a public education, children who are homeless are entitled to the same programs and services as their housed peers, including preschool programs (for example, Head Start, Even Start), early intervention and special education, compensatory education, and after-school and extended-school-year opportunities. This Act further states that simply being homeless is not sufficient reason to separate students from the mainstream school environment (Walter-Thomas, Korinek, McLaughlin, & Williams, 1996).

The most recent amendments to the McKinney Act are incorporated in PL 107-110 (No Child Left Behind Act of 2001) as the McKinney-Vento Homeless Education Assistance Act. This legislation affords protections to and ensures the educational rights of children who are homeless, including those with disabilities.

The enactment of IDEA 2004 specifically addresses the special needs of children who are homeless. This

----

[1] Adapted from R. Gargiulo, 2006. "Homeless and Disabled: Rights, Responsibilities, and Recommendations for Serving Young Children with Special Needs," *Early Childhood Education Journal, 33*(5), pp. 357–362.

legislation incorporates the McKinney-Vento definition of homelessness as well as requiring states to locate, identify, and evaluate children with disabilities who are homeless. Additionally, for students who are homeless with an existing IEP, schools are mandated to provide services as described in the previously developed IEP. Infants and toddlers who are homeless but who have special needs are also eligible to receive early intervention services as appropriate (National Association for the Education of Homeless Children and Youth, 2007).

The Role of Schools. Early childhood special educators need to be especially sensitive to the plight of children who are homeless. Eddowes (1994) once described schools "safe harbors" for these children. Besides offering appropriate educational experiences, schools can also provide special services like bathing facilities, clean clothes, and nutritious meals. The importance of an education for children who are homeless cannot be underestimated. It represents one of the most effective strategies available for overcoming the detrimental effects of homelessness. For children who are homeless, attending school is the most normal activity

they will experience. The classroom is more than just a learning environment, it becomes an island of safety and support, a place to make friends, and a place to have personal space (Driver & Spady, 2004). Yet young students without a permanent address need more than just access to an education; they require individually tailored instructional programs designed to compensate for negative life experiences. At this point in time, an appropriate education is probably the most promising intervention tactic available. It is interesting to note that schools are the *only* institutions in our country that are legally responsible for identifying and serving children who are homeless (National Center on Family Homelessness, 2009). Table 10–2 offers several suggestions of how teachers can meet the needs of children who are homeless. Feature 10–1 lists available sources of additional information on homelessness.

Child Abuse and Neglect

Child abuse and neglect have reached epidemic proportions in the United States. On an almost daily basis, the media expose us to accounts of various acts

TABLE 10–2 What Teachers Can Do to Help Students Who Are Homeless Succeed in School

Students Experiencing Homelessness May	Teachers Can Help By	Strategies
Need positive peer relationships	Facilitating a sense of belonging	• Provide cooperative learning activities. • Assign a welcome buddy to support transition to a new environment. • Provide activities that promote acceptance of diversity. • Maintain a relationship when the student leaves by providing self-addressed stamped envelopes and stationery.
Move frequently and lack educational program continuity	Addressing special learning needs	• Immediately begin to plan for the next transition. • Assess present academic levels quickly. • Provide necessary remediation/tutoring. • Uphold challenging academic expectations. • Contact the school previously attended to help with placement decisions. • Expeditiously follow up on any special education referrals or services. • Remind parents to keep copies of educational records and IEPs to share with a new school upon arrival.

(continued)

TABLE 10–2 **What Teachers Can Do to Help Students Who Are Homeless Succeed in School** *(continued)*

Students Experiencing Homelessness May	Teachers Can Help By	Strategies
Come to class unprepared	Meeting basic needs in classroom	• Provide school supplies if necessary (pencil, paper, etc.) that can be shared with the student privately. • Make sure the student has a chance to have a class job/role. • Avoid the removal of student possessions as a disciplinary measure. • Share a set of texts for each grade level with the local shelter.
Have high levels of depression, anxiety, and low self-esteem due to the stress of homelessness	Addressing these needs and related behavioral considerations	• Reinforce positive behaviors. • Teach and model skills such as problem solving, critical thinking, and cooperative learning. • Support and recognize individual accomplishments. • Increase the frequency distribution of earned reinforcers. • Maintain the privacy of the child. • Let the student know you are glad he/she is in school. • Help the student identify selected work samples and assemble a portfolio. • Enlist support of community organizations and health and social services agencies. • Enlist services of school personnel (e.g., school counselor, school psychologist).
Live in shelters and homes that house more than one family and are often noisy	Compensating in the classroom	• Provide quiet time during school hours. • Have a new student packet containing a few school supplies and a welcome card from the class for all new students. • Allow the child to do homework at school. • Assign the student a personal space. • Have a safe place for student belongings.
Have parents who may be embarrassed by their homelessness	Respecting and supporting parents	• Make parents feel valued as partners in their child's education. • Provide parents with assessment results and related goals and objectives prior to their next move. • Provide an informal support system in which they feel it is safe to discuss parenting issues or concerns. • Allow parents extra time to pay for trips or assist in accessing resources to help pay for special events. • Help parents become familiar with services available for homeless students, including outside agencies.

SOURCE: Adapted from B. Driver and P. Spady, 2004. *What Educators Can Do: Children and Youth Experiencing Homelessness*, Project HOPE—, Virginia, College of William and Mary, Williamsburg, VA.

of cruelty inflicted on children by adult perpetrators. Tragic illustrations of these acts include:

- a father [who] poured lighter fluid on his child's arm and lit it
- a 42-month-old child [who] had been beaten and sexually abused by a babysitter
- a small child [who] was kicked in the face for simply making a noise
- a child [who] was left alone in a locked car on a 90° summer day
- a parent [who] failed to regularly send her child to school
- a mother [who] refused to seek medical care for her children (Gargiulo, 1990, p. 1)

As teachers, we have a legal and, perhaps more importantly, a moral obligation to see that such actions do not continue. Abuse flourishes due to secrecy, privacy, and a lack of attention. Greater awareness and active involvement on the part of teachers can help break the cycle of child abuse and may even save the life of a child.

Definitions. How does one define the terms *abuse* and *neglect?* What might seem to be a simple task is actually quite difficult due to varying accepted practices of child rearing. Societal and community standards generally dictate what is considered abuse. Most people, for example, oppose the beating of children; yet in some families parents use physical punishment as a routine means of disciplining their children. Corporal punishment is still a very common disciplinary strategy in our schools. In fact, 22 states permit school authorities to administer corporal punishment to children (Randall, 2009).

One simple way of distinguishing between physical abuse and neglect is to view the former as an act of *commission*, while the latter implies an act of *omission.*

The four major types of child maltreatment include physical abuse, neglect, emotional abuse, and sexual abuse. Although the definitions of these terms vary according to individual state law, many definitions reflect the following thinking. **Physical abuse** is an act of commission. It refers to an assault on a child designed to cause physical injury or harm. Examples include hitting, kicking, shaking, stabbing, and other nonaccidental inflictions. Spanking is usually considered a disciplinary action; however, if the child is injured or bruised, it can be classified as abusive.

Neglect is an act of omission and involves a variety of caregiver behaviors that include such things as abandonment, inadequate physical supervision, failure to provide basic necessities (shelter, adequate nourishment, attention and affection, clothing), and the failure to provide necessary medical treatment or require a child to attend school.

Emotional abuse is a difficult term to define and can be an act of commission or omission. It is generally distinguished by a constellation of interactions instigated by the caregiver and designed to be psychologically destructive for the child. Verbal attacks on the child's self-esteem and self-image by constant screaming, criticizing, and humiliation illustrate one form of emotional maltreatment. Rejection and inadequate nurturance also define emotional abuse, the effect of which is cumulative.

A description of **sexual abuse**, which is an act of commission, contains two parts: sexual abuse and sexual exploitation. Gargiulo and Metcalf (2010) believe that sexual abuse lives in a veil of secrecy and a conspiracy of silence. It represents the most underreported form of abuse. Sexual abuse includes rape, incest, indecent exposure, and inappropriate fondling, along with sexual exploitation via prostitution or pornography.

Federal statutes also define child abuse and neglect. Unfortunately, like state law, much of the legislation is ambiguous and lacks precision when describing types of child maltreatment.

Prevalence. The number of cases of child abuse and neglect is increasing at an alarming rate. It is difficult, however, to obtain accurate and reliable data because definitions vary from state to state and because there is a significant problem of underreporting. These problems notwithstanding, national surveys reveal that each day, four children die as a result of abuse or neglect, and approximately 2,500 other children are confirmed victims of abuse and neglect (Children's Defense Fund, 2008). An estimated 3.2 million children were alleged to have been abused or neglected in 2007 (U.S. Department of Health and Human Services, 2009). By way of comparison, only 1.9 million cases of abuse or neglect were filed in 1985 and fewer than 700,000 were recorded in 1976 (National Center on Child Abuse and Neglect, 1986).

Child abuse and neglect can occur in all families, disregarding racial, religious, ethnic, and socioeconomic boundaries. Approximately 8 out of 10 perpetrators are parents. Neglect is the most common form of child maltreatment. More than 6 out of 10 child victims are neglected by parent(s) or other caregivers, with approximately 11 percent being physically abused. Preschool children are at significant risk for physical abuse as well as neglect. Almost one out of three victims of abuse or neglect is younger than age four (U.S. Department of Health and Human Services, 2009).

Child Characteristics. Child abuse requires three elements—the perpetrator, the victim, and a precipitating crisis, like the loss of employment or severe health problems. *All* parents have the potential to be abusive, and some children are more vulnerable to abuse and neglect than others. Our focus here is on the role that the child plays in the abuse triangle.

Research (Cosmos, 2001; Goldson, 2001) suggests that children with special needs are particularly vulnerable to abuse. Youngsters with disabilities are typically overrepresented in samples of abused children. Children who are perceived as different or difficult to raise are also at risk for abuse (U.S. Department of Health and Human Services, 2009). According to Gargiulo (1990), some of the specific variables that heighten a child's vulnerability include the following:

- low birth weight
- mental retardation
- prematurity
- orthopedic impairments (cerebral palsy, spina bifida)
- emotional/behavioral disorders
- developmental delays
- provocative or unmanageable behavior (colic, hyperactivity)
- impairment in mother-infant bonding
- language and speech delays
- impaired social skills

An intriguing question that frequently arises is whether a particular characteristic, such as mental retardation or hyperactivity, is the cause or consequence of abuse. A conclusive answer is presently not available. Contemporary best thinking suggests that some youngsters are part of a reciprocal process whereby specific behaviors provoke abuse, which in turn exacerbates the situation and thus gives rise to additional maltreatment. One must remember, however, that a child's characteristics or actions, in and of themselves, do not cause abuse. Specific individual traits are only one factor in the formula for abuse. Child abuse is the outcome of the interplay of parental/caregiver characteristics, cultural factors, environmental considerations, and a precipitating event. It is rare that the etiology of abuse can be linked to a sole condition (Gargiulo, 1990). The interrelationship among the aforementioned variables is illustrated in Figure 10–1.

FIGURE 10–1 A Model of the Interaction of Primary Factors Contributing to Parental Physical Child Abuse

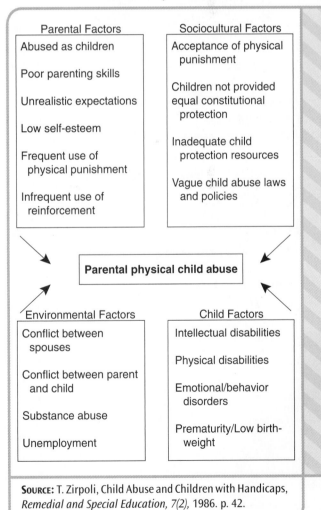

Source: T. Zirpoli, Child Abuse and Children with Handicaps, *Remedial and Special Education, 7(2),* 1986. p. 42.

A Role for Schools and the Early Childhood Special Educator. The toll of abuse and neglect on young children is almost unimaginable. It affects them emotionally, socially, physically, and intellectually (Cosmos, 2001; Hooper & Umansky, 2009). Teachers, however, can play a vital role in the identification and prevention of child abuse and neglect. They may well be the only professionals who have daily and continuous contact with the child. Early childhood special educators are in a unique position, therefore, to intervene and assist in breaking the intergenerational cycle of child abuse and neglect.

Recognizing the signs of abuse and neglect can sometimes be difficult. Table 10–3 provides a list of

TABLE 10–3 Examples of Physical and Behavioral Indicators of Child Abuse and Neglect

Physical Abuse

Physical Indicators
- Bruises, welts, cuts
- Burn marks
- Lacerations and abrasions
- Head injuries
- Skeletal injuries
- Fractures, sprains

Behavioral Indicators
- Fearful of physical contact
- Overly compliant, passive
- Wearing concealing clothing
- Unwillingness to go home
- Wariness of adults
- Behavioral extremes—overly aggressive or very withdrawn
- Lacks reasonable explanation for injury
- Complains about pain or soreness

Neglect

Physical Indicators
- Poor personal hygiene
- Inadequate or inappropriate clothing
- Lack of needed medical/dental care
- Abandonment
- Lack of supervision
- Complaints of constant hunger
- Excessive school absence and/or tardiness

Behavioral Indicators
- Hoarding or stealing of food
- Lethargic, falls asleep in school
- Irregular school attendance
- Rejection by classmates due to offensive body odor
- Dirty clothes, wears same attire for several days

Emotional Abuse

Physical Indicators
Emotional abuse is rarely manifested via physical signs. It is usually associated with other forms of maltreatment. The individual's behavior is often the best clue.

Behavioral Indicators
- Lack of positive self-image
- Low self-esteem
- Depression
- Sleep and/or eating disorder
- Overly fearful, vigilant
- Behavioral extremes—overly compliant/passive or aggressive/demanding
- Poor peer relationships
- Suicidal ideation
- Temper tantrums
- Enuresis

(continued)

TABLE 10–3 **Examples of Physical and Behavioral Indicators of Child Abuse and Neglect** *(continued)*

Sexual Abuse	
Physical Indicators	*Behavioral Indicators*
• Torn, stained, or bloody undergarments	• Sexually sophisticated/mature
• Pain in genital area	• Sexual themes during play
• Presence of sexually transmitted diseases	• Poor peer relationships
• Pregnancy	• Seductive behavior
• Difficulty with urination	• Irregular school attendance
• Presence of semen	• Reluctance to participate in physical activities
• Difficulty walking or sitting	• Infantile behavior
	• Fear of physical contact
	• Statements of sexual abuse

Source: Adapted from R. Gargiulo, "Child Abuse and Neglect: An Overview," in R. Goldman and R. Gargiulo (Eds.), *Children at Risk* (Austin, TX: Pro-Ed, 1990). pp. 19–23.

some of the possible indicators of child abuse and neglect. If a number of these signs are evident or there are repeated occurrences, then you should be alert to the possibility of maltreatment.

Every state has child abuse reporting laws. Teachers, in fact, are mandated reporters. They are legally required to report their *suspicion* of instances of abuse and neglect to the appropriate law enforcement agency or child protective service. The purpose of this legislation is to protect abused and neglected children, not to punish perpetrators. To make a report proof is not necessary. Reasonable cause to suspect maltreatment is all that is required. Educators who act in good faith and without malice are protected from civil or criminal liability. Failure to report can lead to legal problems for the teacher. Fines, misdemeanor charges, and in some instances charges of negligence are possible. Perhaps the greatest tragedy, however, is the child who suffers and possibly dies as a consequence of inaction by a teacher or other professional.

In our opinion, all schools should have a written policy outlining the steps to be taken in recording suspected episodes of abuse and neglect. Schools are also logical places for prevention programs to begin. Examples of such activities include inservice workshops on abuse and neglect for staff and administrators as well as parent education programs (possibly sponsored by the parent–teacher organization)

offering hints and suggestions on child care, behavior management techniques, and parenting skills. Schools can also spearhead community awareness programs on abuse and neglect.

The eradication of child abuse and neglect is not possible. Informed and concerned special educators, however, are vital in attempts to bring this crisis under control. By being informed and vigilant, we can improve the quality of life for many young children with special needs, and maybe the veil of secrecy surrounding child abuse and neglect will be lifted. See Feature 10–2 for sources of additional information on child abuse and neglect.

FEATURE 10–2

Representative Web Resources on Child Abuse and Neglect

- **Child Help USA** http://www.childhelp.org
- **Prevent Child Abuse America** http://www.preventchildabuse.org/index.shtml
- **Child Abuse Prevent Network** http://www.child-abuse.com/
- **Child Welfare Information Gateway** http://www.childwelfare.gov/

Young Children with Special Health Needs

There are a large number of health issues that affect the quality of life of young children. Increasingly, teachers are encountering students with a variety of infectious and chronic conditions. Schools, therefore, are playing larger roles in the health care arena. One result of this expanded role is new professional and personal challenges that now confront the early childhood special educator. Chosen for brief discussion are two contemporary health issues: children with AIDS and children identified as having special health needs ("medically fragile").

Pediatric AIDS. Since the early days of the **acquired immune deficiency syndrome (AIDS)** epidemic in the 1980s, there has been a significant amount of fear and misunderstanding about this disease. Part of the fear about AIDS resides in the fact that, at the present time, it is incurable.

AIDS is caused by the **human immunodeficiency virus (HIV)**. HIV contributes to the breakdown of the child's natural immunity system, leaving the youngster very susceptible to certain infectious and opportunistic illnesses (illnesses that can be serious due to a weakened immune system like chicken pox or influenza). The HIV virus may be spread through sexual intercourse, blood contact, or sharing contaminated hypodermic needles. Pediatric AIDS is usually the result of the child's mother being infected and transmitting the virus to her baby. About 90% of the youngsters diagnosed with HIV acquire the infection from their mothers (Centers for Disease Control, 2009; Spiegel & Bonwit, 2002). Transmission can occur during pregnancy, at birth, and via breastfeeding. Most instances of pediatric AIDS occur in utero (Best & Heller, 2009). Approximately 25% of infants born to HIV mothers are infected (Bell, 2007).

Since the mid 1980s, the Centers for Disease Control has identified about 9,600 cases of pediatric AIDS. Since that time, however, the number of cases has dramatically decreased; only 87 new cases were identified in 2007. This substantial decrease is most likely due to voluntary testing of pregnant women, counseling efforts, and the introduction of effective drug therapy (the use of antiretroviral agents) to combat the HIV virus (Centers for Disease Control, 2009).

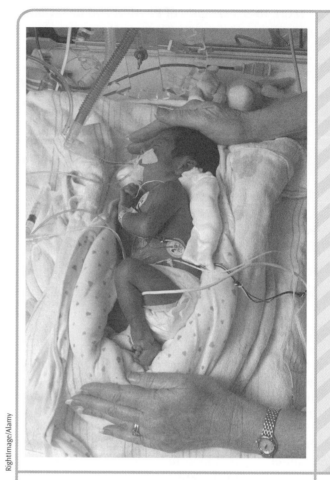

Rightimage/Alamy

Children with special health needs present many challenges to our schools.

According to Gargiulo (2009), "pediatric AIDS is suspected of being a leading infectious cause of intellectual disabilities. At the same time, HIV is the single most preventable cause of infectious mental retardation" (p. 161).

HIV infection is a source of significant stress for families. In fact, Lesar and her colleagues (Lesar, Gerber, & Semmel, 1996) view it as a family disease because it threatens the child's entire caregiving system. The impact of infection has devastating consequences for young children. Although the course of the disease is different for each child and difficult to predict, pediatric AIDS contributes to significant developmental delays and debilitating motor, cognitive, language, and social development. Developmental regression and deterioration are also not uncommon

(Best & Heller, 2009). Some of the other possible adverse outcomes of pediatric AIDS include the following:

- impaired fine and gross motor skills
- chronic bacterial and viral infections
- failure to thrive
- acute diarrhea
- enlarged spleen and liver
- weight loss
- attention deficits
- frequent respiratory problems
- central nervous system damage
- sensory impairments

Early intervention and special education services are almost always necessary for children with AIDS. Some states serve very young children under the category of being at-risk for developmental delay, while older children with HIV receive services via the "Other Health Impaired" label found in IDEA.

Special educators need not worry about contracting AIDS as a result of teaching these children. To date, there has *not* been one reported instance of AIDS transmission from child to classmate or child to teacher in any early childhood program. It is safe, therefore, for children to play with peers who have AIDS and for teachers to serve them. Casual contact such as hugging, touching, coughing, the sharing of clothing items, or even sharing a toothbrush has not been shown to spread the infection (Best & Heller, 2009; Gargiulo, 2009). Of course, appropriate hygiene practices and universal infection control procedures are required, such as wearing disposable gloves when treating a bloody nose, vigorous hand washing (soap and water destroy the HIV virus), and cleaning soiled surfaces like toys, countertops, and bathrooms with a disinfectant like common household bleach.

Young children who are HIV positive or have AIDS are able, in most cases, to participate in early childhood and school-age programs; in fact, the Americans with Disabilities Act (PL 101–336) guarantees this right. All children with HIV infection should, according to the American Academy of Pediatrics, receive an appropriate education designed to meet their evolving needs (American Academy of Pediatrics, 2007). (See Table 10–4 for a checklist of strategies designed to accommodate children with AIDS in the classroom.) There is no logical reason for excluding a student with HIV infection if the youngster's health permits attendance at school (Rutstein,

TABLE 10–4 Teacher Checklist for Accommodating Students With AIDS

- Observe guidelines for confidentiality of information.
- Assess the student for eligibility under IDEA or Section 504.
- Obtain copies of state and local policies for inclusion of students with AIDS.
- Get the facts about AIDS and how it affects learning.
- Assemble a team to develop an individualized family service plan (IFSP) or an individualized education program (IEP) that addresses educational needs and health-related supports.
- Plan modifications of instructional methods and curriculum to meet the student's individual needs.
- Design ways to include the student who has AIDS in typical classroom activities.
- Build flexibility into the student's IFSP or IEP to allow for hospitalizations and frequent absences.
- Arrange for training in infection control procedures (e.g., universal precautions).
- Educate parents about communicable disease policies and the use of universal precautions.
- Answer students' questions about terminal illness

Source: Adapted from K. Kelker, A. Hecimovic, and C. LeRoy, Designing a Classroom and School Environment for Students with AIDS. *Teaching Exceptional Children, 26*(4), 1994. p. 52.

Conlon, & Batshaw, 1997). Some pupils, however, may require alternative instructional programs such as homebound instruction, while in other instances modification of the school program might be necessary due to fatigue or increasingly frequent absences. Most children with AIDS, however, will not require any modifications (Gargiulo, 2009).

Schools and teachers have a unique role and responsibility in our nation's response to the AIDS crisis. Educating our students (and their parents), fellow professionals, and community members about AIDS and HIV infection prevention is an important first step. Accurate information is a powerful tool for combating unwarranted fears. We fully endorse preservice and inservice training experiences for teachers. We also believe that young children should be taught health concepts and good health behaviors such as avoiding contact with blood and washing hands before eating and after toileting. Health care professionals believe that the early years are an appropriate time to begin developing health and safety habits. See Feature 10–3 for additional information about HIV and AIDS.

Students with Special Health Care Needs. Our second example is young children with special health needs (often incorrectly identified as "medically fragile"). This population is growing due to rapid medical and technological advances that are saving lives and improving the quality of life for many of these children. As this population continues to grow, schools will encounter new challenges in service delivery as these children increasingly seek school services. It is very likely, therefore, that you will teach a student with significant health needs at some point during your career. The right of children with complex health care needs to receive an appropriate education in the least restrictive environment is guaranteed by statute (IDEA) and reinforced by substantial legal precedents (e.g., *Irving Independent School District v. Tatro; Timothy W. v. Rochester New Hampshire School District; Cedar Rapids School District v. Garett F.*).

Who are these children who will present early childhood special educators with personal and professional challenges? This question defies a simple

answer. We believe that there are two reasons for this difficulty. The first reason is differences in terminology and the second is the complexity of health issues usually found in this population. Teachers will frequently encounter descriptive labels such as *chronically ill, technologically dependent, medically fragile*, or the IDEA term of *other health impaired*. Contemporary thinking suggests, however, that these labels are inappropriate as they perpetuate stereotypes and imply inaccurate information about the actual health status of these individuals. "Medically fragile is a status," Smith and Tyler (2010) write, "it is not assigned to any specific condition but rather reflects the individual's health situation. Students can move in and out of fragile status" (p. 307). The preferred term, therefore, is **children with special health needs** (Rueve, Robinson, Worthington, & Gargiulo, 2000). This label keeps the primary focus on the child while his or her unique health needs are secondary. We have chosen adopt this term.

As we just observed, part of the problem in defining this population is the diversity of medical conditions embraced by the concept of young children with special health needs. These children do not present a single set of characteristics. Included in this group are students with chronic problems like asthma and those with physical deformities, congenital defects, infectious conditions, heredity difficulties, and life-threatening illnesses (Giardino, Kohrt, Arye, & Wells, 2002). Due to the great variety of conditions represented, generalizations are difficult to make. Yet we feel safe in stating that one of the keys to working with this group of students is for educators to appreciate the highly individualized nature of each child's condition. While pupils might share a similar medical condition—muscular dystrophy, for example—the course and severity of the disease or illness and its impact on the child and his or her family is uniquely personal.

Medical and educational services for young children with special health needs reflect the contemporary belief that early childhood experiences should be as normalized as possible. This philosophy has contributed to the growth of community-based care and the opportunity for these youngsters to attend a variety of early childhood programs in their local communities (Crocker & Porter, 2001). Although young children with special health needs have traditionally not been served by early childhood educators, legal opinions and legislation, coupled with demands from families, have resulted in an increasing number of students seeking services alongside their healthy classmates.

We fully agree with Crocker and Porter (2001), and more recently Downing (2008), who believe that the inclusion of children with special health care needs in early childhood settings should be seen as the norm rather than the exception. Yet such a decision requires that parents, teachers, and other professionals thoughtfully weigh medical opinion about possible harm to the child with the desire to have the child participate in normalized school activities. Any placement decision obviously has both positive and negative features, and the advantages and disadvantages must be carefully considered (Hallahan et al., 2009).

An integral aspect of providing for these children, regardless of the educational setting, is the development of a detailed health care plan (see Figure 10–2). This document, which is a critical element of the student's IEP, "should contain all of the information necessary in order to provide complete medical and educational services to the child with special health needs" (Rueve et al., 2000, p. 16). School personnel must also be prepared for unforeseen circumstances, the "What do I do if" incidents, which hopefully will never materialize. A written plan for potential emergency situations should be created based on the student's particular health needs. (See Figure 10–3 for an example of an emergency medical plan.) We recommend that copies of this plan be located in the classroom and other sites frequented by the child (lunch room, school bus, gymnasium).

Providing an appropriate education to young children with unique health care needs requires collaboration and cooperation with families and the various agencies that provide the necessary services. It also requires open lines of communication with professionals from a variety of disciplines. Services for the child with special health needs, regardless of where they are delivered, is a shared responsibility. Teamwork, flexibility, and the familiar themes of individualized, normalized, and family-focused services also apply to these students. Additionally, in-depth training is frequently required, as early childhood educators are often ill prepared to effectively meet the needs of children with special health needs (Mancini & Layton, 2004; Rueve et al., 2000). Years ago, the Council for Exceptional Children (1988) recommended that preservice training and professional

development activities focus on the following eight components. We believe these suggestions are still valid today.

- Awareness and understanding of student's health care, emotional, and educational needs.
- Knowledge of common medical and health terms.
- Knowledge of medical characteristics including etiology and implications.
- Knowledge of physical, developmental, and emotional characteristics.
- Knowledge of appropriate curricular and environmental modifications.
- Knowledge of the roles and responsibilities of the health care professional in the classroom.
- Knowledge of the importance and necessity for establishing support systems for personnel, students, and families.
- Knowledge of resources for the family. (pp. 5–6)

Regardless of the medical condition presented by the student—be it pediatric AIDS, cancer, or some form of neurological disorder—these children, like all infants, toddlers, preschoolers, and early primary students, have a right to expect high-quality care and beneficial early education experiences from their teachers.

Preparation of Early Childhood Special Educators

It is our opinion that high-quality early intervention and childhood special education programs are the result of many factors, one of which is the quality of the personnel. Good programs for young children with special needs rely on competent teachers. Educators are the key to providing effective services to infants, toddlers, preschoolers, and early primary students with disabilities and their families. Regrettably, there is a nationwide shortage of qualified teachers. With the increase in the number of young children with special needs seeking services, the demand for early childhood special educators has dramatically grown. Teacher vacancies are not uncommon, and some positions are even filled by teachers not fully certified in early childhood special education. A notable lack of trained professionals to work with infants and toddlers with delays and disabilities is also an area

FIGURE 10–2 Sample Individualized Health Care Plan

Student: _____ DOB: _____ Age: _____ Grade/Class: _____

Primary Caregivers: _____ Daytime Phone: _____

_____ Daytime Phone: _____

Primary Health Care Provider: _____ Phone: _____

Date Plan Approved: _____ Frequency of Plan Review: _____ Date Plan Last Updated: _____

Team Members

Team Member Signature	Title	Role/Responsibility	Phone	Alt. Phone (P) or Beeper (B)

Alternate Team Members

AlternateTeam Member Name	Title	Role/Responsibility	Phone	Alt. Phone (P) or Beeper (B)

Training Requirements

Team Member	Health Care Procedure, Assistive Technology, or Medical Equipment Training Required	Frequency of Initial and Ongoing Training	Date of Last Training

Brief Medical History

Current Medical Condition

Positioning or handling requirements:

Precautions/possible adverse reactions to health care procedures:

Restricted activities:

Behavior considerations:

Medical Management

Description of Health Care Procedure	Frequency and Number of Repetitions	Location

(continued)

FIGURE 10–2 Sample Individualized Health Care Plan *(Continued)*

Medical Management Log

Description of Health Care Procedure	Frequency and Number of Repetitions	Location	Date/Time	Authorized Care Giver	Signature of Caregiver

Feeding and Nutritional Needs

Special Feeding Instructions: Amount of Food; Temperature of Food; Number of Feedings, etc.	Nutrition Offered	Frequency and Time	Notable Concerns

Feeding and Nutritional Needs Log

Nutrition Offered	Date	Time	Notable Concerns	Caregiver Signature

Special Equipment and Devices

Assistive Technology Device or Medical Equipment Required	Details on the Use and Maintenance of Apparatus

Transportation Needs

Transportation Needs	Destination	Provider of Transportation	Provider Phone
Transportation to School			
Transportation from School			
Transportation Around School			
Field Trips			
Emergency Transportation			
Other			

Adaptations/Accommodations Req'd: ☐ None ☐ Bus Lift ☐ Seat Belt ☐ Wheel Chair Lockdown ☐ Chest Harness ☐ Booster Seat
☐ Other: _____ Method of Mobility: _____

Family/Caregiver Requests

Health Status Profile Leading to Emergency Interventions

Description of Change/Symptoms of Distress	Interventions

Source: B. Rueve, M. Robinson, L. Worthington, and R. Gargiulo, Children with Special Health Needs in Inclusive settings: Writing Health Care Plans, *Physical Disabilities Education and Related Services*, 19(1), 2000, pp. 17–18.

FIGURE 10–3 Sample Medical Emergency Plan

Student: _____ DOB: _____ Age: _____ Grade/Class: _____

Date Plan Approved: _____ Frequency of Plan Review: _____ Date Plan Last Updated: _____

Emergency Contact Information

Emergency Contact	Relation to Student	Contact for What Type of Emergency?	Daytime Phone	Alt. Phone (P) or Beeper (B)
	Primary Physician			
	Dentist			
	Ambulance			
	EMT			
	Hospital			
	Fire Department			
	Medical Supplier			

Emergency Procedures

Description of Medical Emergency	What To Do	Location of Medication/ Equipment	Transportation Requirement

SOURCE: B. Rueve, M. Robinson, L. Worthington, and R. Gargiulo, Children with Special Health Needs in Inclusive settings: Writing Health Care Plans, *Physical Disabilities Education and Related Services*, *19*(1), 2000, pp. 22.

of growing concern (Klein & Gilkerson, 2000). We envision these critical shortages to continue into the foreseeable future despite attempts by colleges and universities to increase the number of qualified personnel.

Producing a sufficient cadre of well trained and effective professionals is only one of the problems the field is encountering. Another matter confronting early childhood special education is the issue of inclusion of young children with special needs. Research over the past three decades strongly supports the conclusion that integrated early childhood programs are of significant benefit to both children with delays or disabilities and typically developing children (Guralnick, 2001; Sandall et al., 2005). As a result, a growing number of young children with delays and disabilities are receiving services in normalized or natural early childhood settings. Qualified staff, however, are not always available to deliver the needed instruction. For example, of the almost 31,000 teachers serving 3- to 5-year-old children with special needs, approximately 3,700, or 12%, of the workforce are not fully certified (U.S. Department of Education, 2009).

Another concern resulting from the enactment of the No Child Left Behind Act (PL 107-110) is the call for teachers to be "highly qualified" professionals. In order for a special educator to be deemed "highly qualified," he or she must possess full certification as determined by individual states. It is interesting, however, that while this legislation addresses teachers of school-age children, it is silent on the requirements for early childhood special educators to be viewed as highly qualified (Gargiulo, 2009).

Compounding this situation is the fact that the professional qualifications of those who work with young children with special needs greatly vary. Common standards of personnel preparation do not exist; in fact, not all states have a specific certification for early childhood special education. States typically use a wide variety of models or configurations to certify their teachers. In several instances, multiple certification options are available. In one national survey, Lazara, Danaher, and Kraus (2007) found, for example, that 16 states require a special education certificate or license for teachers working with young children with special needs. Eight states allow educators of young children with special needs to possess only a general early childhood certificate that includes some special education requirements. On the other hand,

12 states will certify teachers to work with young children with special needs on the basis of a special education certificate with a preschool special education add-on or endorsement. The age ranges covered by these various certification patterns greatly vary. In some instances, professionals can serve children from birth to kindergarten, birth to grade three, ages 3 to 21, or children between 3 and 8 years of age, among other configurations. The recent work of Stayton and her colleagues (Stayton et al., 2009) echoes these same findings for educators who teach preschoolers with developmental delays or disabilities.

Collectively, we believe that these circumstances have implications for teacher preparation programs. As a profession, we not only need to produce more early childhood special educators who are highly qualified (currently teachers in kindergarten through grade three), we also need to train professionals who can effectively serve young children in inclusive settings. An innovative teacher training program might be one strategy to help alleviate the situation. We issue a call, therefore, for a collaborative or integrative personnel preparation program. We are not the originators of this idea. Support for this model of teacher preparation is growing in both early childhood circles and the field of early childhood special education (Kilgo, 2006; Miller & Stayton, 2000; Stayton & McCollum, 2002). The time is right to question whether we can continue to legitimately prepare early childhood professionals via distinct or fractionalized preparation programs. We think not.

A collaborative teacher training program that prepares professionals to serve *all* young children in the least restrictive or natural environment holds strong promise for improving the delivery of services. Teachers can draw upon effective practices from the fields of early childhood and early childhood special education and thus provide early education services that are both developmentally and individually appropriate in addition to being responsive to the specific teaching and learning requirements of each student. Rather than having distinct preparation tracks, we envision a seamless system for preparing teachers of young children. The blending of professional standards across the two fields would ensure that early childhood educators have the ability to meet the needs of typical students as well as of children with special needs regardless of the type of program in which they are enrolled.

Integrative teacher training experiences dictate that personnel preparation standards be built around mutually agreed-upon critical competencies, common philosophical assumptions, and a common core of knowledge and skills appropriate to all young children. An example of this type of consensus can be found in a document on preparing early childhood professionals developed by the National Association for the Education of Young Children (Hyson, 2003).

The competencies of a well trained early childhood special educator should also reflect the theoretical as well as the research knowledge bases of both early childhood and special education (Division for Early Childhood, 1993/2006). Teachers must be prepared to fulfill their roles as pedagogical experts (Wolery, 1991) and as people who have the primary responsibility of facilitating the child's development in areas of social, motor, communication, cognitive, self-help, and behavioral domains (Klein & Gilkerson, 2000). Teacher education curricula will need to integrate or blend special education content with content from the fields of early childhood education and child development.

Critical to the success of our call is the required collaboration of professional organizations such as the Association of Teacher Educators (ATE), the National Association for the Education of Young Children (NAEYC), and the Division for Early Childhood (DEC) of the Council for Exceptional Children. Fortunately, a shared vision and mutual concern about segregated personnel preparation models has resulted in a joint position statement on personnel standards (see Appendix E). Collectively, these three associations are in a strong position to influence state departments of education who are responsible for the credentialing and licensing of early childhood special educators. Many teacher education programs are exclusively formulated around specific state certification requirements. Thus, state departments of education will have a large voice in whether colleges and universities can develop integrative teacher training programs.

We believe that the time has arrived to put an end to segregated, categorical teacher preparation programs. A collaborative early childhood/early childhood special education teacher training model has the potential to meet the growing need for well trained professionals who have multiple competencies and can deliver high-quality services in a variety of settings. Teachers trained in such a fashion will be well suited to meet the challenges in the workplace of the 21st century.

Summary

We have attempted to identify several challenges that will confront early childhood special educators in the coming years. A growing list of social issues and professional concerns suggests that significant change in early childhood special education programs is on the horizon.

We live in a nation that is rich in its cultural diversity. Our schools are serving growing numbers of young children with culturally and linguistically diverse backgrounds. For some students, entrance into school may represent their first exposure to a culture and a language that is different from that of their home. Because of this, teachers must guard against stereotyping and be certain that ethnicity is not misinterpreted as exceptionality. It is not uncommon for cultural differences to routinely translate into disabilities. Early childhood special educators, therefore, must model respect for and sensitivity to the cultural heritage of their students. For early childhood special education programs to be successful, services must be offered by professionals who are ethnically competent and demonstrate cultural awareness and sensitivity.

A variety of contemporary social ills will result in early childhood special education teachers serving a growing population of students who evidence the deleterious consequences of homelessness, child abuse, pediatric AIDS, and numerous other special health conditions. The causes of many of these problems are beyond the control of the early childhood special educator. Teachers can, however, provide a safe, stable, and nurturing learning environment where children can develop to their maximum potential. As teachers of infants, toddlers, preschoolers, and early primary students, it is our duty to fulfill our role as purveyors of care and education to all youngsters, but especially to those most in need.

Finally, competent teachers are the key to providing effective services to young children with special needs and their families. Unfortunately, there is a shortage of trained personnel. Coupled with this shortfall is the increasing number of young children with special needs who are receiving services in inclusive early childhood settings. In many instances, qualified staff are not available to provide the needed instruction. We believe that this scenario has implications for how we prepare early childhood special educators. We support the concept of a collaborative personnel preparation program wherein competencies, knowledge, and skills appropriate to the fields of early childhood education and early childhood special education are merged into a single model for preparing teachers of young children. An integrative teacher training model has the potential to meet the growing need for well trained teachers who have multiple competencies and can provide high-quality services in a variety of instructional settings.

Check Your Understanding

1. Explain the difference between ethnicity and exceptionality.
2. Why is it important for early childhood special educators to understand and respect the cultural heritage of their students?
3. Provide examples of the four major types of child maltreatment.
4. What role do schools play in providing services to young children with special health needs?
5. Should teachers of young children with special needs have professional preparation in both early childhood and special education? Support your viewpoint.

Reflection and Application

1. Visit several schools in your area. Do these schools serve young children who are homeless? What support systems are available to assist these children and their families? How does the teacher address the educational needs of pupils who are homeless? What would you do if you had a child in your class who was homeless?
2. Interview a school administrator. Does the school have a policy for reporting instances of suspected child abuse or neglect? What is the role of the teacher? Are criminal background checks performed on staff and volunteers?

3. With a group of your classmates, produce a presentation about the characteristics of young children with special health needs. Topics may include a student with juvenile rheumatoid arthritis, muscular dystrophy, cystic fibrosis, AIDS, or epilepsy, among other conditions. Design a health care plan for a young child with one of the preceding examples. How would you explain this child's condition to his or her classmates? How would you organize your classroom to meet the unique needs of this pupil? Are there any particular educational strategies you would incorporate in your classroom? How would you involve the student's family?

References

American Academy of Pediatrics. (2007). *Education of children with human immunodeficiency virus infection.* Policy Statement of the Committee on Pediatric AIDS. Retrieved May 25, 2009, from http://aapolicy.aapublications.org/cgi/content/full/pediatrics;105/6/1358

Barrera, I. (2000). Honoring differences: Essential features of appropriate ECSE services for young children from diverse sociocultural environments. *Young Exceptional Children, 3*(4), 17–24.

Bell, M. (2007). Infections and the fetus. In M. Batshaw, L. Pellegrino, & N. Roizen (Eds.), *Children with disabilities* (6th ed., pp. 61–82). Baltimore: Paul H. Brookes.

Best, S., & Heller, K. (2009). Acquired infections and AIDS. In K. Heller, P. Forney, P. Alberto, S. Best, & M. Schwartzman (Eds.), *Understanding physical, health, and multiple disabilities* (2nd ed., pp. 367–386). Upper Saddle River, NJ: Pearson Education.

CEC Today. (2003). Exceptional and homeless. *9*(6), 1–2, 7, 13, 15.

Centers for Disease Control. (2009). *Pediatric HIV/AIDS surveillance.* Retrieved May 25, 2009, from http://www.cdc.gov/hiv/topics/surveillance/resources/slides/pediatric/index.htm

Children's Defense Fund. (2008). *The state of America's children 2008.* Washington, DC: Author.

Cosmos, C. (2001). Abuse of children with disabilities. *CEC Today, 8*(2), 1, 2, 5, 8, 12, 14, 15.

Council for Exceptional Children. (1988). *Report to the Council for Exceptional Children ad hoc committee on medically fragile students.* Reston, VA: Author.

Crocker, A., & Porter, S. (2001). Inclusion of young children with complex health care needs. In M. Guralnick (Ed.), *Early childhood inclusion: Focus on change* (pp. 399–412). Baltimore: Paul H. Brookes.

Davis, M., Kilgo, J., & Gamel-McCormick, M. (1998). *Young children with special needs: A developmentally appropriate approach.* Needham Heights, MA: Allyn & Bacon.

Division for Early Childhood. (1993/2006). Position statement: *Personnel standards for early education and early intervention.* Missoula, MT: Author.

Downing, J. (2008). *Including students with severe and multiple disabilities in typical classrooms* (3rd ed.). Baltimore: Paul H. Brookes.

Driver, B., & Spady, P. (2004). *What educators can do: Children and youth experiencing homelessness.* Project HOPE—Virginia. Williamsburg, VA: College of William and Mary.

Eddowes, E. (1994). Schools providing safer environments for homeless children. *Childhood Education, 70,* 271–273.

Gargiulo, R. (1990). Child abuse and neglect: An overview. In R. Goldman & R. Gargiulo (Eds.), *Children at risk* (pp. 1–36). Austin, TX: PRO-ED.

Gargiulo, R. (2006). Homeless and disabled: Rights, responsibilities, and recommendations for serving young children with special needs. *Early Childhood Education Journal, 33*(5), 357–362.

Gargiulo, R. (2009). *Special education in contemporary society: An introduction to exceptionality* (3rd ed.). Thousand Oaks, CA: Sage.

Gargiulo, R., & Metcalf, D. (2010). *Teaching in today's inclusive classrooms.* Belmont, CA: Wadsworth/Cengage Learning.

Giardino, A., Kohrt, A., Arye, L., & Wells, N. (2002). Health care delivery systems and financing issues. In M. Batshaw (Ed.), *Children with disabilities* (5th ed., pp. 123–139). Baltimore: Paul H. Brookes.

Goldson, E. (2001). Maltreatment among children with disabilities. *Infants and Young Children, 13*(4), 44–54.

Gollnick, D., & Chinn, P. (2009). *Multicultural education in a pluralistic society* (8th ed.). Upper Saddle River, NJ: Pearson Education.

Graves, S., Gargiulo, R., & Sluder, L. (1996). *Young children.* St. Paul, MN: West.

Guralnick, M. (Ed.). (2001). *Early childhood inclusion: Focus on change.* Baltimore: Paul H. Brookes.

Hallahan, D., Kauffman, J., & Pullen, P. (2009). *Exceptional learners* (11th ed.). Boston: Pearson Education.

Hanson, M. (2004). Ethnic, cultural, and language diversity in service settings. In E. Lynch & M. Hanson (Eds.), *Developing cross cultural competency* (3rd ed., pp. 3–18). Baltimore: Paul H. Brookes.

Hanson, M., Lynch, E., & Wayman, K. (1990). Honoring the cultural diversity of families when gathering data. *Topics in Early Childhood Special Education, 10*(1), 112–131.

Hanson, M., & Zercher, C. (2001). The impact of cultural and linguistic diversity in inclusive preschool environments. In M. Guralnick (Ed.), *Early childhood inclusion: Focus on change* (pp. 413–431). Baltimore: Paul H. Brookes.

Hooper, S., & Umansky, W. (2009). *Young children with special needs* (5th ed.). Upper Saddle River, NJ: Pearson Education.

Howard, V., Williams, B., & Lepper, C. (2005). *Very young children with special needs* (3rd ed.). Upper Saddle River, NJ: Pearson Education.

Hyson, M. (Ed.). (2003). *Preparing early childhood professionals.* Washington, DC: National Association for the Education of Young Children.

Kilgo, J. (Ed.). (2006). *Transdisciplinary teaming in early intervention and early childhood special education.* Olney, MD: Association for Childhood Education International.

Kirk, S., Gallagher, J., Coleman, M., & Anastasiow, N. (2009). *Educating exceptional children* (11th ed.). Boston: Houghton Mifflin.

Klein, N., & Gilkerson, L. (2000). Personnel preparation for early childhood intervention programs. In J. Shonkoff & S. Meisels (Eds.), *Handbook of early childhood intervention* (2nd ed., pp. 454–483). Cambridge, England: Cambridge University Press.

Lazara, A., Danaher, J., & Kraus, R. (Eds.). (2007). *Section 619 profile* (15th ed.). Chapel Hill, NC: National Early Childhood Technical Assistance Center.

Lesar, S., Gerber, M., & Semmel, M. (1996). HIV infection in children: Family stress, social support, and adaptation. *Exceptional Children, 62*(3), 224–236.

Lustig, M., & Koestner, J. (2010). *Intercultural competence: Interpersonal communication across cultures* (5th ed.). Boston: Allyn & Bacon.

Lynch, E., & Hanson, M. (2004). *Developing cross cultural competency* (3rd ed.). Baltimore: Paul H. Brookes.

Mancini, K., & Layton, C. (2004). Meeting fears and concerns effectively: The inclusion of early childhood students who are medically fragile. *Physical Disabilities: Education and Related Services, 22*(2), 29–48.

Miller, P., & Stayton, V. (2000). Recommended practices in personnel preparation. In S. Sandall, M. McLean, & B. Smith (Eds.), *DEC recommended practices in early intervention/early childhood special education* (pp. 77–88). Longmont, CO: Sopris West.

Morrison, G. (2009). *Early childhood education today* (11th ed.). Upper Saddle River, NJ: Pearson Education.

National Association for the Education of Homeless Children and Youth. (2007). *Individuals with Disabilities Education Improvement Act (IDEA) of 2004: Provisions for homeless children and youth.* Retrieved May 24, 2009, from http://www.serve.org/nche/downloads/briefs/idea.pdf

National Center for Education Statistics. (2007). *The condition of education 2007.* Washington, DC: U.S. Government Printing Office.

National Center for Education Statistics. (2008). *The condition of education 2008.* Washington, DC: U.S. Government Printing Office.

National Center on Child Abuse and Neglect. (1986). *Child abuse and neglect: An informed approach to a shared concern.* (No. 20-01016). Washington, DC: Author.

National Center on Family Homelessness. (2008). *The characteristics and needs of families experiencing homelessness.* Retrieved May 22, 2009, from http://www.family homelessness.org

National Center on Family Homelessness. (2009). *America's youngest outcasts.* Newton, MA: Author.

National Coalition for the Homeless. (2008). *Who is homeless? Fact sheet #3.* Retrieved May 28, 2009, from http://www.nationalhomeless.org/factsheets/who.html

Odom, S., & Wolery, M. (2003). A unified theory in practice and early intervention/early childhood special education: Evidence-based practices. *Journal of Special Education, 37*(3), 164–173.

Quality Education for Minorities Project. (1990). *Education that works: An action plan for the education of minorities.* Cambridge, MA: Massachusetts Institute of Technology.

Randall, D. (2009). *States with corporal punishment in school.* Retrieved May 26, 2009, from http://school.familyeducation.com/classroom-discipline/resource/38377.html

Rueve, B., Robinson, M., Worthington, L., & Gargiulo, R. (2000). Children with special health needs in inclusive settings: Writing health care plans. *Physical Disabilities Education and Related Services, 19*(1), 11–24.

Rutstein, M., Conlon, C., & Batshaw, M. (1997). HIV and AIDS. In M. Batshaw (Ed.), *Children with disabilities* (4th ed., pp. 162–182). Baltimore: Paul H. Brookes.

Sandall, S., Hemmeter, L., Smith, B., & McLean, B. (2005). *DEC recommended practices.* Longmont, CO: Sopris West.

Shaw, E., & Goode, S. (2008). *Fact sheet: Vulnerable young children.* Chapel Hill, NC: FPG Child Development Institute, National Early Childhood Technical Assistance Center.

Smith, D., & Tyler, N. (2010). *Introduction to special education* (7th ed.). Upper Saddle River, NJ: Pearson Education.

Spiegel, H., & Bonwit, A. (2002). HIV in children. In M. Batshaw (Ed.), *Children with disabilities* (5th ed., pp. 123–139). Baltimore: Paul H. Brookes.

Stayton, V., Dietrich, S., Smith, B., Bruder, M., Mogro-Wilson, C., & Swigart, A. (2009). State certification requirements for early childhood special educators. *Infants and Young Children, 22*(1), 4–12.

Stayton, V., & McCollum, J. (2002). Unifying general and special education: What does the research tell us? *Teacher Education and Special Education, 25*(3), 211–218.

Tiedt, P., & Tiedt, I. (2002). *Multicultural teaching: A handbook of activities, information, and resources* (6th ed.). Needham Heights, MA: Allyn & Bacon.

U.S. Census Bureau. (2008). *Statistical abstract of the United States: 2009* (128th ed.). Washington, DC: Author.

U.S. Department of Education. (2009). *Twenty-eighth annual report to Congress on the implementation of the Individuals with Disabilities Education Act, 2006* (Vol. 2). Available at http://edpubs.ed.gov/

U.S. Department of Health and Human Services. (2009). *Child maltreatment 2007:* Washington, DC: U.S. Government Printing Office.

Walter-Thomas, C., Korinek, L., McLaughlin, V., & Williams, B, (1996). Improving educational opportunities for students with disabilities who are homeless. *Journal of Children and Poverty, 2*(2), 57–75.

Wolery, M. (1991). Instruction in early childhood special education: "Seeing through a glass darkly . . . knowing in part." *Exceptional Children, 58*(2), 127–135.

Appendices

Division for Early Childhood, Council for Exceptional Children
Professional Standards
Early Childhood Special Education/Early Intervention
October 2008

This document presents the newly validated personnel standards for "professionals" in Early Childhood Special Education/Early Intervention (ECSE/EI). These standards are delineated as Early Childhood (EC) standards for initial preparation. The ECSE/EI standards assume the inclusion of CEC's Common Core standards in personnel preparation for program accreditation.

The terminology that is used in the standards presented below was developed originally in the context of the meetings for CEC's Knowledge and Skills Committee. The purpose was to simplify the wording of the standards for personnel in ECSE/EI and to use terminology that is appropriate for those who serve the populations of children, birth to age 8, and their families.

Terms used in the ECSE/EI Standards:

1. *Infants and Young Children*: all children birth to age 8 years.
2. *Exceptional Needs*: In response to Exceptional Learning Needs (ELN) specified in the CEC standards, "infants and young children with exceptional needs" will be used, and not ELN, since infants and young children, have developmental needs as well as learning needs.
3. *Infants and Young Children with Exceptional Needs*: refers to infants and young children, birth to age 8 years, who have, or are at risk for, developmental delays and disabilities.
4. *Development and Learning*: terms to be used, and in that order, to convey the focus of the following knowledge and skills for personnel—to support the developmental and learning needs of infants and young children, and their families.
5. *IFSP/IEP Family or Educational Plan*: The language of the standards requires spelling out IFSP and IEP. The Knowledge and Skills Committee suggests using "family or educational plan" to (a) simplify the expressions and (b) include Canadian terminology in the standards. DEC respectfully requests the use of "individualized plan" to simplify the language since the IFSP is an educational plan too.
6. *Developmental Domains*: Term to be used to simplify the listing of the five developmental domains specified in federal law—cognitive, communicative, social-emotional, motor, and adaptive development.
7. *Settings for Infants and Young Children*: to avoid lists, these settings refer to home, community-based, and school-based settings.
8. *Developmental and academic content* refers to curriculum.

Standard #1: Foundations

		Chapter									
Knowledge		1	2	3	4	5	6	7	8	9	10
EC1K1	Historical, philosophical foundations, and legal basis of services for infants and young children both with and without exceptional needs.	●	●			●					
EC1K2	Trends and issues in early childhood education, early childhood special education, and early intervention.	●	●			●					
Skills		1	2	3	4	5	6	7	8	9	10
EC1S1	Implement family services consistent with due process safeguards.					●					

Standard #2: Development and Characteristics of Learners

		Chapter									
Knowledge		1	2	3	4	5	6	7	8	9	10
EC2K1	Theories of typical and atypical early childhood development.						●				
EC2K2	Biological and environmental factors that affect pre-, peri-, and postnatal development and learning.		●								
EC2K3	Specific disabilities, including the etiology, characteristics, and classification of common disabilities in infants and young children, and specific implications for development and learning in the first years of life.						●				
EC2K4	Impact of medical conditions and related care on development and learning.										●

(continued)

Standard #2: Development and Characteristics of Learners (*continued*)

Knowledge		Chapter									
		1	2	3	4	5	6	7	8	9	10
EC2K5	Impact of medical conditions on family concerns, resources, and priorities.										●
EC2K6	Factors that affect the mental health and social-emotional development of infants and young children.			●							
EC2K7	Infants and young children develop and learn at varying rates.				●						
Skills		1	2	3	4	5	6	7	8	9	10
EC2S1	Apply current research to the five domains, play and temperament in learning situations.										

Standard #3: Individual Learning Differences

Knowledge		Chapter									
		1	2	3	4	5	6	7	8	9	10
EC3K1	Impact of child's abilities, needs, and characteristics on development and learning.						●		●		
EC3K2	Impact of social and physical environments on development and learning.							●	●		
Skills		1	2	3	4	5	6	7	8	9	10
EC3S1	Develop, implement, and evaluate learning experiences and strategies that respect the diversity of infants and young children, and their families.				●		●			●	
EC3S2	Develop and match learning experiences and strategies to characteristics of infants and young children.				●		●			●	

Standard #4: Instructional Strategies

Knowledge		Chapter									
		1	2	3	4	5	6	7	8	9	10
EC4K1	Concept of universal design for learning.										
Skills		1	2	3	4	5	6	7	8	9	10
EC4S1	Plan, implement, and evaluate developmentally appropriate curricula, instruction, and adaptations based on knowledge of individual children, the family, and the community.						●		●	●	
EC4S2	Facilitate child-initiated development and learning.									●	
EC4S3	Use teacher-scaffolded and initiated instruction to complement child-initiated learning.									●	
EC4S4	Link development, learning experiences, and instruction to promote educational transitions.					●					
EC4S5	Use individual and group guidance and problem-solving techniques to develop supportive relationships with and among children.									●	
EC4S6	Use strategies to teach social skills and conflict resolution.									●	
EC4S7	Use a continuum of intervention strategies to support access of young children in the general curriculum and daily routines.										

Standard #5: Learning Environments and Social Interactions

		Chapter									
Knowledge		1	2	3	4	5	6	7	8	9	10
	None in addition to the Common Core.										
Skills		1	2	3	4	5	6	7	8	9	10
EC5S1	Select, develop, and evaluate developmentally and functionally appropriate materials, equipment, and environments.							●	●		
EC5S2	Organize space, time, materials, peers, and adults to maximize progress in natural and structured environments.							●	●		
EC5S3	Embed learning opportunities in everyday routines, relationships, activities, and places.									●	
EC5S4	Structure social environments, using peer models and proximity, and responsive adults, to promote interactions among peers, parents, and caregivers.							●	●	●	
EC5S5	Provide a stimulus-rich indoor and outdoor environment that employs materials, media, and adaptive and assistive technology, responsive to individual differences.							●	●		
EC5S6	Implement basic health, nutrition and safety management procedures for infants and young children.							●			
EC5S7	Use evaluation procedures and recommend referral with ongoing follow-up to community health and social services.				●						

Standard #6: Language

Knowledge		1	2	3	4	5	6	7	8	9	10
								Chapter			
EC6K1	Impact of language delays on cognitive, social-emotional, adaptive, play, temperament and motor development.								•		
EC6K2	Impact of language delays on behavior.								•		
Skills		1	2	3	4	5	6	7	8	9	10
EC6S1	Support and facilitate family and child interactions as primary contexts for development and learning.								•		
EC6S2	Support caregivers to respond to child's cues and preferences, establish predictable routines and turn-taking, and facilitate communicative initiations.								•	•	
EC6S3	Establish communication systems for young children that support self-advocacy.								•		

Standard #7: Instructional Planning

Knowledge		1	2	3	4	5	6	7	8	9	10
								Chapter			
EC7K1	Theories and research that form the basis of developmental and academic curricula and instructional strategies for infants and young children.						•				
EC7K2	Developmental and academic content.						•				
EC7K3	Connection of curriculum to assessment and progress monitoring activities.				•		•				

(continued)

Standard #7: Instructional Planning (*continued*)

Skills		1	2	3	4	5	6	7	8	9	10
EC7S1	Develop, implement, and evaluate individualized plans, with family members and other professionals, as a member of a team.					●					
EC7S2	Plan and implement developmentally and individually appropriate curriculum.						●				
EC7S3	Design intervention strategies incorporating information from multiple disciplines.									●	
EC7S4	Implement developmentally and functionally appropriate activities, using a variety of formats, based on systematic instruction.									●	
EC7S5	Align individualized goals with developmental and academic content.					●					
EC7S6	Develop individualized plans that support development and learning as well as caregiver responsiveness.					●					
EC7S7	Develop an individualized plan that supports the child's independent functioning in the child's natural environments.					●					
EC7S8	Make adaptations for the unique developmental and learning needs of children, including those from diverse backgrounds.								●		

Standard #8: Assessment

		Chapter									
Knowledge		1	2	3	4	5	6	7	8	9	10
EC8K1	Role of the family in the assessment process.				●						
EC8K2	Legal requirements that distinguish among at-risk, developmental delay and disability.		●								
EC8K3	Alignment of assessment with curriculum, content standards, and local, state, and federal regulations.				●		●				
Skills		1	2	3	4	5	6	7	8	9	10
EC8S1	Assist families in identifying their concerns, resources, and priorities.			●		●					
EC8S2	Integrate family priorities and concerns in the assessment process.				●						
EC8S3	Assess progress in the five developmental domains, play, and temperament.				●						
EC8S4	Select and administer assessment instruments in compliance with established criteria.				●						
EC8S5	Use informal and formal assessment to make decisions about infants and young children's development and learning.				●						
EC8S6	Gather information from multiple sources and environments.				●						
EC8S7	Use a variety of materials and contexts to maintain the interest of infants and young children in the assessment process.				●						
EC8S8	Participate as a team member to integrate assessment results in the development and implementation of individualized plans.				●	●					

(continued)

Standard #8: Assessment (*continued*)

Skills		Chapter 1	2	3	4	5	6	7	8	9	10
EC8S9	Emphasize child's strengths and needs in assessment reports.				•						
EC8S10	Produce reports that focus on developmental domains and functional concerns.				•						
EC8S11	Conduct ongoing formative child, family, and setting assessments to monitor instructional effectiveness.				•						

Standard #9: Professional and Ethical Practice

Knowledge		Chapter 1	2	3	4	5	6	7	8	9	10
EC9K1	Legal, ethical, and policy issues related to educational, developmental, and medical services for infants and young children, and their families.	•	•								
EC9K2	Advocacy for professional status and working conditions for those who serve infants and young children, and their families.										
Skills		**1**	**2**	**3**	**4**	**5**	**6**	**7**	**8**	**9**	**10**
EC9S1	Recognize signs of emotional distress, neglect, and abuse, and follow reporting procedures.										•
EC9S2	Integrate family systems theories and principles to guide professional practice.			•							
EC9S3	Respect family choices and goals.			•							
EC9S4	Apply models of team process in early childhood.					•					

(continued)

Standard #9: Professional and Ethical Practice (*continued*)

Skills		Chapter									
		1	2	3	4	5	6	7	8	9	10
EC9S5	Participate in activities of professional organizations relevant to early childhood special education and early intervention.						●				
EC9S6	Apply evidence-based and recommended practices for infants and young children including those from diverse backgrounds.			●	●		●			●	
EC9S7	Advocate on behalf of infants and young children and their families.			●							

Standard #10: Collaboration

Knowledge		Chapter									
		1	2	3	4	5	6	7	8	9	10
EC10K1	Structures supporting interagency collaboration, including interagency agreements, referral, and consultation.					●					
Skills		1	2	3	4	5	6	7	8	9	10
EC10S1	Collaborate with caregivers, professionals, and agencies to support children's development and learning.					●			●		
EC10S2	Support families' choices and priorities in the development of goals and intervention strategies.								●		
EC10S3	Implement family-oriented services based on the family's identified resources, priorities, and concerns.			●							
EC10S4	Provide consultation in settings serving infants and young children.					●					

(continued)

Standard #10: Collaboration (*continued*)

Skills		Chapter									
		1	2	3	4	5	6	7	8	9	10
EC10S5	Involve families in evaluation of services.				●						
EC10S6	Participate as a team member to identify and enhance team roles, communication, and problem-solving.					●					
EC10S7	Employ adult learning principles in consulting and training family members and service providers.			●							
EC10S8	Assist the family in planning for transition.					●					
EC10S9	Implement processes and strategies that support transitions among settings for infants and young children.					●					

Appendix B

Federal Definitions of Disabilities

Autism means a developmental disability significantly affecting verbal and nonverbal communication and social interaction, generally evident before age three, that adversely affects educational performance. Other characteristics often associated with autism are engagement in repetitive activities and stereotyped movements, resistance to environmental change or change in daily routines, and unusual responses to sensory experiences. The term does not apply if a child's educational performance is adversely affected primarily because the child has an emotional disturbance as defined below.

A child who manifests the characteristics of autism after age three could be diagnosed as having autism if the criteria in this paragraph are satisfied.

Deaf–blindness means concomitant hearing and visual impairments, the combination of which causes such severe communication and other developmental and educational problems that they cannot be accommodated in special education programs solely for children with deafness or children with blindness.

Deafness means a hearing impairment that is so severe that the child is impaired in processing linguistic information through hearing with or without amplification adversely affecting educational performance.

Emotional disturbance is defined as follows:

(i) The term means a condition exhibiting one or more of the following characteristics over a long period of time and to a marked degree that adversely affects a child's educational performance:
   (A) an inability to learn that cannot be explained by intellectual, sensory, or health factors,
   (B) an inability to build or maintain satisfactory interpersonal relationships with peers and teachers,
   (C) inappropriate types of behavior or feelings under normal circumstances,
   (D) a general pervasive mood of unhappiness or depression, or
   (E) a tendency to develop physical symptoms or fears associated with personal or school problems.

(ii) The term includes schizophrenia. The term does not apply to children who are socially maladjusted unless it is determined that they have an emotional disturbance.

Hearing impairment means an impairment in hearing, whether permanent or fluctuating, that adversely affects a child's educational performance but that is not included under the definition of deafness in this section.

Mental retardation means significantly subaverage general intellectual functioning existing concurrently with deficits in adaptive behavior and manifested during the developmental period that adversely affects a child's educational performance.

Multiple disabilities means concomitant impairments (such as mental retardation-blindness, mental retardation–orthopedic impairment, etc.), the combination of which causes such severe educational needs that they cannot be accommodated in special education programs solely for one of the impairments. The term does not include deaf–blindness.

Orthopedic impairment means a severe orthopedic impairment that adversely affects a child's educational performance. The term includes impairments caused by congenital anomaly (e.g., clubfoot, absence of some member, etc.), impairments caused by disease (e.g., poliomyelitis, bone tuberculosis, etc.), and impairments from other causes (e.g., cerebral palsy, amputations, and fractures or burns that cause contractures).

Other health impairments means having limited strength, vitality, or alertness, including a heightened alertness to environmental stimuli that results in limited alertness with respect to the educational environment that

(i) is due to chronic or acute health problems such as asthma, attention deficit disorder or attention deficit hyperactivity disorder, diabetes, epilepsy, a heart condition, hemophilia, lead poisoning, leukemia, nephritis, rheumatic fever, and sickle cell anemia; and

(ii) adversely affects a child's educational performance.

Specific learning disability is defined as follows:

(i) *General.* The term means a disorder in one or more of the basic psychological processes involved in understanding or in using language, spoken or written, that may manifest itself in an imperfect ability to listen, think, speak, read, write, spell, or to do mathematical calculations, including conditions such as perceptual disabilities, brain injury, minimal brain dysfunction, dyslexia, and developmental aphasia.

(ii) *Disorders* **not** *included.* The term does not include learning problems that are primarily the result of visual, hearing, or motor disabilities, of mental retardation, of emotional disturbance, or of environmental, cultural, or economic disadvantage.

Speech or language impairment means a communication disorder such as stuttering, impaired articulation, a language impairment, or a voice impairment that adversely affects a child's educational performance.

Traumatic brain injury means an acquired injury to the brain caused by an external physical force, resulting in total or partial functional disability or psychosocial impairment or both that adversely affects a child's educational performance. The term applies to open or closed head injuries resulting in impairments in one or more areas, such as cognition; language; memory; attention; reasoning; abstract thinking; judgment; problem solving; sensory, perceptual, and motor abilities; psychosocial behavior; physical function; information processing; and speech. The term does not apply to brain injuries that are congenital or degenerative or brain injuries induced by birth trauma.

Visual impairment, including blindness, means an impairment in vision that, even with correction, adversely affects a child's educational performance. The term includes both partial sight and blindness.

SOURCE: Individuals with Disabilities Education Improvement Act of 2004, 34 CFR 300.8 (c). August 14, 2006.

Sample IFSP Form

Sample Individualized Family Service Plan

I. Child and Family Information

Child's Name __Maria Ramirez__   Date of Birth __12-08-07__   Age in Months __30__   Gender __F__

Parent(s)/Guardian(s) __Bruce & Catherine Ramirez__   Address __2120 Valley Park Place__   __Middletown, IN__   __46810__
                                                Street   City   Zip Code

Home Telephone No. __(513) 555-0330__   Worked Telephone No. __(513) 555-1819__

Preferred Language __English__   Translator Appropriate _____ Yes __X__ No

II. Service Coordination

Coordinator's Name __Susan Green__   Agency __Indiana Early Intervention Program__

Address __105 Data Drive__   __Burlington, IN__   __46980__   Telephone No. __(513) 555-0214__
        Street   City   Zip Code

Appointment Date __6-10-10__

III. IFSP Team Members

Name	Agency	Telephone No.	Title/Function
Susan Green	Indiana Early Prevention (EI) Program	513-555-0214	Service Coordinator
Mr. and Mrs. B. Ramirez	N/A	513-555-0330	Parents
Barbara Smith	Indiana EI Program	513-555-0215	Speech/Language Pathologist
Martha King	Indiana EI Program	513-555-0213	Occupational Therapist
Libby Young	Middletown Preschool Program	513-555-3533	Preschool Teacher

IV. Review Dates

Date of IFSP __6-10-10__   Six-Month Review __12-10-10__   Annual Evaluation __N. A.__

(continued)

Sample Individualized Family Service Plan

V. Statements of Family Strengths and Resources

Maria's parents are well educated professional individuals with realistic goals for her educational development. The entire family unit, including her grandparents is committed and motivated to assist her in any way. Because of the family's geographic location, limited resources are available for service delivery at this time.

VI. Statements of Family Concerns and Priorities

CONCERNS

Due to Maria's medical diagnosis of Down syndrome, her parents are concerned about appropriate early intervention services to assist in ameliorating her developmental delays. Additionally, the parents have stated reluctance about a change in Maria's service delivery from her natural environment (i.e., her home) to an inclusive community-based preschool.

PRIORITIES

The priorities that Maria's parents have for her include improving her communication skills, her ability to use utensils, and her toileting skills. They desire services to be delivered at home with the eventual goal of placement with typical children who attend the local kindergarten. Her parents and grandparents want to learn ways in which they can help to facilitate Maria's development in her natural environment.

VII. Child's Strengths and Present Level of Development

Cognitive Skills (Thinking, reasoning, and learning)

Maria's cognitive abilities are commensurate with a 20-month-old child. She's extremely inquisitive and understands simple object concept skills. Imitative play is consistently observed; however, discrimination of objects, persons, and concepts continues to be an area of need.

Communication Skills (Understanding, communicating with others, and expressing self with others)

Communication/language competency skills appear to be similar to that of an 18-month-old toddler. Her receptive language is further developed than her expressive abilities. Primitive gestures are her primary mode of communication. She consistently exhibits a desire/interest to interact with others. Verbal responses primarily consist of vocalizations and approximations of single-word utterances (e.g., ma-ma, da-da, ba-ba).

Self-Care/Adaptive Skills (Bathing, feeding, dressing, and toileting)

Feeding, in general, such as drinking from a cup and finger feeding, is appropriate at this time. A great deal of assistance from caregivers is still required for daily dressing tasks and toileting.

Gross and Fine Motor Skills (Moving) Maria appears to be quite mobile. She is adept at rambling and walking, but needs to improve muscle strength and endurance. She enjoys movement to music. She can scribble, grasp large objects, turn pages of books, and prefers using her right hand while performing tasks. She needs to work on her ability to use utensils and writing tools.

Social-Emotional Development (Feelings, coping, and getting along with others)

Maria is a very happy, affectionate, and sociable child. She enjoys being the center of attention and engaging in interactive games; however, she appears content to play alone. Temper tantrums are triggered by frustration form her inability to communicate. Sharing and turn taking continue to be difficult for Maria.

(continued)

Sample Individualized Family Service Plan

Health/Physical Development (Hearing, vision, and health)

Maria's general health is good, but she has a history of chronic otitis media and upper respiratory infections. Vision and hearing are monitored frequently.

VIII. Outcome Statements

1. Participate in stimulation of all language modalities (visual, auditory, tactile) in order to increase communication competency.

	Strategies/Activities	Responsible Person/Agency	Begin Date	End Date	Frequency of Service	Location	Evaluation Criteria
1.1	Maria will use word approximations combined with consistent guestures for 5 different needs across 3 different people and 2 different settings.	SLP	6-10-10	12-10-10	Once Weekly	Home	Preschool Language Scale
1.2	Maria will use words combined with signs for 5 different needs across 3 different people and 2 settings.	Mom and Dad	6-10-10	12-10-10			Observation samples

2. Maria's daily self-care skills will improve in the areas of dressing and toileting abilities.

	Strategies/Activities	Responsible Person/Agency	Begin Date	End Date	Frequency of Service	Location	Evaluation Criteria
2.1	Maria will push down/ pull up under-garments with minimal assistance.	Mom and Dad Service Coord.	6-10-10	12-10-10	Once Weekly	Home	Observations
2.2	Maria will establish a consistent pattern of elimination.	Mom and Dad Service Coord.	6-10-10	12-10-10	Once Weekly	Home	Recorded data of frequency of elimination
2.3	Maria will spontaneously indicate by gestures and vocalization the need for going to the restroom.	Mom and Dad Service Coord.	6-10-10	12-10-10	Once Weekly	Home	Observation samples

(continued)

Sample Individualized Family Service Plan

3. Maria will develop improved abilities to discriminate auditory/visual stimuli.

	Strategies/Activities	Responsible Person/Agency	Begin Date	End Date	Frequency of Service	Location	Evaluation Criteria
3.1	Indicate by pointing/ verbalizing whether objects are the same or different.	Mom and Dad Service Coord.	6-10-10	12-10-10	Once Weekly	Home	Observations
3.2	Sort several colors and shapes consistently.	Mom and Dad Service Coord.	6-10-10	12-10-10	Once Weekly	Home	Observation samples
3.3	Imitate words and motions in songs upon being given a model.	Mom and Dad Service Coord.	6-10-10	12-10-10	Once Weekly	Home	Observation samples

IX. Transition Plans

If eligible the followings steps will be followed to transition ___Maria Ramirez___ to preschool services on or about ___12-13-10___
 CHILD'S NAME
PROJECTED TRANSITION DATE

1. The service coordinator will schedule meeting with parents to explain transition process and rationale, review legal rights, and ascertain their preferences and need for support.
2. The service coordinator will arrange for Maria and her parents (and grandparents) to visit the center and meet teachers, staff, and children.
3. The service coordinator will arrange for Maria to visit her classroom on at least three occasions in the month prior to her transition date.
4. At least 90 days prior to Maria's third birthday, the service coordinator will convene a meeting to further develop Maria's transition plan.

X. Identification of Natural Environments

The home environment is considered to be Maria's natural environment at this time.

Justification for not providing services in natural environment: Not applicable.

XI. Family Authorization

We (I) the parent(s)/guardian(s) of ___Maria Ramirez___ hereby certify that we (I) have had the opportunity to participate in the development of our (my) son's/daughter's IFSP. This document accurately reflects our (my) concerns and priorities for our (my) child and family.

We (I) therefore give our (my) permission for this plan to be implemented. __X__ ____
 YES NO

Catherine Ramirez	6-10-10	*Bruce Ramirez*	6-10-10
SIGNATURE OF PARENT/GUARDIAN	DATE	SIGNATURE OF PARENT/GUARDIAN	DATE

Appendix D

Sample IEP Form

Individualized Education Program

I. Student Information and Instructional Profile

Student <u>Thomas Jefferson (T.J.) Browning</u> Date of Birth <u>March 3, 2005</u> Student Number <u>000-60-0361</u>

Parent's/Guardian's Name <u>Angela Browning</u> Address <u>141 Boulder Ave. Apt. 16-A</u>   <u>Franklin, SC</u>   <u>42698</u>
                                                              Street   City   Zip Code

Parent's/Guardian's Phone No. <u>803-555-1920</u> Student's Present School <u>Epps Head Start</u> Grade <u>Pre-K</u>

Date of IEP Meeting <u>May 6, 2009</u> Date of Eligibility <u>April 14, 2008</u> IEP Review Date <u>May 6, 2010</u>

Child's Primary Language <u>English</u> Limited English Proficiency <u>No</u> Braille Instruction <u>No</u>
                                                                    Yes/No   Yes/No

Assistive Technology Needs <u>No</u> Language/Communication Needs <u>No</u> Behavior Needs <u>Yes</u>
                           Yes/No   Yes/No   Yes/No

II. Student Performance Profile

T.J. is an energetic, creative five-year-old. He loves outdoor play and has age-appropriate gross motor skills. He demonstrates age-appropriate skills in self-care. Like many of his peers, he still has some difficulty with tying his shoes and buttoning smaller-sized buttons.

T.J is able to communicate his wants and needs. Generally in conveying his message, T.J. uses a lot of gestures to support his verbal language. A language sample conducted on May 1, 2009, indicated that, on average, T.J. was using two- to three-word sentences. Within the classroom T.J. often will not respond to questions asked of him or directives given to him. Classroom observations conducted throughout the school year show that T.J. has the greatest difficulty in answering questions beginning with "Why," "What," and "When." Standardized tests administered on May 1, 2009, place T.J. in the age range of a child 3 years, 4 months and 3 years, 8 months for auditory comprehension and verbal abilities, respectively. Specific areas of difficulty include: vocabulary, recalling details in sequence, language usage, and classification of objects.

T.J. loves to please adults. He is very responsive to praise. T.J. prefers solitary play. He will typically choose activities in which he demonstrates competence. In four out of five opportunities, these activities involve object assembly such as Legos or blocks. T.J. has difficulty playing cooperatively and sharing. Due to his language delays, he tends to rely on aggressive behavior, rather than on verbal interaction, when tying to resolve conflict with his peers. Although T.J. knows the classroom rules, he requires frequent redirection to task. He has a short attention span, usually staying no more than five minutes with any given activity.

(continued)

Visual-motor integration seems to be difficult for T.J. within fine motor activities. He has difficulty copying shapes and designs using pencil or crayon. T.J. is able to cut on a 1/4" straight line, but needs continued practice with cutting other shapes.

Mrs. Browning, T.J.'s mother, states that she is concerned about his ability to communicate and play (interact) with children of his own age at school and at home. She worries about his aggressive behaviors toward his peers at school and church. At home she has noticed that T.J. has difficulty following directions.

The members of the IEP team have identified T.J.'s delayed communication skills, short attention span, poor social interaction, and fine motor skills as areas of concern that impact his achievement in the general education classroom.

III. Program Eligibility

Eligible _____X_____ Not Eligible _____ Area(s) of Disability <u>Language Impairment</u>   <u>Not applicable</u>
                                                                            Primary   Secondary

Rationale for Eligibility ___<u>Delayed receptive and expressive language is significantly below language of same-age peers.</u>___

IV. Measurable Annual Goals and Benchmarks

1. Area. <u>Communication/Language:</u> T.J. will improve his receptive and expressive language skills by responding to teacher inquires using 4- to 5-word sentences 80% of the time given two opportunities to respond.

	Provider	Evaluation Method	Initiation Date	Check Date	Mastery Date
Benchmark #1 T.J. will verbally express his needs using expanded sentences of 4-5 words	General educator Speech/language pathologist	ⓐ Data collection b. Teacher/Text test c. Work samples ⓓ Classroom observation e. Grades ⓕ Other: <u>language sample</u>	9/6/10	1/5/11 5/5/11	_____
Benchmark #2 T.J. will correctly answer "wh" questions (what, who, where, and when)	General educator Speech/language pathologist	a. Data collection b. Teacher/Text test c. Work samples ⓓ Classroom observation e. Grades f. Other: _____	9/6/10	1/5/11 5/5/11	_____

(continued)

Individualized Education Program

2. Area. <u>Cognitive/Language:</u> T.J. will answer teacher questions using appropriate vocabulary 80% of the time on four out of five occasions.

	Provider	Evaluation Method	Initiation Date	Check Date	Mastery Date
Benchmark #1 T.J. will retell simple stories stating at least 3 events in sequence	General educator Special educator	ⓐ Data collection b. Teacher/Text test c. Work samples ⓓ Classroom observation e. Grades ⓕ Other: *tape recorded retellings*	9/6/10	1/5/11 5/5/11	_____
Benchmark #2 T.J. will appropriately use vocabulary associated with the kindergarten curriculum	General educator Special educator	ⓐ Data collection b. Teacher/Text test c. Work samples ⓓ Classroom observation e. Grades f. Other _____	9/6/10	1/5/11 5/5/11	_____
Benchmark #3 T.J. will verbally describe objects found within age-appropriate books	General educator Special educator	a. Data collection b. Teacher/Text test c. Work samples ⓓ Classroom observation e. Grades f. Other: _____	9/6/10	1/5/11 5/5/11	_____

3. Area. <u>Social/Behavioral:</u> *T.J. will exhibit appropriate social interactions with peers and adults 70% of the time given two verbal or visual prompts.*

	Provider	Evaluation Method	Initiation Date	Check Date	Mastery Date
Benchmark #1 T.J. will respond to conflict with peers without aggression	General educator Special educator	a. Data collection b. Teacher/Text test c. Work samples ⓓ Classroom observation e. Grades ⓕ Other *behavior contract*	9/6/10	1/5/11 5/5/11	_____

(continued)

Benchmark #2

| T.J. will follow adult instructions and directions with less than two reminders | General educator
Special educator | a. Data collection
b. Teacher/Text test
c. Work samples
ⓓ Classroom observation
e. Grades
ⓕ Other: *behavior contract* | 9/6/10 | 1/5/11
5//5/11 | _____ |

Benchmark #3

| T.J. will participate in a group activity for up to 10 minutes | General educator
Special educator | ⓐ Data collection
b. Teacher/Text test
c. Work samples
ⓓ Classroom observation
e. Grades
f. Other: _____ | 9/6/10 | 1/5/11
5/5/11 | _____ |

4. Area. <u>Fine Motor:</u> T.J. will write numbers and letters accurately 75% of the time after teacher modeling.

	Provider	Evaluation Method	Initiation Date	Check Date	Mastery Date
Benchmark #1 T.J. will recognizably print his first and last name	General educator	a. Data collection b. Teacher/Text test ⓒ Work samples d. Classroom observation e. Grades f. Other: _____	9/6/10	1/5/11 5/5/11	_____
Benchmark #2 T.J. will print upper- and lowercase letters	General educator	a. Data collection b. Teacher/Text Test ⓒ Work samples d. Classroom observation e. Grades f. Other: _____	9/6/10	1/5/11 5/5/11	_____

V. Supplementary Aids and Related Services

Services/Related Services	Provider	Hours per week	Location
Instructional support	Special educator	2	General education environment
Speech/language therapy	Speech/language pathologist	2	General education environment

Aids/equipment/program modifications needed to attain annual goals and progress in general education curriculum: Not applicable at this time.

Frequency of use: Not applicable.

(continued)

VI. Special Education Placement

Student to be placed in the following least restrictive environment (LRE):

Location of Services	Duration	Extent of Participation
	(No. of hours in location/total no. of school hours)	
General education classroom	35 hours per week/35 hours per week	100%
Special education environments:		
Special day school	_____	
Residential school	_____	
Hospital school	_____	
Homebound services	_____	
Other (e.g. Head Start, preschool program)	_____	
Rationale for placement in setting other than general education class	Not applicable	

VII. Special Services

Physical Education: Regular   X   Adaptive _____

Transportation: Regular   X   Special _____   Not Applicable _____

Is student provided an opportunity to participate in extracurricular and nonacademic activities with nondisabled peers?   Yes
                        Yes/No

Are supports necessary?   No   Describe: _____
                      Yes/No

Rationale for nonparticipation: Not applicable

VIII. Transition (no later than age 16, earlier if appropriate)

Transition Service Needs Focusing on Course of Study	Not applicable at this time
Employment Outcome	Not applicable at this time
Community Living Outcome	Not applicable at this time
Identify Needed Transition Services	Not applicable at this time
Identify Interagency Responsibilities and Community Linkages	Not applicable at this time

(continued)

IX. Assessment Modifications

Is student able to participate in state or district-wide assessments?   <u>Yes</u>
Yes/No

Are modifications required?   <u>No</u>
Yes/No

Identify type of modifications: <u>Not applicable</u>

Rationale for nonparticipation and alternate assessment plan: <u>Not applicable</u>

X. Progress Report

Parents will be informed of child's progress toward annual goals using same reporting methods used for children without disabilities.

Method		**Frequency**
• Written Progress Report	<u>Yes</u> Yes/No	Every <u>6</u> weeks
• Parent Conference	<u>Yes</u> Yes/No	<u>As needed</u>
• Other <u>behavior contact</u> Identify		<u>Weekly</u>
• Other <u> </u> Identify		<u> </u>

XI. Transferal of Rights

I understand that the rights under the Individuals with Disabilities Education Improvement Act will transfer to me upon reaching my eighteenth birthday.

<u>   </u>   <u>   </u>
Student's Signature   Date

XII. Recommended Instructional and/or Behavioral Interventions

<u>Behavior contract designed to reduce frequency of aggressive interactions with peers.</u>

(continued)

XIII. IEP Development Team

Name	Team Member's Signature	Position/Title
Angela Browning	*Angela Browning*	Parent/Guardian
		Parent/Guardian
Patricia Gwin	*Patricia Gwin*	LEA Representative
Ann Martin	*Ann Martin*	Special Education Teacher
Cecelia Watkins	*Cecelia Watkins*	General Education Teacher Student
Melanie Spangler	*Melanie Spangler*	Other: Speech/language pathologist

Personnel Standards for Early Education and Early Intervention

A Position of the Association of Teacher Educators (ATE)

The Division for Early Childhood (DEC)

The National Association for the Education of Young Children (NAEYC)

It is the position of ATE, DEC, and NAEYC that individuals who work with children in early childhood settings must possess, to a degree congruent with their roles, the knowledge and skills for working with young children with special learning and developmental needs and their families. The increasing capacity internationally to provide comprehensive, coordinated services for young children with special learning and developmental needs and their families has significant implications for personnel preparation and credentialing. There is a need to ensure that personnel are both available and adequately prepared to meet the challenges identified by the field. There is a particular need to develop personnel standards that support the practice of inclusion, providing services for young children with disabilities in general early childhood programs and other community-based settings in which typically developing young children are also served. There is also a need to develop personnel standards that support the emerging trend for the development of unified early childhood/early childhood special education teacher training programs and unified state certification. These personnel standards are necessary for individuals functioning in a variety of roles, including but not limited to the following: (a) early childhood educators who work directly with young children in a variety of early childhood settings, who must accommodate children with a range of abilities and special needs, and who must work collaboratively with families and other professionals; (b) early childhood special educators who possess specialized knowledge and skills about young children with disabilities and their families and who may work directly with young children with disabilities or work in a collaborative relationship with early childhood educators, family members, and other professionals serving young children with special learning and developmental needs and their families; and (c) related services professionals who provide consultation and support, as well as direct treatment, to families and other professionals.

In recommending the development of personnel standards that apply to all of these roles, ATE, DEC and NAEYC recognize that the collaboration of professional organizations is critical to this process. The articulation of shared standards will provide a base from which states can develop certification, licensure, and credentialing guidelines. The desirable outcomes will be coherence of state standards and certification guidelines, congruence between personnel standards and standards of recommended practice in early childhood service delivery, an increased probability that services to young children with disabilities are delivered in the context of services to all young children, and that those services are provided by appropriately prepared personnel.

Philosophy and Assumptions Guiding Personnel Recommendations

ATE, DEC and NAEYC recommend that personnel standards be derived from empirically defensible knowledge and clearly articulated philosophical assumptions about what constitutes effective early education and early intervention for young children with special learning and developmental needs and their families. These include the following:

- the uniqueness of early childhood as a developmental phase,
- the significant role of families in early childhood development and early education and intervention,
- the role of developmentally and individually appropriate practices,
- the preference for service delivery in inclusive settings,
- the importance of culturally competent professional actions, and
- the importance of collaborative interpersonal and interprofessional actions.

The Structure of Certification

It is the intention of ATE, DEC, and NAEYC to provide a framework for personnel standards that is sufficiently flexible to allow states to plan within the context of local limitations while also maintaining "content-congruence" (ATE/NAEYC, 1991) with the philosophy and assumptions. In developing a structure for certification standards, the following recommendations are made:

1. State agencies responsible for credentialing, certification, and/or licensure develop standards for all individuals who may be working with young children with disabilities, including at least early childhood educators, early childhood special educators, and related services professionals.

2. As a first step in influencing the credentialing of all individuals working with young children, states develop freestanding certification or licensure guidelines for educational professionals working with young children, and that these be separate from either existing general education or special education certifications. Certification/licensure standards should be clearly delineated for (a) an early childhood professional who will possess knowledge and skills related to general early childhood education as well as a common core of knowledge and skills related to young children with disabilities and their families and (b) an early childhood special education

professional who will possess specialized knowledge and skills related to young children with disabilities and their families, including those related to consultation with team members, as well as common core knowledge and skills related to general early childhood education.

Such separate certifications should be linked clearly to enable professional mobility between roles and should be constructed to support the possibility of unified early childhood/early childhood special education teacher training programs.

3. State certification standards apply to the birth-to-eight age range. Further, recognizing that it is difficult to prepare individuals to be skillful across this broad age range, it is recommended that certification standards incorporate options for subspecializations of birth-t-age three, age three to five, or age five to eight, with the opportunity to specialize in no more than two of these in a preservice program.

Content of Certification Standards

Personnel standards must articulate common core knowledge and skills necessary for all individuals who work with young children with special learning and developmental needs and their families, as well as the specialization knowledge and skills required for each of these roles. The identification of the content of credentialing standards should follow directly from the articulated philosophy and assumptions and reflect the spirit and letter of appropriate federal regulations related to serving young children with disabilities and their families. Credentialing standards should recognized such that graduate-level training is seen as a desirable part of a career ladder for all professionals working with young children and that, as such, it has the potential for improving the quality of services to all young children. Finally, credentialing standards should be outcome based, not course based, and ensure that personnel possess the knowledge and skills to work collaboratively as members of family–professional teams in planning and implementing appropriate services for young children with disabilities in a variety of community settings.

Representative Organizations Concerned with Young Children with Special Needs and Their Families

American Foundation for the Blind (AFB)
11 Penn Plaza, Suite 300
New York, NY 10011
(212) 502-7600
http://www.afb.org/

American Speech–Language-Hearing Association (ASHA)
2200 Research Boulevard
Rockville, MD 20850
(301) 296-5700; (800) 638-8255
http://www.asha.org/

The ARC of the United States
1010 Wayne Avenue, Suite 650
Silver Spring, MD 20910
(301) 565-3842; (800) 433-5255
http:www.thearc.org/

The Association for Persons With Severe Handicaps (TASH)
1025 Vermont Avenue, Suite 300
Washington, DC 20005
(202) 540-9020
http://www.tash.org/

Autism Society of America
7910 Woodmont Avenue, Suite 300
Bethesda, MD 20814
(301) 657-0881; (800) 328-8476
http://www.autism-society.org/

Beach Center on Families & Disability
University of Kansas
3136 Haworth Hall
Lawrence, KS 66045
(785) 864-7600
http://www.beachcenter.org/

Division for Early Childhood (DEC), Council for Exceptional Children
27 Fort Missoula Road, Suite 2
Missoula, MT 59804
(406) 543-0872
http://www.dec-sped.org/

ERIC Clearinghouse on Disabilities and Gifted Education
C/O Computer Sciences Corporation
655 15th Street, NW Suite 500
Washington, DC 20005
(800) 538-3742
http://www.eric.ed.gov/

Federation for Children With Special Needs
1135 Tremont Street, Suite 420
Boston, MA 02120
(617) 236-7210
http://www.fcsn.org/

National Association of the Deaf
8630 Fenton Street, Suite 820
Silver Spring, MD 20910-3819
(301) 587-1788; (301) 587-1789 (TTY)
http:ww.nad.org/

National Association for the Education of Young Children (NAEYC)
1313 L Street, NW Suite 500
Washington, DC 20005
(202) 232-8777; (800) 424-2460
http://www.naeyc.org/

National Coalition for Parent Involvement in Education (NCPIE)
1400 L Street, NW Suite 300
Washington, DC 20005
(202) 289-6790
http:www.ncpie.org/

National Deaf Education Center
Gallaudet University
800 Florida Avenue, NE
Washington, DC 20002
(202) 651-5031
http://clercenter.gallaudet.edu/

National Dissemination Center for Children with Disabilities (NICHCY)
1825 Connecticut Avenue, NW Suite 700
Washington, DC 20009
(800) 695-0285
http://www.nichcy.org/

National Down Syndrome Congress
1370 Center Drive, Suite 102
Atlanta, GA 30338
(800) 232-6372
http://www.ndsccenter.org/

National Down Syndrome Society
666 Broadway, Eighth Floor
New York, NY 10012-2317
(800) 221-4602
http://ndss.org/

National Early Childhood Technical Assistance Center (NECTAC)
Campus Box 8040
University of North Carolina, Chapel Hill
Chapel Hill, NC 27599
(919) 962-2001
http://www.nectac.org/

United Cerebral Palsy Association
1660 L Street, NW Suite 700
Washington, DC 20036
(202) 766-0414; (800) 872-5827
http://www.ucpa.org/

Academic (preacademic) Approach. A model that focuses on reading, writing, arithmetic, and other skills needed in a school setting.

Accessibility. Adaptations of the environment aimed at equalizing participation opportunities for persons with disabilities.

Accommodation. According to Piaget, an alteration of existing cognitive structures to allow for new information; involves a change in understanding.

Accommodation plan (Section 504). Found in Public Law 93-112, a customized plan written by a general educator that is designed to meet the unique needs of a child with a disability.

Acquired immune deficiency syndrome (AIDS). Caused by the human immunodeficiency virus (HIV), which destroys the body's natural immune system; almost always fatal.

Activity area. Organized space within a classroom dedicated to activities based on a theme or developmental domain. Typically designed to accommodate small groups of children and a teacher.

Activity-based instruction. Systematic distribution of teaching and learning across routine activities, planned activities, or child-initiated activities at school and at home.

Activity-based intervention. A curriculum approach that embeds training on a child's individual IFSP or IEP goals and objectives into routine or planned activities.

Adaptability. In family systems theory, this is a concept used to describe a family's ability to change in response to a crisis or stressful situation.

Adapted participation. Use of an alternative means of participation (i.e., orienting head or eye gaze instead of pointing; using a communication board instead of speaking).

Adaptive skills. Those skills that promote independence and facilitate a child's ability to fit into his or her environment.

Age appropriateness. A component of the developmentally appropriate practice (DAP) guidelines, which refers to the need for the learning environment and curriculum to be based on the typical development of children.

Apgar Scale. A screening procedure for newborns given at one minute and again at five minutes following birth to measure heart rate, respiration, reflex response, muscle tone, and color.

Arena assessment. A team process in which one team member conducts the assessment while the other team members observe and contribute.

Assessment. The process of gathering information for the purpose of making a decision about children with known or suspected disabilities in the areas of screening, diagnosis, eligibility, program planning, and/or progress monitoring and evaluation.

Assimilation. In Piaget's terms, the inclusion of new information and experiences into already present cognitive schemes or structures.

At-risk. Describing a child with exposure to certain adverse conditions and circumstances known to have a high probability of resulting in learning and development difficulties.

Auditory trainer. Type of amplification system sometimes used by children with hearing impairments.

Authentic assessment. The process of observing, recording, collecting, and otherwise documenting what children do and how they do it for the purpose of making educational decisions.

Auto-education. In Montessori terms, the self-teaching that occurs as a result of a child independently interacting with a carefully planned environment.

Behavior disorder. A term used to describe a wide variety of social and emotional problems that include, but are not limited to, attention and/or hyperactivity, conduct, and anxiety disorders.

Behavioral approach. A model based on learning principles of behavioral psychology that emphasizes direct instruction through a prescribed sequence of instructional activities.

Biological risk. Young children with a history of pre-, peri-, and postnatal conditions and developmental events that heighten the potential for later atypical development.

Center-based programs. Group-oriented service delivery model for young children with special needs. Intervention and educational services provided in settings other than the child's home.

Child Find. The process of finding and identifying children who have a delay or disability.

Children with special health needs. A general term referring to youngsters with a wide variety of serious and oftentimes unique health care concerns.

Chronosystem. The interaction and influence of historical time on the micro-, meso-, exo-, and macrosystems.

Cochlear implant. A surgical procedure capable of restoring hearing in some individuals with a hearing loss.

Cognitive skills. A child's evolving mental and intellectual ability.

Cohesion. According to family systems theory, this is a concept used to describe the degree of freedom and independence experienced by each family member within a family unit.

Collaboration. The act or process of working together.

Combination programs. A service delivery model for young children with special needs that combines elements of home-based and center-based program models.

Compensatory education. Early experiences and intervention efforts aimed at ameliorating the consequences of living in poverty; goal is to better prepare young children for school.

Communication. The exchange of messages between a speaker and a listener.

Concurrent validity. A type of validity that refers to how well a test correlates with other accepted measures of performance administered close in time to the first.

Construct validity. A type of validity that refers to the degree to which a test addresses the constructs on which it is based.

Content validity. A specific type of validity that refers to how well a test represents the content it purports to measure.

Cooperative teaching. An instructional approach in which an early childhood special educator and a general education teacher teach together in a general education classroom to a heterogeneous group of children.

Criterion-referenced tests. A type of measure used to determine whether a child's performance meets an established criteria or a certain level of mastery within various developmental domains or a set of objectives.

Cultural appropriateness. A teacher's ability to understand each child and his or her unique social and cultural contexts.

Culturally biased assessment. A measure that focuses on skills and abilities of the dominant Western culture and places children from non-Western, nondominant cultures at a disadvantage.

Cultural responsiveness. A complex concept involving the awareness, acknowledgement, and acceptance of each family's culture and cultural values that requires professionals to view each family as a unique unit that is influenced by, but not defined by, its culture.

Culture. The foundational values and beliefs that set the standards for how people perceive, interpret, and behave within their family, school, and community

Curriculum. What is to be learned in an early childhood program; it flows from the theoretical or philosophical perspectives on which the program is based.

Curriculum model. A conceptual framework and organizational structure combining theory with practice, describing what to teach and how to teach.

Curriculum-referenced tests. A type of measure that is used to interpret a child's performance or abilities in relation to specific curricular objectives.

Development approach. A traditional curriculum model based on theories of typical child development.

Developmental age scores. The result from a norm-referenced test for children ages birth through five.

Developmental–cognitive approach. A theory-driven model, based on the work of Piaget, that emphasizes the domain of cognitive skill development.

Developmental delay. A concept defined by individual states when referring to young children with special needs. A delay is usually determined on the basis of various developmental assessments and/or informed clinical opinion.

Developmental domains. The key skill areas that are typically addressed in a comprehensive assessment, including cognitive, motor, self-care, communication, play, social, and emotional skills.

Developmentally appropriate practices. A set of guidelines established by the National Association for the Education of Young Children (NAEYC) to articulate appropriate practices for the early education of young children.

Didactic materials. Instructional items used in Montessori programs.

Disability. An inability to do something; a reduced capacity to perform in a specific way.

Early childhood special education. The provision of customized services uniquely crafted to meet the individual needs of youngsters between three and five years of age with disabilities.

Early Head Start. A federal program providing a variety of services to low-income families with infants and toddlers as well as to women who are pregnant.

Early intervention. The delivery of a coordinated and comprehensive set of specialized services for infants and toddlers (birth through age two) with developmental delays or at-risk conditions and their families.

Eco-map. A drawing or figure used to identify family supports, strengths, and relationships and formal family supports.

Echolalic speech. A condition in which someone repeats what is said rather than generating an original sentence.

Ecological assessment. An assessment that considers all dimensions and requirements of the child's natural environment in determining goals and objectives.

Ecological perspective. The basic tenets of this perspective are that individuals or family units are influenced by the events and experiences that occur in their lives (their ecology), and that these events and experiences can be understood and influenced to promote healthy modes of development and learning in families.

Ecology. The interrelationships and interactions of the various environments or contexts that affect the child and are affected by the youngster.

Eligibility. A comprehensive diagnostic process to determine if a child meets the criteria to be eligible for special services.

Embedding. The process of identifying times and activities when a child's goals *and* the instructional procedures for those goals can be inserted into children's on going activities, routines and transitions in a way that relates to the context.

Emotional abuse. A type of child maltreatment distinguished by caregiver actions that are designed to be psychologically harmful to the youngster.

Empowerment. The process of applying strategies whereby individuals gain a sense of control over their future as a result of their own efforts and activities.

Engagement. Consistent, active involvement with the people (i.e., teachers, parents, classmates), activities (i.e., snack time, play time, group time participation, center selection/participation), and materials (i.e., use of toys, art supplies, water play materials) throughout the child's day.

Environment. The total of the physical and human qualities that combine to create a space in which children and adults work and play together.

Environmental arrangements. Any changes in the environment that are used to facilitate child engagement, such as altering the physical space, altering the selection and use of materials, and altering the structure of an activity.

Environmental risk. Biologically typical children who encounter life experiences or environmental conditions that are so limiting that the possibility of future delayed development exists.

Equilibration. According to Piaget's theorizing, the cognitive process by which a person attempts to balance new information with already existing data.

Established risk. Children with a diagnosed medical disorder of known etiology and predictable prognosis or outcome.

Ethnocentric behavior. The viewpoint that the practices and behavior of one particular cultural group are natural and correct while considering the actions of other groups inferior or odd.

Evidence-based practices. The use of instructional practices that are based upon empirical research.

Exceptional children. Children who differ from society's view of normalcy.

Exosystems. According to Bronfenbrenner, the social systems that exert an influence on the development of the individual.

Expressive language. The ability to communicate one's ideas or feelings through vocalizations, words, and other behaviors used to relay information.

False negative. Designation of a child who needs special services but was not referred by a screening.

False positive. Designation of a child who has been referred by a screening but does not need special services.

Family. A group of people related by blood or circumstances who rely upon one another for security, sustenance, support, socialization, and stimulation.

Family-based practices. Those practices used in early intervention/education designed to have child-, parent-, and family-strengthening and competency-enhancing consequences.

Family-centered practices. A philosophy of working with families, whereby specific techniques and methods are used that stress family strengths, the enhancement of family skills, and the development of mutual partnerships between families and professionals.

Family-directed practices. The term included in the IDEA Amendments that represents family-based practices as mandatory.

Family characteristics. According to family systems theory, this is the component that refers to the dimensions that make each family unique, such as its socioeconomic status, cultural heritage, number of family members, and other distinguishing characteristics.

Family functions. One of the components of family systems theory that refers to a variety of interrelated activities considered necessary to fulfill the collective needs of a family (e.g., affection, economics, recreation, and education).

Family interactions. According to family systems theory, these are the relationships and interactions that occur among and between various family subsystems like the marital subsystem.

Family life cycle. According to family systems theory, the changes that occur in families that influence their resources, interactions, and functions.

Family systems theory. A model that suggests that the family is an interdependent unit; whatever affects one family member has repercussions for the other members of the unit. Adoption of a family systems approach means that professionals focus their attention on the entire family constellation instead of only the child with a disability.

Fine motor skills. The ability to use small muscle groups such as those in the hands, face, and feet.

FM system. A wireless communication system available to children with hearing impairments. Teacher wears a transmitter while the child wears the receiver; allows student to adjust the volume of the teacher's voice.

Formal testing. A type of assessment in which standardized measures are used with a specific purpose in mind, such as screening or eligibility determination.

Formative assessment. Evaluation of children's learning during program operation for the purpose of improving the quality of teaching and overall learning; often conducted at the beginning of the year and ongoing.

Full inclusion. The belief that all children with disabilities should be educated in regular education classrooms in their neighborhood schools. Placements should be age- and grade-appropriate.

Functional approach. A model in which the skills or behaviors are emphasized that have immediate relevance to a child.

Functional behavior analysis. A behavioral approach that seeks to determine the purpose or function that a particular behavior serves.

Functional skills. Those skills that will be useful to a child and will be used often by the child in his or her natural environment.

Generalization. The ability to apply what is learned in one context to different settings, different materials, or different people.

Gifts. A Froebelian term referring to manipulative objects, such as balls and wooden blocks, used as tools for learning in Froebel's curriculum.

Gross motor skills. The type of skills that involve the movement and control of large muscle groups used to function in the environment.

Handicap. The consequences or impact encountered by or imposed on a child with a disability as he or she attempts to function and interact in the environment.

Home-based programs. A type of service delivery model for young children with special needs. Intervention is provided in the youngster's home by the primary caregiver. Professionals make regular visits to work directly with the child and to provide instruction to the caregiver.

Home Start. A derivation of the Head Start program; designed to provide comprehensive services to young children and their parents in the home through the utilization of home visitors.

Human immunodeficiency virus (HIV). The specific virus that causes acquired immune deficiency syndrome (AIDS).

Hybrid family. A family that is different from either family of origin and consists of a blending of cultural and religious origins.

Hypertonic muscle tone. Tight muscles.

Hypotonic muscle tone. Floppy muscles that exhibit resistance to being stretched.

Individual appropriateness. A component of the developmentally appropriate practice (DAP) guidelines that calls for the learning environment and curriculum to be responsive to the individual differences and needs of each child.

Individual transition plan (ITP). Document required by federal law whose purpose is to assist adolescents with disabilities in moving from school to postschool functions.

Individualized education program (IEP). Required by federal legislation. A customized educational plan, constructed by a team, for each child with special needs.

Individualized family service plan (IFSP). A written document mandated by federal law. Designed as a guide for services for infants, toddlers, and their families. Developed by a team of professionals and the parent(s).

Instructional validity. A type of validity that refers to the extent to which the information gained from an assessment instrument would be useful in planning intervention programs.

Intelligence tests. Standardized measures of intellectual functioning that are often referred to as I.Q. tests.

Interdisciplinary. A type of teaming model utilized in delivering services to young children with special needs. Team members typically perform their evaluations independently; however, program development and recommendations for services are the results of information sharing and joint planning.

Interviews. A form of assessment used to gather information from families or other caregivers about a child's abilities; the family's concerns, priorities, and resources; or other relevant information.

Labeling. The assignment of a disability label such as *deaf* or *mentally retarded*.

Language. The use of symbols, syntax, or grammar when communicating with one another.

Learned helplessness. A condition of hopelessness resulting from inconsistent or negative feedback. Persons with learned helplessness feel they have little control over elements of their environment.

Least restrictive environment (LRE). A concept requiring that children with special needs be educated, to the maximum extent appropriate, with their typical classmates. Settings are individually determined for each pupil.

Macrosystems. The ideological, cultural, and institutional contexts that encompass the micro-, meso-, and exosystems.

Mainstreaming. The process of integrating children with special needs into educational settings primarily designed to serve youngsters without disabilities.

Mesosystems. The relationships between the various environments of the microsystems.

Meta-analysis. A comprehensive statistical procedure whereby research studies are evaluated in an effort to ascertain global statistical patterns; they yield "effect size," reported as standard deviations.

Microsystems. As proposed by Bronfenbrenner, the immediate environments in which a person develops, such as a youngster's home and neighborhood.

Milieu strategies. Strategies to facilitate language skills (especially social interaction context) that take advantage of the natural environment (people, materials, activities) to support learning. Milieu strategies include a variety of specific procedures (i.e., time delay, mand-model, incidental teaching).

Mobility. The process of using one's senses to determine one's position in relation to other objects in the environment.

Multidisciplinary team. A type of teaming model utilized in delivering services to young children with special needs. This approach utilizes the expertise of professionals from several disciplines, each of whom usually performs his or her activities independently.

Natural environments. A philosophy that emphasizes providing early intervention in settings viewed as typical for youngsters without disabilities.

Naturalistic observation. A systematic process of gathering information by looking at individuals and their behavior in their environments.

Neglect. A form of child maltreatment; characterized by a variety of caregiver actions that may include failure to provide basic necessities, inadequate physical supervision, or failure to render needed medical treatment.

Normalization. A principle advocating that individuals with disabilities should be integrated, to the maximum extent possible, into all aspects of everyday living.

Norm-referenced tests. A type of measure that provides a score that compares a child's performance to performances of other children from a particular group.

Nuclear family. A family group consisting of, most commonly, a father and mother and their children.

Observational assessment. A systematic process of gathering recordings and analysis of young children's behavior in real-life situations and familiar settings within their environments.

Occupations. A Froebelian concept describing arts-and-crafts-type activities used to develop eye-hand coordination and fine motor skills.

Orientation. The ability to move around in one's environment.

Orthotic devices. Devices used to promote body alignment, stabilize joints, or increase motor functioning.

Outcomes. The *what* (knowledge, skills, abilities, and understandings) that is to be taught to young children with delays or disabilities.

Parent. Any adult who fulfills the essential caregiving duties and responsibilities for a particular child.

Partial participation. Use of only a portion of the response instead of full response (i.e., when told to touch the picture of the tree, a child moves his/her hand in the direction of the correct picture, but does not actually touch the picture).

Peer-mediated strategies. Strategies or approaches that utilize peers (or classmates) to promote learning.

Percentile ranks. The percentage of the same-aged population that performed at or below a given score.

Performance. A child's behavior that is exhibited while putting specific skills into action and is interpreted in relation to the performance of a group of peers of the same age group who have previously taken the same test.

Physical abuse. A type of child maltreatment. An assault on a youngster designed to cause physical injury or harm to the child.

PKU screening. A procedure used to detect the metabolic disorder phenylketonuria (PKU) in infants.

Play-based assessment. A systematic procedure for observing children during play to determine their level of development.

Play-based interventions (strategies). The intentional use of play as the context for implementing interventions.

Portfolio. The format followed during the assessment process which includes the specific skill areas, skills, and/or behaviors to be observed or measured.

Portfolio assessment. A systematic and organized collection of children's work and records of their behaviors, which can serve as evidence to be used to monitor their progress.

Positive behavioral supports. An alternative to punishment; a proactive way of addressing problematic behaviors.

Predictive validity. A type of validity that refers to the extent to which a test relates to some future measure of performance.

Premacking. Arranging sequences of activities so that low-probability (less desirable) behaviors are followed by high-probability (motivating) behaviors.

Prepared environment. An important component in a Montessori classroom; a planned and orderly setting containing specially developed tasks and materials designed to promote children's learning.

Program evaluation. A process that addresses a program's progress in achieving overall outcomes and effectiveness.

Program planning. A procedure used to identify desired goals/outcomes for the IFSP/IEP and intervention.

Program planning assessment. Assessment that focuses on a child's skill level, needs, background, experiences, environmental demands, and interests as the basis for constructing and maintaining individualized programs.

Progress monitoring. The process of collecting information about how children are progressing toward meeting their individual goals and objectives.

Progress monitoring and evaluation. A process of collecting information about a child's progress, the family's satisfaction with services, and overall program effectiveness.

Progressivism. A school of thought founded by John Dewey. Emphasis placed on interest of children rather than activities chosen by the teacher.

Project Follow-Through. A federal program that attempts to continue the gains developed through Head Start. Funding is available for children in kindergarten through the third grade. Children receive educational, health, and social service benefits.

Project Head Start. A federally funded program aimed at young children in poverty; designed to increase the chances of success in school and opportunity for achievement.

Prompts. Any systematic assistance provided to an individual to enable him or her to respond, including verbal, pictorial, and physical cues (such as assistance).

Prosthetic devices. Artificial devices used to replace missing body parts.

Protocol. A format to be followed during an assessment that can include the skill areas on which to focus and/or the specific skills to be observed.

Receptive language. The ability to understand and comprehend both verbal and nonverbal information.

Referral. When a professional comes in contact with a child he or she suspects of having a disability and recommends further assessment.

Regular education initiative (REI). An approach for educating children with special needs; special and regular educators work cooperatively in providing services to pupils with exceptionalities in the regular classroom.

Reliability. The consistency of a test in measuring what it is supposed to assess in a dependable or consistent manner.

Responsivity. The quality of the environment that provides immediate and consistent feedback for child interaction.

Routine-based strategies. The intentional use of predictable routine activities (i.e., snack time, dressing, etc.), transitions (i.e., departure and arrival time, daily transition to the cafeteria, etc.), and routine group activities (i.e., circle time) to implement interventions.

Scaffolding. A Vygotskian concept referring to the assistance rendered to the learner by adults or peers, which allows the person to function independently.

Schema. According to Piaget, a cognitive organizational pattern or framework that provides a foundation for the development of cognitive structures used in thinking.

Scope. The developmental skill and content areas.

Screening. A procedure designed to identify the children who need to be referred for more in-depth assessment.

Section 504. Refers to a section of Public Law 93-112, civil rights legislation aimed at protecting children and adults against discrimination due to their disabilities.

Self-care skills. Those skills that allow a child to independently care for him or herself, are basic for maintaining life, and deal with bodily functions.

Self-fulfilling prophecy. An expectation that individuals who are labeled will achieve at a predetermined level.

Sensitive periods. Stages of development early in life during which, according to Montessori, a child is especially capable of learning particular skills or behaviors.

Sensitivity. A screening instrument's ability to identify children who need additional assessment.

Sequence. The order in which content is taught; sequence is often specified in a developmental progression.

Sexual abuse. A form of child maltreatment in which developmentally immature individuals engage in sexual activities that they do not fully comprehend or about which they are unable to give informed consent. Sexual abuse may also include issues of sexual exploitation.

Social and cultural appropriateness. A component of the developmentally appropriate practice (DAP) guidelines, which calls for curriculum and learning experience to be based on each child's unique social and cultural experiences.

Social skills. Social–emotional skills that refer to a range of behaviors associated with how children interact with others, both adults and peers, and how they react in social situations.

Sound field system. An application system typically used by students with a hearing impairment. Teacher wears a microphone that transmits a signal to speakers strategically placed around the classroom.

Specificity. The capacity of a screening instrument to accurately rule out children who should not be identified.

Speech. The oral motor action used to communicate.

Standardized tests. Tests used during formal testing that are based on the performance of a group of peers of the same age group who have previously taken the same test.

Stereotyping. The generalized belief about members of a cultural group.

Stimulus-control. A behavioral science concept that states that future behaviors are more likely to occur in the presence of specific stimuli while the behavior is initially being reinforced.

Summative assessment. Evaluation of children's learning at the completion of services to see if the goals and objectives of the program were met.

Tabula rasa. Concept attributed to John Locke. Young children seen very much like a blank slate. Learning is not innate but rather the result of experiences and activities.

Task analysis. The process of breaking down a task or skill (i.e., brushing teeth, getting a drink of water, putting on a shirt, turning on a computer, etc.) into sequential steps.

Teacher-mediated. Intervention directed by teachers to promote social interactions.

Tests. Predetermined collections of questions or tasks to which predetermined types of responses are sought.

Time out. A behavioral intervention approach whereby a child is removed from a reinforcing situation for brief periods of time.

Transdisciplinary. A type of teaming model utilized in delivering services to young children with special needs. Building on an interdisciplinary model, this approach also includes sharing of roles and interventions delivered by a primary service provider. Support and consultation from other team members is important.

Transition. The process of moving from one type of educational program or setting to another.

Universally designed curriculum. A curriculum that invites active participation of all children.

Validity. The extent to which a test measures what it was intended to measure.

Zone of proximal development (ZPD). According to Vygotsky, this term refers to the distance between the child's actual development level as determined by independent problem solving and the level of potential development as determined through problem solving under adult guidance or in collaboration with more capable peers.